Law for Advertising, Broadcasting, Journalism, and Public Relations

A Comprehensive Text for Students and Practitioners

LEA's COMMUNICATION SERIES
Jennings Bryant and Dolf Zillmann, General Editors

Selected titles include:

Berger • *Planning Strategic Interaction: Attaining Goals Through Communicative Action*

Bryant/Zillmann • *Media Effects: Advances and Theory in Research, Second Edition*

Ellis • *Crafting Society: Ethnicity, Class, and Communication Theory*

Fortunato • *Making Media Content: The Influence of Constituency Groups on Mass Media*

Greene • *Message Production: Advances in Communication Theory*

Parkinson/Parkinson • *Law for Advertising, Broadcasting, Journalism, and Public Relations: A Comprehensive Text for Students and Practitioners*

Reichert/Lambiase • *Sex in Advertising: Perspectives on the Erotic Appeal*

Shepherd/Rothenbuhler • *Communication and Community*

Singhal/Rogers • *Entertainment Education: A Communication Strategy for Social Change*

Zillmann/Vorderer • *Media Entertainment: The Psychology of Its Appeal*

For a complete list of titles in LEA's Communication Series,
please contact Lawrence Erlbaum Associates, Publishers at
www.erlbaum.com

Law for Advertising, Broadcasting, Journalism, and Public Relations

A Comprehensive Text for Students and Practitioners

Michael G. Parkinson, Ph.D., A.P.R., Attorney at Law
Texas Tech University

L. Marie Parkinson, J.D., Attorney at Law
Texas Tech University

LAWRENCE ERLBAUM ASSOCIATES, PUBLISHERS
2006 Mahwah, New Jersey   London

Senior Acquisitions Editor:	Linda Bathgate
Assistant Editor:	Karin Wittig Bates
Cover Design:	Kathryn Houghtaling Lacey
Full-Service Compositor:	TechBooks
Text and Cover Printer:	Hamilton Printing Company

This book was typeset in 10/12 Times, Italic, Bold, Bold Italic. The heads were typeset in ACaslon Regular, Bold, Italic, and Bold Italic.

Lawrence Erlbaum Associates, Inc., Publishers
10 Industrial Avenue
Mahwah, New Jersey 07430
www.erlbaum.com

Library of Congress Cataloging-in-Publication Data

Parkinson, Michael G.
    Law for advertising, broadcasting, journalism, and public relations : a
comprehensive text for students and practitioners / Michael G. Parkinson, L.
Marie Parkinson.
        p. cm. — (LEA's communication series)
    Includes bibliographical references and index.
    ISBN 0-8058-4975-0 (pbk. : alk. paper)
    1. Press law—United States. 2. Advertising laws—United States. 3.
Public relations and law—United States. I. Parkinson, L. Marie. II.
Title.   III. Series.
KF2750.P37 2006
343.7309'9—dc22
                                        2005035462

Books published by Lawrence Erlbaum Associates are printed on acid-free paper, and their bindings are chosen for strength and durability.

Printed in the United States of America
10 9 8 7 6 5 4 3 2 1

Dedication

In loving memory of our deceased parents:
John Willis Dillon, Helen Francis Parkinson, and Donna Smith Stotts
who taught us the value of education
and
to our surviving parents and stepparents
Jean Carr Dillon and Richard Wesley Parkinson,
who inspired us to persevere
and to
Robert Hawkins Stotts,
who is a major contributor to higher education, especially ours!

The Authors

Michael G. Parkinson is the associate dean for graduate studies in the College of Mass Communications at Texas Tech University. He is accredited by the Public Relations Society of America and is licensed to practice law before the Supreme Courts of Illinois and Oklahoma as well as the U.S. District Court for the Southern District of Illinois and the U.S. Court of Appeals for the Eighth Circuit. He has taught communication and mass communications for more than 30 years and practiced law for 12 years. He has won awards for both his legal writings and his works in mass communications. He also has been recognized by the American Bar Association for excellence in appellate advocacy.

L. Marie Parkinson teaches in both the Department of Political Science and the College of Mass Communications at Texas Tech University. During her 18-year teaching career, she has taught courses in mass communications law, constitutional law, juvenile law, corrections, and the judicial process. She practiced law for more than 20 years and is licensed to practice law before the Supreme Court of Illinois and the U.S. District Court for Southern Illinois. She has been a state prosecutor, a criminal defense attorney, and a civil lawyer, and has tried more than 1,000 cases ranging from traffic tickets to major felonies.

Table of Contents

List of Exhibits   ix

Acknowledgments   xi

Preface   xiii

1

Introduction to the Legal System   1

This chapter provides a background to help the reader understand legal concepts presented in other chapters. It covers government and court structures, sources of law, and legal jurisdiction.

2

Legal Procedure   28

Building on the background provided in chapter 1, this chapter covers legal procedures including categories of law. It describes criminal pretrial, trial, and posttrial procedures, as well as juvenile, civil, and appellate procedure.

3

The First Amendment:
History and Application   60

This chapter describes the difference between liberties and rights. It also explains philosophies used to interpret the First Amendment and explains what rights described in the Bill of Rights must be honored by the states. Standards of judicial review are also introduced here.

4

The First Amendment: Limitations   83

This chapter explains when other legal interests outweigh First Amendment liberties. It introduces time, place, and manner restrictions. It also explains conflicts between free speech and national security and legal control of obscenity. This chapter, and each subsequent chapter, includes a practice note. The practice note here describes some areas of mass communications practice wherein expression may be regulated and also gives some suggestions for how practitioners may anticipate and address conflicts between their interests and laws or ordinances regulating communications.

5

Electronic Media Regulations   111

The history and status of broadcast regulation, with a focus on the trend to deregulation, are described here. Regulation of the business of broadcast is described, as are the prescriptive and proscriptive laws addressing broadcast content. The chapter contains a discussion of indecency control that builds on chapter 4's description of obscenity regulation. The chapter also addresses regulation of cable, satellite, telco, and Internet media. The practice note in this chapter describes the requirements for reporting public service announcements.

6

Access to Places and Information: What You Can Get From Government, It Can Probably Get From You   154

Chapter 6 describes the legal limitations on access by media to governmental facilities and information. A section of this chapter carefully explains the terms *privilege* and *immunity*. The chapter also explains why reporters are subject to subpoenas. The practice note focuses on how to avoid and deal with subpoenas.

7

Access to Trials and Judicial Proceedings   194

Building on concepts introduced in the previous chapter, this chapter explains rules governing access to trials and other judicial proceedings. The chapter includes a specific discussion of changes in access to deportation hearings and the use of secret courts since September 11, 2001.

This chapter concludes with three practice notes that address practical suggestions for reporters seeking access to courthouses, guidelines for reacting to closure orders, and litigation public relations.

8

Means of Access: Law as Entertainment   232

Chapter 8 uses a theatrical analogy to describe the impact of electronic media in courtrooms. Interpretations of current laws covering media access to both trials and executions are addressed. The practice note in this chapter offers suggested legal arguments for media counsel to improve public access to governmental proceedings.

9

Communication Torts   259

Chapter 9 describes the traditional actions in libel, slander, and defamation. It then addresses the modern communication torts of private facts, false light, appropriation, and intrusion. This chapter has two practice notes. The first addresses the misperception that opinion is a defense to defamation. The second explains how employee communication may be a defense to communication torts.

10

Copyright and Trademark   297

Intellectual property law is introduced in chapter 10. The discussion focuses on the impact of copyright and trademark on mass communications professionals. The practice note here addresses works for hire.

11

Contract and Employment Law   327

Chapter 11 begins with an overview of contract law. It then focuses on employment and agency law and explains how those laws create obliga-tions for mass communications professionals and their employers. The chapter concludes with practice notes on an employee's duty to obey and covenants not to compete.

12

Commercial Communication: Rights and Regulations   367

Commercial communication laws are presented to help the reader understand that they regulate more than advertising. Federal Trade Commission regulations are explored, along with cases that apply commercial communications law to advertisers, journalists, and public relations practitioners. We conclude with practice notes describing media, client, and agency liabilities for false or dangerous advertising, and restrictions on political advertising and lobbying.

13

Investor Relations and Financial Press Regulations   407

Chapter 13 begins with a brief introduction to concepts in securities law. It then focuses on specific laws and regulations that impact reporters, public relations practitioners, and advertisers who deal with stock sales. In the practice note we describe legal liabilities of financial reporters and practitioners in investment relations.

Appendices

A   How to Find and Brief a Case   433
B   Sample Case Brief of *Branzburg v. Hayes*, 408 U.S. 665 (1972)   440
C   Sample Documents   470
D   Sample Jury Instructions   478
E   The Constitution of the United States   481

Table of Cases   501
Index   507

List of Exhibits

Exhibit 1.1.   Equitable Remedies   8
Exhibit 1.2.   U.S. District and Circuit Court Locations   10
Exhibit 1.3.   Example of Fragmented Court System. Court Structure of Texas   13
Exhibit 1.4.   The U.S. Federal Courts: A Consolidated System   14
Exhibit 2.1.   Summary of Legal Systems   30
Exhibit 2.2.   Funnel Effect   36
Exhibit 2.3.   Illinois Juvenile Court Act, Purpose   46
Exhibit 2.4.   Texas Juvenile Justice Code Purpose   46
Exhibit 3.1.   Principles of Incorporation   64
Exhibit 3.2.   Selective Incorporation   67
Exhibit 3.3.   Speech and Non-Speech   71
Exhibit 3.4.   Standards of Judical Review   73
Exhibit 4.1.   Philosophies of Constitutional Interpretation   85
Exhibit 4.2.   Forum-Based Review   90
Exhibit 4.3.   Incitement Standard   94
Exhibit 4.4.   Elements and Relief for Torts   95
Exhibit 4.5.   Modified Miller Test   102
Exhibit 5.1.   Six Major FCC Bureaus and Their Functions   116
Exhibit 5.2.   FCC Licensing Processes   121
Exhibit 5.3.   Fairness Doctrine and Corollaries   133
Exhibit 6.1.   Elements and Defenses for Trespass   157
Exhibit 6.2.   Access to Government Property   166
Exhibit 6.3.   Federal Sunshine Act   169
Exhibit 6.4.   Freedom of Information Act   172
Exhibit 6.5.   Electronic FOIA Sites   174
Exhibit 6.6.   Legal Privileges   179
Exhibit 7.1.   Elements for Closure   199
Exhibit 7.2.   Illinois Juvenile Court Right of Access   210
Exhibit 7.3.   Texas Access to Juvenile Proceedings   210
Exhibit 7.4.   Presumption of Openness   213
Exhibit 7.5.   New Colossus   214
Exhibit 7.6.   Court Statement   224
Exhibit 7.7.   Permitted and Prohibited Statements in Litigation PR   226
Exhibit 9.1.   Elements of Defamation   261
Exhibit 9.2.   Requirement for Proof of Harm in Defamation Actions   265
Exhibit 9.3.   Malice Rule   269
Exhibit 9.4.   Example of "Fair" Comment   272
Exhibit 9.5.   Statute of Limitations for Defamation Actions   274
Exhibit 9.6.   Elements of Private Facts   275
Exhibit 9.7.   Elements of False Light   280

Exhibit 9.8.   Elements of Appropriation   283
Exhibit 9.9.   Elements of Intrusion   285
Exhibit 10.1.   Requirements to Create and Enforce a Copyright   299
Exhibit 10.2.   Prohibited Acts   305
Exhibit 10.3.   Copyright Infringement Elements   307
Exhibit 10.4.   Considerations in "Fair Use" Defense to Copyright Infringement   309
Exhibit 10.5.   Trademark Infringement Inquiries   316
Exhibit 10.6.   Requirements for "Works for Hire."   319
Exhibit 11.1.   Elements Required to Create a Contract   328
Exhibit 11.2.   Statute of Frauds: Contracts That Must be in Writing   333
Exhibit 11.3.   Defenses to Contract Obligations   338
Exhibit 11.4.   Terms of Art in Agency Law   343
Exhibit 11.5.   Elements Required to Create an Agency Relationship   344
Exhibit 11.6.   Factors to Identify Independent Contractors   347
Exhibit 11.7.   Factors Used to Determine if Covenant Not to Compete is Overbroad   359
Exhibit 12.1.   The *Bolger* Test Used to Determine if a Message is Commercial Communication   372
Exhibit 12.2.   The *Central Hudson* Test Used to Determine Whether Commercial Speech May Be Subjected to Government Regulation   379
Exhibit 12.3.   FTC Elements of Deceptive Advertising   382
Exhibit 12.4.   Elements of Lanham Act Suit   388
Exhibit 12.5.   Advertisements From *Soldier of Fortune*   396
Exhibit 12.6.   Federal Campaign Expenditure Limitations   399
Exhibit 13.1.   Family Resemblance Test to Determine What is a Security   410
Exhibit 13.2.   Characteristics of Corporations   413
Exhibit 13.3.   Securities Exchange Act Rule 10b-5   417
Exhibit 13.4.   Elements or Cause of Action under Section 14(a)   421
Exhibit 13.5.   Subjects Included in Proxy Solicitations   423
Exhibit 13.6.   Earnings Restatements prior to Sarbanes–Oxley   425

Acknowledgments

We particularly want to thank Marijane Wernsman who graciously proofread many drafts. Her contributions convinced us that most legal documents would be improved if all lawyers were required to have their work reviewed by a journalist.

Preface

A popular Government, without popular information, or the means of acquiring it, is but a Prologue to a Farce or a Tragedy, or perhaps both. Knowledge will forever govern ignorance: And a people who mean to be their own Governors must arm themselves with the power which knowledge gives.[1]

This is not your grandmother's mass communications law book! In fact, we made a deliberate decision not to use the phrase *mass communications law* in the title. The book includes several subjects not usually thought of as mass communications law, but these subjects are important to communications practitioners.

Our more than 40 years of combined teaching experience in several fields motivated us to include background material on history, political science, and legal logics. Laws are not created in a vacuum. To understand law, one must also understand the historical contexts and political pressures that mold its creation and interpretation.

We also have not focused on any one subfield of mass communications, but have tried to respect and present the interests and concerns of four major areas — advertising, broadcasting, journalism, and public relations. If the book has a professional focus, that focus is law. We are both practicing attorneys with more than 30 years' total experience in a wide range of both criminal and civil cases. In this book we present the kind of information and advice we would give a communications practitioner who is a client. We have, for example, included information that may challenge traditional views of journalists' rights and we were careful to include an explanation of laws that may create conflict between advertisers, public relations professionals, and journalists. We have written this book thinking of our readers as we have often thought of our clients—those we would inform, not coddle. Therefore, when the truth is unattractive to one subfield of media practitioners, we do not sugarcoat it. We believe that knowledge and truth make a practitioner and an industry stronger. Shared mythology does not.

Rather than giving multiple examples of individual laws or cases for the reader to memorize, the explanation of legal logics and political philosophies is presented so the reader will understand why our laws were created and what they mean. We believe that a reader who understands the political logics that guide the creation of our laws will be able to interpret law, and a communications practitioner who can interpret law will be able to understand new laws and changes in existing laws without the requirement to memorize individual laws or cases.

Obviously, we do have a point of view and occasionally our commitment to communication liberty is obvious. But, we have focused primarily on what the law is, not what we think it should be. For example, in our approach to briefing cases we advocate ignoring concurring and dissenting opinions that are not part of the law and that often serve only to obfuscate courts' decisions.

While we do present an overview of relevant law, it is important to note that the law differs from jurisdiction to jurisdiction. Furthermore, we can only present a limited introduction to the laws that impact mass communications practitioners; many very important subjects, topics, and areas of the laws have been omitted. This book was written as a survey of the subject, not to provide in-depth coverage of every area of the law. Throughout the book, we repeatedly recommend that communications practitioners should consult a licensed attorney in their jurisdiction who specializes in a relevant area of law.

Text Structure

Footnotes and References

Because of our focus on law, we deliberately chose to use the *Uniform System of Citation*.[2] This is the style and citation guide used universally in legal documents.

Magic Words and Phrases

Because the law is so jargon-driven, each of the chapters includes a list of what we have called "magic words and phrases." To assist the reader in defining and understanding these terms, they are identified in the text in **bold** type.

Cases

Each chapter contains a list of cases. The cases were chosen because they demonstrate or expand on the points made in the chapter and we suggest the conscientious reader brief them. Instructions for finding and briefing the cases are in appendix A and a sample brief is in appendix B.

Practice Notes

Beginning with chapter 4, each chapter has a section titled "Practice Notes." These sections provide information that is applicable to practitioners in one or more of the specific subfields of mass communications or that amplify or explain a concept introduced in the chapter. They are not consistent in their format or content, but all include either very practical suggestions for applying principles from the chapter or an expansion of ideas presented in the chapter.

Underlying History, Political Philosophy, and Questions for Discussion

Rather than providing large numbers of examples and hypothetical legal situations, we have included detailed information on the political philosophies and logics used by governments and courts to establish and interpret law. By applying the legal logics and political philosophies described early in the text to the questions for discussion, the reader should develop a far better understanding of the law than could be achieved by reading examples or hypothetical cases.

Repeated Information

Some readers will notice information from one chapter is often repeated in another and that significantly more detail is included than is presented in books designed exclusively as course texts. The repetition here is not the product of sloppy editing, rather, some information is repeated because we assume some readers will read only those chapters that deal with their interests or that some instructors using the book will assign readings in a different order than they are presented here. Information may be repeated because we want to ensure that someone who reads one chapter can understand the information therein without having to have read the entire book.

We respectfully submit this book with the hope that it will provide a perspective from which mass communications students and practitioners can gain an understanding of the laws and regulations they face every day. Our goal is to provide students, teachers, and professionals alike with greater knowledge of how laws are selected and applied in our system of jurisprudence. We also want to inspire our readers with new insights into the political philosophies that continue to mold and shape the legal terrain that we all must navigate as media practitioners and as citizens in a democratic society.

Notes

1. *EPA v. Mink*, 410 U.S. 73, 110-111 (1973), quoting a letter from James Madison to W.T. Barry, August 4, 1822.
2. HARVARD LAW REVIEW ASSOCIATION, A UNIFORM SYSTEM OF CITATION (17th ed. 2000).

1

Introduction to the Legal System

Certainly, all those who have framed written constitutions contemplate them as forming the fundamental and paramount law of the nation, and consequently, the theory of every such government must be, that an act of the legislature, repugnant to the constitution, is void.

—Chief Justice John Marshall[1]

Overview
Background of Government and Court Structures
Sources of Law in the United States
Other Legal Systems
Types of Courts
Jurisdiction and Venue
Legal Hierarchy and Authorities
Rules for Justiciability

Overview

This chapter begins with an explanation of the legal system and sources of law in the United States. This information is essential to any understanding of the laws that impact the practices of advertising, broadcasting, journalism, and public relations. It also helps the reader interpret and apply the laws described later.

We begin with a brief comparison of governmental systems and a description of sources of law. We then describe legal systems and the types of courts that function both at the federal level and in the individual states. Included in the description of the courts are an introduction to the ideas of jurisdiction and legal authority. We conclude by describing the different types of opinions rendered by the U.S. Supreme Court and the rules of justiciability the court uses to avoid making unnecessary decisions and to avoid interfering with the states and other branches of the U.S. government.

Background of Government and Court Structures

Laws are the principles that structure the relationships between government and the governed and among the people within a society. To understand law, one must first have a feel for the government itself. Therefore, we begin with a cursory explanation of the structure of government so you will have a foundation for a later explanation of our legal system.

Systems of Government

There are three types of governments: the unitary, the confederal, and the federal. The differences among the three are based on how power is distributed and on the placement of sovereignty.

Under a **unitary government**, power rests in a centralized source, which is superior to all citizens and subunits of government. The sovereign, whether it is a single person or a body of rulers, has power over all matters in the society from education to garbage collection.

A **confederal government**, sometimes called a confederacy, is a fairly loose association of sovereign states or units that have joined together for specific purposes. Power in a confederacy flows from the sovereign units to a centralized unit that has very limited authority.

A **federal government** is theoretically a combination of the unitary and confederal systems. Ostensibly, power in a federal system flows both from many sovereign states to a centralized government and from the centralized government to the states. Certain powers are given to the central government by the member states through their subscription to a written constitution. The constitution not only gives sovereign powers to the centralized government, it also binds the member states together. The compact requires subscribing members to accept the delegated authority of the central government.

Most countries today operate under a unitary system of government. These include France, Great Britain, Israel, Egypt, and Sweden. By contrast, a few countries operate or have operated using a confederal system. The United States, as it existed for a short period under the Articles of Confederation, and the southern states under the American Confederacy during the Civil War are historic examples. Switzerland operates under a confederation of sovereign "cantons," and a number of former republics of the Soviet Union have formed a confederal government system called the Commonwealth of Independent States.[2] For more than 200 years, the United States has had a federal government.

It is also important to understand the concepts of power and authority in connection with systems of governance and sovereignty. **Power** is the ability to cause others to modify their behavior and to conform to whatever the power holder wants. Authority is given to a leader or institution by the holders of power. **Authority** allows a leader or institution to compel obedience because of the legitimate position given by the power holders. In the United States, for example, the ultimate power rests with the people. The people can elect or reject all government officials and they have the power to change the form and nature of their government and its Constitutions.[3] However, the government and its officials are given the legitimate authority to compel obedience to our laws.

Sovereignty is the source of power in government. Based on the U.S. Constitution, there are three sovereigns in the U.S. governmental system. These are the national government, commonly called the federal government; the states; and the often overlooked but absolute source of power in a democratic republic, the people. The people have the ultimate power to elect representatives to govern themselves and to change the form and nature of their government and its Constitution.[4]

In the U.S. Revolution, the people of the original 13 colonies took the sovereign power from the British King. Initially, they chose to collectively invest their former colonial governments with this sovereignty in units called "States" and band together under Articles of Confederation. They had effectively moved from a unitary to a confederal government. To further consolidate power and to defend the new country from foreign encroachment, the people, through their state representatives, finally formed the federal democratic republic that is today known as the United States.

The United States is federal in the sense that it operates under two tiers of governance, both of which are sovereigns, the national central government and the individual states. It is democratic in the sense that its leaders are granted authority to act through election by its citizens, and it is a republic in the sense that the people elect representatives who are granted authority to engage in constitutionally specified activities of governance on behalf of their constituents, collectively known as the people.

Under the U.S. Constitution, the people, as sovereigns, gave the central government authority for six specific purposes.

> We the People of the United States, in Order to form a more perfect Union, establish
> Justice, insure domestic Tranquility, provide for the common defense, promote the
> general Welfare, and secure the Blessings of Liberty to ourselves and our Posterity, do
> ordain and establish this Constitution for the United States of America.[5]

The People, through the Constitution, then separated the components of sovereign power into three branches of government. Article I of the U.S. Constitution created a legislative branch. "All legislative powers herein granted shall be vested in a Congress of the United States, which shall consist of a Senate and House of Representatives."[6] Article II created an executive branch. "[T]he executive power shall be vested in a President of the United States of America."[7] Finally, Article III created a judiciary. "The judicial power of the United States, shall be vested in one Supreme Court, and in such inferior courts as the Congress may from time to time ordain and establish."[8]

What is often called the "**Supremacy Clause**" of the Constitution sets out the hierarchy of laws. It says:

> This Constitution, and the laws of the United States which shall be made in pursuance
> thereof; and all treaties made, or which shall be made, under the authority of the
> United States, shall be the supreme law of the land; and the judges in every state shall
> be bound thereby, anything in the Constitution of laws of any state to the contrary not
> withstanding.[9]

Article VI also binds the legislative, executive, and judicial officers of both the national and state governments to support the U.S. Constitution.

> The Senators and Representative before mentioned, and the Members of the several state legislatures, and all executive and judicial officers, both of the United States and of the several states, shall be bound by Oath or Affirmation to support this Constitution.[10]

Our legal system exists within the federal democratic republic established by the U.S. Constitution.

Legal Systems

There are basically two types of legal systems in the world today: code law and common law.

The foundation of **code law** is in statements of religious dogma or in the compilations of written laws, edicts, or decrees from rulers or strong religious leaders. Examples of code law systems include (a) the code of Hammurabi, which is named for the king of Babylonia about 2,000 BC; (b) the Justinian Code, which is the body of Roman law systematized during the reign of the Byzantine Emperor, Justinian I, who reigned from 527 to 565; and (c) the Napoleonic Code, which was the collection of French laws compiled during the reign of Emperor Napoleon Bonaparte from 1804 to 1815. Other types of code laws are those statements of religious laws and principles of living found in the Muslim Quran or in the Christian Bible.

Common law is a more recent legal phenomenon than code law. Common law refers to the system of jurisprudence developed in England from the time of William the Conqueror, approximately 1066, to the present. British common law is based on evolution over time of legal rules, customs, and maxims created by the judiciary. It evolves and changes over time as courts wrestle with and apply the concepts of **precedent** and **stare decisis**. Once the jurisdiction of the British Courts of Law was established by the Magna Carta in 1215, those involved in deciding cases came to the conclusion that cases with similar facts and issues should all have similar results. Courts began consulting older decisions to ensure their decisions followed the principles used before. This consultation of older cases is called "following precedent."

Following **precedent** means relying on previously decided cases to determine the choice and application of laws for current cases. The concept of **stare decisis**, literally to "let the decision stand," is the very foundation of following precedent. Under the principle of stare decisis, judges look for an historic case with facts and issues similar to the one now being adjudicated. The court does not change the laws but applies the holdings from the previously decided cases to the case currently before the court. Although courts can develop new interpretations and applications of the common law to adapt to current situations, real changes in the law are rare. Therefore, the common law is quite stable and sometimes even antiquated.

This text focuses on the common law principles applicable in the United States. But, the distinctions between code and common law remain important today because the global market for mass communications puts practitioners in both code and common law jurisdictions. If one works in any international market, one simply cannot assume activities that are lawful in one's own jurisdiction will be permitted in another. In general, countries that have historically been British colonies have adopted a common law system. Those countries that have histories of strong theocratic governance or intensely centralized governance generally subscribe to code laws. France and a majority of middle-Eastern countries have legal systems based on code laws, while the former and current members of the British Commonwealth, including the United States, use common law as the basis for their legal systems. Even within the United States there is some variation. Louisiana, for example, has a tradition of code law and deference to the Napoleonic Code that influences how some legal decisions are made.[11]

Sources of Law in the United States

Now that we have presented a brief description of our government and legal system we can move to more specific information on law in the United States. At the most basic level, there are four sources of law in the United States: (a) the Constitutions of the United States and of the 50 states, (b) the Statutes of the United States and of the 50 states, (c) treaties made under the authority of the United States, and (d) case law. The distinction between these four sources of law has practical implications for mass communications practitioners. Modification of the U.S. Constitution requires an amendment to be supported by two thirds of both houses of Congress and ratified by three fourths of the states. Therefore, laws based on Constitutional provisions are very stable and difficult to change. Case law, on the other hand, may change relatively easily and quickly.

We should note here that equity, regulations, and ordinances are not sources of law. We address all three of these concepts later, but for now we simply point out that regulations, rules, and ordinances are directives issued by executive agencies or subordinate units of government. They are not laws or sources of law but, in fact, must be permitted or "enabled" by laws. Equity is not a source of law; it is merely a system of remedies. Because rules and regulations are not laws, they may be changed very quickly and practitioners in areas that are heavily regulated must be constantly alert for changes that affect them.

Case law is the most complex source of law and the source that is most pervasive in mass communications. Therefore, we focus our discussion on its three basic components: statutory interpretations, judicial review, and common law.

Statutory Interpretation

Although our elected legislators have been granted the power to enact laws, rather often the statutes they pass are so general or so ambiguous they must be interpreted before they can be applied to real human situations. The onerous task of interpreting statutes has traditionally been left to the courts. If a state legislature, for example, passes and a governor signs into law a statute saying, "[w]hen two trains shall approach each other on the same track, both shall stop and neither shall proceed until the other has passed by," what does that mean? Answering this and the thousands of other questions about the meaning of laws is called statutory interpretation. Decisions regarding the meaning, choice, and applications of our often conflicting or unintelligible laws are presented to the courts by the people being affected.

Judicial Review

There are national statutes, more commonly called federal statutes, and state statutes. **Statutes** are the laws enacted by legislatures and endorsed by the appropriate chief executive. To be valid, all statutes, whether federal or state, must be constitutional. In other words, they must be made in accordance with the U.S. Constitution. State statutes must also be consistent with the appropriate state's constitution.

Judicial review is an action by a court to evaluate whether a statute is consistent with the constitution. The authority for judicial review is implicitly granted by the U.S. Constitution Articles III and VI. The U.S. Supreme Court first enunciated the doctrine of judicial review in 1803.[12] Since that decision, the U.S. Supreme Court has been the arbiter of the constitutionality of governmental actions at both the national and state level. It has become the practice of state supreme courts to decide their own state constitutional issues. If a litigant raises a question regarding the compliance of state action with the U.S. Constitution, then the matter may be heard within the federal court system, possibly by the U.S. Supreme Court.

Common Law

In addition to interpreting statutes and determining the constitutionality of laws, the federal and state courts also develop common law. Common law is based on the system of precedent or stare decisis, a system of using earlier court rulings to provide guidance for current decisions. For a long period in history, most courts looked to English common law as a source because the state legislatures had not yet enacted public laws or statutes in many areas. Thus, continuity between the British Common Law of the 1700s and 1800s and much of the civil law in the United States is particularly apparent in very traditional legal fields like real estate, torts, contracts, commercial paper, and sales of goods. However, over the years, many legal scholars and state legislatures came to the conclusion that the common law needed to be updated and made more relevant and applicable to the U.S. experience. In many cases, both statutes in the United States and the court decisions that are the foundation for common law have altered and superceded the older common laws.

Other Legal Systems

Although equity, rules, regulations, and ordinances are not law, they do impact enforcement of law and have the authority of government. Therefore, it is important for any mass communications practitioner to understand them.

Equity

Equity is a system of remedies that was developed in England. It is close to the antithesis of common law because it permits deviations from rigid enforcement and allows significant judicial discretion. Equity, or more specifically equitable remedies, was developed as a response to the often harsh, unfair, or unjust decisions that resulted from strict application of common law. Where the common law courts could not or would not give truly fair relief, there could be an appeal for justice to the King's Chancellor. The rules and remedies originally applied in these situations have been structured and are now applied in what are called Courts of Chancery. The courts that hear cases in equity are called Courts of Chancery because these actions were originally heard by the King's Chancellor.

Equitable rights and remedies were developed independently from common law. Civil courts of law are limited to awarding money damages, but Courts of Chancery have the authority to grant other remedies to dispense justice. In the United States today, all courts of general jurisdiction are permitted to grant equitable remedies when the appropriate types of cases present themselves. Examples of equitable relief include temporary restraining orders; temporary and permanent injunctions; writs of mandamus; writs of habeas corpus; orders of protection, peace bonds, and specific performance.[13] These remedies are summarized in Exhibit 1.1.

Rules, Regulations, Codes, and Ordinances

In addition to the four sources of law previously discussed, there are several special large bodies or categories of authoritative rules, regulations, codes, and ordinances that often have the force and effect of law. Because of how these rules, regulations, and ordinances originate, they do not rise to the level of law.

Rules and Regulations

When the U.S. Congress or the state legislatures pass laws, they generally designate, within the statutes themselves, a specific executive agency that will be responsible for implementing the law. The specified agency is responsible for creating and enforcing **rules** and **regulations** that give impetus to public policy enunciated in the statute.

Public laws, also called statutes, can only be passed by elected representatives of the people. Rules and regulations are created by executive agencies and may have the force and effect of law, but are not law. The constitutions of the United States and of the individual states give the power to create laws only to the democratically elected representatives of the people. Therefore, only legislators can create law. Executive agencies, appointed by either the president or a state's governor, only have the authority given to them by legislative bodies in statutes. The promulgation, content, purview, and enforcement of rules and regulations are often called "administrative law," although the term *law* used in this context is a misnomer.

Ordinances

As discussed previously, the U.S. Constitution created a federal system of governance. Under this system, the states as original sovereigns possess power over all

Exhibit 1.1.   Equitable Remedies.

Temporary restraining order (TRO)	Emergency order of the court, obtained without the defendant being present, which imposes some requirement or restriction on the actions of the defendant. The requirement has only a short duration.
Temporary injunction	Order of the court restricting the behavior of either party. Usually used to maintain the status quo during the pendency of a court action at law.
Permanent injunction	Order of the court without specified time limit restricting the actions of one party at the request of another party.
Mandamus	Order of a court ordering a public official (or judge of a lower court) to take a specific action that is part of their public office or duties.
Habeas corpus	"Have you the body." A court order to a jailer commanding him or her to bring an inmate before the court and prove the inmate is not held unjustly.
Order of protection	Very similar to a temporary restraining order. It is a court order developed specifically as a remedy for domestic violence.
Peace bond	Remedy developed to prevent future illegal acts. It may require payment of surety to guarantee future good conduct. Violations may also be punished as contempt of court.
Specific performance	A court order directing a party to perform a contractual obligation where money damages do not provide an adequate remedy.

matters within their borders as long as those powers are not granted to the national government by the Constitution.[14] Therefore, each state has a unitary government with a single sovereign and only one source of power. All units of local government are subordinate to the state. Counties, cities, municipalities, wards, parishes, and special districts have no independent authority, power, or existence other than what is specifically granted to them by the state constitution or state law. The type of county government and whether a local government has "home rule," as well as the exact scope of local government is determined by the state constitutions and by the legislatures of the various states. Therefore, directives of local government designated as **ordinances** or codes are similar to the administrative rules and regulations discussed previously. They do not have an autonomous existence of their own and they are not laws.

Types of Courts

In the United States there are two basically independent court systems: the national court system, usually referred to as the federal courts; and the individual state courts. Thus, at any one time there are 51 separate and distinct court systems operating within the United States. Each of these court systems has its own separate power basis or constitution, which describes its structure and authority.

Federal Courts

The U.S. Constitution provides for two types of courts in the national court system: the Article III courts, also known as "constitutional courts" and the Article I courts, also known as "legislative courts." The Constitution creates Article III courts with the following language:

> The judicial Power of the United States shall be vested in one supreme Court, and in such inferior Courts as the Congress may from time to time ordain and establish. The Judges, both of the supreme and inferior Courts, shall hold their Offices during good Behavior, and shall, at stated Times, receive for their Services, a Compensation, which shall not be diminished during their Continuance in Office.[15]

Article I courts are created in Article I, Section 8, which says: "The Congress shall have Power. . . . To constitute Tribunals inferior to the supreme Court."[16]

Federal judges are appointed by the president with the advice and consent of the Senate.[17] Judges appointed under Article III hold their offices for life, during good behavior, and their compensation may not be reduced during their time in office. However, judges in Article I courts do not have similar protection. Therefore, magistrates appointed to serve in legislative courts serve terms with set limits and could conceivably have their compensation reduced or terminated at the whim of Congress.

Article III Courts

The national court system is a three-tiered, consolidated court system. At the lowest level, there are 94 trial courts, called courts of original jurisdiction, where all cases qualified to enter the "federal courts" are originally filed. The number and location of these courts is determined by Congress. The number of these district courts is increased from time to time, based on factors such as the population and the number of cases filed. All states have at least one federal district court. They are identified by the state or the geographic area within a state where they preside. For example, the federal trial court that meets in southern California is referred to as the U.S. District Court for the Southern District of California. In citations this is abbreviated "S.D. Cal."

Exhibit 1.2.   U.S. District and Circuit Court Locations (www.uscourts.gov, retrieved July 14, 2004).

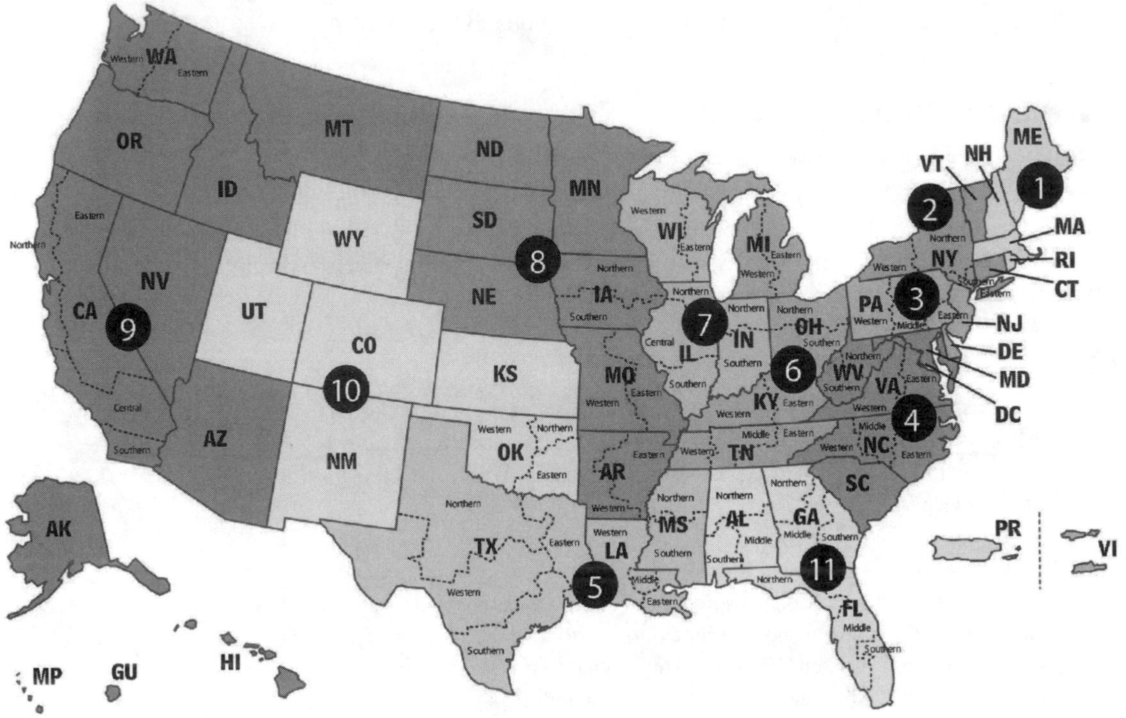

At the intermediate level of the national court system is the U.S. Court of Appeals. This court is divided into 13 circuits. There are 11 numbered U.S. Court of Appeals circuits, a U.S. Court of Appeals for the D.C. Circuit, and a U.S. Court of Appeals for the Federal Circuit. The number and location of the 11 circuits is again determined by Congress based on geography, population, and number of cases filed. Many of the circuits encompass several states. Each of these courts is properly referred to as The U.S. Circuit Court of Appeals for the ————— Circuit. The U.S. Circuit Court of Appeals for the Fifth Circuit for example, presides over federal appeals for the states of Texas, Louisiana, and Mississippi; and the U.S. Circuit Court of Appeals for the Seventh Circuit covers federal appeals for the states of Illinois, Wisconsin, and Indiana. The U.S. Court of Appeals has appellate jurisdiction. In other words, it can review and possibly overturn decisions made by the federal district courts.

At the top level of the national court system is the U.S. Supreme Court, which has original jurisdiction and is the trial court for two categories of cases: those affecting ambassadors and consuls and those in which one of the 50 states is a party.[18] The Supreme Court also has final appellate jurisdiction over virtually all cases presenting issues, based on the U.S. Constitution, federal laws, or treaties.[19]

Other Federal Courts and Tribunals

There are three courts of original jurisdiction, which are lesser or inferior courts whose judges are appointed by the courts they serve, for specific terms. These Article I or legislative tribunals are the bankruptcy courts, which have special and limited jurisdiction only; the U.S. Court of Federal Claims, which is also a specialized and limited court; and the U.S. Magistrates courts. Judges in these courts are generally called magistrates, and help to reduce the workload of cases of the federal district courts.

There are also several extra-judicial or quasi-judicial bodies, boards, and commissions, which serve the federal government, but are not part of the national court system. These are the military courts, both trial and appellate; the Court of Veterans Appeals; the U.S. Tax Court; and hearing officers, referees, or arbiters who work for administrative agencies. These courts, boards, or commissions adjudicate disputes between a government agency and individuals or businesses over the choice and application of the agency's rules and regulations. These hearing boards and commissions are extra-judicial or quasi-judicial in that they are not impartial judges, but work specifically for the various government entities and are paid from agency funds. Although they conduct hearings, they do not follow the rules of evidence and other procedures designed to protect individual rights. Furthermore, rules allow a person or business aggrieved by an agency ruling to sue the agency in the federal court system as a form of appeal. This appeal to the regular courts is typically not available until all administrative remedies have been exhausted. These administrative tribunals function to resolve disputes but are not part of the system of either constitutional or legislative courts, which are the backbone of the U.S. national judicial system.

State Courts

The 50 states each have their own judicial system, which play a significant role in the lives of people in the United States. There are important variations between the individual state judicial systems, making it impossible in one text to explain the composition and function of each state's courts. However, it is vital for the student of mass communications law to have some understanding of the role of the state court systems and their potential impact on the practice of mass communications. Therefore, we present a very general description of state judicial systems, which we hope will help readers understand how their own state court system differs from the federal courts. There are three categories of court systems in the United States today: fragmented, consolidated, and unified. These categories are based on the simplicity or complexity of court structure and on the uniformity of judicial coordination or "voice."

Fragmented Court Systems

Fragmented court systems have more than three layers or tiers of courts, each layer of which can have more than one level within it. Often, the courts within these layers are referred to as major and minor courts. At the bottom tier are several levels of **minor courts** such as municipal courts, justice of the peace courts, magistrate courts, or small claims courts. Jurisdiction of these courts is limited. They may only rule on specific subjects or they may be limited to hearing cases based on local or municipal ordinances. Often, they can only impose limited penalties or fines. Furthermore, the magistrate overseeing these courts often has no formal legal training and no license to practice law. Often, the next level of minor courts within this lower tier will be county courts of limited jurisdiction. These courts usually administer county ordinances, and some uncontested matters such as probate or property disputes. They also hear civil matters where small amounts of money are at issue and may hear appeals *de novo* from the courts below.

Appeals *de novo* refer to cases taken from a court in which no record was made of the proceedings into a court in the next higher level, which will hear the matter again so it may render a decision supported by a record or transcript. Judges in these intermediate trial court levels may or may not be required to have legal training or licenses.

At the upper level of the lower tier of trial courts are often the state district or circuit courts. These courts may be divided into civil and criminal courts, but they are often free to rule on civil matters involving unlimited amounts of money or to impose criminal penalties including incarceration in a state penitentiary or capital punishment. These courts apply state law, not municipal or county ordinances.

Fragmented court systems also have one or more intermediate levels of appellate courts. The lower level appellate courts are often courts of mandatory jurisdiction that are required by state constitution or statute to hear specific types of cases. Some cases may be appealed from these lower appellate courts to the next higher level of appeal, which may also have mandatory jurisdictions. At the top tier of most state court systems will be a state appellate court of last resort, usually called the State Supreme Court. In some states, there is even a division or fragmentation at this highest level of appeal. This division usually requires that civil and criminal cases are heard by two different "supreme courts." Texas and Oklahoma, for example, have this type of **bifurcated supreme court**. In both states, these courts are called the Court of Criminal Appeals and the Supreme Court. The Court of Criminal Appeals exercises final appellate jurisdiction on criminal matters and the Supreme Court hears all final civil and juvenile appeals. Although in most states the highest state court is called the Supreme Court, in New York one set of lower tier trial courts is referred to as Supreme Courts. New York's highest level appellate court is called the Court of Appeals.

As can be seen from this discussion, fragmented court systems, like the one shown in Exhibit 1.3, present some disadvantages, not the least of which is confusion about the court in which a particular type of case should be filed and heard. These courts also are costly to administer because of the duplication of work and caseload.

Consolidated Court Systems

Consolidated court systems, like the U.S. system shown in Exhibit 1.4, have a three-tiered or layered arrangement. The federal courts are a consolidated court system. The courts of original jurisdiction make up the lowest tier, the courts of intermediate appellate jurisdiction are the second tier, and the State Supreme Court sits at the top tier. However, states may rearrange or change the names of these three levels. Illinois, for example, changed its fragmented court structure to a consolidated court system in the 1950s. Each county has its own trial court called a circuit court, which is a court of general

Exhibit 1.3. Example of Fragmented Court System. Court Structure of Texas.

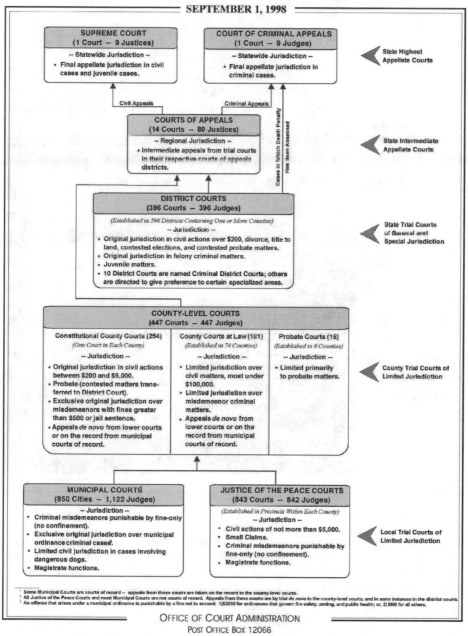

COURT STRUCTURE OF TEXAS
SEPTEMBER 1, 1998

SUPREME COURT
(1 Court -- 9 Justices)
-- Statewide Jurisdiction --
• Final appellate jurisdiction in civil cases and juvenile cases.

COURT OF CRIMINAL APPEALS
(1 Court -- 9 Judges)
-- Statewide Jurisdiction --
• Final appellate jurisdiction in criminal cases.

State Highest Appellate Courts

Civil Appeals | Criminal Appeals

Cases in Which Death Penalty Has Been Assessed

COURTS OF APPEALS
(14 Courts -- 80 Justices)
-- Regional Jurisdiction --
• Intermediate appeals from trial courts in their respective courts of appeals districts.

State Intermediate Appellate Courts

DISTRICT COURTS
(396 Courts -- 396 Judges)
(Established in 396 Districts Containing One or More Counties)
-- Jurisdiction --
• Original jurisdiction in civil actions over $200, divorce, title to land, contested elections, and contested probate matters.
• Original jurisdiction in felony criminal matters.
• Juvenile matters.
• 10 District Courts are named Criminal District Courts; others are directed to give preference to certain specialized areas.

State Trial Courts of General and Special Jurisdiction

COUNTY-LEVEL COURTS
(447 Courts -- 447 Judges)

Constitutional County Courts (254)
(One Court in Each County)
-- Jurisdiction --
• Original jurisdiction in civil actions between $200 and $5,000.
• Probate (contested matters transferred to District Court).
• Exclusive original jurisdiction over misdemeanors with fines greater than $500 or jail sentence.
• Appeals *de novo* from lower courts or on the record from municipal courts of record.

County Courts at Law (181)
(Established in 74 Counties)
-- Jurisdiction --
• Limited jurisdiction over civil matters, most under $100,000.
• Limited jurisdiction over misdemeanor criminal matters.
• Appeals *de novo* from lower courts or on the record from municipal courts of record.

Probate Courts (16)
(Established in 8 Counties)
-- Jurisdiction --
• Limited primarily to probate matters.

County Trial Courts of Limited Jurisdiction

MUNICIPAL COURTS
(850 Cities -- 1,122 Judges)
-- Jurisdiction --
• Criminal misdemeanors punishable by fine-only (no confinement).
• Exclusive original jurisdiction over municipal ordinance criminal cases².
• Limited civil jurisdiction in cases involving dangerous dogs.
• Magistrate functions.

JUSTICE OF THE PEACE COURTS
(843 Courts -- 842 Judges)
(Established in Precincts Within Each County)
-- Jurisdiction --
• Civil actions of not more than $5,000.
• Small Claims.
• Criminal misdemeanors punishable by fine-only (no confinement).
• Magistrate functions.

Local Trial Courts of Limited Jurisdiction

¹ Some Municipal Courts are courts of record -- appeals from those courts are taken on the record to the county-level courts.
² All Justice of the Peace Courts and most Municipal Courts are not courts of record. Appeals from these courts are by trial *de novo* in the county-level courts, and in some instances in the district courts.
³ An offense that arises under a municipal ordinance is punishable by a fine not to exceed: 1)$2000 for ordinances that govern fire safety, zoning, and public health; or, 2) $500 for all others.

OFFICE OF COURT ADMINISTRATION
POST OFFICE BOX 12066
AUSTIN, TEXAS 78711-2066

Exhibit 1.4.   The U.S. Federal Courts: A Consolidated System (www.uscourts.gov, retrieved January 14, 2004).

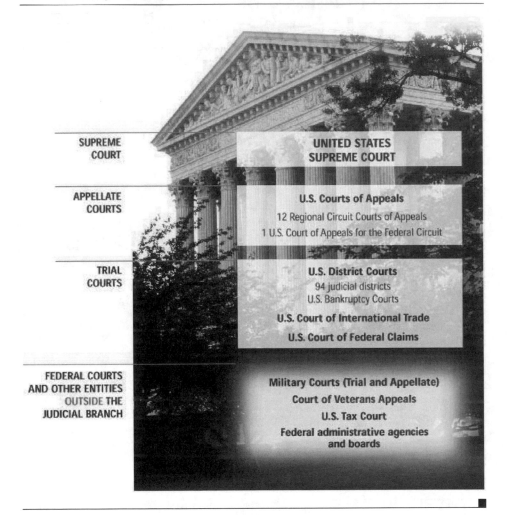

jurisdiction. These circuit courts are arranged into 21 numbered circuits by grouping several counties together according to the population to be served or the caseload. Jurisdiction by the intermediate appellate court level, which are called district courts of appeal, is accomplished by grouping several of the numbered trial court circuits together. The boundaries of the five numbered district courts of appeal are based on population and caseload served, and each encompasses several circuit trial courts. The Illinois State Supreme Court sits as the court of last resort at the top of this type of consolidated court system.

Unified Court System

The federal court system is a consolidated, three-tiered court system that is also unified. A court system is unified if its appellate courts at all levels attempt to speak with a unified or single "voice." Under a unified court system, once an intermediate-level appellate court has delivered an opinion on a legal issue all the other **intermediate appellate** courts treat that holding as mandatory precedential authority and apply it to similar cases. Occasionally, when several of the circuit courts of appeals appear to disagree on the appropriate ruling, the Supreme Court will take the opportunity to set the circuits straight by hearing the next case or group of cases dealing with the issue. The intermediate courts then must defer to the Supreme Court's mandatory authority.

Although the Illinois court system is consolidated, it is not a unified court system. While all five of their district courts of appeal must take as mandatory authority any decision on point made by the Illinois State Supreme Court, or the U.S. Supreme Court, the five individual district courts of appeal treat the opinions of the other four district courts as persuasive authority only. In the federal system, on the other hand, a decision by any court of appeals circuit is deferred to by the other circuits.

Jurisdiction and Venue

The term *jurisdiction* refers to the scope of power granted to a court or other governmental entity. There are many types of jurisdiction, which are discussed below. **Venue** refers to a specific place, court, or judge. Often, these terms are used interchangeably with somewhat confusing results. Venue rules govern where a trial may be held or what court may hear a case. The rules are usually predicated on either where one of the parties resides or where the event that is the subject of the case occurred. Although the U.S. Constitution does not use the term *venue*, it does say criminal trials must be held in the state where the crime occurred. If a crime did not occur entirely within one state, Congress may, by law, direct a location.[20]

When a defendant requests a change of venue, she or he is asking the court to move the location of the trial from the location or court where the case was originally filed to another court or another location. Usually, this is done in order that an impartial jury may be found to try the case.

Types of Jurisdiction

Venue refers to the court or judge who hears a case or to the location where the trial takes place. Jurisdiction is more complex. It may be useful to think of jurisdiction as the power or authority of a court to decide a case. If a court lacks jurisdiction, it lacks any power or authority to make a decision in a case. A lack of jurisdiction compels a court to transfer a case to another court with appropriate jurisdiction or, in some situations, to dismiss the case completely. Any decision a court makes without jurisdiction is void for lack of power or authority. Jurisdiction is one of the few matters that can be raised at any time during the trial or appeal of any case.

In order to try a case, a court must have jurisdiction over the subject matter of the trial and the parties involved and jurisdiction in the appropriate geographic area.

Subject Matter Jurisdiction

Subject matter jurisdiction can be subdivided into two types: general and special or limited jurisdiction. Courts of general jurisdiction may hear any type of case regardless of its subject matter and have the broadest powers. They typically hear and decide both criminal and civil cases. Courts of special or limited jurisdiction may hear and decide only those cases within the authority granted to them by constitution or law. Examples of courts of limited jurisdiction at the national level are the U.S. Bankruptcy Courts, the U.S. Court of International Trade, and the U.S. Tax Courts. State courts of limited jurisdiction include those that hear only juvenile matters, family law matters, county, and/or municipal courts.

Geographic Jurisdiction

The power or authority of a court will also be circumscribed by geographic jurisdiction. For example, the authority of each U.S. District Court is limited to the state or district where it is located. Except for bankruptcy and magistrate courts, the federal courts have general subject matter jurisdiction. However, they are all subject to the geographical limitations of the state or district they serve. Therefore, unless a change of venue has been granted, no court may hear any case in which the cause of action or subject matter of the case took place outside the district of that particular court.

Personal Jurisdiction

Restrictions also apply to a court's jurisdiction over the parties to a case. A defendant cannot be sued or prosecuted in just any court. He or she must have some legal connection to the geographic territory served by the specific court. In other words, the defendant must have engaged in some act or omission that can legally be said to have occurred within that court's geographical jurisdiction. This requirement for personal connection with the court's authority can be met if the defendant contracted to be amenable to suit within a court's boundaries. In addition, before a court has personal jurisdiction over anyone, that person must have been served with notice of the case. There are specific requirements for how such notice must be delivered or "served" on the defendant. Failing to meet any of these requirements means the court does not have personal jurisdiction and it, therefore, cannot render judgment against the defendant.

Federal Court Jurisdiction

There are only three types of federal court jurisdiction: (a) subject matter jurisdiction, (b) federal party jurisdiction, (c) diversity jurisdiction. In order to have a case brought in the U.S. federal court system, a party must present a situation that falls into one of these three categories. To meet the requirement for subject matter jurisdiction, the questions or issues raised in the case must involve the U.S. Constitution, a U.S. **treaty**, or a federal criminal or civil statute. In order to have federal party jurisdiction, a lawsuit or case must be either brought by or against the federal government, its agents, or officers. The third type of federal jurisdiction is based on diversity.

Diversity jurisdiction was established by Congress in 1789 because it recognized that state courts would be biased against citizens from other states or countries or would be biased in favor of their own citizens. Diversity jurisdiction has two requirements, both of which must be present in order for a case to be brought in federal court. The first requirement is based on the citizenship or domicile of the parties. To meet this requirement of diversity of citizenship, the parties to the court action must be from two or more states and/or countries. The second requirement is based on the amount in controversy. To meet this requirement, the amount of damages requested in the case must be at least $75,000.[21]

Original and Appellate Jurisdiction

The Constitution not only sets out the subject matter jurisdiction of the Supreme Court and inferior courts, it also describes original jurisdiction and appellate jurisdiction.[22] **Original jurisdiction** refers to a court's authority to accept initial filings or pleadings. Lawsuits or legal actions must begin in courts with original jurisdiction. These courts are called trial courts because they try cases and decide their outcome.

In the federal court system, the U.S. District Courts are usually the courts of original jurisdiction, which serve as the trial courts. The exceptions are cases involving foreign diplomats and cases wherein one of the 50 states is a party. In these two situations the U.S. Supreme Court exercises original jurisdiction.[23]

Appellate jurisdiction refers to the authority of a court to review decisions of the trial courts. Courts with appellate jurisdiction review lower court decisions to determine whether those decisions are in accordance with the U.S. Constitution, or whether the other applicable laws and rules were properly employed by the trial courts. There are two major functions of appellate courts: (a) to correct errors in the choice, interpretation, or application of the laws to individual litigants, and (b) to make the laws clearer and more consistent.[24]

Trial court orders are often written and lengthy documents. Frequently, they summarize the issues raised by the pleadings, the evidence presented at trial, the findings of fact, and the laws applied by the trial court to reach its decision. These written decisions are always sent to the attorneys and litigants in the case; however, state trial court decisions are not collected and published. In the federal court system, only some of the more important decisions made by the U.S. District Courts are collected and published. On the other hand, appellate decisions at both the state and federal court levels are, with some minor exceptions, collected and published so they may be used as precedents in the future. There are three major purposes for publication of appellate court opinions: (a) to justify the decision to the parties and any other audience, (b) to instruct the lower court on what it must do when reconsidering the case, and (c) to announce the rules of law that determined this decision. Subordinate courts are bound to follow the rule of law or holding in the future.[25]

Appellate jurisdiction is generally based on geography and sometimes the subject matter of the issues being raised on appeal. In the federal court system, appellate jurisdiction is set by Congress. Appellate jurisdiction in each state court system is governed by the appropriate state's constitution.

Appellate jurisdiction can be categorized as mandatory or discretionary. Mandatory jurisdiction over specific subjects or issues or from specific trial courts means the appellate court must hear those cases when they are appealed. If the appellate jurisdiction is discretionary, that means the court may choose whether or not to hear certain cases. This discretionary jurisdiction is exercised by means of an order or **writ of certiorari** issued to the lower court. In order to comply with a writ of certiorari, the lower court is required to certify its complete record of the case and deliver it to the appellate court for review.

Trial and appellate courts can also be categorized based on the number of decision makers at each level. In most trial courts, both in the state and federal systems, a single judge presides over a case. Usually, the judge sits as an impartial "referee" who is responsible for the atmosphere and decorum of the courtroom. The judge also makes decisions relating to motions and objections made by the litigants' attorneys, the choice of law, jury instructions, and the final sentence or judgment in the case. Because jury trials are relatively rare, these single trial court judges usually hear cases as both the trier of fact and the legal decision maker. The major exception to the single judge at the trial court level occurs in the federal court system when three-judge district courts are required to convene by law. These special courts hear three types of cases: (a) certain civil rights cases, (b) cases challenging drawing of legislative districts, and (c) challenges to the constitutionality of "must carry rules" regulating cable television.

Appellate court judges, on the other hand, generally sit in groups of three, five, seven, or nine. The number of judges depends on statute, location, and the type and importance of the case being heard. At the federal level, the number of judges available to sit in these smaller groups varies from 6 judges in the U.S. Court of Appeals for the First Circuit to 28 judges in the Ninth Circuit. The number of judges assigned is based on caseload. Regardless of the number of judges appointed in each circuit, the law provides that cases may be heard by separate three-judge panels, unless the rules of the circuit provide otherwise.[26] The U.S. Supreme Court determines its own rules for the number of justices hearing cases, depending on the type and subject matter of the case. Their panels can range from hearings by one justice to hearings *en banc* by all nine justices. The term *en banc* when used by either state or federal statute or court rules is derived from French meaning "in the bench" and refers to those cases where the entire membership of a court will sit to hear a case. Because of the case and workloads of the appellate courts, decisions to hear cases *en banc* are controlled by the rules of the court. Only cases that address important subjects or have significant precedential value are heard *en banc*.

The U.S. Court of Appeals has appellate jurisdiction over three kinds of cases: tax court appeals, appeals from orders of certain federal administrative agencies, and appeals from the federal district courts, except three-judge district court decisions. Decisions made by three-judge panels in the district courts may be appealed directly to the Supreme Court. The appellate jurisdiction of the U.S. Supreme Court is described in the Constitution.[27] Its review of lower court decisions is almost entirely determined by the court itself. Most cases heard by the high court must be granted permission by the Supreme Court through a writ of certiorari. For a case to move from the highest court of any state to the U.S. Supreme Court, it must present one of three kinds of issues. Such cases must involve interpretation of a provision of (a) the U.S. Constitution, (b) a U.S. treaty, or (c) a federal statute; and the Supreme Court must have granted certiorari.

Additional Types of Jurisdiction

There are two other terms used to describe jurisdiction in the federal and state courts. These concepts help determine whether state or federal courts have jurisdiction over a case. The two terms are federal law and police powers. Police **powers** refer generally to the power and authority retained by the states as sovereigns. This power and authority allows the states to determine their own laws in relation to the safety, health, and general welfare of their own citizens. These state powers include control of education, public safety, health, and welfare matters. **Federal law** refers to those situations where powers have been specifically vested in Congress by the U.S. Constitution[28] or that have been specifically prohibited to the states.[29] In these matters, the national government is said to have **exclusive jurisdiction** and "federal law" supercedes any state laws. There are also some areas involving the states' police powers, where they have exclusive jurisdiction. Examples of exclusive federal jurisdiction include matters of international trade and treaties; regulation of commerce; coining, regulating, and protecting the money supply; establishing and regulating postal service; declaration and financing of wars; establishing uniform rules of naturalization; and uniform laws on bankruptcy. Examples of exclusive state jurisdiction include the establishment and maintenance of systems of general public education; public hospital systems; laws and rules relating to obtaining drivers licenses and driving laws; liquor laws, following repeal of prohibition; laws and rules relating to marriage; and dissolution of marriages, child custody, and distribution of property rights.

Concurrent jurisdiction refers to those subjects and laws wherein both the national government and state governments may exercise simultaneous power to enact and enforce laws. These include pornography, obscenity, indecency, and numerous criminal laws. Prior to the Copyright Act of 1976, both the states and federal government exercised concurrent jurisdiction for the protection of original works of authorship, even though the U.S. Constitution grants power to Congress "(T)o promote the Progress of Science and useful Arts, by securing for limited Times to Authors and Inventors the exclusive Right to their respective Writings and Discoveries. . ."[30] Through the use of common law precedents and statutes, states also attempted to protect rights of original authors and creators of artistic expressions. However, Congress took exclusive jurisdiction and control of copyright matters through the Copyright Act of 1976, effectively preempting all state laws on the subject. There are many situations in which both federal and state laws overlap. Under these circumstances, one individual or group engaging in an activity prohibited by both state and federal law could be prosecuted in either state or federal courts or both. The conspiracy and bombing of the Murrah Federal Building in Oklahoma City by Timothy McVey and Terry Nichols in 1995 is one such example.

Legal Hierarchy and Authorities

Judicial Hierarchy

It may help you understand judicial hierarchy under Articles III and VI, and Amendment X of the U.S. Constitution to think of the courts in this order of significance: (a) the U.S. Supreme Court; (b) the supreme courts of the 50 states; (c) the U.S. Circuit Courts of Appeal; (d) the various courts of appeal for the 50 states; (e) the U.S. District Courts; and (f) the various trial courts and trial levels within the various state court systems. Decisions of courts near the top of this order have greater legal authority than do decisions by lower courts.

Legal Authority

In addition to the "level" of the court, four concepts help determine whether a statement in a court's decision creates a precedent that must be followed in the future. These concepts are mandatory authority, persuasive authority, primary authority, and secondary authority.

Mandatory authority means that a case being cited is dispositive on an issue before a court. Mandatory authority is a statement of law or a holding from a superior court speaking on the same issue. Faced with mandatory authority, lower courts have no discretion at all; they must follow the legal precedent.

It is important to note that mandatory authority "flows" within a single judicial system. For example, for the state trial courts in New York, appellate decisions from the New York courts are mandatory authority. Decisions from an appellate court, or even the supreme court, of another state are not mandatory authority. In both the state and the national court systems, decisions from the appropriate supreme court are mandatory authority over all intermediate courts of appeals and trial courts.

Persuasive authority refers to decisions on points of law from a court on the same level in the hierarchy or from another jurisdiction. Persuasive authority is used only when no higher level court has spoken on the issue.

Primary authority means the law being cited or used to decide a case comes from one or more of the four sources of law: (a) constitutions, (b) statutes, (c) treaties, or (d) case law. In this context, case law includes interpretations, judicial review, and common law precedent.

Secondary authority means the source being cited has persuasive value only and comes from something other than one of the four sources of law. Secondary authority can include such things as learned books and treatises on legal topics, law review articles, or even scholarly studies from outside the legal community. These sources are used only when there is no primary or mandatory authority on point.

Types of Opinions and Their Authority

Because the majority of cases we discuss in this textbook come from the U.S. Supreme Court, it is important to understand how the judgments of that court are reported. The U.S. Supreme Court uses several terms to identify its judgments and the actual disposition of appellate cases, terms usually found at the end of the written opinion of the court. They are almost the very last word or words used by the appellate court in its judgment. In this context, it may be helpful to note that the opinion of the court is reported before any concurring or dissenting opinions. These terms always refer to the decision or judgment of the lower trial or appellate court from whom either certiorari or mandatory appeal was taken and they describe how the lower court's decision is to be treated.

There are five terms used to indicate the legal result of the appeal. The appellate court can **uphold** or **affirm** the lower court decision. It can **reverse** the lower court's decision. Reverse means to overturn the lower court completely. The appellate court can **modify** the lower court's decision by affirming in part and reversing in part; and it can **remand** the case by sending it back to the lower court for further consideration or action. A case is usually remanded with instructions to conduct a new trial or hearing. The appellate court can also **vacate** or totally void a lower court's decision. When the appellate court vacates the lower court's ruling, it dismisses the case completely and nullifies all actions and orders of the lower court. In such a situation, for example, an injunction granted by the lower court would be unenforceable. Often, the terms *reversed* and *remanded* are used together with specific instructions to the lower court about what it must do to correct its errors. Specific instructions are also used when an appellate court modifies or affirms in part and reverses in part the lower court's decision. Often the terms *modify* or *modifies* are not used at all in this context.

Types of U.S. Supreme Court Opinions

While the decisions of the U.S. Supreme Court are mandatory authority over all lower courts, gradations or variations in weight are ascribed to these decisions. The major factor that determines the precedential authority of U.S. Supreme Court decisions is whether a majority of the justices concur with both the holding and the judgment.

Prior to the term of Chief Justice John Marshall, which began in 1801, the High Court delivered seriatim opinions. In a seriatim opinion each justice, in sequence, gave his or her own views on a case and its outcome. Justice Marshall, who was a federalist, initiated the practice of disposing of Supreme Court cases with a single written opinion representing the views of the entire Court. He thought such an opinion would give greater credence and power to the Court as it spoke with one voice, and would minimize the potential for misunderstanding of the Court's decision and reasons. Recently, appointments to the Supreme Court have been politicized. Justices have been appointed by presidents with the specific intention that they will rule consistently with the political or social philosophies of the chief executive who appointed them. Therefore, it has become politically important for justices to indicate when they do not agree with the majority view of the Court. The result of these political influences was the creation of several different types of Supreme Court opinions. Terms used to label Supreme Court opinions include unanimous opinion, majority opinion, dissenting opinion, per curiam opinion, plurality opinion, and concurring opinion.

A **unanimous opinion** is one in which all justices agree on the result, the judgment, and the reasoning. Reasoning is the choice, interpretation, and application of law to the issues in the case. A **majority opinion** is one in which at least five of the nine justices agree on the judgment and the reasoning. When a unanimous or majority opinion is written, one of the justices who most supported the opinion will be assigned to write the opinion and the case will begin with: "J. ——————— delivered the Opinion of the Court." However, following a majority opinion, there will be at least one written **dissenting opinion** in which one justice, who disagreed both with the judgment and with the reasoning in the case, will state his or her reasons for opposing the majority opinion. A **per curiam opinion** is unsigned and signifies either the decision is obvious and no explanation is needed, or the Court is so split over the choice, interpretation, and application of the law they could agree on the result only. It is important to note that in a per curiam decision, the justices do agree on the result or judgment. They simply may not be able to agree on the legal reasoning that supports the judgment. A **plurality opinion** occurs when fewer than a majority subscribe to both the judgment and reasoning in a case. The judgment in a plurality opinion must then be supported by one or more **concurring opinions**, which must agree on the judgment. The concurring opinions may have totally different or additional reasoning to support the judgment.

Per curiam opinions of the second type mentioned and plurality opinions are not supported by the majority of justices. Therefore, they do NOT bind the Court as a statement of policy, constitutional interpretation, or common law. Furthermore, such decisions are NOT mandatory authority on the lower courts and they do not serve as precedent. They are persuasive authority only and usually are used only to guide decisions in that specific case or situation. Per curiam decisions are specifically labeled. Several concurring and dissenting opinions will follow plurality opinions. In some of the more recent cases, it almost appears the Court is returning to the days of seriatim opinions, with concomitant loss of directive power and prestige on the lower courts.[31] On the other hand, majority opinions, regardless of the vote count, are mandatory authority and do bind the courts as policy, constitutional interpretation, and common law.

Rules of Justiciability

Over time, the U.S. Supreme Court has developed special rules of justiciability. These rules are often based on political pressures and are sometimes based upon the need to curtail its own workload. **Rules of justiciability** are used to guide the Court and others to determine whether a case is amenable to judicial decision and if it is in the proper forum. There are six major rules of justiciability. Each one imposes some limit on what cases may be heard by the federal courts. The six rules are labeled case and controversy, mootness, ripeness, standing, political questions, and the abstention doctrine.[32]

The rule that the Court will not make decisions based on hypothetical situations nor give "advisory opinions" is called the **case and controversy rule**. The federal courts will not hear cases or decide issues unless they are between real litigants with a legal cause of action.

With some rare exceptions, the federal courts will not hear cases that are moot. **Mootness** has to do with whether the dispute or controversy has already reached a final determination and is no longer subject to resolution by any court. For example, prior to

Roe v. Wade,[33] federal courts had often refused to rule on abortion challenges because by the time the issue came to court more than the 9-month human gestation period had elapsed. The issue was moot because the plaintiff had either obtained an abortion or the pregnancy had gone to term.

The Court will also not take cases where the controversy has not become ripe. A case is not ripe if the issues in the case have not yet come to a legal impasse. The concept of **ripeness** thus is the opposite of mootness. A case is not ripe if the parties still have opportunities, outside of the courts, to resolve their dispute. For example, in some situations, the Court has refused to take cases challenging the constitutionality of a federal statute because the statute was not yet in effect, because the attorney general had not yet used the statute to charge anyone, or because no violation of the statute had yet occurred.

The federal courts will not take cases where any of the named parties has not been harmed or does not have a personal stake in its outcome. This concept is called **standing** to sue. Historically, for example, the Courts refused to take cases brought by groups such as the Sierra Club who sought to protect the national forests and national parks from logging or other encroachment. The Courts ruled the members of the organization did not and could not personally own these public lands and therefore they were not personally injured by the actions they sought to challenge. Eventually, the Court did change its reasoning and granted standing to groups like the Sierra Club. Standing, in this instance, was based on the members of the organization losing their ability to hike or camp in the parks or view them in pristine, undefiled condition.

Cases covered by the **political questions** rule, more than any others, present perplexing problems for the federal courts. The rule helps sort out the division of powers among the three branches of government. It is also used to protect the Courts' authority and prestige when they will not be able to enforce their decisions because they must rely on the executive branch and willingness of The People to abide by its decisions. The three categories of cases covered by the political questions rule are textual commitment of the issue to another branch of government, lack of judicial standards, and judicial imprudence.

Textual commitment of the issue to another branch of government simply means that the case under consideration presents an issue that is assigned by law or constitution to one of the other three branches of government.[34] **Lack of judicially manageable standards** means that there is no existing rule or standard by which the Court can resolve the dispute presented to it.[35] A number of factors guide the Court's determination of what makes a matter **judicially imprudent**. Colloquially put, judicially imprudent means the question presents a political "hot potato" the Court would rather avoid.[36] The sixth rule of justiciability developed by the U.S. Supreme Court is called the **abstention doctrine**. This rule might also be called the federalism rule because it has been used when appeals were made from the highest state court, and when a litigant is seeking review of the state court's decision by the U.S. Supreme Court. As we have seen previously in this chapter, there are only three possible ways to enter the federal courts. For a case to be heard in the federal courts, it must (a) present a claim based on a provision of the U.S. Constitution, a U.S. treaty, or a federal statute, (b) involve the national government or one of its agents or officers as a party, or (c) involve diversity of citizenship.

Where only a state question is presented in a case that involves only interpretation of a state's constitution or statutes, the decision of the state's highest court is usually final and review by the U.S. Supreme Court is precluded. In these situations, the U.S. Supreme Court abstains from granting certiorari. An exception to the abstention doctrine is made when a case in which a decision made by a state supreme court involves both state and federal questions. In such cases, the U.S. Supreme Court will accept the state court's findings regarding its own constitution and laws, but it will address issues that involve the U.S. Constitution, treaties, or statutes.

Magic Words and Phrases

Abstention doctrine	Justiciability
Affirm	Major courts
Appeals *de novo*	Majority opinion
Appellate judgments/dispositions	Mandatory authority
Appellate jurisdiction	Mandatory jurisdiction
Authority	Minor courts
Bifurcated supreme courts	Modify
Case and controversy	Mootness
Case law	National/federal court system
Codes	Ordinances
Common law	Original jurisdiction
Concurrent jurisdiction	Per curiam opinion
Concurring opinion	Personal jurisdiction
Consolidated court system	Persuasive authority
Constitution	Plurality opinion
Discretionary jurisdiction	Police powers
Dissenting opinion	Political question
Diversity jurisdiction	Power
Equitable remedies	Precedent
Equity	Primary authority
Exclusive jurisdiction	Regulations
Extra-judicial tribunals	Remand
Federal democratic republic	Reverse
Federal governmental system	Ripeness
Fragmented court system	Rules
General jurisdiction	Secondary authority
Intermediate appellate courts	Seriatim opinion
Judicial review	Sovereignty
Jurisdiction	Special or limited jurisdiction

Standing	Treaty
Stare decisis	Unanimous opinion
State court systems	Unified court system
Statute	Unitary governmental system
Statutory interpretation	Vacate
Subject matter jurisdiction	Writ of certiorari
Supremacy clause	

Suggested Cases to Read and Brief

Marbury v. Madison, 5 U.S. (1 Cranch) 137 (1803)
Ashwander v. Tennessee Valley Authority, 297 U.S. 288 (1937)
Colegrove v. Green, 328 U.S. 549 (1946)
Baker v. Carr, 369 U.S. 186 (1962)
Powell v. McCormack, 395 U.S. 486 (1969)
Roe v. Wade, 410 U.S. 113 (1973)
Holtzman v. Schlessinger, 484 F.2d 1307 (2d Cir.1973)
De Funis v. Odegaard, 416 U.S. 312 (1974)
Goldwater v. Carter, 444 U.S. 996 (1979)
Bush v. Gore, 531 U.S. 98 (2000)

Questions for Discussion

1. Why is it important for a mass communications practitioner to understand the distinctions between code law and common law legal systems? What consequences can the international practitioner expect if she or he ignores these differences?

2. Why are the provisions of Article VI, Clause 2 and 3 together with the Amendments IX and X of the U.S. Constitution so vital to the U.S. federal democratic republican system of governance? Why would these provisions be important in understanding the concepts of federal preemption, exclusive, and concurrent jurisdiction?

3. Why is it important to clearly understand the subordinate position of administrative rules, regulations, and the quasi-judicial boards and commissions that administer them? What is their relation to the four sources of law and the judicial systems of both the national and state governments?

4. What are the basic differences between "constitutional" and "legislative" courts? Why did the framers of the U.S. Constitution believe it was so important to grant lifetime tenure to federal judges and justices appointed to administer the "constitutional" courts? What kinds of problems might result if such officials were elected to serve for only 4- or 6-year terms?

5. List and define all the different types of jurisdiction you can, discuss why each is important and whether a different terminology might be developed to distinguish each.

6. Discuss the limited jurisdiction given by Congress to the three-judge district courts and how the three types of cases within their purview relate to each other in importance or to the administration of justice and U.S. public policy.

7. Discuss the components of the judicial hierarchy in relation to mandatory and persuasive authority. Relate these concepts to the types of Supreme Court opinions and the problems that are created when the Court renders less than a majority opinion on a question of national importance.

8. Discuss the concepts of fragmented, consolidated, and unified court systems. How is your state's court system composed? Who is actually served best by each of these systems?

Notes

1. *Marbury v. Madison*, 5 U.S. (1 Cranch) 137 (1803).
2. STEFFEN W. SCHMIDT, MARK C. SHELLY & BARBARA A. BARDES, AMERICAN GOVERNMENT AND POLITICS TODAY 87 (2001-2002 ed., Wadsworth/Thompson Learning 2001).
3. U.S. CONST. amends. IX & X.
4. U.S. CONST. amends. IX & X.
5. U.S. CONST. pmbl.
6. U.S. CONST. art. I, § 1.
7. U.S. CONST. art. II, § 1.
8. U.S. CONST. art. III, § 1.
9. U.S. CONST. art. VI, cl. 2.
10. U.S. CONST. art. VI, cl. 3.
11. James T. McHugh, *Dominant Ideology of the Louisiana Constitution*, 59 ALB. L. REV. 1679 (1996).
12. *Marbury v Madison*, 5 U.S. (1 Cranch) 137 (1803).
13. See, MYRON G. HILL, JR., HOWARD M. ROSSEN & WILTON S. SOGG SMITH'S REVIEW: REMEDIES EQUITY, DAMAGES, RESTITUTION (West Pub. Co. 1974).
14. U.S. CONST. art. I § 10 & amend. X.
15. U.S. CONST. art. III, § 1.
16. U.S. CONST. art I, § 8, cl. 9.
17. U.S. CONST. art II, § 2. cl. 2.
18. U.S. CONST. art III, § 2 cl. 2.
19. U.S. CONST. art. III, § 2, cl 2.
20. U.S. CONST. art III, § 2, cl. 3 & amend. VI.
21. This amount has been changed by Congress several times and is subject to being modified in the future.
22. U.S. CONST. art III § 2, cl. 2.
23. U.S. CONST. art III § 2, cl. 2.
24. FEDERAL JUDICIAL CENTER, STRUCTURAL AND OTHER ALTERNATIVES FOR THE FEDERAL COURTS OF APPEALS 7-9 (1993).
25. LAWRENCE BAUM, AMERICAN COURTS: PROCESS AND POLICY 270 (4th ed 1998).
26. 28 U.S.C § 46 (2003).
27. U.S. CONST. art III, § 2.
28. U.S. CONST. art. I, § 8.

29. U.S. Const. art. I, § 10.
30. U.S. Const. art. I, § 8, cl. 8.
31. See, Craig R. ducat; Constitutional Interpretation 36-37 (7th ed., Wadsworth/Thompson Learning, Inc. 2000).
32. For a summary of these general rules of engagement by Justice Brandeis, see *Ashwander v. Tennessee Valley Authority*, 297 U.S. 288 (1937); Also see *Marbury v. Madison*, 5 U.S. (1 Cranch) 137 (1803), for Justice John Marshall's original views on judicial review and justiciability issues.
33. *Roe v. Wade*, 410 U.S. 113 (1973).
34. See, e.g., *Powell v. McCormack*, 395 U.S. 486 (1969), addressing the power of the House of Representatives to expel but not to exclude a duly elected member; but see *Bush v. Gore*, 531 U.S. 98 (2000), wherein the Supreme Court, not the House of Representatives, decided the 2000 presidential election.
35. See, *Colegrove v. Green*, 328 U.S. 549 (1946); but see, *Baker v. Carr*, 369 U.S. 186 (1962), regarding whether malapportionment violated the guarantee of U.S. CONST. art. IV, § 4 which states: "(t)he United States shall guarantee to every State in this Union a Republican Form of Government."
36. See, e.g., *Holtzman v. Schlessinger*, 484 F.2d 1307 (2d Cir. 1973), regarding use of Congressional appropriations, in violation of the War-Force Military Procurement Act of 1971, to provide military support and assistance to the governments of Cambodia and Laos; and *Goldwater v. Carter*, 444 U.S. 996 (1979), regarding the constitutionality of President Carter's unilateral action in notification of termination of military defense treaty with Taiwan in preparation for normalization of diplomatic relations with the People's Republic of China.

2

Legal Procedure

No person shall be . . . deprived of life, liberty, or property, without due process of law . . .[1]

Overview
Categories of Law and Judicial Procedure
Criminal Procedure
Juvenile Procedure
Civil Procedure
Appellate Procedure

Overview

In chapter 1 we described governmental and legal structures and provided some terms to help you understand the court structure and function. In this chapter, we begin an explanation of how courts really work. We summarize procedures used in criminal, juvenile, civil, and appellate courts.

Legal procedure is not intuitive. It requires significant study to be able to understand and describe the workings of the justice system. In this chapter we hope to provide enough background that you may understand and accurately describe the working of the judicial system. Like the information from chapter 1, this information will help you understand and apply the laws described in the remainder of this text. It will also help you accurately describe court actions you may be required to report.

Judicial procedure is particularly important for mass communications professionals who are often called on to report and interpret trial events and to describe court decisions. As practitioners, we do not perform those tasks well. We hope a careful reading of this chapter allows you to avoid some of the more common mistakes made by others.

Categories of Law and Judicial Procedure

Laws can be categorized as either substantive or procedural. **Substantive laws** are principles for acceptable behavior. They describe the kinds of actions or omissions that are permitted or prohibited. They also describe the punishments that may be imposed for their violation. **Procedural laws** set out the legal rules for determining when and how the substantive laws will be applied. A statute proscribing murder and setting the penalty for murder is an example of substantive law. Procedural laws describe how a person accused of murder is to be treated by the government. They also establish the process for determining whether such a person can be legally held accountable and punished for that crime. In other words, procedural law sets the rules for trials and for appeals.

Procedural law varies depending on the kind of case that is being considered. Of course, procedural law is not identical in every state or jurisdiction. In order to provide a general understanding of how the courts work, we divide legal procedure simply into four major groups: criminal, juvenile, civil, and appellate procedure. The history and characteristics of criminal, juvenile, and civil law are summarized in Exhibit 2.1.

Criminal laws are those substantive laws that are thought to be so important to the maintenance of a stable society that their violation carries serious penalties. Criminal laws are prosecuted in the name of the sovereign, either in the name of the people of the United States or in the name of the people of one of the 50 states. The United States or the individual state is the complainant and the person accused of a crime is the defendant. The government prosecutor has the burden of proof in a criminal case and must show the defendant is guilty **beyond a reasonable doubt**.

Civil laws were developed as part of the common law in England and have evolved through both common law and statute in the United States. Civil laws are enforced through lawsuits brought by a private individual against another private individual. In this context, corporations and some other business entities are "private individuals." The person who initiates the suit is known as the plaintiff and the person against whom the suit is brought is called the defendant or respondent. The burden of proof in a civil case is on the plaintiff, who must prove the elements of his or her case by **a preponderance of the evidence**.

Juvenile laws are a relatively modern legal phenomenon. They relate to the treatment of people under the age of 18 who have committed criminal or antisocial acts, or who are themselves the victims of abuse or neglect. Under British common law, young people were treated just like adults and there is no mention of the rights of young people in the U.S. Constitution. Until the State of Illinois adopted the first juvenile laws in the United States in 1899, typically children either fell directly in the adult legal system or were treated as the property or responsibility of their parents.[2] Occasionally, this resulted in such apparent mistreatment of children that benevolent societies were formed to challenge the judicial treatment of minors. Some of the earliest juvenile laws were actually modeled on laws initiated by the Society for the Prevention of Cruelty to Animals. Contemporary juvenile laws vary from jurisdiction to jurisdiction, but most combine aspects of both civil and criminal law. In some states, principles from sociology, counseling, and education are also applied in juvenile procedure. Juvenile law covers acts of delinquency, status offenses, and child welfare actions. It also involves unusual procedures that are neither

Exhibit 2.1. Summary of Legal Systems

	Criminal	Civil	Juvenile
History	King, lords, and parliament	King, chancellor, and church	SPCA and benevolent societies
Source/authority	Statute	Common law	Statute
Parties	State vs. private	Private vs. private	State as parens patriae
Required proof	Beyond a reasonable doubt	Preponderance of the evidence	Juvenile delinquency—beyond reasonable doubt. To remove from parents—preponderance of evidence and best interest of child
Remedies	Fines, loss of liberty, execution	Money, or equitable remedy	Treatment preferred. Incarceration to age 21 possible. Certification to adult court depends on age and violence.
Jury option	Defendant's choice	Either party can request	If certified as adult, defendant's choice. Otherwise no.

purely criminal nor purely civil. Because of this mixture of purposes and practices, we treat juvenile procedure separately from criminal or civil procedure.

In virtually all legal matters, there is some system for appealing a court's decision. After addressing criminal, juvenile, and civil procedure we describe appellate procedure and provide some additional information on the role of appellate courts and explain how decisions are made on appeal.

Criminal Procedure

Many states and the federal government use four categories of crime. The categorization of a specific crime depends on the state legislature's judgment of the seriousness of the offense and the type of punishment that should be imposed for violations. Anyone responsible for reporting on crime should be familiar with the categories in his or her jurisdiction. The four general categories are felonies, misdemeanors, petty offenses, and juvenile offenses. Because we address juvenile procedure separately, here we only explain the first three.

Felonies are the most serious category of crimes. Felony violations usually carry both heavy fines and significant incarceration. Felony fines generally range from

$2,000 to more than $10,000. Convicted felons are usually incarcerated in state or federal prisons for 3 years to life. In some jurisdictions, capital punishment can also be imposed for some felony violations. Felonies are often classified according to their severity with a number or letter. In most jurisdictions the lesser crimes have the highest numbers. For example, a Class 4 felony is not as serious an offense as is a Class 2 felony. Many jurisdictions add a letter designation, such as "Class X" felony, for the most serious offenses.

Misdemeanors are less offensive crimes. Violation of laws that have been classified by statute as misdemeanors often carry fines of $1,000 or less and/or incarceration for less than 1 year. Incarceration for misdemeanor offenses is usually served in a county or municipal jail, rather than in a state or federal prison.

The classification of **petty offense** is used by some jurisdictions for those crimes that are considered minimal. For example, Illinois classifies minor driving offenses such as speeding, improper lane use, and municipal code or county ordinance violations as petty offenses. Petty offenses are punished by fine only and the fines usually are less than $500. However, some states, as well as the federal government, have placed violations of industrial, corporate, and business regulations in this category. In some instances, fines of $10,000 per violation are possible and each day's violation may be defined as a new violation. Under these circumstances, petty offense fines can be substantial. Some jurisdictions do not use the category of petty offense at all. In those jurisdictions, all crimes are either felonies or misdemeanors.

Pretrial Procedure

Before anyone charged with a crime goes to trial there are several steps of procedural law. These involve investigation, arrest, charging the defendant, and the pleadings that precede trial. Here we omit the investigation and only briefly describe arrest requirements. The judicial procedures of charging the defendant and the pleadings are covered in some detail because these are often the subjects of media coverage and litigation public relations. We include a description of negotiated disposition, sometimes called "plea bargaining," because this process disposes of the vast majority of criminal charges.

Charge Documents

Before a defendant enters the criminal judicial process he or she must be charged with a crime. There are three ways a defendant can be charged: (a) warrantless arrest followed by formal charges, (b) indictment by grand jury, or (c) a prosecutor's information or criminal complaint. In some states, all felonies must be charged by a grand jury and in most states, and in the federal system the most serious crimes are charged by a grand jury.

Warrantless Arrest.   It is important to note the tremendous amount of discretion given to government officials to determine who is brought into the criminal justice system. Law enforcement officials, often, but not always, with the full knowledge and advice of the local prosecutor, decide who will be arrested without a warrant. These individuals may be charged based on the resulting police reports. Arrests that precede such court actions are called **warrantless** arrests. As might be expected, these decisions are often based on things other than whether an individual is actually guilty of committing a crime. Factors determining whether a person is arrested and submitted to the criminal process or is released without any charges at all, are often totally subjective. These factors include, but are not limited to, the officers' on-the-spot perceptions and conclusions about the individual such as demeanor, social class and status, race, gender, age, and past experience with the police. Also, an individual's physical appearance, clothing, neatness, and hygiene are significant predictors of police treatment. Therefore, no one should assume just because a person has been arrested and charged with a crime that she or he is guilty of any illegal conduct.

When a person has been arrested without a warrant, the prosecutor must review the police report and make a decision whether to charge the individual. Usually, this decision must be made within 48 hours. The suspect must then be brought before the nearest magistrate and informed of the pending charges.

Grand Jury Process.   According to the U.S. Constitution "(n)o person shall be held to answer for a capital, or otherwise infamous crime, unless on a presentment or indictment of a Grand Jury."[3] Use of a grand jury to initiate criminal charges against a person is part of the common law system inherited from England. It has been adapted for use in the United States. Depending on the laws of the specific jurisdiction, a **grand jury** may consist of from 1 to more than 30 people who are called by the prosecutor to conduct an official investigation into the commission of crimes. Although in some jurisdictions, justices of the peace and magistrates conduct these proceedings, in most jurisdictions a judge will give the group its official duties and swear the individual members in as part of the panel. The judge rarely has any other official duties except to excuse or disband the group officially when the task is completed. Grand juries are summoned and authorized to conduct investigations over a specified period of time. At the end of its term, a grand jury is disbanded and a new group is sworn in to continue the process. In smaller jurisdictions, where serious crimes rarely occur, grand juries are summoned and convened only when needed. Grand jury members must be paid for their services, but the amount is usually very modest and often only covers or includes meals. Despite the low pay, the process can be expensive.

Unlike trial juries, grand juries are not chosen to be impartial. They are an investigative arm of the prosecution. Prosecutors either subpoena or recommend witnesses to the grand jury and only the prosecutor questions the witnesses who appear. Usually, only those individuals believed to have information about the commission of a crime, including the accused, are called to testify. However, in some jurisdictions, grand juries have been allowed to probe into collateral and tangential matters and some grand juries have been charged with overreaching or corruption for unjustified inquisition into private matters.

Individuals commanded to appear before grand juries by properly served subpoenas must comply or face arrest and contempt charges. Grand jury witnesses may hire an attorney to consult during their testimony. However, private attorneys are not permitted to ask questions or participate in the grand jury inquiry. They may also be required to sit outside the grand jury room. Under these circumstances, their client must ask to consult with the attorney prior to answering suspect or potentially incriminating questions. Witnesses before a grand jury are permitted to use their Fifth Amendment right not to answer any question that might incriminate them.

After the prosecutor has completed his or her presentation before the grand jury, the group convenes in sequestered chambers to decide whether there is sufficient evidence to **indict** or bring criminal charges. The prosecutor will have typically given the grand jury his or her recommendations and the statutory names of the crimes for which **indictments** are requested. The grand jury must decide if it agrees with the prosecutor's request. If the grand jury does find sufficient probable cause against an individual, it returns what is called a **True Bill of Indictment** or a **Bill of Indictment**. Of course, a group of laymen who have only seen witnesses called by the prosecutor typically comply with the prosecutor's recommendations. If insufficient information has been presented to convince the grand jury of probable cause a **No Bill of Indictment** is signed by the members and returned to the prosecutor or supervising judge. A No Bill is **sealed**. Mass communications practitioners should note that grand jury investigations and deliberations are totally secret so that only a **True Bill of Indictment**, which serves as the charge document against defendants in criminal cases, will be filed and made public in court records.

Prosecutor's Information or Complaint.   Although a grand jury indictment is required to bring capital and serious federal criminal charges, that requirement is not imposed on the individual states.[4] In many states, a prosecutor may initiate a criminal charge with a document called a "prosecutor's information" or a "criminal complaint." The title used for the document depends on the jurisdiction and is set by state constitution or statute. Some states still require all serious felonies to be brought by grand jury indictment, whereas others allow either grand jury indictment or criminal complaint, depending on administrative convenience and the prosecutor's need for an investigation using the subpoena power of a grand jury.

While the types of charge documents available to a prosecutor depend entirely on the state's constitution and laws, a prosecutor's information or criminal complaint routinely requires some form of "probable cause hearing" before an impartial judge. Usually called a **preliminary hearing**, this judicial procedure allows an unbiased determination by a detached magistrate who listens to a summary of the state's investigation presented by the prosecutor in the presence of the criminal defendant and his or her attorney. At the conclusion of this hearing, the judge will decide whether or not there is probable cause to believe a crime has been committed and whether the defendant should be held accountable. If the judge decides the defendant should be tried, the defendant is then arraigned on the "prosecutor's information" or "criminal complaint" and is bound over for trial. There are significant differences between jurisdictions regarding requirement and format for the presentation of evidence at a preliminary hearing. Because of the variations in format and evidence, some of these hearings are presumed open and others are closed to the public. These differences and distinctions made by the U.S.

Supreme Court will be discussed in chapter 7 when we address media access to the judicial process.

After an individual is charged with a crime there are still several steps that must be completed prior to trial. The names given these steps and the order in which they are completed may vary from jurisdiction to jurisdiction.

First Appearance

One of the first formal hearings in a criminal case is the **initial appearance** or **first appearance**. At this hearing, the accused is given a written copy of the charges and the court determines whether the accused can hire a lawyer or will need a court-appointed attorney. If the person is still incarcerated, a second appearance or re-appearance will be scheduled quickly. Between the first and second appearance, the accused is given an opportunity to retain counsel. If the accused is indigent, the court typically appoints counsel at the first appearance. At the second appearance, there will generally be a bond hearing to determine flight and public safety risks posed by the accused and to set or deny bond. If bond had already been set by automatic statutory provision or on the arrest warrant, there may be a bond reduction request by the defendant.

Regardless of how criminal charges were brought, most people accused of crimes are permitted to post bond so they may remain free until their trial.[5] For some offenses, bond will be set by statute or the judge may set bond either at a hearing or at the time he or she signs an arrest warrant. Bond either may not be an option or it may be very high, depending on the seriousness of the offense charged and the likelihood the suspect will commit future crimes while released on bond. For cases involving extremely dangerous suspects likely to pose substantial public safety risks, a bond hearing will be set quickly to allow the suspect an opportunity to get an attorney and to permit the prosecutor time to obtain an indictment or further information on the accused.

Arraignment and Plea

The next stage of the criminal process will be for the court to hold an arraignment of the accused. The **arraignment** is a formal reading of the grand jury indictment or prosecutor's complaint. An arraignment always includes a discussion by the judge of the sentencing options for each charged crime and a statement of the defendant's rights in relation to trial. At this time, the defendant is asked to respond with a plea. A **plea** is the defendant's formal legal response to the charges. These are entered on the record.

Plea.   Pleas generally come in one of three forms: depending on the jurisdiction, the defendant may enter a plea of not guilty, nolo contendere, or guilty. If the defendant enters a plea of **not guilty**, the criminal justice process continues. If the defendant enters a plea of **nolo contendere** it means that for this case only, she or he is pleading "no contest" in relation to the charges and the specific facts alleged. A plea of nolo contendere is not an admission of guilt, so it cannot be used against the defendant in any civil case based on the same circumstances. Some states do not permit this plea, but may allow an accused to submit to a **stipulated bench trial** at which his or her attorney will stipulate on the defendant's behalf to the facts alleged for the purposes of obtaining a negotiated disposition of the criminal case. This too is not an admission of guilt and will preserve the defendant's right to contest the facts in any civil suit. If the defendant pleads **guilty**, a trial is not necessary and the judge moves directly to sentencing or any required presentence investigation.

Plea Negotiations.   Many people are amazed to learn that in both federal and state courts 92% to 95% of all criminal convictions result because the defendant pled guilty to obtain a plea bargain.[6] A **plea bargain** is an agreement made between the prosecutor and a defendant. In such agreements, the defendant pleads or stipulates to the facts of the criminal case and the prosecutor agrees to recommend a specific sentence. Sometimes, this agreement includes the reduction of charges to less serious offenses or the dropping of some charges. The prosecutor is always in command of this situation, and his or her decisions are totally discretionary. It is up to the defendant to decide, based on the advice of his or her attorney, whether to accept the plea bargain or to take a chance with a trial.

Once a defendant accepts a plea bargain, there are several ways this may be presented to the court. Often, the plea agreement is presented at the **arraignment** stage discussed earlier. Sometimes both sides wait to review evidence before agreeing to a plea bargain. However, it is up to the judge to approve the terms and conditions of the plea bargain and to enter his or her findings on the record. The judge's findings are based on the nature of the charges, the facts, the defendant's criminal history, the type of victimization, the danger to the community posed by the defendant, and the usual range of sentences for the crime involved. Media, community, and political pressure also influence judges' responses to proposed plea bargains. Judges in most jurisdictions automatically accept a prosecutor's recommended sentence unless some exceptional circumstances are presented by the case. However, in order not to surprise a judge and to avoid unexpected difficulties, foresighted prosecutors and defense attorneys will have had a meeting in chambers with the judge to discuss sentencing recommendations prior to presenting them in open court.

Some judges, as a matter of general practice, and others on special occasion, will mention their own range of routine sentences at the defendant's arraignment. This is done as an implicit offer to the defendant to plead guilty and save the rigor, expense, and inconvenience of a public trial. Sometimes, there even will be an explicit or implied threat that if the defendant proceeds to trial, the judge would have no trouble imposing the maximum sentence allowable by law, but would be willing to impose a significantly reduced sentence on a plea of guilty.

There are opportunities for plea negotiations much later in the criminal process. In most jurisdictions, the defendant has an option to plead guilty up to the time he or she begins to present a defense at trial. This means it is possible for a defendant to go to trial, wait to see what happens during the testimony and cross-examination of prosecution witnesses, and then make a decision to accept a plea bargain. However, this process depends entirely on the prosecutor's discretion.

Exhibit 2.2.   Funnel Effect. (See, LAWRENCE BAUM, AMERICAN COURTS: PROCESS AND POLICY 174 [4th ed. Houghton Mifflin Co. 1998]; THOMAS R. DYE, UNDERSTANDING PUBLIC POLICY 63–64 [10th ed. Pearson Education, Inc. 2002].)

For every 1,000 crimes committed	
Number reported	350
Number arrested	70
Number charged	35
Number sentenced	10.5
Number whose sentence is result of trial conviction	Less than 1

Funnel Effect.   Very few crimes actually result in jail sentences for the perpetrators. Out of every 1,000 crimes committed, only 35% are actually reported. Of the crimes reported, 20% are actually cleared by arrest. Of the crimes in which an identified individual is arrested, 50% are not charged by the prosecutor. Of the other 50% who are charged by prosecutors, 30% actually receive full jail sentences. Thus, only about 10 out of every 1,000 criminals are actually apprehended, charged, convicted, and incarcerated as punishment for their crime.[7] This funnel effect is shown in Exhibit 2.2.

Of those criminals actually convicted and sentenced to incarceration, 96% to 99% of their sentences were the result of the plea bargains. So only 2% to 3% of criminal cases actually go to trial. Furthermore, although the federal and many state jurisdictions have mandatory sentencing laws for some crimes, a prosecutor can avoid these by reducing or dismissing charges or by not bringing them in the first place.

Due Process Protections

For the 5% to 8% of criminal defendants who did not elect to avoid trial through a plea, the system grinds on. The defendant was notified of his or her right to trial at the arraignment. Although there may be additional rights given by state constitution to a person accused of a crime, the U.S. Constitution sets out minimum rights.

> In all criminal prosecutions, the accused shall enjoy the right to a speedy and public trial, by an impartial jury of the State and district wherein the crime shall have been committed, which district shall have been previously ascertained by law, and to be informed of the nature and cause of the accusation; to be confronted with the witnesses against him; to have compulsory process for obtaining witnesses in his favor, and to have the assistance of counsel for his defense.[8]

In addition to the right to a speedy and public trial before an impartial jury, the defendant also has the right to challenge search and arrest warrants and to ask the court to bar the use of evidence obtained without proper warrant.[9] The defendant may also challenge the charge by showing he or she has already been tried for the same actions.[10] Furthermore, the defendant is entitled to use the court's authority to subpoena defense witnesses.[11] Many people, including some legislators, law enforcement personnel, prosecutors, and judges, have referred to these constitutional requirements with terms like *technicality* or *loophole*. However, they are in place to protect citizens who are falsely accused of crimes and they are, under the U.S. Constitution, the supreme law of the land.[12] Exercising all these rights and conducting hearings to ensure the requirements of due process have been met are all part of the pretrial procedure in both federal and state criminal courts.[13]

Rights of Victims and Accuseds

Often, those who are ignorant of the judicial system and the reasons for due process requirements assert that victims of crimes are left out of the criminal process. In a very real sense those people are right.

Our criminal system recognizes that everyone is victimized when any of us becomes a criminal victim. Therefore, criminal charges are not brought by or on behalf of the individual victim. The prosecution of all crime in our society is done in the name of The People of either the United States or of one of the individual sovereign states. Criminal victims are not parties to criminal procedures. They are merely witnesses on behalf of The People. Our criminal procedures recognize that interests of crime victims are represented by the entire might and weight of the sovereign, which uses its resources to catch, try, and punish those accused of crimes. Our criminal system imposes requirements for due process in order to balance or make fair the trial of someone who must defend him or herself against the power of the sovereign. In short, we try to make the system fair by providing protections and resources to the accused.

It may also help to understand the status of crime victims to note that the U.S. Constitution requires that those accused of crime be treated as innocent until after they are proven guilty. They are not given special rights; people accused, but not yet convicted of crimes, are merely given the same rights as every other citizen, including the alleged victim.[14]

It is only after a person accused of a crime in our society has been convicted, following all the rules of **due process**, that he or she becomes a "criminal." Criminals are legally and constitutionally stripped of all civil rights. Criminals have no right to vote, run for most public offices, keep any licenses they may have acquired, and may lose the right to their life, liberty, or property. The Constitution even says they be made "slaves." "Neither slavery nor involuntary servitude, except as a punishment for crime whereof the party shall have been duly convicted, shall exist within the United States, or any place subject to their jurisdiction."[15]

Defenses and Motions

In order to protect the due process rights of the accused, the pretrial stages of criminal proceedings must allow him or her to obtain information about the prosecution's case. He or she must know what witnesses will be called by the prosecution and what their testimony will allege. He or she must also be able to consult with counsel in the formulation of a defense, to make motions concerning the legality of evidence obtained by the state and to obtain defense witnesses. The defendant is also entitled to decide what form of trial will be used.

Discovery.   Both the prosecution and defense are required to exchange all their information in the case including witness lists and contact information, and lists of all evidence to be used. Furthermore, the defense must provide the names and addresses of any alibi witnesses and any written or recorded summaries of their potential testimony. All this is done to ensure both sides are able to thoroughly prepare for trial.

Defenses.   The defense must tell the prosecutor of any affirmative defenses she or he intends to use at trial. The **affirmative defenses** allowed by statute in most jurisdictions are infancy, involuntary intoxication, insanity or mental incapacity, or illness and justifiable use of force or self-defense. The first three affirmative defenses arise from common law, where it was understood that some people do not have the capacity to understand the nature or consequences of their actions. Simply put, they do not comprehend what is "right" and what is "wrong."

The statute that describes each crime will specify a mental state of mind, called under the common law **mens rea**, as one of the elements the prosecution must prove beyond a reasonable doubt in order to convict the defendant. Mens rea elements vary and include frames of mind and connected behavior such as knowingly, recklessly, with wanton disregard for the safety of others, willfully or intentionally. The logic for permitting **infancy, involuntary intoxication,** or **mental incapacity** as a defense is the belief that people suffering from those disabilities cannot form the required state of mind.

In some jurisdictions, an **alibi** may be an affirmative defense. Once a defendant decides to use an affirmative defense, he or she has the burden of proof of that defense by whatever standard has been set by law in the jurisdiction.

The prosecution must prove all of the elements of each crime alleged in the indictment or criminal complaint and must show the defendant committed them beyond a reasonable doubt, but the burden of proof then shifts to the defense to prove any affirmative defenses she or he may have asserted. If the defendant can prove an affirmative defense, the defense bars his or her conviction. The prosecutor must have been given notice of these affirmative defenses so that he or she may prepare to counter them.

Motions.   Several pretrial motions are established by statute or court rules. A **pretrial motion** is a request to the court to either take some action or to order the opposing party to take an action. Pretrial motions may be more easily understood if one simply substitutes the word *request* for motion. Thus, a motion for a speedy trial can be thought of simply as a request for a speedy trial. Pretrial motions include, but are not limited to, motion to dismiss, motion for bill of particulars, motion for a speedy trial, motion for jury trial, motion for substitution of judge, motion for change of venue, motion for joinder of related prosecutions, and motion for severance. There are also numerous motions related to the evidence. These include motions for discovery, a list of witnesses, or production of confessions or statements by the defendant. A motion may also ask to suppress confession or alleged admission, or to suppress evidence illegally seized. Many of these motions will be heard on a special docket to facilitate administration and to expedite the movement of the case to trial or other disposition.

Form of Trial

The prosecution brings the charges and has the burden of proving them in a criminal case. The accused has a right to decide the form of trial he or she will undergo. The Sixth Amendment says the accused has the right to a speedy, public trial by an impartial jury. This has been interpreted by the courts to give the defendant the option to decide whether he or she wants to be tried quickly or to have more time to prepare a defense. Often, this decision is influenced by whether the defendant has been released on bail or is incarcerated while awaiting trial. Most states have statutes setting the time within which a defendant must be tried or the case will be subject to involuntary dismissal. Usually, this period is about 120 days for defendants who are incarcerated and 160 to 180 days for defendants who are free on bond. Both periods are tolled, that is stopped from running, by a defendant's motion for continuance. If the trial deadline is missed for a defendant who has requested a speedy trial, the state may have the option to bring the charges again. This option may be foreclosed by a statute of limitations. **Statutes of limitations** set the time frame during which each type of criminal cases must be brought. After the time specified by the applicable statute of limitations has run, the prosecutor may not charge or try the defendant. The time specified in a statute of limitations relates to the seriousness of the crime involved. More serious crimes have longer time limits. Misdemeanors often have statutes of limitations specifying that charges must be brought within 18 to 24 months. The time ranges upward for more serious offenses. In most jurisdictions, there is no time limit for bringing murder charges. For communications practitioners covering criminal cases it may be helpful to note that the system for calculating time is not the same in all jurisdictions. Some do not begin the statute of limitations count until the crime is discovered and most toll or quit counting during time the defendant is hiding or outside the state's jurisdiction.

In addition to deciding how quickly he or she wants to be tried, the defendant may also decide if he or she wants a jury or a bench trial. In order to distinguish the jury, which sits at a trial, from a grand jury, some jurisdictions refer to these juries as petit juries or trial juries. Trial juries are usually made up of 12 citizens and 2 alternates called by some random selection process from the rolls of registered voters or driver's registration lists. Smaller juries are constitutionally permitted but may never be smaller than 6.[16] The jury's task is to serve as the **trier of fact**. They listen to the evidence presented by the witnesses for the prosecution and the defense, and to any arguments of counsel and they judge the veracity, significance, and weight to be given to each version of the alleged criminal actions of the defendant. The jury decides, based on the instructions on the law given to them by the judge, whether or not the defendant is guilty or not guilty of the offenses charged. A defendant is never found to be "innocent"; nor does a finding of not guilty mean the defendant is "innocent." A finding or **verdict** of **not**

guilty, also called an **acquittal**, simply means the trier of fact did not believe the prosecution proved its case beyond a reasonable doubt.

In some jurisdictions, depending on the crimes and the nature or severity of sentencing possibilities, a defendant who has been found guilty may also have the jury convene to hear factors in aggravation and mitigation in a sentencing hearing. After such hearings, the jury is asked to determine a punishment to recommend to the court. In most jurisdictions, a judge is not bound by the recommendations of the jury, and can impose a different sentence as long as he or she supports the decision with substantial reasons based on the evidence and law. Usually, however, a judge will accept a jury's sentencing recommendation.

In order to receive a bench trial, a criminal defendant must formally waive his or her right to jury trial. At a **bench trial**, the judge tries the case, alone, and sits as both the trier of fact and the legal arbiter who enforces rules of evidence and selects substantive law to apply. At a bench trial, the judge decides whether the state has met its burden of proof and renders one of the forms of verdict described earlier. Finally, the judge who conducts a bench trial also imposes sentence.

Trial Procedure

Obviously, the trial procedure varies significantly depending on whether the defendant has opted for a jury trial or a bench trial. Here, we describe the jury trial, which is more complex. Except for jury selection and jury deliberations, all the procedures described here are also followed in a bench trial.

Jury Selection

Jury selection is the procedure used to select an impartial jury to hear the case. In large jurisdictions, sometimes there will be several hundred people in the **array**, or group of potential jurors. These citizens are called by notice to appear at a specified time and place. In smaller jurisdictions the array may be fewer than 50 people. From this array of potential jurors, **venire men** and **women** are called to sit in the same courtroom to be considered for selection to hear one case. In the smaller jurisdictions, the venire men and women may be the entire array.[17]

Once the potential jurors are convened in a courtroom, and the prosecutor, defendant, and his or her counsel are present, the judge will begin *voir dire*. **Voir dire** is a French term translated by BLACK'S LAW DICTIONARY as "to speak the truth."[18] The specific procedure varies depending on the jurisdiction and the individual judge, but generally a group of potential jurors are called in random order for examination or the entire jury pool will be questioned together, the judge will briefly describe the type of case involved, identify the defendant, prosecutor, and witnesses. The judge will also explain how long the trial is expected to take. Then one by one, the judge will talk with each juror asking for any information that might bias her or him in the case. Often these questions include inquiries into the jurors' experiences with media reports about the defendant or alleged crime. Sometimes a judge will have requested questions from each side in the case and will read them to the potential jurors. The judge may also allow oral questioning by the prosecutor and defense attorney. The lawyers, their assistants, and the defendant all take notes during *voir dire*. They often have a list of the jurors' names and their positions marked on diagrams with comments about each juror's answers to questions. If potential jurors show they are prejudiced and cannot be impartial or for other reasons cannot be qualified to sit on a jury, the judge will thank them for their time, and excuse them.

The judge excuses venire men or women for cause. An excuse **for cause** means that the juror is or should be disqualified for some reason such as prejudice or inability to attend, listen, or see the evidence presented. After all questions have been answered by all venire men and women, a recess will be taken and the attorneys, court reporter, and judge will meet to determine which individuals will serve on the jury panel. During this meeting, the jury selection will be done in a specified order, with each person's name read by the judge or clerk, and the sides alternating in passing on or challenging that juror for cause or by using up one of their preemptory challenges. A limited number of **preemptory challenges** are given to both the prosecution and defense. These permit each side to **strike** the same number of potential jurors without stating any grounds for disqualification. A record is made of these proceedings by the court reporter. Once the appropriate number of jurors and alternates have been selected, the clerk or bailiff will read their names and seat the jurors in the order selected. The remaining veniremen and women are then excused for that session. The jury will be **empanelled** by being sworn to do their duty according to the law. At this point, the actual trial may begin.

Charges and Opening Statement

The trial will begin with an official reading of the charges against the defendant. These are typically read directly from the indictment or criminal complaint. The judge may also tell the jury what to expect during the trial. The jury will be told that the opening and closing statements made by the attorneys are not evidence.

Opening statements by the prosecutor and the defense attorney will include a summary of the case. The prosecutor's statement is usually a chronological explanation of the witnesses and evidence the jury should expect. The prosecutor hopes this will help the jury understand and accept the prosecution's view of the case. Sometimes, the prosecutor or the defense counsel will point to specific witnesses or evidence expected and ask the jury to note a point of proof or a point of weakness in the case.

Presentation of Evidence

After opening statements by both sides and before the prosecution calls its first witness, one of the attorneys may call for the **rule on witnesses**. Sometimes called the rule against witnesses, the procedure is used to prevent witnesses from discussing their testimony with other witnesses, media reporters, or noncourt personnel. It also prevents witnesses from conforming their testimony to that of other witnesses. The rule has two component parts. The first part orders anyone who might be called as a witness to leave the courtroom so they may not hear the testimony of others. The second part involves an order from the judge admonishing witnesses not to discuss their testimony or the testimony of others until after the trial has ended.

Next the prosecution will call its first witness who will be sworn in by the judge or court clerk. The prosecution will continue to present testimony and evidence by asking each witness questions. This interrogation of the witness by the attorney who called them is called **direct examination**. After the prosecutor examines each of his or her witnesses, the defense will have the opportunity to **cross-examine**. The purpose of the cross-examination is to point out defects in the testimony or physical evidence presented, to note the witness' inability to observe or recall, or to cast doubt on the credibility of the witness or the truthfulness of his or her testimony.

At the end of the prosecution's case-in-chief, the defense has an opportunity to present witnesses. These **rebuttal witnesses** are called to refute the testimony of one or more of the prosecution witnesses. They may either offer another view of the events described by the prosecution witness or they may explain why the prosecution witness is biased or unreliable. The prosecutor is allowed to cross-examine each of these defense witnesses in turn. The state may then call the same or additional witnesses. The purpose of this **surrebuttal** is to challenge the defense witness' observations or credibility.

During the testimony, either side may make objections about the evidence or statements being made by a witness. The judge will either **sustain** or **overrule** these objections. Sometimes, there is a sidebar discussion among the attorneys and the judge involving the appropriate rules of evidence; other times court will be recessed and the jury excused while legal arguments are made outside the presence of the jury. These discussions address the reason for the objection and whether the evidence or testimony violates some law or court rule. The discussions are recorded so they may be reviewed by an appellate court.

After the state has presented all its witnesses, the state will **rest**, meaning it is through presenting its case. Just prior to or just after resting, depending on the court's rules, the state will ask that all its physical evidence be admitted. At this time, the jury will be excused and a hearing will be conducted on the record regarding legal arguments by the defense concerning the admissibility of each piece of evidence. A similar procedure will occur after the conclusion of the defense portion of the trial.[19]

Once the prosecution has rested, and its exhibits have been admitted into evidence, the defense may make a **motion for directed verdict** or **verdict for the defendant**. This is done if the defense attorney believes the state has failed to present a **prima facie** case on one or more elements of proof required. Essentially, the defense attorney is saying that even without any defense evidence, the prosecution has failed to prove its case beyond a reasonable doubt. This happens most often if some testimony or physical evidence proffered by the state has been excluded because of an objection by the defense attorney. If the court agrees, there will be a **directed verdict** for the defendant and the jury may be dismissed at that time. If the court denies the motion for directed verdict, the defense will call its witnesses and present its physical evidence following the same rules and procedures used by the prosecution.

Jury Instructions and Closing Argument

After the conclusion of the presentation of evidence, the jury will be excused and admonished not to talk about the case. The judge, court reporter, and counsel will then retire to consider the jury instructions. **Jury instructions** are a set of directives or guide-lines to the jury regarding their duties, rules of deliberation, and statements of law. They also usually include forms for each possible verdict with lines for the jurors' signatures. Each attorney will enter the **jury instruction conference**, with a complete set of jury instructions, often drawn verbatim from sets of patterned instructions published under the authority of the appropriate court.[20] If one of the attorneys believes a current case supercedes an instruction or if there is no patterned instruction that covers the situation being tried, the judge will hear arguments and decide which form of instruction to give the jury. Once the instruction conference is over, the instructions are taken to the judge's bench to be given to the jury.

Court will reconvene and closing arguments will be heard. During their **closing arguments** the prosecutor and defense attorney will each try to convince the jury how the evidence they have heard should be applied to the jury instructions to arrive at the verdict they support. The prosecution will make its **closing argument** first, the defense, second, and the prosecution may be allowed a short rebuttal argument third. Following the closing arguments, the judge will read the jury instructions on the record and charge the jury regarding its duties.

The jury then retires to the jury room to deliberate. Juries can take from 15 minutes to several days to reach a verdict. If the jury becomes deadlocked and cannot reach a unanimous decision, the judge will declare a mistrial. A **mistrial** means the state could try the defendant again. When the jury informs the court by means of a note sent to the judge that it has reached a verdict, court is reconvened. The jury foreperson will hand the form of verdict it has chosen, signed by all 12 jurors, to the bailiff or the clerk who hands it to the judge to read aloud. In some jurisdictions the foreperson reads the verdict aloud. The judge will ask the attorneys if they want the jury **polled**, that is asked individually if this is their verdict, and then the judge will excuse the jury from service in the case.

Following the departure of the jury from the courtroom, there may be a motion for **judgment non obstante verdicto**, often abbreviated "J.N.O.V." The phrase is often translated "judgment not withstanding verdict." This is a request asking the judge to grant a judgment contrary to the jury's verdict. The judge will rule on this after argument by the attorneys, and perhaps on other motions. Depending on the seriousness of the offense and the amount of bond already posted, the judge may revoke bond and have the defendant remanded to the custody of the sheriff to await sentencing. For lesser charges or when there is only low risk that the defendant will flee, the bond may be continued and the defendant remains free pending sentence.

Posttrial Procedure

Following a conviction, the court still must determine sentence and the defendant still may ask for further review of his or her case.

Investigation and Sentencing

Following a conviction, the judge will order a presentence investigation. The **presentence investigation** is usually conducted by a probation officer or other official appointed by the court. It seeks to identify factors that would justify a harsh or light sentence. After receiving a report of the presentence investigation, the judge conducts a sentencing hearing. Sometimes these hearings are lengthy and involve several witnesses. They often give the appearance of being actual re-trials of the case with additional material, such as the defendant's former history of criminality and additional victims testifying. Whether the sentencing hearing is conducted before a judge or a jury depends on the defendant's choice. In death penalty cases, if a jury tried the case, that same jury must be reconvened to hear the sentencing evidence and to determine the defendant's fate. At the conclusion of this hearing, the judge announces the verdict and the sentence and gives the reasoning behind his or her decision, for the record.[21]

After the written judgment, including a sentence imposition, has been filed, an order called a **mittimus** is issued and sent to the warden of the appropriate correctional facility. This order includes the full dates of the sentence. A certified copy of the mittimus will accompany the convicted criminal wherever he or she may be sent within the correctional system, and no warden may accept or detain a prisoner without this order.

Posttrial Motions

Depending on the jurisdiction, there are several posttrial motions available to a convicted defendant. If a defendant feels a plea agreement was not honored or if for some other reason he or she believes the sentence should have been more lenient, the defense may make **motion to reconsider** or to **vacate** the finding and sentence altogether. The defense might also make a **motion for a retrial**, or **new trial**, based on objections to evidence made during the trial. The posttrial motion phase and the appellate process are all controlled by strict time tables and schedules that are established by statutes and court rules in each state or the federal court system.

If these motions fail, the case may be appealed to other courts in the appropriate appellate system for that jurisdiction. The only automatic appeals are those involving the imposition of the death penalty. In most states, those cases go directly from the trial court to the highest court of appeals, bypassing any intermediate courts of appeal.

Postconviction Relief

Historically, many people convicted of crimes in state courts used an equitable remedy called a petition for writ of habeas corpus to gain entry into the federal appellate system. Because of the large number of such petitions, Congress removed this jurisdiction from the U.S. Supreme Court and severely curtailed its use through the Post Conviction Relief Act.[22]

Today, a convicted defendant who has exhausted all state appeals in her or his jurisdiction may use the Post Conviction Relief Act to ask the federal courts to hear his or her case. To take advantage of this option the defendant must have, throughout the pretrial, trial, and posttrial appeals process, consistently raised an issue dealing with fair trial or due process under the U.S. Constitution. Within the permissible time after all state appeals are exhausted, the appropriate petition and supporting portions of the record and findings by the state courts must be sent to the U.S. Circuit Court of Appeals for the appropriate jurisdiction. The Circuit Court of Appeals may or may not grant certiorari in the case, depending on many factors including the seriousness of the constitutional errors alleged and whether it is obvious the defendant would have been convicted anyway.

Juvenile Procedure

Legal procedures developed for juveniles have changed dramatically over time. Today, they vary widely from state to state and from situation to situation. The changes over time are based on evolving attitudes toward children and shifting beliefs about the purpose of juvenile law. Variations from state to state often depend on where a state's legislature falls on the continuum of attitudes toward juveniles.

Today, most people accept the idea that people of different ages should be treated differently. Court rules dealing with children and child witnesses, for example, assume children under a certain age, often 7 years, simply cannot comprehend the nature and consequences of their actions. Courts usually assume that by the time a child reaches the age of 12, his or her cognitive development is adequate to understand the social concepts of right, wrong, good, and bad, and that children should be able to distinguish lying from being truthful.

Some of the original juvenile laws were based on the belief that children, because of their age, lack of knowledge, education, maturity, and judgment, should be treated differently than adults. In some cases, this different treatment was for their own protection; in other situations the different treatment was in the best interest of society. Originally, juvenile offenders were separated from adults when confinement was necessary. This was thought to protect the child offender from adult inmates. Later, completely separate court systems or divisions were developed for juveniles under the age of 18. These separate systems were often designed for rehabilitation because the legislators or courts believed children under the age of 18 were malleable and capable of change. They thought incarceration would not help rehabilitate the juvenile offender and would actually exacerbate the child's antisocial tendencies. Since about the 1980s many jurisdictions have begun to re-think and harden their treatment of 15- to 18-year-old offenders. The increased penalties and more aggressive treatment for juvenile offenders have arisen largely because of the increase in the amount and seriousness of juvenile crime.

In 1899, the Chicago Bar Association described the motivation for the first juvenile court act as an attempt to treat children like a wise and loving parent.[23] Of course, there are significant variations in the approach to juvenile law and the procedures used to adjudicate juvenile matters. The breadth of difference in state's attitudes toward juvenile offenders can be illustrated by comparing the purpose statement in the Illinois Juvenile Court Act and the purpose statement in the Texas Juvenile Justice Code. Those purpose statements are presented in Exhibits 2.3 and 2.4.

Some jurisdictions categorize and place their juvenile court rules within "family law" codes and procedures. For these jurisdictions, juvenile procedure is more like civil than criminal procedure. Other jurisdictions use a system much like criminal law, particularly when addressing alleged juvenile delinquents.

Exhibit 2.3.   Illinois Juvenile Court Act, Purpose (Chapter 705 ICLS 405/1–2, Sec. 1–2 [1] & [2]; formerly Ill.Re. Stat. 1991, ch. 37, para. 801–2).

The Illinois Juvenile Court Act of 1987
Purpose & Policy

(1) The purpose of this Act is to secure for each minor subject hereto such care and guidance, preferably in his or her own home, as will serve the safety and moral, emotional, mental, and physical welfare of the minor and the best interests of the community; . . .

(2) . . . . This Act shall be administered in a spirit of humane concern, not only for the rights of the parties, but also for the fears and the limits of understanding of all who appear before this court.

■

The mechanics of juvenile delinquency and status offense procedures are very similar to criminal procedure. Here, we do not repeat the obvious similarities; rather, we discuss the different purposes of juvenile and criminal law and, where significant, describe difference in procedure. Protection laws share characteristics with both criminal and civil law. Because civil law is discussed in the next section, we only describe the unique characteristics of protection laws.

Exhibit 2.4.   Texas Juvenile Justice Code Purpose (Texas Family Code, Title 3, Juvenile Justice Code, Ch. 51, Sec. 51.01; Ch. 262[l] [1996]).

Texas Family Code –
Juvenile Justice Code
Chapter 51. General Provisions

SEC. 51.01. Purpose and interpretation.
This title shall be construed to effectuate the following public purposes:

(1) to provide for the protection of the public and public safety;

(2) consistent with the protection of the public and public safety:
  (A) to promote the concept of punishment for criminal acts;
  (B) to remove, where appropriate, the taint of criminality from children committing certain unlawful acts; and
  (C) to provide treatment, training, and rehabilitation that emphasizes the accountability and responsibility of both the parent and the child for the child's conduct;

(3) to provide for the care, the protection, and the wholesome moral, mental, and physical development of children coming within its provisions;

(4) to protect the welfare of the community and to control the commission of unlawful acts by children;. . . . .

. . . . (6) to provide a simple judicial procedure through which the provisions of this title are executed and enforced and in which the parties are assured a fair hearing and their constitutional and other legal rights recognized and enforced.

■

Federal and state statutes dealing with juveniles are complicated but can be divided into the following three common categories: (a) laws dealing with young people under the age of 18 years who are accused of committing crimes, also known as juvenile delinquency laws; (b) laws dealing with young people under the age of 18 years who are accused of status offenses; and (c) laws for the protection of children under the age of 18 who are the victims of some form of adult abuse or neglect, or who cannot be controlled by their parents.

Juvenile Delinquency Laws

The first juvenile acts were aimed at getting children away from severely abusive parents; they were also developed with the understanding that delinquent and "wayward" children should be housed and treated differently than adult criminals.

Today, **juvenile delinquency** laws are those that govern people under the age of 18 who have committed an adult criminal offense. In most situations, juvenile delinquents are not prosecuted under criminal laws or by using criminal procedures. There are exceptions for minors at least 15 years of age who are charged with particularly heinous crimes. These individuals may be tried as adults after certification by a judge. Until convicted, no juvenile may be housed within an adult jail or prison population. After a finding of delinquency or conviction, if certified as an adult, adjudicated juvenile offenders under the age of 18 cannot be housed with adult inmates.

When a young person is arrested and charged with a criminal offense, the prosecuting attorney for the appropriate jurisdiction will file a petition for a finding of delinquency. This charge is usually titled: "In the Interest of ————, A Minor." The petition describes the facts justifying the finding of delinquency. It identifies the minor and his or her guardian. In addition, the petition asks that the minor be adjudged a ward of the court. Service of this petition is by summons made upon the minor, and, depending on the minor's age, his or her guardian.

After service of the petition on all parties, the court will appoint a guardian ad litem to represent the interest of the minor. The **guardian ad litem** is usually a licensed attorney but may be a child advocate or a layperson designated as a friend of the court. The guardian ad litem may or may not be the child's attorney, depending on the jurisdiction. He or she is appointed to speak for the minor, whom the court assumes may not be able to speak for him or herself. Sometimes, another lawyer serves as the minor's actual legal counsel. Trials of minors accused of delinquency because of a criminal act are usually conducted by a judge only, but in some states they may be heard before a jury. If the judge or jury finds the minor guilty of the underlying crime, an investigation is ordered to determine the child's family and social situation, education, and criminal or delinquency history. A report of this investigation is given to the court and to the attorneys. This report is somewhat analogous to the presentence investigation in a criminal matter, but focuses more on the best interest of the child and explores treatment or care options. Additional evidence may also be taken at the sentencing hearing where the court decides whether it is in the best interest of society and of the minor to make the juvenile a ward of the court. The end result of this procedure is not a sentence but a disposition. In most states, the trial and decision about whether the minor is a delinquent is called an

adjudication or **adjudicatory hearing**. The sentencing stage is called a **disposition** or **dispositional hearing**. In most states, these two stages must be **bifurcated** or separated by enough time to allow the appropriate background report to be made and reviewed by the judge and the legal representatives involved. A minor who is made a ward of the court may be placed in a juvenile rehabilitation facility, foster care, or returned to his or her guardian with conditions imposed by the court.

Status Offenses

Status offenses relate to actions that would be perfectly legal if done by adults, but that incur penalties when done by minors. Status offenses include violations of truancy laws, minimum driving age laws, curfew laws, underage possession and drinking laws, and the laws prohibiting the purchase and possession of tobacco products. All such laws are a form of legalized age discrimination based on public policy. As an example of the capriciousness of these types of offenses, one might note that laws relating to alcohol and tobacco have recently raised the legal age for purchase, possession, and use to 21, while the Twenty-Sixth Amendment to the U.S. Constitution lowered the voting age from 21 to 18 years, in 1971.

Usually no sanctions are attached to these offenses other than money fines for disobedience by juveniles. Of course, these fines are often paid by the adults whose failure to provide proper supervision significantly contributed to the violations. In part because of the light penalties, there are few procedural protections for minors charged with status offenses.

Laws for the Protection of Children

The third category of juvenile laws, although usually part of the same Juvenile Court Acts that prescribe the processing of juvenile delinquents, deal specifically with young people who have been victimized by their families or living arrangements. These laws are meant to enable the state to remove children from detrimental environments, to treat their illnesses or addictions, and to eventually provide a stable and supportive place for these minors to live and mature. Although state intervention into the lives of young people may remove them from their families, it also recognizes that they are injured children who need treatment, not punishment.

These statutes usually criminalize the actions or omissions of the adults involved and those adults may be tried following the criminal procedures described earlier. The child victims do not, however, become part of the criminal system and actions involving them do not follow criminal procedure. Often, these statutes classify the type of problem or victimization of the young person into three separate categories such as (a) abused, neglected, or dependent minors; (b) minors requiring authoritative intervention, who are beyond the control of their parents or guardians; and (c) addicted minors. The courts have a separate range of placement and treatment options for minors in each of these categories.

Civil Procedure

Although most criminal laws and procedures in the United States are grounded in either Constitutional or Statutory law, many of civil laws and procedures are based on common law case precedents. In both criminal and juvenile cases, it is the government that initiates the action and fills the role of plaintiff. In civil cases, private people or corporations are both the plaintiffs and defendants.

Most states have attempted to create statutes to reflect the common law principles that govern civil law, but much of our civil procedure is still based more on case precedent than on state statutes.[24] This reliance on case precedent is particularly apparent in contract and tort law, which is addressed in chapters 9 and 11.

We assume the honest and conscientious mass communications practitioner will not violate the criminal laws but it is relatively easy for an honest person to become involved in civil matters. Therefore, it is incumbent on the wise mass communications practitioner to become aware of the types of laws, procedures, and court rules in any jurisdiction where he or she may practice. Learning when to obtain the services of competent legal counsel prior to making a legal faux pas and incurring costly liability is wise. Having to hire a lawyer to clean up one's legal obligations after an error is folly. The information contained in this section and throughout this textbook should be used to avoid such problems. When in doubt, always consult competent legal counsel prior to taking any action that may result in serious legal consequences.

Pretrial

Civil law cases are initiated by a plaintiff. The **plaintiff**, also called a petitioner or complainant, is either the victim of misconduct or is the representative of such a victim. The plaintiff has the burden of proving the case against the defendant. The **defendant**, who may also be called the respondent, is the person accused of causing harm to the plaintiff. The standard of proof required in a civil case is **by a preponderance of the evidence**. The charge document used by the plaintiff to initiate the case is called a **petition** or **complaint**, depending on the jurisdiction. Once this document is filed with a court, the court clerk issues a summons, which is attached to the petition. The local sheriff or a local process server delivers the **summons** to the defendant, thereby giving him or her notice of the lawsuit. Each jurisdiction has its own rules for how the summons and complaint must be served on the defendant. This notice of the suit is called **personal service**. In some situations involving businesses, corporations, or fraud by mail or the Internet, **long-arm statutes** provide an alternative method of personal service. Regardless of the rule, a suit may proceed only after it can be proven that the defendant has received legal service of the summons and complaint.

The summons will set a time, usually 30 days, within which the defendant must respond. Generally, the defendant responds by a written appearance through an attorney. The defendant also files a response or answer. The **answer** is a document either denying or admitting the allegations in the complaint. Prior to the answer, the defendant may file motions. For example, in some jurisdictions the defendant may file a demurrer. A demurrer is the legal equivalent of saying "so what" to the plaintiff's complaint. In effect, it says even if the plaintiff can prove all the allegations contained in the complaint, he or she still cannot win the lawsuit. In other jurisdictions, the proper method for raising a question concerning the proper cause of action is called a **motion to dismiss** for failure to state a cause of action. Once the motions have been heard and decided by the court involved, the defendant will be required to file an answer, sometimes called a reply or response.

The defendant's answer may also be accompanied by a **counterpetition** or **counterclaim** alleging the plaintiff caused harm to the defendant. In effect, the defendant can use this technique to sue the plaintiff. If this happens, the plaintiff will then have a specified period to respond to the counterclaims by motion and eventually by answer or reply.

Pleadings refer to the original complaint or petition, the answer, response, or reply and any counterclaims or cross-petitions. **Pleadings** are those legal documents that set out the cause of action and the defendant's response. They establish the legal requirements for any trial on the issues in the case.

Motions deal with procedural matters and such issues as whether or not there is a cause of action to which any response must be made or whether the case should be dismissed, whether discovery has been completed, and whether specific evidence should be considered.

Following the filing of an answer, which is similar to the arraignment phase in a criminal suit, where the defendant has pled not guilty, the next stage in the civil pretrial process is discovery. **Discovery** of evidence in a civil suit may be required by any of the parties through the filing of motions for production of documents and other tangible evidence; **interrogatories**, which are a series of written questions directed to the other side requiring response under written oath; or **depositions**, which require the physical presence of one or more of the opposing parties who appear at the offices of the attorney for the deposing side to answer questions while on record and under oath. Depositions may be taken from any witness listed in the discovery produced by either party. As you may note, because of the Fifth Amendment guarantees against self-incrimination, these methods of inquiry could not be used in a criminal case. In a criminal case, the defendant cannot be required to respond to interrogatories or depositions nor requests for production of personal papers because these requirements could violate the defendant's right against self-incrimination.

Usually near the end of the discovery phase in a civil suit, the parties understand the strengths and weaknesses of their case and are often ready to enter into serious settlement negotiations. Even prior to the completion of discovery, in most civil cases, both sides will have attempted to explore the possibility of settlement without the expense of a trial. The attorneys will send negotiating letters back and forth several times, and there may be many telephone calls or conferences seeking an agreement. Even the courts put pressure on the attorneys to settle their cases. Often, judges require attorneys to attend several pretrial conferences to encourage negotiations. Even fewer civil than criminal cases go to trial. One reason may be cost. In criminal cases, indigent defendants are represented by court-appointed attorneys and the prosecution attorney is also paid by the taxpayers. The motivation to settle civil cases is high, in part because both sides are responsible for their own expenses and, in some states, the losing party must pay the attorneys' fees and reasonable expenses of the winning side.

Occasionally, in a civil suit, **motions** may be made that end the suit without the necessity of further negotiations or trial. One of these is a motion for **summary judgment**, which any of the parties may make if there is no contested issue of fact. The pleadings set out the facts and together with affidavits by the parties or some additional witnesses; they may establish all relevant facts in a case. When this happens, the court may make a ruling that decides the case without having to resort to a trial. Another motion that may result in the settlement of a civil case without resorting to a trial is a **motion for declaratory judgment**. In this situation, one of the parties asks the court to rule on a point of law that may have the effect of ending the suit.

If a trial becomes necessary in a civil case, either side will have had the opportunity, at the time they filed their original or responsive pleadings, to request trial by jury. In some jurisdictions, the party who requests trial by jury in a civil matter is required to pay the trial cost in advance. Unlike a criminal case, where a defendant automatically has a right to a jury trial and must waive that right, the parties in a civil suit must specifically request a trial by jury early in the pleadings phase, or they will forfeit the privilege. Even though one or both parties may have originally made a motion for trial by jury, they may decide and agree to a **bench trial** to lower costs once the discovery phase has been completed.

Trial

Procedures for both jury and bench trials in a civil suit are almost identical to those in a criminal suit, with the exception that the plaintiff's petition and the defendant's answer will serve as the "charge documents" that set the framework for the dispute in the trial. These will be read by the judge at the opening of the trial. These pleadings set forth the elements that must be proven by a **preponderance of the evidence** in a civil suit. These pleadings essentially replace the indictment or criminal complaint, which are read on the record at the beginning of a criminal suit. The trial stages of opening statement, presentation of witnesses, jury instructions, closing argument, and deliberation are the same as were described for criminal trials. Of course, a civil defendant is not found guilty or not guilty. Rather the judge or jury grants a judgment. The trial ruling is for one of the parties and usually specifics an amount of money damages to be paid if the plaintiff is the prevailing party.

Posttrial and Appeal

Should a civil litigant be displeased with the trial outcome, she or he must give **notice of intent to appeal** in most jurisdictions within 30 days following the judgment. This notice, together with a written request for the court reporter to prepare a transcript of the proceedings and for the court clerk to certify the record for the appeal, must be served on all parties within the required time period. There is no automatic appeal of any kind in civil cases. Furthermore, the appellate process is often so expensive that few individual litigants can afford it. All appellate court procedures are based on rules promulgated by the courts in the subject jurisdictions or by the appropriate legislatures.

Appellate Procedure

In some jurisdictions, the rules of appellate procedure are consolidated. In other words, there is one set of appellate procedures for all cases. In other jurisdictions, criminal appellate procedures are attached to or compiled with the jurisdiction's criminal laws and procedures, and civil appellate procedures are found at the end of published civil court rules and procedures. The most important things to note in any appellate procedure, civil or criminal, are the time tables and required notifications that must be strictly followed or an appeal will be barred.

It is possible that both sides in a civil case will cross-appeal. Often, the defendant thinks the judgment was too large and the plaintiff thinks it too small. In a criminal case, the prosecution may not appeal an acquittal because the defendant is protected from "double jeopardy." There are very rare exceptions to this principle. Occasionally, the prosecution will appeal using what is called "a reserve question of law." In this situation, the prosecution does not ask that the acquittal be reversed but asks the appellate court to rule on the law so the decision may be used as precedent in the future. There are also times when the state may appeal rulings prior to or during a trial. This happens most often when a trial judge bars the prosecution from presenting evidence needed to prove one or more of the elements in its case. These pretrial or trial evidentiary appeals are called **interlocutory appeals**. For such an appeal, the trial will be stopped and continued again sometime after the appeals court gives its ruling.

In chapter 1 we discussed the four sources of law. One of these was case law. Case law has three components: **statutory interpretations**, **judicial review**, and **common law**. The legal decisions produced by appeals become the data or rules that form the foundation of common law. Those decisions also provide guidance for statutory interpretation and help readers understand which statutes are and are not constitutional. Therefore, learning to read, interpret, and understand case law should be a major goal of anyone interested in any component of law, especially laws that apply to the practices of advertising, broadcasting, journalism, and public relations.

What Cases Are Reported?

Cases are said to be "reported" if the decision is written and published in an easily available form. In the federal system, only a few of the more important trial court decisions are published, but all appellate decisions are reported. Decisions made in cases of first impression at trials in the federal district courts are most likely to be reported. A **case of first impression** is one that raises a legal question for the first time. Other cases that raise novel questions or that have significant legal ramifications may also be reported. Those few federal district court cases chosen to be reported are published in the **Federal Supplements**. The official abbreviations for the Federal Supplement are "F.Supp. and F.Supp.2d."

The vast majority of reported cases from the federal courts are appellate cases whose decisions are rendered by the Circuit Court of Appeals and the U.S. Supreme Court. Decisions of the Circuit Court of Appeals for all circuits are published in the **Federal Reporters**, which are abbreviated simply "F.," F.2d.," or "F.3d." Decisions of the U.S. Supreme Court are reported in **U.S. Reports**, which is abbreviated "U.S." Decisions from the U.S. Supreme Court are also published in several commercial publications.

What Cases Should You Read?

When deciding which cases to read and cite from those published, do remember the discussion of authority from chapter 1. Some court decisions are mandatory authority and others are only persuasive. For example, a U.S. Supreme Court ruling on a matter of constitutional interpretation is mandatory authority, but a similar ruling from the Court of Appeals is only persuasive when presented to the U.S. Supreme Court.

When selecting a case to read or to cite in support of some principle of common law one must be sure it has not been reversed or modified by subsequent cases. One must also be sure the case cited is the highest authority on that principle of law. Failing to "Shepardize" a case means one may be citing a case that simply is not authority for anything. The term *Shepardize* comes from the use of a table of case citations called *Shepard's Citations*. This citation system is available in most law libraries. It is also available online in several forms. To "Shepardize" a case means to check all the references to that case in later decisions to be sure some later court with higher authority has not modified or reversed its holding. Techniques for checking case citations are described in some detail in Appendix A.

Basis for Appeal

The party who requests an appeal is called the appellant. The appellant typically lost the case in the court below and now seeks a change in that judgment. The appellant must have a "basis for appeal." In other words, he or she cannot simply say the court below was wrong. Some specific issues or questions must be raised on appeal. Therefore, the appellant must have preserved the errors as they are being made by timely objections on the record. This is true regardless of the number or type of errors the appellant wishes to draw to the appellate court's attention. If the appellant did not object to the alleged errors as they occurred, he or she cannot raise those issues on appeal. These objections and appellate issues may relate to decisions about what evidence was admitted, the jury selection, the choice and interpretation of law, or the wording of jury instructions. Actions or decisions of the court to which no objection is made are said to be **waived** for appeal.

There are two major exceptions to this rule. The first and major exception relates to **jurisdiction** of the lower court. No matter how far up the appellate ladder a case may rise, either party may claim lack of jurisdiction, even if the defect was never noticed at the trial court or lower appellate levels. If the court judging the case lacked personal or subject matter jurisdiction, the case must be dismissed. The second exception, which would amount to a violation of the Sixth Amendment in a criminal case, involves the assertion by a defendant that his or her counsel was insufficiently prepared or did not handle the case with the standard of professionalism expected. This error, known as **ineffective assistance of counsel**, may be raised as a constitutional issue at any time. Ineffective assistance of counsel may result in the case being granted certiorari by a federal appellate court, even after the defendant has exhausted his or her state appeals. Often such an error is raised in a postconviction review described in the section on criminal procedure in this chapter.

Standard of Review

The major purpose of all appellate courts is to review the decisions of lower courts, and sometimes those of executive agencies within their purview. The party asking for appellate review is asking the appellate court to rule on errors in law or errors of fact made by the court below. The general **standard of review** in an appellate court is similar to the burden of proof required of the prosecution in a criminal case or the plaintiff in a civil case. These standards help the court decide how much error must be found to justify a change in a decision made by a lower tribunal. These appellate standards are totality of the circumstances, clear and convincing error, against the manifest weight of the evidence, and trial *de novo*. These should not be confused with the standards used by the U.S. Supreme Court to evaluate the constitutionality of governmental actions. Those standards are described in chapter 3.

In most cases appealed directly from the trial court, the reviewing court applies the standard of **clear error**. This means that on at least one of the issues presented for review the lower court made an obvious mistake by allowing evidence to be presented over objection or by refusing to allow relevant evidence to be introduced. Clear error also applies to an obvious mistake by the lower court in the choice, interpretation, and application of the law to the facts of the case. Even if the lower court judge made a clear error, his or her decision is not automatically overturned. The clear error must have affected the trial outcome.

Totality of circumstances refers to a situation in which the mistakes made by the lower court judge were so significant they contributed to an incorrect and therefore unjust judgment, thereby denying the litigants a fair trial. Such situations are labeled "totality of the circumstances" because an unjust decision may result from a single significant mistake or the cumulative effect of several errors. Such trial court decisions will be reversed and, depending on the circumstances, either dismissed altogether, or remanded for a new trial or hearing.

The third standard of review deals with findings made by the trier of fact. Remember the trier of fact is the judge in a bench trial or the jury. The trier of fact at trial actually saw the evidence and heard and saw the witnesses. Because the trier of fact had the advantage of direct contact with the witnesses and evidence, appellate courts are very reluctant to overturn their decisions. Deference to the decisions made by the trier of fact to determine the credibility and weight of the evidence presented by the litigants may be overcome only when the fact-finder has made a decision that is clearly not supported by the record. This standard of review is called "**against the manifest weight of the evidence.**" Usually, such trial court decisions will be reversed and remanded for a new trial.

The last standard of review, **trial *de novo***, is used when the appellate court's jurisdiction extends to the rehearing of executive or administrative agency decisions, or when a reviewing court is not required to defer to the findings of the tribunal being appealed. This is done because the agency hearing boards or commissions do not use rules of evidence and procedural standards by which the state and federal courts try cases, and because administrative arbiters are hired by the agency whose disputes they hear and determine. Therefore, those tribunal's judges are not unbiased magistrates of the courts. The term *de novo* literally means "of new" so that the litigant objecting to a final agency decision has a right to start over and have a new trial, complete with presentation of witnesses and evidence. An appellate court reviewing an agency decision or in any *de novo* evidentiary review generally sends the case back to the agency or district court for additional hearings and findings on evidentiary matters. The appellate court itself conducts no actual evidentiary hearings.

The term *de novo* is also used to describe the standard a superior court uses to review an interpretation of law by a lower court. Because the superior court owes no deference to the lower court, it may simply ignore the lower court's judgment and interpret the law *de novo*.

Evidence on Appeal

Appellate courts will review only those issues raised by the appellant in his or her petition for certiorari. The appellate court considers the briefs filed by both sides and the records certified from lower courts. Briefs, in this context, are written arguments explaining how existing law should be applied to the issues and the record in the case. No witnesses, no evidence, and no new information are presented on appeal.

Learning to Read Case Law

Obviously, to understand how appellate decisions create common law and to know what the law is, one must be able to read the appellate decisions. This task is far more complicated than it might seem. Courts often embed their decisions in esoteric or obscure language. Also, the published court decisions contain editors' comments, clerks' additions, and concurring and dissenting opinions that are not part of the ruling.

The best way to learn to read case law is to understand the various parts of an appellate court opinion and to do a "case brief." A **case brief**, distinguished from an appellate brief, is a summary of the major points contained in each case. Learning to properly read and brief a case is important for a number of reasons. First of all, most errors made by journalists reporting about legal decisions arise because they do not know how to properly "read" or analyze the reports of judicial decisions. Briefing a case forces its reader to organize his or her thoughts and to identify the important parts of the court's decision. A file of case briefs can also be used to identify common law trends and to predict the outcome of future cases.

Most well-written appellate court decisions follow a "formula" that is similar to mathematical equation. It may be useful to think of the appellate decision like the narrative questions used in basic algebra. The decision must be read to identify the variables, and then the variables must be used in an equation to find a solution. There are **seven parts** or variables that should always be included in the appellate decision and in the brief. They are: (a) the **heading**, (b) the **judicial history**, (c) the **facts or factual history**, (d) the **issues**, (e) the **reasoning**, (f) the **holding or decision**, and (g) the **judgment** or **disposition** of the case on appeal. Appendix A explains how those variables can be found and put into a formula that should help identify the legal effect of each appellate decision.

Magic Words and Phrases

Acquittal	Judgment non obstante verdicto
Adjudication	Jury instructions
Admonished	Juvenile delinquency laws
Affirmative defenses	Juvenile status offenses
Against the manifest weight of the evidence	Long-arm statutes
	Mens rea
Answer or reply	Misdemeanors
Appellate procedure	Motion for a retrial
Arraignment	Motion for bench trial
Array	Motion for declaratory judgment
Beyond a reasonable doubt	Motion for directed verdict
Bifurcated hearing	Motion for jury trial
Bill of particulars	Motion to reconsider
Case of first impression	Motions for summary judgment
Challenges for cause	No bill of indictment
Civil laws and procedures	Nolo contendere
Closing statements	Not guilty
Common law	Objections
Counterclaim/cross-petition	Opening statements
Criminal complaint	Overruled
Criminal law	Personal service
Cross-examination	Petition for change of venue
De novo	Petition for discovery
Demurrer	Petition for joinder
Depositions	Petition for severance
Discovery phase	Petition for speedy jury trial
Dispositional hearing	Petition for writ of habeas corpus
Due process of law	Petition or complaint
Empanelled	Petition to suppress evidence or confession
Federal Reporter	
Federal Supplement	Petty offenses
Felonies	Plea bargain
Finding of not guilty by reason of insanity	Post conviction relief
	Posttrial motions and appeals
First appearance	Preliminary hearing
Funnel effect	Preemptory challenges
Grand jury	Preponderance of the evidence
Guardian ad litem	Prima facie case
Indictment	Procedural law
Interrogatories	Prosecutor's information

Rebuttal witness	Summons
Rule on witnesses	Totality of circumstances clear error
Sentencing hearing	Trier of fact
Standard of review	True bill of indictment
Statute of limitations	U.S. Reports
Stipulated bench trial	Venire men and women
Substantive law(s)	Voir dire

Suggested Cases to Read and Brief

In re Gault, 387 U.S. 1 (1967)
In re Winship, 397 U.S. 358 (1970)
McKeiver v. Pennsylvania, 403 U.S. 528 (1971)
Kent v. U.S., 383 U.S. 541 (1966)
Thompson v. Oklahoma, 487 U.S. 815 (1988)
Stanford v. Kentucky, 492 U.S. 361 (1989)

Questions for Discussion

1. Why is it important for practitioners in the field of mass communications to understand the judicial process and different stages in the trials of criminal and civil cases?

2. Why is it important for students and practitioners in the field of mass communications law to learn to read and brief case law?

3. What are the major differences between criminal law and procedure and civil law and procedure? Why are these distinctions important?

4. Why don't the various states and the federal court systems have a uniform set of laws and procedures? Would such a system of uniform laws nationwide be advisable politically, philosophically, and socially? Why or why not?

5. Why are the laws, procedures, and processes for juveniles different from those of adults? In what ways are they different? Why is this important? Should the laws treating juveniles differently from adults be changed? Why or why not?

6. What are the differences in procedure between the charge document titled "indictment" and one titled "criminal complaint"?

7. Why is plea bargaining so prevalent in criminal cases? Should there be so much plea bargaining? What are the benefits from plea bargaining? What are the harms or risks?

8. What is the "funnel effect"? What is the significance of the funnel effect to the criminal justice system and to society?

9. Why might a person plead "guilty" to a crime she or he did not commit? How could an innocent person be found "guilty" of a crime she or he did not commit?

Assuming such cases occur on a regular basis, how might the system be improved to eliminate such grave errors? What are the social consequences of convicting innocent people?

10. Why do we allow the findings of "guilty but insane" or "not guilty by reason of insanity" in addition to findings of "guilty" or "not guilty"? How are these additional findings related to the differential treatment of juveniles in our system of jurisprudence?

11. Why is the system of *voir dire* important in choosing jurors? Discuss the differences between challenges for cause and preemptory challenges. Why can't the jury selection process be significantly shortened by simply calling the next 12 people on the list of venire men and women, and requiring them to sit on the next trial held in any given jurisdiction? Would you want just any 12 people to sit in judgment of your guilt or acquittal at a trial? Would it make any difference if the trial were for speeding or in a case where the death penalty could be imposed on you?

12. Why is it important for those convicted of crimes to have an appellate review of their case? What are the differences among appellate review, postconviction relief, and habeas corpus actions? Why would a person convicted of a serious felony need, or want, a review of his case beyond that of his or her state court system?

Notes

1. U.S. CONST. amend V.
2. See, LARRY J. SIEGEL & JOSEPH J. SENNA, JUVENILE DELINQUENCY: THEORY PRACTICE AND LAW (6th ed. West Pub. Co. 1997).
3. U.S. CONST. amend. V.
4. *Hurtado v. California*, 110 U.S. 516, 538 (1884).
5. See, U.S. CONST. amend VIII.
6. See, LAWRENCE BAUM, AMERICAN COURTS: PROCESS AND POLICY 179 (4th ed. Houghton Mifflin Co. 1998); U.S. DEPT. OF JUSTICE, BUREAU OF JUSTICE STATISTICS (1984).
7. See, LAWRENCE BAUM, AMERICAN COURTS: PROCESS AND POLICY 174 (4th ed. Houghton Mifflin Co. 1998); THOMAS R. DYE, UNDERSTANDING PUBLIC POLICY 63–64 (10th ed. Pearson Education, Inc. 2002).
8. U.S. CONST. amend. VI.
9. U.S. CONST. amend. IV.
10. U.S. CONST. amend. V.
11. U.S. CONST. amend. IV.
12. U.S. CONST. art. VI, cl. 2.
13. U.S. CONST. amend. XIV.
14. U.S. CONST. amends. IV, V, VI & XIV.
15. U.S. CONST. amend. XIII, § 1.
16. *Williams v. Florida*, 399 U.S. 78 (1970); *Ballew v. Georgia*, 435 U.S. 223 (1978), jury of less than six in criminal trial violates U.S. CONST. amends. VI & XIV.
17. See generally, TRIAL HANDBOOK ILL. LAW (West Pub. Co. 2004).
18. Alternate translations include "forced to speak."

19. See generally, 725 ILCS 5/101 et seq. (2004).

20. See, e.g., ILL. S. CT. C. COMM. J. INST., ILL PAT. J. INST. (West. Pub. Co. 2003).

21. See, e.g., ILL. S. CT. R. 601 et seq.

22. 28 U.S.C.S. 2254 (2004).

23. LARRY J. SIEGEL & JOSEPH J. SENNA, JUVENILE DELINQUENCY: THEORY PRACTICE AND LAW 22 (6th ed. West Pub. Co. 1997).

24. See, e.g., 1 AM. JUR. TRIALS 189 (1991).

3

The First Amendment: History and Application

The peculiar evil of silencing the expression of opinion is that it is robbing the human race, posterity as well as the existing generation; those who dissent from the opinion still more than those who hold it. If the opinion is right, they are deprived of the opportunity of exchanging error for truth; if it is wrong, they lose what is almost as great a benefit, the clearer perception and livelier impression of truth, produced by its collision with error.[1]

Overview
Civil Liberties and Civil Rights
Bill of Rights History
First Amendment Political Philosophies
Judicial Review

Overview

The First Amendment to the U.S. Constitution impacts virtually all laws in the fields of advertising, broadcasting, journalism, and public relations. This chapter introduces the basic concepts needed to understand when and how the First Amendment guarantees freedom to communications practitioners and when it restricts the applicability of other laws. Rather than present a chronology of First Amendment interpretations, this chapter is organized around four major concepts that facilitate understanding the meaning and application of the political philosophies that guide interpretation of the First Amendment's provisions by the U.S. Supreme Court.

We begin with an explanation of the difference between civil liberties and civil rights. Familiarity with these concepts is essential to understanding that the First Amendment guarantees freedom of speech and press, not a right of free press or a right of free speech. Furthermore, we explain that the First Amendment does not limit actions by corporations, individuals, and other nongovernmental entities.

Because, on its face, the First Amendment only restricts actions by the federal government, it is important to know how some liberties from the Bill of Rights have been imposed on state governments. Therefore, we provide a brief description of how the Supreme Court has used the concept of selective incorporation to require states to protect only some of the personal freedoms addressed in the Bill of Rights. Next, we describe the political philosophies advocated by commentators or used by the Supreme Court to balance other rights and governmental obligations against freedom of press and speech.

Finally, we describe the standards of judicial review that have been used to determine which of our freedoms is important enough to withstand governmental intrusion. These standards and their applications to laws and other governmental actions that curtail free speech and press provide the substance of constitutional interpretation as it is applied by the U.S. Supreme Court today.

This discussion of history and systems of interpretation is provided to give students and practitioners a foundation for understanding how freedom of speech and the press is enforced and balanced against other liberties and rights. Practical applications of First Amendment interpretations to government regulation of mass communications practitioners are discussed in the next chapter.

Civil Liberties and Civil Rights

Many students and practitioners of mass communications believe the First Amendment requires government to protect their interests or that they, because of their profession, stand in a "special place" in relation to the law. This belief may be the product of professional arrogance or it may result from a simple misunderstanding of what is guaranteed by the First Amendment. To really appreciate what legal actions are required or prohibited by the First Amendment, one must understand that the First Amendment provides "civil liberties," not "civil rights."

The distinctions between the concepts "civil liberties" and "civil rights" have evolved over the history of the United States. The first 10 Articles of Amendment to the U.S. Constitution are commonly referred to as the **Bill of Rights**. However, the term *Bill of Rights* is a misnomer because those amendments describe freedoms and liberties, not rights. Freedoms or liberties are exercised by individual citizens without restrictions from government. A freedom limits the actions of a government vis-à-vis its citizens. It does not actually require any governmental action.

Prior to the American Revolution in 1775, most governments in the world were monarchies or oligarchies and were more often than not extremely despotic. People had little control over their daily lives and the average citizen was completely subservient to the monarchy or anyone to whom the monarch had granted authority. Although there were occasional exceptions to this form of rule,[2] the vast majority of the people in the world suffered under tyrannical forms of government and had absolutely no personal freedoms or rights.

The principles of democracy that underlay the formation of the U.S. government began with the brief forays into self-governance described by the writings of ancient Greek and Roman historians and philosophers. Eventually, ideas about democracy, individual freedoms, and natural human rights found their way into the writings and discourse of 16th- and 17th-century political philosophers like Thomas Locke and Jean-Jacques Rousseau. The writings of these men clearly influenced Thomas Jefferson when he penned the Declaration of Independence in 1776. That document laid the foundation for a sense of civil liberty that is reflected in the U.S. Constitution. In particular, several phrases in the Declaration of Independence make it obvious that the founders of our government intended to create a government that was prohibited from restricting its citizens' liberties. Most obvious among these is the assertion of **unalienable rights**.

> We hold these truths to be self-evident, that all Men are created Equal, that they are endowed by their Creator with certain unalienable Rights, that among these are Life, Liberty, and the Pursuit of Happiness. That to secure these Rights, Governments are instituted among Men, deriving their just Powers from the Consent of the Governed, that whenever any Form of Government becomes destructive of these Ends, it is the Right of the People to alter or to abolish it, and to institute new Government. . . .[3]

In the Declaration of Independence, the term *unalienable Rights* referred to "Life, Liberty, and the Pursuit of Happiness." However, by the time the Bill of Rights was ratified on December 15, 1791, there was a much more extensive listing of our "rights." It was also clear that the framers of the Constitution did not intend, by specifically including some rights within the language of the Bill of Rights, to exclude other personal rights necessary for independent civilized thought and action. According to the Ninth Amendment, "The enumeration in the Constitution of certain rights shall not be construed to deny or disparage others retained by the people."[4]

Following the U.S. Civil War, the Fourteenth Article of Amendment was ratified in 1868. It said, in part,

> No State shall make or enforce any law which shall abridge the privileges or immunities of citizens of the United States; nor shall any State deprive any person of life, liberty, or property, without due process of law; nor deny to any person within its jurisdiction the equal protection of the laws.[5]

This amendment has been interpreted to impose two obligations on the states. First, it compels the states to provide "civil rights" for their citizens. Second, it provides the citizens of each state with "civil liberties."

The civil rights obligation means the states have an affirmative duty to protect their citizens from infringement of some of the rights inuring to them by virtue of their citizenship in the United States. Given the historic context of the Fourteenth Amendment, these obligations have typically involved rights that were denied in states of the former Confederacy, such as freedom from slavery, and voting and educational rights for minority citizens.

The state's obligation to recognize civil liberties arises from the Supremacy Clause of the U.S. Constitution[6] and the Fourteenth Amendment. Taken together, these limit what either the national government or the state governments may do to violate citizens' freedoms described in the Bill of Rights.

Thus, the term **civil liberty** has become synonymous with individual liberties or freedoms against which neither the national nor state government may encroach. The term **civil rights** refers to privileges and immunities guaranteed to U.S. citizens, which the national government and the individual state governments must protect from arbitrary infringement. In the case of civil liberties, government action is prohibited or limited; in the case of civil rights government action is required. The obligation of the national government to protect civil rights is specified in the wording of seven separate amendments to the U.S. Constitution, each of which end with the words, "Congress shall have power to enforce this article by appropriate legislation."[7]

The guarantees of free speech and free press described in the First Amendment are civil liberties, not civil rights. The First Amendment says, "Congress shall make no law . . . abridging the freedom of speech, or of the press."[8] Neither the national government, nor the state governments are required to take any action to protect those liberties. Rather, the governments' obligations are to avoid doing anything that might infringe free speech or press. Because the government is not obligated to take action, there are no laws, based on the First Amendment, that restrict the conduct of any private individual or corporation. In other words, private citizens and private companies are within their legal rights when they deny free speech or limit press freedoms.

Bill of Rights History

Whether civil rights or civil liberties, the states are not required to provide all of the freedoms described in the Bill of Rights. Recognizing how concepts from the Bill of Rights are imposed on states will help explain how conflicts between state laws and First Amendment liberties are resolved.

For well over 100 years, the Bill of Rights was interpreted by the courts to apply only to the actions of the U.S. government, and not to the individual sovereign states.[9] Even after ratification of the Fourteenth Amendment, the U.S. Supreme Court failed, for some time, to recognize that any of the basic rights or liberties stemming from the Bill of Rights restricted actions of the individual states.[10] In fact, it was not until the end of the 19th century that the Supreme Court began to impose the basic requirements of the Bill of Rights on both the federal and individual state governments.

Many in mass communications think the First Amendment and its assurances regarding free speech and free press are now and have always been the paramount freedoms in the Bill of Rights. However, a review of U.S. Supreme Court decisions shows the concepts of "freedom of speech" and "freedom of the press" did not come to have any significant meaning until the 1920s and 1930s. The idea that these rights should be considered clear limitations on governmental actions by either the national or the state governments evolved fairly slowly.

The notion that freedom of speech ought to be recognized as a fundamental liberty was first enunciated by the U.S. Supreme Court in its 1925 decision in *Gitlow v. New York*.[11] By 1927, freedom of speech began to receive effective implementation, rather than simply rhetorical or philosophical support.[12] In 1931, in its decision in *Near v. Minnesota,* freedom of the press from prior restraint was first formally recognized as a fundamental freedom subject to full constitutional protection from restriction by state laws.[13] The process by which the U.S. Supreme Court recognizes a specific freedom as preferred or fundamental so that the freedom is given constitutional protection from state government intrusion was called "a process of absorption" by Justice Cardozo in 1937.[14] This process of absorption is labeled **incorporation** in the social sciences.

Principles of Incorporation

There are at least five principles or paradigms propounded by political scientists to describe the process of incorporation. Each of these paradigms is based on the history of its development, the composition and activism of the U.S. Supreme Court, the wording of the case decisions and dissenting opinions, and the issues or thematic content of the cases chronologically.[15] These paradigms have been grouped by political scientists and named according to the dominant characteristic or judicial philosophy running through a body of cases. Although different titles may be applied, the five paradigms that dominate application of incorporation are (a) case-by-case fairness, (b) selective incorporation, (c) selective incorporation "plus," (d) total incorporation, and (e) total incorporation "plus."[16] These are summarized in Exhibit 3.1.

Case-by-Case Fairness

Some of the first cases following ratification of the Fourteenth Amendment appeared to recognize that individuals born or naturalized in the United States should have the same privileges and immunities regardless of their state of residence. However, very quickly the Supreme Court began to seek a doctrine or test to distinguish those "liberties" without which one could not be fairly said to have received **due process of law**. This decision-making technique is called the case-by-case fairness paradigm of incorporation. **Case-by-case fairness** was totally subjective and was based on the whims of the majority

Exhibit 3.1.   Principles of Incorporation. (What components of the Bill of Rights apply to the states?)

Case-by-case fairness	Selective Incorporation	Selective Incorporation "Plus"	Total Incorporation	Total Incorporation "Plus"
Subjective determination by the Court based on sense of fair play and decency or what would "offend civilized sensibilities" or "shock the conscience"	Court asks if denying a right or liberty described in the Bill of Rights would "violate those fundamental principles of liberty and justice that are the core of our society"	Same as "selective incorporation" plus other rights not mentioned in the Bill of Rights, granted by the court based on the Ninth Amendment	All components of the Bill of Rights that are imposed on the federal government are also imposed on the states	Total incorporation of all components of Bill of Rights imposed on the federal government plus other rights granted by the court based on the Ninth Amendment

of justices serving on the high court at any time. It was a "shoot-from-the-hip" form of jurisprudence that looked at the governmental action, process, or outcome complained of by an individual appellant to determine whether the person had received whatever process seemed fair. The test, if any, used by the court in these cases was whether or not the governmental action "offended civilized sensibilities," "shocked the conscience," or went beyond a community's social sense of "fair play" or "decency." These cases apparently had to reach some emotional cord with a majority of the justices before the decision would require a state to recognize an individual citizen's rights or liberties.[17]

It is interesting to note that economic interests in property and the right to enter into a "contract," no matter how unconscionable or lopsided the terms and bargaining power, were the kinds of "liberties" first incorporated or imposed on the states by the Supreme Court using this case-by-case fairness test.

Selective Incorporation

The **selective incorporation** paradigm of absorption by the Fourteenth Amendment says that the states are obligated to grant only those rights and liberties included in the Bill of Rights that are fundamental principles of liberty. Justice Cardozo first described this principle in his opinion in *Palko v. Connecticut*. The case involved a Fifth Amendment double-jeopardy issue. The appellant, who received a death sentence in a second trial, argued that whatever would be a violation of the original Bill of Rights, if done by the federal government, would be equally unlawful if done by a state. Cardozo responded that there is no such requirement. He said the question to be asked and answered when deciding what components of the Bill of Rights should be incorporated into the Fourteenth Amendment and imposed on the states is, "does it violate those fundamental principles of liberty and justice which lie at the base of all our civil and political institutions?"[18] He went on to say that rights and liberties such as the right to trial by a jury of 12, freedom from double jeopardy, and the right to indictment by grand jury are not so "rooted in the traditions and conscience of our people as to be ranked as fundamental."[19]

The Court then affirmed a state supreme court judgment that allowed a defendant, once tried and convicted of a lesser charge of second-degree murder involving a life sentence, to be retried by the state until it secured a capital conviction of first-degree murder, so long as the trial is "error free" for both sides.

Applying the selective incorporation paradigm, Cordozo did say, in dicta, that free speech and free press were fundamental liberties and the Fourteenth Amendment required their protection by the states.[20] Using this version of the selective incorporation standard, the court found a citizen of any state has the absolute right to speak and complain about not receiving his or her constitutional immunity from double jeopardy—all the way to the gallows. The Fifth Amendment prohibition against double jeopardy was not recognized as a "fundamental freedom" requiring application to state trials until the 1969 case of *Benton v. Maryland*.[21]

Selective Incorporation "Plus"

The **selective incorporation "plus"** paradigm for deciding what parts of the Bill of Rights are imposed on the states by the Fourteenth Amendment is similar to the selective incorporation principle described by Justice Cordozo. It too favors freedoms that are seen as fundamental or rooted in our traditions and conscience. Selective incorporation "plus" expands the parameters of selective incorporation to include rights and liberties not actually mentioned in the Constitution or the Bill of Rights.

The Ninth Amendment to the U.S. Constitution says, in its entirety, "The enumeration in the Constitution, of certain rights, shall not be construed to deny or disparage others retained by the people."[22] Using authority it finds in the Ninth Amendment, the U.S. Supreme Court is free not only to pick and choose from among the various clauses and portions of the Bill of Rights, but also to formulate or acknowledge additional rights not found anywhere in the Constitution. Using the principle of selective incorporation "plus," any right or freedom the court defines as a **fundamental right** can be absorbed by the Fourteenth Amendment and used to restrain state actions.

Total Incorporation

Under the **total incorporation** paradigm any right or liberty mentioned in the Bill of Rights should be applied to the states if there has ever been a court action applying that right or liberty to the federal government. Simply put, under the principle of total incorporation, the states and federal government have exactly the same obligations to honor rights and liberties of their citizens.

Total Incorporation "Plus"

The **total incorporation "plus"** paradigm expands total incorporation just as the selective incorporation "plus" paradigm expanded selective incorporation. Under this paradigm, all of the provisions of the Bill of Rights applied to the federal government are also applied to the states. In addition, as society changes, any additional rights or liberties imposed on the federal government are also applied to the states even if those rights or liberties were not mentioned in the Constitution or Bill of Rights.[23]

A famous line from the comedy duo of Laurel and Hardy seems most appropriate to summarize the various theories of incorporation applied by the U.S. Supreme Court: "What a mess you've gotten us into now, Stanley!" One cannot simply read the Constitution and its amendments and know what rights or liberties must be honored by the states. Regardless of the intent of the framers, through its interpretation and the power of judicial review, the U.S. Supreme Court has applied some provisions of the Bill of Rights to the states while permitting the states to avoid recognizing other liberties and freedoms. Exhibit 3.2 shows the components of the Bill of Rights that states must honor. Freedoms and liberties the states are not required to recognize include all of the provisions of the Second Amendment, dealing with bearing arms; all of the Third Amendment, dealing with quartering of soldiers in individual citizens' homes; the Fifth Amendment right to be indicted by a grand jury in a capital or infamous crime; all of the Seventh Amendment, dealing with jury trials in suits at common law; and the first two clauses of the Eighth Amendment, dealing with the rights against excessive bail and against excessive fines.

Exhibit 3.2.   Selective Incorporation.

Rights and freedoms identified in the Bill of Rights that states are _not_ required to honor

Second Amendment
  Right to bear arms, militia

Third Amendment
  Prohibits quartering soldiers in private homes

Fifth Amendment
  Indictment by grand jury

Seventh Amendment
  Trial by jury in civil matters

Eighth Amendment
  Prohibits excessive bail and fines

Rights and freedoms identified in the Bill of Rights that states are obligated to honor

First Amendment
  Free Speech–_Fisk v. Kansas_, 274 U.S. 380 (1927)
  Free Press–_Near v. Minnesota_, 283 U.S. 697 (1931)
  Freedom of Religion–_Hamilton v Regents of U. of Calif._, 293 U.S. 245 (1934)
  Freedom of Assembly–_DeJonge v. Oregon_, 299 U.S. 353 (1937)
  Separation of Church & State–_Everson v. Board of Ed._ 330 U.S. 1 (1947)
  Freedom of Association–_NAACP v. Alabama,_ 357 U.S. 449 (1958)

Fourth Amendment
  No unreasonable search and seizures–_Wolf v. Colorado,_ 338 U.S. 25 (1949)

Fifth Amendment
  Just compensation–_Missouri Pacific Rwy Co. v. Nebraska_, 164 U.S. 403 (1896)
  No Self-Incrimination–_Malloy v. Hogan_, 378 U.S. 1 (1964)
  No double jeopardy–_Benton v. Maryland_, 395 U.S. 784 (1969)

Sixth Amendment
  Fair Trial and right to counsel–_Powell v Alabama,_ 287 U.S. 45 (1932)
  Right to cross-examine witnesses–_Pointer v. Texas_, 380 U.S. 400 (1965)
  Right to impartial jury–_Parker v. Gladden,_ 385 U.S. 363 (1966)
  Right to speedy trial–_Klopfer v. North Carolina_, 386 U.S. 213 (1967)

Eighth Amendment
  No cruel and unusual punishment–_Robinson v. Calif.,_ 370 U.S. 660 (1962)

Ninth Amendment
  Right to vote–_Reynolds v. Sims_, 377 U.S. 533 (1964)

The rights contained in the Ninth and Tenth Amendments, which are not specific and deal more with the general powers of natural sovereignty and governance by The People, also remain "unincorporated." There are, however, numerous cases in which these amendments have been used to limit expanding federal powers, to expand state's rights, and to increase individual human rights.[24] The First Amendment civil liberties of free speech and free press have been incorporated and individual states are prohibited from infringing those freedoms.[25]

First Amendment Political Philosophies

From the preceding discussion of approaches to selective incorporation used by the U.S. Supreme Court, it is apparent that decisions regarding the treatment of rights and freedoms can be arbitrary. Whether any specific portion of the Bill of Rights has been determined to be a fundamental right or a preferred freedom and is therefore important enough for application to the states turns, to some extent, on the standard of judicial review applied by the court. The standard of review applied depends, in turn, on the political and philosophical views of the court making the decision. Therefore, before proceeding to a discussion of the practical applications of the First Amendment in chapter 4, we describe the major philosophical views about individual rights and liberties. In the next section of this chapter, we describe the standards of judicial review.

First Amendment philosophies have been written into the Constitution, circumscribed by legislation, and interpreted by the courts. They have also become both the topic of political debate and the underlying motive for action by politicians and justices alike. These philosophies can be divided into categories based on the extent to which their proponents believe individuals have absolute rights or only relative rights that must conform to the needs of society. Those who advocate absolute rights are called **absolutists** and those who believe rights are relative and should conform to the needs of society are called **social conformists**.

Absolutists believe that when the First Amendment says: "Congress shall make no law. . . abridging the freedom of speech, or of the press. . ."[26] it means exactly what it says. They believe that no laws can be made by any power or authority on the subject. However, social conformists have generally won this argument by stressing that, because individuals living in social units must adjust their behaviors to correspond with the rights or liberties of others, allowing completely unfettered speech would be tantamount to anarchy or mob rule.

Decisions made by the Supreme Court over the years make it apparent that lawmakers as well as the courts balance individual rights against the needs of society. In effect, they make an accommodation between expressive freedoms and social values. Generally, the Supreme Court cases interpreting freedom of speech have held that individual rights of speech must give way to social values of the time. Values that have superceded free speech include public safety, law and order, protecting the reputations of individuals, protection of children, and public decency or morals. Balancing these social values against free expression has created categories of expression that are not granted First Amendment protection. For example, the Supreme Court has held that fighting words, obscenity, defamation, and threats to national security do not deserve First Amendment protection.

Social scientists have identified the three major philosophies or views used by members of the Supreme Court to identify which forms of expression deserve First Amendment protection. They are the literalist interpretation, the social function interpretation, and the social effects interpretation.[27]

Literalist Interpretation

The literalist interpretation is similar, but not identical, to the absolutist view. An absolutist would argue that there may be absolutely no law restricting free expression. A **literalist** begins by defining what kind of expression should be protected. The literalist philosophy carefully defines **pure speech** to include only natural oral or written expression. It then asserts that all pure speech deserves constitutional protection. Hugo Black was expressing a literalist philosophy on free speech when he said, "Government should do nothing to people for the views they express or the words they speak or write."[28]

To a literalist, any form of expressive conduct that is more than pure speech, including gestures or any activity connected with the process of communicating with others in society, can be subjected to reasonable regulation. Thus, when the natural oral speech of an individual is amplified or aided by media it is no longer pure speech. It has become **speech plus** conduct, which the government may regulate. Likewise, a literalist would protect all forms of natural written expression. But if, after writing his or her thoughts, an individual then tries to copy, reproduce, or disseminate the message to others using any means of distribution, including artificial media, that is conduct, and it can be regulated by government.

However, under the literalist philosophy even governmental regulation of speech plus conduct has limitations. The two major constraints on governmental regulation of speech plus conduct are that any regulation must be politically neutral and that the regulation may not suppress a particular viewpoint. In other words, the regulation may be based on the conduct or format of the expression but must be both content- and viewpoint-neutral.

The next two philosophical perspectives are more paternalistic. Rather than focusing on the medium of communication, the social function and social effects philosophies focus on regulation of expression to protect social conformity or to advance a social agenda.

Social Function Interpretation

The **social function** interpretation begins by looking at the social or political purpose served by the content of an expression. While the literalist would require that any government regulation be content-neutral, the advocate of a social function approach begins his or her analysis by classifying the content as either good or bad. This judgment of the content's merit is based on the court's sense of prevailing social values. Speech content that advances "good" social values is protected. Speech that is determined to be lewd, obscene, defamatory, insulting, or otherwise harmful to "good" social values may be prohibited, controlled, or even punished. Applying this perspective, "What is essential is not that everyone shall speak, but that everything worth saying shall be said."[29]

Under this view, expression that does not advance favored social values is simply defined as non-speech. It is not "worth saying." Such non-speech is not thought to be what the First Amendment was designed to protect and it, therefore, can be regulated out of existence.[30]

Social Effects Interpretation

The final First Amendment philosophy is called the **social effects** interpretation. It is also a subset of the social conformist interpretation. It too, defines expression that serves a proper or legitimate social function as speech that falls under the protection of the First Amendment, and expression that does not advance desired social values as non-speech that deserves no protection from government censorship. Proponents of social effects interpretation add to this approach a very specific view of what social function should be protected. They believe the overriding social purpose of speech is to advance the democratic process. In their view, anything that does not advance the democratic process is non-speech.

Under a social effects interpretation, the protected functions of speech should include the discovery of "truth," serving as a check on governmental excesses, and contributing to social stability by releasing tension in the society as a whole. Therefore, whatever is deemed to be "political speech" should be absolutely protected.

One problem with the social effects interpretation is its reliance on the government itself to decide what speech is politically appropriate. If government views an expression as a breach of the peace, incitement to riot, or some other unlawful act it can be censored or suppressed. Therefore, if the social effects of speech are to challenge the government's power and authority or if the speech is too effective in criticizing the government and advocating change, it may be censored as a threat to public safety or to national security.

Critics of the social effects philosophy note that its application can be quite hypocritical. Its advocates tout the overriding objectives of speech to be of service to the advancement of the democratic process, but courts applying social effects interpretations have allowed governmental suppression of speech and press based on the "political correctness" of the content and the viewpoint being expressed. Opponents of this perspective point to the several instances wherein speech has been restricted when the government itself was the target of the expression and where change in government was the anticipated social effect of the speech.[31] Those critics also note situations wherein the government failed to act to censor, suppress, or punish "hate speech" by individuals or groups who posed a threat of immediate harm to other persons or groups.[32] To its critics, the social effects interpretation allows governmental suppression of political speech based on content determined to pose an immediate threat to public safety or national security. But this protection is only available for the preservation and security of the government itself. Social effects does not provide protection for the people as a whole or protection for specifically threatened members of the populace. In other words, it

Exhibit 3.3. Speech and Non-Speech.

	Social Conformist Interpretation of First Amendment	
	Social Function	**Social Effects**
Speech	1. Currently politically correct 2. Serves important governmental function 3. Informs the public 4. Educates the public 5. Protects the public or 6. Enhances the public morals, health, or welfare	1. Promotes support for the "democratic" process 2. Promotes support for current government [status quo] 3. Promotes "law and order" 4. Promotes social control 5. Promotes "mainstream" U.S. values
Non-Speech	1. Defamatory content 2. Insulting or fighting words 3. Content tends to inflict Injury 4. Lewd, obscene, or pornographic content 5. False or misleading commercial advertising 6. Perjury	1. Content tends to incite an immediate breach of peace 2. Content poses imminent threat to: a. National security, or b. Public safety

provides neither protection of the public safety nor national security; it is only a means by which the government may guard the status quo.

Under the social effects philosophy of judicial interpretation, the Supreme Court has separated mere advocacy of a belief, thought, or idea from incitement to imminent lawless action. Applying what is called the **clear and present danger test**, the Court has found that governmental censorship or criminalization of advocacy or abstract teaching is unconstitutional. The Court has, however, permitted government control and punishment of imminent incitement, which includes preparation for and assistance to some immediate violent or illegal result.[33] This test is described in more detail in chapter 4.

Adding to the criticism of the social effects interpretation, we should note that often a speaker is punished when those who opposed his or her point of view actually created the public disturbance. In effect, this philosophical approach permits opponents of an idea to force its censorship by responding to the idea with violence.[34] The relation between social effects and social function interpretations and the concepts of speech and non-speech are shown graphically in Exhibit 3.3.

Judicial Review

The four sources of law in the U.S. system of jurisprudence were detailed in chapter 1. The concept of judicial review was also discussed as one of the three basic components of case law. In chapter 2, the role of the trial courts was described together with the burdens of proof used to determine whether a criminal or civil plaintiff should win a case. In addition, the role and function of our appellate courts, specifically the U.S. Supreme Court, was discussed, together with the general standards of appellate review. So far in this chapter we have described rules for applying the liberties contained in the Bill of Rights to the states and philosophies of First Amendment interpretation. Now we can combine all these concepts to explain the methods used by the U.S. Supreme Court to determine the **constitutionality** of any law or other governmental action. Pertinent to this topic, questions of constitutionality arise when mass communications professionals challenge local, state, or federal restrictions that may conflict with liberties guaranteed under the First Amendment.

Judicial review is a court-made doctrine that allows the U.S. Supreme Court to determine whether the actions of the other two branches of the federal government or any action of a state government comply with the provisions of the U.S. Constitution. Any statute passed by the legislature, any executive order issued by the president, or any state action that does not comply with the provisions of the constitution are said to be "unconstitutional." Any government action that is unconstitutional is not a valid exercise of governmental power under the supremacy clause of the U.S. Constitution.[35]

The doctrine of judicial review is based on the powers granted by the Constitution itself. Unlike Great Britain, which has an unwritten constitution and incorporates all actions of its parliament in its "living constitution," the United States has a written constitution that mentions only one court as the supreme judicial authority. The U.S. Supreme Court, as the only court mentioned in the Constitution, has from the early history of this country asserted a special oversight power to pass judgment on the constitutional validity of the laws and actions of all other branches of the national government. Since the ratification of the Fourteenth Amendment, the Court has exercised similar power to review state laws for their compliance with the U.S. Constitution. The Articles of the Constitution, upon which this doctrine is grounded, include Article III; Article IV, Sections 1, 2, and 4; and Article VI, paragraphs 2 and 3. These portions of the Constitution combined with the historic duties of the courts in deciding legal disputes through the choice, interpretation, and application of law provide the foundation for judicial review in the United States.[36] The most often cited precedent for judicial review in the United States is the decision in *Marbury v. Madison*.[37] In that decision, Chief Justice Marshall wrote,

> Certainly, all those who have framed written constitutions contemplate them as form-
> ing the fundamental and paramount law of the nation, and consequently, the theory of
> every such government must be, that an act of the legislature, repugnant to the consti-
> tution, is void. . . . It is, emphatically, the province and duty of the judicial department,
> to say what the law is.[38]

When exercising its power of judicial review, the Supreme Court has adopted three standards for determining whether a particular governmental action is in compliance with the U.S. Constitution. These special standards of judicial review, as distinguished from the general standards of appellate review, are used only when the high Court, or

Exhibit 3.4. Standards of Judical Review.

Standard	Reasonableness or Rational Relationship	Strict Scrutiny or Compelling State Interest	Heightened Scrutiny or Intermediate Scrutiny
Question	Is there a reasonable or rational relationship between the challenged governmental action and a legitimate governmental interest?	Does the challenged action involve a protected class like race, religion, or national origin, or a fundamental or preferred liberty like freedoms of speech or press?	Does the challenged action involve a suspect class like gender, truthful advertising, or symbolic speech?
Burden	Burden is on the party challenging governmental action to show there is no legitimate governmental interest or there is no reasonable relation between that interest and the challenged action.	Burden is on the government.	Burden is on the government.
Test	Is law or action overbroad, void for vagueness, arbitrary, or capricious?	There must be a compelling governmental interest and the challenged action must be necessary to meet that interest. The challenged action must also be 1) the least restrictive alternative and 2) narrowly tailored.	There must be an important governmental interest and the challenged means of meeting that interest must be 1) substantially related to the government interest and 2) no broader than necessary to meet the government interest.

some other federal court, must review the actions of other branches of government. Thus, when actions of other branches of the national government or actions by any component of a state government are challenged as being unconstitutional and therefore without validity, the governmental actions in question are judged using one of these three standards. These standards of judicial review, which are summarized in Exhibit 3.4, also set both the appellate burden of proof and specify which of the parties bears responsibility for that proof.

Rational Relationship Standard

The original standard of judicial review applied by the Supreme Court to all cases challenging the constitutionality of government action was called the **reasonableness** or **rational relationship** standard. Under this standard of judicial review, the party challenging the federal governmental action had the burden of proving it was unconstitutional. The government action could be proven unconstitutional by showing either that there was no legitimate governmental interest served by the action or that there was no reasonable or rational relationship between a legitimate government interest and the challenged action.

Under this standard of judicial review, the Court seeks to determine whether or not the challenged governmental action or law imposed burdens or granted benefits in an arbitrary or capricious manner. Another common challenge that originates under this standard is the assertion that a law is overbroad or void for vagueness. Overbroad laws are those that cover so many people or so many actions that they cannot possibly be enforced as written, and laws that are void for vagueness are so imprecise or ambiguous that they cannot be consistently and predictably enforced. Under this standard of review, the challenged actions must either advance no legitimate governmental interest or be so broad or vague that they cannot advance the intended governmental interest. Therefore, it is very difficult to challenge governmental action using the reasonableness standard and most government actions challenged under this standard have been held to be constitutional.

Strict Scrutiny Standard

The Supreme Court's adoption of the strict scrutiny test roughly coincided with the court's adoption of a selective incorporation standard for applying concepts from the Bill of Rights to the states. It seems to have developed as the Court realized that some government actions infringed on liberties set out in the Bill of Rights and that the Bill of Rights could also be applied to state actions under the Fourteenth Amendment. Evolution of the strict scrutiny test also seems to have accelerated in the 1920s at approximately the same time the Court began to apply the fundamental liberties or **preferred freedoms** approach to cases using the First Amendment to challenge restrictions on free speech and free press.

This standard did not emerge fully developed in its first applications, but it became quite well developed as precedent in the 1960s and 1970s. One reason for this delayed development was that its full application depends on the identification of protected classes of citizens. These protected classes were only fully recognized as a result of challenges to the systems of racial segregation and religious discrimination that were frequently challenged from the middle 1950s through the late 1970s. Also, many of the holdings that identified protected classes of citizens and justified careful evaluation of laws impacting them arose from challenges to law enforcement practices associated with searches for evidence and coercing confessions in criminal cases.[39]

The first successful challenges to constitutionality of state government acts were based solely on the **due process clause** of the Fourteenth Amendment. These suits asserted that the Fourteenth Amendment made the entire Bill of Rights applicable to the states. Later cases using this same argument failed because the Supreme Court did not incorporate all protections described in the Bill of Rights under the Fourteenth Amendment. Subsequent successful challenges to the constitutionality of state actions very specifically cite both the Fourteenth Amendment and the amendment from the Bill of Rights that described the constitutional right being asserted.[40] The strict scrutiny standard of judicial review evolved to meet the demands placed on the court by these more complex pleadings. It was developed for use in cases where there were due process challenges against federal actions and laws based on the Fifth Amendment, and for cases that presented equal protection or due process challenges to state laws or actions based on the Fourteenth Amendment and other amendments within the Bill of Rights.[41]

The **strict scrutiny standard of judicial review**, which is also known as the **compelling state interest test** or standard, is used by the high Court when it encounters a case involving what it calls protected classifications or laws that obviously infringe on preferred freedoms or fundamental rights. **Protected classifications** refer to artificial legislative categories used as the basis for laws that discriminate against some groups within our population. It was discrimination against these groups that motivated ratification of the Fourteenth Amendment. The first such protected classification was race; this category has been judicially expanded to include religion, national origin, and alienage. Classifications based on color and creed are often added to this list but those divisions are subsumed under race and religion. Preferred freedoms and fundamental rights are those that involve the due process clauses of either the Fifth or Fourteenth Amendments or that Justice Cordozo in *Palko* said would violate the "fundamental principles of liberty and justice which lie at the base of all our civil and political institutions."[42] Any statutes or other government actions having an adverse effect on these protected classifications or preferred freedoms automatically trigger application and analysis under the strict scrutiny standard.

Once a party challenges the constitutionality of a law or governmental action on the basis of impermissible classifications or violations of a preferred freedom, the government has the burden to prove to the Court that there was both a compelling government interest in applying the law or taking the action and that the means used to achieve the compelling governmental interest meets three criteria. The three criteria are that the means are (a) necessary to accomplish the compelling governmental interest, (b) are the least restrictive alternative available to meet the compelling governmental interest, and (c) narrowly tailored to affect no more people or to limit no more freedom than is necessary. Compelling state interests are those the Court finds to be extraordinarily important and that provide the gravest justification for governmental action. Examples of state purposes found by the high Court to be compelling have been (a) protecting the nation's existence, (b) safeguarding life or limb, and (c) shielding children from lasting emotional harm. Examples of expression considered to be a preferred freedom receiving the highest level of protection have included (a) speech intended to convey political or social ideas or facts, (b) speech that is of fundamental importance to the free flow of ideas and opinions, and (c) expression on matters of public interest and concern.[43]

Heightened Scrutiny Standard

The standard of judicial review most recently developed by the U.S. Supreme Court is called **heightened scrutiny** or **intermediate scrutiny**. It falls between the original reasonableness standard and the strict scrutiny standard. The reasonableness standard requires a party challenging governmental action or legislation to prove there was no reasonable relationship between the duties, benefits, or detriments imposed on an individual and any legitimate governmental interest. The strict scrutiny standard requires the government to prove that its actions were based on a compelling state interest and a close fit between its law or action and that interest. The heightened scrutiny standard requires only an important interest for significant governmental interest. An important interest is more that just legitimate, but not as (major) as a compelling interest. The heightened scrutiny standard also requires more than a reasonable fit between the government's action or law and its interests but does not require the close fit necessary under the strict scrutiny standard.

The **heightened scrutiny standard** was originally developed by the U.S. Supreme Court to deal with a series of state and federal laws and actions that gave benefits to men or operated to the detriment of women. Women have never been included in the Constitution and were not given any constitutional rights, until the 1920 ratification of the Nineteenth Amendment gave them the right to vote. Even after ratification of the Fourteenth Amendment, the Supreme Court has repeatedly refused to grant women equal protection of the laws.

The strict scrutiny standard was adopted, in part, to facilitate enforcement of constitutional protections based on race under the Fourteenth Amendment. Laws and governmental actions that discriminated based on race were granted constitutional protection because the Thirteenth and Fifteenth Amendments specifically referred to "race, color, or previous condition of servitude."[44] The court has subsequently expanded these protections to include religion, national origin, and alienage because those concepts seemed similar in the arbitrariness of their use in legislative classification to those of "race and color." However, gender or sex have not been granted the status of a protected class.

During the late 1960s and early 1970s, activists pointed out that there was not only discrimination in law and governmental action based on race, there was also discrimination based on sex or gender. They argued, if such governmental action imposing burdens based on race or color could be declared to be unconstitutional violations of individual civil rights, the same should be said of legal obstacles based solely on sex or gender. The Supreme Court had no apparent difficulty finding that disparate treatment under the law based on race should be reviewed and analyzed under the strict scrutiny standard of judicial review. It also was willing to expand that standard to cover government discrimination based on religion and national origin. However, the Court did not make the same decision when women challenged the constitutionality of governmental action and asked for equality of treatment under the law.[45]

Presumably, in an effort to compromise between the traditional paternalistic views of women and the changing economic and political roles of women, the U.S. Supreme Court eventually developed the heightened scrutiny standard of judicial review.[46] It has also been argued that a different standard of judicial review was required for gender-based claims of violation of individual freedoms because the Thirteenth, Fourteenth, and Fifteenth Amendments to the U.S. Constitution were ratified. Those amendments specifically recognized equal rights based on racial classifications. The only proposed constitutional amendment guaranteeing equal rights under the laws based on gender has not been ratified.[47]

Development of the heightened scrutiny test can be seen historically in three related U.S. Supreme Court cases decided between 1971 and 1976. In 1971, the Court was confronted with a case challenging differential state benefits for men and women. There the court used a reasonableness standard to overturn the state law. The Court said that in the context of benefit allocation, gender was not a reasonable criterion on which the government might base its decisions.[48] In 1973, the Court reviewed another gender discrimination case. In *Frontiero v. Richardson* the court struck down a federal law providing different spousal benefits to married service-men and service-women. In that case, Justice Brennan, joined by three other members of the court wrote that, "classifications based upon sex, like classifications based upon race, alienage, or national origin, are inherently suspect, and must therefore be subjected to strict judicial scrutiny." Four other justices concurred in the result and held the federal law unconstitutional, but they did not agree that classifications based on sex are inherently suspect and therefore subject to strict scrutiny.[49]

Finally, in 1976 the court heard a case challenging an Oklahoma law that permitted sales of beer to women over the age of 18, but required men to be 21 to purchase beer. In this case, Brennan was again joined by three other justices in a decision that overturned the Oklahoma law. But this time he abandoned the strict scrutiny standard and described the heightened scrutiny standard of judicial review. In this decision, the Court went back to, but reworded, the standard used in the *Reed* decision. The new standard of judicial review was:

> To withstand constitutional challenge, previous cases establish that classifications by gender must serve important governmental objectives and must be substantially related to achievement of those . . .[50]

The heightened scrutiny standard has subsequently been expanded by the Supreme Court and is **now** applied to any challenge to governmental actions or laws involving gender, truthful commercial communication, or symbolic speech. Symbolic speech, in this context, has been held to include draft card burning, wearing clothing imprinted with "fuck the draft," nude dancing, and wearing black armbands. The burden in these cases is on the state. When laws or governmental actions are challenged under this standard, the government has the burden of proving an important governmental interest justified the law or action. Furthermore, the government must prove that the means used to achieve the important governmental interest is both substantially related to achievement of that objective and is no broader than necessary to meet the governmental purpose claimed.[51] Examples of important governmental objectives that have justified regulation of speech include (a) promoting the smooth operation of a government program, (b) protecting community order and tranquility, (c) safeguarding private economic interests, (d) indirectly promoting public health, and (e) upholding basic notions of morality.

In chapter 4 we describe how these standards of judicial review, particularly the standards of reasonableness and heightened scrutiny, have been applied to evaluate limitations on free speech and press.

Magic Words and Phrases

Absolutist	Protected classification
Bill of Rights	Pure speech
Case-by-case fairness	Rational relationship test
Civil liberties	Reasonableness standard
Civil rights	Selective incorporation
Clear and present danger test	Selective incorporation "plus"
Compelling state interest test	Social conformist
Constitutionality	Social effects
Due process clause	Social function
Fundamental rights	Speech "plus"
Heightened scrutiny	Standards of judicial review
Intermediate scrutiny	Strict scrutiny standard
Judicial review	Total incorporation
Literalist	Total incorporation "plus"
Preferred freedoms	Unalienable rights
Privileges and immunities clause	

Suggested Cases to Read and Brief

Benton v. Maryland, 395 U.S. 784 (1969)
Boiling v. Sharpe, 347 U.S. 497 (1954)
Bradwell v. Illinois, 83 U.S. (Wall.) 130 (1873)
Brandenburg v. Ohio, 395 U.S. 444 (1969)
Brown v. Board of Education, 347 U.S. 483 (1954)
Craig v. Boren, 429 U.S. 190 (1976)
Dennis v. U.S., 341 U.S. 494 (1951)

Feiner v. New York, 340 U.S. 315 (1951)
Fiske v. Kansas, 274 U.S. 580 (1927)
Forsyth County, Georgia v. Nationalist Movement, 505 U.S. 123 (1992)
Frontiero v. Richardson, 411 U.S. 677 (1973)
Gitlow v. New York, 268 U.S. 652 (1925)
Goesaert v. Cleary, 335 U.S. 464 (1948)
Gram v. Richardson, 403 U.S. 365 (1971)
Hayburn's Case, 2 U.S. (2 Dall.) 409 (1792)
Hoyiton v. U.S., 3 U.S. (3 Dall.) 171 (1796)
Korematsu v. U.S., 323 U.S. 214 (1944)
Mapp v. Ohio, 367 U.S. 643 (1961)
Marbury v. Madison, 5 U.S. (1 Cranch) 137 (1803)
Miranda v. Arizona, 383 U.S. 436 (1966)
Muller v. Oregon, 208 U.S. 412 (1908)
Near v. Minnesota, 283 U.S. 697 (1931)
Palko v. Connecticut, 302 U.S. 319 (1937)
Plessy v. Ferguson, 163 U.S. 537 (1896)
Reed v. Reed, 404 U.S. 71 (1971)
Schneck v. U.S., 249 U.S. 47 (1919)
Strauder v. West Virginia, 100 U.S. 303 (1880)
Ware v. Hoylton, 3 U.S. (3 Dall.) 199 (1796)
Weeks v. U.S., 232 U.S. 383 (1914)
Yates v. U.S., 254 U.S. 298 (1957)

Questions for Discussion

1. Why is it important for practitioners in the fields of mass communications to understand the distinctions between the concepts of "civil liberties" and "civil rights"? What, if any, differences do these concepts make if one is involved in a federal suit or a state court case?

2. When attempting to legislate racial equality, the courts have adopted a practice called "affirmative action." Under this practice they have ordered businesses or schools to increase the number of minority employees or students. Affirmative action results from the government's obligation to enforce a civil right. If free speech were a civil right, rather than a civil liberty, how would you suggest the government affirmatively guarantee your right of free speech?

3. What is the significance of the theories of incorporation, especially to those practicing in the mass communications fields?

4. What difference does it make whether or not a specific freedom or right has been "incorporated" into the Fourteenth Amendment?

5. Which of the theories of incorporation would you prefer, and why?

6. Why hasn't the Bill of Rights been totally incorporated into the Fourteenth Amendment? What difference does it make? What rights or liberties mentioned in the Bill

of Rights do you think the states should be obligated to honor? What rights or liberties do you think the states should be allowed to avoid?

7. What difference does it make that the framers of the Constitution thought that the right against excessive bail or excessive fines was important enough to be written into the Eighth Article of Amendment, but that the U.S. Supreme Court has not thought it important enough to impose on the states? What if you were being held in jail without bond, or with a very high bail required? What is the significance of this provision to the wealthy accused and to the indigent accused? Should wealth or poverty provide the distinction between those who receive justice and fairness of process in the United States? Why? Why not?

8. What, if any, significance do the various political philosophies held by individual members of the U.S. Supreme Court have as seen in the decisions they make over time?

9. Do you believe in the absolutist, literalist, or the social conformist approach to interpretation of the First Amendment? Why?

10. What, if any, significance does the general acceptance of the doctrine of judicial review have, as it has been applied to cases over the history of the United States? What would happen if we did not have general acceptance of this doctrine? How and by whom would decisions be made about whether governmental actions are fair and just, or whether they are constitutional?

11. Compare the three standards of judicial review developed by the U.S. Supreme Court. What difference does it make whether your particular group or any specific freedom or right is protected classification or a preferred liberty? Why has the Supreme Court decided to consider race, color, national origin, religion, and creed as protected classifications when it does not consider sex or gender classifications in this manner? What differences in the administration of our justice system do these distinctions make? Does it seem fair that equality of opportunity should be denied to some groups on the basis of characteristics over which they have no control?

Notes

1. *Brandywine-Main Line Radio, Inc. v. FCC*, 173 F.2d 16, 19, n.1 (D.C. Cir. 1972), quoting JOHN STEWART MILL, ON LIBERTY.
2. E.g., ancient Athens and various periods during the Roman Empire.
3. DECLARATION OF INDEPENDENCE para. 2 (U.S. 1776).
4. U.S. CONST. amend. IX.
5. U.S. CONST. amend. XIV, § 1.
6. U.S. CONST. art. VI.
7. U.S. CONST. amends. XII, XIV, XV, XIX, XXIII, XXIV, XXVI.
8. U.S. CONST. amend. I.
9. See, *Baron v. The Mayor and City Council of Baltimore*, 32 US. (7 Pet.) 243 (1933), rejecting the plaintiff's contention that city government action taking his land for public use should require just compensation under the Fifth Amendment to the U.S. Constitution.
10. See, *Butchers' Benevolent Assoc. v. Crescent City Livestock Landing and Slaughterhouse Co.*, 83 U.S. (1 Dall.) 36 (1873); *Bradwell v. Illinois*, 83 U.S. (1 Dall.) 130 (1873); *Plessy v. Ferguson*, 163 U.S. 537 (1896).

11. *Gitlow v. New York*, 268 U.S. 652 (1925).

12. See, *Fiske v. Kansas*, 274 U.S. 380 (1927).

13. *Near v. Minnesota*, 283 U.S. 697 (1931).

14. See, *Palko v. Connecticut*, 302 U.S. 319 (1937).

15. Please note that dissenting and concurring opinions may be used to identify the philosophical orientation of justices but they are not legal precedents.

16. See, CRAIG R. DUCAT, CONSTITUTIONAL INTERPRETATION 495–500 (7th ed. Wadsworth/Thompson Learning 2000) for general discussion of principles of incorporation.

17. See, e.g., *Hurtado v. California*, 110 U.S. 516 (1884), saying not all rights are incorporated including the right to grand jury indictment; *Maxwell v. Dow*, 176 U.S. 581 (1900), saying trial by jury of 12 is not required; *Twining v. New Jersey*, 211 U.S. 78 (1908), permitting a judge to call jury attention to defendant's refusal to testify.

18. *Palko v. Connecticut*, 302 U.S. 319, 328 (1937).

19. *Id.* at 325.

20. *Id.* at 324–325.

21. *Benton v. Maryland*, 395 U.S. 784 (1969).

22. U.S. CONST. amend. IX.

23. See, HORACE E. FLACK, THE ADOPTION OF THE FOURTEENTH AMENDMENT (Peter Smith 1908); *Adamson v. California*, 332 U.S. 46 (1947), in particular note Justice Black's and Justice Murphy's dissents.

24. See, e.g., *Roe v. Wade*, 410 U.S. 113 (1973), in which the court used the penumbras of rights under the U.S. Const. amends. IV, V, IX, & XIV.

25. See, e.g., *Near v. Minnesota*, 283 U.S. 697 (1931).

26. U.S. CONST. amend. I.

27. See THOMAS I. EMERSON, THE SYSTEM OF FREEDOM OF EXPRESSION, 6–7 (Random House 1970).

28. HUGO L. BLACK, CONSTITUTIONAL FAITH 45–46 (Alfred A. Knopf, Inc. 1968).

29. Alexander Meiklejohn, *Free Speech and Its Relation to Self-Government*, POLITICAL FREEDOM 26 (Kennikat Press 1948).

30. See, Alexander Meiklejohn, *Free Speech and Its Relation to Self-Government*, POLITICAL FREEDOM (Kennikat Press 1948); *Whitney v. California*, 274 U.S. 357 (1927), see particularly Brandeis' concurring opinion.

31. *Schenck v. U.S.*, 249 U.S. 47 (1919); *Gitlow v. New York*, 268 U.S. 652 (1925); *Dennis v. U.S.* 341 U.S. 494 (1951).

32. See, e.g., *Brandenburg v. Ohio*, 395 U.S. 444 (1969); *Planned Parenthood v. American Coalition of Life Activists*, 244 F.3d 1007 (2001).

33. See, *Yates v. United States*, 354 U.S. 298 (1957).

34. *Feiner v. New York*, 340 U.S. 315 (1951), regarding the "heckler's veto"; see also: *Forsyth County, Georgia v. Nationalist Movement*, 505 U.S. 123 (1992), finding content-based permit fee unconstitutional; *National Socialist Party of America v. Skokie*, 432 U.S. 43 (1977).

35. U.S. CONST. art VI, cl. 2.

36. See, *Hayburn's Case*, 2 U.S. (2 Dall.) 409 (1792); *Ware v. Hoylton*, 3 U.S. (3 Dall.)199 (1796); *Hoylton v. U.S.*, 3 U.S. (3 Dall.) 171 (1796); and *Marbury v. Madison*, 5 U.S. (1 Cranch) 137 (1803).

37. *Marbury v. Madison*, 5 U.S. (1 Cranch) 137 (1803).

38. *Id.* at 177.

39. See, *Weeks v. U.S.*, 232 U.S. 383 (1914); *Mapp v. Ohio*, 367 U.S. 643 (1961); *Miranda v. Arizona*, 384 U.S. 436 (1966).

40. See, *Gitlow v. New York*, 268 U.S. 652 (1925); *Fiske v. Kansas*, 274 U.S. 380 (1927); *Near v. Minnesota,* 283 U.S. 697 (1931).

41. See, e.g., *Brown v. Board of Education*, 347 U.S. 483 (1954).

42. *Palko v. Connecticut,* 302 U.S. 319, 325 (1937).

43. See, e.g., *Thomas v. Collins*, 323 U.S. 516 (1945), labor organizer's speech right superior to requirement to register; *Terminiello v. Chicago*, 337 U.S. 1 (1949), political speaker's rights protected against "fighting words" restriction.

44. U.S. CONST. amends. XIII & XV.

45. See, e.g., *Strauder v. West Virginia,* 100 U.S. 303 (1880); *Korematsu v. United States*, 323 U.S. 214 (1944), rigid scrutiny; *Bolling v. Sharpe*, 347 U.S. 497 (1954), scrutinized with particular care; *Gram v. Richardson*, 403 U.S. 365 (1971), alienage, like nationality or race inherently suspect and subject to close judicial scrutiny.

46. See, *Bradwell v. Illinois*, 83 U.S. (1 Wall.) 130 (1872); *Muller v. Oregon*, 208 U.S. 412 (1908); *Goesaert v. Cleary*, 335 U.S. 464 (1948); See also, *Reed v. Reed.* 404 U.S. 71 (1971), which used a reasonableness standard to overturn state rules giving benefit preference to males.

47. See, Brandon P. Denning and John R. Vile, *Necromancing the Equal Rights Amendment*, 17 CONST. COMMENTARY 593 (2000), the proposed amendment was passed by a two-thirds vote of Congress in 1972 but was ratified by only 34 of the 38 states required.

48. *Reed v. Reed*, 404 U.S. 71 (1971).

49. *Frontiero v. Richardson*, 411 U.S. 677 (1973). Note only four justices concurred in the holding regarding gender as a suspect classification. J. Rehnquist dissented altogether.

50. *Craig v. Boren*, 429 U.S. 190, 197 (1976).

51. *Barnes v. Glen Theatre, Inc.*, 501 U.s. 560 (1991), describes rights of city to consider secondary risks from nude dancing; *Cohen v. California*, 403 U.S. 15 (1971), describes standard for comparing concern for disturbing peace to free speech rights; *Central Hudson Gas & Elect. Corp. v. Public Svs. Comm'n.*, 447 U.S. 577 (1980), describes test for balancing governmental interest and commercial speech rights.

4

The First Amendment: Limitations

It is only an acute ethnocentric myopia that enables the Court to approve the censorship of communications solely because of the words they contain.

—Justice William J. Brennan, Jr.[1]

Overview
Introduction and Review
Time, Place, and Manner Restrictions and Public Fora
Sedition, War, and Clear and Present Danger
The Incitement Test in Civil Litigation
National Security and National Defense
Obscenity and Indecency
Practice Notes

Overview

In chapter 3, we described principles used by the U.S. Supreme Court to selectively apply the individual liberties found in the Bill of Rights to the activities of state governments via the Fourteenth Amendment. We also introduced several philosophies used to interpret the First Amendment and the standards of judicial review used by the U.S. Supreme Court to evaluate the constitutionality of laws and governmental actions. In this chapter, we use that information to describe how the Supreme Court has interpreted and in effect limited the freedoms granted by the First Amendment.

We begin with a very brief review of the absolutist and social conformist approaches to interpretation of First Amendment freedoms. Following this review, we explain how time, place, and manner regulations can be used to restrict expressive behavior. These restrictions are based almost entirely on the concept of speech plus conduct prevalent in the literalist interpretation of First Amendment liberties.

We continue with an analysis of the location-based forum approach to laws involving expressive conduct and explain distinctions between various types of fora. These distinctions affect selection of the standard of review used by the Court to determine whether time, place, and manner restrictions are legitimate and constitutional. Analysis of limitations on communication liberty based on the forum in which the expressive behavior takes place combines concepts from literalist and social conformist interpretations of First Amendment liberties.

Some limitations on First Amendment freedoms are based entirely on communication content. Sections on sedition, war, and the clear and present danger test are included in this chapter both to exemplify situations in which the government may suppress communication because of its content and to warn mass communications professionals that they may be censored or regulated. The incitement standard for civil suits is covered in some detail because it can be used to subject practitioners and their employers to expensive litigation.

Obscenity is defined as non-speech by advocates of the social conformist interpretation. Questions about obscenity and indecency only rarely affect working communications practitioners, so we treat the subject briefly. Application of the philosophies used to interpret First Amendment liberties and the procedure for balancing individual liberties against social interest should allow any mass communications practitioner to predict when obscene communications can be restricted. Indecent communication is somewhat more complex and is addressed in more detail in chapter 5, which deals with telecommunications and electronic media.

Finally, this chapter is the first to include practice notes. These notes describe some areas of mass communication practice wherein expression may be regulated. They also provide some suggestions for how practitioners may anticipate and address conflicts between their interests and laws or ordinances regulating communications.

Introduction and Review

Before we begin describing how the courts have limited free speech and free press, we briefly review the philosophical approaches used to interpret the First Amendment. Chapter 3 introduced the two major philosophies used by the U.S. Supreme Court to interpret free speech and free press issues. Those are the literalist and social conformist philosophies. They are summarized in Exhibit 4.1. Literalists believe there can be no laws restricting natural speech or writing, but as soon as any conduct is mixed with the speech, the conduct may be regulated. Therefore, "pure speech," which is natural oral or written expression, is free from regulation but speech plus conduct may be regulated. The only limitation literalists impose on the regulation of speech plus conduct is that all regulations must be politically neutral and no regulation may discriminate because of the category of speaker or the content of the message.

On the other hand, the **social conformist** approach to freedom of speech and press simply defines some expression as speech and some as non-speech. Under this philosophy, speech enjoys constitutional protection while non-speech does not. Proponents of this philosophical approach also define non-speech as any expression that does not advance a good social goal. Therefore, if they find that oral or written expression does not advance a good social end, it is defined as non-speech and may be controlled or punished by the government. Social conformists are divided into two categories. The **social**

Exhibit 4.1.   Philosophies of Constitutional Interpretation.

Absolutists (Literalists)

"Congress shall make NO law ..."

All pure speech is protected.
  Pure speech is all natural written or oral expression.

All other forms of expression may be regulated, controlled, censored, and possibly punished.

Speech Plus = all forms of human communication that involve some conduct, gesture, or activity added to pure speech. This includes:

1. All media by which pure speech is emphasized, embellished, and disseminated.
2. All communication events, processes, technologies, tools, and implements.

Speech Plus conduct can be regulated – the only two major limitations on government regulation of speech plus are:

1. Any regulation must be politically neutral, and
2. Any regulation must be nondiscriminatory, based on type or category of speaker.

Social Conformists including (includes both social function and social effects)

Look at both purpose and function of the communication and

Classify as either "good" or "bad" based on current view of political correctness.

Permit government regulation or censorship or prohibits government regulation or censorship based on a balance of competing interests.

Use the content of the communication to determine its social function or social effects.

Divide communication into:
  Speech, which deserves constitutional protection and
  Non-speech, which has no protection.

functionalists decide what does and does not advance good social ends based on current social values. The **social effects** advocates say the proper social goal of all "good" speech is the advancement of democratic society or the current government. Therefore, a social effects advocate could justify regulating speech if the content of that speech harmed an interest of the current government.

Application

Applying the literalist interpretation, the U.S. Supreme Court has found restrictions on communication conduct to be permissible as long as those restrictions are content-neutral. These restrictions are typically called the **time, place, and manner** restrictions. However, in order to determine if time, place, and manner restrictions are content-neutral, the Court must obviously consider the content of the message. Doing this requires some application of a social conformist interpretation.

Using the social conformist interpretation by itself, the U.S. Supreme Court has declared that some classes of expression are non-speech. They are without social value because their content does not serve one of the permissible social goals. In the view of social conformists, such non-speech is not what the First Amendment was intended to protect. Non-speech may be prohibited, censored, controlled, and even punished by government. Approximately eight categories of non-speech have evolved from this interpretation: lewd, obscene, or pornographic content; defamatory content; insulting or "fighting words"; expressive content that tends to inflict injury; speech that incites an immediate illegal conduct such as riot or violence; speech that poses an imminent threat to public safety or national security; false or misleading commercial advertising; and perjury. At times, the Supreme Court has applied these categories of non-speech to allow national or state governments to ban it totally and to punish speakers or writers of such communication. In some instances, even those who were merely recipients of non-speech were subject to government action.

Later in this chapter we describe the restrictions on obscenity and in chapter 5 we discuss indecency. Most regulation of obscenity is based on community standards and is left to the individual states. Pornographic expression has been given some protection, as long as it is not obscene, but the creation, distribution, and even possession of child pornography has been declared to be non-speech and totally without First Amendment protection. Profane and indecent expression have been given some protection, but are considered to be "lesser speech" and are subject to rigorous time, place, and manner controls. These are discussed in chapter 5, which deals with regulation of broadcasting.

Defamatory expression, insulting or "fighting words," and expression that tends to inflict injury have been left to the states to regulate primarily through civil laws allowing recovery for proven injury. Some states have allowed "fighting words" to be used as a defense to assault or battery cases, depending on the words and circumstances. Prior to the 1931 Supreme Court decision in *Near v. Minnesota*[2] defamatory speech could not only be censored; speakers and writers could be criminally punished for their utterances. Such expression, because of its falsity, was defined as non-speech and was totally outside the reach of First Amendment protection. In the *Near* decision, the Court ruled that First Amendment protections encompassed defamatory accusations and statements and held that the government itself could not censor or enjoin such publications. However, the Court concluded that the protections of speech and press are not absolute. Therefore, the proper recourse in such cases is through private suits for defamation rather than through government-initiated censorship and criminal punishment.[3]

Oral or written expression that incites an immediate breach of the peace, riot, or other unlawful action, has been determined to be non-speech and not the kind of speech or press that the First Amendment was intended to protect. Therefore, government censorship, arrest of the speakers or writers, and punishment for advocating illegal acts can be constitutional. More recently, the concept of non-speech has been extended to the civil area giving litigants a cause of action against publishers of manuals describing how to complete illegal acts. These suits require that the plaintiff suffer some injury and are based on an "incitement" standard that is described later in this chapter.[4]

Expression that is interpreted to pose an imminent or immediate threat or risk of harm to public safety or national security has, throughout U.S. history, been defined as non-speech. It is therefore censorable and punishable. However, following the creation and application of the **clear and present danger test** in 1919, and since its clear adoption as the prevailing standard in the 1969 case of *Brandenberg v. Ohio*,[5] the Supreme Court has distinguished between mere advocacy of abstract ideas and beliefs, which are now considered to be within the realm of "protected speech," and advocacy of specific illegal activities, which can be prohibited and punished.

Finally, those adhering to the social conformist interpretation of First Amendment issues have determined that both false or misleading commercial advertising and perjury are non-speech and thus can be totally prohibited and punished by the government. Consider also, that prior to the 1975 decision in *Bigelow v. Virginia*[6] all forms of advertising were considered self-serving puffery, and therefore were non-speech and unworthy of any protection under the First Amendment. However, since the decision in *Virginia State Board of Pharmacy v. Virginia Citizens Consumer Council*[7] truthful advertising has been viewed as useful in allowing the public to make "informed" choices about products and services for sale. Commercial communication is now granted limited First Amendment protection under the heightened scrutiny standard discussed in chapter 3.[8]

In summary, it seems apparent that the Supreme Court bases decisions on the social conformist approach to First Amendment interpretation. Clearly, some expressive behavior is being defined as non-speech because of its content, and non-speech is denied First Amendment protection.

It requires careful consideration of both message content and the author's viewpoint to decide what speech is obscene or what commercial messages are false, or whether some expression constitutes an immediate threat to public safety. These decisions are not content neutral and certainly are not consistent with an absolutist or literalist interpretation of the First Amendment. Some would say they are the antithesis of the unalienable human rights so highly regarded by the founders of our nation.

Applying both literalist and social conformist interpretations, the U.S. Supreme Court has created several limitations on the liberties of free speech and free press. In the remainder of this chapter we first explain how the literalist distinction between pure speech and speech plus conduct are used to permit restrictions based on time, place, and manner of speech, or the forum in which the expression takes place. Then we describe limitations based on speech content that are more consistent with the social conformist interpretation of First Amendment liberties.

Time, Place, and Manner Restrictions and Public Fora

It may appear that the social conformist interpretation has been pervasive in U.S. Supreme Court decisions concerning First Amendment liberties. But it would be more accurate to say the Supreme Court has been very eclectic in its interpretations. The Court has employed a combination of both literalist and social conformist approaches to suit the views of the majority of justices on the Court as each individual case has come before it.

Time, Place, and Manner Restrictions

Some permissible restrictions on free expression are based entirely on the time, place, and manner of communication. That is to say laws regulating when one may speak, where one may communicate, or the manner or medium of expression have generally been upheld. For time, place, and manner restrictions to be constitutional they must be absolutely content-neutral. These restrictions permit the conduct used to deliver speech to be regulated but do not permit any regulation that would give preference to one point of view over any other. Applying this standard, the U.S. Supreme Court has upheld restrictions on where charities or religious groups may solicit funds so long as all solicitors are required to follow the same rules.[9] Laws forbidding loudspeakers, prohibiting solicitations in airports, or limiting distribution of literature to specific hours have all been upheld. As long as the restriction does not specify or discriminate based on what is being said, governmental limitations on the time, place, and manner of communications are constitutional. However, the content-neutrality of the law must be absolute. Even laws that might allow some discretion to discriminate against a particular message content or speaker are unconstitutional. In 2002, for example, the U.S. Supreme Court ruled that a village ordinance requiring solicitors to register was unconstitutional. The Court noted the registration process permitted some discretion by the village and could be used to limit communication by some groups.[10] Even the possibility that a public official is given discretion to base a decision on the content of the expression being regulated is enough to make a time, place, or manner restriction unconstitutional. To help evaluate challenges to limitations on free speech based on time, place, and manner, the Court has developed a forum-based approach. It uses the concept of location of the expressive conduct to decide what standard of judicial review to apply.

Public Fora Standards

When evaluating restrictions on time, place, or manner of communication, the Supreme Court has applied the speech plus conduct concept from a literalist interpretation in combination with a social function interpretation to create standards of review based on the forum used for communication. This forum-based approach begins by dividing communication behavior into three categories based on the physical place where they occurred. The Court then applies a different standard of judicial review to governmental restrictions on communication in each of the three categories. These standards of judicial review are used to balance the government's interest in a time, place, and manner restriction of free speech against the speaker's individual right of free speech. These three categories are called traditional public fora, designated public fora, and non-public fora. These fora and the standards of review for each are summarized in Exhibit 4.2.

Traditional Public Forum

If the speaker or publisher chooses to engage in communication plus conduct in areas that have been traditionally available for public expression, such as the public streets, sidewalks, and parks, these locations are called **traditional public fora** by the Court. Some, but not all, public buildings are also public fora, as are some public spaces within government buildings. Whether any public building or public property is a traditional public forum depends on how it is usually used. For example, military buildings and police stations are typically not public fora because of their traditional emphasis on security. Historically, the steps in front of courthouses, capital buildings, and monuments and some government buildings were public fora. When evaluating First Amendment challenges to restrictions of expression in public fora, the Court applies the strict scrutiny standard of judicial review. In order for governmental limitations or regulations on the time, place, and manner of communications in these locations to be valid, the government must show that its laws or limitations are narrowly tailored to achieve a compelling state interest and it must leave ample alternative channels of communication open to users of these venues.[11]

Designated Public Fora

Some locations or media have not been traditionally used for free public expression but have been created or designated for that purpose. For example, most college campuses have a "speakers' corner" or "Free Forum Area" set aside for demonstrations or student speeches. Other examples of **designated public fora** include bulletin boards and what are called metaphysical fora. **Metaphysical fora** are not places but are media that have been created for the expression of ideas. Such metaphysical fora may include student newspapers if the school has surrendered control of the newspaper content. It is also helpful to note that a location or metaphysical forum may be designated a public forum for only a limited purpose, or for use by a limited group of speakers.

The Court also applies the strict scrutiny standard of judicial review when any governmental attempt to regulate communication in designated public fora is challenged. Content discrimination may be permitted if it preserves the purposes of a limited forum; however, viewpoint discrimination is presumed to be impermissible when directed against speech that is within the forum's purpose.[12]

Non-public Fora

The third location-based category used by the Court to select a standard of judicial review for challenges to time, place, and manner regulations on expressive conduct is called a **non-public forum**. This is the largest category of locations where communicative behaviors may be met with both government and private legal restrictions. These places include all remaining public or private property. It includes private property, not designated as public fora, to which owners invite the public, such as shopping malls, restaurants, and business offices. Government properties that are non-public fora include government offices, jails, military bases, mailboxes, and airport terminals. Communication in these non-public fora is evaluated using the reasonableness standard of judicial review.

Therefore, shopping centers and other public retail stores and businesses may impose reasonable time, place, and manner restrictions on communicators wishing to use their facilities, and these limitations may be imposed to minimize disruption of commercial or other business functions of the property owners. In addition, local governments may also impose reasonable ordinances to control activities in these areas. Furthermore,

Exhibit 4.2. Forum-Based Review.

Traditional Public Fora	Designated Public Fora	Non-Public Fora
Venue	**Venue**	**Venue**
Public streets, Sidewalks Parks Some public buildings (and some but not all parts of buildings)	**Location opened by the government for expressive behavior Examples:** Bulletin boards in schools Free fora or speaker corners on college campuses "Metaphysical fora" like student-run newspapers	**All remaining "public property" including private property with public use. Examples:** Shopping malls Government office lobbies Jails & prisons Military bases Airports Mailboxes
Standard of Judicial Review applied to any government regulation of expression in this place.	**Standard of Judicial Review** applied to any government regulation of expression in this place.	**Standard of Judicial Review** applied to any government regulation of expression in this place.
Strict Scrutiny*, which means the burden is on the government to show: 1. the purpose of the regulation is to achieve a compelling state interest, 2. its regulations are narrowly drawn or tailored to achieve the compelling government interest, and 3. the regulation leaves ample alternative channels of communication open.	Strict Scrutiny*	**Reasonableness, which means the burden is on the person challenging the government regulation to show:** 1. no legitimate government purpose is served by the regulation, 2. there is no rational relationship between a legitimate governmental purpose and the regulation, OR 3. the regulation is arbitrary or subject to unreasonable discretion in application.

the national, state, and local governments are not forbidden by the Constitution from controlling use of their own property for conducting their own business. Generally, time, place, and manner restrictions on expressive behaviors in non-public fora must (a) be content-neutral, (b) allow reasonable alternative channels of communication, and (c) be no broader than necessary to serve the government's legitimate purpose. The burden of proof for challenges to communication limitations in non-public fora venues is on the proponent of unconstitutionality, not on the government or property owners.[13]

Sedition, War, and Clear and Present Danger

It should come as no surprise that the U.S. government has, on numerous occasions, sought to control and punish expressive conduct. This is just as true in today's climate of terrorism as it was when the nation faced other periods of crises involving public safety or national security. One of the first acts of the new Congress of the United States was to censor and make punishable by imprisonment any manner of speech or writing critical of the federal government or its elected officials. The Sedition Act of 1798 made it "unlawful to publish false, scandalous, and malicious" information about the government, Congress, or the president. Speech and press that challenged or questioned actions of the fledgling national government or that gave support to a revival of British rule in the United States were seen as treason.[14] Even our first president, George Washington, thought that information and "news" concerning the government should be controlled or "managed" and nothing should be published about the national government that might cast doubt on its legitimacy.[15] However, Thomas Jefferson felt so strongly about the importance of the First Amendment freedoms, even when they involved criticism of our government, that he pardoned the people convicted under the 1798 Sedition Act.[16]

Since that time, several acts by Congress have made it illegal for anyone to speak against governmental actions or to advocate the replacement of our government. Almost all of the statutes limiting free speech have been created during times of perceived national emergencies or war. These include (a) the Espionage Act of 1917, (b) the Smith Act of 1940s, and (c) the USA PATRIOT Act of 2001.[17] In addition, numerous state sedition acts have also found their way to the U.S. Supreme Court for interpretation and review.[18]

Development of the "Clear and Present Danger Test"

In chapter 3, the social effects approach to interpretation of First Amendment liberties was described as a subset of the social conformist viewpoint. Under this view, speech and press are classified based on governmental speculation about the anticipated results of the speech or writing. Governmental control and punishment have generally been found to be constitutional if the government can show that the anticipated results of the challenged communication would be (a) a breach of the peace, (b) an incitement to riot, (c) an incitement to any unlawful action, or (d) an immediate threat or risk to public safety or national security. The **clear and present danger test** was first articulated by Justice Oliver Wendell Holmes in the decision in *Schenck v. United States*.[19] His opinion there elucidates application of the social effects interpretation to seditious communication.

The U.S. Supreme Court unanimously upheld the conviction of Schenck, who was the general secretary of the Socialist Party, under the Espionage Act of 1917. He was charged with conspiracy to violate the act by "causing and attempting to cause insubordination…in the military and naval forces of the United States, and [obstructing] the recruiting and enlistment service of the United States, when at war with the German

Empire." Schenck had used the U.S. Postal Service to distribute leaflets to men who had been drafted for military service. The leaflets quoted the Thirteenth Amendment and equated conscription with slavery. In his opinion affirming Schenck's conviction, Justice Holmes specifically said that our rights and liberties may be interpreted differently depending on national conditions of peace or war.

> We admit that in many places and in ordinary times the defendants in saying all that was said in the circular would have been within their constitutional rights. But the character of every act depends upon the circumstances in which it is done. . .[20]

Justice Holmes described the criteria employed by the Courts to determine the constitutionality of governmental censorship in a time of war. He said:

> The question in every case is whether the words are used in such circumstances and are of such a nature as to create a clear and present danger that they will bring about the substantive evils that Congress has a right to prevent. It is a question of proximity and degree. When a nation is at war many things that might be said in time of peace are such a hindrance to its effort that their utterance will not be endured so long as men fight and that no Court could regard them as protected by any constitutional right.[21]

This statement initiated what is now called the **clear and present danger test**. The test is used to define the point at which speech can trigger serious harm. The Court does not require the government to show that the advocated harm actually occurs. Rather, the language used, by itself, may be sufficient to sustain conviction. It is ironic that just at the point where a speaker's words and message may become truly effective, the government is allowed to suppress the speech and punish the speaker.

Justice Holmes first described the clear and present danger test in 1919 but the majority of the Court did not adopt the test in its present form until its decision in *Brandenburg v. Ohio* in 1969.[22] Between 1919 and 1969, the test went through several permutations. In a dissenting opinion in 1919, Justice Holmes described his belief that people should not be convicted under the expanded Espionage Act of 1918 without proof of specific intent. He said, "It is only the present danger of immediate evil or an intent to bring it about that warrants Congress in setting a limit to the expression of opinion."[23] In 1927, Justice Brandeis stressed that it was the imminence of the danger created and not the strength of advocacy that determines whether free expression can be limited without violating Constitutional rights. Brandeis, with Holmes concurring, wrote:

> In order to support a finding of clear and present danger it must be shown either that immediate serious violence was to be expected or was advocated, or that the past conduct furnished reason to believe that such advocacy was then contemplated.[24]

Brandeis went on to say that "only an emergency can justify repression" and that punishment after communication, rather than censorship, is the preferred remedy even for speech advocating violence or property destruction.[25]

In 1925, Justice Sanford delivered an opinion of the Court affirming the New York criminal anarchy conviction of Benjamin Gitlow. Gitlow was the leader of the Left Wing Section of the Socialist Party and his conviction was based on the publication and dissemination of a statement titled *The Left Wing Manifesto*. The document advocated the overthrow of the government by force and violence. Sanford failed to apply the clear and present danger, but writing for the majority of the Court he did, for the first time, recognize that "freedom of speech and of the press . . . are among the fundamental personal rights and 'liberties' protected by the due process clause of the Fourteenth Amendment from impairment by the States."[26]

Sanford used only the reasonableness standard of judicial review to uphold the constitutionality of the state statute under which Gitlow was convicted. He said, "utterances advocating the overthrow of organized government by force . . . involve such danger of substantive evil that they may be penalized."[27] Under the reasonableness standard, because protecting the government from overthrow is a legitimate governmental interest and there was a reasonable relationship between that interest and restricting speech advocating the violent overthrow of the government, Sanford found Gitlow's conviction appropriate.[28] Unlike the clear and present danger test advocated by Holmes and Brandeis, the Court in this case relied exclusively on the content of Gitlow's message; it did not require any proof of immediate danger to national security or public safety. In his dissenting opinion, Justice Holmes, with whom Justice Brandeis concurred, noted that Gitlow was only accused of publication and that there was no evidence his publication would actually generate real harm.[29]

The clear and present danger test continued to evolve. In a 1951 decision, a plurality of the U.S. Supreme Court applied a restatement of the test used by the U.S. Court of Appeals. In that decision, the Supreme Court was apparently considering the likelihood of harm, not just the message content, when it said,

> In each case (courts) must ask whether the gravity of the "evil," discounted by its improbability, justifies such invasion of free speech as is necessary to avoid the danger.[30]

The Supreme Court finally modified the clear and present danger test to its current form in the 1969 decision in *Brandenburg v. Ohio*. That case dealt with the right of a Ku Klux Klan (KKK) leader to convene and assemble with his group and to advocate messages of hatred and violence toward other people. The Court overturned Ohio's 1919 Criminal Syndicalism Act as unconstitutional under both the First and Fourteenth Amendments. The Criminal Syndicalism Act did not prohibit conduct, but made it a crime to advocate crime, sabotage, or violence or terrorism for the purposes of industrial or political reform. In the per curium decision affirming the KKK's right to meet and speak, the Court said,

> [T]he constitutional guarantees of free speech and free press do not permit a State to forbid or proscribe advocacy of the use of force or law violation except where such advocacy is directed to inciting or producing imminent lawless action and is likely to incite or produce such action . . . we are here confronted with a statute which, by its

Exhibit 4.3. Incitement Standard.

Speech without conduct may not be censored or punished, even if it advocates violence or illegal acts

UNLESS it

| Is intended to incite or produce imminent lawless conduct | and | Is likely to actually incite or produce lawless conduct |

---

own words and as applied, purports to punish mere advocacy. . . . Such a statute falls within the condemnation of the First and Fourteenth Amendments.[31]

Both Justice Black and Justice Douglas concurred with the judgment in *Brandenburg,* but disagreed with the application of the clear and present danger test. Douglas aggressively supported an absolutist interpretation of the First Amendment and said, "The quality of advocacy turns on the depth of the conviction; and government has no power to invade that sanctuary of belief and conscience."[32] In summary, two justices said there should be no limitation of First Amendment speech and press liberties unless there was speech plus conduct; seven justices said speech alone can be censored or punished if it presents a clear and present danger of harmful conduct.

The result of the *Brandenburg* decision was twofold. First, the KKK leader's conviction under the Ohio Syndicalism Statute was reversed and the statute was declared unconstitutional. Second, the decision modified the clear and present danger test into what is now called the **incitement test**. The standard is summarized in Exhibit 4.3. It must be applied to determine whether a state may forbid or prosecute advocacy of force or violation of law. It begins with the assumption that laws punishing mere advocacy are unconstitutional. It permits censorship or punishment of advocacy only if the advocacy (a) is directed to inciting or producing imminent lawless action, and (b) is likely actually to incite or produce violence or illegal conduct.

The Incitement Test in Civil Litigation

During the 1980s, there was a dramatic increase in the number of lawsuits against publishers and broadcasters. Consumers of all kinds of media, along with their parents and heirs, appeared determined to blame media for their own misconduct, stupidity, or bad luck. Many of these suits were frivolous attempts to collect nuisance settlements from well-funded media companies, but some were well grounded in legal concepts. Regardless the motivation for the increase in lawsuits against media, it is important for all mass communications practitioners to understand the logic of legal liability so they can minimize their risk of suit. In chapter 9, we cover the traditional communications torts of defamation, privacy, and publicity, but here we introduce tort liability based on the incitement standard. We have chosen to cover incitement liability here because it is very closely related to the incitement standard developed to deal with governmental actions and because it is not one of the traditional communications torts.

Tort Law

Tort law is one of the many areas of civil law, and civil law is a division of law that permits private individuals and companies to sue one another. While there are variations in tort law from state to state all states do permit suits for simple negligence. For a plaintiff to win a suit in simple **negligence** in most states, he or she must prove five elements by a preponderance of the evidence. Those five elements are (a) the defendant owed the plaintiff a legal duty, (b) the defendant breached that legal duty, (c) the breach was the proximate cause of some injury to the plaintiff, (d) the plaintiff suffered an injury, and (e) the injury suffered by the plaintiff had financial value.

It is not our intention to present a treatise on tort law, but a brief explanation of some basic concepts will help you recognize situations that can create liability and know when you need to seek legal counsel. The legal elements of a tort and available relief are summarized in Exhibit 4.4.

The concept of **legal duty** is situation-specific. It is based solely on what a reasonable person with a normal level of intelligence and experience would do and foresee as a consequence of his or her actions. Every action by any person carries with it a foreseeable risk of harm to others. Everyone owes a legal duty of due care to everyone else based on this risk of harm. If one breaches the legal duty of due care through simple negligent conduct, reckless conduct, or intentional conduct, then the person is held liable for any injury **proximately caused** by his or her actions.

The type of **damages** or the amount of money a plaintiff can recover depends on whether a jury finds that another person was negligent, reckless, or intended to cause harm. Negligence, recklessness, and intentional conduct infer mental states called **scienter** or **mens rea**. **Negligence** refers to failure to exercise reasonable care. A person is **reckless** when he or she shows disregard for the safety of others or gross indifference to

Exhibit 4.4. Elements and Relief for Torts.

Elements that must be proven
- Duty–a legal duty of care owed by the defendant to the plaintiff
- Breach–Failure to meet the duty by the defendant
- Proximate cause–relationship between the breach of duty by the defendant and injury to the plaintiff
- Injury–harm to the plaintiff
- Damages–injury had financial value

Relief

Damages (payment by the defendant to the plaintiff)
- Compensatory: To "make the plaintiff whole"
- Punitive: for gross negligence, recklessness, or intentional act
- Nominal: for small injuries given as a matter of principle

Injunctive relief

the results of his or her actions. A finding of **intentional misconduct** means the plaintiff deliberately engaged in misconduct or actually intended to cause harm.

The type of damages a plaintiff may recover depends, in large part, on the mental state of the defendant. The major types of damages are compensatory, punitive, and nominal.

When one breaches the legal duty of due care, he or she can be held liable for compensatory damages to any person injured. This is true for all three levels of scienter. **Compensatory damages** are the amount of money it takes to make the plaintiff whole. In other words, it is the amount of money required to put the plaintiff back in the same situation he or she would have been in if someone else had not breached his or her duty of care. Compensatory damages include such things as medical expenses, pain and suffering, and lost wages.

Punitive damages are awards of money that are designed to punish the defendant for his or her misconduct. They may be a multiple of the compensatory damages or they may vary with the wealth of the defendant or the egregiousness of his or her offense. Punitive damages are often awarded in situations involving intentional torts or recklessness. Intentional torts are often created by statute to mirror criminal laws and include assault, battery, and wrongful death. These laws permit civil recovery for both compensatory and punitive damages for any harm done. Punitive damages may also be awarded in situations that would not be subject to criminal prosecution but that involve reckless conduct or disregard for foreseeable injury or death.

Nominal damages are token awards made to uphold a legal or ethical principle when there are no financial injuries to compensate and no justification for punitive damages. They are the most problematic and disagreeable to plaintiffs and their attorneys because, while they are based on a finding in favor of the plaintiff, they often produce neither satisfaction nor compensation for the cost of litigation.

In addition to the various types of actual or monetary damages awarded to civil tort plaintiffs, sometimes injunctive relief is also requested and awarded. Injunctive remedies were discussed in chapter 1 where we described the concept of equity. The most common forms of injunctive relief are a temporary restraining order, temporary injunction, and permanent injunction. These are orders from the court for the plaintiff to do something or to refrain from some conduct and are enforceable through the court's **contempt powers**.

Incitement as a Tort

In several cases against media companies, beginning in the late 1970s, the federal district and appellate courts developed case precedents recognizing that personal injury suits based on expression could violate the duty of due care. In these cases, the courts acknowledged that First Amendment freedoms were being limited but they held that traditional common law torts based on negligent conduct were not adequate to provide remedies for injuries caused by expression inciting harmful conduct. To address these suits, the concepts of specific incitement or **negligent incitement** were taken from the *Brandenburg* decision.

When a media representative is accused of inciting harmful conduct, the federal courts determined the plaintiff must meet a stringent burden of proof and must prove that expression by the media representative is responsible for injury to the plaintiff. This heavy burden of proof where media defendants were involved was required to avoid (a) a chilling effect on potentially valuable speech, and (b) a flood of lawsuits based on media content. Media liability in these cases also depends on the nature of the negligent message and facts showing that the medium's communicative behavior incited someone to engage in harmful conduct.[33] These cases involved music lyrics, magazine articles, broadcast documentaries, entertainment shows, and even the alleged cumulative effects of televised program violence. In most of these situations, the cases against the media were dismissed or reversed on appeal when the appellate courts applied the incitement test from the *Brandenburg* decision. Applying the incitement test, appellate courts required plaintiffs to prove the challenged programs or media articles were specifically directed at inciting imminent lawless action and were likely to incite such action.

Suits against the authors or producers of medical advice columns or shows, product-instruction booklets, personal advice publications, or musicians were based on suicides and accidental deaths alleged to have been caused by lyrics, subliminal messages, fad diets, and natural food or poison food descriptions. Both the federal district and appellate courts have dismissed these suits. In such cases, the defendants were generally awarded **summary judgments** because the plaintiff was not able to show the publisher or producer had a **legal duty** to assure the accuracy of its messages. In fact, the courts often ruled there was not even a legal duty for the publishers to investigate the accuracy of their messages. In some of these cases, the courts ruled the plaintiffs had not produced, or could not possibly produce, credible evidence that the words or lyrics were intended to cause imminent suicide or other harm, that injury was a reasonably foreseeable consequence, or that words used actually incited illegal conduct. Therefore, legal claims were barred by the First Amendment.[34] However, when publications provide advice, instructions, or advertising that involves illegal and intentionally harmful activity, the tenor of the cases changes and no First Amendment protection for such speech is found by the courts. When books or advertisements obviously contain information aimed at intentional illegal or harmful activities, the publishers can be held legally liable for damages caused by their publications under two different legal principles. First, publishers in these instances can be held absolutely liable to victims because they aided and abetted the criminal activities that resulted in harm or death. Second, publishers are liable in situations where the advertisement or published material contained a clearly identifiable unreasonable risk of harm to the public. In this context the potential for harm must have been so obvious that it should have alerted a reasonable publisher to the danger.[35]

Based on these cases, the courts now recognize precedent for a **modified negligence standard**. The new standard is applied to suits against media defendants for harm caused by the content of their messages and uses the imminent incitement test from the *Brandenburg* decision. This line of cases also shows how our rights can be limited or expanded once a particular political philosophy is adopted by the Supreme Court. In this instance, the **social effects** interpretation of First Amendment liberties guided the creation of a new legal liability for media.

The general rules applied when media are sued for negligent incitement are based on the foreseeability of the risk to public safety. Generally, publishers and broadcasters are not liable for physical harm caused by advertising or other expression when they had no reason to suspect a defective product or dangerous act was advocated; they can be held liable for actions resulting from the content of their medium only if they knew, or reasonably should have known, of the danger. Also, publishers and broadcasters have no legal duty to investigate products or claims advertised in their media. However, if it is clear from the face of the advertisement or other message that the product, service, or message content presents a public safety risk, the medium containing the message can be held legally liable for any injury that results from the message.

Although the standards and burdens of proof for personal injury cases against media defendants are not always consistent, courts usually excuse media from liability either under the basic negligence law principles or by applying the First Amendment standard developed from the *Brandenburg* incitement test. Finally, media companies are most likely to be held liable for harm when the challenged messages involve commercial advertising, promotions of hazardous or illegal products or services, a danger that is foreseeable to a reasonable publisher, or hateful or depraved expression that is sufficiently detailed and targeted to constitute a threat of bodily harm. These rules are expanded and additional case examples are provided in the practice notes at the end of chapter 9.

National Security and National Defense

When the content of media creates a possible risk to national security or national defense, the Supreme Court has applied exceptions to the strict scrutiny standard of review usually applied to government restrictions on free speech and press. Cases in this area fall into three general categories: (a) where the media gain access to critical information and choose to print it, (b) where government employees who have access to critical information leak it to the press, and (c) wartime access restrictions and censorship. The U.S. Supreme Court has not yet developed a definitive standard of review for these situations, and the outcome of these cases appears to be based on case-by-case review. However, there does appear to be one overall rule. The First Amendment does not guarantee any right of media access, only a right to communicate all but the most sensitive information such as the details of current military operations.

The first case that recognized freedom of the press from government censorship or prior restraint in all but the most exigent circumstances was *Near v. State of Minnesota*.[36] The *Near* case dealt with the constitutionality of a state statute that allowed courts to permanently enjoin, as a public nuisance, any newspaper or other periodical that disseminated malicious, scandalous, and defamatory material. The Supreme Court held such a statute to be an infringement of the liberty of the press guaranteed by the First Amendment. However, in its reasoning, the Court also described the parameters of prior restraint. In that context, the court identified situations in which government censorship may be constitutional.

Justice Hughes, writing for the court, first explained that the main purpose of the First Amendment is to prevent prior restraint and that the First Amendment does not prohibit subsequent punishment for illegal expressions.[37] In dicta, he then described situations in which government censorship would probably be upheld.

> [T]he protection even as to previous restraint is not absolutely unlimited. But the limitation has been recognized only in exceptional cases. When a nation is at war many things that might be said in time of peace are such a hindrance to its error that their utterance will not be endured as long as men fight and . . . no Court could regard them as protected by any constitutional right. . . . No one would question but that a government might prevent actual obstruction to its recruiting service or the publication of the sailing dates of transports, or the number and location of troops. On similar grounds, the primary requirements of decency may be enforced against obscene publications. The security of the community life may be protected against incitements to acts of violence and the overthrow by force of orderly government. The constitutional guaranty of free speech does not protect a man from an injunction against uttering words that may have all the effect of force.[38]

Two cases illustrate the principles underlying governmental censorship of classified or sensitive information. Both cases involve issues that arose in the 1970s. The first of these cases, *New York Times Co. v. United States,*[39] is also known as the Pentagon Papers Case. The second case is *United States v. Progressive, Inc.,*[40] which is also called the Progressive Magazine Case.

In the Pentagon Papers Case, the *New York Times* surreptitiously gained access to a classified study, commissioned by the government, titled "History of the U.S. Decision-Making Process on Viet Nam Policy." The government brought two simultaneous suits in federal district courts requesting a restraining order and permanent injunction to prohibit both the *New York Times* and the *Washington Post*, which had also obtained a copy of the lengthy report, from publishing excerpts. The action against the *New York Times* was brought in the U.S. District Court for the Southern District of New York, and the action against the *Washington Post* was brought in the U.S. District Court for the District of Columbia. Both trial courts refused to grant the restraining orders and the government appealed to the U.S. Court of Appeals. The Court of Appeals for the District of Columbia affirmed the district court's ruling in the *Washington Post* case. However, the U.S. Court of Appeals for the Second Circuit remanded the case against the *New York Times* to the appropriate district court for further hearings. From these mixed decisions, both the government and The New York Times Co. appealed to the U.S. Supreme Courts, which granted certiorari to review the two cases. Justice Brennan, as spokesman for the U.S. Supreme Court said,

> Any system of prior restraints of expression comes to this Court bearing a heavy presumption against its constitutional validity. . . . The government "thus carries a heavy burden of showing justification for the imposition of such a restraint.". . . The District Court for the Southern District of New York in the *New York Times* case and the District Court for the District of Columbia and the Court of Appeals for the District of Columbia Circuit . . . in the *Washington Post* case held that the Government had not met that burden. We agree.[41]

The original orders of both district courts denying the government's request for prior restraint were affirmed.

In 1979, a federal judge for the Western District of Wisconsin granted an injunction against publication of an article in *The Progressive*, a monthly magazine devoted to political issues. The article was written by a freelance contributor and described the U.S. weapons program. The article described the results of the author's research and deductions about the design of the U.S. hydrogen bomb. Having worked to obtain information through the Department of Energy (DOE), but not having access to any classified information, the author submitted the final draft of his article titled, "The H-Bomb Secret: How We Got It, Why We're Telling It," to the DOE for verification of some of its technical information. However, the DOE contended the article contained "restricted data" in about 20% of its text and all of its sketches. According to the DOE, the article, if published as submitted in final draft, would have been in direct violation of the Atomic Energy Act of 1954. The DOE requested deletion of the sensitive material, prior to publication. Both the author and publisher refused to comply with this request.

The district court judge identified three reasons for issuing an injunction against publication of the article. First, the article would give a distinct advantage to any foreign nation that sought to develop its own hydrogen weapon, which could then be used to injure the United States. Second, the publication of restricted data would be analogous to publication of troop movements or locations in time of war, which under the *Near* decision were exceptions to the rule against prior restraints. Third, the government had met its burden under Section 2274 of the Atomic Energy Act. The Act prohibits anyone from communicating, transmitting, or disclosing any restricted data to any person with reason to believe the data could be used to injure the United States or secure an advantage to any foreign nation. The statute also unambiguously defined "restricted data" as all data concerning the design, manufacture, or utilization of atomic weapons. The district judge concluded that the disclosure of such restricted data would create irreparable harm to the United States and that the creation of irreparable harm to the country meets the requirements to issue an injunction.

Many commentators describe The Progressive Magazine Case as precedent for the government's right to censor information that poses an imminent threat of irreparable harm to national security. However, it should be noted that the government finally dismissed its suit against *The Progressive* and the injunction was dissolved, when two separate newspapers published a letter by another researcher who gave detailed construction information about the hydrogen bomb. Even though publication by these newspapers was also in direct violation of the Atomic Energy Act of 1954, neither the *Madison Press Connection* nor the *Chicago Tribune* was indicted by the government. The law-abiding researcher and writer and *The Progressive* were prohibited from publishing information they had obtained by completely lawful means, for a 7-month period while others ignored legal restrictions and disseminated the information to anyone who wanted it. In other settings, this reckless disregard for the consequences of one's actions is defined as either intentional or grossly negligent behavior and can result in large judgments or fines. Why the DOE did not prosecute some publishers for illegal dissemination of restricted data, when they had secured an injunction against another publisher, has never been explained.

Obscenity and Indecency

Limitations on First Amendment liberties based on obscenity and indecency are often called the politics of content and word choice. Obviously, what is obscene or indecent depends no more on the content of a message than it does on the subjective state of mind of the recipient. Recall that under the **social function** subset of the social conformist interpretation of First Amendment freedoms the Supreme Court has predetermined that any obscene expression is non-speech. Therefore, obscene expressions have no First Amendment protection from government censorship or punishment. Further, the definition of obscenity is based on community standards and is often the product of political pressures. Indecent communication enjoys some First Amendment protection, but it is subject to extensive governmental regulation. The definition of indecent speech is based solely on the opinions of current political appointees to federal regulatory agencies and their views are largely motivated by political considerations and the pressures from small factious groups.

In this section, we describe the Court's definition of obscenity and explore concurrent federal and state laws enacted to control the dissemination of allegedly obscene expression. In addition, we introduce the concept of **indecency** as an example of how government censorship and regulatory control can be broadened to include words and phrases widely used in the vernacular speech of millions of Americans.

All laws and regulations are either prescriptive or proscriptive. They either tell us what we must do or what we may not do. Laws and regulations that set standards of behavior to which we must conform are **prescriptive**. Those that prohibit behaviors are **proscriptive**. Criminal laws, for example, are proscriptive. Generally, the U.S. Supreme Court has held that laws providing sanctions for proscribed behavior must be specific enough to inform the people precisely about the type of conduct or behavior to be avoided. Laws that do not give specific descriptions or definitions of the proscribed activities have been held unconstitutional either because of their vagueness or overbreadth. **Vagueness** refers to laws that do not describe or define the prohibited conduct with sufficient specificity to warn members of the public about what behavior will merit punishment. **Overbreadth** applies to laws that are so all encompassing they include a large range of perfectly legal behaviors not meant to be included within the sanctioned conduct. These laws grant too much discretion in their enforcement and may, therefore, also be arbitrary or capricious in their application.

Avoiding vagueness and overbreadth is a problem for all attempts to proscribe and censure obscenity and indecency. The Supreme Court has used the term **obscenity** to refer to a special classification of sexually explicit material considered so offensive that it warrants no First Amendment protection.[42] However, obscenity is so difficult to define that it has caused at least one Supreme Court Justice to proclaim,

> I shall not attempt further to define the kinds of material to be embraced within the short-hand description [of hard-core pornography]; and perhaps I could never succeed in intelligibly doing so. But I do know that when I see it, and the motion picture involved in this case is not that.[43]

Exhibit 4.5.   Modified Miller Test. (*Miller v. California*, 413 U.S. 15, 21-27 [1973]; *Pope v. Illinois*, 481 U.S. 497, 500 [1987].)

The average person, applying contemporary community standards, would find the work as a whole	The "reasonable person" would find that the material as a whole

AND

Appeals to prurient interests by: 1. depicting or describing sexual conduct 2. in a patently offensive way, AND 3. the conduct depicted is specifically defined by applicable state law.	Totally lacks: 1. artistic value 2. political value, OR 3. scientific value.

Obscenity, like beauty, may be strictly in the eye of the beholder. Its definition is totally subjective. Therefore, the Supreme Court has been hard pressed to articulate specific legal standards to determine what written or graphic material is obscene. The current standard used to define obscenity was developed in the 1973 decision in *Miller v. California*.[44] Under the *Miller* test, which is summarized in Exhibit 4.5, material is **obscene** only if the average person, applying contemporary community standards, would find that the work, taken as a whole, appeals to the prurient interests; and the work depicts or describes, in a patently offensive way, sexual conduct that is specifically defined by applicable state law. In addition, the work, taken as a whole, by a reasonable person, must not have serious literary, artistic, political, or scientific value.[45]

All portions of the *Miller* test must be proven in court before material can be labeled "obscene," and be stripped of all constitutional protection. The problems with the *Miller* test are threefold. First, there have been numerous additional cases brought before the U.S. Supreme Court for further definition or clarification of each of its elements. Second, and somewhat ironic, is the fact that any applicable state law that "specifically defines" the type of language or depictions prohibited would be obscene itself. Finally, by allowing the application of "contemporary community standards," the Supreme Court not only permits but encourages arbitrariness or capriciousness in enforcement of obscenity laws. Such overbreadth and ambiguity has always been declared unconstitutional when applying even the lowest standard of judicial review—the reasonableness standard.

In *Miller* and subsequent cases, the U.S. Supreme Court has attempted to define its use of the term "patently offensive" by reiterating that obscenity statutes must specify the depictions of sexual conduct they intended to regulate, control, or prohibit. The government can prohibit those things that are considered to be (a) patently offensive representations or depictions of ultimate sexual acts, whether normal or perverted, actual or simulated, and (b) patently offensive representations or descriptions of masturbation or excretory functions, and lewd exhibitions of genitals.[46] This part of the *Miller* test supposedly prohibits only hard-core representations of sexual conduct, not mere depictions of nudity or the use of sexual terms. In addition, the notion that the work, taken as a whole, must lack serious literary, artistic, political, or scientific value is not to be determined by the contemporary community standards test. It applies the more common legal test that asks what a reasonable person would think or do.

There are significant problems associated with application of the *Miller* test in specific situations. These problems arise from the internal ambiguity of the test and the subsequent decisions attempting to clarifying the test. To apply the *Miller* test, a juror is told to think as an average person and apply his or her contemporary community standards to determine whether the challenged work depicts sexual conduct in a patently offensive way that appeals to the prurient interest. That same juror is then told to switch to the reasonable person standard to judge whether or not the work taken as a whole lacks serious literary, artistic, political, or scientific value. How is this switch accomplished? The test implies that the average person is not a reasonable person and that there are communities where reasonable people do not create the standards of appropriate behavior. Thus seen, the *Miller* test is both ambiguous and impossible to apply. It presents a legally imposed conundrum that not only facilitates governmental censorship and punishment of creative human expression, but which also may be used to shield the obscene messages it intended to proscribe. It is simply too vague and internally contradictory to provide a consistent definitional standard.

Additional problems confront the communications practitioner who while, possessed of the common knowledge that "sex sells" products and services, seeks to steer clear of legal and governmental entanglements. There are a myriad of federal and state laws and a gauntlet of inconsistent Supreme Court cases through which communicators must precariously negotiate. For example, in 1969 the Supreme Court held that the First and Fourteenth Amendments forbid making the private possession and viewing of obscene materials in the home a crime.[47] However, the High Court has also held that state and federal laws are constitutional that make it a crime to mail, import, or transport obscene materials in interstate commerce.[48]

Assuming that a publisher, advertising, or public relations practitioner would want to use sexual content to sell a particular product, and that this legitimate activity requires entry of the product or its advertisements into the "stream" of interstate commerce, the current lack of uniform, legally defined standards for obscenity make it impossible to know what is or is not permissible to depict in each jurisdiction throughout the United States. In addition, the remedies available vary across the country. In some jurisdictions, the penalties include large fines and jail sentences that may be enhanced by charges under the Racketeer Influenced and Corrupt Organization (RICO) statutes. Federal RICO laws, in addition to some state statutes, call for the forfeiture of all property that supported the alleged illegal activity and any property that was purchased with the proceeds from illegal activities.[49]

Statutes also make the transmission of obscene material by broadcast or by cable television illegal; and customs officials may seize and hold any "apparently obscene materials" being imported until a judgment can be obtained declaring the materials to be obscene and enjoining their dissemination.[50] Sections of the Telecommunications Act of 1996 also prohibit obscene communications by telephone for commercial purposes.[51]

Furthermore, professional communicators are confronted by a Federal Postal Statute that allows a postal customer who does not want to receive even "erotic or provocative" advertisements to request the issuance of a postal order that is sent to the "offending" company telling them to stop sending such materials to the postal customer and ordering the company to take the customer off its mailing lists.[52] Of course, it is impossible for an advertiser or publisher to know the preferences of everyone in the target public before making a mass mailing. But, the U.S. Supreme Court has held such statutes to be constitutional on the theory that they allow the consumer instead of government officials to censor the mail because "mailers have no First Amendment rights to communicate through private mailboxes to unwilling recipients."[53]

Thus, the plethora of laws and regulations in the area of sexually oriented expressive materials requires the astute communications practitioner to thoroughly consult with an experienced attorney who specializes in this area of law, before putting creative ability, energy, time, or money into sexually suggestive materials, advertisements, or campaigns.

There is, of course, one reasonably clear area of obscene materials that most can agree should be absolutely prohibited—child pornography. In its 1982 decision in *New York v. Ferber*, the U.S. Supreme Court ruled that the government may prohibit the manufacture, production, and dissemination as well as private possession of child pornography, even in a private home. The court defined child pornography simply as any material showing children engaged in sexual conduct.[54]

Child pornography is prohibited regardless of whether the material is obscene under the *Miller* test. The Court reasoned that because the use of juveniles as pornographic subjects is intrinsically related to sexual abuse of children, the government's interest in safeguarding the physical and mental well-being of children is compelling. Therefore, statutes proscribing child pornography easily pass the strict scrutiny standard of judicial review. What is really being prohibited by these statutes is harm to children, not communication. Thus, federal statutes making it a crime to induce minors to engage in sexually explicit conduct for the purpose of producing visual depictions, where the visual materials are intended for distribution by mail or means of interstate or foreign commerce, are constitutional.[55]

However, when Congress extended the federal law to include the use of computer-generated virtual images in the Child Pornography Act of 1996, the Ninth Circuit Court of Appeals declared that section of the statute overbroad and therefore unconstitutional. The Ninth Circuit Count based its decision on the logic articulated in *Ferber* that the reason child pornography was exempt from the *Miller* test was to protect children from harm. The court ruled the computer-generated images did not harm children and refused to accept the government's speculation that viewing such material provoked child molestors.[56]

Attempts to protect children from viewing pornography have not been nearly so successful. The Supreme Court's 1997 decision ruling the Communications Decency Act unconstitutional and its 2004 decision ruling the Child Online Protection Act overbroad are discussed in chapter 5.

Indecency and the Politics of Words

There are obviously questions concerning the constitutional validity of the *Miller* test applied in obscenity cases. The constitutional flaw of the Miller test arises, in part, from the vagueness and ambiguity inherent in thousands of different community standards. The ambiguity arising from the large number of standards makes it literally impossible for a communications practitioner to have legal notice of what behaviors are proscribed.

This government-sponsored ambiguity is compounded exponentially by the Federal Communications Act of 1934 and its amendments through the Telecommunications Act of 1996. Under these statutes, the U.S. Supreme Court has allowed the Federal Communications Commission (FCC) to regulate expression based on its definition of the term *indecency*. Under these statutes, "(w)hoever utters any obscene, indecent, or profane language by means of radio communication shall be fined not more than $10,000 or imprisoned not more than two years, or both."[57] In 1934, the Federal Communications Act authorized the FCC to enforce the federal statute by means of penalties against broadcasters who violate the statute. These penalties include both huge fines and the denial of licensing.[58]

While predicting what is obscene may be difficult, predicting what is indecent is virtually impossible. The FCC is left to its own devices to fabricate this definition. Furthermore, the definition changes in response to political pressure and public opinion. Because government regulation of indecency is imposed almost exclusively by the FCC, we describe the rules and their enforcement in chapter 5 where we address broadcast regulations.

Practice Notes

The descriptions of First Amendment interpretation and limitations on free speech rights were presented in chapters 3 and 4 to help mass communications practitioners understand the rights they may have to communicate with potential clients and the power of the government to regulate that communication. In chapter 1 we explained that there are four sources of law but that there were also extensive bodies of rules, regulations, and ordinances that may have the force and effect of law. Laws, regulations, and ordinances are all created by different governmental entities. General knowledge of the basic levels of government and the various types of governing instruments is especially important to public relations and advertising practitioners because it enables them to avoid legal problems or at least to anticipate all the possible constraints on campaign activity. For example, some activities such as leafleting, solicitation, door-to-door canvassing, posting signs, and the use of sound equipment may require permits or licenses.

Informed communications practitioners will have done their homework and obtained the proper permit or license well before the activity planned on behalf of a client. Failure to do so may subject a practitioner and his or her client to penalties, fines, and possible prosecution. Of course, having a client fined is not only embarrassing, it is bad for one's business. Practitioners must always make multiple inquiries regarding the local, county, and/or state system of permits and licensing. Applications often involve multiple levels of government, payment of fees, and waiting time. Some require that the practitioner and/or the client appear before a specific board, commission, or committee for a hearing on the requested permit or license. A practitioner should always ask questions, well in advance of any scheduled activity; assume nothing; and, when in doubt, seek competent legal advice!

Depending on the type of campaign activity, placement of posters and signs may cause major problems. These may be subject to time, place, and manner restrictions. The public relations or advertising practitioner must make a comprehensive inquiry regarding restrictions on size, type of sign materials, and placement in buildings and on public rights-of-way. For example, many people assume they may staple signs to telephone or utility poles, or that any sign may be placed on street corners or along curbs. In most jurisdictions, these practices are prohibited. Utility companies must maintain their equipment and workers who use spiked boots to climb their own poles can be injured by staples and signs that cause spikes to lose traction. Additionally, such poles are privately owned by utility companies and are neither "public" nor "designated" public fora. Signs left curbside are subject to control either by local ordinances, property owners, or state departments of transportation regulations. Never place signs or post leaflets without proper permits or permission. Obtain permission in writing on a client's behalf and have multiple copies on file should any questions arise.

Advertising and public relations practitioners also face the necessity of knowing about and complying with all permits and permissions required before distributing leaflets, flyers, brochures, cards, placards, or any other written or printed materials on both public and private property. The placing of pamphlets, leaflets, flyers, or printed advertising or material on vehicle windshields, or the distribution of any other printed literature or advertising materials usually is controlled by local ordinance. The time, place, and manner of such communications can be reasonably regulated by local or state authorities, or by private property owners. Distribution of literature is often strictly prohibited due to the cost of cleanup and disposal of waste. However, the content of the communication can rarely be controlled. Unfortunately, many journalists, advertising, public relations, and other mass communications specialists are often misinformed about the legality, constitutionality, or even the very existence of regulations or laws controlling and licensing such communication activities. The preceding chapter discussion should assist the astute communications practitioner in avoiding legal pitfalls in the publication and dissemination of information to the public.

Magic Words and Phrases

Absolutist	Indecency
Clear and present danger test	Legal duty
Compensatory damages	Mens rea
Contempt power	Metaphysical fora
Damage	Modified negligence standard
Designated public forum	Negligence
Incitement test	Negligent incitement

Nominal damages	Simple negligence
Non-public forum	Social conformist
Obscenity	Social effects
Overbreadth	Social function
Prescriptive laws	Summary judgment
Proscriptive laws	Time, place, manner restrictions
Public fora	Tort law
Punitive damages	Traditional public fora
Scienter	Vagueness

Suggested Cases to Read and Brief

Abrams v. United States, 250 U.S. 616 (1919)
Brandenburg v. Ohio, 395 U.S. 444 (1969)
Braun v. Soldier of Fortune Magazine, Inc., 968 F.2d 830 (11th Cir. 1992)
Dennis v. United States, 342 U.S. 494 (1951)
Gitlow v. New York, 268 U.S. 652 (1925)
Herceg v. Hustler Magazine, Inc., 814 F.2d 1017 (5th Cir. 1987)
Miller v. California, 413 U.S. 15 (1973)
Near v. Minnesota, 283 U.S. 697 (1931)
New York Times Co. v. United States, 403 U.S. 713 (1971)
New York v. Ferber, 458 U.S. 747 (1982)
Rice v. Paladin Enterprises, Inc, 128 F.3d 233 (4th Cir. 1997), *cert. denied* 523 U.S. 1074 (1998)
Schenck v. United States, 249 U.S. 47 (1919)
Stanley v. Georgia, 394 U.S. 557 (1969)
United States v. Progressive, Inc., 467 F.Supp. 900 (W.D.Wis.1979)
Whitney v. California, 274 U.S. 357 (1927)
Yates v. California, 354 U.S. 298 (1957)
Zamora v. CBS, 480 F.Supp 199 (1979)

Questions for Discussion

1. Describe the distinctions between an literalist interpretation and a social conformist interpretation of First Amendment liberties. Does it matter to a mass communications practitioner which interpretation is used by a majority of the U.S. Supreme Court? Why or why not?

2. What categories of communication are considered non-speech by the U.S. Supreme Court under the social conformist approach? What is the significance of a form of communication being considered non-speech? If the content of the communications you use on behalf of a client or in your communications industry employment is determined non-speech what protections may it have from governmental regulation?

3. Under what general sets of circumstances do the decisions in *Near v. Minnesota* and *Schenck v. U.S.* hold that the government may enjoin or use prior restraint against publication by the media? Compare and contrast the types of publications and communications which the government sought to suppress in these cases: *Schenck v. U.S.*, *Abrams v. U.S.*, *Gitlow v. New York*; *Whitney v. California*, *Dennis v. U.S.*, and *Yates v. California*. What, if any, differences existed in the materials that were being suppressed? What factors or criteria explain the different holdings?

4. Compare the decisions made by the U.S. Supreme Court in *New York Times Co. v. U.S.* with that made by the U.S. District Court in *U.S. v. Progressive, Inc.* Why did the District Court enjoin publication in *The Progressive* case? If the case had been reviewed by the U.S. Supreme Court, would there have been a different result? Why or why not?

5. What were the principles of law used by the U.S. Supreme Court in *Brandenburg v. Ohio* to determine the constitutionality of a state criminal syndicalism statute? Describe the subsequent extension of those principles in the civil cases of *Rice v. Paladin Enterprises, Inc.* and *Braun v. Soldier of Fortune Magazine, Inc.*

6. Describe the "forum-based approach" used by the U.S. Supreme Court to determine the constitutionality of governmental regulations of speech and press. What, if any, different standard or test could be used to determine the constitutionality of governmental rules and regulations imposing time, place, and manner restrictions on freedom of expression?

7. What, if any, restrictions should be imposed on those who want to bombard us day and night with their messages, whether commercial, political, or religious? Do the liberties of speech and press belong to the purveyor or the recipient of information? How can these interests be fairly balanced?

8. Describe problems involved when government attempts to censor, prohibit, or punish people for producing or distributing obscene material. Are there less restrictive alternatives available that will recognize the communicator's right to freedom of speech and press, but that, at the same time, protect children and those who do not want to receive such communication? What are they? How could they be enforced?

9. Describe and discuss the concepts of vagueness and overbreadth as they are applied to determine the constitutionality of statutes and regulations. If these concepts are applied to the current test used by the U.S. Supreme Court to determine the constitutionality of restrictions on obscenity, is the test itself constitutional? Why or why not?

Notes

1. *FCC v. Pacifica Foundation*, 438 U.S. 726 (1978).
2. *Near v. Minnesota*, 283 U.S. 697 (1931).
3. *Id.* at 715 & 718–719.
4. *Rice v. Paladin Enterprises,* 128 F.3d 233 (4th Cir. 1997), *cert. denied* 523 U.S. 1074 (1998).
5. *Brandenberg v. Ohio*, 395 U.S. 444 (1969).
6. *Bigelow v. Virginia*, 421 U.S. 809 (1975).
7. *Virginia State Board of Pharmacy v. Virginia Citizens Consumer Council*, 425 U.S. 748 (1976).

8. *Central Hudson Gas & Electric Corp. v. Public Service Comm.*, 447 U.S. 557 (1980).

9. See, e.g., *Heffron v. International Society for Krishna Consciousness*, 452 U.S. 640 (1981).

10. *Watchtower Bible and Tract Society of New York v. Village of Stratton*, 536 U.S. 150 (2002).

11. *Hague v. CIO*, 307 U.S. 496 (1939); *Brown v. Louisiana*, 383 U.S. 131 (1966); *United States v. Grace*, 461 U.S. 171 (1983); *Perry Education Assoc. v. Perry Local Educators' Assoc.*, 460 U.S. 37 (1983); *Ward v. Rock Against Racism*, 491 U.S. 781 (1989); *International Society for Krishna Consciousness v. Lee*, 505 U.S. 672 (1992).

12. *Cornelius v. NAACP Legal Defense & Educational Fund, Inc.*, 473 U.S. 788 (1985); *Rosenberger v. Rector & Visitors of the University of Virginia*, 515 U.S. 819 (1995).

13. *Pruneyard Shopping Center v. Robins*, 447 U.S. 74 (1980).

14. CRAIG R. DUCAT, *CONSTITUTIONAL INTERPRETATION*, 7TH ED. 831 (Wadsworth/Thompson Learning 2000),

15. STEFFEN W. SCHMIDT, MACK C. SHELLEY, & BARBARA A. BARDES, AMERICAN GOVERNMENT AND POLITICS TODAY 2003–2004 ed. 336 (Wadsworth Pub. Co./Thomson Learning 2003).

16. CRAIG R. DUCAT, *CONSTITUTIONAL INTERPRETATION*, 7TH ED. 831 (Wadsworth/Thompson Learning 2000).

17. See also, effects of Title III of Omnibus Crime Control & Safe Streets Act, 18 U.S.C.A. § § 2510–2520 & the Foreign Intelligence Surveillance Act of 1978, 92 Stat. 1783.

18. See, e.g., *Gitlow v. New York*, 268 U.S. 652 (1925); *Whitney v. California*, 274 U.S. 357 (1927); *Brandenburg v. Ohio*, 395 U.S. 444 (1969).

19. *Schenck v. United States*, 249 U.S. 47 (1919).

20. *Id.* at 52.

21. *Id.*

22. *Brandenburg v. Ohio*, 395 U.S. 444 (1969).

23. *Abrams v. United States*, 250 U.S. 616, 628 (1919).

24. *Whitney v. California*, 274 U.S. 357, 376 (1927).

25. *Id.* at 377.

26. *Gitlow v. New York*, 268 U.S. 652, 666 (1925).

27. *Id.* at 668.

28. *Id.* at 670.

29. *Id.* at 673.

30. *Dennis v. United States*, 341 U.S. 494, 510 (1951) quoting *United States v. Dennis*, 183 F.2d 201, 212 (1950).

31. *Brandenburg v. Ohio*, 395 U.S. 444, 447–449 (1969), this is the first type of per curium decision discussed in chapter 2. It was unsigned but supported by the majority of the Court.

32. *Brandenburg*, 395 U.S. at 457.

33. See, *James v. Meow Media, Inc.*, 300 F.3d (6th Cir. 2002); *Herceg v. Hustler Magazine, Inc.*, 814 F.2d 1017 (5th Cir. 1987); *Zamora v. CBS*, 480 F.Supp 199 (S.D. Fl. 1979).

34. See, *Winter v. G.P. Putnam's Sons*, 938 F.2d 1033 (9th Cir. 1991); *Waller v. Osbourne*, 763 F.Supp 1144 (M.D. Ga. 1990).

35. See, *Rice v. Paladin Enterprises*, 128 F.3d 233 (4th Cir. 1997), *cert. denied* 523 U.S. 1074 (1998); *Braun v. Soldier of Fortune Magazine, Inc*, 968 F.2d 830 (11th Cir. 1992).

36. *Near v. State of Minnesota*, 283 U.S. 697 (1931).

37. *Id.* at 714.

38. *Id.*

39. *New York Times Co. v. United States*, 403 U.S. 713 (1971).

40. *United States v. Progressive, Inc.* 467 F.Supp 900 (W.D.Wis.1979).

41. *New York Times Co*, 403 U.S. at 714.

42. See, *Roth v. United States*, 354 U.S. 476 (1957).

43. *Jacobellis v. Ohio*, 378 U.S. 184 (1964), Justice Stewart's concurring opinion.

44. *Miller v. California*, 413 U.S. 15 (1973).

45. *Pope v. Illinois*, 481 U.S. 497, 500 (1987).

46. *Miller,* 413 U.S. at 25.

47. *Stanley v. Georgia*, 394 U.S. 557 (1969).

48. 18 U.S.C. §§1461, 1462, 1464, 1468 & 19 U.S.C. § 1305; *United States v. 12-20 Ft. Reels,* 413 U.S. 123 (1973).

49. *Fort Wayne Books, Inc. v. Indiana*, 489 U.S. 46 (1989).

50. 19 U.S.C. § 1305 (1999).

51. 47 U.S.C. § 223 (1999).

52. 39 U.S.C. § 3008 (1999).

53. *Rowan v. Post Office Dept.*, 397 U.S. 728 (1970).

54. *New York v. Ferber*, 458 U.S. 747 (1982); *Osborne v. Ohio*, 495 U.S. 103 (1990).

55. 18 U.S.C. § 2251 (2002).

56. *The Free Speech Coalition v. Reno*, 198 F.3d 108 (9th Cir. 1999). See also, *Ashcroft v. Free Speech Coalition*, 535 U.S. 234 (2002), 18 U.S.C.A. § 2252A (1999).

57. 18 U.S.C. § 1464 (1927).

58. 47 U.S.C. § § 307, 308, 213 (a)(6) (1999).

5

Electronic Media Regulations

The emphasis must be first and foremost on the interest, the convenience, and the necessity of the listening public, and not on the interest, convenience, or necessity of the individual broadcaster or the advertiser.

—Justice Frankfurter[1]

Overview
Regulation of the Business of Broadcasting
Content Control: What First Amendment Rights?
Practice Notes

Overview

This chapter is divided into two major sections and a practice note. The first section describes regulation of the electronic media. We begin by introducing the principles that guide regulations and a history of the regulations themselves. We also describe the trend and status of deregulation of the industry, and also briefly describe the structure and function of the FCC. Our description of regulation and deregulation focuses on the broadcast industry because it has spawned the most complex regulations and because broadcasting is the electronic medium that most often influences and is influenced by mass communications practitioners. However, we do introduce regulation of cable, telephone, satellite, the Internet, and other electronic media.

The second section of this chapter describes the prescriptive regulations that require content in broadcast media and the proscriptive regulations that prohibit or punish words and content. This chapter is placed at this location in the book because the discussion of indecency requires some familiarity with the court's analysis of obscenity, which was described in the preceding chapter. We conclude the chapter with a practice note that describes the limited requirements for reporting public service announcements (PSAs) and explains how public relations or advertising practitioners may use those requirements to encourage placement of PSAs.

Regulation of the Business of Broadcasting

The power of the U.S. Congress to regulate electronic media comes from the Constitution itself. Article I gives Congress authority to regulate all interstate commerce. It says, in part,

> Section 8. The Congress shall have Power to . . . regulate Commerce with foreign Nations, and among the several States, and with the Indian Tribes. . . . [2] To make all Laws which shall be necessary and proper for carrying into Execution the foregoing Powers, and all other Powers vested by this Constitution in the Government of the United States, or in any Department or Officer thereof.[3]

Obviously, broadcast and other electronic signals cross state lines and are in interstate commerce. Therefore, Congress has exercised its powers of legislation and regulation over the evolving industry. Because of the changes in technology and social uses of electronic media, Congress has been hard pressed to keep up with the ever-changing communications landscape. In many instances, it has not been able to address and adequately supervise the often conflicting needs of commercial enterprise and the consuming public. Further, the proliferation of laws and regulations over the years bears witness to the lack of any comprehensive or consistent congressional policy in the area.

History and Principles of Regulation

Problems with electronic media regulation have been blamed on poor planning, and the inability to predict and adapt to technological and social change. Other problems include a limited budget that required elimination of regulatory oversight. Whatever the reason, regulation of electronic media is one of the most complex and inconsistent areas of governmental control. From the birth of electronic media through the 1980s, the government layered progressively more regulation on the broadcast industry. Since 1980, broadcast and other electronic media have been progressively deregulated. Both regulation and deregulation create problems for mass communications practitioners and we describe both trends here. We begin with a description of the three sets of beliefs about governmental control that have guided regulation of electronic media.

Approaches to Governmental Control

Three different sets of beliefs about the role of governmental regulation have guided decisions about regulation of electronic media. The first of these addresses the proper role of representatives. The second is concerned with the motivation of individual citizens, and the third relates to what is seen as the appropriate goal of governmental regulation.

Legislators deciding how to control electronic media see their proper role along a continuum ranging from the beliefs of Edmund Burke at one end to Andrew Jackson at the other. Burke believed that representatives served the people but did not serve merely as a conduit for their will. He thought legislators should make decisions based on their own informed views rather than on the uninformed opinions of constituents. Jackson, on the other hand, believed that elected officials were obligated to advocate the view held by the majority of their constituents regardless of their motivation. These two models are called the trustee or independent delegate and the instructed or committed delegate styles of representation.

Motivation of individual citizens can also be divided into two categories and decisions about regulation of electronic media may be guided by those views. The terms used to describe these individual motivations are *homo economicus* and *homo politicus*. A citizen motivated by **homo economicus** is self-centered and interested in those governmental policies that maximize his or her immediate personal benefits. Alternatively, citizens motivated by the **homo politicus** philosophy are other-oriented and view governmental decisions in terms of whether or not they obtain the greatest good for the largest number of people. Homo economicus constituents expect control of the electronic media for their own benefit, while homo politicus constituents advocate control for the greater good of society. At various times, the U.S. Congress has responded to both arguments and regulation of electronic media has changed as these different approaches gain and lose influence.

Citizens' views of the appropriate role of government can be divided into three groups based on the individual's attitude toward government and policies: moralistic, traditionalistic, and individualistic. Moralists believe governments are created and instituted among men for the good of the governed. They are likely to also advocate a homo politicus perspective. Traditionalists view government as a vehicle for the advancement of their particular family or group. They are likely to seek Jacksonian representation and to advocate a homo economicus perspective. Individualists see government itself as the problem and would oppose any regulation of electronic media.

Throughout the remainder of this chapter, we discuss how these three beliefs about governmental regulation and representation influence policies and practices governing electronic media.

History of Broadcast Regulations

The first commercial radio station to broadcast in the United States was KDKA in Pittsburgh, Pennsylvania, which went on the air in 1920. At that time, the technology was new and lacked sophistication. Frequency interference was common. Signals overlapped, bled into each other, and, powerful signals completely obliterated others. In many instances, reception of any signal was impossible. Simply put, it was chaos.

In 1912, Congress had created the first Radio Communications Act, but the act predated commercial radio and did not anticipate the problems to come in the 1920s. That act only gave the Secretary of Commerce authority to approve power levels and to regulate assignment of frequencies; it did not specifically give the authority to grant licenses. In the early 1920s, then-Secretary of Commerce Hoover attempted to penalize Zenith Radio Corporation for operating on an unauthorized frequency. The federal courts held that the Secretary had no power to deny licenses, thereby nullifying the 1912 Act's effectiveness.[4]

Because of these problems, a series of National Radio Conferences were held between 1922 and 1925. Those conferences proposed three solutions. The first solution was based on a Jacksonian approach to representation and an individualistic attitude toward government control. That proposal was simply to let the free market take care of the problem. Larger, more powerful broadcasters would be permitted to "jam" the signals of weaker broadcasters until only a few controlling stations remained. Components of this proposal included the idea that the use of a signal frequency would create a kind of "squatter's rights" analogous to the real estate concept of adverse possession and that courts would be called on to decide who had used a frequency longest and with the most success. This proposal was rejected, largely because it was a free-market approach that had created the problem for which a solution was sought.

The second solution proposed was based on a homo politicus belief about personal motivation and a moralistic view of the role of government. That proposal was to have the government step in and create an entire system of public radio broadcasting and transmitting stations. These would be owned and operated by the government itself. However, even the advocates of homo politicus and moralistic approaches to governmental control could not agree on the details of such a system.

Finally, the radio conferences agreed on a compromise that provided for federal governmental control of assignment of radio frequencies but private ownership of broadcast stations and transmission facilities. This compromise resulted in the Radio Act of 1927.

Congress passed the Radio Act of 1927 under its commerce clause powers and included provisions authorizing the newly created Federal Radio Commission to issue licenses. It thus overcame the problems that had made the 1912 Radio Communications Act unenforceable.

The Public Interest Directive

Under the Radio Act of 1927, the newly created Federal Radio Commission was given the authority to issue licenses for use of the channels of radio transmission for only 3 years, "if public convenience, interest, or necessity will be served thereby."[5]

The sponsor of the Act, Congressman White described the importance of the public interest in administration of the Act:

> The recent radio conference . . . recommended that licenses should be issued only to
> those stations whose operation would render a benefit to the public, are necessary in
> the public interest, or would contribute to the development of the art. . . . The broad-
> casting privilege will not be a right of selfishness. It will rest upon an assurance of
> public interest to be served.[6]

The Communications Act of 1934 replaced the Radio Act of 1927. It created the Federal Communications Company (FCC) and continued the Congressional purpose of protecting the public interest. The FCC was entrusted with formulating a unified and comprehensive regulatory system for the industry. Congress sought to regulate all media of electronic communication under the auspices of one authority, which was directed to promote the public interest.[7] Part of the Congressional impetus was the "widespread fear that in the absence of governmental control the public interest might be subordinated to monopolistic domination in the broadcasting field . . . and a desire . . . to maintain, through appropriate administrative control, a grip on the dynamic aspects of" the industry.[8]

It is interesting to note the clarity of vision and purpose behind enactment of the Radio Act of 1927 and its successor the Communications Act of 1934, as these were pronounced in the Congressional record and interpreted by the Supreme Court in 1940 in *FCC v. Pottsville* and in 1969 in *Red Lion Broadcasting v. FCC*. The original communications laws and regulations were passed and promulgated at a time when the industry itself begged for governmental intervention to prevent chaos. Broadcasters wanted a uniform system for frequency assignment and fair trade and business practices for industry development. Congress described its goals to include prohibition of monopolies, establishment and maintenance of federal control over all means of interstate and international communications, and establishment of an atmosphere conducive to communications industry development. Congress also said it wanted to do all of this in a manner that would serve the public interest, convenience, and necessity.

Between 1934 and the passage of the Telecommunications Act of 1996, the public interest doctrine steadily eroded. During this period, the focus of governmental control shifted from the greater good of the listening and viewing public to meeting the political and ideological demands of factious groups. This change was enhanced by major changes in the political philosophies of justices appointed to the U.S. Supreme Court and presidential appointments to the FCC. Congress, too, shifted in response to changes in media technology and the clamoring of special interest groups who demanded ever-increasing governmental control of media content. In the recent past, all branches of government seem to have lost sight of the once-prized public interest directive in an effort to accommodate the interests of competing and often narrow-issue factions.

The FCC: Its Purpose, Tasks, and Divisions

The purpose of the Communications Act of 1934 and later communications laws is

> among other things, to maintain the control of the United States over all the channels of radio transmission; and to provide for the use of such channels, but not the ownership thereof, by persons for limited periods of time, under licenses granted by Federal authority, and no such license shall be construed to create any right beyond the terms, conditions, and periods of the license.[9]

To meet this purpose, Congress created the FCC as an independent regulatory agency. The purview of the FCC includes regulating radio and television broadcasting and regulating all interstate and international communications by wire, satellite, cable, or any other communications technology that involves interstate or international commerce. The FCC and its staff are charged with developing and enforcing communication regulations.

To perform these diverse tasks, the FCC is organized into operating bureaus. Each bureau is subdivided into units, offices, or divisions based on the functions it performs, or policies it must supervise. The six major bureaus of the FCC and their functions are described in Exhibit 5.1.

Exhibit 5.1. Six Major FCC Bureaus and Their Functions.

Media Bureau	1. Controls licensing of:
	   a. Radio broadcasting
	   b. Television broadcasting
	   c. Cable broadcasting
	2. Makes regulations to control:
	   a. Broadcasting business affecting commerce
	   b. Mandatory programming and content
	   c. Proscriptive content and "censorship" rules regarding programming and word choice

Consumer and Govermental Affairs Bureau	1. Engages in consumer education and assistance 2. Coordinates consumer affairs and outreach between all levels of government
International Bureau	1. Coordinates international communications policies 2. Supervises international telecommunication services 3. Regulates domestic and international satellite systems that serve the U.S. market 4. Develops U.S. policy regarding international radio frequencies and orbital locations for communications satellites
Wireline Competition Bureau	1. Extensively regulates interstate wireline telephone and telegraph services 2. Supervises "common carrier" communications services 3. Oversees all connections, terms, conditions, and rates among consumers, carriers, and destinations
Wireless Telecommunications Bureau	1. Regulates and controls all domestic wireless telecommunication services 2. Purview includes cell phones, pagers, personal communication services, and public safety radio communications

Enforcement Bureau	1. Consolidates and coordinates enforcement of all laws and regulations within its purview
	2. Has four divisions:
	   a. Investigations and hearings division
	   b. Market disputes resolution division
	   c. Technical and public safety division
	   d. Telecommunications consumer division

The FCC's mandate to implement the public interest directive for broadcasting is assigned to the Mass Media Bureau. The bureau is charged with three specific tasks: spectrum allocation, band allotment, and channel assignment.

Spectrum allocation involves reservation of portions of the radio spectrum for particular uses such AM, FM, VHF-TV, UHF-TV, emergency services like police and fire communication, aviation, military, and space communication. Band allotment assigns the number of channels or frequencies available. For example, the FM radio band is between 88 and 108 mega-hertz and includes 100 assignable channels. Channel assignment refers to FCC decisions concerning who is permitted to broadcast on a specific frequency. This task includes assignment and supervision of station licenses.

The FCC is also responsible for many other aspects of the communications industry. Its responsibilities include the establishment of technical standards for station operations, enforcing some standards of employment practices, fair trade and commercial practices, and the creation and enforcement of often controversial regulations on the content of communications. FCC and other governmental regulations involving the content of communication and their conflicts with First Amendment liberties are discussed later in this chapter.

Deregulation: Whose Interests Are Really Being Served?

It is not possible to discuss all the regulatory tasks and processes involved in station licensing in one textbook. Therefore, we describe only a few of the procedures used by the FCC to decide the number, quality, and diversity of voices available to the public. The original purpose of the Communications Act of 1934 was retained in the Telecommunications Act of 1996, but the Congressional focus has changed to deregulation. The impetus for this change in focus appears to be budgetary necessity or administrative convenience, and the change is likely to result in a return to monopolistic control of major segments of the communications industry. We present a description of the trend to deregulation focusing on rules as they existed before and after the 1996 Act. Each of these comparisons shows a shift away from the public interest directive.

The FCC and Broadcast Licensing

All local broadcast stations must be granted a license by the FCC in order to operate legally. Generally, stations located east of the Mississippi River have been assigned identifying call letters beginning with the letter "W," while those west of the Mississippi River begin with the letter "K." A license is not required to operate a network because networks own broadcast stations, each of which has been granted a license.

The FCC has authority to assign licenses, frequencies, hours of operation, and power in a manner that is fair, efficient, and provides an equitable distribution of service.[10] In the Communications Act of 1934, these licenses were granted for a 3-year term. The current regulation says that the term of a license is "not to exceed 8 years."[11] Licenses are routinely awarded for the full 8-year term. Under current law, license renewals may be granted from time to time for terms not to exceed 8 years from the expiration date of the previous term and "(n)o renewal of an existing station license in the broadcast or common carrier services shall be granted more than 30 days prior to the expiration of the original license."[12]

License applicants must meet basic qualifications including technical, financial, character, and ownership requirements. Simply put, applicants must have the necessary technical ability to broadcast programs, the operation and managerial capability to construct and run a station, and must be responsible both morally and financially.[13] Of course, it is not necessary for the applicant him or herself to have all the necessary technical skills. The applicant may demonstrate the ability to hire appropriate technicians. The current financial qualification standard is that an applicant must be able to demonstrate the ability to construct and operate a station for 3 months without relying on advertising or other revenues to meet costs. Character of the applicant is the most subjective of the criteria. Applicants have been disqualified for evidence of defective character for misstating facts regarding qualifications, conducting illegal activities on or, in connection with, the station, conviction of drug charges, and fraudulent programming or advertising schemes.

There is no requirement for the Commission to consider the effect of competition on an existing station. The FCC may grant a license to another licensee's competitor even though it results in economic injury to the existing station.[14] The primary objective of licensing is to maximize opportunities for effective use of broadcast frequencies and to provide the greatest service to the public. Licensing is not designed to protect, equalize, or improve the economic or competitive position of an individual licensee.

Prior to 1996, the FCC required each applicant to assess local community needs through an **ascertainment study**. Applicants were expected to prove that there were distinct programming needs currently not being served. They also had to show how the requested license would meet those unsatisfied programming needs. Furthermore, both initial broadcast applicants and renewal applicants were required to demonstrate their awareness of and responsiveness to local programming needs, through consultation with a cross-section of community leaders. The FCC, as part of the deregulation push, dropped all of these requirements during the 1980s.

Contested Applications: Comparative Process to Wealth-Based Allocation

Contested applications result when there are two or more mutually exclusive applicants and only one available license. The FCC's procedures for dealing with contested applications exemplifies the change from regulation to deregulation.

The Old Comparative Process.   When dealing with decisions about assigning a license to one of two or more mutually exclusive applicants, the FCC's original assumption was that the public interest directive was best served when there was diversity in available programming. This assumption was based, in part, on court decisions that said the paramount importance of the needs of the public converted the grant of a license into a "public trust."[15] This assumption motivated a drive to avoid monopolistic control and absentee ownership.

In 1978, the Supreme Court said the FCC may use its licensing authority with respect to broadcasting to "promote diversity in an overall communications market."[16] In that year, the FCC added the goal of increasing participation in station ownership and management by racial minorities and women. In order to meet these objectives, all applicants for licenses were required to present information that included an explanation of how ownership and management would be diversified. Also required was information on proposals for public affairs programming, past broadcast record, and applicant character. The FCC then weighted this information and selected the applicant whom, if granted the license, would best serve the public interest.

Under this procedure, on-site, hands-on owner-managers were preferred because of their direct financial interest, because they were more likely than absentee owners to ensure compliance with FCC rules, and because they would respond better to community needs, interests, and programming preferences. However, a federal circuit court ruled that preference for owner-managers was too arbitrary. The court based its opinion, at least in part, on the observation that other businesses did not insist on integration of ownership and management.[17]

FCC emphasis on assigning broadcast licenses to minorities was supported by court decisions. Responding to a challenge to the FCC's policy emphasizing minority ownership, the U.S. Supreme Court found that "the evidence suggests that an owner's minority status influences the selection of topics for news coverage and the presentation of editorial viewpoint, especially on matters of particular concern to minorities."[18] The Court also said, "(s)afeguarding the public's right to receive a diversity of views and information over the airwaves is therefore an integral component of the FCC's mission."[19] The Court ruled that minority ownership preference was substantially related to the FCC's programming diversity objective, as well as to its diversity in ownership-management objective.

The courts did not support emphasis on broadcast ownership by women. In 1992, the U.S. Circuit Court for the District of Columbia ruled that the FCC's preference in favor of women violated the equal protection rights of male applicants implied in the Fifth Amendment.[20] Judge Clarence Thomas, writing for the Court, agreed that the Supreme Court had found substantial empirical evidence supporting the relationship between minority ownership and a station's editorial and programming practices; however, he opined that no such connection was obvious between the views and programming preferences of men and women and ruled that granting preferences to stations owned by women over those owned by men would not lead to increased programming diversity.

The Move to a Wealth-Based System.   In the 1980s, during the Reagan administration, the FCC began consideration of alternatives to comparative hearings for deciding contested applications. In 1985, the FCC adopted a procedure titled "random selection," which they accomplished using *tie-breaker lotteries*. In 1993, the U.S. Circuit Court ruled the FCC's system of preference for integration of ownership and management was unconstitutional,[21] and the random-selection procedure was approved by Congressional amendments to the Communications Act in the same year.[22] A competitive bidding system, including the tie-breaker lotteries was authorized by Congress in 1996[23] and the procedure mandated by the Balanced Budget Act of 1997.

Currently, the FCC uses a process called **electronic simultaneous multiple-round auctions**. Applicants are still required to meet minimum technical, business, and ownership rules. However, once bidders have these minimum criteria, contested licenses are simply sold to the highest bidder. Money paid for the license goes to the U.S. Treasury. Bidding covers a number of related available licenses, which are grouped together for simultaneous auction. The auctions are conducted via personal computer (PC) and the FCC's Web site. Bids are not sealed and the auctions are conducted in multiple rounds wherein the high bid from the previous rounds compete in the next round of bidding. Four months in advance of each auction, the FCC announces the spectrum and channels to be auctioned. Applicants have 30 days from the announcement to present their applications and a refundable deposit for auction preclearance. The number and type of licenses to be bid on determine the size of the required deposit. These auctions have replaced random selection, lotteries, and the old competitive bid system since July 1, 1997. The only exceptions involve license applications pending in 1997.[24] The authorization for auctions ends on September 30, 2007. This is the date Congress anticipated additional frequencies might be available because of conversion to digital television.[25]

In the statutes authorizing both the random-selection and the competitive bidding system, Congress retained language indicating preferences for minorities and women[26] and even took care to include a definition of what minority groups should receive preference.[27] It said specifically the procedures should

> ensure that small businesses, rural telephone companies, and businesses owned by members of minority groups and women are given the opportunity to participate in the provision of spectrum-based services, and, for such purposes, consider the use of tax certificates, bidding preferences, and other procedures.[28]

Despite this rhetoric, the system currently in place simply sells broadcast licenses to the highest bidder.[29]

Congress has further encouraged purely wealth-driven allocation of licenses by giving the FCC a direct financial interest in the revenues derived from the sale of public airwaves. The successful bidders' payments are deposited in the U.S. Treasury. But those payments are reduced by "offsetting collections" of administrative costs that are assigned directly to the FCC. These costs include salaries and expense accounts and are deposited quarterly to augment appropriations to the FCC.[30]

License Renewals: Old and New Systems Compared

The original Communications Act of 1934 provided for license renewal every 3 years. Today, licenses are renewed every 8 years.[31] Also, under the old system, the FCC could decide not to renew a license if it found that a new applicant would better serve the public interest. Changes in the License granting systems are summarized in Exhibit 5.2.

When evaluating applications for renewal and competing applications for the same license, the FCC had to consider both the old licensee's application and the competing application. When reviewing these renewal applications or competing applications, the FCC considered the same factors used to evaluate new applications. If the old licensee was found to be deficient in any of these categories, the new applicant could be awarded the license. These old rules also required the FCC to consider factors that were material to the public interest directive, and the public being served had a chance to improve its

Exhibit 5.2. FCC Licensing Processes.

Method	Factors and History	Statutory or Regulation	Dates of Use and Current Status
Ascertainment study	Required applicants to conduct survey of community leaders and programming needs.	Regulation only	1940s to 1980s. Not currently used.
Comparative process	Used for selecting licensee from mutually exclusive applicants.	Regulation only	1940s to 1993. Not currently used.
Random Selection used tie-breaker auction	Developed by FCC to determine mutually exclusive application decisions without work of comparative process.	Regulation at first. Became statutory in 1993.	1985 to 1997. Phased out in Telecommunications Act of 1996. Not currently used.
Competitive bidding or electronic simultaneous multiple-round auctions	Authorized by Congress in Telecommunications Act of 1996. Mandated by Balanced Budget Act of 1997. Modified by Auction Reform Act of 2002.	Statutory	Effective July 1, 1997. Currently in use.

broadcasting service each time a license came up for renewal. However, review of these renewal applications required large amounts of administrative staff time as well as time by the applicants who were required to complete a portfolio of performance documents, verifications, information, and materials.

The FCC began to streamline renewal application procedures during the same period of deregulation that led to the creation of an auction system for new licenses. Under the Telecommunications Act of 1996, license renewal became much simpler for license holders. Today, renewal applications must be filed at least 4 months before the expiration date of the license, but "no renewal of an existing station license . . . shall be granted more than thirty days prior to the expiration of the original license."[32] The Act also creates an assumption that licenses will be renewed. It says, in part,

> If the licensee of a broadcast station submits an application to the Commission for the renewal of such license, the Commission shall grant the application if it finds . . .(A) the station has served the public interest, convenience, and necessity (B) there have been no serious violations by the licensee of this Act, or the rules and regulations of the Commission; and (C) there have been no other violations by the licensee . . . which taken together, would constitute a pattern of abuse.[33]

Furthermore, the 1996 Act specifically prohibits consideration of a competitor's application.[34]

In addition, if the Commission finds that the renewal standards have not been met, it can renew the license for a term less than 8 years. The license renewal application may be denied only after notice and an opportunity to be heard, and only if the agency finds that there are no "mitigating factors" to justify lesser sanctions. Furthermore, the FCC may not announce and consider new applications until after this exhausting process.[35]

Ground Rules for Nonrenewal of Licenses

Because a license renewal can only be denied if a license holder violates specific requirements, it would be useful to know exactly how the courts have interpreted those requirements Licenses have been denied for:

1. Lying or making false or misleading statements to the FCC.
2. Violation of alien or foreign ownership rules.
3. Insolvency or bankruptcy.
4. Interference with other stations and/or operating with excessive power.
5. Inadequate or bad equipment.
6. Refusal to allow inspection of station and transmission facilities.
7. Unauthorized transfers of control or assignment of license without FCC authorization.
8. Repeated or major violations of content regulations.
9. Willful or repeated failure to comply with equal candidate access rules.
10. Repeated fraudulent billing of advertisers, or fraudulent promotional schemes.

Competition and financial hardships on older stations are occasionally, but not consistently, considered. Despite the public interest directive, public objections to programming or editorial content of the licensee have never been considered grounds for refusal to grant or renew a license.

The Commission is not required to investigate licensees independently for compliance, but prior to license renewal the FCC must accept petitions to deny applications. Six months prior to the expiration of a license, stations are required to announce, on the air, that their licenses are about to expire, and that informal public comments or formal petitions objecting to the renewal must be filed with the FCC by a particular date. Often at issue, or at least the focus of public attention and FCC interest, is the content of the **local public inspection file**. This file, required by the rules, is kept by the station and is available for viewing during regular business hours, or on any Web site maintained by the station. A station must eventually maintain 10 items in its public inspection file. As of 2005, those items are:

1. A copy of its current FCC license.
2. Copies of any applications, including those for renewal, filed with the FCC.
3. A copy of the current ownership report.

4. Technical maps showing signal range and contours.

5. Copies of materials relating to any FCC investigations.

6. The equal opportunity file showing annual reports of efforts to recruit minority and women as employees.

7. An issues and programs list describing broadcast of information and discussions of specific local concern.

8. A political file listing time requested and provided to candidates for federal office.

9. Children's Television Act reports showing compliance with relevant programming and commercial limits.

10. Copies of written comments by the public during the licensing period.

To be accepted by the FCC, petitions to deny a broadcast license renewal application must set forth specific allegations of fact that are supported by affidavits of persons with personal knowledge, and not by hearsay, rumor, opinion, or broad generalization. The allegations must also be sufficient to show that the petitioners are parties in interest and that the grant of the challenged application would be inconsistent with the public interest, convenience, and necessity.

To be a party in interest, a petitioner must allege that he or she is a listener or viewer of the station, or a resident of the station's service area. A party in interest may also be a responsible representative of the listening public, or have a direct economic interest that will be injured by the renewal. Each petition to deny an application for license renewal must be served on the applicant, as well as the FCC. If the FCC finds that a petition actually presents a substantial and material question of fact, then it will hold a hearing on the matter. If the renewal application survives any challenges, then renewal of the original license must be granted for an additional period up to 8 years. If any petition challenging the renewal is successful, then the FCC will announce that the license is available for reassignment.

Diversity Destroyed: 150 Channels and Nothing's On

In 1943, the U.S. Supreme Court said that the FCC had an affirmative duty to evaluate license and renewal applications. It said the government's role was not merely to serve as a "traffic officer" for license applications.[36] In 1945, the Supreme Court said, it is "axiomatic that broadcasting may be regulated in light of the rights of the viewing and listening audience and that the widest possible dissemination of information from diverse and antagonistic sources is essential to the welfare of the public."[37]

To safeguard the public's right to receive this diversity of views and information over the airwaves, two consistent themes in governmental control of the licensing and business practices of the communications industry emerged—first to avoid the creation of monopolies, and second to encourage diversity of ownership and voices. To avoid the creation of broadcast monopolies the FCC limited the number of licenses any one individual or corporation could hold. To avoid the creation of a combined media monopoly, the FCC restricted cross-ownerships in certain categories of media.

Congress included provisions in the 1996 Telecommunications Act that would permit multiple media ownerships. This provision was included because of anticipation of the transition to digital TV and the increased frequency availability that would result.[38] Anticipating these changes, the FCC has already begun to alter its regulations to modify or eliminate existing limitations on multiple media ownership. These rules are in flux and public objections to media monopolies may motivate reinstatement of some restrictions. Here, we discuss seven of the rules that restricted multiple media ownership. We also describe changes in the rules and their current status.

The **local radio multiple ownership rule** was developed in the 1940s and prohibited any one entity from holding more than one AM station and one FM station in the same market. This prohibition varied with market size and under the Telecommunications Act of 1996, a market-tiered approach permits from five to eight stations per market. For example, a maximum of eight radio stations per owner is allowed in markets with 45 or more commercial radio stations.

The **local TV multiple ownership rule** was enacted in 1999 and allows common ownership of two TV stations in the same market area if (a) at least one station is not among the four highest ranked stations in that market, and (b) at least eight full-power independent TV stations will remain in the market after granting of the dual licenses to one owner. Also, two TV station licenses may be owned by one entity if one of the stations is failing, and there is no other viable purchaser available.

The **radio/TV cross-ownership rule** was developed in the 1970s and was originally referred to as the "one-to-a-market" rule. It is now called the radio/TV **duopoly rule**. The duopoly rule was changed in 1999 to a three-tiered market system: (a) A single licensee may own one or two TV stations combined with not more than six radio stations, if 20 independent stations would remain. (b) A single licensee may own two TV stations combined with up to four radio stations, if 10 independent stations would remain in that market after the merger. (c) A single licensee may only own one TV and one radio station in a single market area, if fewer than 10 independent stations would remain after the merger. Because of FCC interpretation of the 1996 Telecommunications Act, the duopoly rule is being phased out.

The **newspaper/broadcast cross-ownership rule** was developed in 1975 and prohibits the FCC from granting a radio or TV broadcast license to the owner of a daily newspaper serving the same market. The reason for this rule was that such a merger would give too much journalistic power to a single owner. Like the duopoly rule, this rule is being phased out because of FCC interpretation of the 1996 Telecommunications Act.

The **national TV multiple ownership rule** originated in 1953 and limited the total number of stations that could be owned nationwide by a single entity. The original rule was called the "7–7–7 rule," and limited the broadcast licensee to a combination of no more than seven AM, seven FM, and seven TV broadcast licenses. In 1984, this rule was relaxed to a "12–12–12 rule." In 1992, this rule was changed again to allow a single owner to have 30 AM and 30 FM radio station licenses and up to 12 TV station licenses, as long as the combination accounted for no more than 25% of the national market. Some small and minority broadcasters saw this relaxation of the rules as a concession to media conglomerates. Under the 1996 Telecommunications Act (a) all national limitations or caps on nationwide ownership of radio licenses were repealed and the 12 station cap on TV ownership was replaced with a "35% of U.S. market" rule. This means one person may own an unlimited number of radio stations and TV stations reaching up to 35% of all U.S. households. Even this rule has been reconsidered by the FCC, which in 2003 proposed new rules advancing permitting ownership of TV stations reaching up to 45% of U.S. households. As of 2005, Congress has forced reconsideration of the proposed change.

The **dual network rule** was established in the 1940s. It prohibited any entity from operating more than one radio network. The 1996 act permits TV stations to affiliate with more than one broadcast network. But, it prohibits networks created by merger or cooperation between ABC, CBS, NBC, or FOX. The 1996 Act also permits broadcast networks to provide multiple program streams simultaneously, but prohibits any merger of licenses or stations by the "big-four networks."

Statutory license restrictions against foreign ownership have been created by Congress. Specifically, a foreign individual or foreign corporation may own no more than one fifth of a broadcast license. If the license holder is a subsidiary that is owned or controlled by another corporation, the foreign ownership may be one fourth.

Except for the restrictions on foreign ownership, FCC rules are evolving to permit conglomerate broadcast domination. This factor combined with the 8-year licensing and renewal expectancy serves to allow monopolistic control of multiple means of mass communications. Current ownership rules repudiate the "public interest" directive clearly stated in the Communications Act of 1934.

Cable Regulation or Deregulation: That Is the Question

Nearly all consumers receive their television programming through one of three delivery systems: broadcast television, cable, or satellite. We have discussed broadcast regulations. Now we look at some of the obvious and distinguishing characteristics of cable television services. In the next section of this chapter, we describe some of the regulations associated with satellite TV, telephone, and the Internet. We dealt with broadcast in some detail to describe the patterns of regulation and deregulation that apply to all FCC actions. We address cable and the other electronic media more briefly because they follow patterns similar to those described for broadcasting.

Brief History of Cable Television Regulations

Radio and television broadcasting stations transmit electromagnetic signals over the air to be captured for free by any receiving antenna within range, and broadcast stations are supported by advertisers. By contrast, cable television systems distribute their signals to subscribers over a network of coaxial cable, and the primary source of revenue for cable systems is subscriber fees. About 20% of U.S. households rely exclusively on broadcast distribution while more than three times that number receive cable service.[39] Although cable subscribers have to pay for the services, they usually obtain better reception and a wider variety of programming. Currently, 84% of cable systems offer their subscribers at least 30 channels, including programming that is not available on broadcast systems.[40]

Cable began as community antenna television (CATV) systems in the early 1960s. This service was especially attractive in rural areas, long distances from transmitters or where the mountainous terrain blocked signals. CATV systems involved a single operator with a large-capacity antenna atop a hill or mountain who transferred the signal from that antenna via cable to subscribers' homes.

At first CATV systems were left unregulated. Their only legal requirement was to obtain a right-of-way or easement for their cables. The cable system operators were totally free to determine which of the broadcast signals they captured and retransmitted to subscribers and what fees to charge.

Copyright laws were modified to impact the growing cable industry. In 1968, during the ascension of cable television, the Supreme Court evaluated application of the Copyright Act's performance rule and held that "CATV operators, like viewers and unlike broadcasters, do not perform the programs that they receive and carry." [41] Legislative history shows that Congress specifically intended to countermand the Supreme Court's decision when it passed the Copyright Act of 1976. That act specifically designated secondary transmissions of broadcast programs as public performances of those programs. It said owners of copyrighted audiovisual works, such as television programs, have the exclusive right to authorize public performances of those works. [42] However, Congress recognized that requiring each cable system to negotiate separately with every copyright owner whose work was retransmitted by a cable system would be impossible. Therefore, the 1976 Copyright Act granted cable operators a statutory license to retransmit broadcast signals. [43] Essentially, this combination of judicial decision and legislation left cable operators free to retransmit broadcast signals without violating copyrights. However, in order to take advantage of the statutory license to retransmit broadcast signals and to avoid copyright suits, cable operators must submit to the impositions imposed by Congress. These impositions include the **must-carry rule** and requirements for channel dedication.

The **must-carry rule**, imposed by the FCC in 1965, required cable systems to retransmit the signal of any requesting broadcast station that was "significantly viewed" in its local market. There were two major reasons for imposition of this rule. Neither reason involved the public interest directive. First, the FCC feared that cable might undermine free, local broadcasting; the must-carry rule was designed to protect the local broadcaster. Second, the rule was designed to protect newer ultra high frequency (UHF) stations that lacked the signal quality of more established VHF stations. The FCC was concerned that UHF stations not carried by cable would not be able to compete in the advertising market. [44]

Cable operators filed several suits challenging the must-carry rules as an unconstitutional burden on freedom of speech. The U.S. Circuit Court struck down these rules in 1985 and 1987. [45] After several years without carriage obligations, Congress again imposed must-carry rules on cable operators by passing the Cable Television and Consumer Protection and Competition Act of 1992.

The 1992 Cable Act embodied Congress' concern that over-the-air broadcasters were endangered and could not compete for audience and revenue. The new Cable Act rules were challenged on First Amendment grounds in *Turner Broadcasting System,*

Inc. v. FCC in 1994.[46] The Supreme Court held that the must-carry rules were content-neutral restrictions on speech and that they were reviewable using the First Amendment intermediate scrutiny standards.[47] The Court also ruled that the rules served three important governmental interests: (a) preserving local broadcast television, (b) promoting the widespread dissemination of information from a multiplicity of sources, and (c) promoting fair competition in the television programming market.[48] The case was remanded to the three-judge district court for further evidentiary hearings to decide whether the three interests proffered by the government were genuinely advanced by the must-carry rules, and whether the new rules were a narrowly tailored means of promoting these interests. After additional evidentiary hearings, the district court again granted and the Supreme Court upheld summary judgment for the government.[49] The must-carry rule is constitutional and is being enforced.

Channel dedication was imposed by the FCC in 1976. Under these rules cable operators were required to dedicate four of their channels for public, governmental, educational, and leased access. Operators brought several suits to challenge these rules and in 1979 the Supreme Court struck down the requirement.[50] The Court held that "transferring control of the content of access cable channels from cable operators to members of the public . . . transformed cable operators into common carriers."[51] The High Court reasoned that because Congress had prohibited the Commission from imposing common-carrier obligations on broadcasters and that the requirement to dedicate channels for public access did impose common-carrier obligations that would intrude on the cable operator's control over editorial and programming content.[52]

Congress struck back with the Cable Communications Policy Act of 1984. This act revived much of the FCC-created system struck down 5 years earlier by the Supreme Court. The 1984 Act created four impositions on cable programming. First, it compelled cable operators of systems with more than 36 channels to set aside between 10% and 15% of their channels for commercial use by persons unaffiliated with the operator.[53] Cable operators were forbidden from exercising any editorial control over the programming on those leased channels.[54] In return, the 1984 Act exempted operators from criminal and civil liability stemming from programs on leased access channels.[55] Second, the 1984 Act empowered local franchising authorities to ban or regulate the programming on leased access channels if, using the authority's judgment, it was obscene or indecent.[56] Third, Congress authorized local franchising authorities to require, as a condition for a franchise or renewal, that operators set aside channel capacity for "public, educational, or governmental use," known as **PEG channels**.[57] Again, cable operators were forbidden from exercising any editorial control over programming shown on these PEG channels. Operators were relieved of criminal and civil liability for such programming, and both cable operators and franchise authorities were permitted to prohibit programming that was obscene or otherwise unprotected by the U.S. Constitution.[58] Fourth, the 1984 Act required cable operators to provide equipment, commonly known as a "lockbox" to any subscriber who wanted to block a channel during particular time periods, to restrict the viewing of specific unwanted programming.[59]

In summary, cable operators today enjoy the freedom of a statutory copyright license, but are bound by the must-carry rule and a requirement for channel dedication. Restrictions on obscene and allegedly indecent material are addressed in the last section of this chapter.

Satellites, Telcos, the Internet, and Other Things that Go Bump in the Night

This section briefly explores some laws and regulations that impact the most rapidly changing communications media. The focus here is on the difficulty Congress and the FCC have adapting to technological and social change associated with these media.

Selected Material on Satellite Delivery Systems

Direct broadcast satellite (DBS) has recently joined cable and broadcast television as a major conduit for television services. Cable and satellite companies both receive their revenue from consumer fees, and together they serve approximately 80% of the U.S. television market. In the 1980s, satellite reception dishes were 6 to 10 feet in diameter and served primarily rural areas not reached by broadcast and cable. During the 1990s, satellite carriers such as EchoStar and DirecTV developed much smaller dishes and began to compete with cable in urban and suburban areas. In 2005, satellite carriers provide service in each of the nation's 210 television markets and serve 13% to 15% of television households.

Satellites currently used by DBS providers occupy one of three positions in the Earth's orbit, called full CONUS slots, which allow the satellites to transmit a single beam covering the entire continental United States. The FCC licenses the use of 96 frequencies, 32 at each orbital position. Each frequency carries multiple channels. Fifty frequencies are licensed to EchoStar and 46 to DirecTV. Each of these licensees has the ability to carry between 450 and 500 channels through full CONUS satellites. Every channel carried on these satellites is beamed to the dishes of all subscribers, but channels for which subscribers have not paid are blocked by software in the customer's home satellite equipment.[60]

Like cable television, DBS systems originally received little notice and regulation by Congress or the FCC. One of the first major legal hurdles confronting DBS was copyright interpretation. When Congress passed the 1976 Copyright Act, home satellite service did not exist; therefore, the statutory copyright license included in that act only applied to cable systems.[61] Obviously, copyright prohibitions of retransmission of signals would hamper the growth of satellite services.

Congress responded to this problem with the Satellite Home Viewer Act of 1988. As it had done for the cable industry, Congress gave carriers a limited statutory copyright license. The limited copyright license allowed carriers to retransmit signals of distant network broadcast stations to households that were unable to receive adequate over-the-air signals through a conventional antenna.[62] This limited license helped to promote the growth of satellite carriers and expanded viewing options for households outside broadcast stations' transmission area.[63] However, this did not protect retransmission in urban areas.

By the late 1990s, Congress became aware of two major problems in its regulatory scheme. First, cable enjoyed a virtual monopoly in subscription television services in metropolitan areas. This forced cable subscribers to pay whatever cable companies chose to charge. Second, consumers who lived within the broadcast areas of network television stations were ineligible to receive distant network signals via DBS because of limitations in the 1988 Act. Therefore, this audience essentially had no access to network programming.

Congress reacted to these consumer problems and to concerns expressed by the industry by enacting the Satellite Home Viewer Improvement Act of 1999 (SHVIA). SHVIA imposed essentially the same system on satellite broadcasters that had been forced on the cable operators. Congress granted a statutory copyright license in exchange for what are called the carry-one, carry-all rule and the a la carte rule.

The **statutory copyright license** allows satellite carriers to carry the signals of local broadcast television stations without obtaining authorization from the copyright holders of the individual programs aired by those stations.[64] The voluntary decision to carry one local station in a market under the statutory copyright license triggers the mandate to carry all the requesting stations in that market.

The **carry-one, carry-all rule** is similar to the must-carry rule for cable. It took effect on January 1, 2002, and requires DBS systems who choose to take advantage of the statutory copyright license to carry all requesting stations within that market.[65]

The **a la carte rule** is an FCC regulation that put into effect the provisions of SHVIA.[66] It allows satellite carriers to offer local broadcast stations to their subscribers either individually or as part of a single package. The FCC concluded that SHVIA does not require satellite carriers to sell all local television stations in a given market as one package, but that they can offer local stations either as a "package" or "a la carte." However, because of the carry-one, carry-all provision, satellite carriers may not offer their subscribers a package including some, but not all of the local stations in a market, while offering other local stations individually.

The U.S. Circuit Court held that these rules and the statutory provisions of SHVIA that authorized them are constitutional, content-neutral regulations of satellite carriers' speech. The court also found that these rules do not exceed Congress' constitutional powers.[67]

Telcos, Common Carrier Regulation, and Deregulation

Telephone companies (telcos) are covered under the Communications Act of 1934. Unlike broadcasters and cable operators, telcos are regulated as common carriers.[68] Telcos are classified as **common carriers** because they provide two-way, personal communication rather than information or entertainment content for the public. As a passive carrier, they are not responsible for the content of messages they carry. Another justification for treating telcos differently from other communications services was that they were natural monopolies and had to be controlled in the public interest. Original telco regulations prohibited them from discriminating against either the speakers or the messages they carried; they were also required to adhere to published schedules of rates, and they were required to seek permission from the FCC before adding, expanding, or discontinuing services.

The regulatory system that grew over the years was designed to limit abuses of market power and to promote universal service available even in remote areas. Because telcos were thought to be a natural monopoly, regulations prohibited their entry into other markets. Vertical or horizontal integration was also prohibited. Telcos were also forbidden to offer interconnected communications exchanges or to manufacture telecommunications equipment. These restrictions prevented telcos from offering retransmission of television programming even though the optical fibers adopted by telcos could provide better signal service than the coaxial cable used by most cable television systems. Telephone companies are also subject to public utility regulation by the states. The effect of all this regulation was often to prohibit rather than stimulate competition, and consumers complained about service quality and pricing.

The Telecommunications Act of 1996 changed the regulatory quagmire. Two of the seven titles of the 1996 Act attempt to reconfigure the telephone industry.

Title I of the act promotes competition in local telephone markets. It allows Bell-operating companies to provide long-distance service and to manufacture telecom equipment. However, the act continues subsidies for rural phone service and other special interest customers. It also gives states a major voice in enforcing the federal regulations.

Title III of the Telecommunications Act of 1996 deals with cable services. The act repealed the telco–cable cross-ownership restrictions. It allows telcos to own cable television systems within their phone service area and also allows cable companies to provide telephone service. Furthermore, the new statute authorized telcos to offer video services either by distributing programming as a CATV system or by establishing an open video system for disseminating programming as a common carrier. As common carriers, they are prohibited from discriminating in the rates charged for the same services.[69]

The Internet and the Misnomer "Internet Law"

Today's Internet began in 1969 as a military program called the Advanced Research Project Agency Network (**ARPANET**). The network was designed to enable the military, defense contractors, and universities conducting defense-related research to communicate with one another by redundant computer channels. ARPANET no longer exists, but it was the model for development of civilian networks that, when linked with each other, now enable millions of people to communicate and exchange virtually limitless information.[70] The civilian Internet retains the redundancy and lack of central control that was the major characteristic of ARPANET.

Countless private servers and several major commercial online services offer access to their own proprietary networks and links to the much larger resources of the Internet. The Internet's World Wide Web is located nowhere, but is available to everyone in the world. No single organization controls membership in the Web, nor is there any centralized point from which individual Web sites or services can be blocked.[71] Any individual, group, organization, or government—from the complete idiot to the incredible genius—can place any kind or amount of information on the Web, from the patently fabricated to the profoundly wise. These characteristics of the Internet make it virtually impossible to regulate effectively.

The phrase *Internet law* is often used to describe the huge number of laws passed by Congress in its attempts to control Internet use. However, careful analysis of these laws reveals that they are all attempts to apply existing legal principles to a new technology. Simply put, Internet law is a misnomer. There is no special category of law that is unique to the Internet. There are only attempts to modify and apply existing law to a rapidly changing technology and an evolving pattern of information access.

In the next section of this chapter, we describe Congress's attempts to apply obscenity and indecency law to the Internet. That discussion should demonstrate the difficulty of applying existing law to a new medium. Other areas of existing law that are being applied to the Internet include copyright, defamation, and privacy. In each of these areas, the redundancy and breadth of the Internet creates problems for regulation and enforcement.

Content Control: What First Amendment Rights?

The need for governmental assignment of broadcast frequencies led communications entrepreneurs in the 1920s and 1930s to exchange many of their communication freedoms for access to a specific channel. Initially, governmental control was justified by the view that the airwaves are the property of the collective people and are a scarce resource. In this context, it not only made sense, it was necessary for the government to control frequency assignment. However, in exchange for licenses to use frequencies, the government imposed obligations on the licensees. Today, governmental control of electronic media has become ubiquitous. It has expanded to include not only the mode of communication but also the content, viewpoint, and even the very language used on the licensed frequencies.

We describe the growth of both proscriptive and prescriptive regulations of electronic media content. In the section dealing with prescriptive content we begin with early regulations that were motivated by a paternalistic concern for the greater public good. These early regulations sought to compel presentation of a diversity of viewpoints in a fair and balanced manner. We show how those concerns, represented primarily by the fairness doctrine, have evolved into requirements that largely serve the interests of special groups including Congress itself. In our discussion of proscriptive control, we describe the efforts by Congress and the FCC to prohibit and control media content they define as indecent.

The Politics of Regulation: Prescriptive Content Rules

Just as the FCC has developed multiple ownership rules, so too there are multiple rules prescribing media content. Here, we discuss two major sets of prescriptive rules. First, we present the fairness doctrine and its corollaries. Then, we explain the specific statutes that prescribe broadcast content.

Fairness Doctrine

The **fairness doctrine** originated early in the FCC's efforts to implement the public interest directive. The public interest directive was inspired by specific language in the Communications Act of 1934, which said the FCC should use its licensing power to encourage programming and fair trade practices that were in the public's interest. The fairness doctrine, on the other hand, is not identified by specific statutory language. It was motivated by the results of FCC reports on licensee responsibilities and editorializing that were written between 1946 and 1949.[72] The doctrine had two components. First, it required broadcasters to give coverage to controversial issues of public interest. Second, it required coverage of those controversial issues to be fair. The requirement for fairness included an obligation to permit presentation of conflicting views. Balance was required but equal treatment was not. Because the fairness doctrine replaced an earlier FCC policy prohibiting broadcast editorials, it was perceived as increasing the communication rights of licensees.[73] The **personal attack corollary**, the **Cullman corollary**, the **political editorial corollary**, and the **Zapple doctrine** all modified the fairness doctrine. These corollaries and doctrines are described in Exhibit 5.3.

The Equal Opportunity Rule

The fairness doctrine was eventually abandoned as regulations and policies of the FCC evolved. However, several statutes apply the same principles that motivated the fairness doctrine. For example, Section 315 of the Communications Act of 1934 says,

> if any licensee shall permit any person who is a legally qualified candidate for any public office to use a broadcasting station, he shall afford equal opportunities to all other such candidates for that office in the use of such broadcasting station . . . provided that the licensee shall have no power of censorship over the material broadcast.

The section goes on to say that the act does not impose any affirmative obligation on any licensee to allow use of its station by any candidate.[74] In 1959, Congress amended Section 315 to clarify this requirement. The 1959 amendments specifically said that the appearance of a political candidate in a bonafide newscast, interview, or documentary did not create an obligation for the broadcaster to provide the candidate's opponent an equal opportunity to use the broadcast station.

The 1959 amendments also codified the "fairness doctrine" and its corollaries by reminding broadcasters that the news coverage use exemptions did not relieve them of the obligation to operate in the public interest and to afford reasonable opportunity for the discussion of conflicting views on issues of public importance.[75]

Subsequent amendments require a **lowest unit charge** for political candidates. Lowest unit charge means that political candidates must be charged the lowest rate charged any advertiser for the same class, time, and period of advertising. In addition, the amendment requires that broadcasters maintain records of all requests for political advertising and the time, class, and charges for all such advertising. These records must be available for public inspection for two years. Other amendments address content and identification requirements.

Exhibit 5.3. Fairness Doctrine and Corollaries.

Common Name	Description	Statute or Regulation	Time of use
Fairness doctrine	Developed by the FCC to implement public interest directive. Two components: 1. Broadcasters must cover controversial issues. 2. Broadcasters must give fair and balanced coverage.	Regulation at first, later codified by amendments to 47 U.S.C. § 315(a) in 1959	1949–1987
Personal attack corollary	Required licensees to provide notice and an opportunity to reply to any attack on the character or integrity of an identified person or group. In order to trigger the right of reply, the original criticism had to be part of a presentation of views on a controversial issue of public importance.	Regulation. See, 47 C.F.R. § 73.1920	1949–1987
Cullman corollary	Required broadcasters to provide coverage of controversial issues and to provide coverage of all views on those issues even if no sponsor would pay for the required programming. In other words, the broadcaster could be required to provide free airtime for opposing views or to cover issues that no sponsor would support.	Regulation. See, *Cullman Broadcasting Co.*, 40 FCC 576 (1963)	1963–1987
Political editorial corollary	If a licensee endorsed or opposed a candidate in an editorial, this rule required the licensee to notify the opposing candidates within 24 hours after the editorial was broadcast. The opposing candidates had to be informed of the time of the editorial and be given a transcript or tape. The rule also required that they be given a reasonable opportunity to appear and respond.	Regulation. See, 47 C.F.R. §§ 73.123, 73.300, 73.598, and 73.679	1968–1987
Zapple doctrine	Also known as the "quasi-equal opportunities rule," requires that a licensee who sells time to the political supporters of one legally qualified candidate during an election campaign period also make comparable time available to his or her opponents.	Regulation interpreting statute. See, 23 FCC 2d 707 (1970), letter to Nicholas Zapple.	1970–present

The FCC has interpreted the phrase *equal opportunities* to mean that there must be no discrimination in rates, facilities, practices, or services rendered to candidates. This does not, however, require a station to donate time to a candidate who cannot afford advertising comparable to that paid for by his or her opponent.[76]

The equal opportunities requirement is often mislabeled the "equal time rule." Section 315 does not require that the time made available to a candidate be equal to that used by another candidate. In each case the services, including airtime, must be comparable in terms of the candidate's exposure to the broadcaster's audience.[77]

Section 315 also prohibits licensees from censoring or editing the material broadcast under the equal opportunities rule. However, the section has also been held to create immunity from liability for defamatory statements made by the candidates.[78]

In 1971, the Federal Election Campaign Act added the **reasonable access rule for federal candidates** to the Communications Act of 1934.[79] In unambiguous language, this amendment authorizes the Commission to revoke a broadcaster's license "for willful or repeated failure to allow reasonable access to, or to permit purchase of reasonable amounts of time for the use of a broadcasting station by a legally qualified candidate for federal elective office on behalf of his candidacy." This amendment created a new affirmative right of access to broadcast media for individual candidates for federal elective office. Under challenge from CBS, the Supreme Court upheld the act and ruled that it did not violate the broadcaster's First Amendment right to control its own editorial content.[80]

This new "reasonable access rule for federal candidates" differs significantly from the older "equal opportunities rule." Compliance with the old rule was necessary to assure license renewal and some time had to be given to political issues. But, no individual candidate could claim a personal right of access to any broadcast station unless his or her opponent was first allowed to use the station. Furthermore, there was no distinction between federal, state, and local election candidates.[81] In contrast, the new "reasonable access rule for federal candidates" applies only to candidates for federal office and grants them a special right of access to broadcast stations. Violation of this rule can be punished by license revocation. However, under this amendment, stations are not required to give airtime to federal candidates. The candidate must pay for the time requested, without reference to whether an opponent has secured time.[82] The equal opportunity rule still applies to candidates for state and local office.[83]

Special Interest Mandates

Although the reasonable access rule for federal candidates is a logical development from the fairness doctrine and equal access rule, it is also the first of several FCC and Congressional mandates that defer to special interests. Obviously, a rule that compels broadcasters to sell airtime to candidates for federal office but provides no such right for state or local candidates was created to serve the interest of the members of Congress who passed it. Subsequent acts passed to cater to special interests include the sponsorship identification rule, the video programming accessibility rule, and the children's programming requirements. Each of these requirements provides some benefit to the general public, but each also provides greater protection or access for a specific group.

The fairness doctrine, its corollaries, and the equal access rule have all repeatedly been upheld by the U.S. Supreme Court. The Court has ruled they are valid exercises of authority by the FCC and that they are constitutional under the First Amendment.[84] In addition, the Supreme Court has held that the 1959 amendments to the 1934 Communications Act codified the fairness doctrine.[85]

As recently as 1969 the Supreme Court endorsed the fairness doctrine saying,

> It is the purpose of the First Amendment to preserve an uninhibited marketplace of ideas in which truth will ultimately prevail, rather than to countenance monopolization of that market, whether it be by the government itself or a private license. . . . It is the right of the public to receive suitable access to social, political, esthetic, moral, and other ideas and experiences which is crucial here. That right may not constitutionally be abridged either by Congress or by the FCC.[86]

In 1970, the FCC said that, "the fairness doctrine is a term of art and the thrust of the doctrine as developed by the Commission and codified in law by 47 U.S.C. § 315 does not require equality, but reasonableness.[87]

Despite more than 50 years of commitment to the fairness doctrine, in 1987 the FCC did a total about-face. There was no change in legislation or common law, but the FCC eliminated the fairness doctrine from its interpretation of broadcast licensee's responsibilities to "operate in the public interest." Contradicting its own 1970 statement, the FCC now says the fairness doctrine was not codified or required by Section 315.[88]

The FCC gave three reasons for its break with Congressional mandates, legislative history, U.S. Supreme Court decisions, and its own 50-year history of public interest directive enforcement. These reasons were a volatile and changing economy, a dramatic increase in media outlets since 1959, and the belief that the fairness doctrine "chilled speech."[89]

What has survived from the fairness doctrine are (a) the Zapple doctrine and equal opportunity rule, which protect politicians' rights of reply and right to lowest unit cost advertising and (b) the reasonable access rule for federal candidates, which guarantees Congressional and presidentia candidates access to political advertising when they run for election.

Since 1987, content control of the broadcast media, whether prescriptive or proscriptive, has become increasingly punitive and driven by special interest groups. The access rule, which mandates access to use a licensee's programming for all members of Congress and the presidential and vice-presidential candidates, affects very few people. There are only 537 federal elective positions available.[90] Here, we describe three other special interest mandates: (a) the sponsorship identification rules, (b) the closed-captioning requirements, and (c) the children's television mandates. None of these are optional for broadcast licensees, and all make specialized demands on programming content that require extra expense to accommodate. These expenses must be born by the broadcasters, advertisers, or subscribers.

Sponsorship identification was initiated in the 1960s and has been modified several times.[91] This regulation requires that a broadcaster identify the sponsor of programming or advertising at the time the sponsored material airs. Sponsorship includes direct or indirect payment of money, services, or anything of value in exchange for the broadcast of any material. Sponsors of paid political television advertisements, concerning candidates for public office, must be identified in letters at least 4% of the vertical picture height and the identification must air at least 4 seconds. This is called the 4×4 rule.[92] When a broadcaster accepts film, tape, or transcripts in exchange for a broadcast on any controversial issue, the broadcaster must identify the sponsor of the film, tape, or transcript. An announcement identifying the sponsor must be made both at the beginning and end of a broadcast that lasts more than 5 minutes.[93] This regulation requires the licensee to exercise reasonable diligence to identify and disclose the true identity of individuals or groups for whom airtime is purchased.[94] Sponsorship information must be kept as part of the licensee's public inspection file for 2 years.

Although it might seem that sponsorship identification regulations would benefit the entire public, this regulation is actually designed to protect two small groups. Consumers of commercial advertising already know that broadcast programming is sponsored and commercial advertisements identify their sponsors. This rule gives special care to political advertisements. The regulation was created to notify political opponents when their rights are triggered under the "equal opportunities use" and "reasonable access for federal candidates" rules. Even the application of this rule to commercial advertising benefits the competing advertisers and not the general public. The rule permits competitors to keep track of each other's claims so that they can pursue unfair trade practices and false advertising. None of these requirements benefit the general public. In chapter 12, we explain that consumers rarely have standing to sue for false advertising or unfair trade practices.

Video programming accessibility is covered in Section 613 of the broadcast licensing statutes.[95] That section requires both closed-captioning and video description to benefit the hearing and visually impaired. The statute provides for inquiries by the FCC and authorizes regulations and establishment of industry deadlines. It also provides exemptions for requirements that would impose an undue burden on video programming providers.

It is impossible to determine how many people in the public are served by this requirement. Even if we had numbers showing how many people would benefit from closed-captioning or audio descriptions, there is no public record of the number of exemptions granted because of undue burden. Clearly, this provision was not enacted with the general public in mind. It was created to accommodate a very small special interest audience that was not being served by the capitalistic broadcast industry. There is no provision for reimbursement for this mandated accommodation and costs must be passed on to the greater audience by the industry in the form of increased advertising or subscription fees.

Children's programming rules address the following four separate problems or topics: (a) commercialization and advertising requirements that we address in chapter 12; (b) child pornography and exploitation, which was discussed in chapter 4; (c) keeping children away from media pornography, which we describe later in this chapter; and (d) children's programming mandates, which is the topic of our inquiry here.

The Children's Television Act of 1990 requires the FCC, when conducting its broadcast license renewal reviews, to consider whether licensees have served the educational and informational needs of children. The FCC must evaluate both the overall programming and the programming specifically designed to serve the special needs of children.[96]

In 1996, the FCC adopted a "quantitative approach" to determine licensee compliance. Since then, licensees have been required to provide 3 hours per week of "core programming." **Core programming** is defined as programming (a) serving the educational and informational needs of children 16 and under, (b) that is aired between 7 a.m. and 10 p.m., (c) that is regularly scheduled each week, and (d) that is at least 30 minutes long.[97] In addition, the core programming must be described in a written report and a program guide indicating the age groups for which programs are intended.[98] The regulation contains some hedging. For example, the FCC may include "specials, PSAs, short-form programs, and regularly scheduled nonweekly programs with a significant purpose of educating and informing children" as part of core programming.[99] All licensees who operate commercial AM, FM, TV, or Class A TV stations are required to maintain a public inspection file and FCC regulations mandate 17 sets of material that must be included in that file.[100] AM and commercial FM radio stations are exempted from these requirements but there is a separate and detailed regulation dealing with noncommercial broadcast stations.[101] These regulations address educational accreditation and school system transmission authorization as well as licensing and reporting requirements.

All the other prescriptive mandates we have discussed were made without any provision for funding from the FCC or Congress. The mandates for children's programming has some limited support. As part of the Children's Television Act, Congress established a National Endowment for Children's Educational Television.[102] The purpose of the endowment was "to enhance the education of children through the creation and production of television programming specifically directed toward the development of fundamental intellectual skills."[103] Congressional findings included in the act recognized that "children's programming is aired too infrequently either because public broadcast licensees and permittees lack funds or because commercial broadcast licensees and permittees or cable television system operators do not have the economic incentive."[104]

The National Endowment for the Arts provides grants for production of children's educational programming that cover up to 75% of the production costs. The resulting programming is made available only to public television and noncommercial licensees and permittees for a period of 2 years. Thereafter, it is to be made available to commercial television licensees, or cable television system operators for a fee. However, commercial operators may not interrupt the programming with commercial advertising.[105]

The Word Police: Proscriptive Content Regulations

The previous section described prescriptive content regulations. These are rules that tell communications professionals what they must say. This section addresses proscriptive rules, which tell mass communications professionals what they cannot say. Such laws are often referred to as censorship.

According to BLACK'S LAW DICTIONARY, "censorship" is "the denial of a right of freedom of the press and freedom of speech, and of all those rights and privileges which are had under a free government." According to FUNK & WAGNALLS' STANDARD COLLEGE DICTIONARY, a "censor" is "an official examiner of manuscripts, plays, etc., empowered to suppress them, wholly or in part, if politically or morally objectionable." It says the verb "to censor" means "to act as a censor of; to delete or to suppress." Section 326 of the Communications Act of 1934, states:

> Nothing in this Act shall be understood or construed to give the Commission the power of censorship over the radio communications or signals transmitted by any radio station, and no regulation or condition shall be promulgated or fixed by the Commission which shall interfere with the right of free speech by means of radio communication.

Contrary to the clear working of this section, the FCC issued an order in 1963 saying that the statute authorized the commission to prohibit a licensee from broadcasting material that is coarse, vulgar, suggestive, or susceptible of indecent double meaning.[106] In addition, Congress has moved a section into the U.S. Criminal Code that says, "(w)hoever utters any obscene, indecent, or profane language by means of radio communications shall be fined not more than $10,000 or imprisoned not more than 2 years, or both."[107] Simply put, despite language specifically prohibiting censorship, the U.S. government does censor electronic media. The one limitation on the authority to censor is a "safe harbor" between 10 P.M. and 6 A.M. during which only obscene, but not indecent, material may be prohibited.

The Communications Act of 1934 and its more recent counterpart, the Telecommunications Act of 1996, are replete with conflicting protections and proscriptions. Not only do many of the statutes and FCC regulations conflict with one another, they often conflict with the Commission's rhetoric prohibiting censorship. Many also conflict with the First Amendment itself.

Here, we look at government censorship and control of the modes and content of communications, in spite of and contrary to admonitions contained in the First Amendment. We specifically describe attempts to control indecent communications by Congress and the FCC in four media: broadcasting, cable television, telephone "dial-a-porn," and Internet services.

We also see how the proliferation of new communications technologies has confronted legislators, regulators, and would-be censors with a major enigma. Not only do legislative changes lag significantly behind technological innovations, but quite often Congressional attempts to control speech in a new format are overturned because they are unconstitutional. Furthermore, the very technology that frustrates legislative control often provides its own solutions. Several of the media that Congress and the FCC seek to control have created their own methods of customer selection and exclusion that resolve the very problems Congress seeks to address through legislation. Even more frustrating for legislators is the fact that the technological solutions often are created and implemented more quickly that the courts can review legislation.

Before we begin our discussion of specific attempts to control media content, we review some basic principles from chapters 3 and 4. These concepts and rulings on First Amendment liberties provide a background for evaluating proscriptions on media content.

Review of First Amendment Principles

In 1931, the U.S. Supreme Court, in *Near v. Minnesota*, provided guidance on both prepublication censorship, also called prior restraint, and postpublication punishment of disfavored speech. The court ruled that prior restraint is unconstitutional and also noted that the prospect of severe sanctions could deter publication in the first place and therefore operated as a form of prior restraint or censorship,[108] The Court also ruled that without a finding of actual harm, the only possible purpose for punishment of speech or publication was governmental suppression or censorship.[109] Both prior restraint and threats of post-speech punishments have a "chilling effect" on speech and both are violations of the First Amendment. The *Near* decision has never been reversed or overturned and is still part of U.S. case law.

Recall from chapter 3 that there are two different approaches to interpretation of First Amendment liberties. They are the literalist and social conformist. The literalist approach says that any government suppression of speech must be based on the conduct associated with the speech and may not discriminate because of the content of the message or the viewpoint expressed. The social conformist approach permits control of "non-speech," but prohibits viewpoint regulation. Obscenity is non-speech; indecent communication is speech and has First Amendment protection. Regardless of the interpretational approach, the First Amendment prohibits any governmental action that regulates speech based on the viewpoint of the speaker, and neither approach would permit content regulation unless the communication fits in one of the categories defined as "non-speech."

Finally, recall the concepts of vagueness and overbreadth. Vagueness refers to proscriptive laws that do not describe or define the prohibited conduct with sufficient specificity to warn members of the public about what behavior will merit punishment. Thus, the term *vagueness* refers to laws that are so imprecise or ambiguous that they cannot be consistently and predictably applied. The term *overbreath* refers to laws that are so all-encompassing that they include a number of innocent or legal behaviors not meant to be proscribed. Vague or ambiguous laws are often said to be under inclusive. Laws that suffer from overbreadth are said to be over inclusive. Laws in both categories violate the Fifth and Fourteenth Amendment requirements for due process.

Indecency Regulations and the Broadcast Media

Congressional and FCC control of allegedly indecent speech has been vague and may be overbroad. The FCC has claimed authority to regulate speech that does not rise to the level of obscenity but that the FCC thinks is indecent. The commission claims this authority because of a U.S. Code provision that prohibits the use of "obscene, indecent, or profane language by means of radio communications."[110] The FCC has combined the authority from this statute with principles analogous to the law of nuisance that was overturned in *Near v. Minnesota* to create sanctions on indecent communication. In 1978, in *FCC v. Pacifica Foundation,* the U.S. Supreme Court upheld sanctions imposed by the FCC for indecent, but not obscene, material aired by a broadcast licensee.[111] The FCC now exercises the power to decide whether a broadcast was actually indecent and then to issue sanctions against a broadcast station that violates the prohibition. Sanctions range from informal warnings to formal removal of a license.

In *Pacifica*, the Supreme Court reviewed a ruling by the FCC that sanctioned a radio station for airing a 12-minute program titled *Filthy Words*. The FCC review was initiated by a listener complaint about the satiric program, in which a comedian reviewed a list of colloquial expressions for body parts, sexual acts, and excretory functions. The program was aired on a Tuesday at approximately 2 p.m.

The FCC contended that it never intended to place an absolute prohibition on indecent language, but only sought to "channel" it to times of day when children most likely would not be exposed to it.[112] The commissioners were divided on the basis for their order.[113] The U.S. Circuit Court, which reversed the FCC order, was not able to agree on an opinion and, even the U.S. Supreme Court, in its plurality opinion, could not agree on the legal rationale for its judgment. Everyone on the Commission, on the Circuit Court of Appeals, and on the Supreme Court unanimously agreed, however, that the monologue was not obscene. The only agreement among the justices in the plurality opinion was that the FCC did have the authority to require that material it found to be indecent be "time channeled" to periods when children were unlikely to be in the audience.

Three additional situations exemplify the arbitrary enforcement in the area of broadcast indecency. The first was an order issued by the FCC in the same year as the *Pacifica* case. The FCC found that it could not require censorship of the word "nigger" used in a political announcement because the U.S. Code "prohibits censorship of broadcast matter by the Commission" and also "prohibits a radio or television station from censoring use by legally qualified candidates of its facilities."[114]

The second situation involves another 1978 FCC order. The FCC's order in this case found that "discussions of sex are not per se obscene and may not be automatically prohibited." The commission also ruled that the occasional use of an expletive does not warrant sanction. Furthermore, the FCC found that it was the individual licensee's responsibility to decide what programming is appropriate or suitable for airing to audiences, and when.[115]

One final case exemplifies the continuing confusion faced by broadcasters caused by the FCC's lack of consistent interpretation and enforcement of statutes and regulations. In 1996, the FCC combined three cases before the U.S. Circuit Court. All related to efforts of a candidate for federal office to air political advertisements portraying images of aborted fetuses during periods when children were likely to be in the viewing audience.[116] Both television stations and citizens' groups requested that the FCC render a declaratory ruling. These complaints raised two questions. First, what, if any right or obligation does a broadcast licensee have to channel political advertisements that it reasonably and in good faith believes are indecent to times when children are unlikely to be in the audience? Second, do broadcasters have any right to time channel material that is not indecent, but may be otherwise harmful to children?[117]

In 1994, responding to the original complaints, the FCC issued a Memorandum Opinion and Order with four conclusions. First, the FCC concluded that the challenged advertisement was not indecent. Second, it found there was evidence that the images in the advertisement could be psychologically damaging to children. Third, it concluded there was nothing in the federal candidate access rules that precluded a broadcaster from exercising some discretion to protect children from harmful political advertisements. Finally, the FCC concluded that time channeling was not censorship and was not prohibited.[118]

The Court of Appeals vacated the FCC's ruling. The court ruled that content-based time channeling violated the reasonable access requirement and thus denied the candidate the access to the broadcast media envisioned by Congress. The court said specifically,

> Not only does the power to channel confer on a licensee the power to discriminate between candidates, it can force one of them to back away from what he considers to be the most effective way of presenting his position on a controversial issue lest he be deprived of the audience he is most anxious to reach.[119]

We learn at least eight lessons from these cases. First, channeling is a form of censorship, based on content discrimination between speakers. Second, exerting coercive pressure on a speaker who wishes to avoid channeling has a chilling effect on speech that frustrates full and unrestrained discussion of issues. Third, qualified candidates for any political office can require broadcast stations to air material that reasonably has been found to be harmful to children. Fourth, all political advertisements take precedence over children's interests not to be confronted with indecent words or harmful material. Fifth, both the FCC and the appellate courts discriminate based on viewpoint and message content to determine who has access to prime time and who must be "time-channeled." Sixth, both speakers and broadcast licensees bear the burdens of these arbitrary and changing rules. Seventh, the FCC requires licensees to serve as the government's censors by proxy when it requires them to "time channel" indecent material or face sanctions such as loss of licenses. And finally, after dispensing with the "fairness doctrine" in 1987, the FCC no longer considers the rights of the public as paramount. Currently, an oligarchy of special interest groups determine the political correctness of the content of broadcast programming.

In the most recent cycle of FCC programming censorship, the newly appointed members of the Commission have expressed their personal ire and emotional involvement. Rather than being unbiased regulators serving the entire public, the FCC currently punishes or proscribes content its members find personally objectionable. The Commission's news release of October 2, 2003, even advocated treating each indecent utterance, distinct conversations, or program segments as a separate event to which the highest fines available to the agency will be applicable. One commissioner said, "This will substantially increase our fines, which by statute are capped at an inadequate level, so they will be more commensurate with the offenses." This statement demonstrates the willingness of the Commission to ignore the intent of Congress. Furthermore, the policy of increasing penalties without Congressional authorization cannot help but have a chilling effect on some speech. Although the speech punished may be indecent and offensive, the law requires every speaker be granted the liberties guaranteed under the First Amendment. A commission or an individual commissioner who feels free to express his disdain for Congress publicly is obviously not considering those liberties.

V-Chip Technology, Program Ratings Systems, and Viewer Choices

We mention one other item in the confusing world of government control of broadcast programming. The Telecommunications Act of 1996 presented the television broadcast industry with two mandates. The first was the "V-chip" requirement. It required the installation of programming-blocking technology by 2000 on all new televisions with screens larger than 13 inches.[120] The second was a requirement for the broadcast industry to create a system of ratings, which parents and others could use to exercise their own personal censorship through their V-chip equipment.[121] Despite reluctance from the industry, government pressure coerced a ratings system that was finally approved by the FCC in 1998. In effect, Congress felt compelled to create legislation facilitating the same control that people with functioning brains already exercised with the power and channel change buttons. In spite of all the time and effort invested in this system, only about 17% of households that have television sets with V-chip equipment actually use the technology.[122]

Congressional Censorship of Telephone Communications

Long before its 1996 overhaul of the Communications Act of 1934, Congress attempted to control adult communication on the telephone. In 1989, the Supreme Court declared the first of these attempts unconstitutional. The Court's decision in *Sable Communications of California, Inc. v. FCC* unanimously struck down legislation that attempted to ban allegedly indecent communications over the telephone by adult consumers of dial-a-porn sites.[123]

Congress had used the often successful governmental justification of protecting minors and unconsenting adults from sexual expression of any kind. The Court said that although protection of minors was an important governmental interest, sexual expression that is allegedly indecent, but not obscene, is also protected by the First Amendment, and any governmental action suppressing such communications must be narrowly tailored to serve the specific governmental interests proffered.

Since the inception of telephone communications in the United States, telecos have always been considered common carriers. Common carriers are required by law to accept and transmit all communications submitted to them, and may not discriminate between speakers or messages. However, in the challenged legislation, Congress required the telcos to ban or block all communications to dial-a-porn sites. Anyone who wanted access to such a site had to specifically request access to the site in writing.

In striking down this form of censorship called **reverse blocking**, the Supreme Court noted that callers seeking dial-a-porn services had to perform the affirmative act of dialing a specific number in order to receive the communications. Therefore, they would not be surprised by the message content. The Court said that a complete ban on all such communication was overbroad and that less restrictive alternatives were available to protect the governmental interests involved. The Court suggested that the dial-a-porn services could be required to verify the adult status of callers before initiating adult communications. Examples of protective devices offered included preselected code words, special PIN numbers, or credit card numbers.

It is interesting to note that Congressional and FCC solicitude toward the special needs of children is often more rhetorical than real. During the same time frame in which Congress had adopted its ban on adult dial-a-porn telephone communications, the FCC dropped its long-standing prohibitions of commercial content and advertising placement in children's programming. The Commission justified the elimination of this children's protection policy by stating that it was consistent with the FCC's general de-emphasis of quantitative guidelines and the importance of advertising as a support mechanism for the presentation of children's programming.[124] In other words, the FCC thought it was more important to protect broadcasters' profit interests than to protect children. This is not to imply that profit-making is bad in a capitalistic society, but to show that when there is a choice between business interests and children's interests, profit often prevails.

Congressional Attempts to Censor Internet Communications

In 1996, Congress enacted the Communications Decency Act (CDA). This act was one of several titles in the Telecommunications Act of 1996 and attempted to control adult communication on the Internet. The CDA criminalized the transmission of both obscene and indecent communications via any interactive computer service that could be accessed by any person under the age of 18.[125] In 1997, the Supreme Court struck two of the three major sections of this title because they violated the First Amendment.[126]

The Supreme Court acknowledged that Congress can totally prohibit obscene communication because it is "non-speech" and therefore outside the protection of the First Amendment. However, adult communication that is merely indecent is protected by the U.S. Constitution. The overturned sections were found unconstitutional for a variety of reasons. They were void for vagueness because they totally failed to define what was meant by the term *indecency*. This made it impossible for Internet speakers to know what communication was prohibited. Furthermore, Congress had included a definition for *obscene material* that failed to comport to the High Court's own definition in the case of *Miller v. California*. The Court also ruled that the breadth of the coverage of the two sections effectively suppressed a large amount of speech that adults have a constitutional right to receive. The beleaguered Supreme Court emphasized the theme running through all its decisions stating:

> It is true that we have repeatedly recognized the governmental interest in protecting children from harmful materials. But that does not justify an unnecessarily broad suppression of speech addressed to adults. As we have explained, the Government may not "reduce the adult population . . . to only what is fit for children." "Regardless of

the strength of the government's interest" in protecting children, "the level of discourse reaching a mail box simply cannot be limited to that which would be suitable for a sandbox."[127]

The Supreme Court said that although the government certainly has an interest in protecting children from potentially harmful materials, the CDA was a content-based prohibition on speech. For such a statute to withstand constitutional challenge, the means used by the government had to be narrowly tailored to achieve its stated purpose. The Court noted that user-based software costing only $40 could be used by parents to prevent their children from accessing materials. The Court was not persuaded that the CDA was narrowly tailored to achieve its goals and said, "(t)he interest in encouraging freedom of expression in a democratic society outweighs any theoretical but unproven benefit of censorship."[128]

Undaunted in its attempt to criminalize protected adult speech, Congress passed the Child Online Protection Act, known as COPA, one year later.[129] COPA attempted to impose criminal penalties including a $50,000 fine and 6 months in prison for knowingly posting, for commercial purposes, to the World Wide Web content that is "harmful to minors." While COPA did contain a lengthy definition of its terms, the Supreme Court affirmed a preliminary injunction preventing its enforcement because the statute likely violated the First Amendment.[130] The Court reasoned that because content-based prohibitions, enforced by severe criminal penalties, have the constant potential to be a repressive force in the lives and thoughts of a free people, to guard against that threat the Constitution demands that content-based restrictions on speech be presumed invalid.[131] The High Court agreed with the Third Circuit that had ruled the "community standards" language in COPA, used as part of its definitional scheme, by itself rendered the statute unconstitutionally overbroad.[132] The Supreme Court agreed with the District Court's reasoning that there were plausible and less restrictive alternatives for the protection of minors. The less restrictive alternatives included blocking and filtering software.[133]

Congressional Attempts to Suppress Adult Speech on Cable Television

In a case that was cited as precedent in the court's review of COPA, the Supreme Court reviewed a challenge to programming content on the Playboy Cable Channel. The case involved enforcement of Section 505 of the Telecommunications Act of 1996, which was also Title V of the CDA.[134] That statute made cable television operators the licensed censors of adult expression in their medium. Section 505 required cable television operators who provided channels primarily dedicated to sexually oriented programming either to fully scramble or otherwise fully block those channels or to limit transmission of such programs to the **safe harbor** hours of 10 p.m. to 6 a.m., when children were unlikely to be in the audience.

Because of "signal bleed," which allowed part of the scrambled programs to be partially heard or seen, 69% of cable operators adopted the time channeling approach. Because 30% to 50% of all adult programming is viewed prior to 10 p.m., the result of time channeling was a dramatic reduction in audience for the Playboy Channel.[135]

The Supreme Court affirmed a district court's finding that Section 505 was unconstitutional. Its enforcement was permanently enjoined. The district court found that Section 505 imposed a content-based restriction on speech. It also concluded that, although the interests advanced by Congress in protecting children were compelling, the government could further those interests in a less restrictive way. For example, under Section 504 of the Telecommunications Act cable operators could be required to block undesired channels at individual households upon request.[136]

The Supreme Court pointed out that this case rested on the key difference between cable television and the broadcast media. Cable systems have the capacity to block unwanted channels on a household-by-household basis. Allowing the consumer to choose target blocking of unwanted programming enables the government to support parental authority without affecting the First Amendment interests of speakers and willing listeners.[137]

Our final case exemplifying Congress' attempt to control non-obscene, adult programming deals with earlier legislation in which cable operators were essentially used as censors. Congress enacted the Cable Television Consumer Protection and Competition Act in 1992. This act includes three separate sections at issue in our discussion. Section 10(a) of the act permitted a cable system operator to prohibit the broadcasting on **leased access channels** of programming that the operator reasonably believed to describe or depict sexual or excretory activities or organs in a patently offensive manner.[138] Leased access channels are those that federal law required a cable system operator to reserve for commercial use by unaffiliated third parties. Section 10(b) of the act required cable system operators who decided to permit such "patently offensive programming" to both segregate such programming on a single channel and also to block that channel from viewer access unless the viewer requested access in advance and in writing.[139] Finally, Section 10(c) of the act essentially permitted a cable system operator to prohibit the broadcasting of such programming on public access channels or PEGs.[140]

In *Denver Area Educational Telecommunications Consortium, Inc. v. FCC* [141] the Supreme Court held that (a) cable operators may ban indecent programming from leased channels but not from public access channels, and (b) the signal scrambling and advance consent requirements are unconstitutional. The High Court found that these mandates substantially burdened the First Amendment rights of viewers by requiring advance planning and forcing people to reveal their identities to cable operators who could disclose lists of their adult programming subscribers. Furthermore, the protection of children from viewing patently offensive material could be achieved by much less restrictive alternatives available to cable subscribers through the current technology of V-chips and lockboxes.[142]

Practice Notes

The 1934 Communications Act required license renewal every 3 years. Broadcasters applying for licenses and for renewal were required to demonstrate that they would or had operated in the public interest. Under that system, the FCC could refuse to renew a license if it found a new applicant would better serve the public interests. One method for demonstrating this commitment to the public interest was willingness to contribute time for announcements or advertising for charities and other organizations operating for the public good. The announcements or advertisements were called PSAs. Needless to say, broadcasters were highly motivated to accept PSAs when they had to submit to license renewal every 3 years and might lose their license if a competitor offered to do more for the public good.

Today, licenses are renewed every 8 years[143] and for most broadcasters the public interest directive is only a memory. The Telecommunications Act of 1996 did away with much of the motivation for broadcasters to provide time and facilities for PSAs. However, even in today's market, PSAs are still aired and there is significant legal motivation for their use.

License renewal applications are no longer competitive but applicants must still show that they meet minimum standards. One of these standards is a demonstration that the "station has served the public interest, convenience and necessity."[144] Also, the current procedure provides for public comment and objection to a renewal application by interested parties. This public input is facilitated by a requirement for each station to maintain a public inspection file that contains, among other things, an issues and programming list and a Children's Television Act report.[145]

Stations applying for any change in their permit, including license renewal, are required to make the following announcement frequently, and well in advance of their renewal review.

> On [date of last renewal grant] [Station's call letters] was granted a license by the Federal Communications Commission to serve the public interest as a public trustee until [expiration date].
>
> Our license will expire on [date]. We must file an application for renewal with the FCC [date four calendar months prior to expiration date]. When filed, a copy of this application will be available for public inspection during our regular business hours. It contains information concerning this station's performance during the last [period of time covered by the application].
>
> Individuals who wish to advise the FCC of facts relating to our renewal application and to whether this station has operated in the public interest should file comments and petitions with the FCC by [date first day of last full calendar month prior to the month of expiration].
>
> Further information concerning the FCC's broadcast license renewal process is available at [address of location of station's public inspection file] or may be obtained from the FCC, Washington, DC 20554.[146]

The application described in this announcement must contain some materials from the public inspection file.[147] One such requirement is a political file that records political candidate's requests for advertising and response time under either the equal opportunities rule or the reasonable access for federal candidates rule.[148] The application and inspection file must also include an issues program list. This list identifies programs the station has aired and time provided to address community issues. It must report the date, time, and duration of these programs.[149]

The Children's Television Act Report must also be included in the inspection file. This report describes programming efforts made by the licensee to serve the educational and informational needs of children under 16.[150] The Children's Television Act has been interpreted to count PSAs as part of the core programming for children.[151] Finally, letters and suggestions from the public must be included in the application and inspection file.[152]

Under today's rules, it would be extraordinary for a station's renewal application to be denied based on a failure to operate in the public interest. However, the application process can be bothersome for broadcasters. Public objection or complaints make the process more difficult and avoiding that difficulty should motivate the broadcasters to action. Advertising and public relations practitioners may be able to take advantage of this motivation.

Because of the political file requirement, practitioners representing politicians should find broadcasters receptive to requests for either lowest unit cost advertising or airtime for response to attacks. The issues program list requirement may encourage an amenable response to requests for news or public service coverage of controversial issues of public concern. Finally, mass communications practitioners representing schools, children's groups, or educational interests may be able to take advantage of the Children's Television Act Report. In order to serve the broadcaster's needs in the area of children's programming, the duration of the program is important. Traditional brief PSAs may help some, but longer educational or instructional programs will be more attractive.

In summary, the 30-second PSA may be aired today only because broadcasters are generous and community-spirited, but a careful advertising or public relations practitioner can tailor his or her messages to provide an actual service to the broadcaster. Obviously, those messages are more likely to find free airtime.

Magic Words and Phrases

A la carte rule	Equal opportunities rule
ARPANET	Fairness doctrine
Ascertainment study	Homo economicus
Carry-one, carry-all rule	Homo politicus
Common carriers	Leased access channels
Core programming	Local public inspection file
Cullman corollary	Local radio multiple ownership rule
Dual network rule	Local TV multiple ownership rule
Duopoly rule	Lowest unit charge
Electronic simultaneous multiple-round auctions	Media bureau
	Must-carry rule

National TV multiple ownership rule	Reasonable access rule
Newspaper/broadcast cross-ownership rule	Reverse blocking
	Safe harbor
PEG channels	Sponsorship identification
Personal attach corollary	Statutory copyright license
Public interest directive	Tie-breaker lotteries
Radio/TV cross-ownership rule	Zapple doctrine

Suggested Cases to Read and Brief

Action for Children's Television v. FCC, 821 F.2d 741 (D.C.Cir. 1987)
Ashcroft v. ACLU, 124 S.Ct. 2783, 2789 (2004)
Bechtel v. FCC, 10 F.3d 875 (D.C.Cir. 1993)
Becker v. FCC, 95 F.3d 75 (1996)
CBS, Inc. v. FCC, 453 U.S. 367 (1981)
CBS, Inc. v. Democratic National Committee, 412 U.S. 94 (1973)
Denver Area Educational Telecommunications Consortium, Inc., v. FCC, 518 U.S. 727 (1996)
Farmers Educational & Cooperative Union of America v. WDAY, Inc., 360 U.S. 525 (1959)
FCC v. National Citizens Committee for Broadcasting, 436 U.S. 775 (1978)
FCC v. Pacifica Foundation, Inc., 438 U.S. 726 (1978)
FCC v. Pottsville Broadcasting Co., 309 U.S. 134 (1940)
Fortnightly Corp. v. United Artists Television, Inc., 392 U.S. 390 (1968)
Hoover v. Intercity Radio Co., 286 F. 1003 (D.C.Cir. 1923)
Kennedy for President v. FCC, 636 F.2d 432 (1980)
Lamprecht v. FCC, 958 F.2d 382 (D.C. Cir. 1992)
Paulsen v. FCC, 491 F.2d 887 (1974)
Red Lion Broadcasting Co., Inc. v. FCC, 395 U.S. 367 (1969)
Reno v. ACLU, 521 U.S. 844 (1997)
Sable Communications of California, Inc. v. FCC, 492 U.S. 115 (1989)
Satellite Broadcasting v. FCC, 275 F.3d 337 (4th Cir. 2001)
Syracuse Peace Council v. FCC, 867 F.2d 654 (D.C.Cir. 1989)
Turner Broadcasting System, Inc. v. FCC, 512 U.S. 622 (1994)
Turner Broadcasting System, Inc., v. FCC, 520 U.S. 180 (1997)
U.S. v. Playboy Entertainment Group, Inc., 529 U.S. 803 (2000)

Questions for Discussion

1. Recall the concepts of homo politicus, homo economicus, moralistic, traditionalistic, and individualistic political cultures. How do these principles relate to the public interest directive?

2. What trend appears to guide the changes in the ownership rules? How do these changes relate to the interest of the public and the public interest directive?

3. Describe the changes in the fairness doctrine. Today, how does the FCC guarantee programming fairly represents all interests in our society?

4. What was the original purpose of the comparative process rules? What factors were used by the FCC to determine which applicant would receive the contested license? How are the same decisions made today?

5. Discuss the processes for granting and renewing licenses under the Communications Act of 1934. How are the same decisions made today? What impact do you think these changes will have on programming content and media ownership?

6. Describe the differences between the equal opportunities rule and the reasonable access rule. Who benefits from the reasonable access rule?

7. Does society as a whole benefit from children's programming? In what way? If society does benefit, why must broadcasters be mandated to carry such programming or to curb commercialization of children's TV? If society does not benefit, why is children's programming prescribed?

8. Describe the technologies involved in broadcast, cable, and satellite TV. How do copyright laws and licenses, must-carry rules, carry-one, carry-all, and a la carte rules relate to each of these technologies?

9. Describe the sequence of statutes and cases relating to Congressional attempts to control indecent communication on the Internet. Is there a way to control access by minors that does not violate the First Amendment? If so, describe the law that would survive a First Amendment challenge.

Notes

1. *FCC v. Pottsville Broadcasting Co.*, 309 U.S.134 (1940).
2. U.S. CONST. art. I, § 8, cl. 3.
3. U.S. CONST. art. I, § 8, cl. 18.
4. *Hoover v. Intercity Radio Co.*, 286 F. 1003 (1923).
5. 47 U.S.C. § 307 (2001.)
6. *Red Lion Broadcasting Co., Inc. v. FCC*, 395 U.S. 367, 381 (1969), quoting 67 CONG. REC. 5479.
7. *FCC v. Pottsville Broadcasting Co.,* 309 U.S. 134, 137 (1940).
8. *Id.* at 138–139.
9. 47 U.S.C.§ 301 (2001).
10. 47 U.S.C. § 307 (2001).
11. 47 U.S.C. § 307(c) (2001).
12. 47 U.S.C. § 307(d) (2001).
13. *Regents of University System of Georgia v. Carroll*, 338 U.S. 586 (1950).
14. *FCC v. Sanders Bros. Radio Station,* 309 U.S. 470 (1940); *Regents of University System of Georgia v. Carroll*, 338 U.S. 586 (1950); but see, *Busse Broadcasting Corp. v. FCC*, 87 F 3d 1456 (D.C.App. 1996).
15. *McIntire v. William Penn Broadcasting Co.*, 151 F.2d 597 (1945).

16. *FCC v. National Citizens Comm. for Broadcasting*, 436 U.S. 774, 794 (1978).
17. *Bechtel v. FCC*, 10 F.3d 875, 880 (D.C.Cir. 1993).
18. *Metro Broadcasting, Inc. v. FCC*, 497 U.S. 547, 581 (1990).
19. *Id.* at 568.
20. *Lamprecht v. FCC*, 958 F.2d 382 (D.C.Cir. 1992).
21. *Bechtel*, 10 F.3d 875.
22. 47 U.S.C. § 309 (2001).
23. 47 U.S.C. § 309(j) (1996).
24. 47 U.S.C. § 309(i)(5) (2001).
25. 47 U.S.C. §§ 309(i)(11) & (14)(A) (2001).
26. 47 U.S.C. §§ 309(i)(3)(A) & (B) (2001).
27. 47 U.S.C. §§ 309(i)(3)(C)(ii) (2001).
28. 47 U.S.C. § 309(i)(3)(D) (2001).
29. 47 U.S.C. § 309(i)(5) (2001).
30. 47 U.S.C. §§ 309(j)(8)(A)&(B) (201).
31. 47 U.S.C. § 307 (c) (2001).
32. 47 U.S.C. § 307(d) (2001).
33. 47 U.S.C. § 309(k)(1) (2001).
34. 47 U.S.C. § 309(k)(4) (2001).
35. 47 U.S.C. § 309(k) (2)&(3) (1996).
36. *National Broadcasting Co. v. United States*, 319 U.S. 190, 215 (1943).
37. *Associated Press v. United States*, 326 U.S.1, 20 (1945).
38. 47 U.S.C. § 309(i)(D) (2001).
39. 16 FCC Rᴄᴅ. 6005 (2001).
40. *Satellite Broadcasting v. FCC*, 275 F.3d 337, 344 (2001).
41. *Fortnightly Corp. v. United Artists Television, Inc.*, 392 U.S. 390, 400–01(1968), interpreting the Copyright Act of 1909.
42. 17 U.S.C. § 106(4) (2001).
43. See 17 U.S.C. § 111(c)(1976).
44. *Satellite Broadcasting v. FCC*, 275 F.3d 337, 345 (2001).
45. *Quincy Cable TV*, 768 F.2d 1434, 1463 (D.C.Cir. 1985); and *Century Communications Corp. v. FCC*, 835 F.2d 292, 293 (D.C.Cir. 1987).
46. *Turner Broadcasting System, Inc. v. FCC*, 512 U.S. 622 (1994).
47. *U.S. v. O'Brien*, 391 U.S. 367 (1969).
48. *Turner*, 512 U.S. at 662–663.
49. *Turner Broadcasting System, Inc., v. FCC*, 520 U.S. 180 (1997).
50. *FCC v. Midwest Video Corp.*, 440 U.S. 689 (1979).
51. *Id.* at 700–701.
52. *Id.* at 707–709.
53. 47 U.S.C. § 532(b).
54. 47 U.S.C. § 532(c)(2).
55. 47 U.S.C. § 558 (amended in 1992).
56. 47 U.S.C. § 532(h) (2001).
57. 47 U.S.C. § 531 (2001).
58. 47 U.S.C. §§531 (e), amended in 1992; 544 (d)(1) (2001).
59. 47 U.S.C. § 544(d)(2) (2001).
60. *Satellite Broadcasting v. FCC*, 275 F.3d 337, 345 (4th Cir. 2001).
61. 17 U.S.C. S§ 111(c)(1976).

62. 17 U.S.C. § 119(a)(2)(B)(1988), amended 1994 and in 1999.

63. *Id.*

64. 17 U.S.C. § 122(a) (1999).

65. 47 U.S.C. § 338 (a)(1)(1999).

66. 47 U.S.C. § 338(g) (2000).

67. *Satellite Broadcasting v. FCC,* 275 F.3d 337, 367 & 370 (4th Cir. 2001).

68. 47 U.S.C. §§ 201–226 (1992).

69. 47 U.S.C. § 202 (2004).

70. *Reno v. ACLU,* 521 U.S. 844, 849–850 (1997).

71. *Id.* at 850–853.

72. 13 F.C.C. 1246 (1949).

73. *Mayflower Broadcasting Corp.* 8 FCC 333 (1940).

74. 47 U.S.C. § 315 (1934).

75. Act of September 14, 1959, § 1, amending 47 U.S.C. § 315(a). See also, *Red Lion Broad-casting Co., Inc. v. FCC*, 395 U.S. 367, 382 (1969)

76. *Paulsen v. FCC,* 491 F.2d 887, 889 (1974), quoting Use of Broadcast Facilities by Candidates for Public Office, 35 Fed. Reg. 13048, 13060 (1970).

77. 34 FCC 2d 510 (1972).

78. *Farmers Educational & Cooperative Union of America v. WDAY, Inc.,* 360 U.S. 525, 531 (1959).

79. *CBS, Inc. v. FCC,* 453 U.S. 367, 377 (1981); 47 U.S.C. § 312(a)(7) (1971).

80. *CBS, Inc.,* 453 U.S. at 377.

81. *Farmers Educational & Cooperative Union v. WDAY, Inc.,* 360 U.S. 525, 534 (1959).

82. *CBS, Inc.,* 453 U.S. at 382 (1981), quoting *Kennedy for President v. FCC,* 636 F. 2d 432, 446–450 (1980).

83. 69 FCC 2d 2209, 2290 (1978).

84. See, *Red Lion Broadcasting Co, Inc. v. FCC,* 395 U.S. 367 (1969); *Farmers Educational & Cooperative Union of America* v. *WDAY,* 360 U.S. 525 (1959); *CBS v. Democratic Nat'l Committee,* 412 U.S. 94 (1973); *FCC v. League of Women Voters of California,* 468 U.S. 364 (1984).

85. See, *Red Lion Broadcasting Co., Inc. v. FCC,* 395 U.S. 367, 382 (1969); *CBS v. Democratic National Committee,* 412 U.S. 94, 114 n.12 (1973).

86. *Red Lion,* 395 U.S. at 390.

87. 25 FCC 2d 283 (1970).

88. *Syracuse Peace Council v. Television Station WTVH,* FCC 87–266, adopted August 4, 1987. See also, *Complaint of Syracuse Peace Council Against Television Station WTVH, Syracuse, New York,* FCC 88–131, adopted March 24, 1988.

89. See, *Syracuse Peace Council v. FCC,* 867 F.2d 654 (D.C. Cir. 1989); *Arkansas AFL-CIO v. FCC,* 11 F.3d 1430, 1441 (8th Cir. 1993).

90. 435 representatives, 100 senators, the president, and vice-president.

91. 47 C.F.R. 73.1212 (2003).

92. 47 C.F.R. 73.1212 (a)(2)(ii)(2003).

93. 47 C.F.R. 73.1212(d)(2003).

94. 47 C.F.R. 73.1212 (e)(2003).

95. 47 U.S.C. § 613 (1996).

96. 47 U.S.C. §§ 303 a, 303 b, 394 (1991).

97. 47 C.F.R. 73.671(c)(1)-(4) (1996).

98. 47 C.F.R. 73.671 (c)(5) & (6)(1996).

99. 47 C.F.R. 73.671 n.2 (2001).

100. 47 C.F.R. 73.3526 (2003).

101. 47 C.F.R. 73.503 (2001).

102. 47 U.S.C. § 394 (1990).

103. 47 U.S.C. § 394(a) (1990).

104. Act Oct.18,1990, P.L.101-437, Title II, Sec. 202, 104 Stat. 997.

105. 47 U.S.C., Sec. 394 (b)(1)(A)&(b) (2003).

106. *Balmetto Broadcasting Co.*, 24 FCC 2d 434 (1963).

107. 18 U.S.C. § 1464 (2003).

108. *Near v. Minnesota*, 283 U.S. 697, 711 (1931).

109. *Id.* at 709.

110. 18 U.S.C. § 1464 (2001).

111. *FCC v. Pacifica Foundation*, 438 U.S. 726, 731–732 (1978).

112. *Id.* at 732.

113. *Id.*

114. *Complaint by Julian Bond*, 69 FCC 2d 943 (1978), interpreting 47 U.S.C.S. §§ 315 & 326 (2001).

115. *WGBH Educational Foundation*, 69 FCC 2d 1250 (1978).

116. *Becker v. FCC*, 95 F.3d 75 (1996).

117. *Id.* at 77.

118. *Id.* at 77–78.

119. *Id.* at 83.

120. 47 U.S.C. § 303 (w)(1)(1996).

121. 47 U.S.C. § 303(x)(1996).

122. Jim Rutenberg, *Survey Shows Few Parents Use TV V-Chip*, New York Times, July 25, 2001 at E-1.

123. *Sable Communications of California, Inc. v. FCC*, 492 U.S. 115 (1989).

124. *Action for Children's Television v. FCC*, 821 F.2d 741, 744 (D.C.Cir. 1987).

125. 47 U.S.C. §§ 223(a) & 223(d)(1996).

126. *Reno v. American Civil Liberties Union*, 21 U.S.844 (1997).

127. *Reno v. ACLU*, 521 U.S. 844, 875 (1997).

128. *American Civil Liberties Union*, 521 U.S. at 885.

129. 47 U.S.C. § 231 (1998).

130. *Ashcroft v. ACLU*, 124 S.Ct. 2783, 2789 (2004).

131. *Id.* at 2788.

132. *Id.* at 2789.

133. *Id.* at 2791–2792.

134. 47 U.S.C. § 561 (1996).

135. U.S. v. *Playboy Entertainment Group, Inc.*, 529 U.S. 803, 809 (2000).

136. 47 U.S.C. § 560 (1996).

137. *Playboy Entertainment*, 529 U.S. at 815.

138. 47 U.S.C. § 532(h) (1992).

139. 47 U.S.C. § 532(j) (1992).

140. 47 U.S.C. § 531 note (1992).

141. *Denver Area Educational Telecommunications Consortium, Inc. v. FCC*, 518 U.S. 727 (1996).

142. *Id.* at 759–780.

143. 47 U.S.C. § 307 (c) (2001).

144. 47 U.S.C. § 309(k)(1) (A) (2001).
145. 47 U.S.C. § 307(d) (2001).
146. 47 C.F.R. 73.35801 (d)(4)(i) (2003).
147. 47 C.F.R. 73.3526 (2003).
148. 47 C.F.R. 73.3526 (e)(6) (2003).
149. 47 C.F.R. 73.3526 (e)(11)(i) (2003).
150. 47 C.F.R. 73.3526 (e)(11)(iii)(2003).
151. 47 C.F.R. 73.671 n.2 (2001).
152. 47 C.F.R. 73.3526 (e)(9) (2003).

6

Access to Places and Information: What You Can Get From Government, It Can Probably Get From You

The right to speak and publish does not carry with it the unrestrained right to gather information.

—Justice Earl Warren[1]

Overview
Access to Private Property
Access to Government Property
Access to Governmental Decision-Making Processes
Access to Governmental Information and Records
Misused Terminology: Getting it Straight
Access by Government and Others to Media Information
Practice Notes

Overview

The First Amendment has been consistently interpreted to mean that although there is a fundamental freedom to communicate and publish information after it is obtained, there is no right of access by the public or press to information. Therefore, the First Amendment cannot be used as a lever to force disclosure of information, no matter how newsworthy it may seem, from any source, private or public.

This chapter discusses many of the problems faced by mass communications professionals who seek to gather information from private and public sources. It also explains obligations mass communications practitioners have to provide information in response to court orders.

The first section deals with media access to private property or information. In a much longer second section, we address problems associated with obtaining access to governmental facilities, government decision-making processes, and government records. We include a description of a series of Supreme Court cases dealing with the issues of government ownership and management of its own property. Next, we summarize the federal Sunshine Law and similar open meeting laws enacted by the states. Then we turn to the topic of access to government information and records, including the Freedom of Information Act (FOIA) and similar state access statutes. The clash of interests inherent when government agencies must collect private information about individuals in order to perform its various functions is described when the **Privacy Act of 1974** is introduced and juxtaposed against the FOIA.

We then begin our explanation of how government may force information disclosure from media with the definition and analysis of seven terms and concepts. These terms and concepts are privilege, immunity, "shield law," defense and affirmative defense, exemption, exception, and protection. This terminology is important to understand the remainder of this chapter and subsequent chapters. In the next section, we describe the problems faced by reporters when government officials and others seek information from the media through the use of subpoena powers.

The final part of the chapter includes several practice notes that focus on how to avoid and deal with subpoenas.

Access to Private Property

This chapter concerns the clash of many competing interests. One of the major freedoms inherent in the American form of government is the **right of privacy**. The rights of citizens to be let alone by government and not to have others intrude into their private lives, businesses, and affairs is implicit in both the Fourth and Ninth Amendments. Yet, when some common disaster befalls any person or group, curious members of the public as well as the media descend in great numbers to view and report on the horrors that can suddenly happen to anyone at any time. Whether compelled by a sense of compassion or morbid curiosity, the public and press want to see what has occurred. Another set of competing interests comes into play when a newsworthy event occurs on private land whose owner wishes to occupy and enjoy her or his property free from public intrusion. This competition of interests is exacerbated because the public and the press seem to believe they have a right to go onto or across private property in order to gain access to the scene of a newsworthy event.

It is incumbent on all who work in mass communications to understand and respect the right of citizens to enjoy their privacy and their private property. The U.S. Supreme Court has repeatedly said that the First Amendment does not guarantee any right to media personnel that is different than that of the general public.[2] The general public does not have a right of access to private property; ergo, neither do members of the media.

Responding to an argument that denying media access to private property would restrict the free flow of information, Justice Warren wrote,

> There are few restrictions on action that could not be clothed by ingenious argument
> in the garb of decreased data flow. For example, the prohibition of unauthorized entry
> into the White House diminishes the citizen's opportunities to gather information he
> might find relevant to his opinion of the way the country is being run, but that does not
> make entry into the White House a First Amendment right.[3]

Justice Warren also explained that private property owners may deny access to their land and the government may limit travel to protect safety; the First Amendment has nothing to do with such situations.[4]

Public access to private property, in most jurisdictions in the United States, is still controlled by the application of common law principles. The modern communication torts are covered in chapter 9. However, many of those laws are expansions and extensions of the tort of trespass so it is important to understand the concept. It is also important to understand that the laws regarding trespass are applicable to reporters and their agents who go on private property to gain access to newsworthy events.

The simple, common law definition of **trespass to private property** or land is the intentional, unauthorized entry on property rightfully possessed by another.[5] Each state jurisdiction has its specific definition of trespass from either common law interpretations or statute. But most have only two fundamental requirements, which are "a rightful possession in the plaintiff and unlawful entry upon such possession by the defendant."[6] Under these laws, anyone, including members of both the public and media, can be sued for the civil tort of trespass to property, or prosecuted under the criminal statutes of any state, or both. "The First Amendment does not insulate a person from liability for unlawful trespass."[7] The elements of trespass are summarized in Exhibit 6.1.

The most common defense to either civil or criminal liability for trespass to real property is consent. If, prior to the entry onto land owned or occupied by another, an individual obtains consent of the property owner, this permission to enter constitutes a complete defense to the tort or crime of trespass. There are two recognized types of consent: express and implied. **Express consent** results from invitation by the landowner or person occupying the land or by specific authorization by these individuals to be on the property. Implied consent is a bit more complex, and includes the concept or "doctrine of custom and usage." **Implied consent** generally applies to situations wherein the public is invited onto property for the purpose of conducting business or for some specific reason intended by the property owner. Implied consent would extend to those areas, days of the week, and times of day that are covered by signs on the premises or by the pattern of use permitted by property owners in similar situations. If an individual goes beyond the scope of the implied consent given, he or she is trespassing.[8] Trespassing in an implied consent situation results from (a) entering into areas specifically marked "private," "employees only," or "no admittance beyond this point"; (b) wandering into clearly non-public rooms or spaces on the premises; (c) staying beyond the hours posted for invitees; (d) engaging in activities inconsistent with those of normal invitees; and

Exhibit 6.1.   Elements and Defenses for Trespass.

Element	Explanation
Intentional	May include accidental entry if defendant stays beyond notice or reasonable realization that he or she has entered property of another.
Unauthorized	Without express or implied consent. See defenses below.
Entry on Property	Simply means crossing the boundary of another's land or property. May include entry by misrepresentation.
Possessed by another	Rental property or loaned property is included May specifically include hotel rooms and rented conference rooms.

Defense	Explanation
Express consent	Specific permission to enter from the person in rightful possession of the property. Note a land owner may not give permission to enter property he or she has rented to another.
Implied consent	Permission to enter is implied by the common use of the property. Usually applies to retail businesses. Does not include permission to enter non-public areas and areas posted as non-public. May be revoked with notice or for: Activities not normally part of implied consent Staying beyond normal hours of invitation.

(e) staying on after specific notice to leave. Effective notice to leave may be oral or posted by sign.

"Wrongful conduct following an authorized entry upon land can result in trespass."[9] Even if one has been given express consent, this is revoked by any behavior that goes beyond the scope of consent. Further, express consent can be revoked by overstay (a) the period given, (b) failing to leave after notice, (c) entering an unauthorized area or, (d) engaging in activities inconsistent with the express consent. Specifically, secret videotaping or other covert behaviors involving subterfuge or snooping are trespass in most jurisdictions. In some jurisdictions, obtaining **entry by misrepresentation** is trespass and can negate any express or implied consent. In other jurisdictions it does not, but any conduct beyond what is implied by the consent, such as secret photography, filming or taping of activities, will subject an individual to charges of trespass.[10] "The First Amendment is not a license to trespass, to steal, or to intrude by electronic means into the precincts of another's home or office."[11]

In addition, no one may assume that just because consent has been given to one person, that consent extends to others. Specifically, media that have been invited to ride with police, firemen, or other emergency personnel may not accompany them onto private property without the property owner's permission.[12] Even though law enforcement or emergency personnel have given their consent to ride along and film their activities and private parties give implied or specific permission for the police to enter their homes, this permission does not extend to the media. Media personnel can be, and have been, sued by these private property owners for trespass as well as for invasion of privacy, which is discussed more fully in chapter 9.

Even on public land, access may be legally denied. When newsworthy events occur on public property, such as highways, schools, or government buildings, law enforcement authorities may govern access. Often, such areas will be closed in the interest of public safety, for the purposes of search and rescue operations, or to preserve evidence. Access in these situations often may only be had from a legal vantage point on the ground or in the air. The reporter must always obtain private landowner or occupant permission, regardless of why he or she seeks entry to private land. Emergency personnel are charged with granting or denying access to public property, and can arrest noncompliant reporters or any nonessential members of the public for any number of crimes. The laws of most jurisdictions do not have exceptions for media access independent of public access. Some law enforcement authorities do have agreements with members of the media to whom they issue courtesy press passes. However, these agreements are discretionary; there is no legal obligation to issue or to recognize a press pass.

Those who go into crime scenes or disaster areas without express permission of law enforcement personnel may be arrested for criminal trespass, disobeying a police officer, interference with police investigation, interference with rescue operations, or obstruction of justice. In short, media representatives have no greater right of access to private property or accident scenes than do any other citizens. Permission and good relations with emergency personnel are a reporter's only protection.

Access to Government Property

In chapter 1, we defined the concepts of *power*, *authority*, and *sovereignty*. **Sovereignty** refers to one who is or who holds the ultimate supreme power in a state. Both the federal government and the 50 state governments are sovereigns. As sovereigns, our various governmental jurisdictions have sole ownership, control, possession, and exclusive management rights to the property owned by them. This is true even though such property is simultaneously said to belong to The People, whose tax monies purchased and maintain it. Merely because government property has a public purpose or use does not mean that the whole or any part is open to the public or media. Public and media access to government property is determined by the sovereign government based on whatever use best serves the property's purpose and meets the standards of public safety, national security, or state police power interests. The laws of both civil and criminal trespass to government lands or chattels apply to the public and media personnel alike. If members of the public or press trespass on government property, they have violated the government's proprietary interest and government policy and thus open themselves to prosecution. "Governmental entities are empowered to regulate property under their control in order to preserve the property for the use to which it is lawfully dedicated."[13] "The First Amendment does not shield newspersons from liability for torts and crimes committed in the course of news-gathering."[14] "The State, no less than a private owner of property, has power to preserve the property under its control for the use to which it is lawfully dedicated."[15]

The Supreme Court's ruling that there is no First Amendment right of access to government places or information does not conflict with the fact that the High Court has also fairly consistently held, at least in the past 50 years, that once the media have gathered information, the Constitution, with few exceptions, prohibits prior restraint of publication by the government. Therefore, it is very important for mass communications practitioners to be aware continually of the legal distinction between the First Amendment freedom of the press, which is a freedom to publish, and the ability of the press and public to gather, obtain, or acquire information, which is not guaranteed by the First Amendment. As seen in chapters 3 and 4, "freedom of the press" has been interpreted to include the right to publish legally obtained, non-obscene, non-defamatory, non-inciteful material without governmental restraint. Even illegally obtained material or material that falls into the unprotected areas of non-speech can be published with recognition and acceptance of the consequences, such as criminal and civil liability. "The prevailing view is that the press is not free to publish with impunity everything and anything it desires to publish."[16]

Competing Interests and Examples

Numerous cases have been brought to court because the public and media have sought access to government-owned and controlled places. These cases emphasize the clash of interests between the governmental entity, the interests of the people being served by the facilities, the business interests of the media attempting to gain access, and the more generalized interests of the public.

Cases that involve attempts by the media to gain access to government-owned and operated facilities usually arise when media access has been thwarted by a statute, rule, or regulation and/or by the specific application of a statute, rule, or regulation by some public official. Sometimes, the media actually interpose public interests as part of their arguments for access, at other times the public has actually pushed for regulations confining the media to certain locations or parameters of operation. Cases involving access to polling places by the media to conduct "exit polls" offer pertinent examples.

Polling Places

The 1988 case of *Daily Herald Co. v. Munro*[17] involved media plaintiffs who were challenging a Washington State statute that prohibited exit polling within 300 feet of a polling place. The law was amended in 1983 from an older law that prohibited exit polling within 100 feet. While recognizing the compelling interests of the people and states in "maintaining peace, order, and decorum at the polls and in preserving the integrity of their electoral processes," the Court of Appeals found that polling places were traditional public fora and the regulation of speech covered was content-based because it involved the discussion of voting.[18] The court then applied the strict scrutiny standard of review to the state statute and said, "(a) content-based statute that regulates in a public forum is constitutional only if it is narrowly tailored to accomplish a compelling government interest."[19] After finding the statute was "content-based, overbroad, and not the least restrictive means of advancing the state's legitimate interest of keeping peace, order, and decorum at the polls" and that there were "no alternative channels of communication [existing]. . . to gather the type of information obtained through exit polling," the court ruled the statute "unconstitutional on its face."[20]

A similar case involved a Georgia statute, which made it a misdemeanor punishable by imprisonment of up to 1 year or a fine of up to $1,000 or both for any person to "conduct any exit poll or public opinion poll with voters on any primary or election day within 250 feet of any polling place." The federal District Court permanently enjoined the operation of the statute beyond 25 feet of the exit of any building in which a "polling place" is located. In this case, the statute had been enacted in reaction to voter complaints after the 1984 national election.[21]

In still another case, the U.S. Supreme Court upheld the constitutionality of a Tennessee statute involving a 100-foot "campaign-free" zone from the entrance to polling places. In that case, the High Court said,

> (W)e reaffirm that it is the rare case in which we have held that a law survives strict scrutiny. . . . Here, the State, as recognized administrator for elections, has asserted that the exercise of free speech rights conflicts with another fundamental right, the right to cast a ballot in an election free from the taint of intimidation and fraud. . . . we hold that requiring solicitors to stand 100 feet from the entrances to polling places does not constitute an unconstitutional compromise.[22]

In summary, it appears laws forcing exit pollsters to remain 250 to 300 feet from the polls cannot survive constitutional challenge while prohibitions forcing those soliciting votes to remain at least 100 feet from the polls are constitutional.

Jails, Prisons, and Inmates

Cases involving public and media access to jails, prisons, or prisoners for the purposes of observing and reporting on prison conditions and the treatment of inmates as well as interviewing specifically named prisoners all produce the same conclusion. Prisoners have no specific First or Fourteenth Amendment rights that are violated by procedures confining them to communications with their family, friends, ministers, and legal counsel. Any right of access by the public and media can be limited to public tours of the facilities and visits subject to strict restrictions imposed for institutional safety. The media, depending on the jurisdiction, may also be allowed to speak with randomly selected inmates as they tour the facilities. However, the media have no greater right of access to prisons or prisoners than does the general public; neither the public nor the media have any specific First or Fourteenth Amendment right of access to specifically named inmates for interviews.[23] Statements of legal authority supporting state and prison regulations prohibiting face-to-face interviews with specifically designated inmates, made by the U.S. Supreme Court, include the following:

> It has generally been held that the First Amendment does not guarantee the press a constitutional right of special access to information not available to the public generally. . . . Newsmen have no constitutional right of access to the scenes of crime or disaster when the general public is excluded. Similarly, newsmen have no constitutional right of access to prisons or their inmates beyond that afforded the general public.[24]

Military Facilities

Governmental control of access to military facilities via the authority vested in base commanders is absolute, regardless of whether or not these regulations might arguably violate First and Fourteenth Amendment rights. Three cases serve as examples.

Cafeteria & Restaurant Workers Union v. McElroy[25] involved a female employee who worked as a short-order cook for a food services contractor at the Naval gun factory in Washington, DC. Her security clearance was cancelled, her identification badge was confiscated, and she was refused further admission to the base. Therefore, she could not perform her job. The commander of the installation denied her request for a hearing or even to explain the reason why she had failed to meet security requirements. Her union filed suit, on her behalf, in U.S. District Court, based on the alleged denial of her Fifth Amendment right to due process. The complaint was dismissed and this decision was affirmed through the U.S. Supreme Court. The two issues the Supreme Court addressed were (a) was the commanding officer of the gun factory authorized to deny the woman's access to the gun factory in the way he did? and (b) did his action in excluding her deprive her of any right derived from the Constitution?[26] The Supreme Court ruled the commander was authorized to deny access and that the petitioner was not deprived of any constitutional rights. The Court's legal analysis is instructive because it typifies the reasoning involved in all military installation access cases.

> The control of access to a military base is clearly within the constitutional powers granted to both Congress and the President. . . . The power of a military commandant over a reservation is necessarily extensive and practically exclusive, forbidding entrance and controlling residence as the public interest may demand. It is well settled that a post commander can, in his discretion, exclude all persons other than those belonging to his post from post and reservation grounds. . . . [He may] in his discretion, exclude private persons and property therefrom, or admit them under such restrictions as he may prescribe in the interest of good order and military discipline.[27]

Greer v. Spock involved several individuals seeking access to a U.S. Army post for political campaigning. This suit involved two separate interest groups. The first group all claimed to be candidates for national political office who had been denied permission to enter Fort Dix, New Jersey, to distribute campaign literature and discuss political issues with Army personnel. The second group had been evicted from the post on a number of occasions for distributing political literature. Both groups filed suit in U.S. District

Court. They sought an injunction against the enforcement of post regulations based on an asserted violation of their First and Fifth Amendment rights.[28] The U.S. Supreme Court granted certiorari to review the case after the District Court had denied a preliminary injunction and the Court of Appeals reversed and prohibited the military authorities from interfering with political speech and leafleting in the areas of Fort Dix that were open to the general public. The Supreme Court reversed this decision and confirmed its opinion that the rules and regulations issued and enforced by base commanders cannot be challenged under the First Amendment. The Court reasoned:

> The guarantees of the First Amendment have never meant that people who want to propagandize protests or views have a constitutional right to do so whenever and however and wherever they please. The State, no less than a private owner of property, has power to preserve the property under its control for the use to which it is lawfully dedicated. . . . A necessary concomitant of the basic function of a military installation has been the historically unquestioned power of [its] commanding officer summarily to exclude civilians from the area of his command.[29]

Finally, the Supreme Court listed a number of federal statutes and regulations that prohibit the military from engaging in political activities or appearing to influence the political lives of service men and women. According to the Supreme Court, the purpose of these statutes is to "insulate [the military]. . . . from both the reality and the appearance of acting as a handmaiden for partisan political causes or candidates."[30]

JB Pictures, Inc. v. D.O.D. also addresses public and media access to military facilities.[31] This case also exemplifies problems created by conflicting interests when a government policy is chosen with the specific concerns of a small group of the public in mind rather than the interests of the U.S. people as a whole.

JB Pictures involved a change in Department of Defense (DOD) policy that moved the site of arrival for soldiers killed abroad and any ceremonies or services connected therewith to sites near the families of the deceased. This policy also provided the families with veto power over press coverage of these events. The point of entry for deceased soldiers beginning in 1983 was Dover Air Force Base, Delaware. Dover was the site of the only mortuary jointly operated by the military services.[32] In 1991, in connection with Operation Desert Storm, military policy for the return of war dead was significantly changed. The DOD stopped ceremonies or services at Dover and held them at the deceased service member's home duty station. This new policy also permitted media coverage only "if the family so desires."[33]

The DOD explained its new policy saying it was trying to reduce the hardship on the bereaved, who might otherwise have felt obliged to travel to Dover for the arrival ceremonies.[34] Media representatives were not permitted to view the arrival of war dead and concomitant ceremonies but the policies allowing civilian access to other activities on the base, including departure activities for outgoing military personnel and supplies to the Persian Gulf remained in place.

A disgruntled group including the plaintiff media organization, several other media groups, and individual reporters, as well as veterans' organizations, challenged the new

Dover access policy in the U.S. District Court for the District of Columbia. The suit was based on the First Amendment but took the unusual approach of claiming that the new DOD policy constituted impermissible "viewpoint discrimination."[35] The **viewpoint discrimination** argument was predicated on the idea that allowing the media and public access to view and gather information about outgoing troops supplies and activities led to the transmission of a substantially different message than the message produced by viewing images of caskets of deceased soldiers. The former purportedly carried an implicit pro-war attitude and the latter an implied anti-war viewpoint.[36]

The district court dismissed the complaint, finding no First Amendment violation. On appeal, the U.S. Court of Appeals for the District of Columbia affirmed the decision of the lower court. The appellate court applied a **balancing test**, which considered the competing interests supported by the new government policy and those allegedly disadvantaged by the denial of access. The court categorically rejected the viewpoint discrimination argument. In its reasoning, the court noted that the DOD policy applied to all members of the media and public regardless of their views on the war or the U.S. military. The court also said that viewpoint discrimination could be claimed in virtually any situation restricting access to government facilities and that accepting the argument would require public access to all venues and events absent a special government justification. The tradition of limited access to military bases was also noted, as was the fact that the policy did not impede newsgathering because other sources of information remained available. Finally, the court noted that the governmental interest in protecting grieving families was consistent with limiting press access to funeral services and that the press had only a right of speech, not a right of access.[37]

> The Circuit Court then concluded with its holding and judgment: Because the access policy at Dover does not violate the First Amendment's guarantees of freedom of speech and of the press, and because the complaint does not embrace a claim based on the right to engage in on-base speech, the judgment of the district court is Affirmed.[38]

Access Permitted by Government Must Not Discriminate

As we have seen, the cases dealing with access to military and other governmental facilities are often based on distinctions that require a balancing of competing interests. Also, the interests involved in access to government places, functions, or processes cannot be easily condensed into just those of the government on one side versus the public and press combined on the other side. There are often at least two types of media interests that need to be considered in First Amendment freedom of access cases; there are also at least two forms of public interest involved. Media interests arise from their roles as businesses and as sources of public information. There are also two major categories of publics in access cases: (a) the people, whose powers of self-government require information as the basis for decision making; and (b) the public as a mass audience seeking entertainment.

Most cases dealing with access to governmental facilities lump the competing interests of the public and press together vis-à-vis the interests of the government. The media are viewed as representatives of the people and are allowed no greater access than the public. The Supreme Court, in a simplistic "all for one, and one for all" scheme, views their competing interests as one and the same. The Supreme Court's mantra comes straight from its decision in *Zemel v. Rusk* wherein it said: "[i]t has generally been held that the First Amendment does not guarantee the press a constitutional right of special access to information not available to the public generally."[39]

However, the courts have also held that once the government does grant even limited access to its facilities, information, and processes, it may not discriminate based on either the viewpoint of those seeking access or the content of their communication. The First, Fifth, and Fourteenth Amendments require the government to provide or deny access to everyone equally. In its 1972 decision in *Police Department of the City of Chicago v. Mosley,* the U.S. Supreme Court struck down a city disorderly conduct ordinance that prohibited picketing near schools, except for "the peaceful picketing of any school involved in a labor dispute."[40]

Justice Marshall, writing for the Court, expounded on the requirement of equality of access to communications fora, and the concomitant Constitutional limitations on governmental abridgment of First Amendment freedoms of speech and press.

> Necessarily, then, under the Equal Protection Clause, not to mention the First Amendment itself, government may not grant the use of a forum to people whose views it finds acceptable, but deny use to those wishing to express less favored or more controversial views. And it may not select which issues are worth discussing or debating in public facilities. . . . Once a forum is opened up to assembly or speaking by some groups, government may not prohibit others from assembling or speaking on the basis of what they intend to say.[41]

Once it opens its facilities to limited access by the public and press, the government is prohibited from restricting admission on the basis of the content of expressive activity allowed to be conducted therein. In addition, the government, acting through its officials and agents, must also grant equal access to all who fit within the categories of individuals or groups it has admitted to its forum. The district court decision in *Borreca v. Fasi* serves as an illustration of this principle. In that case, Fasi, the mayor of Honolulu, directed his staff to keep, Borreca, a city hall reporter, out of the mayor's office. This directive also excluded the reporter from general news conferences given by the mayor on at least four occasions. The mayor also instructed city officials not to talk to the reporter. The mayor objected to Borreca because he thought the reporter was "irresponsible, inaccurate, biased, and malicious in reporting on the mayor and the city administration."[42] In granting the reporter's request for a preliminary injunction, the district court discussed the requirements of the First Amendment and the equal protection clause of the Fourteenth Amendment:

> Requiring a newspaper's reporter to pass a subjective compatibility–accuracy test as a condition precedent to the right of that reporter to gather news is no different in kind from requiring a newspaper to submit its proposed news stories for editing as a

condition precedent to the right of that newspaper to have a reporter cover the news. Each is a form of censorship.[43]

A third decision describes the **equality of access doctrine**. *Sherrill v. Knight* involved a reporter who was denied a White House press pass because of a recommendation by the Secret Service.[44] Clearly, the governmental function of protecting the president of the United States is of paramount importance, and seems to fit somewhere between the absolute control of access, which can be exercised by a military base commander as seen in *Cafeteria & Restaurant Workers Union v. McElroy*,[45] and the access to jails and prisons cases illustrated by *Pell v. Procunier*.[46] The problem in the *Sherrill* case was that there were no published or internal regulations describing the criteria for a White House press pass, there was no procedure for explaining the basis for denial, and there was no opportunity for a reporter to respond or refute a false allegation.

Sherrill had all the prerequisite press pass credentials, including a pass for the House and Senate press galleries and the fact that he had been employed as the Washington correspondent for *The Nation* since 1965. He resided in the Washington, DC, area and his editor confirmed that he needed to report regularly from the White House. Sherrill was summarily denied a White House press pass and all his attempts to find the reasons for this denial were refused. He even filed a Freedom of Information Act request to which the Secret Service claimed an exemption.

Sherrill filed suit in Federal District Court, basing his complaint on a violation of his First and Fifth Amendment Constitutional rights. Sherrill challenged the system under which his application had been denied, including the lack of procedures for notification, opportunity for rebuttal, and final written summary of the bases for denying the press pass. He did not challenge the authority of the Secret Service to determine clearance, or the decision made to deny him the credential; he challenged the apparent arbitrariness of the decision in his case, compared with the 1,589 other reporters who had been granted press passes. He also challenged the lack of due process involved in the decision-making system.

The District Court granted Sherrill two types of relief. First, it required the Secret Service formulate specific standards by which applications are to be judged. Second, it required the creation of procedures for handling requests for press passes.[47] However, on appeal by the Secret Service, the Circuit Court determined that the courts should leave the standards by which applications are judged to the Secret Service because of the importance to national security and of the continuing safety of the president. The Circuit Court said the Secret Service is uniquely qualified to make such determinations and reviewing courts should accord them appropriate deference and wide latitude in such matters.[48]

The appellate court's reasoning is instructive because it creates case law rules governing access to government facilities. The first of these rules says the government has absolute power to grant or deny access to its places, processes, and information. The second rule says that once the government grants access to a designated location or to a specific group, for expressive behavior, the First, Fifth, and Fourteenth Amendments prohibit the government from arbitrarily denying access to otherwise qualified members

Exhibit 6.2.   Access to Government Property.

The government, as a sovereign land owner, has no obligation to provide access to its land, [*Green v. Spock*, 424 U.S. 823, 836 (1976)] and

The press has no greater right of access to government property than does the general public, [*Zemel v. Rusk*, 381 U.S. 1, 16 (1965)] but

Once some class or group of the public is admitted to any government property, the government may not discriminate against members of that class or group based on their viewpoint or expression while there, [*Mosley v. Rusk*, 408 U.S. 93, 95-96 (1972)] but

Providing special treatment or access for one person does not create an obligation to provide that same treatment for everyone. [*Snyder v. Ringgold*, 40 F.Supp 2d 714, 715-717 (D. Md. 1999)]

∎

---

of the group. Finally, the government must provide due process to any otherwise quali-fied member of the group who is denied access.[49]

Access Granted by Government Neither Prohibits Nor Requires Preferential Treatment

The principles governing access to government property are summarized in Exhibit 6.2. Once access to government facilities or information has been granted, equality of access must be given to all members of the groups that have been admitted. However, the gov-ernment is not prohibited from granting exclusive access in some situations nor is it required to give preferential treatment to everyone within the category. Although this may appear to violate the requirement for equality of access, some members of the class may receive specialized treatment. Granting preferential treatment to one member of the class does not create a requirement that preferential treatment be accorded to everyone else in the class.

This conceptual distinction is partially illustrated by the appellate court in the *Sherrill* decision where the court explains a **corollary to its equal access doctrine**.

> The First Amendment's protection of a citizen's right to obtain information concern-ing the way the country is being run does not extend to every conceivable avenue a citizen may wish to employ in pursuing this right. Nor is the discretion of the Presi-dent to grant interviews or briefings with selected journalists challenged. It would cer-tainly be unreasonable to suggest that because the President allows interviews with some bona fide journalists, he must give this opportunity to all.[50]

The second part of this corollary to the court's "equal access doctrine" is that grant-ing preferential treatment or exclusive access to one member of the media, does not mean the government must give special, preferential, or exclusive treatment to all reporters. This part of the access to government judicial interpretation scheme is illustrated by the decision in *Snyder v. Ringgold*. Snyder was a journalist in the Baltimore area who worked in both print and television media. She sued Ringgold, the police public relations officer, for tortious interference with prospective economic relations. Snyder based her claims on the First and Fourteenth Amendments to the U.S. Constitution, as well as the corresponding state constitutional sections and state law. She claimed her right to obtain information had been denied because Ringgold, in his official capacity, had refused to give exclusive access to police investigations and had limited her access to police officials to specific times and places.[51] In her complaint, Snyder failed to mention that, from the police perspective, she had been a royal pain and was viewed as a source of harassment. She paged the public relations officers needlessly many times during the weekends when they were off duty for information about police scanner calls and, in violation of confidentiality agreements, she had printed information obtained from police records and investigations.

An initial district court order temporarily required Ringgold to give Snyder access to all police information and interviews that were given to any other members of the media. After a complicated appeal, the decision was remanded for hearing before a different district court judge. The new judge dissolved the injunction and granted summary judgment in favor of the police department. In his decision, the judge delineated the legal principles applicable in the case:

> No reporter has a right of access to a particular interview, exclusive story, or off the record statement. Snyder, therefore, is not seeking equal access to public information, but the kind of preferential treatment that public officials can provide to certain journalists, and that, in Ringgold's opinion, she does not merit. While a constitutional right to equal access for members of the press may well exist, extending the right to encompass preferential treatment would completely change the longstanding relationship and understanding between journalists and public officials. . . . I find that Ringgold's actions did not violate Snyder's First Amendment or Fourteenth Amendment rights.[52]

In short, a reporter would be well advised not to annoy the public relations office, especially if it represents local law enforcement.

Access to Governmental Decision-Making Processes

Under the federal system, two independent types of sovereign powers exist concurrently—the federal government and the 50 state governments. The sovereign powers of each concurrent jurisdiction are subdivided into three branches: (a) the legislative branch, charged with making the laws; (b) the executive branch, charged with implementing and enforcing the laws; and (c) the judicial branch, charged with interpreting and reconciling the laws with the constitutions. Because each of these branches and all of their subdivisions are invested with power delegated by the U.S. Constitution, they have the option of deciding whether or not to grant access to their facilities, their processes, and their information. That is to say that each branch may independently decide how much access or information they give and may decide to whom they will grant access or information.

For almost two centuries, the national government and the individual state governments operated in virtual secrecy. The people, who are theoretically the third sovereign in our system of representative democratic government, simply could not challenge decisions made by any of the branches of all 51 sovereign governments. Because there was no way to require government to divulge information, the people had no way to gather the information necessary to evaluate governmental action or to hold government officials accountable.

Beginning in the 1940s, increasing pressure was placed on legislators in both the national and state governments to grant statutory access to the major decision-making bodies, so that people could observe how their government worked. This pressure was increased by numerous media organizations, which had the ability to capture public and government attention. Other sources of pressure to release government information came from the secret bombings in Cambodia during the Viet Nam military campaign and allegations of spying on citizens by the government during the Nixon administration. Congress was finally convinced that some public access to the meetings of decision-making bodies should be accommodated.

Federal Open Meetings Law: The "Sunshine Act"

In 1976, the "Government in the Sunshine Act" became law. In the declaration of policy and statement of purpose at the beginning of the **Sunshine Act**, Congress announced its new public policy:

> It is hereby declared to be the policy of the United States that the Public is entitled to the fullest practicable information regarding the decision-making processes of the Federal Government. It is the purpose of this Act to provide the public with such information while protecting the rights of individuals and the ability of the Government to carry out its responsibilities.[53]

The Act provides that all meetings of federal agencies headed by a "collegial body" must be open to public observation, with 10 exceptions.

> Members shall not jointly conduct or dispose of agency business other than in accordance with this section. Except as provided in subsection (c), every portion of every meeting of an agency shall be open to public observation.[54]

The term *meeting* is defined by the act as a quorum of a **collegial body** that has been appointed by the president with the advice and consent of the Senate, that is gathered for the purpose of taking action on behalf of the agency, where such deliberations will result in joint action conducting or disposing of official agency business.[55]

The federal Sunshine Act covers at least 50 federal agencies or commissions, but applies only to the executive branch. It leaves many government agencies, commissions, committees, and boards out of its coverage. Specifically, it does not apply to Congress or to the judiciary.

Agency meetings at which specified matters are discussed are exempt from the requirement for openness. The subjects that justify private meetings are:

1. National defense and foreign policy secrets.
2. Personnel practices.
3. Trade secrets and privileged or confidential commercial or financial information.
4. Accusing any person of crime or involving formal censure.
5. Personal information involving clear invasion of privacy.
6. Investigatory records compiled for law enforcement purposes.
7. Reports on oversight of financial institutions.
8. Information where premature disclosure would significantly frustrate agency actions or threaten the stability of financial institutions.
9. Meetings on topics about which federal statutes preclude disclosure.
10. Meetings that concern subpoenas, lawsuits, arbitration, formal agency adjudications, or determinations made on record after an opportunity for hearing.

Meetings that may be closed and those that must be open are compared in Exhibit 6.3.

Exhibit 6.3. Federal Sunshine Act.

Meetings that must be open	Meetings that may be closed
All meetings of a quorum of a collegial body, appointed by the President, gathered to take action or vote. UNLESS the body is meeting to discuss one of the listed topics that are exempt.	Any meeting of the judicial branch
	Any meeting of Congress or Congressional committees
	Any meeting covering one of the excepted topics. Those topics are:
	1. National defense or foreign policy secrets.
	2. Personnel practices.
	3. Trade secrets.
	4. Accusing anyone of a crime.
	5. Information that would invade privacy.
	6. Law enforcement investigations.
	7. Oversight of financial institutions.
	8. Any information for which premature disclosure would cause harm.
	9. Any topic for which disclosure is precluded by law.
	10. Any discussion of subpoenas, lawsuits, etc.

The Sunshine Act also requires all affected agencies and commissions to give public notice, at least 1 week before the meeting, of the time, place, and subject matter of the meeting. The notice must also state whether the meeting is open or closed to the public, and must provide the name and phone number of the official of whom the public may inquire about the meeting.[56] This information is required to be submitted for publication in the **Federal Register**.

When the Sunshine Act is violated, any person may bring a suit for declaratory judgment, injunction, or other appropriate relief in the district courts of the United States within a period of from 60 days prior to the meeting to 60 days after the meeting that allegedly violated the act. The agency bears the burden of proof supporting its actions. However, the courts are not authorized to set aside, enjoin, or invalidate any agency action, except that of improperly closing a meeting or withholding transcripts, recordings, or minutes of a meeting not authorized to be withheld under the act. Additionally, the court may assess attorney fees and other litigation costs reasonably incurred by any party who prevails in such a suit. Furthermore, costs may be assessed against any plaintiff where the court finds that a suit was initiated primarily for frivolous or dilatory purposes.[57]

State Open Meeting Laws

The history and provisions of state open meeting laws vary from state to state. Alabama was the first state to enact open meeting legislation. In 1907, Alabama prohibited executive or secret sessions of specifically listed boards, commissions, or courts, except "when the character or good name of a woman or man is involved."[58] Florida became the second state to pass open meetings legislation in 1967.[59] During the 1960s, many other states also created such legislation, and, as of 2005, all 50 states have some form of open meeting law prohibiting specified commissions, boards, agencies, or other policy-setting groups from conducting secret meetings or going into executive session. All provide for some exemptions to this requirement.

Most state open meeting laws have two major requirements: (a) entities subject to the laws must provide advance public notice of their meetings, including time and location; and (b) governmental entities must actually conduct their meetings openly. Meetings are generally defined to include any gathering of a quorum necessary to make binding decisions whenever official business is discussed or a vote is taken. The nature of the discussion, not the location, usually controls. Based on these general rules, it is clear that the public and media have a right to witness the process their government goes through in making actual decisions, and that decision-making entities cannot sidestep the open meetings laws by calling their sessions "social gatherings," "fact-finding sessions," or "retreats." They are not allowed to adjourn and reconvene the quorum at a golf course, restaurant, bar, restroom, or some secluded vacation spot.

Many of the state open meeting laws also require governmental entities covered to post a formal agenda prior to the meeting. These agendas may be published in a local newspaper where other legal announcements are made, on a bulletin board outside the meeting room, or both. However, many laws also provide that anyone having business with the governmental entity will need to request a spot on the agenda, and some entities will not entertain business that has not been posted on the agenda because that would preclude public notice of the subject matter.

Remedies for violations of the open meeting laws vary depending on the jurisdiction. These may include (a) injunctions or writs of mandamus requiring the entities to open their meetings, and/or to provide transcripts of those meetings improperly closed; (b) voiding the governmental actions taken at improperly closed meetings; (c) providing that successful plaintiffs with a valid challenge receive reasonable attorney fees and costs of bringing suit against the violating agency; or (d) providing criminal misdemeanor penalties for knowing or deliberate violations of the acts.

Even in jurisdictions with open meeting laws, public meetings often involve votes with little or no discussion or hearings that are obviously only performances. Most state open meeting laws lack the legal "teeth" to motivate compliance. They usually neither punish commissions or boards who meet in secret nor void the decisions made at secret meetings. Therefore, the laws are only as effective as the willingness of government officials to honor their intent.

Access to Governmental Information and Records

Laws governing access to records, documents, and information actually preceded the Sunshine Act. These laws were motivated by the public frustration with governmental recalcitrance that motivated the open meeting laws.

Federal Access Statute: Freedom of Information Act

The first federal Freedom of Information Act (FOIA) was passed in 1946 under the title "Administrative Procedure Act." It required that every federal agency

> shall separately state and currently publish in the Federal Register (1) descriptions of its central and field organizations including delegations by the agency of final authority and the established places at which and methods whereby, the public may secure information or make submittals or requests.[60]

The original act also required that any covered agency make available for public inspection all of its final opinions or orders in the adjudication of cases and make available to "persons properly and directly concerned" all matters of official record.[61]

Despite this attempt by Congress to require the agencies under its control to release information, the statute was flawed and almost impossible to enforce. It provided no operational definitions for its major terminology. Furthermore, if only those persons "properly and directly" concerned with information could have access to official records, then the general public and media were precluded from access. Public and media pressure on Congress for access to government information was fueled by government secrecy during the Korean conflict, the McCarthy-era inquisition, the secret spying and wiretapping by governmental agencies on members of the civil rights movement

Exhibit 6.4.   Freedom of Information Act.

Material that may be obtained under the FOIA	Material that may not be obtained under the FOIA
Documents produced, written, commissioned, or ordered by any agency within the executive branch of the U.S. government, AND any documents in the possession of any agency within the executive branch of government. Documents include papers, electronic databases, recordings, and photographs.	Anything produced by or in the possession of the judiciary or legislative branches of government. Presidential records Items for personal staff convenience Anything covering a topic on the following list: 1. National security 2. Agency internal rules and procedures 3. Material exempt by federal statutes 4. Trade secrets 5. Inter- or intra-agency memos and letters 6. Personal and medical information 7. Law enforcement investigations 8. Financial institution regulation 9. Oil and gas well information.

and Vietnam protest organizations. Responding to these pressures, the **Freedom of Information Act** was proposed in the Senate in 1965. The Senate bill passed without debate and was referred to the House, which passed the Senate bill without revision and without a dissenting vote on June 20, 1966. The FOIA was signed into law by President Lyndon B. Johnson on July 4, 1966, and became effective on July 4, 1967, as an amendment to the Administrative Procedure Act.[62]

Further amendments were required to address response times and costs of information requests. Congress adopted the amendatory legislation, which clarified exemptions and specified the time frame within which covered agencies must respond, in 1974. President Ford refused to sign the new amendments to the FOIA because he felt they were unconstitutional and unworkable.[63] Both houses overrode his veto with bipartisan support for a workable and effective FOIA[64] and created the requirements that are summarized in Exhibit 6.4.

Selected Sections of the FOIA

The FOIA creates a system of presumptive availability to the public and media of all government documents and records. There are nine statutory exemptions and three exceptions to the presumption of availability. The FOIA covers most executive branch agencies, except for the president and his or her immediate staff and advisors. It covers the Federal Trade Commission, which is an independent regulatory agency, as well as certain executive branch departments including the Department of Defense, the

Department of Justice, the Federal Bureau of Investigation, the Central Intelligence Agency, the National Aeronautics and Space Administration, and some government-controlled corporations like the U.S. Postal Service. The FOIA does not cover Congress itself or the judicial branch.

The types of records covered by the FOIA include (a) agency-generated documents that are in the agency's actual possession, and (b) documents that were written, commissioned, or ordered by the agency. Types of records excepted from coverage by the FOIA include presidential records and items of personal agency staff convenience, such as phone messages or calendar notes, unless they are used for official agency business. Records that were neither generated by the agency nor are in the agency's possession also are not subject to the FOIA. The term *records* is interpreted broadly to include any reproducible form of documentary information, such as papers, electronic databases, films, sound recordings, and photographs.

There are nine categories of exemptions to the FOIA. The provisions of the FOIA do not apply to matters that are

> (1)(A) specifically authorized under criteria established by an Executive order to be kept secret in the interest of national defense or foreign policy and (B) are in fact properly classified pursuant to such Executive Order; (2) internal rules and practices of an agency; (3) specifically exempted from disclosure by other federal statute(s); (4) trade secrets and commercial or financial information [privileged or confidential]; (5) inter-agency or intra-agency memos or letters; (6) personal and medical files [& similar files which constitute a clearly unwarranted invasion of personal privacy]; (7) records or information compiled for law enforcement purposes; (8) records related to the supervision or regulation of financial institutions; (9) geological and geophysical information and data, including maps, concerning oil & gas wells.[65]

The FOIA provides that if a part of any requested information is exempt from disclosure, any "reasonably segregable portion" of a record shall be provided to a requesting individual, after deletion of the exempt sections.[66] The amount of information deleted must be indicated at the place in the record where it occurs, unless even that indication would harm any interest protected by the exemptions to the act.

The Electronic Freedom of Information Act Amendments

After the FOIA passed, the number of requests for information increased dramatically. By the early 1990s, agencies were overwhelmed and the public, the media, and the agencies themselves were all frustrated by delays and costs. Responding to this frustration, in 1996 Congress passed the Electronic Freedom of Information Act Amendments. A statement issued by President Clinton when he signed the amendment explains its purpose and motivation.

> The legislation I sign today brings FOIA into the information and electronic age by clarifying that it applies to records maintained in electronic format. This law also

Exhibit 6.5.   Electronic FOIA Sites.

Sample of Web pages created under The Electronic Freedom of Information Act Amendments of 1996

Air Force	www.foia.af.mil/
Department of Justice	www.usdoj.gov/04foia
Department of Labor	www.dol.gov/dol/foia/main.htm
Department of State	http://foia.state.gov/
Environmental Protection Administration (EPA)	www.epa.gov.foia/
FBI	http://foia.fbi.gov/room.html
Federal Communications Commission (FCC)	www.fcc.gov.foia/
NASA	www.hq.nasa.gov.pao/foia/

> broadens public access to government information by placing more material
> on-line. . . . In a period of government downsizing, the numbers of requests continue
> to rise. . . . The result in many agencies is huge backlogs of requests. . . . This legislation
> extends the legal response period to 20 days. More importantly, it . . . establishes
> procedures for an agency to discuss with requesters ways of tailoring large requests
> to improve responsiveness. This approach explicitly recognizes that FOIA works best
> when agencies and requesters work together.[67]

Several of the Web pages created under the electronic FOIA are listed in Exhibit 6.5.

The FOIA and the Privacy Act of 1974

The federal government collects huge amounts of data about private citizens in the United States and abroad. Most of this information comes from Social Security records, medical records, police files, licensing files, and passport and visa records. Other information is gathered in the context of FBI and CIA investigations. Any of this information could compromise the financial security or privacy of any citizen. In the late 1960s and early 1970s, the American public became uncomfortably aware that thousands of individuals had been secretly investigated and spied on by the FBI and that President Nixon had a "political enemies list" about whom his staff had gathered private information. In this context, after having passed the FOIA amendments of 1966, **The Privacy Act** became law on December 31, 1974.[68]

The Privacy Act limits access, under the FOIA, to government records about individuals. It says, in part,

> No agency shall disclose any record which is contained in a system of records by any
> means of communication to any person, or to another agency, except pursuant to a
> written request by, or with the prior written consent of, the individual to whom the
> record pertains.[69]

Access to these records is only permitted for very specific governmental use. It is clear from a reading of the limited exceptions to the Privacy Act that it was enacted to prevent use of the FOIA to obtain information about specific individuals.[70] The Privacy Act prevents members of the public and media from using the FOIA as a conduit to intrude into the private homes, businesses, or confidential papers of citizens. It is clearly one thing for the public to have access to government decision-making processes and records, it is quite another to force the populace to divulge private, confidential information to the government, which could then be exposed to public scrutiny.

State Access to Records Statutes

Most states have followed the federal FOIA initiative and have enacted some form of open records statute. These tend to cover most statewide governmental agencies and also include the records of local governmental units, including counties, cities, municipalities, school and special districts. As with the federal statute, state open records laws do not cover the legislative branch itself not the court system. In some states, agency, board, commission, and committee records are presumed open with specifically enumerated exceptions or exemptions. In other states, the statutes list the specific governmental bodies, entities, or agencies that must open their records to public inspection and copying, with exceptions to the types of records subject to public access. The typical exceptions include vital statistics like birth and death records. Typically, adoption and welfare records are also exempt, as are questions for professional license exams and academic records. Usually, any record that involves private or confidential information is not accessible.

How well records are maintained, how they may be retrieved, and fees for search and copying depend solely on the jurisdiction involved and the cooperation of the agency or governmental entity heads. Some administrative or bureaucratic department heads fully believe in governmental availability and openness; others actually try to avoid public contact and believe that public and press inquiries are either threatening or intrusive into their domain. Some believe public inquiries actually interfere with the real mission of their governmental entity.

Misused Terminology: Getting It Straight

Before we discuss how government officials may extract information from media, it is important to establish some basic terminology. Many mass communications practitioners seem to believe they have special privileges that do not inure for other citizens. This misunderstanding may arise from misuse of terminology, particularly the word *privilege*. What are more accurately called statutory shields, immunities, defenses, exemptions, exceptions, or protections are often described with phrases like: "fair comment privilege," "fair report privilege," public record privilege," "truth and fair comment privilege," "neutral reportage privilege," "First Amendment reporter's privilege," "qualified reportorial privilege," and "limited First Amendment privilege." None of these phrases properly use the word *privilege*.

Privilege

At law, the term **privilege** has a very specific meaning. It refers to particular types of communications or information about which certain parties cannot be forced to testify. In other words, certain persons are "privileged" from testifying if called before a judge, jury, tribunal, or investigative body or from being forced to disclose materials such as letters, papers, or documents because their communications are legally exempt from public scrutiny. Two types of testimonial privileges have been carried over from British common law and have been used continuously in both federal courts and in all U.S. state courts. These are attorney–client privilege and spousal privilege. Spousal privilege is more accurately called the "husband and wife privilege during coverture." Additionally, there is only one Constitutional privilege in the United States—the Fifth Amendment privilege, which says, "no person . . . shall be compelled in any criminal case to be a witness against himself."[71] The Supreme Court has confirmed that the only constitutional privilege is the one against self-incrimination.

> Until now the only testimonial privilege for unofficial witnesses that is rooted in the Federal Constitution is the Fifth Amendment privilege against compelled self-incrimination. We are asked to create another by interpreting the First Amendment to grant newsmen a testimonial privilege that other citizens do not enjoy. This we decline to do.[72]

It is also important to understand that the common law privileges arose to protect the confidentiality of the sources of information and were based on overwhelmingly important public policy concerns. Thus, spousal privilege was unmistakably significant to ensuring the legal sanctity of marriage. It gives both husbands and wives, as sources and keepers of confidences during coverture, the privilege of not having to reveal, or of fearing that the other spouse will be compelled to disclose, those intimate details to which each may become privy about the other. Attorney–client privilege on the other hand, is based on the client's confidential communications to his or her attorney. This privilege protects the client's private revelations to the attorney. Furthermore, it is only the client's communications that are in fact privileged. This privilege prohibits the attorney from disclosing confidential information, unless and until the client authorizes disclosure. The attorney does not "own" the privilege; the client does. Attorney–client privilege was developed because it is in the public interest that an attorney be able to zealously and effectively represent the client. If an individual client is not encouraged to disclose everything to his or her attorney in any case, then proper representation under the advocacy system is not possible.

Finally, the framers of the U.S. Constitution were led by the insistence of at least five of the ratifying states to add the Bill of Rights to the U.S. Constitution. The framers were very mindful of the potential abuses of unlimited government against its individual citizens. They recognized the need to limit the potential of those in the majority to suppress and the liberties of minority groups not in power. Therefore, the framers agreed on a series of constraints against governmental actions, which were in the first

10 amendments. Although it does not use the word *privilege*, the Fifth Amendment creates the only Constitutional privilege. Courts in all 50 states must recognize the privilege against self-incrimination because this right has been incorporated under the Fourteenth Amendment, if not contained in the individual state constitutions.

The U.S. Constitution actually uses the words *privilege* and/or *privileges and immunities* four times. However, in these contexts, the framers were clearly referring to legal concepts that have since been identified with more definitive legal terms. For example, Article I, Section 6 of the Constitution says,

> The Senators and Representatives shall . . . in all Cases, except Treason, Felony and Breach of the Peace, be privileged from Arrest during their Attendance.[73]

This statement means that members of Congress are immune from arrest while attending their respective sessions; and the word *privileged*, in this context clearly refers to what today would be called an *immunity*. Immunity, as is discussed in detail later in this section, is a special exemption from arrest, suit, prosecution, or other application of law.

The word *privilege* also appears in Article I, Section 9: "The Privilege of the Writ of Habeas Corpus shall not be suspended unless when in Cases of Rebellion or Invasion the public Safety may require it."[74] Here, the Constitution uses the word *privilege* as it was used in British common law. In British common law, the "privilege of habeas corpus" was the name given to a class of special writs or orders made by the monarch or his chancellor. These privileges were extended as special favors to someone being held prisoner, in return for money or exceptional service. Such writs or special orders were directed to a jailor or warden and required him to bring a prisoner before the chancellor or the king for a new determination of sentence. The framers of the U.S. Constitution were clearly fearful of the infinite power of the national government to seize and imprison people for indefinite periods. The use of the word *privilege* in this case refers to the opportunity for any citizen or person subject to the jurisdiction of the United States to petition the appropriate court or governmental body to release them from improper imprisonment, or at least to have their loss of personal liberty questioned.

Finally, the phrase *privileges and immunities* appears in both Article IV, Section 2, and in the Fourteenth Amendment, Section 1. In both locations, the terms refer to the same legal concepts. Article IV, Section 2 says, "the Citizens of each State shall be entitled to all Privileges and Immunities of Citizens in the several States";[75] and the Fourteenth Amendment says, "No State shall make or enforce any law which shall abridge the privileges or immunities of citizens of the United States."[76] In both of these sections, the Constitution not only incorporates the specifically enumerated privilege of the writ of habeas corpus, and the testimonial privilege against self-incrimination granted by the Fifth Amendment, but also requires that all such privileges and immunities as may be granted by any state to any of its citizens must be granted to all of its citizens as well as to those of any other state who may come within its jurisdiction. The type of privileges and immunities delineated in this context refer to civil liberties like the right to vote and the right to use the courts to obtain remedies for legal wrongs, as well as the right to any specific immunities, exemptions, exceptions or defenses that may be extended by the laws in each state.

In addition to the common law spousal privilege, the attorney–client privilege, and the Fifth Amendment Constitutional privilege against self-incrimination, the federal courts have recognized several presidential privileges. These presidential privileges and their development are thoroughly described in *In re Sealed Case (Espy).*[77] **Presidential privilege** can be divided into two types: (a) absolute, which involves the President's role as the director of international and foreign affairs for the United States, and (b) qualified, which involves the president's role as the chief executive of the United States including his or her communication with internal White House staff, directors, and cabinet members. This qualified executive privilege applies to policymaking by the chief executive.

The qualified executive privilege can be further divided into two general categories: (a) the deliberative process privilege and (b) the presidential communications privilege. The deliberative process privilege is derived from British common law under which information exchanged between the monarch and the prime minister and his or her immediate executive staff members are exempt from public disclosure through the subpoena or other judicial hearing processes. To qualify for such exemptions, the communication must be pre-decisional, and must be deliberative, that is, it must be made during the policymaking process. If the subject statement only involves decisions that have already been made, it is not privileged. Also, statements of fact are not privileged unless they are inextricably intertwined with policymaking deliberations.

The presidential communications privilege relates to statements associated with decision making by the president of the United States. This privilege is rooted in the U.S. Constitution and its principle of separation of powers. Although qualified, this privilege does provide protection against disclosure by requiring those seeking the information to prove a "focused demonstration of need." The privilege covers all written or oral utterances by presidential advisors in the course of preparing advice for the president, even when these communications are not made directly to the president. It covers statements and writings by the president or presidential advisers and any information or messages they solicited and/or received in the preparation of communication on behalf of the president. In order to fall within the purview of the presidential communications privilege, any communication must have been created or delivered in the course of advising the president on official government matters. Furthermore, the deliberative process executive privilege and the presidential communications privilege are qualified because they must meet very specific criteria before the statements are privileged. The criteria are (a) the communication must have been in the course of performing the specific function of advising or preparing advice for the president, (b) the communication must specifically relate to official governmental matters, (c) the communication must deal with a legal subject matter, and finally (d) the communications must be between top cabinet members, White House staff directors, advisors, and their immediate staff.

In summary, *privilege*, in this context, relies on the source of the communication for its legitimacy and application. Communications that fall under the privilege are confidential and their disclosure cannot be compelled by a subpoena or at any hearing or trial where one privy to such information may be called to testify.

Exhibit 6.6.   Legal Privileges.

These are the only privileges recognized by law in the United States		
Privilege	Legal Authority	Jurisdiction where applicable
Attorney–client Husband–wife	Common law	Throughout United States
Self-Incrimination	U.S. Constitution	
Absolute presidential privilege (in role as director of international affairs)	U.S. Constitution	
Qualified presidential deliberative process privilege (in role as CEO of U.S.)	Common law	
Qualified presidential communication privilege (in role as CEO of U.S.)	Implied from U.S. Constitution	
Clergy–penitent	State common law or statute	Only in the state where it is law.
Physician–patient Psychotherapist–patient		
State Statutory Privilege[a]	State "Shield laws"	

[a]Depending on operation within each individual state with a state statutory privilege, this may be more accurately labeled an immunity, a defense, or a protection.

The six testimonial privileges currently recognized throughout the United States are spousal privileges attorney–client privileges the presidential foreign affairs privilege, the Fifth Amendment privilege against compelled self-incrimination, the deliberative process executive privilege, and the presidential communications executive privilege. The first four privileges are absolute and no one may testify about covered information unless the privilege is waived by the source of the communication. The last two privileges are qualified because only communication that meets very specific criteria is qualified for the privilege.

Statutory or Evidentiary-Based Privileges

There are three additional qualified testimonial privileges that may be recognized by statute, or by the rules of evidence, in some jurisdictions. These are the clergy–penitent privilege, physician–patient privilege, and psychotherapist–patient privilege. The exact nature, extent, qualifications, and limitations on such privileges are described in the statutes or the rules of those jurisdictions that recognize them.

All the legal privileges are summarized in Exhibit 6.6.

Immunity

While privilege addresses communication or information that is protected from disclosure, immunity refers to an exemption for certain people. Under appropriate circumstances, those people are exempt from the normal operation of law. Individuals who have been granted an **immunity**, either by operation of common law, the U.S. Constitution, statute, or by governmental action in a specific case, are inoculated from being brought into court to answer for their actions or communications. Essentially, such individuals cannot be held liable for actions or communications covered by their immunity. This immunity may apply to criminal and/or civil law depending on the extent and source of the immunity granted. Immunity is a way of legally saying, "you can't touch me on this matter, action, or communication because I have a special form of exemption from liability."

The term *immunity* should be used to describe the exemption from arrest enjoyed by representatives and senators during and going to and from their respective sessions. Federal legislators are also immune from lawsuits that might stem from the content of their debates in Congress. The immunity in these situations is absolute, but the immunity does not apply to communication made outside of official speeches or debates made in either House, during their sessions.

The president of the United States also has an absolute immunity from damages for liability relating to his or her official acts while in office. Cabinet members, White House executive staff, and presidential aides have only qualified immunity from lawsuits resulting from their official duties on behalf of the president. These immunities are situation-specific, are narrowly construed, and may not relate to or involve any illegal activities or concealment of such activities, and apply only to top-level cabinet, staff, or advisory aides acting in their official capacities.

Additional immunities have been granted to some public officials. These have been granted by common law in some jurisdictions, by some state constitutions, or by state statutes. All appointed judicial officers of the United States, including justices, judges, magistrates, and federal prosecutors have an absolute immunity for all actions taken or made within the scope of their official duties. State appellate court judges, trial court judges, and prosecutors, as well as state attorneys general, also have absolute immunity for actions within the scope of their official duties. Depending on the jurisdiction, some state governors and legislators are also granted absolute immunity for actions that are part of their official duties. Other public officials, either elected or appointed, may be granted qualified or limited immunities by their state constitution, statutes, or common law. In most jurisdictions, law enforcement officers, whether elected or appointed, are also given qualified immunity or limited immunity. When an official has been granted a qualified immunity, this usually refers to those actions taken by them under "color of law" or within the scope of their duties. When an official has been granted a limited immunity, the immunity only applies to specific duties or tasks. Immunity may also be limited to a maximum judgment amount. For example, a police officer may be immune from liability for an automobile accident while on duty but the limited immunity may not apply to intentional or reckless misconduct; or a police officer may be immune for liability over $100,000. These limited immunities are determined by statute in each jurisdiction.

One final category of immunities is the **prosecutorial grants of immunity**. These immunities may only be given by a federal or state prosecutor in a criminal case. They are given selectively to individuals who have been called as witnesses in criminal proceedings and who may refuse to testify by exercising their Fifth Amendment right against compelled self-incrimination. If individuals are granted prosecutorial immunity, their testimony cannot be used against them. Therefore, they cannot claim a Fifth Amendment privilege. Another type of individual who might receive a prosecutorial grant of immunity is someone already under indictment or who has been charged with a crime. If such an individual is able to implicate others or give law enforcement authorities information about other crimes, he or she may be given immunity in exchange for testifying.

Prosecutorial immunity can only be granted by a prosecutor, never by law enforcement officers. Furthermore, there is no right to this immunity, it is granted entirely at the discretion of prosecutors.

Prosecutors may grant three types of immunity: use immunity, derivative use immunity, and transactional immunity. **Use immunity** protects an individual from prosecution for crimes in which she or he may implicate herself or himself in the requested testimony. **Derivative use immunity** protects the witness from prosecution for crimes described in the requested testimony and from the use of information that could be derived from the testimony. In other words, the prosecution cannot even use information derived from the testimony to support prosecution of the witness. **Transactional immunity** provides the greatest protection from prosecution for the witness. It includes all the protection included in use and derivative use immunity and, in addition, protects the witness from prosecution for any crimes that are related to the crimes described in the testimony or that might be investigated because of the testimony.

Shield Law

The term **shield law** usually refers to one of two types of state statutes. The first type of shield law grants a limited or qualified protection from testifying to some class of individuals. The second type of shield law limits media liability or provides an affirmative defense for defamation when there has been a retraction of a defamatory statement. It is imperative to note that all shield laws are state statutes. That means that such laws vary from state to state and that none are available through or imposed by the U.S. Constitution or statutes.

The first type of shield law is designed to protect specified groups of potential witnesses. The laws may exempt them from the requirement to testify or it may prohibit disclosure of their identity. These witnesses are not shielded because their information is privileged but because lawmakers are convinced the witness needs protection. Such shield laws include child witness protection laws, rape victim identification or protection laws, and media shield laws. Not all states have media shield laws and the protections they provide vary, but where such laws exist, they often protect reporters from being required to reveal the names of confidential sources.

According to the U.S. Supreme Court, the proper terminology for state laws that grant limited and qualified exemptions from testifying to journalists is **state statutory**

privileges.[78] This terminology is more appropriate than the often used "media shield law." When referring to state statutory privileges, the appropriate state statute should be cited because the laws vary significantly from jurisdiction to jurisdiction.

Defense and Affirmative Defense

Often the word *privilege* is misused to describe defenses. For example, the following labels are used in both mass communications and legal literature: "fair comment privilege," "fair report privilege," and "public record privilege." Obviously, none of these fit in any of the six legally recognized privileges. A more appropriate legal term for these protections is *affirmative defenses*.

In chapter 2, we briefly introduced the concept of defenses and listed some of the more common affirmative defenses. A defense can be as simple as denying the charge of the prosecution or plaintiff. An **affirmative defense** is a justification or "legal excuse." While the prosecution in a criminal case or the plaintiff in a civil case is responsible for proving the charge, the defendant is responsible for pleading and proving an affirmative defense. In other words, the burden of proof shifts to the defendant who raises an affirmative defense. Affirmative defenses and their requirements vary from jurisdiction to jurisdiction. However, in most jurisdictions affirmative defenses in criminal matters include an alibi, infancy, involuntary intoxication, mental incapacity, and self-defense. Civil cases also have affirmative defenses that are created by statute or case law in each jurisdiction. For example, in some jurisdictions there is a public records defense to a suit for public disclosure of private facts. Often, commentators on mass communications law erroneously describe affirmative defenses with the word *privilege*.

Exemption versus Exception

Another set of terms, often confused with each other, are *exemption* and *exception*. This is especially a problem when legislators exempt a class of people or actions from the prescription or proscription of a new law. The term **exemption** should be used to refer to a specific class of things, activities, people, or information, that would normally fall within the operation of any particular law, but to which lawmakers have made the law inapplicable. The term exception, on the other hand, should be used to describe a specific class of things, activities, people, or information that is inadvertently or purposefully omitted from coverage within the law itself. Exemptions would normally be included within the coverage of the law, but have been defined out of the application or operation of the law in a selective type of immunity. Exceptions were never included within the coverage or application of the law in the first place.

Protection

The term *protection* is helpful to describe the resolution of conflicts between liberties described in the Bill of Rights and the powers of sovereign government. The liberties and rights identified in the first 10 amendments as well as those applied to the states by selective incorporation are **protections**. The First Amendment provides protection from governmental abuses or abridgement of our freedoms of speech and press. Rather often, based on the context of the material, the term *protection* should be substituted for that of *privilege* to give the correct meaning. The term *privilege* should never be used to describe a right or freedom. The term *privilege* should be used only to refer to one of the six specific testimonial exemptions recognized by law in all U.S. jurisdictions or one of the three additional testimonial exemptions created by the rules of evidence in some jurisdictions. The term *state statutory privilege* should be used when referring to exemptions created by a state's shield law or when a state jurisdiction recognizes a testimonial privilege for reporters.

There is *no* First Amendment testimonial privilege, qualified or limited. Also there is no federal statutory testimonial privilege for journalists or reporters.[79] No other types of privileges are recognized under the laws of the United States or of any state. No reporter or medium of mass communications has any special privileges or immunities different than or distinct from those granted to any other citizen, unless they are specifically defined and granted by state statute. Those protections are properly referred to as state statutory privileges.

Access by Government and Others to Media Information

One reason for the lengthy explanation of appropriate terminology is to help the reader understand that the obligations of reporters and media to honor summons and subpoenas are not limited by any constitutional privilege. Some mass communications practitioners seem to think that the media possess special rights or liberties that other U.S. citizens do not. Phrases often misused to label those concepts include "First Amendment reporter's privilege," "qualified reportorial privilege," and "limited First Amendment privilege." Obviously, these are not properly called privileges; further, the use of these phrases implies a special federal protection or exemption for media that does not exist. Media privilege was alleged as a defense in *Branzburg v Hayes* in 1972. In a five-to-four majority decision, the U.S. Supreme Court ruled there is no such privilege:

> The issue in these cases is whether requiring newsmen to appear and testify before
> state or federal grand juries abridges the freedom of speech and press guaranteed by
> the First Amendment. We hold that it does not.[80]

Some commentators on mass communications law downplay the importance of this opinion. Some describe it as a plurality opinion because Justice Powell wrote a concurring opinion. It was a majority opinion and has been cited as such and quoted repeatedly by the Supreme Court itself in countless subsequent cases dealing with media issues. The High Court's subsequent reliance on *Branzburg* shows its importance and the esteem in which it is held as precedential authority. Justice Powell's concurring opinion supported the Court's reasoning and results. It was really used by Powell as a vehicle for a scathing attack on Justice Stewart's dissenting opinion. Stewart had attempted to imbue the decision with much broader scope and impact than it really had. Additionally, Justice Stewart's dissent has been erroneously quoted, misread, and misused by many as though it was the opinion of the Court. Some commentators also read the description of subpoena requirements in *Branzburg* as the enumeration of criteria for some kind of "reportorial privilege." As is described later in the discussion of the practical application of *Branzburg*, these alleged privileges are simply a description of the limitations imposed on all subpoena requests. They do not create any special treatment or protection for reporters. Only state statutes grant any immunity to communication professionals. Not all states grant this immunity, and even when it is granted, the immunity is limited.

If Any Protection Is Available to Allow Journalists Immunity From the Effect of Subpoenas, It Must Be Granted by State Constitutions or Statutes

The *Branzburg* decision involved four separate cases, consolidated for hearing. Each case raised the same First Amendment issue and all involved newspersons who had been subpoenaed before different grand juries investigating crimes in their areas. One case had arisen under the laws of the Commonwealth of Massachusetts, one from a federal grand jury under the auspices of the Northern District of California, and two involved petitioner Branzburg who had been subpoenaed by two separate county grand juries investigating drug crimes in Kentucky.[81]

What is most interesting in the two cases involving Branzburg himself is that at the time of the case, Kentucky, which was the scene of the crimes Branzburg witnessed and about which he had written several articles, had a state statutory privilege. That state law said,

> No person shall be compelled to disclose in any legal proceeding . . . before any grand or petit jury . . . the source of any information procured or obtained by him, and published in a newspaper.[82]

The Kentucky Court of Appeals interpreted the phrase "source of any information" in its own statute as "affording a newsman the privilege of refusing to divulge the identity of an informant who supplied him with information, but held that the statute did not permit a reporter to refuse to testify about events he had observed personally, including the identities of those persons he had observed."[83] The U.S. Supreme Court also pointed out that at the time of the case in 1972, "(a) number of States have provided newsmen a 'statutory privilege' of varying breadth, but the majority have not done so, and none has been provided by federal statute."[84] Despite all this, the U.S. Supreme Court refused to recognize or create any special privilege for reporters or media.[85]

Practical Applications of the Branzburg Decision

Because there is no First Amendment testimonial privilege, and because there is no federal shield law granting any testimonial protection to the press, members of the media who are subpoenaed to testify, to give depositions, or to reveal certain of their notes, records, or collections of information, must rely on other sources of law to provide them with legal protection. Differences between decisions evaluating whether journalists enjoy a state statutory limited or qualified testimonial privilege to refuse subpoenas depend on a number of factors.

If the case is brought in a state court, that court will apply the laws, rules, and case precedents of its own jurisdiction. If the state has a state statutory privilege for reporters, the courts of that jurisdiction will be bound to apply the statute, as well as any appropriate case precedent. There is no federal statute recognizing any type of testimonial privilege for reporters, and the Supreme Court in *Branzburg* and all subsequent cases has refused to recognize any First Amendment privilege for reporters. However, the federal courts will generally apply the laws of the state wherein they sit when reporters request protection from subpoena. The application of state law by federal courts is based on the concepts of federalism and of "comity" or judicial courtesy. The variation in federal decisions regarding reporter protections arises from this application of state law. Many observers confuse this variation based on comity for inconsistent deference to the *Branzburg* decision. Those observers simply fail to recognize that federal courts are often called on to apply state laws and procedures.

Even if there is a state statutory privilege for reporters in the state where a federal court sits, the court will probably apply *Branzburg* and find no testimonial privilege exists for reporters in criminal cases involving grand jury or prosecutor's subpoenas. This is because the federal courts are part of a "unified" judicial system, headed by the U.S. Supreme Court, and the Court's decision in *Branzburg* is mandatory authority for all federal courts. Our judicial system provides as much judicial and procedural fairness as possible for defendants in criminal matters. Therefore, if a federal court is ruling on the request for media information by a defendant in a criminal case, the court will probably apply a balancing test that considers three factors: (a) the relevance and need by the defendant for the information sought from the media; (b) whether or not the defendant has access to the same information by alternative means, and has exhausted those other means; and (c) whether the reporter actually possesses the information requested by the defendant. If a defendant cannot show the requested information is relevant, there is no reasonable alternative source of the information and that the reporter has the information, the subpoena will be quashed. In any criminal case, no court will allow a subpoena to stand if it has not been issued in good faith, or if it has been issued for purposes of harassment, or as a "fishing expedition" for any information that it might produce. A court faced with any of these situations will either grant a motion to quash the subpoena totally, or will issue a protective order limiting the type and amount of material subject to the subpoena. This procedure and these rules apply to any person who has been subpoenaed to give testimony or bring materials before a grand jury, or as a witness in a trial, whether or not the person is a reporter. This is not "reportorial privilege"; it is a protection granted to every citizen.

In civil cases, similar considerations will be made. The same rules for the protection of witnesses from harassment or from mere "fishing expeditions" will be applied. However, a distinction will generally be made depending on whether the reporter or media organization is a party to a suit, or is simply being called as a witness, and whether the suit involves defamation or one of the other communication torts.

Clearly, if a reporter and his or her media organization is a defendant in a communication tort suit, the plaintiff will be given the opportunity to subpoena the reporter's notes, the editor's notes, memoranda between staff regarding the matter involved, and any tapes, transcripts, or recordings made in the matter including the names of sources.[86] This is because the plaintiff has the burden of proof and would be entitled under the rules of evidence to depose the sources, the reporters, the editors, and other people with relevant knowledge about the matters alleged. Again, the courts will issue protective orders when the subpoenas are too broad in the categories of information they seek, or appear to be merely probing for general information, or when they constitute harassment. This type of protection from overreaching or harassment by subpoena is available to anyone, not just media parties or witnesses.

In other types of civil suits, especially where the reporter is not a party, but is subpoenaed for deposition as a witness, the courts are more likely to protect the reporter and his or her information. In these situations, the court will look to the parameters of any state statutory privilege as well as whether the information sought has been provided to the reporter under a promise of confidentiality. Nonconfidential material and sources, if relevant to a material allegation or matter of proof in civil cases, will receive less protection. However, depending on whether there is some statutory protection, the courts may still require disclosure of information, testimony, or evidence, if the requesting party to a suit can show (a) the information sought is actually possessed by the reporter, (b) the information is materially relevant and necessary to prove or disprove an element in the case, (c) the information cannot be obtained through an alternative source, and (d) the party has presented proof of the unsuccessful effort to obtain the information by alternative means. These factors present a heavy burden of proof on the party seeking the information through the subpoena process. Usually, the courts will grant a reporter's motion to quash in such cases because the party issuing the subpoena cannot meet these stringent requirements.

Methods of Dealing with Subpoenas and Consequences of Failure to Comply

There are two basic types of subpoenas: a general **subpoena**, which requires the person served to appear at a specific place and time to give personal testimony, and a **subpoena duces tecum**, which requires the person served to collect and present specified material and/or information and to appear with the material at a designated time and place. All subpoenas are backed by the contempt powers of the courts that issued them. However, judges themselves do not issue subpoenas. Subpoenas are issued by the clerks of the courts at the request of a grand jury, a prosecutor, a defendant in a criminal case, or one of the parties to a civil case. Additionally, state and federal legislatures and legislative committees have subpoena powers, as do many administrative agencies.

Penalties for failure to comply with a subpoena are generally stated on the subpoena itself and can include criminal or civil contempt citations by the judicial, legislative, or administrative body that issued the subpoena. **Criminal contempt** is usually used by the government as a penalty for gross or egregious behavior in failing or refusing to respond to a subpoena, or to other orders of a court. It is usually reserved for those situations in which the subpoenaed witness, by his or her repeated conduct, exhibits defiance toward the dignity and power of a court. The person charged with criminal contempt will be given a bill of particulars laying out the specific charges, and will have the opportunity, in a hearing or trial, to defend him or herself. If convicted of criminal contempt, an individual will face a range of sanctions from fine to imprisonment. These sanctions are obviously punitive. The offense and possible penalties will be defined by statute.

Civil contempt is purely coercive. It applies the threat of imprisonment to a recalcitrant witness. Any time a person who has been duly served with a subpoena fails to appear as ordered, the court will issue a warrant, and law enforcement authorities will arrest and take the individual before the judge. If the person cannot show good cause for neglect of the legal duty, he or she may be held in contempt of court. If a person does appear in answer to a subpoena, but refuses to testify or to bring the materials and information requested, the same procedure may be followed. People held in contempt, even in civil cases, may be incarcerated, but any decision to incarcerate is usually preceded by numerous warnings. The person jailed for civil contempt is usually told he or she will be freed from imprisonment by asking to appear before the court and by complying with the subpoena. If an individual refuses to comply, he or she may remain in jail until the matter before the court is ended, and the civil order of contempt becomes moot. In some cases, the judge will also levy a fine for a specified amount per day of failure to comply with the court's order.

Practice Notes

Suggestions to Avoid Problems with Subpoenas

If Served with a Subpoena

The appropriate legal response to a subpoena or subpoena duces tecum is to contact your editor or supervisor immediately, and take the subpoena(s) to legal counsel. Be sure that you understand what the subpoena is asking you to do and what information it is asking you to produce. Determine the nature, extent, and scope of the material or information required to be presented by the subpoena. Comply whenever possible and/or with whatever material you feel you can present that is not covered by your state's statutory privilege or that is not irrelevant, harassing, or overreaching. If, after careful consultation with your attorney, you determine that you cannot comply with the subpoena, or if you wish to claim a state statutory privilege, or you could comply, but only partially, your attorney will need to file a motion to quash the subpoena on your behalf. Your attorney may also request a protective order. This must be done prior to the appearance date on the subpoena. Additionally, you must be prepared to comply personally with the subpoena and appear with your attorney on the day scheduled, unless a hearing on your motion is set for another time. If the judge, after a hearing on your motion to quash, orders you to comply, you must do so within the time frame specified by the order. If you still feel you cannot comply, you will need to appeal to the court asking that the order be vacated, and/or get a continuance of the case, or stay of the order pending your appeal to the proper court. Your attorney may also need to file a motion for a protective order, writ of prohibition and/or mandamus requiring the trial court judge to vacate his prior orders or quashing the subpoena. All of these steps and motions will be done, based on the laws and procedures of your particular jurisdiction.

Try to Avoid Actions that Will Subject You to Subpoena or Summons

The most important thing a reporter can do is become aware of behavior that might subject him or her to a subpoena to testify or to a summons as a party to a lawsuit concerning confidential sources or information. Obtain a copy of any state statutory privilege law and learn the circumstances and conditions under which a reporter may be protected from divulging confidential or nonconfidential sources or information. If you have any questions about the law, its applicability to specific situations, or its scope, consult competent legal counsel. Also, be sure you discuss the ramifications of any agreements you make with your editor. Remember she or he is your principal. When you act as an agent for your employer you also obligate them. This obligation is discussed in detail in chapter 11.

Unless you are sure you understand the obligations you are creating, do not promise confidentiality to any source. Understand the distinction between a promise of confidentiality regarding the identity of a source and of confidentiality regarding information provided by a source. Understand the Kentucky Appellate Court's finding of distinction in the *Branzburg* case between the law's protection of a reporter from disclosure of the identity of a source versus the requirement that a newsperson testify about both illegal conduct she or he observed and the demand for the identities of the alleged criminals engaged in the observed conduct.

If you feel you must promise confidentiality to a source in exchange for special information or material, then realize that you are creating a verbal contract with that source, and recognize the potential consequences of your actions for yourself and your employer. If you divulge the source's identity or confidential information after making such a promise, several things could happen, depending on the existence and scope of protections offered in your jurisdiction. First, if you personally observed criminal conduct, or you know the identity of the individuals involved, you can be subpoenaed by a grand jury or prosecutor to divulge that information, and a judge will probably order you to testify about what and whom you observed. If you refuse, you can be fined for contempt of court, and jailed for the duration of the proceeding, or until you agree and comply. However, if you respond to a subpoena in a criminal investigation or case, and testify about the individuals, to whom you promised confidentiality, they could sue you and your employer for breach of contract. In addition, you could possibly be arrested as an accessory to the criminal activity, as an aider and abetter, as a co-conspirator, or for obstruction of justices depending on the criminal statutes in your jurisdiction.

If you merely got the information concerning criminal activity from a source to whom you promised confidentiality, and did not personally observe the conduct involved, then, your state's statutory privilege law may provide you some protection, depending on its interpretation by the courts. If you received defamatory information from a source to which you promised confidentiality, and you publish the information, you and your employer can be sued for defamation. If, to defend yourself from defamation charges, you divulge the name of your source, you and your organization can also be sued for breach of contract by the source.

Also, by promising confidentiality to a source, you may obtain insider information on organized crime, government corruption or malfeasance by a public official, which when included in your exclusive report could result in awards, accolades, and promotions. On the other hand, if you decide to reveal the source or information for which you have promised confidentiality, you and/or your employer could face several types of civil suits.[87] Finally, if you absolutely refuse to divulge any information, despite court order to testify, you may face jail time and a hefty fine. On the bright side, however, if you have to sit in jail, you'll have time to write that next award-winning story!

Magic Words and Phrases

Affirmative defense	Privacy Act of 1974
Balancing test	Privilege
Civil contempt	Privileges and immunities
Collegial body	Prosecutorial grant of immunity
Contempt	Protection
Corollary to the "equal access doctrine"	Public meeting
Criminal contempt	Right of privacy
Entry by misrepresentation	Shield law
Equality of access doctrine	Sovereignty
Exception	State statutory privilege
Exemption	Subpoena
Express consent	Subpoena duces tecum
Federal Register	Sunshine Act
Freedom of Information Act (FOIA)	Transactional immunity
Immunity	Trespass to private property
Implied consent	Viewpoint discrimination
Presidential privilege	

Cases to Read and Brief

Borreca v. Fasi, 369 F. Supp. 906 (D. Haw. 1974)
Branzburg v. Hayes, 408 U.S. 665 (1972)
Burson v. Freeman, 504 U.S. 191 (1992)
Cafeteria & Restaurant Workers Union v. McElroy, 367 U.S. 886 (1961)
Dietemann v. Time, Inc., 449 F.2d 245 (9th Cirt. 1971)
Greer v. Spock, 424 U.S. 828 (1976)
Hanlon v. Berger, 526 U.S. 808 (1999)

In re Sealed Case (Espy), 121 F.3d 820 (D.C. Cir. 1997)

JB Pictures, Inc. v. D.O.D., 86 F.3d 236 (D.C. Cir. 1996)

Pell v. Procunier, 417 U.S. 817 (1974)

Police Department of the City of Chicago v. Mosley, 408 U.S. 92 (1972)

Sherrill v. Knight, 569 F.2d 124 (D.C. Cir. 1977)

Snyder v. Ringgold, 40 F.Supp.2d 714 (D.Md. 1999)

Special Force Ministries v. WCCO T.V., 584 N.W.2d 789 (Minn.App. 1998)

Stahl v. Oklahoma, 665 P.2d 839 (Ok.Crim.App. 1983)

The Daily Herald Co. v. Munro, 838 F.2d 380 (9th Cir. 1998)

Wilson v. Layne, 526 U.S. 603 (1999)

Zemel v. Rusk, 381 U.S. 1 (1965)

Questions for Discussion

1. There are common law defenses for most communications torts for newsworthy information. For example, you can defend against a lawsuit for revealing private facts by showing the information revealed was newsworthy. Do you think there should be a similar defense for trespass to property? For example, should a reporter be able to enter private land to cover a plane crash, without the permission of the landowner?

2. Can you explain how police officers and firefighters are permitted to enter private property without permission, but reporters are not given the same freedom?

3. *Daily Herald Co. v. Munro*[88] and *National Broadcasting Co., Inc. v. Cleland*[89] both permitted exit polls near polling places, but 4 years later the U.S. Supreme Court, in *Burson v. Freeman,*[90] upheld a law prohibiting campaigning near polling places. If political speech enjoys particular protection, how can you explain these apparently contradictory decisions?

4. Do you agree with the decision in *JB Pictures, Inc. v. D.O.D*?[91] Should military commanders be allowed to prohibit reporters from covering the return of deceased U.S. soldiers? Should the families of those soldiers be permitted to decide whether their funerals may be covered by media? Explain your position and offer arguments in its support.

5. Because prisoners and inmates are already isolated from society, how can we know if they are being abused if reporters are not permitted access? Do you believe jails and prisons should be closed to reporters? Why or why not?

6. Explain why the U.S. Supreme Court would have a different presumption about public and press access to grand juries and trials. What is it about those two procedures that justifies different rules of access?

7. Consider the cases of *Sherrill v. Knight*[92] and *Borreca v. Fasi.*[93] Do you believe a public relations officer should be able to "cut off" a reporter who is difficult to deal with? If you are a journalist, can you think of reasons a reporter would frequently call a police public affairs officer on weekends and at night or might offend a city politician? If you are a public relations major, can you think of ways to deal with a difficult reporter short of terminating her or his access to information and interviews?

8. Why do you think the word *privilege* is misused so often? Do you think there should be a "reportorial privilege" that excuses reporters from testifying? If such a privilege existed, would career criminals be motivated to enter the profession of journalism?

9. If you have seen any public meeting, from a congressional hearing to a city council meeting, have you ever noticed that decisions appear to be almost automatic? Is it possible the collegial body's members have discussed the matter in private? How would you write a law to prevent the private "premeetings" that are apparently part of some political decision making?

10. Look at any of the FOIA Web pages for government agencies. Do you find it easy to access information? Do you think these will help ease the burden on FOIA requests for information? Why or why not? How would you suggest improving them?

Notes

1. *Zemel v. Rusk*, 381 U.S. 1, 17 (1965).
2. *Branzburg v. Hayes*, 498 U.S. 665, 684 (1972).
3. *Zemel*, 381 U.S. at 16–17.
4. *Id.* at 15–16.
5. *Special Force Ministries v. WCCO T.V.*, 584 N.W. 2d 789, 792 (Minn.App. 1998).
6. *Garvis v. Employers Mut.Cas.Co.*, 497 N.W.2d 254, 259 (Minn. 1993).
7. *Dietemann v. Time, Inc.*, 449 F.2d 245, 249 (9th Cir. 1971).
8. *Special Force Ministries,* 584 N.W. 2d at 792.
9. *Id.*
10. See, *Dietemann v. Time, Inc.*, 449 F.2d 245 (9th Cir. 1971).
11. *The Florida Star v. B.J.F.*, 491 U.S. 524, 535 (1989).
12. See, *Ayeni v. Mottola*, 35 F.3d 202 (2d Cir. 1984); *Wilson v. Layne*, 526 U.S. 603 (1999); *Hanlon v. Berger*, 526 U.S. 808 (1999).
13. *Greer v. Spock*, 424 U.S. 828 (1976).
14. *Stahl v. Oklahoma*, 665 P.2d 839, 841 (Ok.Crim.App. 1983).
15. *Gree*, 424 U.S. at 836.
16. *Branzburg v. Hayes*, 408 U.S. 665, 683 (1972).
17. *Daily Herald Co. v. Munro*, 838 F.2d 380 (9th Cir. 1988).
18. *Id.* at 385.
19. *Id.*
20. *Id.* at 386.
21. *National Broadcasting Co., Inc. v. Cleland*, 697 F. Supp. 1204, 1208 (N.D.Ga. 1988).
22. *Burson v. Freeman*, 504 U.S. 191, 211 (1992).
23. *Pell v. Procunier*, 417 U.S. 817 (1974).
24. *Id.* at 833–834.
25. *Cafeteria & Restaurant Workers Union v. McElroy* 367 U.S. 886 (1961).
26. *Cafeteria & Restaurant Workers Union v. McElroy* 367 U.S. 886, 889 (1961).
27. *Id.* at 891–893.
28. *Greer v. Spock*, 424 U.S. 828 (1976).
29. *Id.* at 836–839.
30. *Id.* at 839.
31. *JB Pictures, Inc. v. D.O.D.*, 86 F.3d 236 (D.C. Cir. 1996).

32. *Id.* at 238.

33. *Id.*

34. *Id.*

35. *Id.*

36. *Id.* at 239.

37. *Id.* at 239–241.

38. *Id.* at 242.

39. *Zemel v. Rusk*, 381 U.S. 1, 16 (1965).

40. *Mosley v. Rusk*, 408 U.S. 93, 94 (1972).

41. *Id.* at 95–96, internal citations omitted.

42. *Borreca v. Fasi*, 369 F. Supp. 906 (D.Haw. 1974).

43. *Id.* at 909–910.

44. *Sherrill v. Knight*, 569 F.2d 124 (D.C. Cir. 1977).

45. *Cafeteria & Restaurant Workers Union v. McElroy*, 367 U.S. 886 (1961).

46. *Pell v. Procunier*, 417 U.S. 817 (1974).

47. *Sherrill*, 569 F.2d at 126.

48. *Id.* at 130.

49. *Id.* at 129–131.

50. *Id.* at 129.

51. *Snyder v. Ringgold,* 40 F.Supp 2d 714, 715–717 (D.Md. 1999).

52. *Id.* at 718.

53. Pub.L. 94-409, Sec. 2, (1976); 5 U.S.C., Sec. 552(b) (1977).

54. 5 U.S.C.S. § 552b(b) (1977).

55. 5 U.S.C.S. § 552b(a)(2) (1977).

56. 5 U.S.C.S. § 552b(e)(1) (1977).

57. 5 U.S.C.S. §§ 552b(h)(1)(2) and (i) (1977).

58. Ala.Code, § 13A-14-2, formerly Sec. 1192 (1907).

59. Fla.Stat.Ann., § 286.011 (1967).

60. 5 U.S.C.A. § 1002 (1946).

61. 5 U.S.C. § 1002 (c) (1946).

62. Pub.L. No 89-487; 5 U.S.C. § 552 (1967).

63. 20 Cong. Rec. 36243–36244.

64. 20 Cong. Rec. 36622–36633, 36865–36882.

65. 5 U.S.C. § 552(b)(1–9) (1999).

66. 5 U.S.C. § 552(b) (unnumbered paragraph following 9) (1999).

67. 5 U.S.C. § 552, as amended by P.L. 104–231, 110 Stat. 3048.

68. 5 U.S.C. § 552a (1974).

69. 5 U.S.C.A. § 552a(b) (1974).

70. 5 U.S.C.A. § 552b(b)(3)(6) & (7) (1974).

71. U.S. Const. amend. V.

72. *Branzburg v. Hayes*, 408 U.S. 665, 689–690 (1970).

73. U.S. Const. art I, § 6.

74. U.S. Const. art I, § 9.

75. U.S. Const. art IV, § 2.

76. U.S. Const. amend. XIV, § 1.

77. *In re Sealed Case (Espy)*, 121 F.3d 820 (D.C. Cir. 1997).

78. *Branzburg v. Hayes*, 498 U.S. 665, 689 (1972).

79. See, e.g., *Cohen v. Cowles Media Co.*, 501 U.S. 663, 669 (1991).

80. *Branzburg*, 408 U.S. at 667.

81. *Id.* at 667–677.

82. Kentucky Revised Statutes § 421.100(1962); *Branzburg v. Hayes*, 408 U.S. 665, 669 (1972).

83. *Branzburg*, 408 U.S. at 669.

84. Seventeen states had provided newsmen with a statutory privilege: Alabama, Alaska, Arizona, Arkansas, California, Indiana, Kentucky, Louisiana, Maryland, Michigan, Montana, Nevada, New Jersey, New Mexico, New York, Ohio, and Pennsylvania. *Branzburg v. Hayes*, 408 U.S. 665, 669 n.27 (1972).

85. *Branzburg*, 408 U.S. at 669–690.

86. See, e.g., *Herbert v. Lando*, 441 U.S. 153, 165–166 & 171 (1979).

87. E.g., *Cohen v. Cowles Media Co.*, 501 U.S. 663, 671 (1991).

88. *Daily Herald Co. v. Munro*, 838 F.2d 380 (9th Cir. 1988).

89. *National Broadcasting Co., Inc. v. Cleland*, 697 F. Supp. 1204, 1208 (N.D.Ga. 1988).

90. *Burson v. Freeman*, 504 U.S. 191 (1992).

91. *JB Pictures, Inc. v. D.O.D*, 86 F.3d 236, 238 (D.C. Cir. 1996).

92. *Sherrill v. Knight*, 569 F.2d 124, 129 (D.C. Cir. 1977).

93. *Borreca v. Fasi*, 369 F. Supp. 906 (D.Haw. 1974).

7

Access to Trials
and Judicial
Proceedings

Legal trials are not like elections, to be won through the use of the meeting hall, the
radio, and the newspaper.[1]

Overview
Introduction to Fair Trial versus Free Press
Restrictions on Access: Gag Orders, Restrictive Orders, and Closure Orders
Access to Criminal Pretrial and Posttrial Procedures and Records
Access to Other Hearings and Trials
Practice Notes

Overview

In chapter 6, we described how law could either limit or facilitate access to government
facilities and information. We also explained how law and subpoenas are used to access the
information held by media representatives. Because there is no constitutionally required
access to government facilities, mass communications practitioners must obtain permission to enter and cover courts and their records. In this chapter, we focus specifically on
access to courts and other judicial proceedings by the public and press. The unique problems associated with cameras and recording devices are addressed in chapter 8.

This chapter is divided into six parts. The first part explains the conflict between the
First Amendment freedoms of speech and press and the Sixth Amendment requirement
to provide fair and impartial trials. This conflict is often called the "fair trial versus free
press dilemma." In this section, the rights of people accused of crime are juxtaposed
against the rights of the public and press to be present during trials.

The second part of this chapter explains when trial coverage may be restricted
and describes the judicial processes from which the press and public may be excluded.

We also describe the proper nomenclature for three techniques used by trial courts to control court decorum and to protect the judicial process from media influence.

The third section covers public and press access to various criminal trials, and the fourth section describes access to pretrial and posttrial stages and to court records. This section describes the stages in the overall judicial process to show why some phases and records must be closed.

The fifth part of the chapter looks at miscellaneous hearings and trials. Here, we cover special rules for juvenile and family matters and describe the extraordinary variation in access to civil trials. We also cover the unique problems of access created by national security concerns since September 11, 2001.

In the practice notes, we provide practical suggestions for reporters who seek access to courthouses, personnel, records, and procedures. We also offer specific guidelines to follow when covering a trial and a motion for closure is made. The final practice note describes limitations on litigation public relations.

Introduction to Fair Trial versus Free Press

To understand how public access to trials can conflict with litigants' rights, one must first understand how trials work. We introduced trial procedure in chapter 2. Here, we expand that description to focus on the aspects of trials that can be altered by public or media presence.

Adversarial versus Inquisitorial Trial System

The framers of the U.S. Constitution chose to adopt an adversarial rather than an inquisitorial trial system. In an **inquisitorial judicial system**, the judge acts as investigator, prosecutor, and as ultimate decision maker who determines guilt or innocence of an accused, as well as any sanctions to be imposed. Additionally, the judge may interrogate any person, including the accused.

On the other hand, in an **adversarial judicial system**, there are three roles, each played by a separate individual. These roles are prosecutor, defense attorney, and judge. In civil trials, these roles are the plaintiff's attorney, the defendant's attorney, and the judge. The prosecution and the defense are deliberately set at odds, each as an advocate for one side of the case. The judge sits as a referee, deciding what rules and what procedures to apply. Under the adversarial system, it is assumed that the truth will win if each side is encouraged to support his or her position with the greatest zeal possible. It is also assumed that witnessing the conflict between prosecution and defense will lead the trier of fact to the truth; and that, in the final analysis, justice will be done. For such a system to work, it is essential that the judge or jury be free from any outside influence and that an absolutely consistent procedure always be used.

Justice Requires Procedural Due Process

Trials are conducted in order to discover truth and to do justice. There is no objective way to verify whether the trial was successful. Simply put, if we had an independent or objective measure of truth or justice we would not need a trial. Because we cannot guarantee that justice has been done in any specific case, we must rely on the **procedural due process** by and through which a person accused of a crime can receive the opportunity to obtain justice. We presume that if a person accused of a crime has received the opportunity to obtain justice, then the victim and society as a whole will also receive justice. This opportunity to obtain justice is called *due process* or *procedural due process*. It relies completely on providing every defendant a consistent trial procedure.

The Fourth, Fifth, Sixth, and Eighth Amendments provide guidelines to help guarantee consistent trial procedures in criminal matters, and most, but not all, of these procedural requirements are incorporated into the due process clause of the Fourteenth Amendment and are, therefore, imposed on the states. In order to ensure a fair and impartial trial that follows due process, the jury must receive all of its information about the case from the trial participants. Because the media are not subject to the procedural rules of due process, it is important that judicial decision making be completely isolated from media reports. Without this isolation, jurors may be influenced by uncontrolled news coverage and the consistency of due process will be lost.

Conflict of Interests Inherent Between First and Sixth Amendments

The Sixth Amendment requires the government to provide a fair and impartial trial and the judicial system creates a fair trial by guaranteeing procedural due process. However, news coverage does not follow procedural due process and the First Amendment prohibits the government from restricting press freedom. This conflict is the heart of the fair trial versus free press dilemma. Simply put, it is impossible to have a truly fair trial that is covered by a completely free press. The Sixth Amendment guarantees an accused a fair trial by a panel of "impartial, 'indifferent' jurors . . . as a basic requirement of due process . . . [and requires that any]. . . verdict must be based upon the evidence developed at the trial."[2] However, this right conflicts with First Amendment liberties of the press and speech.

At common law, the conflict between fair trial and free press was resolved easily. Fairness of the trial always outweighed freedom of the public and press to access pretrial and trial processes.[3] Trial courts understood and carefully enforced the rights of an accused to a fair trial by an unbiased jury. They took action to control the consequences of sensationalistic reporting or publication of evidence that would be inadmissible at trial. Also, until recently, the Sixth Amendment right to a fair trial belonged exclusively to the accused in a criminal proceeding. The Sixth Amendment says, "In all criminal prosecutions, *the accused shall enjoy the right* to a speedy and public trial, by an impartial jury of the State and district wherein the crime shall have been committed . . ." [emphasis added].[4]

Conflict between the provisions of the First and Sixth Amendment have motivated changes in the interpretation of the rights of accuseds and the freedoms of the press. Here, we review these changes and summarize how requirements for a fair trial and free press are currently balanced.

Near the beginning of every criminal action, the court tells the defendant of his or her rights and explains these rights on the record. This is done before the court accepts any waiver of rights by the defendant and makes it clear that these rights belong, under the Constitution, exclusively to the accused. In *Gannett Co. v. DePasquale,* the High Court considered a defendant's unopposed motion to exclude the public and press from his pre-trial suppression hearing.[5] The hearing involved an allegedly involuntary confession and certain physical evidence the state wanted to use at trial. The Supreme Court upheld the exclusion of the press and public from the pretrial proceeding. The sole issue presented in that case was "whether members of the public have an independent constitutional right to insist upon access to a *pretrial judicial proceeding,* even though the accused, the prosecutor, and the trial judge all have agreed to the closure of that proceeding in order to assure a fair trial" (emphasis added).[6] In its decision, the Supreme Court first described the purpose and importance of suppression hearings. It said,

> The whole purpose of such hearings is to screen out unreliable or illegally obtained evidence and insure that this evidence does not become known to the jury. . . . Publicity concerning the proceedings . . . could . . . inform potential jurors of inculpatory information wholly inadmissible at the actual trial.[7]

The Court went on to explain the danger to the fairness of a trial when pretrial publicity thrusts into public consciousness prejudicial material alleged about an accused, which would be wholly inadmissible at the actual trial. Then the Court explained that these rights specifically guaranteed by the Sixth Amendment, applicable to the states via the Fourteenth Amendment, are personal to the accused.

> Among the guarantees that the Amendment provides to a person charged with the commission of a criminal offense, and to him alone, is the "right to a speedy and public trial, by an impartial jury." The Constitution nowhere mentions any right of access to a criminal trial on the part of the public; its guarantee . . . is personal to the accused. . . . There is not the slightest suggestion there is any correlative right in members of the public to insist upon a public trial.[8]

The Court also recognized the strong societal interest in public trials by citing several advantages to openness in court proceedings. These included (a) improving the quality of testimony, (b) inducing unknown witnesses to come forward with relevant testimony, (c) causing all trial participants to perform their duties more conscientiously, and (d) generally providing the public with an opportunity to observe the judicial system at work.

Gannett Co. v. DePasquale dealt with a pretrial suppression hearing. Its holding does not apply to trials themselves. One year after the *DePasquale* decision, the Supreme Court considered the "narrow question . . . [of] whether the right of the public and press to attend criminal trials is guaranteed under the United States Constitution."[9] The decision was made in *Richmond Newspapers v. Virginia,* a case involving a defendant who was standing trial on a murder charge for the fourth time. His first conviction had been reversed on appeal, and two subsequent trials had ended in mistrials. At the beginning of his fourth trial, the Virginia trial court granted the defense counsel's unopposed motion that the trial be closed to the public. Two *Richmond Newspaper* reporters were present in open court when the **trial closure order** was granted, but neither reporter objected at the time. Later in the day, the newspaper filed a motion to vacate the closure order and requested a hearing. The trial court denied the newspaper's motion and the following day, with the press and public excluded, the court granted a defense motion to strike the prosecution's evidence, released the jury, and entered a finding that the defendant was not guilty.

In *Richmond Newspapers,* a plurality of the Supreme Court held that "the right to attend criminal trials is implicit in the guarantees of the First Amendment . . . (a)bsent an overriding interest articulated in findings, the trial of a criminal case must be open to the public."[10] The Court reasoned that under the Ninth Amendment, several rights not specifically enumerated among the Bill of Rights had been considered to be implicit in enumerated guarantees. In its examples the Court listed (a) the rights of association, (b) the rights of privacy, (c) the right to be presumed innocent, (d) the right to be judged by a standard of proof beyond a reasonable doubt in a criminal trial, and (e) the right to travel. The Court went on to state that "without the freedom to attend such trials, which people have exercised for centuries, important aspects of freedom of speech and of the press could be eviscerated."[11]

The Supreme Court distinguished its decision in *Richmond Newspapers v. Virginia* from that in *Gannett Co. v. DePasquale*, noting that the *Gannett Co. v. DePasquale* decision only addressed hearings on pretrial motions.[12]

In *Richmond Newspapers,* the Supreme Court held that there is a qualified implicit First Amendment right of the public and press to attend criminal trials, and that the right is applicable to the states via the Fourteenth Amendment. It based this conclusion primarily on the common law in England and at the time of the adoption by the U.S. Constitution and Bill of Rights. This application of historic rights of access to places traditionally open to the public, is similar to the Court's forum-based approach to time, place, and manner decisions about First Amendment Freedom of Speech Clause issues. This application has become a common thread, connecting its decisions involving public and press access to the judicial system, and is woven throughout the remainder of this chapter as well as chapter 8.

The *Richmond Newspapers* decision dealt with a trial closure order that was based on a Virginia statute authorizing trial closure at the discretion of the judge when requested by the parties. A plurality of the Supreme Court found this statute a violation of the First and Fourteenth Amendments. The Court specifically ruled that a trial court could not close criminal trials, absent (a) an overriding interest articulated in its findings, (b) which supported such a closure, and (c) specific inquiry by the trial court about whether alternative solutions would have met the need to ensure trial fairness. In dicta, the Court also suggested that there were several alternatives to closure that a trial court should consider. Those were (a) excluding witnesses from the courtroom, (b) sequestration

Exhibit 7.1.   Elements for Closure (*Richmond Newspapers v. Virginia*, 448 U.S. 555 [1980]; *Globe Newspaper Co. v. Superior Court*, 457 U.S. 596 [1982]).

If a judicial procedure is presumed open, before a court may order it closed all of the following conditions must be met:

1. There is an overriding governmental interest in closure.
2. The closure is essential to meet that interest.
3. The closure is narrowly tailored to meet the interest.
4. All three of the above must be shown on the record in the trial or hearing.

of witnesses during trial, and (c) sequestration of jurors. The elements required to overcome the presumption that trials one after are summarized in Exhibit 7.1.

The Supreme Court's decision in *Richmond Newspapers* granted the public and press a qualified implicit right of access under the First Amendment to criminal trials. However, two major questions loom before trial courts after *Richmond Newspapers*. The first is, how can the courts balance the explicit Sixth Amendment rights of an accused to a trial by an impartial jury with the new qualified implicit right of the public and press to attend criminal trials? The second question is, how can a trial judge control courtroom decorum and ensure that information given to jurors will come only from properly admitted testimony and exhibits in the face of pretrial and trial disclosures of inadmissible evidence by the press and public?

Restrictions on Access: Gag Orders, Restrictive Orders, and Closure Orders

Traditionally, trial courts have used three methods to control pretrial publicity or prevent the impact of prejudicial, inadmissible, and false or inaccurate material regarding a case or an accused from tainting a jury panel. The U.S. Supreme Court has ruled some of these permissible and some unconstitutional. They are gag orders, restrictive orders, and closure orders.

Gag Orders: Unconstitutional Prior Restraint

The most stringent attempt by trial courts to control the flow of pretrial information is the use of a **restraining order** to forbid media coverage. Often pejoratively referred to as **gag** or **muzzle orders**, such orders forbid the media to report specific facts or to cover specific topics. These orders have almost uniformly been declared unconstitutional under the First Amendment. In a line of cases beginning with the 1931 landmark decision in *Near v. Minnesota*,[13] the Supreme Court has held that **prior restraint** against media publication of information already in its possession, no matter how it was obtained, is unconstitutional on its face or bears a heavy presumption against its constitutionality.[14]

The Supreme Court directly addressed the issue of prior restraint in relation to widespread news coverage of a pending murder trial in *Nebraska Press Association v. Stuart*.[15] In that case, the trial judge made the mistake of allowing the public and press to be present at an open preliminary hearing in a murder case. The judge then entered an order restraining the news media and wire services from publishing or broadcasting accounts of an alleged confession. The restraining order also precluded publication of "other facts 'strongly implicative' of the accused."[16]

The Supreme Court said the issue it granted certiorari to decide in *Nebraska Press Association* was "whether the entry of such an order . . . violated the constitutional guarantee of freedom of the press."[17] The Supreme Court saw several problems, including the trial court's inability to control the actions of newspapers and broadcasters outside its jurisdiction, which could also reach potential jurors.

The Supreme Court began its analysis by noting the requirement that jurors cannot be subject to outside influences from the media. It continued by pointing out that cases dealing with the First Amendment have held freedom of the press is not an absolute right but, "that prior restraints on speech and publication are the most serious and the least tolerable infringement on First Amendment rights."[18] Next, the Supreme Court applied a standard from earlier rulings on prior restraint. Using this standard, it examined the restraining order to determine whether "the gravity of the 'evil,' [to be avoided] discounted by its improbability, justifies such invasion of free speech as is necessary to avoid the danger."[19] The Court then developed a three-pronged test to determine whether the facts supported prior restraint on publication, which it described as "one of the most extraordinary remedies known to our jurisprudence."[20] The test applied by the Court considered:

> (a) the nature and extent of pretrial news coverage; (b) whether other measures would be likely to mitigate the effects of unrestrained pretrial publicity; and (c) how effectively a restraining order would operate to prevent the threatened danger. The precise terms of the restraining order are also important.[21]

After applying its test to the pretrial record, the Supreme Court concluded that the trial judge had met only the first part of its test in that he was indeed justified in concluding that there would be "intense and pervasive pretrial publicity . . . [and the] publicity might impair the defendant's right to a fair trial."[22] But, the trial court had not considered other measures to protect the defendant's rights and had not explored whether the restraining order would be effective. The Supreme Court also found the trial court's prohibition regarding implicative information was too broad and too vague to survive the protections we give First Amendment freedoms.[23] The Supreme Court ended with its holding, saying,

> We hold that . . . the order entered in this case prohibiting reporting or commentary on judicial proceedings held in public . . . is clearly invalid . . . and the judgment of the Nebraska Supreme Court is therefore . . . Reversed.[24]

Simply put, it is unconstitutional for a judge to order media not to print or broadcast information they already have from legal sources.

Posttrial Publication Restraints Also Unconstitutional

Restraining orders prohibiting media disclosure of information obtained in criminal cases are prior restraint and are prohibited by the First Amendment; so too are state statutes that punish posttrial publication violations. Several cases by the Supreme Court have addressed the constitutionality of state statutes aimed at protecting certain classes of defendants, victims, or sources of information about pending investigations or criminal cases. In 1978 the Supreme Court, in *Landmark Communications*, held that the First Amendment guarantees of freedom of speech and press prohibited enforcement of a state law punishing third parties, including the media, for publishing truthful information regarding proceedings of the Virginia Judicial Inquiry and Review Commission.[25] The law purported to protect the confidentiality of judges under investigation. The Supreme Court did not hold the entire statute unconstitutional. Rather, the High Court said its application to the press, who were not participants in the proceedings, was unconstitutional.

The Supreme Court decision in *Smith v. Daily Mail* held a West Virginia statute to be an unconstitutional violation of the First Amendment.[26] The statute made it a crime for a newspaper to publish the lawfully obtained names of youths charged as juvenile offenders. The statute was ruled unconstitutional because it only restricted publication of the names of juvenile delinquents by newspapers, and did not restrict the electronic media or any other form of publication. While the statute might serve a state interest of the highest order in attempting to protect juvenile offenders from publicity that would have a harmful impact on their rehabilitation, the means chosen by the statute to accomplish its goals could not satisfy constitutional requirements.

The 1990 decision in *Butterworth v. Smith* struck down as an unconstitutional violation of the First Amendment, applicable to the states via the Fourteenth Amendment, a Florida statute that prohibited grand jury witnesses from disclosing their own testimony after the grand jury investigation had ended. The Court reiterated its reasoning from *Landmark Communications* saying, "(o)ur prior cases have firmly established . . . that injury to official reputation is an insufficient reason for repressing speech that would otherwise be free."[27] The Court also held the First Amendment precluded a state from imposing damages for publication of a rape victim's name; and in *Oklahoma Publishing Co. v. Oklahoma County District Court* the Supreme Court held that a state could not constitutionally enjoin the publication of a juvenile offender's name.[28]

Similarly, the Supreme Court has held, in a number of cases, that state courts cannot constitutionally assert and exercise their common law powers to punish, by contempt, out-of-court publications that were critical of their handling of pending cases. Several state courts, in response to such criticism, had held reporters, editors, cartoonists, publishers, and an elected sheriff guilty of criminal contempt charges after finding their statements had obstructed the orderly and fair administration of justice in pending cases. The types of speech viewed by these local courts as contemptuous involved (a) thinly veiled threats of possible legal and other consequences if a preferred decision was not made,[29] (b) two editorials and one cartoon highly critical of a local court's handling of a series of pending criminal cases,[30] (c) vitriolic attacks by a newspaper on a Texas non-lawyer judge's decision in a forcible entry and detainer case still pending at the time of the articles,[31] and (d) a written press statement by a local sheriff criticizing a county judge's special charge and instructions to a grand jury investigating alleged bloc voting by African Americans.[32]

In its judicial review of these contempt convictions, the Supreme Court applied the clear and present danger test to determine whether the gravity of the evil to be prevented would outweigh or overcome the restrictions on speech and press. In *Bridges v. California* the Court restated and applied the doctrine it first enunciated to fit these circumstances in 1919 in *Schenck v. United States*:

> The clear and present doctrine requires a weighing of the evidence and a determination 'whether the words used are used in such circumstances and are of such a nature as to create a clear and present danger that they will bring about' a substantial interference with the orderly administration of justice.[33]

The Supreme Court found that courts must have power to protect the interests of prisoners and litigants before them from unseemly efforts to pervert judicial action, but it also found that the right of courts to be free from intimidation, in these cases, did not outweigh freedom of the press. Therefore, the contempt citations were all overturned.

Restrictive Orders Against Trial Participants

Court orders restraining members of the media from publishing lawfully obtained information are unconstitutional. However, there is no general prohibition against court-imposed restrictions on trial participants, court personnel, or law enforcement officers. It is inaccurate to refer to such orders as gag orders. They do not involve prior restraint on the right to publish information. Orders prohibiting trial participants, court personnel, and police from disclosing information are more accurately called **nondisclosure orders** or **restrictive orders**. Because the courts recognize the need to ensure cases are not tried in the "press," such orders against trial participants are constitutional and are enforceable by both civil and criminal contempt proceedings. **Nondisclosure orders** have consistently been upheld and listed as one of several methods that may be used to prevent improper information from reaching potential jurors or tainting the testimony of witnesses. Trial courts can legitimately enforce **restrictive orders** against all law enforcement personnel, judicial personnel, courthouse employees, parties in a case, attorneys in a case, witnesses in a case, and jurors.

In summary, a restraining order issued against media disclosure of lawfully obtained information is unconstitutional prior restraint or censorship. However, restrictive or nondisclosure orders against trial participants and their staffs are not an abridgement of their First Amendment rights because the very nature of their positions as participants within the judicial system requires them to keep information confidential. Nondisclosure orders also have no impermissible effects on freedom of the press. Although the media are free to publish the information they gather, they have no Constitutional right to gather information. The government, as sovereign, is entitled to refuse to give information to the public or the press. This means that public relations practitioners representing the courts or law enforcement agencies have no legal duty to provide releases or information in response to press inquiries.

Closure Orders

Since its 1980 decision in *Richmond Newspapers* the Supreme Court has interpreted the First Amendment to give an implied and qualified right of public access to attend criminal jury trials.[34] This is not an absolute right but it does belong to the public, including members of the media. Under this ruling, a court may close a criminal trial only when closure is required to protect a defendant's Sixth Amendment right to a fair trial, or when some other overriding consideration requires closure. This ruling may conflict with state statutes mandating trial closure during trials of sex offenses or involving victims under the age of 18. Such statutes are sometimes referred to as **witness protection laws** or **shield laws**, but should not be confused with the state statutory privilege laws sometimes applied to media described in chapter 6.

In the 1982 case of *Globe Newspaper Co. v. Superior Court*, the Supreme Court addressed a Massachusetts statute that had been construed by the Massachusetts Supreme Judicial Court to require exclusion of the public and press during the testimony of minor victims in sex offense cases. The U.S. Supreme Court agreed that the state's interest in safeguarding the physical and psychological well-being of a minor witness was compelling. But, it held the statute was unconstitutional because the state had not shown that the mandatory closure statute was **narrowly tailored** to serve that interest. According to the Supreme Court, the trial court had to determine whether a closure order was narrowly tailored to meet the state interest on a case-by-case basis. A **blanket statutory closure rule** is an unconstitutional violation of the First and Fourteenth Amendments. The Court said that a trial court must weigh various factors in such cases before ordering a trial closure. Those factors include (a) the minor victim's age, (b) the victim's psychological maturity and understanding, (c) the nature of the crime, (d) the desires of the victim and his or her willingness to testify despite the presence of the press, and (e) the interests of parents and relatives of the victim.[35]

It is important to remember that the criminal jury trial is the culmination of a long series of steps, many of which have taken place well before the public and press have been granted access to the victim's testimony at trial. The Supreme Court's 1980 plurality decision in *Richmond Newspapers* granted only a qualified and limited right of access for the press to criminal trials. It is useless and confusing to attempt to generalize from the *Richmond Newspapers* decision. In the first place, the *Richmond Newspapers* opinion was a plurality decision, which means it is not mandatory authority and is less likely to be followed than are other Supreme Court decisions. Second, the situation in *Richmond Newspapers* was unusual because it involved closing the defendant's fourth trial for the same crime. Finally, it dealt only with a criminal trial closure and the court offered no ruling on closure of other judicial procedures.

Since the *Richmond Newspapers* decision, the court has issued several opinions dealing with public access to specific pretrial procedures. Access to judicial proceedings for both the public and media vary depending on the particular judicial procedure involved. The next section of this chapter addresses access to specific pretrial and posttrial procedures.

Access to Criminal Pretrial and Posttrial Procedures and Records

Here we summarize decisions regarding access to pre- and posttrial procedures. This material is arranged following the chronology in which the procedures would be encountered by a typical criminal defendant. In order to understand these rules, it is imperative that any reporter who covers court proceedings knows the proper terms for the various judicial procedures used in their jurisdictions, as well as those generally used by the federal and state courts.

Search Warrant Materials

There is no First Amendment right of access to search warrant materials. Most jurisdictions have statutes or court rules requiring these documents to be sealed because the government's case on behalf of the people would be totally compromised if these materials were made public.

There is no U.S. Supreme Court decision on point. However, the U.S. Court of Appeals for the Ninth Circuit, in a case of first impression, held "the First Amendment does not establish a qualified right of access to search warrant proceedings and materials while a preindictment investigation is still ongoing."[36]

Grand Jury Proceedings: Secrecy Is a Functional Requirement of the Process

The secrecy of grand jury proceedings, processes, and records has always been vigorously protected by the courts. In *Butterworth v. Smith* the U.S. Supreme Court described the history of the grand jury process and also explained the importance of secrecy to its proper function:

> We consistently have recognized that the proper functioning of our grand jury system depends upon the secrecy of the grand jury proceedings. In particular, we have noted several distinct interests served by safeguarding the confidentiality of grand jury proceedings.[37]

The Court went on to list reasons for grand jury secrecy. Those reasons included (a) encouraging and protecting witnesses, (b) preventing the flight of those under investigation, and (c) protecting the reputation of people who are investigated and exonerated.

In *Illinois v. Abbott*, the U.S. Supreme Court even refused disclosure of federal grand jury materials to an Illinois State Attorney General because he failed to show "particularized need." Relying on Rule 6(e) of the Federal Rules of Criminal Procedure, the Court emphatically stated that the Attorney General of the United States is not permitted to disclose any grand jury proceedings to a state attorney general unless he or she is directed to do so by a court. In that case, the court stressed both the importance of secrecy to the grand jury process, and the fact that these interests must be protected even after the termination of criminal proceedings.[38]

Preliminary Hearings: California Style Presumed Open, Others Presumed Closed

In *Press-Enterprise Co. v. Superior Court*, the issue was "whether the petitioner had a First Amendment right of access to the transcript of a preliminary hearing growing out of a criminal prosecution."[39] The U.S. Supreme Court held that "the qualified First Amendment right of access to criminal proceedings applies to preliminary hearings *as they are conducted in California*" (emphasis added).[40] The case involved the unusual California procedures wherein the prosecutor has a choice of securing a grand jury indictment or a finding of probable cause following a preliminary hearing. However, even when an accused has been indicted by a grand jury, she or he has an absolute right to an elaborate preliminary hearing before a neutral magistrate. The U.S. Supreme Court limited its narrow holding to preliminary hearings as they are conducted in California because **California-style preliminary hearings** are "*sufficiently like a trial* to justify the . . . conclusion"(emphasis added).[41] California-style preliminary hearings are also unusual because they give an accused the right to personally appear and be represented by counsel and also allow cross-examination of hostile witnesses, presentation of exculpatory evidence, and exclusion of illegally obtained evidence.

In most states, a preliminary hearing is a perfunctory procedure presided over by a judge who hears a general summary of the investigation conducted by the police and then decides whether there is sufficient probable cause to bind a defendant over for trial. The defendant has a right to appear at the hearing with counsel, but the defense counsel is allowed only a limited cross-examination of the witnesses presented by the prosecution. The only witnesses are almost always the law enforcement officers who were in charge of the investigation and who are permitted give their interpretations of multiple hearsay statements that are impossible to cross-examine. The defense is not allowed to present evidence or witness testimony. These non-California-style preliminary hearings serve the same function as a grand jury and have not been presumed to be open to the public or press.[42] Opening a non-California-style preliminary hearing to the public and press would be just as damaging to the concept of a fair trial by an impartial jury as would be opening grand jury proceedings to the public and press.

Motions to Suppress Evidence or Confessions: Closed by Motion of Defendant; Otherwise Presumed Open

In our discussion of control of the right to a public trial we described the case of *Gannett Co. v. DePasquale*. In that decision, the U.S. Supreme Court upheld exclusion of the public and press from hearings on a defendant's motions to suppress evidence. The closure motion in that case was made by the defendant and was unopposed by the state.[43] Five years after the *DePasquale* decision, the High Court rendered a decision on "the extent to which a hearing on a motion to suppress evidence may be closed to the public over the objection of the defendant."[44]

Waller v. Georgia dealt with the prosecution's use of court-authorized wiretaps of telephones by Georgia police in an investigation of an illegal lottery. These wiretaps formed the basis for search warrants that were followed by indictments against several defendants. In *Waller*, it was the prosecution that requested closure of the pretrial hearings on the defendant's motions to suppress the wiretaps and evidence. The defendants were co-conspirators and they objected to the closure. Over these objections, the trial court closed the suppression hearing to all but witnesses, court personnel, the parties, and the lawyers. The prosecution contended that information in the wiretap tapes would either invade the privacy rights of innocent, unindicted persons or would provide warning to still unindicted potential defendants.

On appeal, the U.S. Supreme Court first ruled that when a defendant objected to closure of a motion hearing there was a heavy presumption of openness. The Court then said,

> The presumption of openness may be overcome only by an *overriding interest based on findings* that *closure is essential to* preserve higher values and is *narrowly tailored* to serve that interest. The interest is to be articulated along with findings specific enough that a reviewing court can determine whether the closure order was properly entered. (emphasis added)[45]

The High Court went on to say that the trial court had failed to give proper weight to the defendant's Sixth Amendment right to a public trial. It remanded the matter to the Georgia courts with instructions to hold new and public suppression hearings.[46]

The result of these decisions is that hearings on pretrial motions to suppress may be closed on motion by the defendant. But if the defendant objects to closure, pretrial suppression hearings are presumed open and may be closed only if the court finds an overriding government interest based on findings on the record and that the closure is essential and narrowly tailored to meet that government interest. [47]

Voir Dire Jury Selection Proceedings Presumed Open

Press-Enterprise Co. v. Superior Court involved a trial for the rape and murder of a teenage girl.[48] The decision in that case contains a statement of the current qualified right of access to voir dire proceedings. Before the voir dire phase of the trial began, Press Enterprise Company moved that the jury selection process be open to the public and press. The state opposed the motion because of the nature of the crime and the fact that both the state and defense counsel would ask personal and private questions of the potential jurors. During voir dire potential jurors would be asked questions such as whether they or close relatives or friends had been raped and/or sexually assaulted. The state argued that if the press were present, the potential jurors would not be as candid and forthcoming because these very private matters would be reported to the general public. The trial judge agreed and although he permitted the press to attend the general voir dire proceedings, which lasted only 3 days, he closed the "individual" voir dire proceedings that took approximately 6 weeks. Additionally, after the jury was empanelled, Press Enterprise Company moved for release of a complete transcript of the voir dire proceedings. Both the prosecution and defense objected, and the trial court again denied the motion. Finally, after the defendant had been convicted and sentenced to death, Press Enterprise Company made and the trial court denied a second request for release of the voir dire transcript.

The case ultimately reached the U.S. Supreme Court, which ruled that there could be some circumstances in the jury selection process, when interrogation might touch on "deeply personal matters . . . [that prospective juror would have] legitimate reasons for keeping out of the public domain"[49] and that would rise to the level of a compelling interest. However, the U.S. Supreme Court ruled that the trial court failed to articulate its findings of overriding interest on the record and that it had also failed to consider alternatives to closure. In dicta the Supreme Court offered two narrowly tailored alternatives the trial court had not considered. Instead of sealing the entire voir dire transcript, they suggested the trial judge seal only those parts of the transcript necessary to preserve the anonymity of individuals to be protected. The High Court also suggested deleting the names of jurors whose responses might lead to invasion of privacy.

Sentencing Hearings: Open versus Presentence Investigation Reports: Closed

There is a qualified implicit First Amendment right of the public and press to attend criminal trials. This right was first recognized in *Richmond Newspapers v. Virginia*[50] and the reasoning has since been expanded to cover the sentencing hearings that follow trials in most jurisdictions. However, there is no right of access to all documents connected with criminal proceedings. For example, representatives of the media have, on numerous occasions, attempted to gain access to the confidential presentence investigation reports, provided for by federal rules and by the individual states in their statutes or court rules.[51]

In *U.S. v. Corbitt*, a district court authorized disclosure of a defendant's presentence investigation report. The judge based his decision on the **common law right of access** to judicial records, not on any First Amendment right of access to criminal trials. However, the U.S. Court of Appeals vacated the district court order and remanded the case for reconsideration under the "appropriate legal principles."[52] Before discussing the differences that may arise in obtaining access to judicial proceedings as opposed to judicial records, and the legal theories of access as selected and applied in the *Corbitt* example, it is important to understand the purpose of presentence investigation reports.

Presentence investigation reports are required by statute in most states and by the federal courts following a criminal felony conviction. In many jurisdictions, the court also may order a presentence investigation and report prior to sentencing a defendant convicted of a misdemeanor. Whether the conviction follows a trial or a plea, the sentencing judge needs to know as much as possible about the background of the defendant, the victim, and the circumstances of the case to ensure that the sentence will fit the crime and the criminal.

Presentence investigations and reports are generally conducted and prepared by the probation divisions of the court within a 30- to 60-day period following conviction or plea. The presentence investigation involves several interviews, background checks, and document searches. It may also involve psychological tests and drug or alcohol rehabilitation evaluations.

Originally, under the federal rules as well as those of many states, neither the defendant nor his attorney was given access to these reports. They were given to the judge and then sealed in the court files.[53] Although presentence investigation reports generally do not contain sentence recommendations, they often contain information about availability of treatment and other community resources for the defendant, including those available within the corrections department.

The Federal Rules of Criminal Procedure were amended in 1983 to make these reports available to the defendant and her or his attorney and to allow the defendant to challenge the accuracy of factual statements contained in them. Also, the defendant is not allowed to challenge evaluations made by the professionals who assessed him or her.[54] Finally, under the Federal Rules, and those of most state jurisdictions, presentence investigation reports, although part of the record, are sealed and can only be opened on court order. Some states give potential parolees access to their own confidential presentence investigation reports, but these reports are uniformly confidential and are not accessible by the public or media.

The issue before the U.S. Court of Appeals in *U.S. v. Corbitt* was "whether, and under what circumstances, a district court may release the presentence investigation report of a criminal defendant to members of the news media."[55] Corbitt, who had been a police chief for a small town in Illinois, was indicted in a federal district court for extortion and accepting bribes to permit criminal activities while he was sheriff. After Corbitt pleaded guilty, the federal district judge imposed a sentence lower than was recommended in the presentence report. The decision to be lenient was apparently based on a large number of letters from both elected and appointed public officials in Corbitt's community. The media and many in the community wanted to know which officials had requested leniency, especially because many of the letters were reportedly written on official letterhead.

Pulitzer Community Newspapers, the publisher of the local newspaper that had covered the case, requested release of the presentence report and the testimonial letters relied on by the judge during the sentencing hearing. The defendant and the government both objected to disclosure of the presentence report and the defendant also objected to release of the letters. The district court judge authorized disclosure of the defendant's presentence report based on his interpretation of the common law "right of access to judicial records." The judge did order some portions of the report **redacted** to protect the privacy of the defendant and others.

Pulitzer relied on two separate legal principles to seek release of the presentence report: (a) the common law right to inspect and copy judicial records and (b) the First Amendment right of access to criminal proceedings. The appellate court agreed that the

U.S. Supreme Court had recognized a "common law right of access" to judicial records. However, the Circuit Court determined that this was a "flexible concept" and that there was no common law right of access to documents that have traditionally been kept secret for important policy reasons.[56] The Court of Appeals then listed several public policy concerns that would justify keeping presentence investigation reports closed. The Court repeatedly compared the importance of keeping the presentence investigation reports confidential with the reasons for sealing of search warrant applications and grand jury secrecy.[57]

Responding to Pulitzer's argument asserting a "First Amendment right" of access to criminal proceedings, the Circuit Court determined that the First Amendment provided no broader right of access to presentence reports than was available under the common law. The Court then applied the "experience and logic test" from *Press Enterprises v. Superior Court.* That test first decides whether any stage of a criminal proceeding should be opened to the public by asking if the place and process have historically been open to the press and general public and if public access would play a significant positive role in the functioning of the process.[58] The Circuit Court also determined that the presentence investigation report was a separate part of the criminal process and that there was a major distinction between the presumptive openness of sentencing hearings and the assumed confidentiality of presentence reports. Finally, the Circuit Court found that

> disclosure would constitute a positive hindrance to the probation office's performance of its obligation to provide the sentencing court with a comprehensive analysis of the defendant's character.[59]

Therefore, a First Amendment right of access would not attach to presentence reports. In summary, sentencing hearings are presumed open but access to the presentence investigation report is closed.

Access to Other Hearings and Trials

Most attempts by media to access trials and court records involve criminal matters. However, there are a number of other court actions that warrant public and press attention. Juvenile and family court and civil trials have their own rules. Since September 11, 2001, interest in national security and deportation hearings has grown and access to those matters do not follow the principles described earlier.

Juvenile Courts and Family Law Courts

In chapter 2, we described different types of judicial process. There we noted that juvenile law covers accusations of delinquency, status offenses, and child welfare. Because the laws and rules in these matters vary by jurisdiction, mass communications practitioners must be fully acquainted with the laws and court rules in their area before attempting to gain access to juvenile proceedings and records.

Exhibit 7.2.   Illinois Juvenile Court Right of Access (705 ILCS 405/1-5 [1991]).

Rights of Parties to Proceedings
(6) The general public except for the news media and the victim shall be excluded from any hearing and, except for the persons specified in this Section only persons, including representatives of agencies and associations, who in the opinion of the court have a direct interest in the case or in the work of the court shall be admitted to the hearing. However, the court may, for the minor's safety and protection and for good cause shown, prohibit any person or agency present in court from further disclosing the minor's identity.

Except for divorce or dissolution of marriage cases, most hearings dealing with children are closed and the records sealed. Even in divorce cases, when matters are heard relating to the custody of children, some jurisdictions close court access to those not involved directly in the case. These laws are to protect the children, which is seen as a compelling governmental interest. Additionally, because the Supreme Court has not and usually does not address state juvenile court matters, there is no High Court decision addressing attempts by media to access juvenile or family courts. Therefore, state courts develop their own rules for dealing with cases and records involving children.

As a very general rule, those states that deal with children using the treatment philosophy described in chapter 2 do not permit public or press access to juvenile hearings or records. Those states whose legislators and constituents have rejected the treatment philosophy and do not believe young people can be redirected into proper social behavior tend to focus on punishment. Access to juvenile delinquency hearings and records in these states usually follow the same rules that are applied to criminal procedures. Illinois and Texas are examples of these two approaches. Their laws governing access to juvenile hearings are shown in Exhibits 7.2 and 7.3.

Each state has its own rules regarding these matters. However, in most jurisdictions access to court proceedings is restricted to those people connected with the case. Also, in most jurisdictions, records relating to adoption, parentage, custody, and guardianship are closed or sealed to protect the confidentiality of the minors involved. Not only will

Exhibit 7.3.   Texas Access to Juvenile Proceedings (Tex Fam Code, Title 3, Ch. 54, §54.08 [1997]).

Chapter 54 § 54.08 Judicial Proceedings, Public access to court hearings
(a) Except as provided by this section, the court shall open hearings under this title to the public unless the court, for good cause shown, determines that the public should be excluded. . .
(c) If a child is under the age of 14 at the time of the hearing, the court shall close the hearing to the public unless the court finds that the interests of the child or the interests of the public would be better served by opening the hearing to the public.

the records be sealed or in some way made inaccessible to public and press, but usually the state freedom of information laws will exempt such records from disclosure.

Most jurisdictions have expungement statutes that provide additional protection for the confidentiality of minors. Under these statutes individuals with juvenile records are able to apply to ask the court for an order expunging or destroying all law enforcement and court records. Usually this request may only be made after the juvenile becomes an adult and only after a specified length of time without additional offenses. Reporters should be aware of the procedure in their jurisdiction, including whether or not a record is kept of such expungement petitions and their results.

Public and Press Access to Civil Trials and Records: Presumed Open

The only place the U.S. Constitution mentions the concept of civil suits is in the Seventh Amendment, which says, in part,

> In suits at common law, where the value in controversy shall exceed twenty dollars, the right of trial by jury shall be preserved, and no fact tried by a jury shall be otherwise reexamined in any Court of the United States, than according to the rules of the common law.[60]

The U.S. Supreme Court has not addressed the issue of a Constitutional right of the public and press to attend civil trials or to access civil court records. However, each time a case has questioned access to civil trials in a Circuit Court of Appeals, the court has applied the reasoning developed for criminal trials in *Richmond Newspapers* and its progeny.[61] Using that reasoning the appellate courts have always found that the civil trial in question should be open. This pattern of ruling that civil trials are presumed open carries through both federal and state courts that have reviewed closure of civil courts.[62] However, it is not necessary to rely solely on the presumption of openness for criminal trials that the U.S. Supreme Court found was implicit in the First Amendment. Public and press rights of access to civil court proceedings are also found in several state constitutions and statutes, as well as state common law.[63]

In addition, the U.S. Supreme Court, in *Nixon v. Warner Communications,* has addressed a related matter. In that case, the High Court ruled on the common law rights to access exhibits subpoenaed from third parties in a civil case. The Court recognized a right to documents from civil trials saying,

> It is clear that the Courts of this country recognize a general right to inspect and copy public records and documents, including judicial records and documents.[64]

However the Court also noted that this right is limited and qualified, saying,

> It is uncontested, however, that the right to inspect and copy judicial records is not absolute. Every court has supervisory power over its own records and files, and access has

been denied where court files might have become a vehicle for improper purposes . . .
the decision as to access is one best left to the sound discretion of the trial court . . . to
be exercised in light of the relevant facts and circumstances of the particular case.[65]

Civil trials and court records are presumed open. But, to avoid confusion and
embarrassment, it is important for any mass communications practitioner, attempting to
enforce the common law concept of public access, to understand the difference between
the "open access to courts" provisions contained in most state constitutions and the concept of public access to proceedings and records. Open access to courts refers to the
common law principle that courts should be open to everyone who has a grievance recognized by the civil laws. This principle exists to allow citizens to seek redress of legal
wrongs through the courts. This is very different from the idea that the general public or
the press should have access to trials or court records involving matters in which they
are not parties. Just because a state's constitution, statutes, or court rules have an open
access to courts provision does not mean that public access to proceedings and records
can be assumed. Without specific language granting public access to proceedings and
records, such access may be left entirely to the discretion of each court within the jurisdiction. A table summarizing what matters are usually presumed open or closed is presented in Exhibit 7.4.

Special Hearings and 9-11

As is expressed in Exhibit 7.5, the United States is a nation of immigrants. Our national
motto is *E Pluribus Unum*, Latin for " From Many, One." From the Declaration of Independence until the *Chinese Exclusion Case* in 1889, immigration was open to virtually
all foreign nationals or their descendants. Today, the United States accepts more immigrants than all other nations of the world combined. Until approximately 1965, most
immigrants to the United States came from Europe and England. Today, most immigrants come from Asia and Latin America, and approximately 8% of the U.S. population is foreign-born.[66]

Deportation Hearings: Presumed Open Unless the Creppy
Directive Is Imposed

The *Chinese Exclusion Case* first recognized the government's broad sovereign
authority over immigration. But in that decision, the Supreme Court also "acknowledged
that Congress' power over immigration matters was limited by 'the Constitution
itself.'"[67]

The first general immigration act in the United States was passed in 1882. From that
time to the present, a distinction has been made between legal procedures that close
entry, called "exclusion" hearings, and "deportation" hearings. **Deportation hearings**
have historically been open to the public. In fact, since 1965, Immigration and Naturalization Service regulations have explicitly required deportation proceedings to be "pre-
sumptively open."[68] These hearings are open because the people involved have usually
already begun to behave as citizens or residents of the United States. The U.S. Supreme

Exhibit 7.4. Presumption of Openness.

	Presumed Open √	**Presumed Closed** ×
Prior to filing of "charge document(s)"	× Report of Crime × Possible identification of suspect(s) × Investigation × Surveillance & wire-tapping (with or without warrant) × Search & seizure (with or without warrant) × Line-up or show-up × Arrest (with or without warrant) × Gathering, testing, and processing of evidence	
Subsequent to filing of "charge document(s)"	× Grand jury proceedings × Filing of indictment, prosecutor's complaint or information × Arrest and processing of accused √ First or initial appearance √ Setting of bond √ Determinations of indigency & determination or appointment of counsel × Preliminary hearings if not charged by indictment (note exceptions for "California style" preliminary hearings.) √ Arraignment × Discovery × Motions √ Motion hearings (Note: Most are open, but some are closed. For example, motions to suppress are closed at defendant's request.) √ Pretrial docket settings and trial readiness calls √ Waiver(s) of Sixth Amendment rights (speedy trial, public trial, jury trial) × Plea bargaining process √ Plea bargain acceptance	
Trial	√ Jury or bench Trial	
Posttrial (If convicted)	× Revocation of bond & taking into custody × Presentencing investigation & report √ Sentencing trial or hearing × Mittimus to custody of sheriff or warden × Executions in capital punishment cases	

Court recognized this status in its 1982 decision in *Landon v. Plasencia* where it said, "once an alien gains admission to our country and begins to develop the ties that go with permanent residence, his constitutional status changes accordingly."[69] Justice Murphy's concurring opinion in *Bridges v. Wixon*, which was later adopted by the full court, said,

Exhibit 7.5.   New Colossus.

The first lines of the poem titled the "New Colossus" inscribed at the base of the Statue of Liberty in New York Harbor read:

Bring me your tired, your poor, your huddled masses yearning to breath free, The retched refuse of your teaming shores, Send These. I lift my lamp beside the Golden Door.

∎

> Once an alien lawfully enters and resides in this country he becomes invested with the rights guaranteed by the Constitution to all people within our borders. Such rights include those protected by the First and Fifth Amendments and by the due process clause of the Fourteenth Amendment. None of these provisions acknowledges any distinction between citizens and resident aliens.[70]

Although a deportee possesses vested due process rights, non-citizens seeking entry to the United States stand on a different footing. They (a) have no ties to the United States, (b) are therefore not considered to be persons within the meaning of the Fifth Amendment, (c) have no right to due process, and thus (d) "(w)hatever process the government affords them, no matter how minimal, illusory, or secret, is due process of law, beyond the scope of judicial review."[71]

The clear distinction between exclusion proceedings where participants have no rights to due process and deportation proceedings whose participants have such rights was blurred in 1996. In that year, Congress passed the Illegal Immigration Reform and Immigrant Responsibility Act and changed the nomenclature of "exclusion" and "deportation" proceedings, referring to both as **removal hearings**.[72] The rights of deportees were further eviscerated following the September 11, 2001, terrorist attacks on the World Trade Center and Pentagon. On September 21, 2001, Chief Immigration Judge Creppy issued a directive to all U.S. immigration judges requiring closure of **special interest** cases. The **Creppy directive** requires that all proceedings in such cases be closed to the press and public, including family members and friends. The record of the proceeding is not to be disclosed to anyone except a deportee's attorney or representative. If the file contains classified information it may not even be released to the deportee's attorney. This restriction covers all information including even confirming or denying whether such a case is on the docket or is scheduled for a hearing. Under the Creppy directive, the Office of the Chief Immigration Judge, under the direction of then Attorney General Ashcroft, designates cases to be "special interest cases." Those cases are conducted in secret and are closed to the public and press.[73]

Sixth Circuit Review of Creppy Directive

The first challenge to the Creppy directive is described in *Detroit Free Press v. Ashcroft*. Rabih Haddad was scheduled for a deportation hearing for allegedly overstaying his tourist visa. Haddad's attorney, his family, several newspapers, and Congressman John Conyers all tried to attend Haddad's hearing. On the day of the hearing, without prior notice, security guards informed them that the hearing was closed. The Department of Justice designated Haddad's case as a "special interest case" because an Islamic charity he operates was suspected of supplying funds to terrorist organizations. Haddad was denied bail, detained, and remains in the government's custody. Subsequent hearings were closed to the public and press, and the deportee was transferred to Chicago for additional proceedings.[74]

Three separate suits, including one by the media, sought a declaratory judgment against the Creppy directive. The media suit charged the directive violates their First Amendment right of access to deportation proceedings. They asked for an order opening the proceedings and granting access to transcripts of previous proceedings.[75] The U.S. District Court granted the media requests and ruled that blanket closures of deportation hearings in "special interest" cases are unconstitutional.

The Department of Justice appealed the district court's decision to the U.S. Court of Appeals for the Sixth Circuit. The government argued that it had plenary authority over both substantive immigration issues, such as who may enter the United States, and nonsubstantive issues, such as deportations. The Court of Appeals disagreed and found that in nonsubstantive issues, like the deportation hearing for Haddad,

> where a non-substantive immigration law involving a constitutional right is at issue, the Supreme Court has always recognized the importance of that constitutional right, never deferring to an assertion of plenary authority.[76]

Furthermore, the Sixth Circuit found that the media plaintiffs had a First Amendment right of access. Once there is such a right, government closure of judicial proceedings can only be defended using the principles from *Globe Newspaper.*

> Under the standard articulated in *Globe Newspaper*, a governmental action . . . that curtails a First Amendment right of access "in order to inhibit the disclosure of sensitive information" must be supported by a showing "that denial is necessitated by a compelling governmental interest," and is narrowly tailored to serve that interest.[77]

The court agreed that preventing terrorism is a compelling government interest but ruled the Creppy doctrine is so broad it violates the requirement that closure orders be narrowly tailored to serve the government's interest.

> The Creppy directive does not apply to 'a small segment of particularly dangerous' information, but a broad, indiscriminate range of information, including information likely to be entirely innocuous. Similarly, no definable standards used to determine whether a case is of 'special interest' have been articulated. Nothing in the Creppy directive counsels that it is limited to "a small segment of particularly dangerous individuals." In fact, the Government so much as argues that certain non-citizens known to have no links to terrorism will be designated "special interest" cases. Supposedly, closing a more targeted class would allow terrorists to draw inferences from which hearings are open and which are closed.[78]

The court concluded by expressing its commitment to democratic values and First Amendment rights. It then affirmed the district court order and required that the hearing be open for public scrutiny.[79]

Third Circuit Review of the Creppy Directive

In a case almost identical to *Detroit Free Press*, the U.S. Court of Appeals for the Third Circuit, in a two-to-one decision, reached a completely different result. In *New Jersey Media Group, Inc. v. Ashcroft* the Federal District Court in New Jersey granted a media plaintiffs' request for an order enjoining the Attorney General from denying access to "special interest" deportation hearings.

As they had done in *Detroit Free Press v. Ashcroft*, the government appealed this decision. The U.S. Circuit Court of Appeals for the Third Circuit heard this appeal. The Third Circuit agreed that the principles of *Richmond Newspapers* and *Globe Newspaper* should be applied but when applying those principles they reached a radically different decision than had the Sixth Circuit. The Third Circuit found that there was no First Amendment right to attend deportation proceedings.[80] The Third Circuit simply bowed, without questioning, to the government's experience and allowed some deportation cases to be labeled "special interest" cases, which could be closed forever from public or press scrutiny. In its decision the Third Circuit noted that they were aware of the dangers associated with granting the executive branch authority to essentially abrogate constitutional liberty but said they were "unable to conclude that openness plays a positive role in special interest deportation hearings at a time when our nation is faced with threats of such profound and unknown dimension."[81] In effect the court granted the government authority to violate the First and Sixth Amendment because of their fear of terrorist threats. The court also noted "although there may be no judicial remedy for these closures, there is, as always, the powerful check of political accountability on Executive discretion."[82] Obviously, there can be no check on executive discretion when the executive branch operates in secrecy and the public is denied information about its actions.

Although the Sixth Circuit had noted that "democracies die behind closed doors" and that "The Framers of the First Amendment 'did not trust any government to separate the true from the false for us.' They protected the people against secret government,"[83] the U.S. Supreme Court denied certiorari to North Jersey Media Group.[84] In summary, today the Department of Justice may, completely at its discretion, declare a deportation hearing a "special interest" matter and thereby close the proceedings and records to any public or media access.

Expansion of the Creppy Directive

Limitations on media access to deportation matters has been expanded further by an interim Department of Justice rule that "authorizes immigration judges to issue **protective orders** and seal documents relating to law enforcement or national security information in the course of immigration proceedings."[85] The rules authorize an immigration judge to restrain deportees and their attorneys from disclosing specified information for an indefinite period of time. This means the protective orders remain in effect until they are "vacated by the immigration judge," and "any information submitted subject to the protective order . . . shall remain under seal as part of the administrative record."[86] This rule appears to violate prior U.S. Supreme Court decisions that have held that prohibitions against disclosure for indefinite periods are unconstitutional when applied to one's own information and testimony.[87]

The absolute secrecy of these hearings is guaranteed by a combination of an indefinite protective order and the requirement for all participants to sign a **memorandum of understanding** that is enforced with the court's power to punish perjury as a criminal offense. This procedure was described in *U.S. v. Lindh.*

In that case, the government was prosecuting the defendant for allegedly contributing services to al Qaeda. The defendant, through his right of discovery, requested reports of interviews with detainees that contained information he could use in his defense. The government requested a "protective order" regarding detainee interview reports. In effect, the government wanted assurance that the information in the reports would not be released by the defendant or his attorney. In its review of the government's request for a protective order, the district court described the scope and significance of government procedures to guarantee the secrecy of its report,

> (I)t appears that the government's interests can be adequately protected and defendant's concerns accommodated by requiring defendant's investigators or expert witnesses to sign a memorandum of understanding. . . . By signing such a "memorandum of understanding" a defense investigator or expert would declare under penalty of perjury under the laws of the United States that she or he had (I) read and understood the protective order pertaining to these unclassified documents and materials and (II) agreed to be bound by the terms of the protective order, would remain binding during, and after the conclusion of these proceedings. Defendant, by counsel, would then be required to file, ex parte and under seal, any such memorandum of understanding promptly, and prior to the disclosure of any unclassified protected information to the investigator or expert.[88]

It is difficult to image a more thorough or effective procedure to deny public and media access to information about the actions of government. However, the next section demonstrates that our government has a more vivid imagination than most mass communications practitioners. It describes an even more effective denial of media access to government information.

Secret Courts: FISA and the "Un-Patriotic Act"

Beginning in the early 1970s, the United States established secret courts. The special interest deportation hearings may be closed to the public and the media and their records may not be accessible. But, the secret courts are so inaccessible that even their meeting times and locations are not revealed. Furthermore, they simply have no records to request. The media are completely denied access to these courts and the public has no way to be informed about the actions and procedures of these courts. Here we briefly describe the history of these courts and what little is publicly known about their function.

The Fourth Amendment to the U.S. Constitution guarantees citizens the right to be free from unreasonable search and prohibits search or arrest warrants without probable cause established before a court. It says,

> The right of the people to be secure in their persons, houses, papers, and effects, against unreasonable searches and seizures, shall not be violated, and no Warrants shall issue, but upon probable cause, supported by Oath or affirmation, and particularly describing the place to be searched, and the persons or things to be seized.[89]

The secret or special courts were created to circumvent the Fourth Amendment requirement for the government to secure search warrants based on probable cause. Their sole function appears to be to issue search warrants for electronic eavesdropping.

Throughout our history, both the U.S. Congress and state legislatures have avoided or circumvented the Fourth Amendment requirements in order to provide stronger crime control and national security. Since September 11, 2001, the Department of Justice has requested and Congress has passed significant legislation in the name of national security. Much of this legislation has come at tremendous cost to individual liberty and to public and media access to information about our government.

The first step toward our current special court system began with the passage of the Omnibus Crime Bill in 1968. The bill was designed to assist the FBI and Department of Justice in their efforts to control organized crime. It authorized electronic eavesdropping or "wiretapping." The bill did contain a provision that specifically required the government to secure warrants based on probable cause and "set forth the detailed and particularized application necessary to obtain such an order as well as carefully circumscribed conditions for its use."[90] However, Supreme Court decisions have noted that the requirement for a warrant is limited to investigations of domestic crime. The FBI and Department of Justice, because they are agencies of the executive branch, are also charged with protecting national security. Supreme Court decisions have specifically noted that there is no requirement for a warrant or for a demonstration of probable cause if an agency of the executive branch is investigating a foreign intelligence matter.[91]

The different requirements for permission to conduct electronic eavesdropping in domestic crime and foreign intelligence matters are explained in detail in *United States v. United States District Court*. The Supreme Court's decision in that case also lays the foundation for the creation of the secret courts.[92] The case involved the bombing of an office of the CIA in Ann Arbor, Michigan. The Department of Justice used an unauthorized wiretap in the investigation of the crime and the Supreme Court was eventually called on to evaluate the propriety of the government action. The Court framed the issue as "Whether safeguards other than prior authorization by magistrate would satisfy the Fourth Amendment in a situation involving national security."[93] In its decision, the Court first explained the importance of protecting the First and Fourth Amendment rights of people who may be targeted for surveillance for their unorthodox political beliefs and then held that surveillance without prior authorization by a neutral magistrate was unlawful in a domestic situation.[94]

In dicta the court offered possible solutions to the problem confronted by government agencies investigating domestic crimes and national security matters. Specifically, the Court suggested that Congress could enact legislation based on a sliding scale of Fourth Amendment protections to be applied depending on the purpose of the surveillance. The Court suggested that surveillance of ordinary crime should receive full Fourth Amendment protection. Surveillance involving domestic security may receive less protection and surveillances where foreign powers are involved should receive even less protection. The Supreme Court then suggested the creation of a "special court" to hear cases involving domestic security and foreign powers. The Court said,

> It may be that Congress, for example, would judge that the application and affidavit showing probable cause need not follow the exact requirements of [The Omnibus Crime Control Act, based on Fourth Amendment standards] but should allege other circumstances more appropriate to domestic security cases; that the request for prior court authorization could, in sensitive cases, be made to any member of a specially designated court . . . and that the time and reporting requirements need not be so strict. . . .[emphasis added][95]

Congress accepted the suggestion and passed the **Foreign Intelligence Surveillance Act (FISA)** in 1978.[96] FISA created a system of "specially designated courts" whose function is to issue warrants for surveillances involving domestic and national security.

"Secret Courts" in the United States: No Access by Public or Media

Based on the guidance from the Supreme Court in *United States v. United States District Court*, the Foreign Intelligence Surveillance Act prohibits wiretapping without prior judicial approval when the target of the surveillance is a U.S. citizen, a lawfully present resident alien, or any incorporated or unincorporated domestic organization. The act also provides civil and criminal penalties for violations. However, there is no requirement to show probable cause to investigate anyone, regardless of his or her citizenship or residency status, if that person is believed to be engaged in intelligence operation for a foreign power or acting as an agent for a foreign power. Further, there is no requirement for probable cause for surveillance of anyone associated with a "secret group" subject to National Security Agency investigation.

Under this act, warrants for electronic surveillance are obtained from a special court comprised of judges who are selected by the chief justice of the Supreme Court. These judges are not subject to public appointment and, unlike other federal judges, their appointment is not subject to the advice and consent of the Senate. This court convenes in closed hearings, sees no one but prosecution and government applicants, issues only ex parte orders, does not publish its decisions, and no private person or media representative is permitted to observe its procedures. "Between 1979 and 2001, reports to Congress show that the FISA courts approved, without modification, 14,031 of 14,036 surveillance applications."[97]

The power of the FISA courts was expanded by the Uniting and Strengthening America by Providing Appropriate Tools Required to Intercept and Obstruct Terrorism Act of 2001. This act, also known as the USA PATRIOT Act, includes a provision permitting surveillance whenever the FBI certifies that a significant purpose of the investigation is to obtain foreign intelligence materials.[98] According to some commentators, this provision is now being used to obtain warrants from the secret FISA courts when the primary purpose is criminal investigation, not intelligence gathering.[99] In the final analysis, we now have a special judicial system that exists solely to approve surveillance of U.S. citizens and resident aliens alike, which is not subject to any public or press scrutiny.

Practice Notes

We present two practice notes. The first offers practical suggestions for reporters seeking access to trials and other judicial proceedings. The second explains legal limitations on the efforts of public relations practitioners attempting to influence trial outcome or preserve the reputation of a client involved in litigation.

Gaining Access to Trials

Establish Rapport with Courthouse Personnel

It may be helpful to remember that whenever you seek access to either court records or court procedures, you will need the cooperation of the courthouse staff. As a journalist it is expected that you think your job is important and that you have values associated with your profession. But when you cover a court, you are entering a world with somewhat different values and expectations. To secure information and access, you need to be aware of their rules. People who work in a courthouse, from the clerks and secretaries to the judges, are all busy and their jobs are important. A media request for information or records access may seem inconsequential to a clerk who has just dealt with a mother who lost custody of her children or a lawyer preparing to defend a client from imprisonment. We have heard numerous courthouse conversations about reporters and almost none of them were remotely flattering. What we suggest here may seem like common sense but following these suggestions would improve the behavior of most reporters covering the judicial system. Following them will also improve your chances of securing the information you need to do your job.

First, learn to talk the talk. Any reporter assigned to cover the legal system must first become familiar with the terminology and the court rules of his or her jurisdiction. You cannot object to a court action or even request a court record without knowing what to call it. Also, you are more likely to get information and cooperation from people if you know their titles and names. Understand that judges have virtually unlimited power in many courthouses, so always address them with deference and as "Your Honor" when in court and as "Judge" when outside court.

Second, learn to walk the walk. Your demeanor, appearance, and conduct will mark you as someone who "fits in" the courthouse or as an outsider. If you spend time in a courthouse you will notice two dominant groups of people: the court staff including judges, lawyers, and clerks, and those outside the system including criminal defendants and "observers." The court staff is typically given access, courtesy, and assistance not afforded the outsiders. The staff also behaves and dresses in ways that "mark" them as part of the system. If you model their behavior and appearance you are more likely to be treated well.

No matter how rushed, frustrated, or even aggravated about your assignment you may be, always be friendly, courteous, and respectful. Dress well, and be well groomed, especially if you are attending a court proceeding. Business attire is always correct. If you have a suit, wear it to cover court proceedings. A white shirt and tie with black trousers or conservative skirt and blouse is acceptable. Women should not wear high heels, short skirts, or low-cut tops. Navy, gray, and black are always good conservative colors to wear for court. Do not wear jeans and try to find loafers or oxford shoes rather than tennis shoes. If your organization has shirts or blazers with a company logo, these are also appropriate. Beware of streaked hair or hair colors not found in nature and try to cover any tattoos or unusual body piercings. Many judges simply refuse to admit people to court wearing shorts or jeans and some even refuse to admit women wearing slacks. Simply put, there is no such thing as too conservative. This may seem extreme but anything that puts you outside the norms of courtroom behavior will make your job more difficult.

Learn the court's security and attendance rules. Most courthouses today have a clearance system that makes airport security seem casual. In order to preserve decorum, many judges do not permit more observers in their courtroom than the seating will accommodate. That means if you are assigned to cover a trial you will have to pass through security in time to get to the designated courtroom before the seats fill.

Well in advance of any court hearing you need to cover, find your way to the courthouse and reconnoiter. Know how long it takes to park and get through security, and whether you need to get a press pass issued specifically by court security. Be prepared to have your fingerprints, photograph, and ID taken. You may not be permitted to carry metal objects, including your computer, so on your first trip to court, take only your notebook, pen, photo ID, press pass, and minimal keys. It may be helpful to have a neck ID or badge.

Prior to any hearing you may cover, it is helpful to learn how the docket is handled, when it is printed and posted each day, and where. If there is a system for e-mailing the docket, get on the list. Find out what requirements they may have for accessing or copying dockets and court files. What are the costs for copying per page, how long does it take, do they allow verbal requests, or must requests be in writing? Knowing all of these procedures makes you look like you belong and will help you get the information you need when you need it.

Once you are comfortable with the terminology and the procedures, get to know the people involved. Their cooperation will be essential. Ask about any problems reporters have had with any currently sitting judge. Learn the specific nature of the problems, if and how they were resolved. Learn the judge's names, their generally assigned courtrooms, and the types of cases they usually hear.

Ask the clerk and/or assistants for the names of the judges, their secretaries, assistants, or reporters. If at all possible, take some time to "hang out" in the clerk's office and see how the clerk handles the legal secretaries, attorneys, judges, and general public members who come in with questions or papers to be filed. This may take time, but find out who actually does the most work in the clerk's office and who is the most knowledgeable and helpful. This personal work on your part and development of a good rapport with the clerk's office will be a great asset to you in your future reporting. If judges who appear to be on break or seem to have some free time to chat with the clerk personnel, come in to the clerk's office, introduce yourself, or ask one of the clerk's assistants to introduce you to the judge. Obviously, do not interrupt conversations, but observe how the judge treats the staff and how they interact with him or her.

Ask if there is a time when you could meet the judges' assistants, secretaries, and/or court reporters. Be sure you concentrate on times that are convenient for them, not for you. You might also ask to meet the judges, when they are in chambers and are in a long recess or lull in the court docket.

Discuss your position, your employment, your assignment, and then ask the judge how she or he interprets the *Richmond Newspapers* presumption of openness of criminal trials and whether and under what circumstances they have had to close proceedings. Also, inquire about the openness of civil trials and hearings, and of juvenile cases. Listen and take notes, don't argue, but ask for clarification of any of the situations that might have arisen where the judge closed a trial or hearing. Ask the judge how you might proceed should you be in his or her courtroom when one of the parties makes a motion for closure, and as a reporter you feel the proceedings should be open. Listen and take copious notes. Ask how the judge wants you to proceed should you wish to obtain his or her permission to bring cameras and other recording devices or equipment to a hearing or trial. Discuss the local rules, and any cases and problems she or he may have had in the past and how they were resolved, or how they might be resolved in the future. Be gracious and thank the judge for his or her assistance and suggestions.

If you can find the time, attend a few hearings or trials you do not have to cover. Be there often enough that you are perceived by the courthouse staff to be a regular or court watcher. Meet and talk with the bailiffs, security staff, marshals, and/or sheriff and deputies about any crowd and/or media control problems they have had, and how these are handled. This information will help you when special circumstances arise. Ask their advice on how to proceed to get the story, but stay unobtrusive and out of the way. Most of the time events in court are routine and take long periods of time waiting for court to convene. Your patience and the rapport you build and support with your regular presence, reasonable attitude, and polite behavior toward all court personnel will pay off when the "big" case occurs or when you need some preferential treatment.

Be aware that in many jurisdictions, particularly small towns or county courthouses, there is a ritual among court staff of exchanging token holiday gifts. We realize some journalists may see these exchanges as unethical but it is impossible for a journalist covering a courthouse to function without asking for assistance from the court staff, and giving a box of cookies, candies, or fruit as a "thank you" for help is an excellent rapport enhancer. Failing to at least offer a sincere gesture of thanks may cost you future help. Judges cannot accept gifts, but leaving a basket of "goodies" with the judge's administrative assistant and/or court reporter will be appreciated. Rest assured that the judge will get some of your thank-you gift as well.

What To Do If/When Confronted by a "Closure Order"

First, be prepared. For example, ask your editor, supervisor, or someone who has covered the courts in your area if there have been any court closures in the past. Learn the circumstances of those closures and the outcome of any objections to closure. It would be helpful to find the transcripts of any hearings on closure orders so you will know what motions worked and what failed. The transcripts will allow you to learn the wording of any objections to closure orders. Additionally, it would be wise to ask your editor or supervisor if your organization has counsel on retainer and whether you should meet him or her.

If there is a standard procedure used by your organization for dealing with court closure, get a copy of the suggested steps and wording of objections to closure. Carry that procedure with you along with contact information for your attorney. If you are the least bit shy, practice the steps and the wording before a mirror, with a steady, firm, loud voice, until you are satisfied that you can stand in a crowded courtroom and speak confidently, but politely, to address the court.

If you are in court when one of the litigants makes a motion to close the hearing or trial, listen carefully as the motion is made. What reasons are they giving, what is the response by the other litigant's counsel, what is the judge's response and/or questions? Is the motion being set for hearing on another day or time, which will give you time to alert your editor, supervisor, and legal department? Does it appear that the judge is taking everything under consideration and is conducting the hearing on this motion for closure at this time?

If you have established the rapport with the court and this particular judge, proceed as she or he suggested you should in your initial meeting. If you have not met with this judge and it appears he or she is about to summarize findings supporting closure you have two courses of action. Wait until it appears all the arguments on the motion have been made by the attorneys, and at that point you may either continue waiting to see what the judge's findings of fact, and actual ruling will be on the record. Your second option is to interpose an objection at the end of all the arguments by counsel, but before the judge announces his or her decision on closure. To be recognized and relate your objection to closure of the court proceedings stand and/or raise your hand, introduce yourself, and state your objection. If your organization does not provide such guidance we recommend the statement produced by the Gannett Company. It is a straightforward and simple request for a continuance to permit your organization's attorney time to object to the closure. That statement is reproduced as Exhibit 7.6.

Don't be argumentative; be deferent and respectful. Use phrases like, "with all due respect to the Court," "thank you, Your Honor," "may I ask for clarification of your order, Your Honor." Always remember that you are addressing a person invested with one third of the sovereign power of your state or of the United States. Your exercise of your qualified implied First Amendment right of access to court hearings and trials is extremely important, but so is your freedom from being jailed for contempt of court. Never laugh, and never swear. Be assertive but not arrogant. Being free to exercise your rights from prison is not an appropriate goal at this juncture, and being jailed for contempt will not vindicate your freedom of speech and press. Immediately, outside of the

Exhibit 7.6.   Court Statement (used with permission of Gannett Co., Inc).

Your Honor, I'd like to address the Court on the Motion to close the courtroom. My name is _____ and I am a reporter for _____. It is my understanding that a hearing must precede your decision to close this proceeding, and that I and the newspaper have the right to present arguments at that hearing. If you will grant a reasonable time, I'd like to contact my editor and the newspaper's lawyer, so that we may present our arguments properly. May I have that time, please, your Honor. Thank you very much.

If the court denies the recess, continue as follows:

If the court will not take a brief recess, then, on behalf of the (your newspaper), I request that my objection and a brief statement of the legal issues be made a part of the record in the case.

courtroom, phone your editor, supervisor, and/or legal counsel and explain what has happened. Either there will be a recess, and your organization's attorney will need to be present to intervene and argue for access to this hearing or trial, or your counsel may take other steps to seek reconsideration of the closure order, or to begin an appeal.

Litigation Public Relations

One of the fastest growing areas of public relations practice is litigation public relations. Both lawyers and public relations firms have recognized the "court of public opinion" can be as important as the courtroom itself.[100] Many people believe anyone charged with a crime is probably guilty and a similar majority seems to believe corporations who are sued by consumer groups are always engaged in wrongful behavior. Furthermore, with the growth of Court TV, cable news, and tabloid journalism, it is not uncommon for a high-profile criminal defendant or a large corporation to be so victimized by pretrial publicity they cannot locate a truly impartial jury. In this environment, "smart lawyers have little choice but to engage in litigation public relations to provide their clients with every advantage."[101] Of course, good public relations practices can help anyone, including a criminal defendant or civil litigant, address false accusations but it is not our purpose here to make recommendations about how public relations tactics should be used. However, we do want to ensure that any reader who practices litigation public relations is aware of the legal limitations on what they may or may not do.

As a practical matter, anyone engaged in litigation public relations should realize that plaintiffs and, in particular, prosecutors have a significant advantage. The party who initiates charges has the opportunity to describe investigations and/or to make accusations before a complaint is filed or charges brought. During the time before any legal actions are begun there are few, if any, legal restrictions on what information may be given to the press. However, even during these pretrial stages inflammatory publicity can lead to prejudice that might cost your attorney's client his or her case.[102] As soon as complaints or charges are filed significant legal restrictions on public relations can be imposed. Because defendants often do not even know they are parties to a legal proceeding until they are arrested or served, they may not have any opportunity to publicly respond to the publicity directed against them.

Judges in most jurisdictions are free to issue restraining orders or non-disclosure orders and otherwise control the conduct of attorneys, parties, and witnesses in trials and pretrial proceedings. A litigation public relations practitioner representing any of these trial participants will be governed by the restraining orders and would be well advised to honor the limitations imposed by the court.

In addition to specific orders issued by a judge in a trial, there are some general rules that must be followed by anyone working for an attorney. In most jurisdictions, these same rules would apply to the attorneys' clients and to witnesses who will be called by the attorneys. Under the doctrine of *respondeat superior*, if you are a public relations practitioner hired by an attorney and you violate the rules of attorney conduct, your attorney employer can be held liable for your misconduct. Obviously, this is not a great way to endear yourself to your client.

In 1991, the U.S. Supreme Court reviewed a Nevada rule prohibiting attorneys from making extra-judicial statements to the press. Although the Court ruled the specific Nevada rule void because it was too vague, the Court did state that its decision did "not call into question the constitutionality of other States' prohibitions upon an attorney's speech that have a substantial likelihood of materially prejudicing an adjudicative proceeding."[103] Simply put, rules prohibiting attorneys or their agents from attempting to influence potential jurors or witnesses through public relations are constitutional if they are clearly stated.

Most states either use the rules governing trial publicity adopted by the American Bar Association (ABA) or some variation of the ABA rules. We therefore focus our discussion on the publicity that is prohibited by those rules. Although the ABA rules do provide useful guidelines, you should consult counsel in your local area to identify specific rules that apply there. The ABA rules say:

> A lawyer shall not make an extrajudicial statement that a reasonable person would
> expect to be disseminated by means of public communication if the lawyer knows or
> reasonably should know that it will have a substantial likelihood of materially preju-
> dicing an adjudicative proceeding.[104]

For the purpose of the rules, an adjudicative proceeding is any civil matter that may go to a jury trial or any criminal matter that could result in incarceration of the defendant.

The kind of statements the rules say would materially prejudice a trial or hearing include the kind of information that might lead a potential juror to form an opinion about the defendant's guilt or liability. The prohibited topics listed in the left column of Exhibit 7.7 seem reasonably obvious. Comments about witness reliability, lie detector tests, opinions about guilt, inadmissible evidence, and pleas would all lead a potential juror to form opinions about the proper trial outcome. One prohibited comment seems worthy of particular note. It is improper for a lawyer or anyone representing a lawyer to say that a defendant has been charged with a crime unless that statement also says that all defendants

Exhibit 7.7.   Permitted and Prohibited Statements in Litigation PR (ABA Model Rule 3.6).

When talking about a civil matter that could be tried by a jury or a criminal matter that could result in incarceration

Do NOT talk about	You may state, *without elaboration*
The character, credibility, reputation, or criminal record of a witness or the defendant	The general nature of the claim or defense
The results of any test, including a lie-detector test or whether anyone has agreed or refused to take a test	Information contained in a public record
Any opinion about the guilt or innocence of a defendant or suspect	The general scope of any investigation in progress
Any information that a lawyer reasonably believes will not be admissible at trial	The name of the defendant—UNLESS it is prohibited by law
Any statement that a defendant has been charged with a crime UNLESS you also say that all defendants are presumed innocent	A request for assistance in obtaining evidence Schedule and result of any hearings A warning when there is reason to believe there is a public danger
In a criminal matter—any plea agreement or the possibility of a plea	In a criminal matter only: 1. Name, residence, occupation, and family status of the accused 2. Information needed to apprehend an accused at large 3. If an arrest has been made, the time and place of arrest 4. Identity of investigating and arresting agency and length of investigation.

are presumed innocent until proven guilty. This requirement is imposed because it has been observed that most people do not assume innocence. In fact, most people seem to believe incorrectly that a person charged or indicted by a grand jury is guilty.

The kind of information that can be used in litigation public relations is limited to straightforward statements of fact with two exceptions. If it is necessary to protect the public safety, statements may include a warning. For example, the police can describe a suspect and say that he is armed in order to help citizens protect themselves from danger. Also both sides in criminal and civil matters are permitted to ask for assistance obtaining evidence. You could, for example, give the time and location of a traffic accident and ask that any witnesses contact you. Some jurisdictions also permit lawyers or their agents to respond to publicity that might prejudice their client.[105] The provisions permitting a response to harmful publicity almost always requires that the person responding have done nothing to encourage the publicity to which he or she is responding.

Finally, journalists covering trials should note that these restrictions on communication are often imposed on virtually everyone who has accurate information about a trial. Most jurisdictions prohibit press contact by court personnel, clerks, bailiffs, secretaries, and court reporters and many also restrict communication by attorneys, parties, and witnesses. As a practical matter, what this means is that very often the only people willing to talk to journalists about a trial either do not have any useful information or violate the law themselves. In a combined 32 years of legal practice we have never read a news report about a trial that did not contain a significant factual error. The dearth of informed and honorable sources may have something to do with this.

Magic Words and Phrases

Adversarial judicial system	Presentence investigation
Blanket statutory closure rule	Prior restraint
California-style preliminary hearings	Procedural due process
Common law right of access to records	Protective orders
Creppy directive	Redacting
Deportation hearings	Removal hearings
FISA courts	Restraining order
Gag order	Restrictive order
Inquisitorial judicial system	Shield laws
Memorandum of understanding	Special interest cases
Muzzle order	Suppression hearings
Narrowly tailored	Trial closure order
Nondisclosure order	Witness protection laws

Suggested Cases to Read and Brief

Bridges v. California, 314 U.S. 252 (1941)
Bridges v. Wixon, 316 U.S. 135 (1945)
Butterworth v. Smith, 494 U.S. 624 (1990)
Chinese Exclusion Case, 130 U.S. 581 (1889)
Craig v. Harney, 331 U.S. 367 (1947)
Dennis v. United States, 341 U.S. 494 (1951)
Detroit Free Press v. Ashcroft, 303 F.3d 681 (6th Cir.2002)
Gannett Co. v. DePasquale, 443 U.S. 368 (1979)
Globe Newspaper Co. v. Superior Court, 457 U.S. 596 (1982)

Illinois v. Abbott & Assoc., Inc., 460 U.S. 557 (1983)

Landmark Communications, Inc. v. Virginia, 435 U.S. 829 (1978)

Landon v. Plasencia, 459 U.S. 21 (1982)

Near v. Minnesota, 283 U.S. 697 (1931)

Nebraska Press Association v. Stuart, 427 U.S. 539 (1976)

New York Times v. United States, 403 U.S. 713 (1971)

Nixon v. Warner Communications, Inc., 435 U.S. 589 (1978)

North Jersey Media Group, Inc. v. Ashcroft, 308 F.3d 198 (3d Cir. 2002)

Press-Enterprise Co. v. Superior Court, 478 U.S. 1 (1986)

Press-Enterprise Co. v. Superior Court of California, 464 U.S. 501 (1984)

Richmond Newspapers, Inc. v. Virginia, 448 U.S. 555 (1980)

Schenck v. United States, 249 U.S. 47 (1919)

Smith, Judge v. Daily Mail Publishing Co., 443 U.S. 97 (1979)

Times Mirror v. United States, 873 F.2d 1210 (9th Cir.1989)

United States v. Lindh, 494 F.Supp.2d 739 (A.D.E.D.V. 2002)

United States v. Corbitt, 879 F. 2d 224 (7th Cir.1989)

Waller v. Georgia, 467 U.S. 39 (1984)

Williams v. New York, 337 U.S. 241 (1949)

Wood v. Georgia, 370 U.S. 375 (1962)

Questions for Discussion

1. Why do you believe the United States adopted an adversarial rather than an inquisitorial judicial system? Describe advantages for both systems.

2. The U.S. judicial system places extraordinary emphasis on due process. Are there other ways to ensure a fair trial or to guarantee that justice is done? Does due process guarantee that the truth is always found in a trial?

3. Many states have laws protecting child witnesses and witnesses who are victims of sexual assault. The government interests for these acts are to protect the witness from embarrassment and harassment and to encourage witnesses so that criminals may be prosecuted. If you were a judge, how would you protect the government interests while at the same time guaranteeing that any court closure was narrowly tailored to meet the government interest?

4. Often, police departments will request that courts be closed during the testimony of undercover police officers. The government interest expressed is to protect the officers from retaliation by criminals or to protect ongoing investigations. If you were a reporter covering a trial where a motion was made to close the trial for the protection of an undercover police witness, how would you react? If you were the judge, how would you balance the government's interest against the implied and qualified First Amendment right of the press to cover a trial of public interest?

5. Why do you believe "gag orders" prohibiting media from publishing information are unconstitutional while restraining orders prohibiting court personnel and trial participants from talking to media are constitutional? If restraining orders are

constitutional where do you think reporters get their information? Are available sources reliable and well informed in trials where a restraining order has been entered?

6. Why are grand juries presumed closed while trials are generally presumed to be open?

7. Why are California preliminary hearings presumed open while other forms of preliminary hearings are presumed closed?

8. Why are sentencing hearings generally open but presentence investigation reports are almost always sealed from the public and press?

9. If you were a U.S. legislator, how could you fashion a law that would both protect the First and Fourth Amendment rights of citizens while protecting national security in a time of terrorist threat? Is the FISA court and the closure of "special interest" deportation hearings a good idea? Why or why not?

10. If statements about evidence, confessions, and prejudicial information are prohibited by the ABA Model Rules, how do litigants in "high-profile" cases manage to get so much information in the media? Also, how do you think the media gets as much information about evidence as they do?

Notes

1. *Bridges v. California*, 314 U.S. 252, 271 (1941).
2. *Nebraska Press Assn. v. Stuart*, 427 U.S. 539, 551 (1976).
3. See, *Bridges v. California*, 314 U.S. 252, 283 (1941).
4. U.S. Const. amend VI.
5. *Gannett Co. v. DePasquale,* 443 U.S. 368 (1979).
6. *Id.* at 370.
7. *Id.* at 377.
8. *Id.* at 380.
9. *Richmond Newspapers v. Va.,* 448 U.S. 555 (1980).
10. *Id.* at 580–581.
11. *Id.* at 576.
12. *Id.* at 564.
13. *Near v. Minnesota*, 283 U.S. 697 (1931).
14. *New York Times Co. v. U.S.*, 403 U.S. 713 (1971).
15. *Nebraska Press Assn. v. Stuart,* 427 U.S. 539 (1976).
16. *Id.* at 541.
17. *Id.*
18. *Id.* at 559.
19. *Dennis v. United States,* 341 U.S. 494, 510 (1951).
20. *Nebraska Press Assn.* 427, U.S. at 562.
21. *Id.*
22. *Id.* at 562–563.
23. *Id.* at 568.
24. *Id.* at 570.
25. *Landmark Communications, Inc. v. Virginia*, 435 U.S. 829 (1978).
26. *Smith v. Daily Mail*, 443 U.S. 47 (1979).
27. *Butterworth v. Smith*, 494 U.S. 624, 634 (1990), citing *Florida Star v. B.J.F.*, 491 U.S. 524 (1979).

28. *Oklahoma Publishing Co. v. Oklahoma County Dist. Court,* 430 U.S. 308 (1977).

29. *Bridges v. California,* 314 U.S. 252 (1941).

30. *Pennekamp et al. v. Florida,* 328 U.S. 331 (1946).

31. *Craig v. Harney,* 331 U.S. 367 (1947).

32. *Wood v. Georgia,* 370 U.S. 375 (1962).

33. *Bridges,* 314 U.S. at 261, quoting *Schenk v. U.S.* 249 U.S. 47 (1919).

34. *Richmond Newspapers v. Virginia,* 448 U.S. 555 (1980).

35. *Globe Newspapers Co. v. Superior Court,* 457 U.S. 596, 608 (1982).

36. *Times Mirror v. United States,* 873 F.2d 1210, 1214 (9th Cir. 1989).

37. *Butterworth v. Smith,* 494 U.S. 624, 630 (1990), internal citations omitted.

38. *Illinois v. Abbott & Assoc., Inc.,* 460 U.S. 557, 564 (1983).

39. *Press-Enterprise Co. v. Superior Court,* 478 U.S. 1, 3 (1986).

40. *Id.* at 10.

41. *Id.* at 12.

42. See, e.g., *El Vocero de P.R. v. Puerto Rico,* 508 U.S. 147 (1993).

43. *Gannett Col. V. DePasquale,* 443 U.S. 368 (1979).

44. *Waller v. Georgia,* 467 U.S. 39 (1984).

45. *Id.* at 45.

46. *Id.* at 50.

47. *Press Enterprise Co. v. Superior Court,* 464 U.S. 501, 510 (1984).

48. *Id.*

49. *Id.* at 511.

50. *Richmond Newspapers v. Virginia,* 448 U.S. 555 (1980).

51. See, e.g., 18 U.S.C. § 3661.

52. *U.S. v. Corbitt,* 879 F. 2d 224 (7th Cir. 1989).

53. *Williams v. New York,* 337 U.S. 241 (1949).

54. Fed. R. Crim. P. 32(c); Rule 32 (c)(2)(A); Rule 32 (c)(3).

55. *Corbitt,* 879 F. 2d at 226.

56. *Id.* at 228.

57. *Id.* at 232.

58. *Id.* at 228.

59. *Id.* at 229.

60. U.S. Const. amend. VII.

61. See, *Richmond Newspapers v. Va.,* 448 U.S. 555 (1980); *Globe Newspaper Co. v. Superior Court,* 457 U.S. 596 (1982).

62. See, *NBC Subsidiary (KNBC-TV), Inc. v. Superior Court of Los Angeles County,* 20 Cal. 4th 1178 (1999) for a detailed analysis and review of lower court cases on point.

63. See, Jack B. Harrison, *Comments: How Open is Open? The Development of the Public Access Doctrine Under State Open Court Provisions,* 6 U.Cin.L.Rev. 1307 (1992) for a review of the public access doctrine and three models describing state approaches to access.

64. *Nixon v. Warner Communications, Inc.,* 435 U.S. 589, 580 (1978).

65. *Id.* at 598–599.

66. Thomas R. Dye, Understanding Public Policy 198-201 (10th ed. Pearson Education, Inc. 2002).

67. *Chinese Exclusion Case,* 130 U.S. 581, 604 (1889).

68. 8 C.F.R. § 3.27; *Detroit Free Press v. Ashcroft,* 303 F.3d 681, 701 (6th Cir.2002).

69. *Landon v. Plasencia,* 459 U.S. 21, 32 (1982).

70. *Bridges v. Wixon*, 326 U.S. 135, 161 (1945); also, see: *Reno v. American-Arab Anti-Discrimination Committee*, 525 U.S. 471 (1999).

71. *Ex rel.Mezei,* 345 U.S. 206, 212 (1953), internal citation omitted.

72. 8 U.S.C. § 1229a; see, *Zadvydas v. Davis*, 533 U.S. 678, 693 (2001), which says historical and legal distinctions still remain.

73. *Detroit Free Press v. Ashcroft*, 303 F.3d 681, 683-4 (2002).

74. *Id.* at 683.

75. *Id.* at 684.

76. *Id.* at 688.

77. *Id.* at 705.

78. *Id.* at 692.

79. *Id.* at 710.

80. *North Jersey Media Group, Inc. v. Ashcroft*, 308 F.3d 198, 204-205 (2002), *cert. denied* 538 U.S. 1056 (2003).

81. *Id.* at 220.

82. *Id.*

83. *Detroit Free Press v. Ashcroft*, 303 F.3d 681, 683 (2002).

84. *North Jersey Media Group, Inc. v. Ashcroft,* 538 U.S. 1056 (2003).

85. 67 FED. REG. 36799; *Detroit Free Press v. Ashcroft*, 303 F.3d 681, 708 (2002).

86. 67 FED. REG. 36799; 8 C.F.R. § 3.46(f)(3); *Detroit Free Press v. Ashcroft*, 303 F.3d 681, 708 (2002).

87. See, *Butterworth v. Smith*, 494 U.S. 624 (1990).

88. *U.S. v. Lindh*, 198 F. Supp.2d 739, 742-743 (A.D.E.D.V. 2002).

89. U.S. CONST. amend. IV.

90. *U.S. v. U.S. District Court*, 407 U.S. 297, 301-302 (1972); 18 U.S. C. § 2510-2520 (1968).

91. See, e.g., *Berger v. New York*, 388 U.S. 41 (1967). *Katz v. U.S.,* 389 U.S. 347 (1967).

92. *U.S. v. U.S. District Court*, 407 U.S. 297 (1972).

93. *Id.* at 309.

94. *Id.* at 313–314.

95. *Id.* at 323.

96. 92 Stat. 1783 (1978).

97. Ann Beeson, *On the Home Front: A Lawyer's Struggle to Defend Rights After 9/11*, THE WAR ON OUR FREEDOMS: CIVIL LIBERTIES IN AN AGE OF TERRORISM 299–300 (Richard C. Leone & Greg Anrig, Jr., eds., Century Foundation Books 2003).

98. Pub. L. 107-51. 115 Stat 272 § 218 (2001).

99. See, e.g, William F. Zieske, *Demystifying the USA Patriot Act*, 92 ILL.BAR J. 82, 86 (2004). Jeremy C. Smith, *The USA Patriot Act: Violating Reasonable Expectations of Privacy Protected by the Fourth Amendment Without Advancing National Security*, 82 N.C.L. REV. 412 (2003).

100. Robert Shapiro, *Secrets of a Celebrity Lawyer*, COLUMBIA JOURNALISM REVIEW, 25 (Sept./Oct. 1994).

101. Fraser Seitel, THE PRACTICE OF PUBLIC RELATIONS 9TH ED. 169 (Pearson Education, Inc. 2004).

102. See, *Stroble v. California*, 343 U.S. 181 (1952), discussion of pretrial publicity by a prosecuting attorney.

103. *Gentile v. State Bar of Nevada*, 501 U.S. 1030, 1034 (1991).

104. 3.6 ABA MODEL RULES OF PROFESSIONAL RESPONSIBILITY.

105. See, e.g., Colorado Rules of Professional Responsibility 3.6(c) as amended 1998.

Means of Access: Law as Entertainment

It has generally been held that the First Amendment does not guarantee the press a constitutional right of special access to information not available to the public generally.[1]

Overview

Clash of Competing Interests: The Courts, the Media, and Multiple Publics

Trials as Theater, Trials as Farce

No Access to a Tragedy: Government Executions

Practice Notes

The Final Act

Overview

Chapter 6 addressed access to information and places; chapter 7 focused specifically on access to judicial proceedings. This chapter describes problems associated with the medium of access. Specifically we describe laws and rules that restrict recording devices in courtrooms and other venues controlled by the government. Here we also describe the conflict between journalists who seek access to governmental processes in order to share information with the public, and media who seek access to trials and other governmental processes as a form of public entertainment.

This chapter is divided into four parts. The first brief section describes the conflicts between different interests that motivate requests for electronic recording of court procedures and other governmental processes. Here we describe the growth of trial coverage as entertainment rather than journalism and explain how this trend influences laws and rules governing cameras and recording devices in governmental proceedings.

The second part of this chapter builds from the approach to trials as entertainment and uses the metaphor of a play to describe how cameras and recording devices transform the media from mere observers into participants in trials. The trial process is described with an analogy to an original stage play performed before a live audience. We use this analogy to show how the entire nature of a trial, seen as reality theater, is substantively changed by the introduction of cameras and recording. We also explain how the perception of the "play" is altered by cutting and editing for transmission to an absentee audience. In this section we trace the evolution and current status of prohibitions against cameras and other recording equipment in courtrooms.

The third section introduces the trends in coverage of executions. Here we explore why media are not permitted to record executions and why the public is denied access to what was historically a very public event. We present arguments and legal trends from the last public execution in the United States in 1937 through the limited transmission of the Timothy McVeigh execution in 2001. The practice note in this chapter offers suggested legal arguments for media and their counsel who seek to improve public access to governmental proceedings through media recording and transmission of these events. In a final paragraph, we return to the theatrical analogy to illustrate how executions might be covered.

Clash of Competing Interests: The Courts, the Media, and Multiple Publics

As described in chapter 7, the government may restrict or totally prohibit access to its facilities and procedures, particularly courtrooms and prisons. Furthermore, the cases on access to governmental facilities and procedures uniformly hold that access by the public and media does not mean access by any method the public and media choose for themselves.[2] The government may completely control the **means of access** to its facilities. Therefore, even if the government permits public or media access to a court or prison, it may prohibit the use of cameras or recording devices. The government may specify the number of cameras and/or the type of equipment permitted. It can also screen or control equipment operators.

Courts Versus the Media and the Public

The Supreme Court, in *Zemel v. Rusk* and later cases, ruled that the press has no greater right of access to trials and court proceedings than does the general public.[3] This means literally that if media are permitted to bring their cameras and recording devices into a courtroom, then the public would also be permitted to bring their equipment. Permitting access for media equipment would, therefore, open the door for unrestricted access by amateur photographers and court observers. The response of many courts to this possibility has been the teleological argument that unlimited access is intolerable, therefore, all access will be denied. Of course, the courts' interests are preserving court decorum and guaranteeing that the parties involved in litigation receive a fair and impartial trial, but courts are only one part of the sovereign government. The people who pay taxes to support the government and who suffer themselves to be regulated by the government are also sovereign and the interests of the people often conflict with the courts' desire for impartiality and decorum.

The People, as sovereigns, have the right to change and control the government. They cannot reasonably exercise this right unless they have access to, or information about, the processes of their government. This right does not depend on the First Amendment. For example, the Ninth Amendment says, "(t)he enumeration in the Constitution of certain rights shall not be construed to deny or disparage others retained *by the people*" [emphasis added][4] and the Tenth Amendment says "(t)he powers not delegated to the United States by the Constitution, nor prohibited by it to the States, are reserved to the States respectively, *or to the people*" [emphasis added].[5] Taken collectively, these amendments grant the people access to the processes of their government and to information about governmental actions. If the media are **surrogates** or representatives of the people, they would have the same rights of access and information.

In addition to conflicts between the interests of the courts and the people, there are conflicts among multiple interests of different publics and within the media themselves. Public interests can be divided into a need for information in order to function as voters and responsible citizens and a desire for the titillation and entertainment associated with "court watching." Media interests include both a journalistic drive to inform readers and viewers about the functioning of the court system and an economic drive to recruit audience. There is also a conflict between the media, who often claim to be the representatives of the "public" and the public who has not elected the media and who may or may not share a particular medium's biases, perspectives, or interests. Courts often resolve requests to record court proceedings with a simple logic of balancing the court's interests against the combined interests of media and the public. There are multiple conflicts between the interests of the government and several subsets of the public and media.

The Public versus the Media

Often, courts' refusal to permit recording of trials occurs because media representatives have presented virtually all cases seeking permission to record or photograph trials. Those representatives have taken a professionally chauvinistic approach and the court has responded negatively. The media has presented itself as the surrogate of the people and the Supreme Court has apparently accepted this view of media participation. The *Zemel* decision ruled that the media and public have the same rights of access. When confronted with a media petitioner, the court weighs its governmental interest against the asserted right of the media to record governmental proceedings. If the court finds the media's interests are outweighed by the government's interests, both the media and public are denied access.

No one, other than the press itself, has elected media to be the surrogate or representative of the people. Nor is it the role, duty, or prerogative of the media to educate the public. Neither the public nor the press is the primary beneficiary or steward of First Amendment liberties. Each has rights independent of the other. The liberties mentioned in the First Amendment belong severally and collectively to the people and to the media. Therefore, neither the media litigants, on their own behalf, nor the courts in deciding qualified implied First Amendment access cases, should act to deny the public at large access to its government.

Media litigants' claim of a special privilege to record or photograph trials actually thwarts public access to these government procedures. By inviting the courts to define who may qualify as members of the press, these litigants invite judicial interpretation of who may enjoy First Amendment liberties. This activity itself is an abridgment of freedom of speech and press. Furthermore, some commentators see the media's attempt to set themselves apart from the population at large as a request for the creation of a special class of citizens to whom the government grants superior rights. Such a grant is specifically prohibited by Article I and by the Thirteenth and Fourteenth Amendments to the Constitution.[6] From a practical perspective, these arguments either permit or force courts to deny public access to trials. Perhaps if media litigants presented themselves as part of the people who have a right of access to their government rather than as a separate class who deserve special privileges, they might literally and figuratively "get somewhere."

Courts' willingness to deny media, and therefore public access to trials is facilitated by the conduct of some media representatives and by the contemporary merger of journalism and entertainment. Courts should see the need for citizen information about the process of government as a compelling interest. However, courts are unlikely to favorably evaluate the need for entertainment or media revenue.

Journalism versus Entertainment: Media and Publics

Under the *Zemel* doctrine, the court sees only two competing interests in access cases—those of the government on one side; and those of the public and media combined on the other. There are at least two types of media interests and two forms of public interest. These often compete with each other and all four must be weighed against the governmental interest involved in access cases. Media interests can be categorized as commercial and journalistic. **Commercial interests** drive programming that increases audience and advertising revenue. **Journalistic interests** relate to media as gatekeepers of information to be disseminated to the public audience. There are also two categories of publics whose interests arise in access cases. The publics can be labeled "the people" and the mass audience. The people are the sovereigns whose interest in self-government motivates them to use the media to gather and receive information to serve as the bases for intelligent decision making. The mass audience uses the media for entertainment and catharsis.

Commercial media interests tend to cater to the mass audience and journalistic media interests serve the people. Only the media as an industry seems to have the money, motivation, and ability to challenge denial of access to trials and other governmental proceedings. As we discuss decisions regarding permission to record or film trials and other events, it should be noted that often the courts respond to requests for access for journalistic purposes with a concern for the commercial and entertainment use of that access. Commercial interests and entertainment value are typically given little consideration when weighed against a defendant or litigant's right to an impartial trial. Perhaps separating these interests would lead to more success for journalists seeking permission to record trials.

Trials as Theater, Trials as Farce

Shakespeare observed that "All the world's a stage and All the men and women merely players: They have their exits and their entrances; And one man in his time plays many parts."[7] That observation is nowhere more true than in a trial. Historically, trials have been public performances. Under what was called the "Rule of Publicity," attendance at trials in pre-Norman England was mandatory for all freed men. It was assumed that having all citizens attend a trial would be part of the punishment of the guilty and would help vindicate the innocent.[8] Eventually, trial attendance became discretionary but service on juries is still a duty of citizenship. Our founding fathers assumed that being asked to judge one's peers was only one step removed from judging oneself.

Because Anglo-American trials have evolved as a form of public performance, comparing them to live theater helps to understand their function. Furthermore, seeing a trial as theater explains some of the issues confronted by judges who are asked to permit cameras and recording devices to intrude on the performance. This analogy is submitted to the thoughtful reader to provide a vehicle through which he or she may compare the competing interests involved when this most solemn of governmental proceedings becomes confused, in the minds of many, with entertainment and commercial venture.

Trials are very formal, stylized procedures used by a government to communicate serious messages to the trial participants and any spectators. All jury trial courtrooms in the United States are laid out in a similar pattern. The architecture and furnishings create a "stage" on which a reality play unfolds.

Each courtroom has a railing that defines the "stage" or area for performance. This railing, known as "**the bar**," also serves to keep non-actors or non-trial participants on the outside as mere spectators. The bar is analogous to a proscenium arch in a theater setting. Inside the bar, there are very specific sections, marked out by railing, space dividers, and levels or platforms. Each of the "players" has a specific place from which to enact his or her role.

In all courtrooms, the highest point in the room is reserved for the most important "player" in the drama to be presented—the judge. The judge's place is called **the bench** and is usually flanked from behind and on either side by wooden paneling or other materials to mark his or her importance. Usually, some crest, flag, or other icon of authority is placed immediately above or near the judge.

To one side of the judge, usually on a lower level, and often slightly in front of the judge's bench, but still within the framework of the judge's area, is a lone chair in a space where the witness will sit and perform on command. This space is called the **witness box**. At approximately 90° to the judge's bench and several feet from the witness box will be another space delineated by a lower railing or paneled area. This area, called the **jury box**, often contains two levels with rows of chairs sufficient to accommodate at least 12 people.

Usually near the jury box, and significantly behind it, will be chairs for bailiffs, who will play the roll of escorts and protectors for the jury panel. In front of and facing the bench, in the middle of the space provided inside the "bar," two large tables will be placed with significant space between them. Each large table will have at least two chairs behind it, facing the "bench." These tables will also be at a right angle to the jury box. Depending on the rules of the court, the prosecution attorney will sit together with his or her assistants at one table, and the defendant and his or her attorneys and their assistants will sit at the other table. Often, these two tables are separated by a podium and/or lectern from which the attorneys address the judge or witnesses. Other times, a lectern will be built into the area just below the judge's bench and near the witness box. The judge's bench, the witness box, and the lecterns will all be equipped with microphones, and/or there will be one microphone placed on each of the two litigants' tables.

Usually, there will be a number of chairs inside the bar, but with their backs to or just against the bar. These are for attorneys' assistants or law enforcement personnel in charge of order and safety. Someplace near the witness box and near the bench will be a chair and small table where the official court reporter will sit. The reporter will label and file exhibits and record the testimony. The clerk of the court will also have a reserved space, either built into the bench area or just outside it. The clerk will assist the judge and the reporter in retrieving court documents and in collecting and protecting the evidence submitted.

Outside the bar there will be seats for observers. These seats are for the spectators to the reality play. Those seated there are not participants or actors in the play. One indication of the exclusion of these observers is the fact that some of the major players in the trial are even positioned with their backs to the observers. The jury, the only official audience for the play, is positioned inside the bar.

Five major roles are played in this courtroom theater. Four players have major speaking parts, and there are numerous small bit or walk-on parts. His or her placement, height, and prominence in the courtroom theater make it obvious the judge is the most important player. The judge is also the only player who consistently wears an official costume, traditionally including a somber black robe. The role of judge is divided into several subparts. The judge plays a gatekeeper in that the other players must have permission from the judge before they may perform their roles. The judge also plays referee in that she or he determines the timing and rules by which each play will be regulated. The judge also decides what "props" may be introduced as evidence by the other players.

The role of "fact finder" may be played by either the judge or a jury. If the "play" is a jury trial, the fact finder is a jury, who must sit attentively and watch the play unfold before rendering their formal critique or verdict. The jury has only one speaking part, that of a foreman. The jury foreman is selected by the jury from its members during the critical analysis of the play called "jury deliberation." This phase occurs after the last "scene" in the play has been presented, and the judge informs the jury of the rules by which they must critique the play and determine the results. Once the jury has concluded its critical analysis and identified the winners and losers, the foreman, in his or her brief speaking part, responds to a question by the judge. The judge will either ask the foreman to announce the final results or the foreman will be asked to hand a critique sheet to the judge who will read it aloud. The verdict then becomes part of the record that has been prepared throughout the performance by the official court reporter.

Voir dire, or jury selection, is analogous to an audition casting the parts of the jury members. Convening, selecting, and empanelling a jury is expensive and time-consuming for the major actors in a trial. Despite the care taken in jury selection, juries can be unpredictable. Therefore, the judge critiques the majority of courtroom plays. The judge instructs the jury and may even take the role of fact finder from the jury.

There are three additional roles in these trials or plays. The main "protagonist" is called the prosecutor in a criminal trial and the plaintiff's attorney in a civil trial. It is the prosecutor's job to cast and direct witnesses who will, if the prosecutor is clever, re-enact facts through their testimony and evidence. The "antagonist" in this drama is the defense attorney who represents the interests of a defendant. His or her major task is to cast doubt on the performance of the prosecution's witnesses by questioning them or by presenting contradictory evidence and testimony. The defendant plays another major part, but in a criminal trial this part is often nonspeaking. Other "bit" players include the bailiffs and clerks but their participation is more analogous to that of theater ushers than to actors.

This reality play is not performed for its entertainment value; it is performed solely for the benefit of the judge or jury acting as fact finder because their decisions determine who wins and loses. While the format and performance of a trial is analogous to a play, it is absolutely serious and very real. Winners in civil trials may receive substantial sums of money and losers in criminal trials may even die as a result of the trial's outcome.

Seats are always provided in a courtroom outside of the bar or "proscenium arch," but the play will be performed whether anyone chooses to watch or not. The audience does not participate in any way and their presence is completely irrelevant to the performance and outcome. Finances, incarceration, and even life or death are decided despite the interest or disinterest of the public or press. In fact, spectators can, and often do, cause disturbances that interfere with the smooth presentation of the drama by the principals.

The purpose of courtroom drama is not and never has been the entertainment of the spectators, nor is the response of the spectators relevant to a trial's outcome. The sole purpose of this reality play is the resolution of disputes between the players. Also, each trial or hearing is presented as an original work, written, produced, and choreographed by the judge, prosecutor, and defense attorney. It falls to the person who plays the role of judge to direct the original production as objectively as possible, without subjecting the jury to distractions that might take their concentration away from the presentation of the case, which they alone must critique and score.

The Play Changes: Enter the Media, Cameras Rolling

Typically, the producers of live theatrical performances forbid cameras and recording devices. They understand that recording a play alters the quality of the performance. The presence of the cameras, the movement of the camera operators, the noise of shuffling about, and the lighting necessary to film or tape are all distracting, not only to the actors, but also to the audience. When actors know they are being filmed or taped their demeanor changes. Actors especially, like the players in a trial who are not used to being recorded, will become nervous. They forget lines, lose concentration, and may not be able to continue their roles. Furthermore, the presence of cameras changes the performance of the play itself. The camera operators become the producers of the play and by their presence create something different from what was intended by the playwright, the director, and the actors.

Anyone who has had the opportunity to appear on stage in the live performance of a play and who has also had the opportunity to perform before a camera knows about these critical distinctions in the substantive nature of the stories and messages they convey. Trials, like live plays, are meant to be one-time performances. Their scenes are presented only once; there are no retakes or replays. The interplay between the actors is critical to the outcome and is changed or distorted by distraction or recording. In a play, altering the outcome may impact the reviews or upset the audience. In a trial, altering the outcome can alter the litigants' lives. If producers forbid cameras at live plays, it seems reasonable for judges to forbid cameras at trials.

Access to a Farce: The *Estes* and *Sheppard* Case Examples

The first time the U.S. Supreme Court was asked to address the question of whether a person convicted of a crime "was deprived of his right under the Fourteenth Amendment to due process by the televising and broadcasting of his trial" was in the 1965 case of *Estes v. Texas*.[9] In that case, the defendant, who was ultimately convicted of swindling, had been granted a change of venue because of the notoriety created by massive pretrial publicity. The defendant asked the trial court to prohibit radio and television broadcasting and news photography in the courtroom. A 2-day hearing on the defendant's request was conducted in the presence of trial witnesses and veniremen. News photographs were taken in the courtroom and the hearing was also carried live on television and radio. There were 12 cameramen and cables were strung across the courtroom. Broadcasters placed three microphones in the courtroom, including one on the judge's bench, one aimed at the jury box, and one at the counsel table. The appellate court noted that the profusion of cameramen and equipment caused considerable disruption.[10] After this 2-day media event, the judge denied the defendant's motion to prevent televising of the trial.

During the 3-day trial, cameras were confined to a special booth in the back of the courtroom. However, there were continuous problems with the filming and broadcasting of the trial. Because of objections by defense counsel, the judge had to invent rules to govern the live broadcasting and still photography. Live telecasting was prohibited during opening and closing arguments of the state and the return of the jury's verdict, but even these events were broadcast live on radio. On one occasion, videotapes of the pretrial hearings were rebroadcast in place of the "late movie."[11] The defendant was convicted and the Texas Court of Criminal Appeals affirmed his conviction. The U.S. Supreme Court granted certiorari to review the case for constitutional error.

This appeal was heard prior to the decision in *Richmond Newspapers* and the Supreme Court considered an argument that the First Amendment "extended a right to the news media to televise from the courtroom, and to refuse to honor this privilege is to discriminate between the newspapers and television." The High Court responded to this argument saying,

> (t)he television and radio reporter have the same privilege. All are entitled to the same rights as the general public. The news reporter is not permitted to bring his typewriter or printing press.[12]

Later in its reasoning, the Supreme Court said,

> As has been said, the chief function of our judicial machinery is to ascertain the truth. The use of television, however, cannot be said to contribute materially to this objective. Rather, its use amounts to the injection of an irrelevant factor into court proceedings. In addition experience teaches that there are numerous situations in which it might cause actual unfairness.[13]

The Supreme Court went on to delineate seven problems presented by cameras in the courtroom. The first problem the court identified is the potential impact of cameras and filming on the jurors themselves. The second is impairment of the quality of witness testimony. Third, broadcasting testimony will permit later witnesses to alter their testimony in response to what has already been said. The fourth problem is the impact of courtroom television on the roles of the defendant and his attorney. Broadcasting may cause distractions and intrusions into the confidential attorney–client relationship and tempt the defense attorney to play to the public audience, thereby depriving the accused of effective representation. The fifth problem is the destruction of the accused and his case in the eyes of the public. The sixth problem is the involvement of the courts in commercialism, voyeurism, and sensationalism when notorious cases are selected for broadcast by the media in order to generate advertising revenue. The final problem identified by the court is that media coverage can shape public opinion and thus strip the accused of a fair trial.[14]

The Supreme Court reversed the conviction in *Estes* and, quoting Justice Holmes from the 1907 decision in *Paterson v. Colorado*, ruled that to be constitutional, a conviction must be based on "evidence and arguments in open court, and not by any outside influence, whether of private talk or public print."[15] The next Supreme Court decision to address cameras in the courtroom was *Sheppard v. Maxwell*.[16] Dr. Sam Sheppard was convicted by an Ohio trial court of murdering his wife. His conviction was affirmed through the Ohio Supreme Court. The U.S. Supreme Court denied his initial application for appeal in 1956, but after serving approximately 8 years in prison, he filed a habeas corpus petition in the U.S. District Court. Sheppard prevailed in the district court but lost in the court of appeals. Finally, the U.S. Supreme Court granted certiorari to review the case. The issue before the Supreme Court was,

> whether Sheppard was deprived of a fair trial in his state conviction for the second-degree murder of his wife because of the trial judge's failure to protect Sheppard sufficiently from the massive, pervasive, and prejudicial publicity that attended his prosecution.[17]

The appeal listed several pages of media abuses but here we focus only on those relating to cameras in the courtroom. First, a television station was permitted to set up broadcasting facilities next door to the jury room, making newscasts from this room throughout the trial and during jury deliberations. Second, television cameras lined the sidewalks and steps in front of the courthouse where trial participants were interviewed. Third, the corridors outside the courtroom were clogged with cameras and reporters filming the trial participants and interviewing witnesses whenever they entered or left the courtroom. These interviews disclosed trial testimony. Fourth, movement of the media representatives into and out of the courtroom often caused so much confusion that, despite an amplification system installed in the courtroom, witnesses and counsel had difficulty being heard. Fifth, an interview with the judge as he entered the court was broadcast to the public. Sixth, television cameras were used to photograph prospective jurors during selection of the jury. Seventh, daily records of the proceedings including the testimony of each witness were often broadcast on the nightly news.[18]

The U.S. Supreme Court quoted from the Ohio Supreme Court to describe the trial atmosphere:

> Murder and mystery, society, sex, and suspense were combined in this case in such a manner as to intrigue and captivate the public fancy to a degree perhaps unparalleled in recent annals. Throughout . . . circulation-conscious editors catered to the insatiable interest of the American public in the bizarre. . . . In this atmosphere of a "Roman holiday" for the news media, Sam Sheppard stood trial for his life.[19]

The U.S. Supreme Court went on to state: "(i)ndeed, every court that has considered this case, save the court that tried it, has deplored the manner in which the news media inflamed and prejudiced the public."[20] After a thorough discussion of the problems presented by cameras in the courtroom, and a listing of some of the techniques the trial judge might have used to control media behavior, the High Court concluded with the following admonitions:

> Neither prosecutors, counsel for defense, the accused, witnesses, court staff nor enforcement officers coming under the jurisdiction of the court should be permitted to frustrate its function. Collaboration between counsel and the press as to information affecting the fairness of a criminal trial is not only subject to regulation, but is highly censurable and worthy of disciplinary measures.[21]

Finally, the U.S. Supreme Court held that "Since the state trial judge did not fulfill his duty to protect Sheppard from the inherently prejudicial publicity. . . This case is remanded to the District Court with instructions . . . that Sheppard be released from custody."[22]

Current Rules for Courtroom Recording

The U.S. Supreme Court, both prior to and since its decision in *Richmond Newspapers*, has consistently ruled that any right of access to judicial proceedings does not include a right to bring "things" into the courtroom. The qualified and implied right of the public and press to be physically present during trials is grounded in the First Amendment. However, people have rights, things do not. Just as they are permitted to impose dress codes and to forbid weapons, courts are permitted to refuse to allow spectators to bring disruptive equipment into the courtroom.

Our courts have the obligation as part of the sovereign government to provide a forum for the resolution of legal disputes, and enforcement of the laws. Access to the courts, whether as a litigant or a general spectator, has always been circumscribed by a set of rules. The requirements of the particular type of work done by our courts set parameters within which all who seek admission must abide.

As part of its tasks, each trial court must make a contemporaneous record of its proceedings for possible appeal of its decisions to higher courts. This is accomplished by court appointment of specially trained individuals called "certified court reporters" who have the responsibility for maintaining exact records on each proceeding. These records include transcripts of argument and testimony, and any physical evidence. There is only one **official record** of each court hearing or trial. No additional recording devices can be allowed, unless by specific authorization of the court. Any extraneous equipment or recording devices threaten the sanctity of the official records in a case. This requirement for only one record was made particularly apparent by the Supreme Court in its decision in *Nixon v. Warner Communications*. In that decision the court ruled very specifically that media have no right to copy or broadcast taped evidence.[23]

Having reviewed two cases where cameras and recording devices destroyed judicial decorum and the environment necessary for a fair trial, it should be obvious how such equipment can threaten the proper function of a court.

Use of Cameras Is Prohibited in Federal Courts

Applying the same standards that were articulated in *Chandler v. Florida*, the federal courts have established rules banning cameras.[24] The currently effective federal rules of criminal procedure prohibit use of cameras in all federal courts. These rules are grounded on the federal courts' consistently negative experience with recording devices and their use by media. Historically, the first trial at which the negative impact from the media's use of cameras in the courtroom was clearly observed was the Hauptman trial for the kidnapping and murder of the infant son of famous aviator Charles Lindbergh. Apparently, the breach of proper courtroom decorum caused by the activities of the media spectators was so egregious that it spawned the first rules prohibiting the use of cameras in the courtroom. Subsequent experiences with cameras in courtrooms has led to their continuing prohibition in federal courts.

> Former Rule 53 of the Federal Rules of Criminal Procedure said,
> The taking of photographs in the courtroom during the progress of judicial proceedings or radio broadcasting of judicial proceedings from the courtroom shall not be permitted by the court.

The amended version of **Rule 53** of the Federal Rules of Criminal Procedure says,

> Except as otherwise provided by a statute or these rules, the court must not permit the taking of photographs in the courtroom during judicial proceedings or the broadcasting of judicial proceedings from the courtroom.[25]

The amended language is not a substantive change. It simply modifies the syntax and terminology to delete the word radio and to apply the prohibition to all broadcasting by either radio or television. The exceptions clause provides for conformity with other federal statutes or rules that might allow for "video teleconferencing" as a form of trial communication, thereby involving "broadcasting" in one sense. The rule has not been interpreted to permit public mass communications broadcasting of any courtroom proceedings.

Use of Cameras Is Discretionary in State Courts

In 1981, the U.S. Supreme Court considered the issue of "whether, consistent with constitutional guarantees, a state may provide for radio, television, and still photographic coverage of a criminal trial for public broadcast, notwithstanding the objection of the accused."[26] This decision came in the case of *Chandler v. Florida* wherein the Court reviewed the constitutionality of an experimental program that permitted electronic media to cover all judicial proceedings in Florida, without reference to the consent of participants. Florida did impose specific standards on the technology and the conduct of operators.[27] The case arose because the two appellants, former policemen, had been convicted of crimes by a jury during this experimental program. The defendants consistently objected to the presence of the camera, televising, and broadcasting of their trial, asserting they were deprived of a fair and impartial trial.[28]

The appellants argued that "the televising of criminal trials is inherently a denial of due process."[29] However, the U.S. Supreme Court affirmed the convictions and found "no evidence in the trial record to indicate that the presence of a television camera had hampered appellants in presenting their case or had deprived them of an impartial jury." The trial record indicated the televised coverage of this trial was very limited. It included less than 3 minutes of coverage and covered only the prosecution's side of the case.[30] The appellants did not show any evidence of prejudice by the coverage, no matter how lopsided it may have been.

The U.S. Supreme Court recognized that, under the concept of **federalism**, it has no supervisory authority over state courts, and limited its review to deciding whether there was a constitutional violation. The High Court ruled, "that the Constitution does not prohibit a state from experimenting with the program . . . [permitting courtroom cameras]."[31]

The U.S. Supreme Court noted the following major principles were used to reach its conclusion: (a) there is no constitutional right to have witness testimony recorded and broadcast; (b) the guarantee of a public trial is a safeguard against any attempt to employ our courts as instruments of persecution, but it confers no special benefit on the press; (c) the Sixth Amendment does not require that the trial, or any part of it, be broadcast live or on tape to the public; and (d) the requirement of a public trial is satisfied by the opportunity of members of the public and press to attend the trial and to report what they have observed.[32] These four points remain the consistent foundation upon which all U.S. Supreme Court cases have grounded their refusal to mandate or prohibit the use of cameras in the courtrooms across the United States. State courts are free to create their own rules for allowing or prohibiting cameras in the courtroom so long as the presence of recording devices and their operators do not deny the litigants their Constitutional right to a fair and unbiased trial.

State jurisdictions vary considerably in whether or not and to what extent cameras are allowed in their courtrooms. Although many state statutes and court rules prohibit cameras in the courtroom, a number of states have embarked on experiments with cameras in their trial or appellate courts. Often, these experiments result in a negative experience involving a notorious crime or trial and the states revoke the privilege of access to trials by recording device. Thus, the rules within the various state jurisdictions are in constant flux.[33]

Selling Tickets for Admission

There are proposals in some states that will essentially turn courtroom access into a commercial enterprise. Under these proposals the court would charge a **trial broadcast fee** to media. One of the more prominently debated proposals suggests that such fees could be used to compensate crime victims.[34] Of course, challenges to these proposals include the assertion that they would impose an improper tax on the media, that they create a means for the court to discriminate based on content, they discriminate in favor of well-funded media, and that they discriminate against media as a whole.[35]

Those who advocate the sale of trial broadcast rights for the benefit of crime victims fail to recognize the very purpose of the courts. Crime victims have always had access to the criminal courts for vindication and retribution for the offenses committed against them, and to the civil courts for the collection of damages or compensation. The state is not an insurer for the risks of living in society, nor are the courts the insurance agents. More important, no one taking part in this discussion seems to realize that any such venture will make it seem like "justice is for sale" in the court system. Trials will truly become commercial events, and the media will have paid for permission to be present, to film and broadcast whatever portions they can sell to their advertisers. Trial participants will have their likenesses and their voices appropriated for commercial purposes by both the courts and the media, without just compensation and without their consent or authorization. Also, if the media purchase broadcast rights, they will be free to edit the trial. Because live trials are typically long, boring events, editors will pick and choose from the witnesses and rearrange the trial presentation to appeal to a commercial audience. Court TV will become reality TV. The long tradition of live, uncensored, singular courtroom trials presented exclusively for the purpose of finding the "truth" and the administration of justice will be destroyed. Even the appearance of justice will be for sale.

The proposal that media should pay for broadcasting trials provides concrete evidence that many courts do not separate the entertainment and commercial interests of media from the journalistic motivation to inform the public. Furthermore, these proposals fail to acknowledge that the right to trial publicity does not belong to the court. The right of trial access belongs to the public or the people as a whole and the right to a fair and impartial trial belongs to the litigants.

No Access to a Tragedy: Government Executions

The practice of killing individuals in the name of the people has been a recognized means of asserting government control in virtually every country of the world. Capital punishment evolved under British common law and was integrated into the U.S. Constitution. It is specifically mentioned in the Fifth Amendment.[36] During the 20th century, Great Britain, France, and many other countries around the world abandoned capital punishment as barbaric, uncivilized, or cruel. Also, the Eighth Amendment prohibits **cruel and unusual punishment**[37] and during a brief period during the 1970s, the U.S. Supreme Court found that the arbitrary and capricious manner in which the death penalty was applied in some states violated the Constitutional rights of the condemned.[38] However, today the U.S. government and approximately two thirds of the individual state governments use capital punishment as the ultimate sanction for the most severe violations of law.

Traditionally, capital punishment has been defended and justified as a **deterrence** of crime and a tool for protecting society. One major aspect of the effectiveness of the death penalty has been public observance of its administration.[39] Contemporary criminal justice theory suggests that for any punishment to operate as an effective deterrence of crime, that punishment must have three characteristics. Those characteristics are certainty, swiftness, and severity. Our system of justice is deliberately biased to protect the rights of people accused of crime. This frustrates certainty of punishment. Our guarantees of fair and impartial trials and our system of appeals make swift punishment impossible. Therefore, the only component of deterrence possible is the severity of the punishment. Simply put, if punishment is to deter crime effectively, it must be severe. Death is certainly a severe penalty. But, for the death penalty to be perceived as a severe punishment and to act as a deterrent, its administration must be observed by those it is intended to deter. In other words, actually seeing the condemned die should frighten potential criminals into compliance with the laws. Furthermore, if the people, in whose name these government killings are performed, are to remain informed about the efficiency, effectiveness, and humanity or cruelty of the techniques used in their name, they must be able to observe executions. Without this knowledge, citizens cannot know whether the procedures they have authorized are cruel and unusual or are effective deterrents to crime. Such knowledge is essential to any informed debate on the propriety of capital punishment.

Despite the importance of public knowledge about executions, they have become increasingly secret. In the United States, the severity of sanctions for crime has varied. Correctional theories have also run the gamut from reformatories to penitentiaries and from rehabilitation to incarceration. Even the means of administering capital punishment has evolved along with social sensibilities and our notion of what is "severe." Traditionally executions in both England and the United States were public spectacles. For example, the city of Tyburn in England hosted 50,000 public executions from 1196 to 1783. The Old Bailey, a famous English courthouse, was the site of executions from 1783 to 1868. Large and disorderly crowds viewed these executions, including one in 1807 that numbered more than 40,000.[40] The last "town square" execution in the United Sates took place in 1937 when approximately 500 people watched a hanging in Galena, Missouri. The year before, thousands had observed a public hanging in Owensboro, Kentucky.[41] Today, both the federal government and all states that use capital punishment conduct executions in secure and private facilities and impose severe restrictions on public access.

Public and Media Rights to Attend Executions

In 1890, the Supreme Court last addressed the issue of a public right to attend executions. In *Holden v. State of Minnesota*, the High Court ruled that state legislatures may restrict attendance at executions for the public good. The Supreme Court has not issued any decision directly addressing the right of the public or media to attend executions since that time or since its decisions in *Press Enterprise Co. v. Superior Court* and *Globe Newspaper Co. v. Superior Court*. In both *Press Enterprise* and *Globe Newspaper,* the court identified a three-part test to determine whether historically open governmental procedures could properly be closed. The three parts of the test are (a) whether an overriding governmental interest exists, (b) whether it is necessary to preserve higher values, and (c) whether the closure is narrowly tailored to serve the governmental interest. Each of these three factors must be found on the record to justify closure. Because executions were historically open to the public, it seems reasonable to assume the court would use these criteria to guide any request to attend an execution by media or the public today.

In one of the few federal cases on point, subsequent to the *Press Enterprise* and *Globe Newspaper* decisions, the U.S. Court of Appeals for the Ninth Circuit in 1998 reviewed a decision by the District Court for the Northern district of California. The district court had issued an injunction permitting witnesses to view an entire execution by lethal injection. The court of appeals began its analysis with an excellent summary of the history of executions in California. That history helps predict how courts may react to requests for media access to executions.[42]

California had public hangings until 1858 when the state legislature passed a statute moving executions inside county jails and requiring at least 12 reputable citizens to attend.[43] Even when the executions were closed to the general public, the witnesses were given access to the events surrounding the execution including the condemned's demeanor, his final minutes, and final words.[44] When hanging was used as a method of execution, until 1936, witnesses could observe "the condemned's assent up the gallows to the fall of the trap door." When California changed its method of killing to lethal gas in 1937, witnesses were allowed to observe from the time the condemned was put in the gas chamber "until pronouncement of death."[45] Apparently, the first lethal gassing executions were so repugnant that the eyewitness media reports created widespread public debate over both the form of execution and the use of capital punishment itself.[46] In 1992, when California switched its method of killing solely to lethal injection, regulations were issued limiting witness observation of the execution. These limited viewing rules allowed spectators to enter the observation room adjoining the execution chamber only after the condemned had been strapped to a gurney and intravenous tubes had been inserted into his or her arms. The observable portion of the execution took only a few minutes and did not include the period of at least 20 minutes when the execution staff prepared the condemned for execution.[47] Witnesses were selected by the warden and included physicians, necessary law enforcement personnel, and family, friends, and clergy requested by the condemned. Of 50 spaces in the observation room, 17 were given to members of the media.[48]

Petitioners in the case objected to the limited time for viewing and sought an injunction permitting them to view the entire execution procedure including the insertion of the intravenous tubes and restraint of the condemned on the gurney.

Appeal of this case came in two stages. Initially, the district court ordered the warden of San Quentin Prison to permit the media to view the entire execution, but the circuit court reversed that decision on appeal. On appeal, the warden argued that the limited viewing protected staff safety and security by hiding the identity of execution staff and thereby protecting them from retribution. The circuit court agreed that concern for prison staff safety and security was a significant government interest. However, the appellate court also remanded the matter to the district court to determine if the procedure limiting press access to a few minutes was, in fact, narrowly tailored to meet the government interest or if it was an **exaggerated response**.

The district court then held a 2-day hearing, during which the court compared evidence on the current execution procedures and the one used during executions by lethal gas. After the trial, the court found that "restricting public access to view lethal injection executions to a degree greater than that afforded to view lethal gas executions *is an exaggerated response* to defendants' safety concerns (emphasis added)."[49] The court then issued a permanent injunction against the prison, ordering them to allow uninterrupted viewing of executions from the moment the condemned enters the execution chamber to the time he or she is declared dead.

In the second stage of the appeal, the Ninth Circuit was again asked to reverse the decision of the district court. This time, the appellate court upheld the trial court's decision. They ruled that the limitation on execution attendance was

> motivated, at least in part, by a concern that the strapping of a condemned inmate, the injection of intravenous lines or other aspects of a lethal injection execution would be perceived as brutal by the public, and . . . was prompted by considerations other than legitimate concerns for prison personnel safety.[50]

Both the district and circuit court ruled that concerns for protection of the execution staff's identity could be met by permitting them to wear surgical garb, including cap, mask, and gloves.[51] The circuit court concluded saying,

> We therefore hold that *the public enjoys a First Amendment right to view executions* from the moment the condemned is escorted into the execution chamber, including those "initial procedures" that are inextricably intertwined with the process of putting the condemned to death (emphasis added).[52]

Access to Executions by Electronic Media

The 1890 Supreme Court decision in *Holden v. State of Minnesota,* which allowed states to restrict access to executions, was based almost entirely on concerns for crowd control and public safety.[53] Obviously, the advent of broadcasting makes it possible to permit public viewing of an execution without any requirement for crowd control. The U.S. Supreme Court has not addressed the issue since the advent of broadcast technology. However, some recent cases from the U.S. Court of Appeals have addressed restrictions on access to executions by electronic media.

In 1977, the U.S. Court of Appeals for the Fifth Circuit addressed the issue of "whether a news cameraman can require the State of Texas to permit him to film executions in state prison for showing on television."[54] This issue arose on appeal from

Garrett v. Estelle. Garrett was a reporter for a Dallas television station who had requested permission to film the first execution in the state since 1964. His request was denied and shortly thereafter the Department of Corrections created a media policy permitting access to executions by a **press pool**, providing facilities where additional media representatives could view a simultaneously closed circuit telecast of the execution, and access to death row inmates for interviews.[55] Shortly after its creation the media policy was repudiated because it violated the state's Code of Criminal Procedures. That code prohibited press access to death row inmates and press attendance at executions.[56]

Garrett sued and the U.S. District Court declared that section of the Texas Criminal Code denying reporter access to condemned inmates to be an unconstitutional violation of the First and Fourteenth Amendments. The district court also ordered that the proposed policy for press pool viewing of executions reinstated, and ordered that Garrett be allowed to witness and film executions that he could then televise a later time.[57] Texas appealed only part of the district court's decision. The state objected to the requirement to permit Garrett to film the executions.[58] Texas never argued that filming, recording, or televising executions was not in the public interest or violated the security interests of the Department of Corrections or the privacy rights of the condemned.

This decision preceded the U.S. Supreme Court decisions in *Richmond Newspapers* and other cases that ultimately recognized an implicit First Amendment right for the public to attend trials and hearings. Therefore, the only decisions the Circuit Court could rely on were *Holden v. State of Minnesota, Zemel v. Rusk, Branzburg v. Hayes, Pell v. Procunier,* and *Saxbe v. Washington Post Co.*[59] *Holden v. Minnesota* held that a state legislature could restrict public access to executions and the other four cases all held that the press had no greater right of access to, or privileges from, governmental processes than do members of the general public.

The *Garrett* appeals court repeatedly cited the reasoning used by the Supreme Court in the four later cases, regardless of the arguments used to challenge the Texas prohibition of filming executions. Relying on the reasoning from *Holden v. State of Minnesota*, the Circuit Court simply ignored the possibility that the public might have a right of access and deferred to the state's contention that televising an execution would amount to conducting a public execution, a practice Texas discontinued in 1920. The court ruled that,

> the First Amendment does not guarantee the press a constitutional right of special access to information not available to the public generally. Therefore, Garrett cannot find his right to film Texas executions in the First Amendment.[60]

The circuit court reversed the district court and denied Garrett access to film or record executions.

In 1993, the Ninth Circuit reviewed a request to videotape a hanging in Washington State. The request to videotape the hanging of an inmate named Dodd came from another inmate named Campbell, who was also condemned to hang. Campbell argued that the tape would be the best possible evidence that hanging is cruel and unusual punishment. He wanted the tape to present as evidence in the appeal of his own death sentence. Although this case does not directly address media access to executions, it does show the court's reaction to one of the most powerful arguments for access. Ultimately, even Campbell's request was denied.[61]

After discussing some concerns associated with the fact that Dodd's case was still in a habeas corpus review, the Ninth Circuit ruled "the evidentiary value of the tape was doubtful, while the infringement upon comity concerns and privacy interests was serious."[62] The district court had apparently supported its decision by finding that (a) the evidentiary value of such a videotaped recording was dubious and unnecessary for an informed ruling on whether hanging constitutes cruel and unusual punishment in violation of the Eighth Amendment, (b) the condemned's "privacy and dignity" during the actual execution might be affected by the placement of cameras and microphones necessary to create a permanent audiovisual record of the event, and (c) the condemned prisoner had not given his consent to having his execution recorded. The circuit court agreed with each of these arguments and further said, "Campbell desires the evidence for its sheer emotional impact."[63] As discussed earlier, the history of the administration of capital punishment that was summarized in *California First Amendment Coalition v. Woodford* noted that California abandoned the gas chamber in response to public outcry after witnesses saw a gas chamber execution in the 1930s. It appears the circuit court in *Campbell v. Blodgett* feared a similar public response to factual information. Furthermore, the court's sudden solicitude for the alleged "privacy rights" of a condemned prisoner seems disingenuous. A condemned prisoner is one of the few citizens who have virtually no rights. He or she does not even have the right to live. His or her privacy rights are violated by public access to judicial proceedings, safety regulations of prisons requiring strip and cavity searches, and the presence of state witnesses at the execution itself.

Finally, we address the execution of Timothy McVeigh. McVeigh was sentenced to death after a federal district court found him guilty of bombing the Murrah Federal Building in Oklahoma City on April 19, 1995. He was convicted of the murder of 168 men, women, and children and it is difficult to imagine a figure for whom there was less public sympathy or whose public execution would have created greater catharsis. In 2001, two media organizations requested permission to record and broadcast his execution on the Internet.[64]

McVeigh was scheduled for execution at the U.S. prison in Terre Haute, Indiana. Bureau of Prisons regulations specify who is permitted to attend federal executions. Those rules allow a U.S. marshall, the warden, necessary personnel and attorneys, not more than 6 people selected by the prisoner, and not more than 8 citizens and 10 representatives of the press selected by the warden to attend executions.[65] Attorney General Ashcroft had already approved considerable deviation from these rules when he agreed to allow the survivors, victims' families, and certain other designated counselors and governmental representatives to view a closed circuit transmission of the execution. This transmission originated at the federal prison in Terre Haute and was broadcast to a facility in Oklahoma City where the bombing had taken place. This broadcast was permitted with a stipulation that no temporary or permanent recording would be made. Further, federal regulations provide that "no photographic or visual or audio recording of the execution shall be permitted."[66]

Entertainment Network, Inc. (ENI) filed its action as intervener together with Liveontheweb.com, Inc. They requested declaratory and injunctive relief challenging the constitutionality of the federal regulation that prohibited photographic, audio, and visual recording devices at federal executions. They also asked to be allowed to serve as the media pool witness to the execution. Specifically, they asked to bring a small camera to the witness chamber of the execution room, to record and simultaneously broadcast the execution via the Internet to the public or in the alternative, to be given access to the live audiovisual transmission of the execution and to be permitted to broadcast that communication. The Bureau of Prisons denied the request, citing three governmental interests. First, they wanted to avoid sensationalizing the event. Second, they sought to maintain prison security and good order. Third, they argued the Internet broadcast would violate the privacy interests of the condemned.[67]

The district court determined that the issue presented by the case was "whether the Bureau of Prisons' challenged regulation . . . violates ENI's First Amendment right to videotape and broadcast the execution of Timothy McVeigh."[68] The court ruled that the prohibition did not violate the First Amendment.

In its reasoning, the court focused on prior cases on prisoner rights and challenges to regulations of prisoners.[69] From these rulings, the court fabricated rules that could be employed to determine the reasonableness of a prison regulation governing matters affecting the rights of both prisoners and outsiders. Applying these rules, the court accepted the Bureau of Prison's assertion of three governmental interests and denied the request for an Internet broadcast.

Unlike the Ninth Circuit opinion in *California First Amendment Coalition v. Calderon*, the district court in *Entertainment Network, Inc. v. Lappin* did not explore whether the total prohibition on recording or broadcasting executions was an exaggerated response to the governmental interests or was, in fact, narrowly tailored to meet those interests.

What is most disconcerting about the McVeigh case is that the U.S. Attorney General had already provided for an exception to the Bureau of Prisons rules prohibiting photographic, visual, or audio recording of executions. By waiving the Bureau rules, and providing for the private viewing of the execution by means of a closed circuit transmission to the victims and surviving families in Oklahoma City, but refusing to waive the rules for ENI, the Attorney General violated the First and Fifth Amendments. As an officer of the federal government, he arbitrarily discriminated in favor of a small interest group while simultaneously denying the same benefit of access to both the media and the people of the United States.

Practice Notes

In this section, we summarize the problems experienced by the public and media attempting to gain access to governmental facilities, decision-making processes, and proceedings. We also provide some suggestions for arguments that might secure greater media access. Here, we draw together the lessons learned in chapters 6, 7, and 8 to provide insight into the issues associated with governmental and judicial denial of media access.

Six factors or concepts guide this analysis:

1. The federal government and individual state governments are sovereigns.
2. As sovereigns the governments are not required to permit any access at all.
3. Once a sovereign grants access it must be done without discrimination against any group, but general access does not require or prohibit specialized or preferential treatment for individuals.
4. Granting access to people does not require granting access for things including recording equipment.
5. Courts do attempt to balance governmental interests including interests in protecting the rights of litigants.
6. The courts currently view the interests of the public and media as one and the same and balance those collective interests against the interests of the government.

With these six principles in mind, we offer the following suggestions.

Use the Balancing of Interests Standard to Greater Advantage

Media, as big businesses, often have both the financial resources and a commercial incentive to challenge access limitations. However, media plaintiffs generally assert their interests in one of two ways. They assert a right of access by motion to intervene in an existing suit, sometimes called an interpleading, or they initiate suit against a governmental entity.

When media enter cases as third-party intervenors, their position is more difficult than when they sue a governmental entity directly. This is because in intervenor cases the courts must consider at least three competing interests, while in individual suits usually only two interests are presented. The three interests in the intervenor suit are the interests of the two original litigants and the new interest presented by the intervenor. Typically, courts consider the interests of the original litigants and the governmental interest in a fair, unbiased trial process as more important than those represented by media intervenors. Being an intervenor, although necessary in many situations, weakens the media's position.

Regardless of how an access suit is initiated, the argument that the media are the representatives of "the people" weakens the media's case. Making this argument has encouraged the courts to combine the interests of the media and the entertainment-seeking public and to balance that combined interest against whatever governmental interest supports closure of governmental process or records. The courts give no greater right of access to the media than they give the general public. If a court has not chosen to give the public access to governmental records, processes, or procedures, the media will also be denied access. When media organizations initiate suits against governmental entities or agencies, media plaintiffs need to argue that there are more than just two competing interests, that of the government on one side balanced against the combined interests of the media and the public on the other. Media petitioners must learn how to break the teleological reasoning used by courts that results in the consolidation of two very distinct interests of the public and the media. The courts must be convinced that the vastly greater weight of the arguments falls on the side of the media plaintiff simply because the greater public interest also resides there.

Broaden the Scope of Interests Involved in Media Suits

One method by which media petitioners might achieve greater success in obtaining access to government places, processes, and procedures is to join with named groups as co-petitioners. Such groups should have clear standing based on the interests they represent. This type of coalition including public and media groups was successful in *California First Amendment Coalition v. Woodford* where the Ninth Circuit granted access to California executions.[70] The importance of both forming a coalition and using arguments for the interest of each coalition member can be seen in *JB Pictures, Inc. v. Department of Defense*. The case dealt with a challenge to a military policy denying access to ceremonies associated with the return of deceased servicemen and women. In that case, the plaintiffs created a coalition of several media organizations, individual reporters, and veterans' organizations, but they failed to advance all of the available First and Fifth Amendment arguments.[71] They also failed to bring in a citizen's group to represent the broad interests of the people in being fully informed about the war and the full costs in terms of the human lives lost.

Furthermore, although this coalition effort was commendable, it concentrated its focus on only two of at least four interests and constitutional arguments. Even the court of appeals that reviewed the case suggested that the claim advanced by the coalition was based solely on the media's interest in a right of access for newsgathering. The circuit court hinted that had the group made the additional First Amendment argument for a right to engage in speech on the base, the outcome might have been different.[72]

Develop a Wider and More Comprehensive Vision of the Constitution

Media petitioners and their legal counsel who initiate "right of access to government" suits need to use not only the full range of competing interests, but also a comprehensive vision of the Constitutional rights involved in each case. Again, the *JB Pictures* case is an example. Rather than simply concentrate on the single issue involving the right of media access to newsworthy events, the coalition of plaintiffs also included a "viewpoint discrimination" argument in their suit. However, they failed to accentuate all of the interests represented by their coalition because they did not argue for a right to engage in speech on the base. Thus, they lost the advantage that adding alternative constitutional arguments could have provided. By myopically concentrating on the qualified implied First Amendment right of access for newsgathering, they forgot that freedom of speech was a separate interest to be weighed and considered against the government's asserted interests in protecting the privacy rights of the surviving family members.

Raising the free speech issue would also have allowed the plaintiffs in *JB Pictures* to incorporate more and stronger arguments. For example, a Fifth Amendment argument based on denial of due process was available. The government had, for at least the previous 10 years and two wars provided the public and the media with a "designated public forum" at the ceremonies for returning war dead. The DOD closed that public forum without asserting any compelling state interest. This violated not only the First Amendment but also the Fifth Amendment's due process clause.

Remember, that the only interest asserted by the government for its promulgation of the new policy was to protect the surviving families' "qualified implied rights of privacy" and to avoid imposing the hardship of traveling to Delaware for arrival ceremonies. Qualified, implicit rights, in this case stemming from the Fourth Amendment in relation to the surviving family members, never trump substantive First Amendment rights of speech nor their denial without due process under the Fifth Amendment. Arguments combining the qualified implicit First Amendment right of access for newsgathering, plus the unqualified First Amendment freedom of speech rights, plus the withdrawal of the designated public forum without a compelling governmental interest, and the denial of due process in violation of the Fifth Amendment should have won the case.

Media plaintiffs seem to believe that the only significant Constitutional protections come from the First Amendment. In suits to open access to governmental places, processes, procedures, and records, they need to remember to bring all of the possible Constitutional provisions to bear. These can be argued as alternative theories of recovery or in combination to persuade the courts of the weight and societal value of the substantive and procedural arguments for openness versus the asserted governmental interests in closure or secrecy.

Coalitions arguing for open access should use both the free speech and free press clauses of the First Amendment combined, when available, with the due process clause of the Fifth Amendment. In addition, innovative coalitions should also bring the atrophied Ninth Amendment into play to convince the courts that the range of rights possessed by the media, the public, and particularly The People under the qualified implied First Amendment rights of access, should be expanded.

In both state and federal venues, media plaintiff coalitions should remember that the equal protection clause of the Fourteenth Amendment applies to their rights. Finally, in all state courts, media coalitions need to think comprehensively. In addition to any available arguments based on the U.S. Constitution and Fourteenth Amendment, media plaintiffs should base their suits and arguments additionally and alternatively on their own state constitutions, statutes, and common law. These state laws often include expanded recognition of the interests represented by the media and the public. In addition, state courts are often more amenable to openness in government access cases. Remember it is state legislatures, not the U.S. Constitution or Congress, that created state statutory privileges for media.

The Historic Right of Access to Executions Reinstated via Media Pools

Executions are particularly ripe for a complete and collective argument for media access to governmental processes. The precedent set by Attorney General Ashcroft's waiver of the Bureau of Prisons' rule against videotaping or transmissions of executions could be used to reopen public access to federal executions. Three of the four arguments asserted by the government to support denying ENI's request to broadcast the execution of Timothy McVeigh were waived by the attorney general when he permitted broadcast of the execution from Terre Haute to Oklahoma City. The only compelling governmental interest that was not waived is the concern for institutional and staff safety and security. Reopening federal executions to viewing by the people will require suit by a well-selected coalition of media and public interest groups. That group should be able to use successfully the exaggerated response reasoning from the Ninth Circuit's decision in *California First Amendment Coalition v. Woodford*, together with an agreement to appoint one media pool representative with limitations on equipment and operator screening. The media must be careful to submit their argument for right of access to federal executions by fully exploiting the rights of all possible competing interests, including their own as a surrogate for the people. Here, because of the pool requirement, the concept of media as surrogate for the people seems quite strong. In addition, the media coalition must be prepared to present the broadest range of constitutional arguments possible. Finally, a wide range of public policy arguments must be woven into this history-making case. Under the Eighth Amendment, the only way to advance continued social and governmental support for capital punishment, or to produce informed rejection of capital punishment, mandates public access to executions. Deterrence depends on public exposure to executions and informed decisions require knowledge that can only be produced by observation.

Access to executions does not present publicity concerns, such as those inherent in the pretrial and trial phases, because there is no jury or trial to prejudice. Neither should there be any concern that one prescreened camera and operator would be disruptive or interfere with the process. Institutional safety and order concerns can be accommodated by V-chip or other controls foreclosing inmate access to the transmissions. Institutional staff and victim privacy rights are accommodated when the camera concentrates solely on the condemned and the execution staff wear surgical garb. Finally, the condemned has no privacy or any rights remaining other than to be used by the society to set an example. This is the sole function that the condemned have traditionally served in our legal system.

The Final Act

The trial has concluded, the sentence has been pronounced, the appellate procedures have been exhausted, substantive due process has been served, the execution order has been signed, there are no pardons, reprieves, or stays left, the opportunity for "justice" has arrived, there are no roles left to play, the final Act has ended, the dénouement is at hand, The People await.

Enter the condemned, center stage. The lights go down, the stage is empty and dark, save for the camera in one room, viewing through a glass into the next at the lone occupant in the spotlight, until the light goes dim and then out—down curtains.

Executions are a tragedy for all the people of the United States, yes—a sensation for entertainment purposes, no!

Magic Words and Phrases

Bar	Means of access
Bench	Official record
Commercial interests	Press pool
Cruel and unusual punishment	Rule 53 (Federal Rules of Criminal
Deterrence	Procedure)
Exaggerated response	Surrogates of the people
Federalism	Trial broadcast fee
Journalistic interests	Witness box
Jury box	

Suggested Cases to Read and Brief

California First Amendment Coalition v. Calderon, 150 F. 3d 976 (9th Cir.1998)
California First Amendment Coalition v. Woodford, 299 F.3d 868 (9th Cir.2003)
Campbell v. Blodgett, 982 F.2d 1356 (1993)
Chandler v. Florida, 449 U.S. 560 (1981)
Entertainment Network, Inc. v. Lappin, 134 F.Supp.2d 1002 (2001)
Estes v. Texas, 381 U.S. 532 (1965)
Garrett v. Estelle, 556 F.2d 1274 (5th Cir.1977)
Holden v. State of Minnesota, 137 U.S.483 (1890)
Thornburgh v. Abbott, 490 U.S. 401 (1989)
Turner v. Safley, 482 U.S. 78 (1987)

Questions for Discussion

1. One argument against permitting recording devices in a courtroom is that those devices would create a second record of the trial. On appeal, trials are always reviewed based on the official record. Would having a second, unofficial record make appeals easier or more difficult? Would it make them fairer or would it discriminate against defendants who could not afford to create a second record? What other arguments can you think of to support or oppose permitting observers to make an independent record of the trial?

2. Opponents of cameras in the courtroom have argued that cameras impair witness testimony, distract attorneys, and draw the jury's attention from the testimony and evidence. First, do you believe cameras do, in fact, cause these detrimental effects on a trial? Second, if you were a judge, how could you control the use of cameras in your courtroom to avoid these problems?

3. The Supreme Court has ruled that citizens have a right to attend most trials but today most people do not have the time or ability to leave other responsibilities to attend trials that may take several days or weeks. Would broadcasting trials today serve the same purpose that public attendance served 50, 100, or 200 years ago? If you support

the idea of broadcasting trials, how would you ensure the experience is the same for those who view a broadcast and those who actually attend?

4. Many courts simply assume that televising a trial equates to denying the litigants a fair and impartial trial. Do you agree? Why or why not?

5. Do you agree with the proposal in some states to charge a trial broadcast fee? Explain the advantages and disadvantages of a program that charged broadcasters a fee for recording trials. When you answer this question consider the issue from the perspective of a broadcaster, a print journalist, and a criminal defendant.

6. Remember that the U.S. Supreme Court, in *Zemel v. Rusk*,[73] has ruled that the media have no greater right of access to trials than the general public. With that in mind, if you were a judge in a state that has agreed to sell broadcast rights to trials to the news media, could you refuse to sell broadcast rights to a company called "Lurid TV" that you know gathers trial recordings only to sensationalize the events for commercial distribution? How would you respond if you received so many requests to broadcast a trial that the cameras would not leave room for live spectators?

7. Whether you support or oppose capital punishment, describe one argument for and one argument against permitting broadcast of executions. If you oppose capital punishment be sure to explain both why broadcasting would advance and harm the interests of those who oppose the penalty. If you support capital punishment be sure to explain both why broadcasting would advance and harm the interests of those who support the penalty.

Notes

1. *Pell v. Procunier*, 417 U.S. 817, 833 (1974).
2. *Sherrill v. Knight*, 560 F.2d 124, 129 (D.C.Cir. 1977).
3. *Zemel v. Rusk*, 381 U.S. 1 (1965).
4. U.S. CONST. amend. IX.
5. U.S. CONST. amend. X.
6. U.S. CONST. art. I § 9, cl. 8; amends. XIII & XIV.
7. William Shakespeare, AS YOU LIKE IT. Act II, Scene VII.
8. *Near v. Minnesota*, 448 U.S. 555, 568 (1980), quoting Sir Frederick Pollocks, THE EXPANSION OF THE COMMON LAW 31–32 (1904).
9. *Estes v. Texas*, 381 U.S. 532, 534–535 (1965).
10. *Id.* at 536–537.
11. *Id.* at 537–538.
12. *Id.* at 539–540.
13. *Id.* at 544–545.
14. *Id.* at 549–550; See also, *Nichols v. District Court*, 6 P.3d 506 (Ok.Crim.App.2000) where the highest Oklahoma court of criminal appeals, relying in part, on *Estes*, found that televising or recording a criminal trial over the objection of a defendant would violate the state constitutional guarantee of due process.
15. *Estes*, 381 U.S. at 551, internal citation omitted.
16. *Sheppard v. Maxwell*, 384 U.S. 333 (1966).
17. *Id.* at 335.

18. *Id.* at 345.

19. *Id.* at 356, internal citation omitted.

20. *Id.*

21. *Id.* at 362.

22. *Id.* at 363.

23. *Nixon v. Warner Communications*, 434 U.S. 591 (1978).

24. *Chandler v. Florida*, 449 U.S. 560 (1981).

25. U.S.C.S. FED. RULES CRIM. PRO. R 53 (2004).

26. *Chandler*, 449 U.S. at 562.

27. *Id.* at 565-566 (1981).

28. *Id.* at 567.

29. *Id.* at 570.

30. *Id.* at 568.

31. *Id.* at 582–583.

32. *Id.* at 569.

33. See, *Estes v. Texas*, 381 U.S. 532 (1965), J. Harlan's concurring opinion for a summary of the history of ABA Cannon 35 proscribing photographic and broadcast coverage of courtroom proceedings; *In re: Petition of Post-Newsweek Stations, Florida, Inc., for Change in Code of Judicial Conduct*, 370 So.2d 764 (Fla.1979), for a report on its 1-year pilot program permitting electronic media coverage of judicial proceedings; Christo Lassiter, *An Annotated Descriptive Summary of State Statutes, Judicial Codes, Canons, and Court Rules Relating to Admissibility and Governance of Cameras in the Courtroom*, 86 J. CRIM. L. & CRIMINOLOGY 1019 (1996).

34. Stephen D. Easton, *Cameras in Courtrooms: Contrasting Viewpoints: No Pay, No Play: Trial Broadcast Fees are Constitutional*, 49 S.C.L. REV. 73 (1997).

35. *Id.*

36. U.S. CONST. amend.V.

37. U.S. CONST. amend. VIII.

38. See, e.g., *Bell v. Ohio*, 438 U.S. 637 (1978); *Coker v. Georgia*, 438 U.S. 584 (1977). But see, *Jurek v. Texas*, 428 U.S. 262 (1976); *McGautha v. California*, 402 U.S. 183 (1971).

39. See, *California First Amendment Coalition v. Woodford*, 299 F.3d 868, 875 (9th Cir. 2003), for a discussion of the tradition of public access to executions.

40. *California First Amendment Coalition v. Woodford*, 299 F.3d 868, 875 (9th Cir.2003).

41. *Id.*

42. *California First Amendment Coalition v. Calderon*, 150 F.3d 976 (9th Cir.1998).

43. *Id.* at 978.

44. *Id.*

45. *Id.* at 978–979.

46. *Id.* at 979.

47. *California First Amendment Coalition v. Calderon*, 150 F.3d 976 (9th Cir.1998).

48. *Id.* at 978.

49. *California First Amendment Coalition v. Woodford*, 299 F.3d 868, 871 (9th Cir.2002).

50. *Id.* at 880.

51. *Id.* at 885.

52. *Id.* at 877.

53. *Holden v. State of Minnesota*, 137 U.S. 483 (1890).

54. *Garrett v. Estelle*, 556 F.2d 1274, 1275 (5th Cir. 1977).

55. *Id.* at 1276.

56. *Id.*
57. *Id.* at 1277.
58. *Id.*
59. *Holden v. State of Minnesota*, 137 U.S. 483 (1890); *Zemel v. Rusk*, 381 U.S. 1 (1965); *Branzburg v. Hayes*, 408 U.S.665 (1972); *Pell v. Procunier*, 417 U.S. 817; (1974); *Saxbe v. Washington Post Co.*, 417 U.S. 843 (1974).
60. *Garrett,* 556 at F.2d. at 1279.
61. *Campbell v. Blodgett*, 982 F.2d 1356 (1993).
62. *Id.*
63. *Id.* at 1369.
64. *Entertainment Network, Inc. v. Lappin*, 134 F.Supp.2d 1002 (S.D.Ind. 2001).
65. *Id.* at 1007, citing 28 C.F.R. Sec. 0.96 Further federal regulations provide that "no photographic or visual or audio recording of the execution shall be permitted."
66. 28 C.F.R., Sec. 26.4(c) (2001).
67. *Id.* at 1007–1008.
68. *Id.* at 1009.
69. See, *Turner v Safley*, 482 U.S. 78 (1987); *Thornburgh v. Abbott*, 490 U.S. 401 (1989).
70. *California First Amendment Coalition v. Woodford*, 299 F.3d 868 (9th Cir.2002).
71. *JB Pictures, Inc. v. DOD*, 86 F.3d 236 (D.C.Cir. 1996).
72. *Id.* at 241.
73. *Zemel v. Rusk,* 381 U.S. 1 (1965).

9

Communication Torts

Freedom of speech has been reduced to a tool, like the Roto-Rooter's snake that periodically is plunged down the sewer line to ensure the free flow of commerce through the pipes.[1]

Overview
Defamation
Private Facts
False Light
Appropriation
Intrusion
Practice Notes

Overview

As part of the discussion of the incitement standard in chapter 4 we introduced some concepts of basic tort law. Here we expand those concepts and explain the specific torts that are traditionally called communication torts. Defamation, private facts, false light, appropriation, and intrusion are often called the *communication torts* because they are the civil legal actions most often pursued by private citizens who feel they have been wronged by journalists, advertisers, public relations practitioners, and photographers. Defamation has a long history that has evolved from English common law. Private facts, false light, appropriation, and intrusion appeared as causes of actions for the first time in the late 19th century and are often referred to as *modern communication torts*.[2] Of course, what is "modern" is relative. Both case law and statutes describing the modern communication torts have been evolving for more than 100 years. Defamation law is the amalgamation of centuries of common law, U.S. Constitutional interpretation, and individual state laws. It is, therefore, extraordinarily complex. Some legal scholars argue that defamation is virtually useless as a means of protecting private citizens who are wronged by sloppy or dishonest media coverage.[3] These same scholars often argue defamation is less important than privacy because defamation laws only protect individual citizens, whereas privacy laws protect the entire society against intrusions by government and media.[4] Despite these arguments, we begin with an explanation of defamation because we believe understanding the basic concept of defamation provides a good foundation for an explanation of more modern communication torts.

The basic concept of defamation is simple and easy to understand, and basic understanding is all that is required for an honest and careful communications practitioner to protect him or herself. We begin with a very basic introduction to defamation, move to more complicated components, and then to modern communication torts. We conclude with two practice notes, the first of which addresses the misperception that opinion is a defense to defamation and other communication torts. The second practice note explains how employee communication may be a defense to communication torts for public relations practitioners.

Defamation

Defamation is a combination of the two even older torts of libel and slander. Slander is the use of the spoken word to injure the reputation of another person or to expose the person to public contempt or disgrace. Libel is the use of written communication to cause the same kinds of harm to another person. Historically, the distinction between libel and slander was significant. In the societies where these common law actions evolved, most people could not write, so written words seemed more powerful or more truthful and were therefore more likely than speech to cause harm. Prior to the advent of devices for recording speech, the spoken word was ephemeral and usually spoken insults or lies did not have the same potential for harm as did written language. With modern recording and broadcast media and the high rates of literacy in the United States, the distinction between libel and slander has become trivial. In nearly all circumstances, libel and slander are combined into a single action called defamation. With very few exceptions, we treat libel and slander under the single label of *defamation.*

One has committed the civil offense of defamation when he or she, with intent, communicates an untrue and defamatory statement about another and identifies the person or entity defamed. In many jurisdictions, there is also a criminal offense called defamation. Criminal defamation has the same elements as civil defamation but usually adds a requirement to show willful intent to harm and actual financial harm.

You may notice the tautology of using "makes a defamatory statement" as part of the definition of defamation. This confusion arises because defamation was an element of both libel and slander, and defamation is also the term adopted by most jurisdictions to describe the combination of libel and slander.

The order in which the elements of defamation are presented in Exhibit 9.1 is unusual, but we find this structure useful, because it permits the statement of the elements in a single sentence most students find easier to remember than a list of otherwise unrelated words. It may help to think of defamation as:

> An *untrue statement, about the plaintiff* that *defames the plaintiff,* and is *communicated* to a third party *by the defendant* with *intent by the defendant.*

Exhibit 9.1. Elements of defamation (the plaintiff must prove all six to win an action for defamation).

Element 1	Untrue statement
Element 2	About the plaintiff
Element 3	That defames the plaintiff
Element 4	Communicated or published
Element 5	By the defendant
Element 6	With intent by the defendant

Untrue Statement

Some careful legal scholars may question the inclusion of falsehood or "untrue statement" as an element of defamation. We acknowledge that historically falsehood was not an element of defamation. Under common law, the plaintiff was not required to prove the statements made about him or her were not true. Rather, truth was what is called an affirmative defense and it could be raised by the defendant. For example, under traditional common law, if a newspaper ran an article saying the local mayor was corrupt, the mayor could sue for defamation. The newspaper could defend against the action by the mayor by proving the statement was true. In effect, the newspaper, which is the defendant in this example, would have to prove the mayor really was corrupt. This affirmative defense differs from an element because the defendant must initially raise the question of truth and the defendant must prove the statement is true.[5]

Falsehood as an Element

Initially the U.S. Supreme Court began to impose the burden of proving falsehood only on plaintiffs who were public figures.[6] The Supreme Court also applied this burden on private citizens in 1986. In its decision in *Philadelphia Newspapers, Inc. v. Hepps*,[7] the Court addressed an allegation of defamation by the owner of a convenience store chain. The story alleged the storeowners used ties to crime syndicates to influence the state's laws. The trial judge instructed the jury the plaintiffs had to prove the statements made against them were not true and the jury returned a verdict for the defendant newspaper. This verdict was, at least in part, the result of the plaintiff's inability to prove it actually did not have ties to organized crime. The Pennsylvania Supreme Court reversed and remanded the case saying the defendants had to prove the statements were true. The Pennsylvania Supreme Court was using the traditional affirmative defense logic. In effect, the court said falsehood is not an element of defamation, but rather that truth is a defense the defendant must prove. The case was then appealed to the U.S. Supreme Court, which agreed with the trial court and not with the Pennsylvania Supreme Court.[8] In *Hepps*, the U.S. Supreme Court did not entirely overturn the notion of affirmative defense, but did leave us with a rule that says if the plaintiff is a public figure or if the subject of the allegedly defamatory statement is a matter of "public concern," then the plaintiff bears the burden of proving falsehood.[9] The careful communications professional should note that the defendant still bears the burden of proving his or her statements are true where both the plaintiff is private figure and the subject matter is not a matter of public concern.[10] We, therefore, think it reasonable to include "untrue statement" in the list of elements for defamation.

The definition of a public figure and the concept of matters of public interest also are essential to differentiating levels of intent. The terms *public figure* and *matter of public interest* are defined and discussed in the section on intent later in this chapter.

How Much "Truth" is Required?

In order to prove a statement is not true, it is not enough to show that there are minor inaccuracies. For example, slight variations in terminology or minor errors in quotations are not enough to make a statement false. As long as the gist or general meaning of the statement is accurate, it is legally "true." An example of this principle of the "gist of the truth" can be seen in the case of *Strada v. Connecticut Newspapers, Inc.*[11] During the reelection campaign of William Strada, a state senator, the defendant newspapers ran a story describing his relationship with criminals. The story specifically said Strada had taken trips with the criminals to Las Vegas and New Orleans. At trial, both parties agreed Strada had never taken the trips to Las Vegas or to New Orleans, but he had gone to Reno with an alleged criminal named DePoli. The court ruled that inaccurately stating the destination of the trip did not change the fact that the assertion was essentially true. They said, "The sting of this excerpt . . . does not arise from the trip location . . . but rather from the fact that the plaintiff had taken a trip in some way connected with DePoli."[12] As long as the component of the statement that caused the defamation or harm is accurate, the statement is "legally" true.

This same principle applies to minor modifications of quotes. Of course, the courts are not judging journalistic or agency/client ethics; they are only determining what is true for the purpose of defending against an allegation of defamation. For the purpose of defending against defamation, "[i]f an author alters a speaker's words but effects no material change in meaning," then the statement or quotation is still legally true.[13]

Communication professionals are not free to alter information in a way that gives a false impression. In fact, even if the statements made are technically true, they may be "legally" false if they lead a reasonable reader to an inaccurate conclusion. If accurate statements are made but details necessary to clarify or explain are omitted and the omissions create a false impression, the statement, as a whole, may be an "untrue statement" for the purposes of proving defamation.[14]

About the Plaintiff

Of course, for a plaintiff to sue for defamation, he or she must prove the untrue statement is actually about him or her. If the statement mentions the plaintiff by name or title, this element is easily met. If a newspaper article says, "the mayor of Smallville is corrupt," the statement is about whomever holds the office of mayor at the time of publication. If the statement says, "John Doe is a thief" and your name is John Doe, the article is about you unless there are so many people named John Doe that there might be some other conclusion. This element only becomes complicated when the allegedly defamatory statement is about a group of people.

A very general rule is that individual members of a small group may sue for defamation when the group is defamed, but individual members of a large group cannot. This leaves the question, how large is a large group? Very often the judge in such a case will simply ask the jury to decide if people reading or hearing the allegedly defamatory statement would think it is about the plaintiff. One case helps to make the point that members of fairly large groups may be individual plaintiffs when the group is defamed. An article in a 1958 issue of *True* magazine described the dangers of amphetamine use by college athletes. The article contained the allegation that the University of Oklahoma's 1956 national championship football team took steroids by nasal inhalant and included the copy:

> Speaking of football teams, during the 1956 season, while Oklahoma was increasing its sensational victory streak, several physicians observed Oklahoma players being sprayed in the nostrils with an atomizer. And during a televised game, a close-up showed Oklahoma spray jobs to the nation.[15]

Evidence showed the inhalant used by the Oklahoma football players contained spirit of peppermint, not steroids. Spirit of peppermint was used to help fatigued players combat dry mouth and its use did not violate any law or athletic regulation.

Although there were more than 75 players on the football team, only one, a second-string fullback named Dennit Morris, sued the publisher for defamation. One issue addressed by the state Supreme Court was whether the statement was "about the plaintiff." The court in that case ruled the group was small enough and Morris was so well associated with it that he would be recognized as a member of the group and would be harmed by the defamatory statement.[16] The U.S. Supreme Court later denied certiorari, effectively leaving the state court ruling in place.

In 1952, Crown Publishers in New York offered a book for sale that was aggressively critical of Neiman-Marcus, a Texas department store. The Neiman-Marcus Corporation and three different groups of its employees sued the publisher for defamation. The three groups of employees were 9 models, 15 salesmen, and 33 saleswomen. The book alleged the models and saleswomen at the store were prostitutes and the salesmen were engaged in illegal homosexual activities. Much of the case turned on whether the groups of employees could be plaintiffs because none of them had been identified by name. The New York District Court that heard the case ruled the nine models could be plaintiffs because they were all the models at the store at the time of the publication. The court dismissed the suits by the salesmen and saleswomen because the store was so large the sales staff was constantly changing, and the salespeople had not shown they were employed at the time of the publication or the alleged defamation.[17] In short, the plaintiff must be able to prove both that he or she is a recognized member of the group and that he or she was a member of the group at the time referred to in the defamatory statement.

One final problem for plaintiffs proving they have been identified is unique to government employees. In its decision in *New York Times v. Sullivan*,[18] the U.S. Supreme Court ruled political or government officials do not have the same right to be protected from defamation as do private citizens. Some courts have expanded this ruling to say that when a government agency is criticized its individual members cannot sue for defamation. For example, in the Virginia case of *Dean v. Dearing*,[19] the Virginia Supreme Court ruled an individual policeman could not sue for defamation for a statement saying his police department was corrupt, even though the department only had five to eight members. The logic for this exception for government officials or agents seems to be to protect the right to comment on and criticize the government.

Defames the Plaintiff

To win an action in defamation, the plaintiff must show that he or she has been defamed. Remember this dual use of the word *defame* is a product of the merger of the actions of libel and slander and that defamation can mean both the legal action resulting from the merger of libel and slander and the specific element of harm that is required in such actions. In the context of the required element of harm, to be defamed means to be injured by a communication that damages reputation or social standing. Such communication may cause other people to ostracize the plaintiff or it might cause potential customers, clients, or patients to withhold their business. Furthermore, the harm of the communication can vary with the context. For example, if a plumber was called an incompetent writer that is probably not defamatory. We do not expect plumbers to write well, so being called an incompetent writer would not damage the professional reputation of a plumber. If the same communication was uttered referring to a journalist or public relations practitioner, it could be defamatory because being thought of as an incompetent writer would harm the professional reputation of the professional communicator. Some statements would damage the reputation of any citizen. For example, being called a cheat, thief, or murderer would defame almost anyone. What makes a communication defamatory is that someone hearing it would reasonably understand the reputation of the plaintiff has been damaged.

In all civil actions, the plaintiff must prove some kind of harm was done by the defendant. In most actions the harm must be financial. In other words, to win most civil suits the plaintiff must show he or she actually lost money or something of value in order to win. Defamation differs from most civil actions in that it may not be necessary to show actual financial harm. The harm may be assumed. The assumption of harm has evolved along with a complex set of terms and rules. Given how difficult it would be to prove the financial value of reputation or social standing, it is easy to see how different courts through time have found justification for assuming harm.

The rules for assumed harm vary from state to state, but there are some general principles that apply in most jurisdictions. These rules were evolving long before libel and slander were combined into defamation, so they still do vary depending on the medium of communication. If the communication is in a relatively permanent medium, like writing, it is treated as libel. If the communication is an ephemeral form like speech, it is treated like slander.

For the purpose of deciding whether or not to require some proof of harm, libel is divided into the categories of *libel per se* and *libel per quod*. *Libel per se* is a statement that "on its face" obviously harms the reputation of a subject. The statement "Student John Doe is a cheat" is an example of libel per se. *Libel per quod* only damages the subject's reputation if other information is known. For example the statement "Student John Doe worked on his homework with Student Sally Smith" is only defamatory if the person reading the statement knows that students who work together are cheating. *Libel per se* is more direct, more likely to injure and, in most jurisdictions, can be prosecuted without any evidence of financial harm. In most jurisdictions, a plaintiff pursuing an action in *libel per quod* must show some measurable financial harm unless the allegation fits in a very narrow list of historic topics that included accusations of

1. criminal conduct,
2. moral turpitude,
3. infection with a loathsome disease,
4. professional incompetence, or
5. unchastity of a woman.

In defamation actions that arise from a spoken communication, the rules in most jurisdictions require proof of some financial harm unless the communication made one of the very specific accusations just listed.

One way to determine whether or not the plaintiff must prove actual financial harm is to work through the requirements for proof of harm described in Exhibit 9.2. First, ask yourself, "Is the communication permanent or ephemeral?" If the communication is in writing or some other permanent medium, then ask if it is *libel per se* or *libel per quod*. If it is *libel per se*, there is no need to prove financial harm. If the statement is *libel per quod* it is treated the same as communications in ephemeral media like speech. Plaintiffs

Exhibit 9.2. Requirement for Proof of Harm in Defamation Actions.

Libel	*Per Se:* No need to prove actual damage or *Per Quod:* treated like slander
Slander	Statement involves: criminal conduct, moral turpitude, "loathsome disease," misconduct in profession, or unchastity of a woman or Must prove actual damage

challenging statements that are either *libel per quod* or slander need not prove financial harm if those statements include one of the five specific allegations listed. If the statement is *libel per quod* or slander and does not include one of the five specific allegations then the plaintiff must prove financial harm.[20]

It may be helpful to remember these rules evolved in a society where women who were unchaste were unlikely to be able to marry and when marriage was thought of as the only appropriate social role for a woman. Also, "loathsome diseases" were sexually transmitted diseases and highly contagious diseases. Accusations involving such diseases were socially devastating when the technology to cure them did not exist.

One final note about harm is worth mentioning. Without a proof of financial harm a plaintiff may win a defamation lawsuit, but then he or she may receive only a token award from the court. In today's litigious world, such an award means the plaintiff may not even recover her or his attorneys' fees and court costs. In short, such actions are only worthwhile if the plaintiff can afford to lose money to repair his or her reputation.

Communicated or Published

No matter how vicious, untruthful, or hurtful a statement is, it cannot be defamation unless it is communicated to a third party. The logic behind this principle is that if a statement is only delivered to the person defamed, he or she will know the statement is not true and there will not be any harm to his or her reputation. Communication to a third party may take the form of publication, broadcast, or simply a loud voice. The element of "communication or publication" is met if the defamatory statement is delivered by the defendant to anyone other than the plaintiff him or herself. For example, a college professor could privately accuse a student of cheating. Even if untrue and very hurtful, this accusation is not defamation if it is delivered privately to the student. The same statement or accusation delivered in front of a class full of students has been communicated and would meet this one element of defamation. The communication has to be made by the defendant. If the student accused of cheating tells his or her fellow students about the accusation, this is not communication because the defendant professor did not do it. The defendant must intend to communicate the defamatory statement. If, for example, the professor sent an e-mail to the student and the student's roommate intercepted the message and read the accusation, the defamatory statement probably has not been communicated because the professor did not intend to deliver it to anyone other than the student involved.

The intent to communicate does not require the defendant to communicate the message deliberately to a third party. The intent requirement can be met if there is a reckless lack of care by the defendant. Extending the example of the professor accusing the student of cheating, if the professor makes the accusation in a very loud voice that is overheard by other students or faculty, the professor has communicated the accusation because of his or her recklessness.

Where there is foreseeable repetition of a message there is communication. Those in the professions of journalism, public relations, advertising, and photography should foresee that their written and graphic work will be shown to others. For legal purposes, almost everything those in these professions say and do is communicated. Thus, they should anticipate that even internal memoranda, draft articles, campaign proposals, or story boards will be circulated and therefore meet the legal definition of communication.

Generally speaking, reporting or repeating a statement that has already been made public does not constitute a new communication.[21] This principle is often called *republication* and its application to communications professionals is discussed in greater detail under defenses later in this chapter. For now, note that to avoid communicating defamatory information, communication professionals should avoid repeating statements that appear false.

One final issue about communication should be discussed. If a publisher produces a book, magazine, or newspaper in one state and then distributes the same material either in another state or in another medium of communication, is the distribution in a second state a new communication or simply a continuation of the original communication? This question becomes important where the victim of defamation wants to either pick a friendly state in which to sue or wants to sue several times in the hopes of receiving a larger judgment. Most states have adopted the "single publication rule." This rule means each repetition or redistribution of a statement is not a new communication or a new act of defamation. However, there are exceptions to this rule. For example, in its decision in *Keeton v. Hustler Magazine* the U.S. Supreme Court allowed a New York resident to sue *Hustler Magazine* in New Hampshire. *Hustler's* corporate headquarters are in Ohio and the first "communication" of the allegedly defamatory statement was made in Ohio. The plaintiff chose to sue in New Hampshire because that state has particularly "plaintiff-friendly" defamation laws. In their decision, the justices reasoned that *Hustler* deliberately took advantage of the economy of New Hampshire and therefore made a "communication" in New Hampshire that was subject to the suit.[22] The Florida Supreme Court also ruled that where a newspaper is distributed in multiple counties within the state a plaintiff may initiate a defamation action in any county where an allegedly defamatory statement is communicated.[23] In both of these cases, the courts ruled that the plaintiff can only sue for one communication of the alleged defamatory statement but did rule the plaintiff could choose a friendly venue where the communication was disseminated.

By the Defendant

The requirement to prove the defendant made the allegedly defamatory statement is the simplest of the elements of defamation. In very rare circumstances, a professional communicator may find his or her work has been modified by an editor or publisher. These modifications can raise questions about who actually made the challenged statement. However, virtually all defamation cases bring a claim against the publication or broadcaster of the statement. We discuss the concept of *respondeat superior* in more detail in the chapter on employment law. For now, we simply say, if you are the publisher, managing editor, or chief executive of any medium of communication and the medium contains a defamatory statement, you are probably responsible.

It should also be noted that republication or repeating a defamatory statement could create a new liability. In other words, if a reporter, or other communications practitioner, quotes a defamatory statement made by another person, the communications professional may be liable for making the statement if he or she intended to cause harm or had reason to know the statement was not true. This principle of republication is addressed in more detail in the section on defenses to defamation.

With Intent

To a lawyer, intent does not mean the same thing that it does to most laymen, so we begin this section by explaining the legal concept of intent. At law, intent simply means having the appropriate state of mind. For example, if you are driving and are hit by another car you may be able to sue the driver of the other car and force him or her to pay for the damage to your car. Such suits require that you prove an intent on the part of the other driver. In most jurisdictions, the intent you have to prove is called negligence. You do not have to prove the other driver actually intended to hit your car; you only have to prove that he or she was negligent. *Negligent* means not being as careful as you should be. For cases in defamation, each state has created its own standard for intent. Some states require only a showing of negligence and require no proof of intent at all. Those states that require no proof of intent presume if the statement is defamatory and untrue, the "intent" element has been met.

In 1964, the U.S. Supreme Court began to standardize the requirement for intent in its decision in *New York Times v. Sullivan*.[24] Although the *Sullivan* decision did create a national standard for intent, it certainly did not simplify the standard.

The *Sullivan* case arose at the height of the U.S. Civil Rights Movement. The facts of the case involve a full-page advertorial run by a civil rights group in *The New York Times*. Part of the advertorial described police reaction to a peaceful civil rights demonstration at Alabama State University in Montgomery. It said, "truckloads of police armed with shotguns and teargas" surrounded peaceful demonstrators and the authorities padlocked the university dining hall in an attempt to starve the protestors into submission. Some of the statements in the advertorial were not true; for example, the university dining hall had never been padlocked. L.B. Sullivan, the police commissioner of Montgomery at the time of the advertorial, sued *The New York Times* for defamation. Under Alabama law, at the time, Sullivan did not have to prove any intent on the part of *The New York Times*. The trial courts in Alabama returned judgment for Sullivan and awarded him $500,000. The U.S. Supreme Court granted certiorari and in its decision said the Alabama law violated the U.S. Constitution because it failed to protect free speech and a free press. Specifically, the Supreme Court said there was a constitutional obligation to protect the right to criticize public officials.[25]

In the decision in *New York Times v. Sullivan*, Justice Brennan created what is called the "malice rule." The rule is summarized in Exhibit 9.3. It prohibits a public official from collecting any damage in a defamation action arising from a statement about his or her official conduct unless the statement was made "with knowledge that it was false or with reckless disregard of whether it was false or not."[26]

The Supreme Court's decisions in *Curtis Publishing Co. v. Butts* and *Associated Press v. Walker* expanded the malice rule to cover public figures as well as public officials.[27]

Exhibit 9.3.   Malice Rule.

Plaintiff Type	Plaintiff Defined	"Standard of Intent"
Public official	Elected or appointed government official with apparent authority or who is subject to independent public interest	Malice: Defendant knew the statement was not true or recklessly disregarded whether it was true or false
Public figure	Person who *voluntarily* puts him or herself in the public interest	
Private person	Person who is *involuntarily* involved in a matter of interest or who is not involved in a public matter at all	States set their own standard

This expansion of the malice rule was clarified by the Supreme Court in *Gertz v. Robert Welch, Inc.*[28] Gertz was a lawyer who represented the family of a juvenile who had been shot by a Chicago policeman. Welsh was the publisher of the John Birch Society newsletter who wrote a very colorful article accusing Gertz of being a communist and the head of a criminal conspiracy against the police. In its decision, the U.S. Supreme Court ruled private citizens who do not voluntarily involve themselves in matters of public interest are not required to prove malice in order to win defamation lawsuits. The Court left the standard of "intent" in these cases entirely in the hands of the states. The decision in *Gertz v. Welch* did include one other ruling. The Court there said that plaintiffs may not receive punitive or presumed damages unless there is proof of malice. In other words, if there is no proof of malice, the plaintiff can only recover the value of what he or she actually lost because of the defamation.[29]

Who Is a Public Official or Public Figure?

Obviously, high-ranking government officials are public officials, but there are questions about how far down the "chain of command" one may be before he or she is no longer a "public official." For example, should a file clerk in a government office be given the same protections against acts of defamation as the president of the United States? In its decision in *Rosenblatt v. Baer,* the U.S. Supreme Court answered that question. The Court ruled a public official is a person who has or appears to have "substantial responsibility for or control over the conduct of public affairs,"[30] or "[such] importance that the public has an independent interest in the qualifications and performance of the person."[31] The first of these tests is often called the "apparent government authority test" and the second is the "independent public interest test."

Defining public figures has proven somewhat more difficult, but generally a public figure is a person who voluntarily puts him or herself in a position that meets the independent public interest test. For example, in its decision in *Curtis Publishing v. Butts,*[32] the Supreme Court ruled a major college football coach had voluntarily accepted a position that created public interest in his qualifications and performance. In the *Associated Press v. Walker* decision, the Supreme Court ruled a person who became an active and public opponent of school desegregation had voluntarily put himself in the public interest.[33] In *Gertz v. Welch,* the Court further noted that public figures give up their right to status as a private person only in the context of the public matter in which they are voluntarily involved.[34] Gertz was an attorney and in the courtroom he was a public figure. However, Welch made untrue statements about things outside the courtroom, including Gertz' politics and private beliefs. The Court ruled the entire life of a public figure is not open to comment or criticism. The requirement to prove malice only applies to statements made about the specific matters in which the public figure volunteered to involve him or herself.

Finally, we should emphasize the fact that a person must have volunteered to become a public figure. He or she must have accepted a job or taken an action that drew the public's attention. The Supreme Court has ruled that people who are forced into the public eye by news coverage are not public figures.[35] Even people who hire public relations counsel to respond to the false allegations against them are not public figures.[36]

Defenses and Immunities

One may defend against any legal action, including defamation, by showing the plaintiff failed to prove one of the required elements. In addition to this defense there are affirmative defenses and immunities. Affirmative defenses and immunities can be used to avoid judgment even if the plaintiff does prove all elements of defamation. Remember, for example, that falsehood may be an element or truth may be an affirmative defense, depending on the circumstances and jurisdiction of a trial for defamation.

The words *privilege* and *immunity* are often confused or used interchangeably by those not being careful about the distinction. Often, affirmative defenses to defamation are described using the words privilege and absolute privilege when the appropriate term is *immunity.*[37] This confusion may arise from the wording of Article I, Section 6 of the U.S. Constitution which says, in part: "Senators and Representatives shall . . . be privileged from arrest during their attendance at the session of their respective houses." This phrase is the basis for one of the immunities from prosecution for defamation. Here, we are careful to use the words as they are most commonly defined in contemporary law.

Absolute Immunity

An absolute immunity from prosecution for defamation arises from Article I, Section 6 of the U.S. Constitution. This Constitutional provision has been interpreted to guarantee legislators freedom from prosecution for anything said in Congressional debates. This protection is given to legislators to ensure they are completely free to present all arguments for and against proposals. The immunity has been extended to judges and judicial proceedings[38] and to the executive and administrative branches of government.[39] Because of this immunity, a person who is subjected to even the most egregious insults cannot sue most government officials for defamation. This protection extends to legislators, mayors, judges, and even heads of government agencies.

While the protection is very broad, it does not protect these government officials everywhere. The immunity is only available for statements made in the context of official duties. The U.S. Supreme Court made this limitation very clear in its 1979 decision in *Hutchinson v. Proxmire*.[40] The defendant in the case was then Senator William Proxmire. The senator publicly ridiculed wasteful government spending by presenting what he called the "Golden Fleece" award. One of his Golden Fleece awards was given to Dr. Ronald Hutchinson, the director of research at a mental hospital. Hutchinson had received a government grant to study aggression in primates. In a speech on the Senate floor, in a news release, and in a newsletter he mailed to constituents, Proxmire referred to Hutchinson's studies with phrases like "monkey business" and "transparent worthlessness." In short, Proxmire's statements were unquestionably defamation of a professional research scholar like Hutchinson. Hutchinson sued Proxmire for defamation. The suit was dismissed by the trial court and the Court of Appeals also ruled for Proxmire. The logic for granting the judgments against Hutchinson was that Proxmire's statements were immune from prosecution because they were made in his capacity as a senator. The U.S. Supreme Court reversed, saying:

> A speech by Proxmire in the Senate would be wholly immune and would be available to other Members of Congress and to the public in the Congressional Record. But neither the newsletters nor the press release was 'essential to the deliberations of the Senate' and neither was part of the deliberative process.[41]

This holding has been applied to all immunity for government officials. Statements made by officials as part of their official duties or statements that are necessary for debate and deliberation in a government function are immune from suit for defamation. However, government officials acting beyond the scope of their official duties are not immune from suit for defamation.

Qualified Immunity

Several categories of communication have immunity from prosecution for defamation unless the defendant acts with malice. For example, communications between employers and employees, letters of reference, and statements in police reports cannot be the basis for suits in defamation unless the person making the statements did so for the purpose of harming the plaintiff.[42]

The courts have extended qualified immunity to the news media because of the interest in public oversight of government and large private organizations. To enjoy immunity, a reporter must be describing some public activity of a government official or public figure. Many jurisdictions do not grant immunity to reports of allegations contained in court documents before those documents are brought before a judge. Information in complaints, affidavits, and other pretrial documents therefore do not enjoy qualified immunity.[43] Also, there is no immunity to report the statements of government or corporate executives until after the executive takes some public action.[44]

To have qualified immunity, statements reported must be public and must be accurately reported. Therefore, statements made in private meetings or closed hearings cannot be reported with immunity. Also, errors in quotations or even omissions of critical information can void the qualified immunity if the error or omission creates a false impression. It is not necessary to provide verbatim quotes, but a reporter must be careful not to change the meaning of the quotes or to put the report in a context that will create a false impression.[45]

Finally, qualified immunity is lost if the report is made for any reason other than to inform a public with a reasonable need to know. To determine if the immunity is lost for this reason, the courts look to the motivation of the reporter. Obvious misstatements of facts and financial gain by the reporter are evidence he or she did not report the statement for the purpose of informing a relevant public.[46]

Fair Comment and Nonverifiability

Historically, there was a common law defense for expression of opinion. As we explain in the practice notes at the end of this chapter, the opinion defense was totally eliminated by the U.S. Supreme Court in 1990.[47] What remains of the old opinion defense is a right to make "fair comments" and a defense for statements whose truth or falsity cannot be verified. The fair comment defense is related to the malice rule articulated in *New York Times Co., v. Sullivan.*[48] It effectively protects fair comments about public officials, public figures, and matters of public interest. Today, statements of either fact or opinion about public people or public matters are protected unless the plaintiff can prove those statements were made with the intent to harm or with a reckless disregard for the truth.[49] Exhibit 9.4 is an example of how critical such fair comments have been.

In the last two decades, another defense has effectively replaced opinion. In *Milkovich v. Lorain Journal Co.*, the U.S. Supreme Court ruled there was no "exemption

Exhibit 9.4.   Example of "Fair" Comment (*Cherry v. Des Moines Leader*, 114 Iowa 298, 86 N.W. 323 [1901]).

One of the most colorful comments made by a reporter or critic was held to be protected as "fair comment" by the Iowa Supreme Court. The case involved a critique of a vaudeville act in 1901. The critique by Billy Hamilton of the Odebolt Chronicle is reproduced below.

Effie is an old jade of 50 summers, Jessie a frisky filly of 40, and Addie, the flower of the family, a capering monstrosity of 35. Their long skinny arms, equipped with talons at the extremities, swung mechanically, and anon waived frantically at the suffering audience. The mouths of their rancid features opened like caverns, and sounds like the wailings of damned souls issued therefrom. They pranced around the stage with a motion that suggested a cross between the *danse du ventre* and fox trot – strange creatures with painted faces and hideous mien. Effie is spavined, Addie is stringhalt, and Jessie, the only one who showed her stockings, has legs with calves as classic in their outlines as the curves of a broom handle.

for anything that might be labeled opinion"[50] but went on to say only statements whose truth or falsity could be verified can be the basis for suits for defamation. Simplifying a very complicated decision, the court said that because the plaintiff must prove a statement is false in order to win an action in defamation, it is impossible to win an action in defamation if the statement, by its very nature, cannot be proven false.[51] The court then went on to give examples of the kinds of statements that cannot be proven false. These statements included descriptions of a negotiator's motivations, figurative language, rhetorical hyperbole or overstatements, parodies, and statements under emotional distress that could not reasonably be interpreted as assertions of fact.[52] It appears as long as the communicator is careful to make statements that cannot be proven factually untrue, he or she has a defense to defamation.

Retraction

If a communicator realizes he or she has made a defamatory statement, it may be possible to reduce the risk of suit by retracting the statement. However, retraction is not a complete defense. In virtually all jurisdictions, a retraction, to be effective, must be communicated quickly and with the same prominence as the original defamatory statement. Furthermore, retractions do not provide a complete defense; they only mitigate or reduce the kinds of damages a plaintiff may recover from the defendant. The effect of retractions are governed by individual state laws usually called "retraction statutes." These statutes vary widely but most say that if an adequate retraction is published, the liability of the defendant is reduced. In other words, if the defendant loses a lawsuit for defamation, he or she will not have to pay as much to the plaintiff.[53]

Statutes of Limitations.   In most jurisdictions, defamation is what is called a "disfavored" action. The courts find suits for defamation difficult to adjudicate so they impose barriers to make them more difficult to initiate. In many jurisdictions, the major barrier is a short statute of limitations. Statutes of limitations set a limit on the amount of time the plaintiff has to initiate the lawsuit. A 2-year statute of limitations, for example, means that after the allegedly defamatory statement is published, the plaintiff has 2 years to begin his or her lawsuit. If 2 years pass and the plaintiff has not filed suit, he or she is barred from ever suing the defendant.[54] Most torts have a statute of limitations of 2 years. As can be seen in Exhibit 9.5, many jurisdictions set a much shorter limit for bringing actions in defamation.

Private Facts

Actions in libel and slander, which are combined under the label *defamation,* were created by common law decisions and have a very long history. During that long history, complex rules have evolved for defamation. Private facts, on the other hand, is a relatively recent legal invention. Some authors suggest it began with a law journal article published in 1890[55] and other authors trace its formation to an English case involving Prince Albert in 1848.[56] Whatever its origins, the civil action to protect private facts is, by legal standards, so new that it is often called a modern communications tort.

Exhibit 9.5.   Statute of Limitations for Defamation Actions.

Please note that the way "time" for the statute of limitations is counted varies from state to state. For example, some states begin counting when the defamatory communication is published and some when the plaintiff learns of the defamation.

One Year or less	Two Years	Three Years or more
Arizona	Alabama	Arkansas
California	Alaska	Massachusetts
Colorado	Connecticut	New Hampshire
Georgia	Delaware	New Mexico
Illinois	Florida	Rhode Island
Kansas	Hawaii	Vermont
Kentucky	Idaho	
Louisiana	Indiana	
Maryland	Iowa	
Michigan	Maine	
Mississippi	Minnesota	
Nebraska	Missouri	
Nevada	Montana	
New Jersey	North Dakota	
New York	South Carolina	
North Carolina	South Dakota	
Ohio	Washington	
Oklahoma		
Oregon		
Pennsylvania		
Tennessee		
Texas		
Utah		
Virginia		
West Virginia		
Wyoming		

The key difference between defamation and the tort of publication of private facts is that truth is not a defense nor is falsehood an element. In other words, a defendant can be sued for publishing private information even if the publication is completely accurate. The tort is based on an evolving belief that some accurate information is so private its publication should be prohibited. One of the earliest applications of this principle was in the "Red Kimono" case. The plaintiff in that case was Gabrielle Melvin who, prior to 1919, had been a prostitute famous for wearing a red kimono. She was accused of killing one of her clients but was acquitted at trial. Following the trial she reformed, married and, in the words of the court, "at all times lived an exemplary, virtuous, honorable and righteous life."[57] In 1925, Dorothy Reid and other defendants sued by Melvin owned a company that made a motion picture titled *The Red Kimono*. The film used Melvin's real maiden name, Gabrielle Darley. Furthermore, in advertisements for the movie the defendants said the movie was "the true story of Gabrielle Darley." All this was done without the knowledge or consent of Melvin.

> [Because of] the production and showing of the picture, friends of appellant [Melvin] learned for the first time of the unsavory incidents of her early life. This caused them to scorn and abandon her and exposed her to obloquy, contempt, and ridicule, causing her grievous mental and physical suffering.[58]

Melvin's suit against the film's producers was dismissed by the trial court, which said that because the events were accurately depicted, Melvin had no cause of action against the producers. The California Appellate Court disagreed and ruled Melvin's right to protect private facts about her life had been violated. This, and other cases in the early 1900s, established a plaintiff's right to sue defendants who revealed private facts even when the defendant's statements are true.

Generally, authors of legal articles describe four elements in actions for revealing private facts. Those elements, summarized in Exhibit 9.6, are publicity, private matter, highly offensive information, and not newsworthy.[59] Here, we present those elements in a slightly different form in order to facilitate comparison with defamation. The elements, as we present them, expressed as a sentence are:

> A *private fact, about the plaintiff* that *would be highly offensive to a reasonable person*, is *communicated to a large group by the defendant* with *intent by the defendant.*

Exhibit 9.6. Elements of Private Facts (the plaintiff must prove all six to win an action for revealing private facts).

Element 1	Private fact	Reasonable person would keep private This plaintiff did keep private Is not newsworthy
Element 2	About the plaintiff	
Element 3	Highly offensive to a reasonable person	
Element 4	Communicated or published to a large group	
Element 5	By the defendant	
Element 6	With intent by the defendant	

What Is a Private Fact?

Remember the primary difference between defamation and actions for private facts is that one may sue for revealing private facts even if the information is true. But, if plaintiffs could sue for any true statement it would be virtually impossible to communicate anything. Therefore, a plaintiff can sue for revealing private facts only if the information is truly private.

The prohibition against revealing private facts is based on the idea that the press "cannot be said to have any right to give information greater than the extent to which the public is entitled to have information."[60] For the past 75 years, courts have ruled consistently that the public is not entitled to have information a reasonable person would keep private, that the plaintiff did keep private, and that is not newsworthy. We address each of the three components of a private fact separately.

Reasonable Person Would Keep Private

Unfortunately, there is no simple rule to identify what kind of information a reasonable person would keep private. Information that has been held to be reasonably private usually focuses on sexual or criminal conduct[61] but has included such innocuous information as the style and color of undergarments[62] and eating disorders.[63]

As a practical matter, it should be noted the courts have consistently required the plaintiff to prove the information he or she seeks to protect would be offensive to reasonable people. Furthermore, when confronted with a question about what kind of information reasonable people would keep private, the courts have consistently said "it is for the trier of fact to determine."[64] This means, "what a reasonable person would keep private" is what the plaintiff can convince a jury, or the judge in a bench trial, a reasonable person would keep private. This is not an easy burden for a plaintiff to bear. Perhaps as a result of this burden, it is rare for any information that is not obviously offensive and private to be the basis for a successful action for revealing private facts.

Did Keep Private

Not only must the plaintiff prove a reasonable person would keep the subject facts private, he or she must also prove the subject facts were actually kept private. Certainly, a child molester would keep his or her sexual proclivities private. But many communities and news organizations post the names, addresses, and criminal records of such individuals on Web sites or other public media. This is not a violation of the child molester's privacy because the molester did not keep the information private. The molester made the information public by his or her criminal conduct, arrest, and the creation of a public record of conviction. No information already contained in public records is private. "There is no liability when the defendant merely gives further publicity to information about the plaintiff which is already public."[65]

It seems obvious that one may repeat information from the public record about a child molester, but other, less intuitive rulings hold that any information already public may be used without violating a right of privacy. For example, the name of rape or assault victims may be used if that name is already in a public record.[66] Also, images already available for public view can be used without invading a person's privacy. For example, a local television station may broadcast the image of a poorly maintained house if the image could be seen by the public from the street.[67] The media can also use the image of a woman exposing her breasts if she engaged in the act in a way that showed no intent to keep the act private.[68]

Not Newsworthy

In 1940, the U.S. Court of Appeals for the Second Circuit ruled "at some point the public interest in obtaining information becomes dominant over the individual's desire for privacy."[69] Since then, courts have consistently ruled that even information a reasonable person would keep private and which is, in fact, kept from the public does not meet the legal definition of "private facts" if the information is legitimately newsworthy. When courts determine what is newsworthy, they are admonished not to edit journalists aggressively[70] and not to impose their standards of taste on the media.[71] Rather, when defining newsworthiness, the courts look for matters of legitimate public interest.

While the courts have provided some guidance to help determine what is and what is not newsworthy, this element, much like what a reasonable person would keep private, is not clearly defined. The Federal Court of Appeals for the Ninth Circuit ruled information is not news if it only is "prying into private lives for its own sake" and further said information that "serves no legitimate public interest…is not deserving of protection."[72] The courts of California have also said information that is "not of legitimate public concern" is not newsworthy.[73]

One way to help identify the kinds of information that is "newsworthy" is to review the facts of some specific cases. One of the first cases in this area was *Sidis v. F-R Pub. Corp.*, which involved a feature titled *Where Are They Now?* in the *New Yorker* magazine. The article described the eccentric lifestyle of a former child prodigy who graduated from Harvard at the age of 16. The Court of Appeals ruled the public's interest in a person who had been a celebrity in the past made the story newsworthy even though the former prodigy made extraordinary efforts to keep his current life private and unremarkable.[74] In its decision in *Cinel v. Connick,* a U.S. Appellate Court ruled the public's legitimate interest in the immoral conduct of a Catholic priest outweighed the priest's right to keep videotape of his homosexual acts private.[75] The Georgia Supreme Court ruled the public's interest in the identity of a woman who fought off and killed a potential rapist outweighed the woman's privacy right.[76] A federal Appellate Court in Washington, DC, ruled the results of a drug test on a police officer could be a matter of legitimate public interest preventing the officer from suing for violation of his privacy when the results were publicized.[77] Finally, a Florida Appellate Court ruled a nude picture of a woman can be newsworthy if it is relevant to a story of public interest.[78]

Just like the requirement to prove a reasonable person would keep the information private, the courts have ruled the plaintiff has the burden of proof for this component of private facts. The plaintiff must prove the information was not newsworthy.[79] In other words, for this element, a communications professional is probably safe from suit for revealing private facts if the facts involve the kind of information typically covered in news media in the community where the action would be tried.

Finally, it should be noted that the lives of public figures are typically newsworthy. When deciding whether someone is a public figure for the purpose of deciding whether facts about them are newsworthy, one need apply a somewhat different standard than when identifying public figures for applying the malice rule in defamation actions. To apply the malice rule the voluntary status of the person is important. For private facts, the issue is whether there is legitimate public interest in the activities of the person involved. Therefore, whether the person has become a celebrity by choice or because of events over which he or she has no control, the person becomes a public figure, in this context, because of interest about him or her.[80] However, even a public figure may legitimately keep parts of his or her life private. The information for which newsworthiness is claimed must have some reasonable relation to the arena in which the person has become a public figure. For example, information about the moral standards of a priest or a police officer's illegal conduct does fit within the sphere of their public life, [81] but descriptions of a past love affair are not within the public life of a person accused of sedition.[82]

About the Plaintiff

Because the gravamen of actions for revealing private facts is individual privacy, the plaintiff must be able to show that the public will know the information is specifically about him or her.[83] Unlike actions in defamation, this means statements about groups may not violate a right to protect private facts regardless of how small the group might be.

As a result of this requirement to prove invasion of the privacy of a specific individual, the heirs of a person whose privacy is invaded cannot sue on behalf of the estate.[84] As a practical matter, this means communications professionals writing about deceased subjects are usually safe from suit for private facts.

Highly Offensive

To sustain an action in defamation the plaintiff had to prove the information revealed defamed him or her and harmed his or her reputation. The parallel element in an action for revealing private facts is the requirement that the plaintiff prove the information is highly offensive. In an attempt to make this requirement more specific, the Court of Appeals for the Second Circuit said the information must "be so intimate and so unwarranted in view of the victim's position as to outrage the community's notions of decency."[85] Many times, the courts apply exactly the same tests to determine what a reasonable person would keep private and to determine what information is highly offensive.[86] Just like the information seen as reasonably private, this information usually involves sexual misconduct or criminal activity.[87]

Communicated to a Large Group

The element for communication or publication in a defamation action could be met by showing that the defamatory statement had been communicated to any third party. In actions for revealing private facts, the plaintiff must prove that "the public" has been made aware of the information. In fact THE RESTATEMENT OF TORTS uses the word *publicity* to label this element. The Restatement says publicity "means that the matter is made public, by communicating it to the public at large, or to so many persons that the matter must be regarded as substantially certain to become one of public knowledge."[88]

Publicity does not depend on the medium used to disseminate the information; the element of publicity or communication to a large group is met if the information is disseminated in any medium sure to reach the public.[89] Publication in a newspaper, broadcast on television, posting on a well-read Web site, or even the development of a widespread rumor is "communication to a large group." Professional communicators should note the courts have uniformly held that release of information in any medium of mass communication meets this requirement.[90] Virtually all the plaintiff needs to show to prove he or she has met this element is to show that the information appeared in a newspaper, magazine, or media broadcast.

Revealed by the Defendant

Unlike defamation where "republication" of a defamatory statement may not be actionable in suits, for revealing private facts the issue is who first delivered the private information to "the public." Therefore, a communications professional who is given accurate information by a third party could be successfully sued for revealing private information if he or she was the first person to communicate the information to a large group by publishing it in a newspaper or other mass medium.

With Intent by Defendant

The requirement for intent or state of mind for defamation was complicated and varied depending on whether the plaintiff was a public or private figure. Although the standard of intent required varies from state to state, all require more than simple negligence. Most states require the plaintiff prove "knowing or reckless falsity in the publication." Furthermore, the U.S. Supreme Court has ruled there is a Constitutional requirement for malice or reckless disregard for the truth in matters involving public figures or matters of public interest. The High Court said:

> A negligence test would place on the press the intolerable burden of guessing how a
> jury might assess the reasonableness of steps taken by it to verify the accuracy of
> every reference to a name, picture, or portrait.[91]

Defenses

Basically, the same defenses are available for publication of private facts that were available for defamation. Except, of course, truth. Proving the statement is true is not a defense for revealing private facts.

Other defenses that might be available include waiver and consent. Consent of the plaintiff means he or she gave the defendant permission to publish the private facts. Consent may be either express consent in the form of an oral or written release or implied consent in the form of "Conduct which is reasonably understood by another to be intended as consent."[92]

Express consent is the easier of the two defenses to prove and express consent cannot be withdrawn or modified if the person giving the consent later changes his or her mind.[93] Even express consent is limited to the specific terms of the consent. In other words, one cannot secure consent to use the private information for one purpose or in one medium and then later use that information differently. Both express and implied consent are limited to the purpose and medium for which they were given. For example, a model who gives express permission to have a private photograph published in a book has not consented to having that photograph appear in a newspaper[94] and a private citizen who allows a photograph to be taken by a newspaper photographer has not consented to having that photograph used years later in the context of another story.[95]

False Light

The first cases for false light appeared in the 1950s. Since then, almost all cases have dealt with using a photograph taken in one situation to illustrate another situation or inaccurately identifying the people in a photograph.[96]

False light is similar to defamation because both require the plaintiff to prove the information communicated is untrue and that it is communicated to others.[97] But false light differs from defamation because defamation is designed to protect the reputation of the plaintiff while false light protects the plaintiff from emotional distress or mental anguish.[98] To win an action in false light, the plaintiff only needs to prove a false impression is created and that the false impression would offend a reasonable person. Therefore, in many instances plaintiffs may be able to win actions for false light when they could not win a suit for defamation.

It should also be noted that some states have rejected actions in false light because they are so similar to defamation.[99] In the jurisdictions that do recognize actions in false light, the elements are fairly standard and typically involve distortion, embellishment, or fictionalization of photographs or video. The elements of false light are listed in Exhibit 9.7. Expressed as a sentence those are:

Exhibit 9.7.   Elements of False Light (the plaintiff must prove all six to win an action for false light).

Element 1	Creation of a false light or false impression
Element 2	Of the plaintiff
Element 3	That would offend a reasonable person
Element 4	In publicity presented to the public
Element 5	By the defendant
Element 6	With malice or reckless disregard for the truth by the defendant

The creation of a *false light* or false impression *of the plaintiff* that would *offend a reasonable person* in *publicity* presented to the public *by the defendant* with *malice or reckless disregard for the truth* by the defendant.

Creation of False Light

For an action in false light, the plaintiff does not have to prove a specific untrue statement. Rather, he or she must show the information or image, as presented by the defendant, created a false impression or put the plaintiff in a false light in the eyes of the public. For example, a Chicago newspaper published a story describing the 25 suicide attempts of Evelyn Daly, but the article was accompanied by a photograph of another woman. The woman in the photograph successfully sued the newspaper because the presence of her picture with the article titled "Suicide Fiend" gave those who knew her the impression she was the subject.[100] A false impression does not have to be negative. Baseball pitcher Warren Spahn sued a publisher who falsely reported that Spahn had received military decorations for valor.[101]

Identification of Plaintiff

Because actions for false light require communication to a large group, the plaintiff must be identifiable not only to a few people who know him or her well but must be identified by a large group. This requirement is met if the defendant uses the plaintiff's name, photograph, or even a description that the public will recognize.[102]

That Would Offend

It is the trier of fact, the jury or the judge in a bench trial, who must determine whether the impression created by the false light communication would offend a reasonable person.[103] The question the trier of fact must ask is, "Would a reasonable person in the same circumstances be highly offended by the impression created?"[104] Most cases identifying this level of offensiveness have involved impressions of sexual or moral misconduct or misidentifying the responsible party in an accident or crime.[105]

Presented to Public

This requirement is identical to the fourth element of actions for revealing private facts. The defendant must have delivered the information, photographs, or images that created the false light to a large enough group to create an impression in the mind of "the public."[106]

Communicated by Defendant

This requirement is identical to the fifth element in actions for revealing private facts. It should be noted that just like defamation and private facts actions, here the plaintiff cannot be the person who communicates the damaging information. If, for example, the defendant showed information to a small group of people and created a false impression of the plaintiff, the plaintiff cannot then repeat the same information to a larger group and thereby meet the requirement that false light publicity has reached a large public.[107]

With Malice or Reckless Disregard for the Truth

The requirements for intent or state of mind in actions for false light are well established. In two different decisions, the U.S. Supreme Court ruled for all actions in false light, regardless of whether the plaintiffs are public or private persons, the plaintiff must prove the defendant acted with actual malice or with reckless disregard for the truth.[108]

Defenses

Obviously, an action can be defended by showing the plaintiff failed to prove the required elements. In this context, defenses include truth and absence of malice. In addition, affirmative defenses include waiver or consent, which were discussed under private facts and immunity. Immunity from prosecution can also arise when the information that creates the false light is in a protected venue. Such venues include documents filed in courts and private reports.[109] Also a defense for fair comment, much like that available for suits in defamation, has been recognized.[110]

Appropriation

The tort of appropriation protects us from improper use of our name or likeness by others. This tort is sometimes referred to as the "right of publicity." Possibly because the word *publicity* has been associated with the tort, a common misconception exists that it is closely related to the practice of public relations or that it involves a right to secure news coverage or publicity. As seen in this brief summary of appropriation law, it is only tangentially related to the practice of public relations and it has almost nothing to do with a right to receive publicity.

There is extraordinary variation in appropriation law from state to state. Some states have created a common law action for appropriation. In other states, the legislatures passed statutes recognizing the tort. Some states have refused to recognize even a right to prevent the use of names or photographs in advertising or on packaging.[111] Most of the appropriation statutes prevent the use of names or likenesses for commercial purposes without express consent.[112] Whether based on common law or statute, actions in appropriation exist primarily to prevent the commercial use of a person's name or likeness without payment or permission.[113]

The elements for defamation, private facts, and false light are all very similar. However, appropriation and intrusion protect different kinds of interests, and the elements for these two torts are different than those for defamation. In most jurisdictions, the elements for appropriation are:

> The *use of the plaintiff's name or image, without consent* of the plaintiff, for the *financial benefit* of the defendant. Those are also listed in Exhibit 9.8.

Exhibit 9.8.   Elements of Appropriation (the plaintiff must prove all three to win an action for Appropriation).

Element 1	Use of plaintiff's name or image
Element 2	Without consent from the plaintiff
Element 3	With financial benefit to the defendant or harm to the plaintiff

Because intent is usually assumed, it is not an element of appropriation. The minimal intent requirement in appropriation is usually met simply by showing the defendant used the plaintiff's name or image.[114] The courts and legislatures seem to think it is impossible for a plaintiff to use the image or name of another person "accidentally."

Use of Plaintiff's Name or Image

The key to deciding if a plaintiff's name or image has been used is whether the plaintiff can be recognized by the general public. It is not enough for the plaintiff to be able to recognize his or her own image. Others must be able to recognize the image or name and associate it with the plaintiff.[115] There is no need for the plaintiff to be well known. Average citizens have been successful in actions for appropriation where their name was used in advertisements.[116]

If it is recognizable, a person's "image" can be taken by the use of his or her photograph, video, painting, or even a voice.[117] The use of look-alikes or sound-alikes can also constitute a taking of a plaintiff's image when their use gives the impression the plaintiff him or herself was actually represented.[118]

Without Consent

Of course, anyone may consent to the use of his or her name or image. Just as was discussed earlier, consent may be either express or implied. In most actions for appropriation, there either was no consent, there are questions about an implied consent, or the challenged use of the plaintiff's name or image is not within the scope of the express consent. Because these cases typically arise from commercial use of the plaintiff's name or image, anyone producing advertisements or commercial communication would be well advised to secure a specific written release, prepared by competent legal counsel, from everyone whose name or image is used.

Financial Benefit to Defendant

Remember the interest being protected by appropriations law is the plaintiff's right to be paid for his or her image. Therefore you may be able to use a celebrity's name or image so long as there is no financial benefit or harm. However, the financial "benefit" element can be proven even if the defendant does not profit. The element is met if there is a financial loss on the part of the plaintiff. Use of the plaintiff's name or image in some way that dilutes her or his ability to sell it to others is a "financial benefit." For example, if a plaintiff's image is used in a message endorsing a charity or social movement, the plaintiff's ability to secure payment for endorsement of another cause would be destroyed, thus meeting the requirement for financial benefit.

Furthermore, the financial benefit may be indirect. It is not necessary to sell the image of the plaintiff or to use his or her name in a commercial advertisement. If another person's name or image is used to advance a political cause or even to solicit donations to a charity, their likeness is being appropriated because people are normally paid or rewarded for those uses of their image.[119]

Defenses

Defenses to appropriation include incidental use and newsworthiness. Incidental use is a use that is so small or trivial that it neither adds to the value of the medium in which the image or likeness was used nor damages the interests of the plaintiff. The defense for newsworthiness arises from the courts' desire to protect the right of the media to comment on matters of public interest. We have discussed the concept of newsworthiness before, but there are some unique problems created by the interaction of newsworthiness and appropriation law. One of these problems is the use by the news media of the name or likeness of a celebrity to promote sales of a newspaper or to recruit audience for a television or Web news broadcast. Generally, the courts have permitted news media to use the names and images of news subjects to advertise the media, even if those subjects are celebrities.[120] However, the courts have ruled for celebrities suing the news media if the use of their name or likeness implied a specific endorsement of a medium. For example, *Forum* magazine ran advertising copy in its own pages saying that the singer and actress Cher gave information to *Forum* she would not give to the magazine's competitors. Cher, who had neither given consent nor the described information to *Forum*, sued for appropriation of her name and won judgment against the magazine.[121]

Finally, the newsworthiness defense cannot be used to excuse broadcast of an entire entertainment act, regardless of how short that act may be. In 1977, the U.S. Supreme Court ruled even the First Amendment right of the media to comment on and describe matters of public interest was outweighed by the appropriation of an entire entertainment act. The decision came as the result of a local television station's broadcast of a 15-second performance by a human cannonball.[122] In effect, the court said that the media could not use their rights to completely appropriate the plaintiff's act and source of income.

Intrusion

Intrusion is the simplest of the communications torts. The only complicated part of intrusion is understanding what it has to do with communications. Actions for intrusion are not based on how information is used or how it is communicated. Rather, actions for intrusion are based entirely on how the information was gathered. If a communications professional gathers information by invading or intruding upon physical space where the plaintiff had a reasonable expectation of privacy or by taking information the plaintiff could reasonably expect to be private, that is intrusion.

Exhibit 9.9.   Elements of Intrusion (the plaintiff must prove all three to win an action for intrusion).

Element 1	Intentional intrusion
Element 2	In the personal space or information of the plaintiff
Element 3	In a way that would offend a reasonable person

Trespass was described in chapter 6. One simple way to define intrusion is to think of it as the use of any information that was acquired by an act of trespass.

The elements of intrusion are listed in Exhibit 9.9. Expressed as a sentence, they are:

Intentional intrusion into the *personal space or information* of the plaintiff in a way that would *offend a reasonable plaintiff.*

Intentional Intrusion

Because the tort requires intentional intrusion, a person who accidentally walks through the wrong door or inadvertently stumbles upon information has not committed intrusion. Of course, a person who finds him or herself accidentally in the private milieu of another must leave as soon as the invasion is apparent. Even if the defendant accidentally stumbled into the private area, if he or she does not leave quickly, that is still intrusion.[123]

Personal Space or Information

As a general rule, personal space is any place where a person would not expect to be observed. Private homes, offices, and hospital rooms have all been ruled personal spaces in this context.[124] However, places that can be viewed from the street or other public areas usually are not personal space. For example, even a reporter observing the inside of a home through a window from the street may not have committed intrusion if he or she did not stay too long or use exotic optical equipment.[125]

It is also important to remember that actions for intrusion can be based on intrusions into private information or seclusion. For example, a newspaper columnist who published a plaintiff's phone number and encouraged readers to call was found liable for intrusion because the resulting phone calls intruded upon the plaintiff's expectation of privacy.[126] Intrusion also covers hacking into computer data in which the plaintiff had a reasonable expectation of privacy.[127]

It is also intrusion if deception is used to gain access to personal spaces or personal information. For example, a reporter who enters a home or office with a secreted camera or audio recorder has met the element of violation of personal space.[128]

Offend a Reasonable Person

Like most legal requirements that require a judgment about what a reasonable person would do or think, this element is usually left for the trier of fact to determine.[129] To provide some guidance about what juries or judges think would offend a reasonable person, the following examples are provided. Uninvited attendance at a private party by a reporter who took notes and photographs was held to offend a reasonable person.[130] Entering a private home or office while it is vacant has also been judged to offend a reasonable person.[131] However, courts have ruled going through trash left some distance from a plaintiff's hospital room and interviewing neighbors to secure information about a plaintiff would not offend a reasonable person.[132]

Defenses

Of course, a communications professional accused of intrusion may defend him or herself by showing the plaintiff cannot prove the elements of the action. In other words, he or she can show the intrusion was not intentional or the place intruded upon was not personal space or the intrusion would not offend a reasonable person. However, there appear to be no affirmative defenses or immunities for intrusion. It is imperative, particularly for reporters, to understand neither truth nor newsworthiness is a defense to intrusion. No matter how much public interest there may be in subject, neither trespass nor intrusion into personal space or information can be defended.

It should be noted that one element of intrusion is the actual invasion of the personal space or information. This means if one person invades the personal space of another, he or she is liable for intrusion. But if the person who invaded the space gives information gained in the intrusion to a reporter who publishes the information, the reporter is not liable for the intrusion. In *Pearson v. Dodd* the U.S. Circuit Court described this limited liability for intrusion. The case involved an employee of Senator Dodd who improperly searched the senator's private files, copied information, and gave the information to Jack Anderson, a reporter who, in turn gave the copies to Drew Pearson, who published the documents. Even though Pearson knew the documents had been improperly obtained, the Circuit Court ruled he was not liable for intrusion.[133]

Practice Notes

The Opinion Defense: A Dangerous Fantasy for Journalists

Some mass communications practitioners are under the dangerous misimpression that simply labeling their comments as "opinion" provides a defense to defamation.[134] This simply is not true.

The belief may have gained credence because in 1984 a circuit court decision described a set of criteria, called the "Ollman test," to be used to determine whether a statement is or is not an expression of opinion.[135] This determination was important because in 1984 there was a common law defense to defamation for statements of opinion.

But, 6 years after the *Ollman* decision, in 1990, the U.S. Supreme Court reviewed an Ohio decision that had recognized the opinion defense. The U.S. Supreme Court noted the Ohio courts had applied the Ollman test[136] but immediately after its discussion of the Ollman test the Court said:

> We granted certiorari, 493 U.S. 1055 (1990), to consider the important questions raised by the Ohio courts' recognition of a constitutionally required "opinion" exception to the application of its defamation laws. **We now reverse.** [emphasis added][137]

In its decision, the Supreme Court described its rationale for refusing to recognize an opinion defense. In that context, the Court said,

> If a speaker says, "In my opinion John Jones is a liar," he implies a knowledge of facts which lead to the conclusion that Jones told an untruth.... Simply couching such statements in terms of opinion does not dispel these implications; and the statement, "In my opinion Jones is a liar," can cause as much damage to reputation as the statement, "Jones is a liar."[138]

One year later, the Court made its ruling absolutely clear and completely dispelled any hope that opinion might be a defense in defamation. In *Masson v. New Yorker Magazine, Inc.*, the Supreme Court said, "Last term in *Milkovich v. Lorain Journal Co.*, we refused to create a wholesale defamation exception for anything that might be labeled opinion."[139]

Prefacing defamatory statements with "in my opinion" or putting opinion editorials or advertorials on the opinion page of a newspaper or otherwise putting a statement in the social or journalistic context of opinion is not a defense to defamation.

Employee Communication Defense: Possible Help for Public Relations Practitioners

Public relations practitioners working in internal or employee communications are often called on to explain why employees are terminated or how employee misconduct motivated changes in employer policy. Such communications could lead to a suit based on one of the communications torts described in this chapter. It may be helpful to know that in many situations, communications directed to employees by, or on behalf of, employers are immune from suit for defamation, private facts, or false light.

Many courts have ruled when two parties share a common business interest in information or share a need to know information in order to perform their jobs, that information cannot be defamatory. For example, courts in Connecticut, Delaware, Indiana, and Mississippi have all recognized a defense they call a "qualified privilege" for communication between employers and employees.[140] The defense, which the court erroneously called a privilege, has also been described by the U.S. Supreme Court.[141] While there are variations in how the defense is applied, it does provide an affirmative defense to communications torts in almost all jurisdictions in the United States.

In order to qualify for this defense, the communication must be limited to information that is necessary for the employees to do their jobs. It must be a "statement of fact honestly believed to be true…and with the honest intention to perform a duty."[142] The defense is lost if the damaging information given to employees goes beyond that necessary to help them do their jobs or if it is given to employees who do not need the information. The defense is also lost if the information is disseminated with actual malice.

Actual malice, in this context, is different than the legal malice that was required for defamation of public figures. Legal malice includes intentional harm or reckless disregard for the truth. Actual malice requires ill will or an actual intent to improperly harm the person who is the subject of the communication.[143]

The kinds of communication that have been protected from communications torts by this defense include information given in meetings, employee interviews, and internal memoranda explaining why another employee was demoted, suspended, or terminated.[144] The U.S. Circuit Court of Appeals has ruled that explaining the termination of an employee in a news release involved too broad an audience, showed the malice that would defeat the defense[145] and other courts have found malice when the employer included fabricated allegations about employee misconduct[146] or when a nonstandard medium involving a very large audience was used to communicate derogatory information.[147]

In short, an employee communications practitioner may be protected if he or she is delivering derogatory information to employees that will help them meet the objectives of their employment or dispel rumors that interfere with productivity. But these protections vary by jurisdiction and you should always have local legal counsel check any communication that might be defamatory.

Magic Words and Phrases

Absolute immunity	Gravamen
Affirmative defense	Hacking (in intrusion)
Apparent government authority test	Harm
Appropriation	Identifies plaintiff (what is required)
Communication or publication	Immunity
Consent	Implied consent
Defamation (two definitions)	Implied endorsement
Defense	Incidental use (in appropriation)
Element	Independent public interest test
Employee communication defense	Intentional intrusion
Express consent	Intrusion by deception
Fair comment	Invasion
False light	Legally true
Falsehood	Libel
Financial benefit (in appropriation)	*Libel per quod*

Libel per se	Public official
Loathsome disease (in defamation)	Public records (in private facts)
Look-alike	Publicity
Malice (actual malice & legal malice)	Reckless disregard for the truth
Modern communications torts	Recognized by the general public
Moral turpitude (in defamation)	Retraction statute
Negligence	Single publication rule
Newsworthy (in private facts)	Slander
Offensive to a reasonable person	Sound-alike
Opinion defense	Tort
Private facts	Trier of fact
Privilege	Truth
Professional incompetence (in	Unchastity of a woman (in defamation)
defamation)	Waiver
Public figure	Waiver (and consent)
Public matter	

Suggested Cases to Read and Brief

Barr v. Matteo, 360 U.S. 564 (1959)

Cantrell v. Forest City Publishing Co., 419 U.S. 245 (1974)

Cher v. Forum Int'l., Ltd., 692 F.2d 634 (9th Cir.1982), *cert. denied* 462 U.S. 1120 (1983)

Cox Broadcasting Corp. v. Cohn, 420 U.S. 469 (1975)

Crump v. Beckley Newspapers, Inc., 173 W.Va. 699, 704, 320 S.E.2d 70. 75 (W.Va. 1983)

Curtis Publishing Co. v. Butts and *Associated Press v. Walker*, 388 U.S. 130 (1967)

Dun & Bradstreet, Inc. v. Greenmoss Builder, Inc., 472 U.S. 749 (1985)

Fawcett Publications, Inc. v. Morris, 1962 OK 183; 377 P.2d 42, 47 (1962), *cert. denied* 376 U.S. 513 (1964)

Gertz v. Robert Welch, Inc., 418 U.S. 323 (1974)

Gregoire v. G.P. Putnam's Sons, 298 N.Y. 119; 81 N.E.2d 45 (1948)

Hinerman v. Daily Gazette Co., Inc., 188 W.Va. 157, 423 S.E.2d 560 (1992), *cert. denied*, 507 U.S. 960 (1993)

Hutchinson v. Proxmire, 443 U.S. 111 (1979)

Keeton v. Hustler Magazine, Inc., 465 U.S. 770 (1984)

Masson v. New Yorker Magazine, 501 U.S. 496 (1991)

McSurely v. McClellan, 753 F.2d 88 (D.C.Cir 1985), *cert. denied* 474 U.S. 1005 (1985)

Melvin v. Reid, 112 Cal.App. 285, 297 P. 91 (1931)

Milkovich v. Lorain Journal Co., 497 U.S. 1 (1990)

Neiman Marcus v. Lait 107 F. Supp 96 (S.D.N.Y. 1952)

New York Times v. Sullivan, 376 U.S. 254 (1964)

Onassis v. Christian Dior-New York, Inc., 122 Misc.2d 603, 472 N.Y.S.2d 254 (Sup.Ct.1984)

Pearson v. Dodd, 410 F.2d 701 (D.C.Cir. 1969), *cert. denied* 395 U.S. 947 (1969)

Philadelphia Newspapers, Inc. v. Hepps, 475 U.S. 767 (1986)

Sidis v. F-R Pub. Corp., 113 F.2d 806, 809 (2d Circ. 1940), *cert. denied* 311 U.S. 711 (1940)

Time Inc. v. Hill, 385 U.S. 374, 397 (1967)

White v. Fraternal Order of Police, 909 F.2d 512, 528 (D.C. Cir. 1990)

Wood v. Hustler Magazine, Inc., 736 F.2d 1084 (5th Cir.1985), *cert. denied* 469 U.S. 1107 (1985)

Questions for Discussion

1. Several reality television shows involve what could be called "ambush entertainment." These programs involve unannounced confrontations with accused criminals or people accused of being unfaithful to a spouse or paramour. Could the victims of these "ambush" confrontations successfully sue the production companies for defamation, false light, intrusion or appropriation? Why or why not?

2. Some television shows like *American Idol* and *Weakest Link* often include insulting or derogatory comments about a participant's talent or intelligence. Could people appearing on these shows sue the production companies or the person who insulted them for defamation or any other communication tort? Why or why not? Specifically, consider whether there is an implied consent given by people who appear on these shows.

3. Many news media do not use the names of rape victims. Is there any legal prohibition against using the names of victims of sexual assault? Could a state, without violating the First Amendment, create a law that prohibits the use of the names of victims of sexual assault?

4. Could a rape victim whose name is revealed by a news medium sue for intrusion, private facts, or appropriation? Why or why not?

5. Is a rape victim, an accused rapist, or a convicted rapist a public figure? Why or why not?

6. For this question, assume you are a public relations practitioner working for a company that just discharged a large number of employees for embezzling company funds. If the company's executive officer asked you to write an article explaining why the people were discharged, would you discourage him or her from publishing the article? What would you need to know in order to decide if the article could be defended from a suit for defamation, private facts, or false light with the "employee communication" defense?

7. In the same situation described in question 6, what would be different if the company's executive officer asked you to write a news release for the local media? If you wrote the release and it was published in the local newspaper, what defenses

might you use if the fired employees sued you for defamation, false light, or private facts?

8. Would the situation be different if you worked for a government agency that fired employees for embezzlement?

9. Assume you work for an advertising agency and one of your clients wants you to produce a radio commercial with a voice that sounds exactly like a famous actress. If you use the commercial, could the actress sue you for appropriation? Could she sue your client? What, if anything, can you do to protect yourself and your client from the suit?

10. Assume you are a reporter for a statewide newspaper. While at a reception honoring ex-convicts who have become successful in reputable professions, you meet a former convict of the state penitentiary who tells you that inmates in the prison are routinely beaten and food or money sent to them by their relatives is often stolen by the guards. In order to protect yourself from a lawsuit for defamation by the prison warden or guards, how carefully do you have to check your facts before writing the story? Are the prison guards public officials or public figures? If the guards are not public figures, do you have to be more careful than you would have to be if they were not?

11. Assume you are a public relations practitioner developing a campus brochure for a large state university. To illustrate your brochure you take several photographs of the campus and students. One of the photographs is of an attractive couple holding hands. If you use that photograph without the consent of the couple, can they sue you for appropriation? Why or why not? If the two people in the photograph are both married to other people, can they sue you for intrusion, false light, or private facts?

12. If the couple described in question 11 saw you with your camera and carefully posed while you took the photograph, have they waived their right to sue you if you use the picture in the campus brochure? Why or why not?

13. Again, assume you are the public relations representative of a state university preparing a campus brochure. If you took a photograph from the top of an administrative building that showed hundreds of students and faculty walking across campus, could the people in that photograph sue for appropriation if the picture was used in a fundraising campaign for the university?

14. A political commentator, referring to the president of the United States, in a national television broadcast said, "In my opinion, he is a neo-Nazi, fundamentalist Christian religious bigot." Can the president win a lawsuit for defamation? Why or why not? What defenses could the commentator use if he or she were sued? Is the fact that the commentator prefaced his comment with "In my opinion" important? Why or why not?

Notes

1. Gerry Spence, *The Sale of the First Amendment*, 75 A.B.A. J., 52, 54 (1989).
2. See, e.g., Samuel D. Warren & Louis D. Brandeis, *The Right to Privacy*, 4 HARV. L. REV. 193 (1891).

3. See, e.g., Gerry Spence, *The Sale of the First Amendment*, 75 A.B.A. J., 52 (1989).

4. W. Page Keeton et al., PROSSER AND KEETON ON THE LAW OF TORTS § 111 (5th ed. 1984).

5. See e.g., 2 William Blackstone, COMMENTARIES ON THE LAWS OF ENGLAND 94 (19th ed. 1852).

6. See, e.g., *Garrison v. Louisiana*, 379 U.S. 64 (1964).

7. *Philadelphia Newspapers, Inc. v. Hepps,* 475 U.S. 767 (1986).

8. *Id.*

9. *Id.* at 776.

10. *Dun & Bradstreet, Inc. v. Greenmoss Builders, Inc.* 472 U.S. 749 (1985).

11. *Strada v. Connecticut Newspapers, Inc.,* 193 Conn. 313, 477 A.2d 1005 (1984).

12. *Id* at 1009–10.

13. *Masson v. New Yorker Magazine*, 501 U.S. 496, 516-17 (1991).

14. See, e.g., *Gannett Co., Inc. v. Re*, 496 A.2d 553 (Del. 1985).

15. *Fawcett Publications, Inc. v. Morris*, 1962 OK 183; 377 P.2d 42, 47 (1962), *cert. denied* 376 U.S. 513 (1964).

16. *Id.*

17. *Neiman Marcus v. Lait,* 107 F. Supp 96 (S.D.N.Y. 1952).

18. *New York Times v. Sullivan*, 376 U.S. 254 (1964).

19. *Dean v. Dearing,* 263 Va. 485; 561 S.E.2d 686 (2002).

20. William L. Prosser, TORTS 763 (4th ed. 1971).

21. See, e.g., *Gregoire v. G.P. Putnam's Sons*, 298 N.Y. 119; 81 N.E.2d 45 (1948); and *Mc-Cutcheon v. State*, 746 P.2d 461 (Alaska 1987).

22. *Keeton v. Hustler Magazine, Inc.*, 465 U.S. 770 (1984).

23. *Firstamerica Dev. Corp. v. Daytona Beach News-Journal Corp.*, 196 So.2d 97 (Fla. 1966).

24. *New York Times v. Sullivan*, 376 U.S. 254 (1964).

25. *Id.* at 273–276.

26. *Id.* at 279–280.

27. *Curtis Publishing Co. v. Butts* and *Associated Press v. Walker*, 388 U.S. 130 (1967).

28. *Gertz v. Robert Welch, Inc.*, 418 U.S. 323 (1974).

29. *Id.* at 349–350.

30. *Rosenblatt v. Baer*, 383 U.S. 75, 85 (1966).

31. *Id.* at 86.

32. *Curtis Publishing*, 388 U.S. U.S. 130.

33. *Associated Press v. Walker*, 388 U.S. 130 (1967).

34. *Gertz v. Welch*, Inc., 418 U.S. 323 (1974).

35. See, e.g., *Wolston v. Reader's Digest Assn., Inc.* 442 U.S. 157 (1979).

36. See, e.g., *Time, Inc. v. Firestone*, 424 U.S. 488 (1976).

37. See, e.g., *Briscoe v. LaHue*, 460 U.S. 325 (1983); *Buckley v. Fitzsimmons*, 509 U.S. 259, 277 n.8 (1993).

38. See, e.g., *Buckley v. Fitzsimmons*, 509 U.S. 259 (1993).

39. See, e.g., *Barr v. Matteo*, 360 U.S. 564 (1959).

40. *Hutchinson v. Proxmire*, 443 U.S. 111 (1979).

41. *Id.*

42. See, e.g., *Garziano v. E.I. EuPont De Nemojurs & Co.*, 818 F.2d 380 (5th Cir. 1987).

43. See, e.g., *Sanford v. Boston Herald-Traveler Corp.*, 318 Mass. 156, 61 N.E.2d 5 (1945).

44. See, e.g., *Phillips v. The Evening Star Newspaper Co.*, 424 A.2d 78 (D.D. 1980), *cert. denied* 451 U.S. 989 (1981).

45. See, e.g., *Schiavone Constr. Co. v. Time, Inc.*, 847 F.2d 1069 (3d Cir. 1988).

46. See, e.g., *Lavin v. New York News Inc.*, 757 F.2d (3d Cir. 1985); *Mastandrea v. Lorain Journal Co.*, 65 Ohio App.3d 221, 583 N.E.2d 984 (Ohio App. 1989), *cert. denied*, 498 U.S. 822 (1990).

47. *Milkovich v. Lorain Journal Co.*, 497 U.S. 1 (1990).

48. *New York Times Co., v. Sullivan*, 376 U.S. 254 (1964).

49. See, *New York Times v. Sullivan*, 376 U.S. 254, 279-280 (1964); *Curtis Publishing Co. v. Butts* and *Associated Press v. Walker*, 388 U.S. 130 (1967); *Gertz v. Welch*, 418 U.S. 323 (1974).

50. *Milkovich*, 497 U.S. at 18.

51. *Milkovich*, 497 U.S. at 16.

52. *Milkovich*, 497 U.S. at 16–18.

53. See, e.g., *Hinerman v. Daily Gazette Co., Inc.*, 188 W.Va. 157, 423 S.E.2d 560 (1992), *cert. denied*, 507 U.S. 960 (1993).

54. See, e.g., *Gregoire v. G.P. Putnam's Sons*, 29 N.Y. 119, 81 N.e.2d 45 (1948).

55. Samuel D. Warren & Louis D. Brandeis, *The Right to Privacy*, 4 HARV. L. REV. 193 (1890).

56. *Prince Albert v. Strange*, 2 DeGex & Sm. 652, 64 Eng. Rep. 293 (V.C. 1848).

57. *Melvin v. Reid*, 112 Cal.App 285, 286; 297 P. 91 (1931).

58. *Id.*

59. Samuel D. Warren & Louis D. Brandeis, *The Right to Privacy*, 4 HARV. L. REV. 193 (1890); RESTATEMENT SECOND OF TORTS § 652D (1977).

60. *Virgil v. Time, Inc.* 527 F.2d 1122, 1128 (9th Cir. 1975) *cert. denied* 425 U.S. 998 (1976).

61. See, e.g., *Hawkins by and through Hawkins v. Multimedia, Inc.*, 288 S.C. 569, 344 S.E.2d 145, *cert. denied* 479 U.S. 1012 (1986); *Melvin v. Reid*, 112 Cal.App 285, 287; 297 P. 91 (1931); *Briscoe v. Reader's Digest Assn.*, 4 Cal.3d 529, 483 P.2d 34 (1971).

62. *Daily Times Democrat v. Graham*, 276 Ala. 380, 162 So.2d 474 (1964).

63. *Barber v. Time, Inc.*, 348 Mo. 1199, 159 S.W.2d 291 (1942).

64. *Briscoe v. Reader's Digest Assn.*, 4 Cal.3d 529, 543, 483 P.2d 34 (1971).

65. *Virgil v. Time, Inc.* 527 F.2d at 1126.

66. *Cox Broadcasting Corp. v. Cohn*, 420 U.S. 469 (1975); *Macon Telegraph Pub. Co. v. Tatum*, 263 Ga. 678, 436 S.E.2d 655 (1993).

67. *Wehling v. Columbia Broadcasting System*, 721 F.2d 506, 509 (5th Cir. 1983).

68. *California Superior Court Judge Dismisses Lawsuit Against Mantra Films and Joe Francis*, BUSINESS WIRE, Nov. 25, 2003.

69. *Sidis v. F-R Pub. Corp.*, 113 F.2d 806, 809 (2d Circ. 1940) *cert. denied* 311 U.S. 711 (1940).

70. *Ross v. Midwest Commmunications, Inc.*, 870 F.2d 271, 275 (5th Cir. 1989) *cert. denied* 493 U.S. 935 (1989).

71. *Neff v. Time, Inc.*, 406 F. Supp. 858, 860 (W.D.Pa. 1976).

72. *Virgil v. Time, Inc.* 527 F.2d 1122, 1129 (9th Cir. 1975) *cert. denied* 425 U.S. 998 (1976).

73. See, *Forsher v. Bugliosi*, 26 Cal.3d 792, 808-809, 608 P.2d 716 (1980); *Briscoe v. Reader's Digest Assn.*, 4 Cal.3d 529, 541-544, 543, 483 P.2d 34 (1971); *Kapellas v. Kofman*, 1 Cal.3d 20, 34-39, 459 P.2d 912 (1969)

74. *Sidis v. F-R Pub. Corp.*, 113 F.2d 806 (2d Circ. 1940), *cert. denied* 311 U.S. 711 (1940).

75. *Cinel v. Connick*, 15 F.3d 1338, 1345-1346 (5th Cir. 1994).

76. *Macon Telegraph Pub. Co. v. Tatum*, 263 Ga. 678, 436 S.E.2d 655 (1993).

77. *White v. Fraternal Order of Police*, 909 F.2d 512, 528 (D.C. Cir. 1990).

78. *Cape Publications, Inc., v. Bridges,* 423 So.2d 426, 427-428 (Fla.Dist.Ct.App. 1982), *cert. denied*, 464 U.S. 893 (1983).

79. *Diaz v. Oakland Tribune, Inc.*, 139 Cal.App.3d 118, 128-129, 188 Cal.Rptr. 762 (1983).

80. See, e.g., *McSurely v. McClellan*, 753 F.2d 88 (D.C.Cir 1985), *cert. denied* 474 U.S. 1005 (1985).

81. *Cinel v. Connick,* 15 F.3d 1338, 1345-1346 (5th Cir. 1994); *White v. Fraternal Order of Police*, 909 F.2d 512, 528 (D.C. Cir. 1990).

82. *McSurely v. McClellan*, 753 F.2d 88 (D.C.Cir 1985), *cert. denied* 474 U.S. 1005 (1985).

83. *Tureen v. Equifax, Inc.,* 571 F.2d 411, 482 and nn. 48, 49 (8th Cir. 1978).

84. *Livsey v. Salt Lake County*, 275 F.3d 952 (10th Cir. 2001).

85. *Sidis v. F-R Pub. Corp.*, 113 F.2d 806, 809 (2d Circ. 1940), *cert. denied* 311 U.S. 711 (1940).

86. *Daily Times Democrat v. Graham*, 276 Ala. 380, 162 So.2d 474 (1964); *Barber v. Time, Inc.*, 348 Mo. 1199, 159 S.W.2d 291 (1942).

87. *Melvin v. Reid*, 112 Cal.App 285, 287; 297 P. 91 (1931); *Briscoe v. Reader's Digest Assn.*, 4 Cal.3d 529, 483 P.2d 34 (1971); *Hawkins by and through Hawkins v. Multimedia, Inc.*, 288 S.C. 569, 344 S.E.2d 145, *cert. denied* 479 U.S. 1012 (1986).

88. Restatement Second of Torts § 652D (1977).

89. *Virgil v. Time, Inc.,* 527 F.2d 1122, 1125-1126 (9th Cir. 1975), *cert. denied* 425 U.S. 998 (1976).

90. *Tureen v. Equifax. Inc.*, 571 F.2d 411, 418 (8th Cir. 1978).

91. *Time, Inc., v. Hill*, 385 U.S. 374, 389 (1967); See, also, *Roshto v. Hebert*, 439 So.2d 428, 432 (La.1983).

92. *McCabe v. Village Voice, Inc.*, 550 F.Supp. 525, 529 (E.D. Pa. 1982).

93. *Morgan v. Hustler Magazine, Inc.*, 653 F.Supp. 711 (N.D. Ohio 1987).

94. *McCabe v. Village Voice, Inc.*, 550 F.Supp. 525 (E.D.Pa. 1982).

95. *Crump v. Beckley Newspapers, Inc.*, 173 W.Va. 699, 704, 320 S.E.2d 70. 75 (W.Va. 1983).

96. See, e.g., *Leverton v. Curtis Pub., Co.*, 192 F.2d 974 (3d Cir.1951); *Peay v. Curtis Pub. Co.*, 78 F.Supp. 305 (D.D.C.1948); *Gill v. Curtis Pub. Co.*, 38 Cal.2d 273, 239 P.2d 630 (1952) .

97. See, e.g., *Wood v. Hustler Magazine, Inc.*, 736 F.2d 1084 (5th Cir.1985) *cert. denied* 469 U.S. 1107 (1985).

98. *Prescott v. Bay St. Louis Newspapers, Inc.*, 497 So.2d 77, 80 (Miss. 1986).

99. See, e.g., *Renwick v. News & Observer Pub. Co.*, 310 N.C. 312, 326, 312 S.E.2d 405, 413 (1984), *cert. denied* 469 U.S. 858 (1984); *Cain v. Hearst Corp.*, 878 S.W.2d 577, 579 (Tex. 1994).

100. *Wandt v. Hearst's Chicago American*, 129 Wis. 419, 109 N.W. 70 (1906).

101. *Spahn v. Julian Messner, Inc.*, 21 N.Y.2d 124, 233 N.E.2d 840 (1967), *appeal dismissed* 393 U.S. 1046 (1969).

102. *Brauer v. Globe Newspaper Co.*, 351 Mass. 53, 217 N.E.2d 732 (1966).

103. See, e.g., *Braun v. Flynt*, 726 F.2d 245, 252 (5th Cir.1984), *cert. denied* 469 U.S. 883 (1984).

104. See, e.g., *Machleder v. Diaz,* 801 F.2d 46, 58 (2d Cir.1986), *cert. denied* 479 U.S. 1988 (1987); *Braun v. Flynt*, 726 F.2d 245, 252 (5th Cir.1984), *cert. denied* 469 U.S. 883 (1984).

105. See, e.g., *Braun v. Flynt*, 726 F.2d 245, 252 (5th Cir.1984), *cert. denied* 469 U.S. 883 (1984); *Leverton v. Curtis Pub. Co.,* 192 F.2d 974 (3d Cir.1951).

106. See, e.g., *Moore v. Big Picture Co.*, 828 F.2d 270 (5th Cir.1987); *Polin v. Dun and Bradstreet, Inc.*, 768 F.2d 1204 (10th Cir.1985); *Reed v. Ponton,* 15 Mich.App. 423, 166 N.W.2d 629 (1968).

107. *Moore v. Big Picture Co.*, 828 F.2d 270 (5th Cir.1987).

108. See, *Time, Inc. v. Hill*, 385 U.S. 374 (1967); *Cantrell v. Forest City Publishing Co.*, 419 U.S. 245 (1974).

109. See, e.g., *Lee v. Nash*, 65 Or.App 538, 671 P.2d 703 (1983); *Devlin v. Greiner*, 147 N.J.Super. 446, 371 A.2d 380 (1977).

110. *Bichler v. Union Bank & Trust Co.*, 745 F.2d 1006 (6th Cir.1984) (en banc).

111. See, e.g., *Roberson v. Rochester Folding Box Co.*, 171 N.Y. 538, 64 N.E. 442 (1902).

112. See, e.g., California, Florida, Kentucky, Massachusetts, Nebraska, New York, Oklahoma, Tennessee, Utah.

113. *Roberson v. Rochester Folding Box Co.*, 171 N.Y. 538, 64 N.E. 442 (1902); *Onassis v. Christian Dior-New York, Inc.*, 122 Misc.2d 603, 472 N.Y.S.2d 254 (Sup.Ct.1984).

114. See, e.g., *Douglass v. Hustler Magazine, Inc.*, 769 F.2d 1128, 1140 (7th Cir.1985) *cert. denied* 475 U.S. 1094 (1986).

115. See, e.g., *Rawls v. Conde Nast Pub., Inc.*, 446 F.2d 313 (5th Cir.1971), *cert. denied* 404 U.S. 1038 (1972).

116. *Canessa v. J.I. Kislak, Inc.*, 97 N.J.Super. 327, 235 A.2d 62 (1967).

117. See, e.g., *Pavesich v. New England Life Ins. Co.*, 122 Ga. 190, 50 S.E. 68 (1905), *Welch v. Mr. Christmas, Inc.*, 57 N.Y.2d 143, 440 N.E.2d 1317 (1982); *Kimbrough v. Coca-Cola/USA*, 521 S.W.2d 719 (Tex.Civ.App.1975).

118. *Onassis v. Christian Dior-New York, Inc.*, 122 Misc.2d 603, 472 N.Y.S.2d 254 (Sup.Ct.1984).

119. See, e.g., *Hinish v. Meier and Frank Co.*, 166 Or. 482, 113 P.2d 438 (1941).

120. See, e.g., *Booth v. Curtis Pub., Co.*, 15 A.D.2d 343, *aff'd* 11 N.Y.2d 907, 182 N.E.2d 812 (1962); *Namath v. Sports Illustrated*, 48 A.D.2d 487 (1975) *aff'd* 39 N.Y.2d 897, 352 N.E.2d 584 (1976); *Guglielmi v. Spelling-Goldberg Prods.*, 25 Cal.3d 860, 603 P.2d 454 (1979).

121. *Cher v. Forum Int'l., Ltd.*, 692 F.2d 634 (9th Cir.1982), *cert. denied* 462 U.S. 1120 (1983).

122. *Zacchini v. Scripts-Howard Broadcasting Co.*, 433 U.S. 562 (1977).

123. RESTATEMENT SECOND OF TORTS § 652B (1977).

124. See, e.g., *Miller v. National Broadcasting Co.*, 187 Cal. App.2d 1463 (1986); *Ritzmann v. Weekly World News, Inc.*, 614 F.Supp. 1336 (N.D.Tex.1985); *Rawlins v. Hutchinson Pub. Co.*, 218 Kan. 295, 543 P.2d 988 (1975); *Mark v. King Broadcasting Co.*, 27 Wash.App 344, 618 P.2d 512 (1980).

125. *Mark v. King Broadcasting Co.*, 27 Wash.App 344, 353, 618 P.2d 512, 519 (1980), *aff'd. sub. nom. Mark v. Seattle Times*, 96 Wash.2d 473, 498, 635 P.2d 1081, 1094-1095 (1981), *cert. denied* 457 U.S. 1124 (1982).

126. *Harms v. Miami Daily News, Inc.*, 127 So.2d 175 (Fla.App.1961).

127. John A. McLaughlin, Comment, *Intrusion Upon Informational Seclusion in the Computer Age*, 17 J. MARSHALL L. REV. 831, 843 (1984).

128. See, e.g., *Dietemann v. Time, Inc.*, 449 F.2d 245 (9th Cir.1971).

129. See, e.g., *Rafferty v. Hartford Courant Co.*, 36 Conn.Sup. 239, 416 A.2d 1215 (1980; *Harms v. Miami Daily News, Inc.*, 127 So.2d 715 (Fla.App.1961).

130. *Harms*, 127 So.2d 715.

131. *Gonzales v. Southwestern Bell Tel. Co.*, 555 S.W.2d 219 (Tex.Civ.App.1977); *Pearson v. Dodd*, 410 F.2d 701 (D.C.Cir.1969), *cert. denied* 395 U.S. 947 (1969).

132. *Nicholson v. McClatchy Newspapers*, 177 Cal.App.3d 509 (1986); *Froelich v. Werbin*, 219 Kan. 461, 548 P.2d 482 (1976).

133. *Pearson v. Dodd*, 410 F.2d 701 (D.C.Cir. 1969), *cert. denied* 395 U.S. 947 (1969).

134. See, e.g., Don Pember & Clay Calvert, MASS MEDIA LAW 227–228 (McGraw-Hill 2005–2006 ed. 2004).

135. *Ollman v. Evans*, 750 F.2d 970 (D.C.Cir. 1984).

136. *Milkovich v. Lorain Journal Co.*, 497 U.S. 1, 10 (1990).

137. *Id.*

138. *Id.* at 18–19.

139. *Masson v. New Yorker Magazine, Inc.*, 501 U.S. 496, 515 (1991).

140. *Toprosyan v. Boehringer Ingelheim Pharmaceuticals, Inc.*, 234 Conn. 1, 622 A.2d 89 (1995); *Tacket v. Delco Remy Div.*, 678 F.Supp. 1387 (S.D.Ind.1987), applying Indiana law; *Garziano v. E.I. DuPont De Nemours & Co.*, 818 F.2d 380 (5th Cir.1987); *Gonzalez v. Avon Products, Inc.*, 609 F.Supp. 1555 (1985), applying Delaware law; *Batista v. Chrysler Corp.*, 454 A.2d 286 (Del.Super.Ct.1982).

141. *Barr v. Matteo*, 360 U.S. 564 (1959).

142. *Garziano v. E.I. DuPont De Nemours & Co.*, 818 F.2d 380, 387 (5th Cir.1987).

143. *Batista v. Chrysler Corp.*, 454 A.2d 286, 292 (Del.Super.Ct.1982).

144. *Tacket v. Delco Remy Div.*, 678 F.Supp. 1387 (S.D.Ind.1987); *Garziano v. E.I. DuPont De Nemours & Co.*, 818 F.2d 380 (5th Cir.1987); *Batista v. Chrysler Corp.*, 454 A.2d 286 (Del.Super.Ct.1982).

145. *Barr v. Matteo*, 256 F.2d 890 (1958).

146. *Toprosyan v. Boehringer Ingelheim Pharmaceuticals, Inc.*, 234 Con. 1, 622 A.2d 89 (1995).

147. *Gonzalez v. Avon Products, Inc.*, 609 F.Supp. 1555 (1985).

10

Copyright and Trademark

[T]he plaintiff . . . was the author, inventor, designer, and proprietor of the photograph . . .
to which he gave visible form.[1]

Overview
Introduction to Copyright
Creation of Copyrights
Ownership of Copyright
Prohibited Acts
Copyright Infringement
Defenses
Trademark
Practice Notes

Overview

This chapter describes the rights and obligations associated with copyrights and trade-marks. Although there is a significant body of related international and state law, we focus on those laws that would impact a mass communications practitioner working in the United States. Most international agreements on intellectual trade apply a concept called *national treatment*. National treatment means that a country provides authors from other countries the same protection given its own citizen authors. Because of national treatment, the protections afforded intellectual creations vary significantly from country to country. Treaties like the Berne Convention impact the enforcement of rights in the United States, so they are mentioned, but practitioners working outside the United States or those who work with materials produced outside the country are encouraged to seek legal counsel.

We have also omitted coverage of a number of related state laws. Most states, for example, have laws addressing unfair trade practices, misappropriation, and fraud. All of these laws could be used to protect the creative work of authors or artists. Because of the variations in these laws, they are simply beyond the scope of a single text.

We work from the assumption that most of our readers are primarily concerned about protecting works created in the United States from plagiarism by competitors in the United States. Therefore, this chapter focuses primarily on U.S. copyright protection. We also provide a brief overview of protections given to trademarks, service marks, and trade dress because experience shows that many practitioners in advertising and public relations are involved in creation and application of those items.

Introduction to Copyright

Article I, Section 8, Clause 8 of the U.S. Constitution grants Congress the power to promote science and the arts by giving authors and inventors exclusive rights to their writings and discoveries. The rights of inventors to their inventions are called *patents* and the rights of authors to their writings are called *copyrights*. Collectively, patents, copyrights, and trademarks are called **intellectual property**. The very words used to describe these rights are significant. Copyright is a right to prohibit copying. It is not the right to prohibit another author from independently creating a similar or identical document. Intellectual property is property. It can be bought and sold just like other kinds of property. It is called intellectual property because it is the product of intellectual creativity, not simply hard work. Each of these ideas is explained in more detail later in this chapter but it may facilitate understanding to keep the concepts of *copy*, *property*, and *intellectual* in mind as you read this chapter. It may also help to note that the notions of *author* and *writing* have been expanded to include *artists* and their *art*. Therefore, the work of graphic artists, musicians, and photographers can all be protected by copyright. As we introduce the section on trademark, we explain why trademarks are not covered under copyright law.

The first U.S. copyright laws were passed in 1790. They were revised in 1831, 1870, 1909, and 1976. In addition, when the United States ratified the **Berne International Convention** in 1989, that action modified some of the copyright laws, particularly those dealing with the requirements for notice. As we discuss copyright law, we focus on the law as it exists as of this writing, but some copyrights created prior to the 1976 act and prior to the 1989 accession to the Berne Convention are still in effect. Materials copyrighted prior to 1976 and between 1976 and 1989 have different protections and requirements than do materials copyrighted in 2005.

Creation of Copyrights

Before an author or artist can protect work from being copied he or she must create a copyright. The requirements to create a copyright are listed in Exhibit 10.1. Generally, a **copyright** is created the instant an original work is reduced to a tangible form and the author can prohibit others from copying his or her work by either an actual or implied notice.[2] Registration is not required to create a copyright. However, it is necessary to register a copyright before the author can obtain statutory damages and attorney fees in an infringement suit. For this reason, we include registration in our discussion of the requirements for copyright creation.

Exhibit 10.1. Requirements to Create and Enforce a Copyright. (Registration not required to create copyright but is required for enforcement.)

Original Work

Reduced to Tangible Form

Notice – Implied or Actual

Registration

What Is an Original Work?

There are two major limitations on what is legally an original work. First, the work must be creative. Second, the work must be intellectual and not **utilitarian**. If they involve significant intellectual creativity, some reproductions or copies are treated as original works.

Original Work Must Be Creative

The key to intellectual originality is **creativity**. Works cannot be copyrighted simply because the author was the person who originated them. The work must have been creatively original, not simply the product of hard work. It may help you understand this concept to remember the idea that copyrights are *intellectual* property. Time, sweat, and effort are not intellectually creative. In 1991, the U.S. Supreme Court delivered an opinion that emphasizes the distinction between effort and the creativity required to make something an original work. A commercial publisher of telephone books simply copied the listings from a rural telephone company's directory and the telephone company sued for copyright violation. It is difficult to imagine a written work that takes more time and effort than the creation of an accurate telephone directory, but the Supreme Court ruled the listings in such a directory cannot be copyrighted because they are not original works. The Court said, "The *sine qua non* of copyright is originality. To qualify for copyright protection, a work must be original to the author."[3] The Court ruled the Feist Directory could legally take the work of the telephone company and republish the same information without violating copyright laws because there was nothing creative in the creation of the original directory. In order to be creative, a directory or database would have to be organized in some creative way or include novel language or material. Following this general rule, collections of court cases cannot be copyrighted nor can typefaces.[4]

Utilitarian Items Are Not Original

There is an historic distinction between utilitarian objects and the creative works that can be copyrighted. This distinction arises primarily from the separate references in the Constitution to authors and writing in one clause and to inventors and discoveries in another. Many courts have ruled that objects that can be patented should not also enjoy copyright protection.[5] This philosophical and legal distinction had little meaning to those of in mass communications until technology began to merge utility and creativity in the form of computer programming. Because some works may involve computer programming or application, we briefly describe when such utilitarian works may or may not be copyrighted.

Dealing with a low-technology work, the U.S. Supreme Court described how utility and creativity might merge in the case of *Mazur v. Stein* in 1954.[6] The case dealt with an attempt by a sculptor to use copyright law to protect statuettes he designed for use as bases for lamps. The courts below rejected his claims, saying the lamps were utilitarian and therefore could not be copyrighted. The Supreme Court ruled the statues themselves could enjoy copyright protection even though they were designed to be used as lamp bases. Art incorporated into the moving parts on a watch face has also been permitted a copyright.[7]

The fact that utilitarian works were denied patents led many to think that computer programs could not be protected by copyright. Congress resolved this concern with the 1980 amendments to the Copyright Act. Those amendments added language protecting computer programs as original works and defined programs with the following language: "[A] set of statements or instructions to be used directly or indirectly in a computer to bring about a certain result."[8] Furthermore, the U.S. Court of Appeals for the Third Circuit said that even when embedded in a utilitarian chip, a computer program is a copyrightable creative work if it is original and meets the definition given by the 1980 amendments to the Copyright Act.[9] Some of the difficulty deciding how to deal with programs embedded in computer chips was resolved when Congress passed the Semiconductor Chip Protection Act in 1984. That act mixes principles from copyright and patent law to protect products that may be both utilitarian and creative.[10]

Even with these decisions and laws, courts are occasionally confronted with programs, not in chips, that incorporate both utilitarian and creative components. For example, a program that produces outlines may have utilitarian components such as pull-down menus or printing commands and these may not be copyrightable, but the same program may have specific language or instructions that can be copyrighted.[11] Some other components of computer programs, like what is often called the use and feel of the programs, have been denied copyright protection. These aspects are not reduced to written codes[12] and may be denied protection because they are utilitarian and therefore not original work. They may also be denied copyrights because they have not been reduced to a tangible form.

Copies or Reproductions May Be Original

One form of original work that seems contrary to common sense is the reproduction or copy. Courts have consistently held that a copy can be an original work if the reproduction introduces interpretation or elements of originality. This view of original work arose at a time when hand copying was the usual form of reproduction. It was solidified in application of copyright law to photography. Ours is not the first time in which courts have attempted to apply old law to new technology. Just as contemporary courts are trying to find how to separate utility and creativity in computer programs, courts in the past had to wrestle with then new technology like photography. One of the first cases applying copyright law to photography was *Barrow-Giles Lithographic Co. v. Sarony*.

The plaintiff had taken a portrait of Oscar Wilde and the defendant copied that photograph. The facts of the case were not disputed. The defendant admitted copying plaintiff's work but defended his actions by saying that a photograph was merely a mechanical copy of a natural image and lacked the originality required for copyright. In other words, the defendant said that one cannot copyright a photograph because it is not an original work. The Supreme Court ruled photographers, by posing their subjects, arranging background and costume, and selecting lighting, do add their own originality and creativity to photographs.[13] Working from this logic, a later Circuit Court case said, "no photograph, however simple, can be unaffected by the personal influence of the author, and no two will be absolutely alike."[14] In short, a photograph, even though it is only a copy of nature, has enough creativity to be an original work and can be copyrighted.

Because of the principles established for photography, we know that some copies can be copyrighted. But the element of creativity must be more than just a trivial modification. In 1951, the U.S. Court of Appeals ruled that an engraver's copy of an old art master had enough creativity to be copyrighted but that simple colorization of the engraver's work was too trivial to justify a new copyright. The court said that an author must contribute "something more than a merely trivial variation. . . ." He must contribute "something recognizably his own."[15]

For those in mass communications, this means that news photographs, video, or audiotape of news, and courtroom sketches may all be copyrighted.[16] Probably more important to most mass communications practitioners, it also means an original interpretation or new expression of facts can be copyrighted. The copyright of news reports or expressions of facts are somewhat complicated by the requirement that copyrighted material must be reduced to a tangible form so that **pure ideas** or information cannot be copyrighted. That distinction between expression and ideas is addressed in the next section.

Reduced to a Tangible Form

In order to copyright any work, that work must be in some **tangible form**. The form can be any medium including writing, painting, sculpture, photography, or magnetic recording.[17] The Copyright Act even includes language saying works may be "fixed in any tangible medium of expression now known or later developed."[18] The act also says materials are protected by copyright as soon as they are reduced to a tangible form.

The requirement for a tangible form means ideas, facts, or pure information cannot be copyrighted because they are not tangible. What can be copyrighted is the physical expression of the ideas, facts, or pure information. For example, if an individual has an idea for a word-of-mouth public relations campaign, even if that campaign is implemented, the idea or concept cannot be copyrighted. What could be copyrighted is the written plan or instructions for the campaign.

If a reporter invests his or her time and energy in research to identify information for a groundbreaking story on political corruption, he or she cannot copyright the facts in the story. Only the tangible form of the story itself can be copyrighted. Another reporter could read the story, rewrite it, and add his or her own elements of creativity in the way the facts are expressed.

Copyright is available for the form of expression of an idea but not for the idea itself.[19] The principle that ideas cannot be protected by copyright was made obvious by the U.S. Supreme Court in a ruling involving an author who developed a unique accounting system and described the system in a book he copyrighted. The Court ruled other accountants could use his system or ideas; they just could not use the expression or the language he had used to describe the system in his book.[20] What is protected by copyright is not an idea but the exact tangible form in which it is expressed.

Furthermore, if there is only one way to express an idea, one may not even be able to copyright one's tangible writings. For example, Frank Morrissey developed an idea for a sales promotion contest based on customers' social security numbers. He even wrote the rules for the contest and registered those rules for copyright. After attempting to sell his idea to several companies, one of those companies began to use the promotional scheme without paying him. Morrissey sued for copyright infringement because a promotion for Tide soap used a copy of the rules he had registered. The court held that the promotional contest idea was not tangible and could not be protected by copyright. Even more damaging to Morrissey, the court held that the rules for the contest could only be expressed in a limited number of ways and therefore even the rules could not be copyrighted because they were simply an idea, not a form of expression.[21] In a more contemporary case, the U.S. Court of Appeals ruled the Windows system used on most personal computers cannot be copyrighted. The court ruled the system of "icon-driven" computer controls originated by Macintosh is a pure idea and there are only a limited number of ways computer controls and screen images can express the idea. Therefore, Microsoft Windows programs are free to adopt ideas and control features developed by Macintosh without violating any copyright laws.[22]

Notice

Notice simply means including markings, language, or specific admonitions to the viewers of material that the author does not intend to surrender his or her rights to the intellectual property. Without notice, a person seeing a document or photograph might innocently assume the work is available for public use. In the United States, the requirements for notice were fairly formal and rigid until 1976. Specifically, a notice had to include three elements: (a) the word *copyright*, the abbreviation "C" or "Copr.," or the symbol ©; (b) the date of publication; and (c) the name of the copyright holder.[23] Each of these elements serves a simple and logical function. First, the word or abbreviation for copyright tells the reader or viewer that the author prohibits unauthorized use of the material. Second, the date allows a reader to determine if or when the copyright will expire. Third, the name of the copyright holder helps the reader locate the copyright holder in order to seek permission to use the copyrighted material.

From 1976 to 1989, the requirements for notice gradually eroded. The date of the most recent Copyright Act was 1976; the date the Berne Convention on intellectual property was implemented in the United States was 1989. If there is reason to determine the requirements for notice for material first published between those dates, one would be advised to consult an attorney.[24] Prior to 1976, the rule was straightforward. Formal notice was required.

Since 1989, the rule has been consistent if not quite so simple. An original work published today is still protected by copyright even though it does not include formal notice. However, the absence of notice does make it more difficult to pursue an action for infringement. If a work is published without notice, a viewer who copies it may claim a defense called *innocent infringement*. An innocent infringer is one who uses the material without knowing it was copyrighted.

Copyright infringement can be prosecuted either as a civil matter between the copyright holder and the person making unauthorized copies or as a criminal matter in which the government asserts its authority. The penalties for criminal copyright are greater and obviously there are advantages to having the government pursue someone who has improperly taken one's materials. However, criminal copyright violation must be "willful."[25] Someone who can claim innocent infringement will probably escape the government's involvement. Furthermore, even in civil cases, the defense of innocent infringement may reduce the amount of damages a defendant is ordered to pay a wronged copyright holder.[26] In summary, a notice statement may not be legally required but it costs virtually nothing to add and provides both some legal protection and convenience.

Registration

As noted previously, registration is not a requirement to create a copyright. The copyright is created the instant an original work is reduced to tangible form.[27] However, registration is required before an author may sue someone for infringing on that copyright[28] and there are limitations on damages that occur prior to the date of registration. For example, if someone copies and sells your work after the date of registration, you may be entitled to attorneys' fees and statutory damages. If that person copies and sells your work prior to the date you register the copyright, you will not be able to recover your attorneys' fees and you cannot recover the statutory damages. You will have to prove the amount of your loss to establish the damage the defendant will be required to pay you.[29]

For most works, the requirement to register a copyright is simply the completion of a form, the payment of $30, and submitting one copy of an unpublished work or two copies of a published work. The procedure is outlined and the forms are available from the U.S. Copyright Office online at www.copyright.gov. If you believe you have written a Pulitzer Prize-winning article, a Clio-winning advertisement, or a Silver Anvil-winning public relations campaign, it certainly seems worth the minor expense of protecting your rights by registering the work.

Ownership of Copyright

Remember that copyrights are intellectual property and property can be sold, inherited, or simply given away. Therefore, the copyright holder is often not the author of the copyrighted work. However, the **duration** of the copyright is, in many cases, a function of the life of the author rather than the copyright holder. Since the first Copyright Act in 1909, the duration of copyright ownership has been gradually increased. Most copyrights established today are valid for the life of the author of the copyrighted material, plus 75 years.[30] If the work is co-authored, the copyright is enforceable for the life of the last surviving author, plus 75 years.[31] One exception, which is explained later in the practice notes, applies to works for hire. Works for hire are written by an employee or are written under contract for another person. The copyright for works for hire can be valid for as long as 120 years.[32] An excellent summary of copyright duration is online at http://www.copyright.cornell.edu/training/hirtle_public_domain.htm.

If one is negotiating for the purchase or sale of a copyright, he or she should note that any contract to transfer a copyright must be in the form of an express and written contract.[33] It should also be noted that simply buying a work does not give the new owner a copyright in the work. The copyright must be sold separately.[34] This means, for example, that purchasing an original Mark Twain manuscript does not give the purchaser the right to copy or to publish that manuscript.[35]

Even a bona fide purchaser may not have perpetual ownership of the copyright. The 1976 Copyright Act created a right to "terminate transfer."[36] Under this provision, an author who sells his or her copyright can terminate the transfer during a 5-year period that begins 35 years after the copyright is sold. This right even extends, in some cases, to relatives of the author who may inherit the right of **termination of transfer**. The provision was created to help authors who sell rights to literature or songs early in their career and only later learn that they will be worth much more than was originally paid. This right to terminate transfer does not apply to works for hire.

Ownership of co-authored works is somewhat complicated and we can only present a simplified summary of the rules governing them here. Generally, the copyright is owned by the author who wrote or created the first part of the work, unless there was some intent on the part of the authors to create a **joint work**.[37] Also, where one person compiles the works of several other authors into one piece, copyright of the resulting compilation is owned by the compiler.[38] Where the authors intended to create a joint work, the co-authors are owners "in common" of the copyright. Owners in common, in this context, have a duty to report any use of the copyright to the other authors, to share any profits, and not to do anything that would damage the rights or interests of the other co-authors. Works produced under contract with an agency or as an employee of an agency or news medium are discussed in the practice notes to this chapter.

Prohibited Acts

If your work is protected by copyright, what can you prohibit others from doing with that work, and what are you prohibited from doing with the copyrighted works of others? This section answers those questions. Copyrighted material may not be copied, used to create derivative works, distributed, performed, displayed, or transmitted digitally without the permission of the copyright holder. Each of those concepts requires some explanation. These prohibited acts are listed in Exhibit 10.2.

Exhibit 10.2.   Prohibited Acts. (Actions that may not be done without a copyright holder's permission.)

Reproduction – Copying

Creating a Derivative Work

Distribution

Performance

Display

Digital Transmission

■

Reproduction

Reproduction means just what it sounds like. Copyrighted material may not be copied or reproduced without the permission of the copyright holder. There is an exception for "fair use" of the material and we discuss those exceptions later in this section in the discussion on defenses. In addition to the defenses associated with fair use, there are also two exceptions in the Copyright Act that specifically permit copying protected material. One such exception is provided for broadcast media. They are permitted to make very short-term or temporary copies for delayed broadcast.[39] There is also an exception that allows the legitimate purchaser of a computer program to copy the programs for the sole purpose of repair or maintenance.[40]

It should also be noted that what is prohibited really is copying, not the creation of an identical work. In other words, if someone through independent work and creativity writes an article exactly like one that is already copyrighted, they have not "copied" it. This point may best be made by describing the facts in *Columbia Broadcasting v. DeCosta*, which involved a television show titled *Have Gun Will Travel*. The show's main character was named Paladin. Paladin wore a black outfit featuring a holster with a knight chess piece in silver and displayed a calling card that read, "Have Gun, Will Travel, wire Paladin San Francisco." Prior to the time the television show first aired, Victor DeCosta performed at parades and other events throughout New England as a character he named Paladin. DeCosta's Paladin wore a black outfit featuring a knight chess piece in silver and he used a calling card that read, in part, "Have Gun, Will Travel, Wire Paladin. . . ." The Court of Appeals ruled that even though the two characters were virtually identical, CBS had not copied DeCosta's creation. The ruling was based on several factors but chief among them was that the similarities were not the result of copying DeCosta's creation. Rather, the court found the two characters, including their calling cards, were independently created.[41] DeCosta lost his suit for copyright infringement.

Derivative Works

The prohibition against **derivative work**s was originally designed to prevent copying copyrighted work in another medium. For example, it prohibited copying an engraving or drawing onto ceramic tiles.[42] Today, this prohibition covers such derivative works as translations, abridgements, or condensations. Specifically, it prohibits reproduction in "any form in which a work may be recast, transformed, or adapted."[43] The kinds of derivative works prohibited include copying a tape to a CD format,[44] translation into another language,[45] or the production of plot outlines.[46] The prohibition against derivative works is designed to prevent a creative but dishonest person from making a copy with some minor variation in medium. Simply put, one cannot reproduce copyrighted material even if it is copied into another medium or language or it is copied with some modifications that do not involve significant creativity.

Distribution

The prohibition against **distribution** is limited by what is called the first sale doctrine. The **first sale doctrine** "provides that nothing in [The Copyright Act] shall be deemed to forbid, prevent, or restrict the transfer of any copy of a copyrighted work the possession of which has been lawfully obtained."[47] If the copyright holder sells a book, article, or work of art, the new owner can resell that object, but cannot copy it or sell copies of it. The new owner has a right of "first sale" but not subsequent sales.[48]

In addition to this first sale, a copyright holder can "distribute copies of phonorecords . . . to the public by sale or other transfer of ownership, or by **rental, lease, or lending** . . . [emphasis added]."[49] This right is limited to the copyright holder. In other words, only the author of the work or someone to whom the author has assigned the right may distribute records by rental, lease, or lending. This limitation on distribution applies to electronic recordings, computer programs, and other media.[50] As a practical matter, many publishers charge libraries a higher price for books or journals than those same publishers charge private purchasers or subscribers. This higher price is often imposed to cover the copyright holder's fee for giving permission to distribute their work by rental, lease, or lending.

Performance

Obviously, a playwright or composer of music would expect to be paid for the performance of his or her work. **Performances**, without the permission of the copyright holder, are prohibited. However, there are several exceptions to the prohibition against performance. For example the Copyright Act specifically permits radio stations to play records, tapes, and CDs without paying royalties for the performance.[51] Also exempt are not-for-profit displays of some art work.

It should be noted that performance for commercial purposes is almost always prohibited and the courts' definition of commercial is very broad. As early as 1916, the U.S. Court of Appeals, for example, noted that performing a song in a restaurant had a commercial purpose even though no fee was paid for the audience to hear the song.[52] Even if the commercial motivation is indirect, such as making the environment of a restaurant more attractive to customers, that may be commercial purpose and the user of copyrighted art or music should secure the permission of the copyright holder before using his or her work in such a venue.

Display

As described under performance, usually the not-for-profit display of one piece of art, which one owns, does not violate the rights of a copyright holder. However, it should be noted that the advent of computer and electronic display capabilities complicates even this simple rule. Today, the owner of art who is not the copyright holder may display only one image of the work in one location at a time. This rule would prohibit, for example, placing an image of the artwork on a Web page.[53]

Digital Transmission

In addition to prohibitions against displaying copyrighted material in multiple locations via the Internet, a recent modification of the Copyright Act also prohibits digital transmission of performances. In 1995, the Copyright Act was modified to give copyright holders the right to limit or to be paid for digital transmission of their work over the Internet. It should be noted that taping for private or home use is probably not covered by this prohibition, but any commercial use does appear to violate the rights of the copyright holder.[54] It should also be noted that provisions of the Copyright Act specifically outlaw decrypting or in any way circumventing attempts to prevent copying.[55]

Copyright Infringement

In order to sue someone successfully for infringing on copyright, one must prove the existence of a valid copyright, that one actually owns the copyright, and the person sued has committed one of the prohibited acts described earlier. Although registration may not be required to create a copyright, it is required before one can sue for copyright infringement. These elements are shown in Exhibit 10.3.

To prove the prohibited act, one may only have to show that the person had access to the work and that he or she produced something that is substantially similar.[56] In effect, the courts will usually assume if someone ever saw the work and then produced something just like it, they probably copied it. But, if the new work has significant differences from the original, one may have to prove the person both saw and specifically copied the

Exhibit 10.3. Copyright Infringement Elements. (All elements. including each component required for creation of a valid copyright, must be proven.)

Valid Copyright	Original Work
	Tangible Form
	Notice – implied or actual
	Registration
Ownership	
Prohibited Act	

work.[57] What is prohibited is copying the form of expression, not the idea. Therefore, when looking for similarity, it is similarity in the language or form used, not similarity of the concepts or ideas, that is important. However, copyright "cannot be limited literally to the text, else a plagiarist would escape by immaterial variations."[58]

Comparing two cases may help explain what is and what is not prohibited as copyright infringement. In 1977, the U.S. Court of Appeals ruled a McDonald's advertising campaign used cartoon characters that were improperly copied from Sid and Marty Kroft's television show *H.R. Puffinstuff*. The court ruled that similarity in cartoon character appearance, costume, and mannerism was enough "content" to justify a suit for copyright infringement.[59] Much earlier, another Court of Appeals ruled the title *Gone with the Wind* was not content but was simply an idea and the use of the title by someone other than the copyright holder was not infringement.[60] In order to win an action for copyright infringement, the judge or jury must find there was some copying of a form of expression. In effect, they must find significant similarity in the form, language, or expression to succeed in a copyright infringement suit.

Intent or state of mind is not an element for copyright infringement. In other words, one person who profits from another person's misuse of copyrighted material can be sued for copyright infringement. This is called **vicarious infringement**. One can also unconsciously infringe upon a copyright.

Vicarious infringement usually arises because the owner of a theater hires a performer who has improperly taken copyrighted material from another.[61] For a defendant to lose a suit for vicarious infringement, he or she must have profited from the infringement. The suit usually is to recover the profits made by the defendant as a result of the misuse of the copyright holder's work. In 1971 and 1972, "bootleg" copies of the Charlie Chaplin movie *Modern Times* were shown on the campus of Columbia University by a student group that charged admission for the showing. The copyright holder sued Columbia University for vicarious infringement, but the suit failed because Columbia had not profited from the infringement. The university had allowed the student group to use the room without charge and the profits from the showing went only to the student group.[62] Internet service providers (ISPs) are also exempt from liability for this kind of vicarious infringement.[63] Because the ISPs may charge for use of its system, one might think the ISP would profit from its use to transmit copyrighted material. The logic for exempting ISPs seems to be the fact that they, like all common carriers, simply charge for the use of their system, not for the transmission of specific images or material. Similarly, suits against manufacturers of recording devices have typically failed because those manufacturers do not profit from the reproduction of specific copyrighted material.[64]

Finally, it should be noted that one can be liable for a completely unconscious copying of copyrighted material. In 1976, a federal District Court ruled that George Harrison of the Beatles improperly used two "motifs" of three and four notes in his composition "My Sweet Lord." Those motifs came from the Chiffon's song, "He's So Fine." The court ruled that even though Harrison had not intended to copy the Chiffon's song "his subconscious mind" knew the motif would work because it had worked before.[65] You may be held liable for other people improperly using copyrighted material and you can be held liable for the acts of your "unconscious mind." It seems obvious there is no defense to copyright infringement based on a lack of intent.

Defenses

Lack of intent may not be a defense to copyright infringement, but there are significant defenses. The most common of these is fair use. Other defenses include the allowances for parody and satire. Under the principle of **fair use**, people are allowed some limited use of, including a right to reproduce, copyrighted material.

Fair Use

The Copyright Act gives several examples of fair use and even identifies four criteria that should be used to determine what is fair use. However, the act does not provide a specific definition of fair use.[66] The four criteria used to determine what is and what is not fair use are:

1. Purpose and character of the use.
2. Nature of the copyrighted work.
3. Proportion taken.
4. Economic impact of the use.

None of these considerations is, by itself, a total defense to copyright infringement. Rather, the court will look at how the four come together to justify use of the copyrighted material.

The application of these considerations is so complex that the U.S. Court of Appeals referred to fair use determinations as the "most troublesome in the whole of copyright law."[67] We try to make this area somewhat less "troublesome" by addressing each of the four considerations separately.

Purpose and Character of the Use

Purpose and character of use refers to the reason the copyrighted material was taken or used. This consideration does overlap significantly with the fourth factory economic impact. Generally, when the motive for copying or otherwise using copyrighted material is to make money, the courts have not found it to be fair use. The Copyright Act specifically

Exhibit 10.4.   Considerations in "Fair Use" Defense to Copyright Infringement.

Purpose & Character of Use

Nature of Work

Proportion Taken

Economic Effect

lists teaching, criticism, news reporting, and scholarship as examples of fair use[68] and, as long as uses for these purposes are not motivated by financial gain, the courts have generally permitted them as fair use. For example, the Court of Claims permitted the copying of entire articles from medical journals for use in interlibrary loan programs when the articles were used for medical research or study.[69] But, the court refused to permit copying articles or chapters from textbooks or encyclopedias.[70] The reason for the distinction was that the courts saw the purpose for copying the medical journal articles as advancing scholarship in medicine, whereas they found the encyclopedia articles had been copied to circumvent requirements to pay for the books themselves. They also found the purpose of the original works was significant. The medical journals had been produced to advance research while the textbooks and encyclopedia had been produced specifically for sale to schools.

Uses of copyrighted material for parody, criticism, and news coverage have also been permitted. Key to fair use for these purposes is not using more of the original copyrighted work than is absolutely necessary to produce the **parody**, criticism, or news report.[71]

If there is a single and simple summary of the test for purpose and character of work, it is that a profit motive destroys the defense of fair use. If the copyright holder can show the copyright infringer is motivated solely by profit, the defense of fair use will fail.[72]

Nature of Work

It seems to fly in the face of the purpose of copyright but courts have consistently ruled that some kinds of works are meant to be copied. For example, there is an implied permission for copying some reference works and particularly books of forms.[73] Other works whose nature implies they are intended to be copied include databases, directories, and tables of formulas.[74] These are the same kind of works that often are not afforded copyright protection in the first place because they are more works of diligence than works of creativity. It should also be noted that fair use is not a defense to using works that have not been published.[75]

Proportion Taken

In some commercial copy facilities, there are signs above the copy machines prohibiting copying more than a specified number of pages from a copyrighted work. These signs may be an attempt to provide a defense against copyright infringement. But, there is no defense based on a specified number of pages that may or may not be copied. A customer at the copy center might be able to defend copying several pages from a novel the length of *War and Peace* but he or she could not defend taking even two lines of a haiku poem. Section 107 of the Copyright Act says that one must consider both the qualitative and quantitative **proportion taken.** What may not be copied is the "heart" or "valuable part" of the copyrighted work. In a song one cannot copy the part that makes the song memorable or that "gave it popular appeal."[76] One case even held that taking as little as 1% of a copyrighted work is too great a proportion to be a fair use.[77]

In addition to considering the proportion of the copyrighted work that is copied, courts have also considered what percentage of a new work is copied from previously copyrighted material. This concept is often called **reverse proportionality**. Under this principle, even if the defendant only copied a small part of the original work, he or she would lose the defense of fair use if the copied material was the majority of what they presented as their own work.[78]

Economic Effect

The U.S. Supreme Court ruled that **economic effect** is the most important consideration when evaluating a defense of fair use.[79] Of course, economic motivation also overlaps with the purpose of the use, which adds even more to its importance.

To determine economic effect, the court will try to determine both whether the person who improperly took the copyrighted material profited from the taking and whether the taking caused some economic harm to the copyright holder. In other words, if one uses someone else's copyrighted material, one may cause an economic effect even if one does not charge for or make money from the use. By using another person's materials, one may harm their market for the material. Such economic effect has been found, for example, where McDonald's used a cartoon character in its commercials. The court ruled that the use made it difficult or impossible for the copyright holder to sell its cartoon characters to other companies.[80] If you are using another person's creative work, even if you are not making money, you may hurt their economic situation and you would be well advised to secure their permission before using their work.

Parody, Satire, and News

Parody, satire, and news fit neatly under the fair use consideration of "purpose of use," but they often stand alone as defenses even without review of the other three considerations. Therefore, we discuss them independently, but briefly.

Courts have typically permitted use of copyrighted material in parodies and satires of the original material, even where the parody is done for profit. The logic for allowing this defense is that authors typically do not license or permit parodies of their work and they just as rarely use their own work for parody. In short, there seems to be no harm to the author occasioned by parody. However, for parody to be a defense, the parody must use no more of the original work than is necessary.[81]

News coverage is carefully protected by the courts and where there is any conflict with the First Amendment, the courts are loath to impose even copyright restrictions. In addition, information cannot be copyrighted. Only the form of expression enjoys copyright protection. Therefore, if a reporter uses his or her own language or film to describe an event, there is no copyright infringement. In some very limited circumstances, the courts have even permitted the use of copyrighted material in news coverage. For example, a U.S. District Court permitted use of a copyrighted film of the Kennedy assassination when it determined the film was the only way to express the newsworthy idea being reported.[82] Reporters should not rely on this defense. Situations in which copyrighted material is the only way to express an idea are very rare and the use of protected works is severely limited. One of these limitations is that reporters may use only so much of copyrighted material as is absolutely necessary to communicate the newsworthy idea.[83]

Trademark

Copyrights are intellectual property, as are trademarks, service marks, and trade dress. Trademarks are the logos, icons, symbols, or even titles associated with products in trade. Trademarks can also include short slogans associated with products in trade.[84] For example the white script "Coca-Cola" on a red background is a trademark of the famous soft drink company. So too the phrase "things go better with Coke" could be a trademark for the company. **Service marks** are like trademarks, but they are associated with services rather than products for sale. An example of a service mark might be the word "Kelly" in green, associated with the Kelly temporary services company. **Trade dress** refers to elements of packaging or product modification that are associated with particular brands or companies. To qualify as trade dress, these modifications or elements must be done solely for the purpose of product identification. The pink color of Owens-Corning fiberglass and the familiar shape of a Coca-Cola bottle are examples of trade dress. Trade dress cannot include functional elements of packaging. A handle on a paint can, for example, is not trade dress. Trademarks, service marks, and trade dress are all governed by the same basic rules. For the sake of simplicity here, we collapse all three under the one label of *trademark*.

Although copyrights, patents, and trademarks are all intellectual property, some very significant differences exist between the laws that govern patents and copyright on one hand, and trademarks on the other. Copyrights and **patents** are governed by federal law, while trademarks are primarily regulated by state law. Copyrights can be bought and sold like other property, but **trademarks** are rights "appurtenant" to products and cannot be sold without affecting the product or business with which they are associated.[85] Finally, a copyright is created simply by reducing an original idea to a tangible form while the creation of a trademark requires the creation of an association between the trademark and a product in the public mind.

The U.S. Constitution makes specific provisions for copyright and patents and most copyright and patent law is consolidated under federal authority.[86] Trademarks are not mentioned in the Constitution and attempts to create federal laws to regulate trademarks have been declared unconstitutional.[87] As a result, trademarks are controlled by a combination of state laws and some federal laws. The federal laws only control how trademarks are used in interstate commerce. The federal government's registry of trademarks is only a listing of state-recognized trademarks.

Purpose of Trademarks

Originally, trademarks were created to give notice to customers about the origin of the goods they purchased.[88] However, they have evolved to do more than identify the manufacturer; they now are markers of company goodwill and often are representative of the public's attitude toward a product or company.[89]

Particularly important to practitioners in public relations and advertising, courts have ruled that trademarks are (a) indications of product origin, (b) guarantees of quality, and (c) marketing and advertising devices.[90] In effect, a trademark can be the symbol of a company's goodwill and the quality of its products. Advertising campaigns are often based on the consumers' identification of a trademark with a quality product and public relations campaigns may use the public's positive perception of a trademark associated with a company that has been a good corporate citizen. Both advertising and public relations professionals, therefore, benefit from protecting their clients' trademarks.

How Trademarks Are Created

Until recently, in order to create a trademark legally, it had to be used. Some association had to be created in the public mind between the trademark and the product or service before anyone had the right to prohibit others from using the trademark.[91] Today, it is possible to register an "intent to use" a trademark.[92] However, this registration depends on the registrant submitting a sworn statement that no other company or person has established a right to use the trademark and that she or he will actually begin using the trademark. In other words, one has to swear that no one else has a common law right to the trademark and that one will establish a common law right very soon. Again, the common law right to a trademark is established by its actual use and the creation of an association between the product and the trademark in the collective mind of the public.

Registration of trademarks, by itself, does not establish a right to the trademark. The registry is administered by the U.S. Patent and Trademark Office but rights to trademarks are established by state laws. The registry is only a listing of trademarks that have been established under state laws.[93] In most states, the right to a trademark is established by use of the trademark and the establishment of an association between the mark and a product or service.[94] Although registration with the federal government does not create a right in the trademark, it does have some significant advantages. First, registration provides notice to any future user of the trademark. If a trademark is registered, no one can later begin using the same trademark and argue that they did not know it had already been used. The registration and subsequent publication of the trademark in the government's "Official Gazette" is legal notice to everyone of a claim to that trademark.[95] Other advantages of registration are (a) access to the federal court system for enforcement of the copyright, (b) use of the registry to help establish the trademark in foreign countries, and (c) assistance from the U.S. Patent and Trademark Office in challenges to use of the trademark by foreign companies. Instructions for registering a trademark are available at www.uspto.gov.

It should also be noted that registration of trademarks must be renewed every 10 years. This requirement helps identify marks that have been abandoned and may be available for use by a new company or product.[96]

What Trademarks May Not Be Registered

Generally, the U.S. Patent and Trademark Office will register any trademark that is eligible for protection under state laws. The regulation says, "No trademark by which the goods of the applicant may be distinguished from the goods of others shall be refused registration."[97] However, law is rarely that simple. There are several categories of marks or terms that cannot be registered or used as trademarks.

Existing Trademarks

Obviously, marks already in use by another product or company cannot be registered.[98] It may be permitted for two products or companies in geographically distant areas to use the same mark if the use does not create any confusion in the minds of the consuming public.[99] Approval of the registration or adoption of an "old" trademark depends on whether the old mark has been abandoned and on the likelihood that the new use will create confusion, mistake, or deceit in the marketplace.[100] When trying to determine the likelihood of confusion, mistake, or deceit, the courts will consider seven factors. They are:

1. Similarity of the marks.
2. Similarity of the products with which the trademark will be associated.
3. Geographic areas where the old and new trademarks will be used.
4. Degree of care consumers use in selecting the products or considering the trademarks.
5. How strongly the old mark is associated with a product in the minds of consumers.
6. Actual confusion by consumers.
7. Whether the applicant for the new mark intends to create confusion.[101]

In the past, a drug company was denied a trademark for a motion sickness cure called "bonamine" because the name was too similar to "Dramamine," which was an already existing trademark for a motion sickness remedy,[102] but Toyota Motors was permitted to register the name Lexus for its luxury car despite objections by Mead Data, which had earlier registered the trademark "Lexis."[103] The Court reasoned that because only about 1% of the public knew "Lexis" was a legal database and because there were differences in both spelling and pronunciation, the two trademarks were dissimilar enough to justify registration of both.

Descriptive Terms

Words or terms that simply describe a product cannot be used as trademarks. The logic for this seems to be that permitting a company to protect the use of a term like *parking lot*, which simply describes a business, would effectively eliminate any competitor from describing his or her business.[104] **Descriptive terms** that acquire a secondary meaning are, however, permitted. A descriptive term acquires a secondary meaning when it becomes so associated with a particular product that it is no longer seen as descriptive. For example, in 1980 Miller Brewing Company argued that the word "lite" had become so associated with its light beers that it was no longer a descriptive term, but had acquired a secondary meaning that now meant "Miller Lite." A U.S. District Court agreed. [105] Abercrombie & Fitch Company has also had problems with an attempt to enforce the trademark "safari." The U.S. Court of Appeals ruled that Abercrombie & Fitch had succeeded in establishing a secondary meaning for "safari shirts" as a trademark for a particular style of shirt the company first sold, but that the word "safari" was simply descriptive and could be used by competitors to describe other products, including other garments. [106]

Some terms that were originally trademarks for specific products have become descriptive because of public use. These include "aspirin," which was originally a trademark associated with Bayer Company[107] and "cellophane," which was originally a trademark associated with a particular plastic product manufactured by DuPont. [108] Because they have become descriptive in common use, these terms are no longer protected as trademarks.

Geographic Descriptions

Similar to descriptive terms, names of towns, places, or other geographic locations cannot be used as trademarks. The apparent reason for this limitation is to avoid the impression that a product is manufactured in a specific location. When evaluating challenges to trademarks that include geographic locations, the courts have consistently asked whether the consuming public would think the goods associated with the trademark originated in the place identified by the mark. [109] Locations that are so obscure that few people recognize them and names that have long been associated with a particular product are permitted.

Surnames

As a matter of policy, surnames have been denied trademark protection. One reason seems to be that if a surname was protected by trademark, another individual with the same name could not use his or her own name in business. The rule here seems to be that if a word is primarily a surname in the mind of the public it cannot be registered as a trademark. [110]

Obscene or Offensive Trademarks

Although we can offer no discussion on the propriety of a government agency simply making its own determinations about what is or is not offensive, the Patent and Trademark Office does exercise the authority to reject trademarks that include sexual innuendo or religious connotations it finds offensive. Trademark applications for bras called "bubby traps," and "Messias" wine have been rejected along with some creative but suggestive advertising slogans. [111]

Antidilution of Trademarks

In the past, trademarks were denied registration and protection only if they were used and had established a connection with a product similar to the one for which registration was sought. In other words, the trademark "Flying R" could be registered for a new rotisserie grill even if "Flying R" already was an established trademark for a rotary engine because the products were dissimilar. Today, courts recognize that trademarks must be protected so companies may move into new fields, protect their reputation from association with inferior goods of any kind, and protect the public from confusion or mistake about who manufactures a product.[112] Therefore, the use of trademarks that are so similar they could confuse the consuming public or dilute the good reputation of a company are prohibited even if they are on very dissimilar products.[113] Although courts have recognized this "**antidilution**" principle for nearly 50 years, it was first incorporated into the Copyright Act in 1996.[114] Today, any practice that could deceive consumers about the source of products is prohibited.[115]

Enforcement of Trademarks

Although not "elements" in the true sense of that word, courts do make nine inquiries to evaluate claims of trademark infringement. These are listed in Exhibit 10.5. All relate to the probability that the use of the challenged trademark will deceive consumers.[116]

The first inquiry is whether the marks themselves are similar in appearance, sound, or the impression they create. In other words, will the consuming public be likely to confuse the two marks? The second inquiry asks whether the marks are used on similar products or services. The assumption is that marks on similar products are more likely to be confused. Third, the court will inquire if the products on which the marks are used are bought and sold in similar channels. Channel, in this context, includes both the geographic area where the products are traded and the kind of stores or systems for sale. For example, machine equipment sold only through large distributors are in a different channel than are products sold in retail stores. The

Exhibit 10.5.   Trademark Infringement Inquiries. (These are not actually elements but are questions the court will ask to help determine whether a new trademark violates the rights of another trademark holder.)

- Similarity of the trademarks
- Similarity of the goods or services
- Similarity of the trade channels
- Is sale impulse or analyzed
- Strength of existing trademarks
- Actual consumer confusion
- Number of similar marks
- Time of use
- Variety of goods associated with trademark

fourth inquiry asks whether the products marked are typically purchased on impulse or if they are carefully analyzed purchases. The assumption is that impulse purchases are more likely to be influenced by the reputation of the product's trademark. Fifth, the court will evaluate the strength of the competing or established trademarks. A trademark that is not well established or recognized by a large portion of the consuming public is more easily challenged. Sixth, the court will look for evidence of actual consumer confusion. Obviously, if consumers are actually confused, it suggests the marks are deceiving purchasers. The seventh inquiry asks whether there are other similar trademarks on similar products. The assumption here is that if there are already a number of similar trademarks on products in the market, the addition of one more trademark will not add significantly to the confusion. Eighth, the court will look for evidence to show that the two marks have both been used for some time. If, in fact, there is concurrent use of the two marks without consumer confusion, the court is more likely to permit the continued use of both. Finally, the court will look at how many different kinds of products are associated with the trademarks. If a company uses a single trademark on a great many different products, the courts are likely to see a new use of that trademark by another company as potentially confusing to consumers.[117]

Defenses

Defenses to trademark inquiry fall into three categories. First, one may defend a trademark infringement by demonstrating that the challenged trademark is not similar to the one held by the complaining party. Second, one could argue that the person challenging cannot hold a trademark because his or her trademark falls into one of the prohibited categories—descriptive terms, geographic descriptions, surnames, or offensive terms.

The third defense is **abandonment**. Most common law rulings held that a trademark that had not been used for 20 years had been abandoned. The pace of business today is somewhat faster and a trademark not used for 10 years may be available for use by a new applicant. In fact, the U.S. Patent and Trademark Office requires reregistration of trademarks every 10 years.[118]

Failing to reregister a trademark certainly is evidence the trademark has been abandoned. Other actions that show abandonment include failing to control or challenge the use of the trademark by other companies and licensing the trademark without controls. One example of such licensing gone amiss can be seen in the challenges to Nintendo's use of a gorilla that looked like "King Kong" in the video game "Donkey Kong." The trademark character "King Kong" was owned originally by the author of a book from 1932. It was licensed to RKO Pictures for a 1933 film titled *King Kong*. Later, rights to the character and name were transferred to Universal Pictures for a 1975 remake of the motion picture. When Universal attempted to sue Nintendo for infringing on the "King Kong" trademark, the courts simply could not determine who owned and who had abandoned the mark.[119]

To avoid appearing to abandon a trademark, one would be well advised to take every opportunity to challenge its use by others. Courts do appear to look at both use of the trademark by others and any indication of the trademark holder's intentions. Challenging misuse and attempting to contract for control of the use of a copyright both provide evidence of the trademark holder's intentions.[120]

Practice Notes

Works produced for other people often fit in a category called *works for hire* and are covered by some unusual copyright laws. Most mass communications professionals are employed by or under contract with newspapers, broadcast stations, advertising agencies, public relations agencies, or public relations departments and their work is often work for hire. Because so much of what is produced by mass communications professionals is work for hire, it is important for a book on mass communications law to address those rules in some detail.

What Is a "Work for Hire"?

Anything produced by an employee while working within the scope of his or her employment is a **work for hire**.[121] The U.S. Supreme Court has ruled that, for this purpose, an employee is anyone acting within the scope of his or her employment who is doing the normal work of his or her job while under the supervision and control of an employer. Specifically, the courts look at three factors to determine if a person is an employee in this context. The most obvious of these is an agreement for payment. Other factors include the employer's right to assign tasks to an employee and the employer's right to set working hours and to control the employee's work. Independent workers who are not employees tend to own their own tools, set their own hours, and are free to hire assistants.[122] The Supreme Court's definition of employee would cover most reporters, advertising, and public relations practitioners. Our editors or agency directors can usually assign us tasks, set our working hours, and edit or review our work. Therefore, in most traditional mass communications environments, we are employees and our work is work for hire.

Stringers and independent advertising or public relations practitioners may not be employees. However, as shown in Exhibit 10.6, they may produce work for hire. Such contract workers are covered by a different section of the Copyright Act. That section says work produced by an independent contractor is "work for hire" only if the work was done under a written contract and if it also fits in one of the following 10 specific categories:[123]

1. Contributions to collected works.
2. Parts of motion pictures or audiovisual productions.
3. Translations.
4. Supplementary works like forewords, illustrations, and prefaces.

Exhibit 10.6.   Requirements for "Works for Hire."

Employee acting with scope of employment			
Or			
Contract Worker	With a written contract	Performing one of these tasks	Contribution to a collective work
			Part of movie or audiovisual work
			Translation
			Supplements (e.g., preface, illustrations)
			Compilation of other works
			Instructional text
			Tests
			Answers to tests
			Atlas
			Sound recording

5. Compilations of other works.
6. Instructional texts.
7. Tests.
8. Answers to tests.
9. Atlases.
10. Sound recordings.

If there is no written contract or if the work does not fit in one of the 10 specific categories, the work is not work for hire. Note specifically that despite what a contract may say, the work cannot be work for hire if it does not fit in one of the 10 categories listed in the Copyright Act.[124] Because stringers or independent reporters usually prepare their work before approaching a potential media buyer, they have no contract and since news releases are not one of the categories listed in the Copyright Act, their work does not appear to be work for hire. The status of work by independent advertising and public relations professionals depends entirely on the existence of a written contract and the kind of work being done.

Why Is "Work for Hire" Important?

There are two reasons why it is important to know if what you are doing is work for hire. First and probably most important is that the copyright for work for hire does not belong to the author. It belongs to the employer. In other words, if you write or produce something that is work for hire you cannot copyright it and you cannot benefit from the sale of the copyright. Your employer owns the copyright and only he or she can sell it.[125]

Second, the duration of copyright for most works is related to the life of the author. Because the copyright for works for hire does not belong to the author, his or her life is not used to calculate the copyright duration. Copyright for works for hire last 120 years from the creation of the work or 95 years after the first publication of the work, whichever term is longest.[126]

Magic Words and Phrases

Abandonment of trademark	Parody
Antidilution of trademark	Patents
Berne Convention	Performance
Copyright	Proportion taken (and fair use)
Creativity	Pure idea
Derivative work	Reverse proportionality
Descriptive terms	Service mark
Distribution	Tangible form
Duration of copyright	Termination of transfer
Economic effect	Trade dress
Fair use	Trademark
First sale doctrine	Utilitarian
Intellectual property	Vicarious infringement
Joint work	Work for hire

Suggested Cases to Read and Brief

Abercrombie & Fitch Co. v. Hunting World, Inc., 537 F.2d 4 (2nd Cir.1976)

Alfred Bell & Co. v. Catalda Fine Arts, Inc., 191 F.2d 99, 102 (2ndCir.1951)

American International Pictures, Inc. v. Foreman, 576 F.2d 661, 663 (5th Cir.1978)

Apple Computer, Inc. v. Franklin Computer Corp., 714 F.2d 1240, 1245 (3rd Cir.1983), *cert. dismissed* 464 U.S. 1033 (1984)

Apple Computer, Inc. v. Microsoft Corp. 35 F.3d 1435 (1994), *cert. denied* 513 U.S. 1184 (1995)

Baker v. Selden, 101 U.S. 99 (1879)

Bright Tunes Music Corp. v. Harrisongs Music, Ltd., 420 F.Supp. 177, 180 (S.D.N.Y.1976)

Burrow-Giles Lithographic Co. v. Sarony, 111 U.S. 53, 55 (1884)

Campbell v. Acuff-Rose Music, Inc., 510 U.S. 569 (1994)

Chamberlain v. Feldman, 300 N.Y. 135, 89 N.E.2d 863 (Crt.App.N.Y.1949)

Cmty. For Creative Non-Violence v. Reid, 490 U.S. 730, 751 (1989)

Coca-Cola Co. v. Seven Up Co., 497 F.2d 1351, 1354 (Cust. & Pat.App.Bd.1974)

Columbia Broadcasting System, Inc. v. DeCosta, 377 F.2d 315 (!st Cir.1967)

Feist v. Rural Telephone Service Co., Inc., 499 U.S. 349, 345 (1991)

Ferguson v. National Broadcasting Co., 584 F.2d 111 (5th Cir.1978)

Goldstein v. California, 412 U.S. 546 (1973)

Hanover Star Milling Co. v. Metcalf, 240 U.S. 403 (1916)

Harper & Row, Publishers, Inc. v. Nation Enterprises, Inc. 471 U.S. 539 (1985)

Herbert v. Shanley Co., 229 F.340 (2nd Cir.1916)

In re E.I. DuPont DeNemours & Co., 476 F.2d 1357 (Cust. & Pat. App.1973)

In re Societe Generale Des Eaux Minerales De Vittel, 824 F.2d 957 (Fed.Cir.1987)

Mazur v. Stein, 347 U.S. 201 (1954)

Mead Data Central, Inc. v. Toyota Motor Sales, U.S.A., 875 F.2d 1026 (2nd Cir.1989)

Morrissey v. Proctor & Gamble Co. (379 F.2d 675 (1st Cir.1967)

Reddy Communications v. Environmental Action Foundation, 477 F.Supp. 936 (D.D.C. 1979)

Roy Export Co. v. Trustees of Columbia University, 344 F.Supp. 1350 (S.D.N.Y. 1972)

Shapiro, Bernstein & Co. v. Jerry Vogel Music Co., 221 F.2d 569 (2nd Cir.1955)

Sid & Marty Kroft Television Productions, Inc. v. McDonalds Corp., 562 F.2d 1157 (9th Cir.1977)

Sony Corp. of America v. Universal City Studios, Inc., 464 U.S. 417 (1984)

Thrifty Rent-A-Car System v. Thrift Cars, Inc. 831 F.2d 1177 (1st Cir.1987)

Time, Inc. v. Bernard Geis Associates, 293 F.Supp. 130 (1968)

U.S. v. Steffens, 100 U.S. 82 (1879)

Universal City Studios, Inc. v. Nintendo Co., Ltd., 578 F.Supp. 911 (S.D.N.Y.1983)

Walt Disney Productions v. Air Pirates, 581 F.2d 751 (9th Cir.1978)

Williams & Wilkins v. United States, 487 F.2d 1345 (Ct.Cl.1973), aff'd 420 U.S. 396 (1975)

Zacchini v. Scripps-Howard Broadcasting Co., 433 U.S. 562 (1977)

Questions for Discussion

1. Article I, Section 8, Clause 8 of the U.S. Constitution gives the government the authority to protect authors and inventors. Article I, Section 8, Clause 3 of the Constitution gives the federal government the authority to encourage and control interstate commerce. Why do you think the Supreme Court said Congress had the authority to regulate the intellectual properties of copyright and patent but did not allow federal control of trademarks, which are also intellectual property and are intimately associated with commerce?

2. As a public relations practitioner you invest hundreds of hours creating a list of reporters and editors. Your list includes information on the news preferences of those journalists and contact information. Can you copyright the list? If so, how? If not, why not?

3. If you are an advertising practitioner and you have an original idea for an advertising campaign that you believe has the potential to influence purchasing decisions

and to be very valuable, can you copyright that campaign to prevent other advertising professionals from using it? If you do not believe it can be protected, why? If you believe you can copyright it, what would you have to do to create that copyright?

4. Some popular advertisements involve repetitions of portions of competing advertising copy and outright criticism of the competitor's advertisements. Do these "reaction" advertisements violate the copyrights of the original advertisement's creators? If so, why? If not, why not?

5. Some cases from the mid- to late-1800s found that photographs are not copies of natural events but rather are creative works and therefore are original works that can be copyrighted. Do you believe a photograph is always creative? If so, why? If not, explain when a photograph might not be creative?

6. Courts have ruled that photographs are always creative but in some cases, including *Apple Computer, Inc. v. Microsoft Corp.*,[127] courts have ruled that some computer programs cannot be copyrighted. Do you agree with this reasoning? If you do agree, explain how photographs and computer programs differ. If you do not agree, explain why you think the courts reached the conclusions that some computer programs are not original or are "pure ideas."

7. If you are a reporter writing an article on a local theater company's production of *Hamlet*, how much of *Hamlet* can you quote verbatim in your article? How would you decide how much of the play you could reproduce?

8. Explain the concept of reverse proportionality. Why is this idea important to someone writing very brief summaries of television shows or movies for a local newspaper?

9. Define and give some examples of trade dress. In what context is trade dress important to practitioners in advertising and public relations?

10. If you were contracted by a company that is introducing a new line of clothing designed specifically for college-age women, how would you decide what to call that line of clothing? In particular, how would you determine if the name you are considering is already a trademark for some other company? How would you decide if the name you are considering could be registered as a trademark?

11. If geographic terms are prohibited as trademarks, how do you think airlines like Southwest, Northwest, American, and Allegheny can protect the marks associated with their companies? How can universities named after the state where they are located protect their names and service marks?

12. If you are a reporter for a major newspaper and decide to write a novel about your experiences and the people you have met, can you copyright that novel or is it "work for hire"? Explain why you think it is or is not "work for hire."

13. If you start your own public relations firm specializing in political representation and work for several different clients in local- and state-level elections, how can you protect your work so that your clients cannot use your copy, slogans, and graphics designs in future campaigns without your permission?

Notes

1. *Burrow-Giles Lithographic Co. v. Sarony*, 111 U.S. 53, 55 (1884).
2. 17 U.S.C.A. § 102(a) (2002).
3. *Feist v. Rural Telephone Service Co., Inc.*, 499 U.S. 349, 345 (1991).
4. *Matthew Bender & Co. v. West Publishing Co.*, 158 F.3d 693 (1998); *Adobe Systems v. Southern Software, Inc.*, 45 U.S.P.Q.2d 1827 (1998).
5. U.S. CONST. art. I, § 8; *Brown Instrument Co. v. Warner*, 161 F.2d 910 (1947).
6. *Mazur v. Stein*, 347 U.S. 201 (1954).
7. *In re Yardley*, 439 F.2d 1389 (1974).
8. 17 U.S.C.A. § 101 (2002).
9. *Apple Computer, Inc. v. Franklin Computer Corp.*, 714 F.2d 1240, 1245 (3d Cir.1983), *cert. dismissed* 464 U.S. 1033 (1984).
10. 17 U.S.C.A. § 902 (2002).
11. *Brown Bag Software v. Symantec Corp.*, 960 F.2d 1465 (9th Cir. 1992).
12. *Computer Associates International, Inc. v. Altai, Inc.*, 982 F.2d 693 (1992).
13. *Burrow-Giles Lithographic Co. v. Sarony*, 111 U.S. 53, 55 (1884).
14. *Jewelers Circular Publishing Co. v. Keystone Pub. Co.*, 274 Fed. 932, 934 (S.D.N.Y. 1921).
15. *Alfred Bell & Co. v. Catalda Fine Arts, Inc.*, 191 F.2d 99, 102 (2d Cir. 1951).
16. *Time Inc. v. Bernard Geis Associates*, 293 F.Supp. 130 (1968).
17. *Goldstein v. California*, 412 U.S. 546 (1973).
18. 17 U.S.C.A. § 102(a) (2002).
19. *Johnson Controls, Inc. v. Phoenix Control Systems, Inc.*, 866 F.2d 1173 (1989).
20. *Baker v. Selden*, 101 U.S. 99 (1879).
21. *Morrissey v. Proctor & Gamble Co.* 379 F.2d 675 (1st Cir. 1967).
22. *Apple Computer, Inc. v. Microsoft Corp.* 35 F.3d 1435 (9th Cir. 1994), *cert. denied* 513 U.S. 1184 (1995).
23. 17 U.S.C.A. 401(b) (2002).
24. 17 U.S.C.A. § 405(a) (2002).
25. 17 U.S.C.A. § 506 (2002).
26. 17 U.S.C.A. § 504 (2002).
27. 17 U.S.C.A. §§ 102(a), 408(a) (2002).
28. 17 U.S.C.A. § 411(a) (2002).
29. 17 U.S.C.A. § 412 (2002).
30. 17 U.S.C.A. § 302(a) (2002).
31. 17 U.S.C.A. §302(b) (2002).
32. 17 U.S.C.A. § 302(c) (2002).
33. 17 U.S.C.A. § 204 (2002).
34. 17 U.S.C.A. §§ 202, 204 (2002).
35. *Chamberlain v. Feldman*, 300 N.Y. 135, 89 N.E.2d 863 (Crt. App.N.Y. 1949).
36. 17 U.S.C.A. § 203 (2002).
37. *Shapiro, Bernstein & Co. v. Jerry Vogel Music Co.*, 221 F.2d 569 (2d Cir. 1955).
38. 17 U.S.C.A. § 201 (2002).
39. 17 U.S.C.A. §§ 111(b), (c) (2002).
40. 17 U.S.C.A. § 117 (2002).
41. *Columbia Broadcasting System, Inc. v. DeCosta*, 377 F.2d 315 (1st Cir. 1967).
42. *Mirage Editions, Inc. v. Albuquerque A.R.T.* Co. 856 F.2d 1341 (9th Cir. 1988); contra, *Lee v. A.R.T. Co.* 125 F.3d 580 (7th Cir. 1997).

43. 17 U.S.C.A. § 101 (2002).

44. 17 U.S.C.A. § 106 (2002).

45. *Stowe v. Thomas*, 23 F.Cas. 201 (E.D.Penn. 1853).

46. *G. Ricordi & Co. v. Mason*, 201 F. 184 (S.D.N.Y. 1912).

47. *American International Pictures, Inc. v. Foreman*, 576 F.2d 661, 663 (5th Cir. 1978).

48. *Lee v. A.R.T. Co.*, 125 F.3d 580 (7th Cir. 1997).

49. 17 U.S.C.A. § 106(a) (2002).

50. 17 U.S.C.A. § 109(b) (1) (2002).

51. 17 U.S.C.A. §§ 106(4), 114 (2002).

52. *Herbert v. Shanley Co.*, 229 F.340 (2d Cir. 1916).

53. 17 U.S.C.A. § 109(b) (2002).

54. 17 U.S.C.A. § 1008 (2002).

55. 17 U.S.C.A. §§ 1201 et. seq (2002).

56. *Ferguson v. National Broadcasting Co.*, 584 F.2d 111 (5th Cir. 1978).

57. *Bleistein v. Donaldson Lithographing Co.*, 188 U.S. 239 (1903).

58. *Nichols v. Universal Pictures Corp.*, 45 F.2d 119, 121 (2d Cir. 1930).

59. *Sid & Marty Kroft Television Productions, Inc. v. McDonalds Corp.*, 562 F.2d 1157 (9th Cir. 1977).

60. *Warner Brothers Pictures, Inc. v. Majestic Pictures Corp., 70* F.2d 310 (2d Cir. 1934).

61. See, e.g., *Dreamland Ball Room v. Shapiro, Bernstein & Co.*, 36 F.2d 354 (7th Cir. 1929).

62. *Roy Export Co. v. Trustees of Columbia University*, 344 F.Supp. 1350 (S.D.N.Y. 1972).

63. 17 U.S.C.A. § 512 (2002).

64. See, e.g., *Sony Corp. of America v. Universal City Studios, Inc.,* 464 U.S. 417 (1984).

65. *Bright Tunes Music Corp. v. Harrisongs Music, Ltd.*, 420 F.Supp. 177, 180 (S.D.N.Y. 1976).

66. 17 U.S.C.A. § 107 (2002).

67. *Dellar v. Samuel Goldwin, Inc.*, 105 F.2d 661, 662 (2d Cir. 1939).

68. 17 U.S.C.A. § 107 (2002).

69. *Williams & Wilkins v. United States*, 487 F.2d 1345 (Ct. Cl. 1973), *aff'd* 420 U.S. 396 (1975).

70. See, e.g., *MacMillan v. King*, 223 862 (D.Mass. 1914).; *Encyclopedia Britannica Educational Crop v. Crooks*, 447 F.Supp. 243 (W.D.N.Y. 1978).

71. See, e.g., *Campbell v. Acuff-Rose Music, Inc.* 510 U.S. 569 (1994); *Zacchini v. Scrippts-Howard Broadcasting Co.*, 433 U.S. 562 (1977).

72. *Wainwright Securities, Inc., v. Wall Street Transcript Corp.*, 558 F.2d 91 (2d Cir. 1977).

73. See, e.g., *American Institute of Architects v. Fenichel*, 41 F.Supp. 46 (S.D.N.Y. 1941).

74. See, e.g., *New York Times Co. v. Roxbury Data Interface, Inc.* 434 F. Supp. 217 (D.N.J. 1977).

75. See, e.g., *Harper & Row, Publishers, Inc. v. Nation Enterprises, Inc.* 471 U.S. 539 (1985).; *Salinger v. Random House, Inc.*, 811 F.2d 90 (2d Cir. 1987).

76. See, e.g., *Robertson v. Batten, Barton, Durstine & Osborne, Inc.*, 146 F.Supp 795 (S.D.Cal. 1956); *Williams & Wilkins v. United States*, 487 F.2d 1345 (Ct.Cl. 1973), *aff'd* 420 U.S. 396 (1977).

77. *Meeropol v. Nizer*, 560 F.2d 1061 (2d Cir. 1977).

78. See, e.g., *Walt Disney Productions v. Air Pirates*, 581 F.2d 751 (9th Cir. 1978).

79. *Harper & Row Publishers, Inc. v. Nation Enterprises, Inc.,* 471 U.S. 539 (1985).

80. *Sid & Marty Kroft Television Productions, Inc. v. McDonalds Corp.*, 562 F.2d 1157 (9th Cir. 1977).

81. See, e.g., *Campbell v. Acuff-Rose Music, Inc.*, 510 U.S. 569 (1994).; *Berlin v. E.C. Publications, Inc.*, 319 F.2d 541 (1964).

82. *Time, Inc. v. Bernart Geis Associates* 293 F.Supp. 130 (S.D.N.Y. 1968).
83. *Zacchini v. Scripps-Howard Broadcasting Co.*, 433 U.S. 562 (1977).
84. *Coca-Cola Co. v. Seven-Up Co.*, 497 F.2d 1351, 1354 (Cust. & Pat.App.Bd.1974).
85. *Hanover Star Milling Co. v. Metcalf*, 240 U.S. 403 (1916).
86. U.S. Const. art. I, § 1
87. *U.S. v. Steffens*, 100 U.S. 82 (1879).
88. *Time, Inc. v. Motor Publications, Inc.*, 131 F.Supp. 846 (D.Md. 1956).
89. *Scott Paper Co. v. Scott's Liquid Gold Inc.*, 439 F.Supp. 1022 (D.Del.1977), *reversed* 589 F.2d 1225 (3d Cir. 1978).
90. *Reddy Communications v. Environmental Action Foundation*, 477 F.Supp. 936 (D.D.C. 1979); also see, *Allied Maintenance Corp. v. Allied Mechanical Trades, Inc.* 399 N.Y.S.2d 628 (N.Y. 1977).
91. 15 U.S.C.A. § 1051 (2002).
92. 15 U.S.C.A. § 1051(b) (2002).
93. www.uspto.gov, retrieved June 5, 2004.
94. See, e.g., *Thrifty Rent-A-Car System v. Thrift Cars, Inc.* 831 F.2d 1177 (1st Cir. 1987).
95. 15 U.S.C.A. § 1062 (2002).
96. 15 U.S.C.A. §§ 1058, 1059 (2002).
97. 15 U.S.C.A. § 1052 (2002).
98. *Modular Cinemas of America, Inc. v. Mini Cinemas Corp.*, 348 F.Supp. 578 (S.D.N.Y. 1972).
99. 15 U.S.C.A. § 1070 (2002).
100. 15 U.S.C.A. § 1052(d) (2002).
101. *International Kennel Club v. Mighty Star Inc.*, 846 F.2d 1079 (7th Cir. 1988).
102. *G.D. Searle & Co. v. Chase Pfizer & Co.*, 265 F.2d 385 (7th Cir. 1959).
103. *Mead Data Central Inc. v. Toyota Motor Sales, U.S.A.*, 875 F.2d 1026 (2d Cir. 1989).
104. See, e.g., *Park'N Fly, Inc. v. Dollar Park & Fly*, Inc., 469 U.S. 189 (1985).
105. *Miller Brewing Co. v. Falstaff Brewing Corp.*, 503 F.Supp. 896 (D.R.I. 1980).
106. *Abercrombie & Fitch Co. v. Hunting World, Inc.*, 537 F.2d 4 (2d Cir. 1976).
107. *Bayer Co. v. United Drug Co.*, 272 F. 505 (S.D.N.Y., 1921).
108. *DuPont Cellophane Co. v. Waxed Products Co.*, 85 F.2d 75 (2d Cir. 1939).
109. See, e.g., *Prestwick, Inc. v. Don Kelly Building Co.*, 302 F.Supp. 1121 (D.Md. 1969); *In re Societe Generale Des Eaux Minerales De Vittel*, 824 F.2d 957 (Fed.Cir. 1987).
110. *In re Hutchinson Technology, Inc.*, 852 F.2d 552 (Fed.Cir. 1988).
111. *In re Riverbank Canning Co.*, 95 F.2d 327 (Cust.&Pat.App. 1938).; *In re Sociedade Agricola E. Comercial Dos Vihnos Mesias, S.A.R.L.*, 159 U.S.P.Q. 275 (Trademark Tr. & App. Bd. 1968); see also *Bromberg v. Carmel Self Service, Inc.*, 198 U.S.P.Q. 176 (Trademark Tr. & App. Bd. 1978) rejecting, "Only a breast in the mouth is better than a leg in the hand," as a trademark for a chicken restaurant.
112. *Scarves by Vera, Inc. v. Todo Imports Ltd.*, 544 F.2d 1167 (2d Cir. 1976).
113. *Allstate Insurance Co. v. Allstate, Inc.*, 307 F.Supp. 1161 (N.D.Tex. 1969). Dealing with an insurance company and a car wash.
114. 15 U.S.C.A. § 112(c).
115. 15 U.S.C.A. § 1125 (1999).
116. 15 U.S.C.A. § 1125 (2002).
117. *In re E.I. DuPont DeNemours & Co.*, 476 F.2d 1357 (Cust. & Pat. App. 1973).
118. 15 U.S.C.A. §§ 1958, 1059 (2002).
119. See *Universal City Studios, Inc. v. Nintendo Co., Ltd.*, 578 F.Supp. 911 (S.D.N.Y. 1983) and the decision affirming the district court decision at 746 F.2d 112 (2nd Cir. 1984).

120. See, e.g., *Beech-Nut Packaging Co. v. P. Lorillard Co.*, 273 U.S. 629 (1927); *Sheila's Shine Products Inc. v. Sheila Shine, Inc.*, 486 F.2d 114 (5th Cir. 1973).

121. 17 U.S.C.A. § 101 (2002).

122. *Cmty. For Creative Non-Violence v. Reid*, 490 U.S. 730, 751 (1989).

123. 117 U.S.C.A. §§ 101, 201(b) (2002).

124. *Reid*, 490 U.S. at 738, note the category for sound recordings was added to the Copyright Act after the decision in this case.

125. 17 U.S.C.A. § 101 (2002).

126. 17 U.S.C.A. 302(c) (2002).

127. *Apple Computer, Inc. v. Microsoft Corp.*, 35 F.3d 1435 (9th Cir. 1994), *cert. denied* 513 U.S. 1184 (1995).

Contract
and Employment Law

The publisher of a newspaper has no special immunity from the application of general laws. He has no special privilege . . .[1]

Overview
Contract Principles
Employment and Agency Law
Rights and Obligations that Result from Agency
Practice Notes

Overview

Contracts are used in virtually every arena of mass communications practice. Consider the release and waiver defenses in defamation and copyright infringement, for example. A release is a contract. Well drafted, that contract or release can save you from a successful lawsuit. Poorly drafted, the release may not provide any defense at all. Principles of contract law also cover the purchase of all the goods and services used in our profession, including our own professional services. When bartering our skills and effort for payment from our employers or clients, we all are using principles of contract law. In short, virtually everything we do in mass communications is covered by some component of contract law.

Contract law is extensive and complicated; we do not even attempt to cover all of its nuances here. What we do is present some basic concepts to help you understand how and when a contract may be created or enforced. In particular, we discuss the requirements for written contracts, problems associated with contracting with minors, and how to avoid unwittingly entering into a contract. We also provide enough background so readers will understand the concepts behind employment agreements, which are, we believe, the most important application of contracts in most mass communications practices. In the discussion of employment contracts, we include a summary of the concept of agency because it seems particularly important to those working in advertising and public relations. The discussion of employment law also summarizes the limited protection of whistleblowers and employers' rights to terminate.

Through this brief introduction to the topic, we hope to help you understand when and why contracts are important. We certainly do not aspire to teach you enough that you can draft and evaluate contracts. Our objective is to give you enough information so that you know when you are forming a contract and to know when you should seek the advise of counsel to draft a contract properly or to evaluate a contract obligation.

Contract Principles

In the copy of BLACK'S LAW DICTIONARY on our desk, the definition of the word *contract* begins on page 394 and ends on page 397.[2] Obviously, it would take far too long to explain all the intricacies of contracts. For our purposes here, we simply note that a contract is a legally enforceable agreement between two or more people. As you read this chapter you may note that some of the cases cited date back to the 15th century. Some of the very earliest questions presented to courts involved contracts and many of the principles of contract law were formed at times when many parties were illiterate and when business practices and concerns were very different than they are today. The antiquity of some decisions and principles still followed may contribute to the complexity of contract law. Here we concentrate on contemporary issues and law as it exists in the 21st century.

Elements of a Contract

The elements required to create a contract are well established but each require some explanation. They are shown in Exhibit 11.1. Most authors say that a contract is created when two parties have a **meeting of the minds** and there is consideration. The meeting of the minds means that the parties agree to be bound and the agreement is specific enough to be enforceable. Many jurisdictions use the concepts of *offer* and *acceptance* to show this meeting of the minds. So it can be said that a contract is created when an offer and acceptance shows the parties have agreed to be bound, and when there is consideration.

Usually an agreement or meeting of the minds is formed in negotiations. Those negotiations take the form of one party making an offer or proposing terms of an agreement and the other party either rejecting or accepting those terms. If the offer is rejected,

Exhibit 11.1.   Elements Required to Create a Contract.

Meeting of the Minds	Offer and Acceptance
	Consideration

there is no contract. If the offer is accepted and there is also consideration, the parties have a contract.

Offer

For an **offer** to be sufficient, it must be so specific that all the other party need do for both to understand exactly what is expected is to say "I agree." Therefore, offers may not be conditioned on things beyond the control of the person making the offer. For example, if your friend says, "I will give you $20 to wash my car if my parents send me money this week," you may not have a meeting of the minds because neither of you really knows whether the parents' check will arrive. As a practical matter, if you seek to form a contract, keep your offer very specific. For example, "I will pay you $20 immediately after you wash my car today."

Offers may be express or implied. Express offers are presented either orally or in writing and detail the terms of the offer. Implied offers are communicated by the conduct of the offeror.[3] If your sorority or fraternity held a charity car wash, your conduct in putting up signs, actually washing cars, and accepting payment is an implied offer. A person could simply drive his or her car in and say, "I accept." From the person's conduct, it would be obvious he or she was saying "I accept your offer to wash my car for the price stated on the sign." When evaluating implied offers, it is important to note that conduct does sometimes create the impression of a gift rather than an offer. What must be made clear in the implied offer is the idea that the offeror does expect to be paid for the service rendered. In the example given earlier, the sign stating the price and the act of accepting payment gives this impression. However, one does need to be sure that the expectation of payment is known to everyone. If one is providing services to a church, synagogue, or mosque, for example, the organization may expect that those services are donated rather than presented as part of a negotiation for payment. The test for an implied contract is "Would a reasonable person expect the conduct to create an obligation to pay?"[4]

Many advertising messages also create an offer. For an advertisement to be a legally valid offer, it must contain enough specificity to be enforceable. Everyone who functions in a capitalistic society knows that if a product is advertised for sale at a particular price not everyone who sees the advertisement could possibly accept the offer. No store is expected to have an unlimited supply of goods and no one is expected to sell goods today for prices that were advertised years ago.[5] However, if an advertisement contains language like "first come, first served," it is specific enough to constitute a legally binding offer and the advertiser may be contractually bound to honor the advertised price and terms to a reasonable number of customers who fit the category "first come."[6] Offers may also be withdrawn at any time before they are accepted. This means that if someone mistakenly advertises a product far below market value, the offer can be voided by advertising a withdrawal of that offer as long as it is done before customers arrive at the store to accept the offer.[7] It should be noted that in order to avoid charges of fraud or deceptive advertising, the original advertisement must be an honest mistake and an honest effort must be made to communicate withdrawal of the offer.

Acceptance

An **acceptance** must be a simple accession to the original offer. If the acceptor adds terms or modifies the offer in any way, that is not an acceptance. It is a new offer.[8] In order to be binding, an offer must be so specific that all the other party need do for both to understand exactly what is expected is to say "I agree." If the other party says "I agree but . . .", then the parties may not understand exactly what is expected. Furthermore, the person who made the original offer may not accept the new terms or conditions. This exchange of offer and acceptance, often called *contract negotiations*, is not complete until all the contract's terms are fully understood and the final party in the exchange simply says "I agree."

The person making the offer may also specify the form of the acceptance. He or she could say, "I offer to sell you my car for $100, but you have to accept by standing on your head." Of course, offers like this are extraordinarily unusual, but offers that contain terms like "you must accept in writing" or "you must accept within 30 days" are very common and those conditions are absolutely enforceable. An acceptance that does not comply with the terms specified in the offer is not a binding acceptance. Also, the intent to accept is completely irrelevant. In order to accept an offer, one must communicate that acceptance to the person who made the offer.[9] Even signing a written acceptance is not a legally enforceable acceptance. Where a written and signed acceptance is required, it must actually be delivered to the offeror before the "meeting of the minds" is complete.[10] Delivery does not need to be physical. For example, you may accept by placing your acceptance in a mailbox[11] or by sending it by telegraph or fax.[12] The standard is that you have effectively delivered the acceptance as soon as you put it beyond your control.[13] In other words, as soon as you no longer have the power to stop the acceptance from reaching the offeror you have accepted. Since you cannot legally stop a letter once it is mailed and you cannot stop a telegram, fax, or e-mail transmission once it is sent, those are effective acceptances. If it is possible to "overtake" the acceptance you can withdraw it. You might, for example, mail an acceptance, but before it reaches the offeror, you could call or e-mail her or him and withdraw your acceptance. When you seek to withdraw an acceptance in this way, you must be able to prove that your withdrawal actually reached the offeror before your acceptance. Remember, as soon as the acceptance is received, the "meeting of the minds" part of contract formation is complete and you cannot simply "change your mind."[14]

To illustrate the rules of offer and acceptance, consider the case of William Lyon who attempted to purchase an advertising company in 1985. Edward Sherman owned an advertising company called Adgraphics. Sherman, through a real estate agent, offered to sell his business. Lyon attempted to accept the offer but in his acceptance he proposed a price lower than Sherman's offer. Lyon's proposal was not an acceptance; it was a counteroffer and it did not create a contract; it started the negotiations anew. At this point, Sherman could have simply said "I agree" and created a contract on the terms proposed by Lyon, but he did not. Sherman made still another counteroffer proposing a new price. Lyon liked this last offer and attempted to accept. First, he signed the offer indicating his acceptance. Then he had his signature notarized to prove his commitment. He then took the signed and notarized acceptance to Sherman's broker at 9 a.m. the next morning. Just before Lyon arrived with acceptance, Sherman called his broker and withdrew his offer. The state court of appeals that reviewed the case said that Lyon had not successfully accepted because he did not deliver his acceptance to Sherman before the offer was withdrawn.[15] In this case, Lyon took the acceptance to Sherman's broker himself. Therefore, the acceptance was never out of his control right up to the minute when he arrived at Sherman's broker who told him the offer was withdrawn. Had Lyon placed the acceptance in the mail the night before, his acceptance would have been placed beyond his control before Sherman withdrew the offer and today Lyon would probably be the owner of an advertising business.

Consideration

In addition to a meeting of the minds, a contract must involve an exchange of consideration. That means that something of value must be given to the bargain by each of the parties. Put another way, a **bare promise** by one person or a gift from one person to another is simply not enforceable because it is not a contract.[16] A common mistake made by mass communications practitioners may help illustrate the requirement for mutual consideration. Often, communications professionals ask subjects, news sources, and others for releases. Sometimes, these agreements carefully explain that the subject gives permission to use his or her image or information and that the subject agrees not to sue the reporter or photographer for use of the information or image. Frankly, such a release is not worth the cost of the paper to produce it. Unless the reporter or photographer also agrees to give something of value, the release, which is a contract, is not enforceable. It is only a "bare promise."

If a teacher promises to give a student his or her car, no matter how specific that promise may be and no matter how specifically both parties understand the terms of the promise, the student cannot enforce that promise unless it also involves a commitment of something of value from the student. However, the requirement for consideration does not require an equal exchange. If the teacher was extraordinarily generous, he or she might agree to sell the student the car for $1. If the student accepted that offer and both parties understood it to be a legitimate offer, a legally binding contract could be created. Many contracts begin with language that says something like:

> For consideration of $1, in hand paid, the receipt and sufficiency of which is hereby acknowledged.

This language is included because the person who drafted the contract wanted to be sure it was binding. The language guarantees that the person who signs the contract has acknowledged that she or he has received something of value from the party to whom a promise was made and that the consideration was sufficient to justify enforcement of his or her contractual obligations.

Legal texts are full of odd examples like exchanges of estates for peppercorns. The only requirement is that both parties invest something in the exchange. A contract exchanging payment for naming a child after the offeror was upheld[17] and, in one of the best-known and bizarre exchanges, a contract exchanging an uncle's estate for a nephew's promise to refrain from drinking, smoking, and playing cards was upheld.[18] For those in mass communications, it is important to note that intangibles like information or publicity can also be consideration. If one agrees to exchange publicity on behalf of the source for the source's permission to use his or her photograph, mutual consideration occurs. Even more important, if one agrees not to divulge the source's name in exchange for information, the agreement not to divulge the source's name is consideration and the information is consideration. This contract exchanging information for silence can be legally enforceable.

Some contracts, often called **executory contracts**, are exchanges of promises to do things of value in the future. These too can be legally binding. Returning to the example of the generous teacher with the car: if he or she promises to give the student the car the first of next month if the student promises to take out the trash each day for the next 2 weeks, a mutually binding executory contract to perform those acts has been created.

There are some restrictions on the obligations that may be exchanged. Of course, a valid contract obligating a party to perform an illegal act or to do something that is literally impossible or completely beyond the person's control cannot be created. One of the most common mistakes made in attempts to construct contracts is to include a past event as consideration. For example, a reporter cannot enforce a promise made by his or her editor to pay a bonus for exceptional reporting in the previous year. Since the reporter has already done the work for last year, he or she is not putting anything of value into the contract being created today.[19]

Requirement for Written Contract

When we listed the elements required to create a contract, we said absolutely nothing about the physical form of the contract. Under most circumstances there are no requirements for a specific form. Contracts may be implied by conduct, they may be express and oral or they may be expressed in writing. There are, however, some situations in which contracts cannot be enforced unless they are written. This requirement for written contracts is called the **Statute of Frauds**. Both the Uniform Commercial Code and the Restatement of Contracts list six kinds of contracts that must be written, but these requirements do vary from jurisdiction to jurisdiction. The contract types are listed in Exhibit 11.2. For example, some jurisdictions add contracts that cannot be performed within the lifetime of one party and some permit oral leases for up to 1 year.[20]

Most of these are irrelevant to the mass communications professionals but others often do impact our business. For example, many public relations and advertising campaigns take more than 1 year to complete. Contracts for goods with clients, suppliers, and contributing professionals in these campaigns should be written. Other contracts requiring a writing that are seen in mass communications include office leases. Often, when a public relations or advertising contract is transferred from one agency to another, the acquiring agency is asked to accept obligations created by the old agency. These contracts also should be written. Generally, there is a logic to deciding what

Exhibit 11.2.   Statute of Frauds: Contracts that Must be in Writing.

- Contract of an executor or administrator to answer for a duty of the decedent
- Contract to answer for the duty of another (Suretyship)
- Contract made upon consideration of marriage (Prenuptial Agreement)
- Contract for sale of an interest in land
- Contract that is not to be performed within one year
- Contract for sale of goods over $500

contracts should be written. The longer the term of the contract, the more likely the parties are to forget the original agreement and the more complex the agreement the more likely it is that a misunderstanding will arise. For both long-term and complex agreements, a written contract will keep all the parties informed and honest and, if necessary, will help a judge decide what terms were actually part of the agreement.

Most people think of a written contract as some monstrously complex document filled with the ritualistic language lawyers use to confuse laymen. The Statute of Frauds requires only "a writing." It does not require a specific form of writing and it does not require professional language. All that is required is a permanent record that is understandable and that specifies the terms of the agreement. Things that have been used to meet the requirement for a writing include a letter,[21] a telegram,[22] a receipt,[23] an invoice,[24] a check,[25] or even the minutes of a meeting at which the agreement was discussed.[26] What a judge is typically looking for is some evidence that records the agreement so that she or he does not have to rely on the memory and testimony of the parties.

Even for contracts that are covered by the Statute of Frauds there are times when a written contract is not required. These are times when other evidence serves the same purposes that would be served by a written document. Part performance meets this requirement. **Part performance** occurs when one party does what he or she believes the contract required and the other party accepts those goods or services. When this happens, the courts typically will say that accepting the goods or services is the same as accepting the contract and the actions of the parties substitute for the written contract.[27] The reason for requiring a written agreement is to help understand what agreement the parties reached. When the terms of the contract can be determined from the parties' conduct, the court does not need the document.

Finally, the writing can be communicated by electronic means. We may think of the Internet as presenting novel legal questions but some of those same questions have been addressed when courts were confronted with much older technology. More than 130 years ago, courts were asked to decide if written contracts could be created through electronic media. Dealing with the then-new technology of the telegraph, a New Hampshire Appellate Court set a precedent that is still in place. That ruling said the medium used to communicate thought to paper is irrelevant. What matters is that the parties to the contract caused their thoughts to be reduced to some tangible form.[28] A legally enforceable and written contract can be created by telegraph and it can be created by e-mail.

Contract Limitations

Some people cannot form contracts or, if they do enter into contracts, are given the right to avoid their contractual obligations. People without the capacity to form binding contracts can create problems for several communications practices. One of the most common is the problem of securing a binding contract of release from a child. Less likely to be an issue in the practice of mass communications are limitations on contracting with people who are mentally incompetent and contracts that deal with prohibited subjects.

Contracting with Minors

Historically, people under the age of 21 were considered too young to understand the significance of their agreements. Today, most jurisdictions have lowered this age to 18 to be consistent with voting laws.[29] When a minor enters into a contract, he or she is free to **disaffirm** that contract and completely avoid its obligations. Although the minor can avoid her or his obligations under the contract, an adult party to a contract with a minor is obligated to meet his or her contract duties. In most jurisdictions, that means a minor can avoid contract payments or providing goods and services even if the other party has fully performed her or his duty under the contract.[30] For example, a minor can disaffirm a release or contract not to sue.[31] An advertising producer using a model under the age of 18 or a photographer securing a release from a subject under 18 could conceivably pay for a release and then have the model or subject sue for damage to her or his reputation or for lost profits. One should be very careful when contracting with a minor.

Contracting with minors is further complicated by the fact that some states even allow a minor who lies about his or her age to escape contract obligations.[32] The only solutions to this problem are to avoid contracts with anyone who even might be young enough to disaffirm a contract or to consult with local counsel to learn the rules for contracting with minors in your jurisdiction. Finally, there are some contracts that even minors may not disaffirm. Contracts for necessities like food and shelter cannot be disaffirmed in most jurisdictions. Also, minors who are conducting their lives as adults, called emancipated minors, cannot disaffirm contracts in most jurisdictions. Evidence that minors might be emancipated include marriage, full-time employment, and living outside their parents' homes.

Contracting with People who Are Mental Incompetents

It is at least possible that an ethical practitioner in a field of mass communications may have to form a contract with a person who is mentally incompetent. A reporter, for example, might need a release from a homeless person who is mentally ill or a public relations practitioner might have to contract with an intoxicated client. Because these situations seem unusual, we treat this area very briefly.

In most jurisdictions, the test for mental incompetence is whether the person forming the contract is able to understand what he or she is doing. If he or she does not understand the terms of the contract, that person cannot form the requisite "meeting of the minds."[33] This is a difficult standard to prove or to challenge, so it is advisable to seek legal advice for the rules in one's jurisdiction before entering into a contract with anyone who seems mentally incapacitated or confused. Finally, it should be noted that in most jurisdictions, the mental incapacity must be involuntary. That means if you volunteer to make yourself incompetent through drug or alcohol use you may not be able to avoid obligations under contracts you enter into while intoxicated.

Contract Subject Limitations

Unless there is some policy reason, people are usually allowed to contract for anything they like. Policy justifications have been used to prohibit contracts for illegal acts, for usurious interest rates, or to contract away some legal rights. Most of these limitations do not impact mass communications professionals but one seems worthy of note. In many jurisdictions it is illegal to contract away the implied warrant of merchantability. In other words, no matter what kind of release or contract you try to fashion, you cannot avoid the obligation to guarantee that products are fit for the purpose for which they are sold. Other limitations imposed for policy reasons include an obligation to disclose very specifically the terms of a contract.[34] People working in public relations and advertising need to be careful that advertisements and messages about commercial products disclose any sale terms that limit liability based on how a product can be used.

Acceptance, Breach, and Remedies

Once a contract is created, each party has an obligation to deliver the consideration she or he put into that agreement. Acceptance, in this context, refers to the one party's acknowledgment that the other party has delivered the consideration. Acceptance is particularly important to people in mass communications because often the consideration they put into contracts is their work as writers, photographers, or electronic producers. Usually, they agree to produce "acceptable" writing or "appropriate" photography or "workmanlike" productions. The other party to the contract may refuse to accept the work by saying it does not meet his or her standards. We therefore begin this section by describing the standards of acceptance for subjective or artistic works.

Acceptance of Performance

If the consideration in a contract is money or specific goods, then the contract obligation is performed when that money or the goods are delivered. If the consideration is some kind of performance that is subject to fancy, taste, or judgment courts have given a great deal of discretion to the person to whom that consideration is owed. For utilitarian services like auto repair, the standard of acceptance is reasonable performance. A court trying to evaluate the performance asks itself, "Would a reasonable person accept this performance?" Usually, those in mass communications are not contracted to provide utilitarian services. They are more likely to contract to provide artistic work like writing, photography, and electronic productions. In these cases, the standard is "honest evaluation."[35] The person deciding whether to accept the performance is not obligated even to be reasonable. He or she is only required to be honest when interpreting the work.[36] Although an individual may have a contract to provide reporting, advertising, or public relations services for a year, if the quality of the writing, advertising production, or public relations work is not satisfactory, in the honest judgment of the client, he or she could cancel the contract before the year is over.[37] For artistic types of work, all that is required to avoid payment is that the work does not meet the expectations of the employer.[38] Finally, it is important to note that when hiring an expert or tradesman in a particular professional field, the employer is legally entitled to assume that tradesman is competent in his or her trade.[39] This means that even in a contract where the subjective judgment standard of approval is not used, the acceptance may still be withheld if the work is not done to the standard of a competent professional. To avoid problems with having your work rejected, an individual should not describe him or herself as a writer, photographer, or researcher unless he or she really is a competent tradesman in those fields.

Breach and Remedies for Breach

Breach is the legal term used to describe the situation when one party meets his or her obligations under a contract and the other does not. If, for example, you contract to sell your textbook to a fraternity brother for $50 and you deliver the book but he does not pay the $50, he is in **breach of contract**. Most questions concerning breach of contract are not so simple. They often involve partial performance, for example only delivering some of the textbooks you agreed to sell to your roommate, or the existence of some term in the contract that creates a condition for performance. Conditions are created by statements in the contract like, "I will pay you if I get the advertising contract." Contracts subject to conditions or suits for partial performance are often complicated and their analysis usually requires the assistance of an attorney. If the other party to a contract breaches her or his obligations there are several options, called remedies.

One remedy is **specific performance**. To exercise this option you must sue in equity to secure a court order that compels the other party to actually meet his or her obligation under the contract. Specific performance is only available when the other party's obligation involves some truly unique object or action. The most common application of specific performance is to enforce contracts for the sale or lease of real estate. Courts have consistently ruled that one office, home, or farm cannot be substituted for another. Examples of contracts in the practices of mass communications that could be enforced by an order for specific performance might include contracts not to compete and contracts for exclusive information. If someone has contracted not to compete with your business or to provide exclusive information, your attorney could ask a court to enter an affirmative injunction demanding that they actually give you the information or refrain from competition with your business. In part, because it involves a great deal of the court's resources to enforce such actions, specific performance may be difficult to obtain and is usually impossible when the breach can be corrected by payment of money. It should also be noted that because of the abhorrence in the United States to indentured service, specific performance is never required for personal service contracts. In other words, even if you have already paid someone, a court will not order that person to work for you. This does not mean the person you have paid completely escapes his or her liabilities. The individual may be ordered not to work for anyone else, not to compete with you and to return your money but, he or she will not be ordered specifically to work for you.[40]

The court may also either grant rescission of the contract or construct a new contract called a **novation**. If the contract is rescinded, that relieves each party of all their obligations to the other. Simply put, if a rescission is granted because the other party did not perform his or her obligation, you are not required to make payment or perform any other act that the contract may have required of you. A novation is a new contract, written by the court. This is done where there was a partial performance or if some condition prevents one party from meeting his or her obligations. The principle that guides a novation is *quantum meruit*. **Quantum meruit** means "as much as he deserves" and refers to the practice of courts to require payment for the value of actual services or goods delivered. Assume, for example you contracted to write, in exchange for $1,000, a unique news release for each of 10 newspapers as part of a public relations campaign, but you only completed 8 of the releases. A court exercising the principle of *quantum meruit* would not excuse payment to you, but would require that you be paid the fair value of the eight releases you actually delivered. It is important to note that under the doctrine of *quantum meruit* the court may not order a payment of the amount expected or for any subjective or emotional value. The court will award only the actual market value of the goods or services actually delivered, less any damage or loss caused by your failure to complete your obligation.[41]

Other remedies include payment for detrimental reliance losses. This is significant in public relations and advertising because it may result in an order to pay more than the original contract required. **Detrimental reliance** losses are money spent or value lost by one party because that party relied on the contract performance of the other. In public relations, such a loss might occur if a client contracts with you to provide publicity and encourage attendance at a business opening. If the client pays caterers, agrees to pay extra staff, and incurs other obligations relying on your publicity and you fail to notify the target publics, the client may not only refuse to pay you, he or she may also sue you for the money spent preparing for the crowd that never appeared.[42]

Lost bargain or expectation damages are like reliance losses because they can lead to a requirement to pay more than the original contract obligation. **Expectation damages** are the money a contract party would have made had the contract been honored. Such a situation can arise when you contract to perform part of a larger campaign or project. You may contract with an advertising agency to produce the Web page for an agency client and your Web page may be part of an expensive campaign being done for the client by the agency. If you fail to produce the page and the agency loses the client, you might be obligated for the loss of the entire campaign contract.[43]

Because there are several options for determining damage in the event of contract breach, many contracts contain clauses called **liquidated damages**. Liquidated damages are predetermined remedies for breach. When such a clause is included in the contract the parties decide, as part of the negotiations, what would be a reasonable payment for a breach and they include a description of this payment in the contract. Liquidated damages must be a reasonable reflection of the loss that will result from breach. Some people have attempted to create punitive clauses or requirements to pay exorbitant amounts in the event of a contract breach. Most courts reject these punitive damage clauses and refuse to enforce them.

Before we leave the idea of damages, we should note that even when another party breaches a contract you do have a **duty to mitigate damage**. If your subcontractor fails to produce the Web page for which you contracted you cannot simply sue him or her for the loss of your client. You do have a duty to try to find another Web designer. Before you can sue anyone for breach of contract, you must show that you have performed your obligations under the contract and that you have made every reasonable effort to lower or "mitigate" the damage caused by their breach.

Defenses

The simplest defense to an allegation that someone breached a contract is to show that there was no contract. Therefore, defenses include the absence of an offer, an acceptance, or mutual consideration. Demonstrating that one of the parties lacks the legal **capacity to contract** is also a valid defense to a suit for breach of contract. So if an individual can show that he or she was underage, mentally incapacitated, or incompetent, he or she may be able to avoid obligations under an alleged contract. Other defenses include mistake, impossibility, fraud, and duress. These defenses are summarized in Exhibit 11.3.

Exhibit 11.3.   Defenses to Contract Obligations.

Defense		Remedy or Result
No contract because of	No offer No acceptance No consideration	There is no enforceable obligation
Lack of capacity to contract because of	Infancy Voluntary mental incapacity	Infant can disaffirm There is no enforceable obligation
Illegal act or purpose		No enforceable obligation
Mistake	Mutual	There is no contract; all obligations are void
	Unilateral	Relief depends on circumstances
Fraud		Contract is void
Duress because of	Improper threat that would induce a reasonable person to agree to contract	Contract is void

Mistake

The defense of **mistake** is based on a misunderstanding of facts that prevented an informed meeting of the minds. In effect, it is an assertion that there never was a valid contract. The term *mistake,* as used in contract law, does not mean what most laymen think when they hear the word *mistake.* A mistake is not simply an error in judgment or a poor decision; it must be a mistaken understanding about some fact.[44] Furthermore, to be a legal defense to a contract obligation, a mistake must be an honest misunderstanding about facts that is so significant that it prevents the contract parties from creating a meeting of the minds.[45] Mistakes may be mutual or unilateral. A **mutual mistake** occurs when both parties to the contract do not understand facts that are essential to their agreement and a unilateral mistake occurs when one party misunderstands but the other party is accurately aware of all the facts. When describing mutual mistake, contract teachers in law school typically use the example of a contract to sell a cow that both parties believe is barren and unable to bear calves. Such a cow is far less valuable than one who is fertile and can bear calves. When, after the sale of the supposedly barren cow, it gives birth to a calf both the buyer and seller realize they made a mistake about the cow and her value. The result of this mistake is that the contract for sale is void. The buyer must return the cow and calf, and the seller must return the purchase price. They simply did not have a contract because they did not have a meeting of the minds.[46]

Today, there is some variation in how mutual mistakes are treated from jurisdiction to jurisdiction, but generally, if the mistake is about a fact that is central to the contract agreement and if the mistake was not caused by the party who seeks to void the contract, the mistake will nullify the entire contract. Just like the situation with the barren cow, all the exchanged goods and payments must be returned and any services rendered are paid for based on *quantum meruit.*[47]

Where the mistake is unilateral, courts do not seem as willing to void the contract. If, for example, someone miscalculates the fee for a public relations campaign, he or she may not be able to void the contract and seek a higher payment even though he or she made an honest mistake. Even in these situations, the decisions are not consistent. For example, some jurisdictions do permit revision of contracts if bids were produced under a great deal of time pressure. Some courts believe that if one party puts the other under so much pressure that the probability of mistake is increased, he or she should not benefit from mistakes created by that pressure. On the other hand, if work has begun or if a party has invested resources in reliance on a mistaken bid before he is told of the mistake the contract may be enforced as agreed.[48]

Impossibility

A contract is "impossible" when some event occurs that prevents one party from meeting his or her contract obligation. Obviously, if one of the parties dies or becomes disabled it may be impossible for him or her to perform.[49] The destruction of property necessary for the contract performance also makes the contract impossible. For example, if a public relations practitioner contracts for a display space at a convention in order to present a client's new products, he or she cannot hold the convention center liable for not meeting their contract obligation if the center burns to the ground before the convention.[50] Because contracts may not require illegal conduct, if the laws change after a contract is formed such that the contract obligation would now require an illegal act, then the contract has become impossible.[51]

It is not necessary that the obligation be absolutely impossible. In fact, many judges and legal commentators use the term *impracticability* rather than the word **impossibility** to describe this defense. However, a contract obligation cannot be escaped simply because it has become more difficult or more expensive. Increased cost alone does not make a contract obligation either impossible or legally impractical. Individuals are required to use alternative means of meeting their obligations if they are available. If, for example, your computer equipment crashes while you are attempting to complete an advertising or public relations campaign you may be required, at your own expense, to rent or purchase new equipment and to pay your staff overtime to complete a contracted project. Increased cost and inconvenience are usually not a defense. In some extreme cases, courts have ruled that massive increases in cost do make contract performance legally impracticable but all of these cases involve increased expenses of several times the original costs.[52]

Fraud and Duress

Fraud is the intentional creation of a unilateral mistake. It is a misrepresentation that creates such a significant misunderstanding in the mind of the other party that a meeting of the minds is impossible. It voids the contract completely and may justify other remedies including multiple damages. Multiple damages mean that the party who committed the fraud may be required to pay double or triple the actual damage suffered by the other party.

Duress is the use of threat to induce a person to enter into a contract. The threat must be so significant that it deprives the other party of his or her "free will."[53] In order to use duress as a defense to avoid a contract obligation, four elements must be proven. First, there must have been a threat. Second, the threat must have been improper. Third, the threat must have actually induced the person to agree to the contract, and finally the threat must have been sufficiently grave that it would induce a reasonable person to agree to the contract.[54] Usually, the party who wants to use duress as a defense has the burden of proving all four of these elements.

Although warranties, releases, and other contracts are important in the professions of mass communications, we believe it is the employment contract that is most important to mass communications practitioners. The remainder of this chapter focuses on problems and issues associated with employment contracts.

Employment and Agency Law

Employment and agency deal with the responsibilities employees and employers owe one another. Employment law includes concepts like the prohibitions against discrimination and sexual harassment and requirements to provide handicapped access and work place safety. Although these are certainly important, they are beyond the scope of this book. We limit our discussion of employment law to those components that are particularly important, if not unique, to people working in mass communications.

Those individuals who work as reporters, advertising executives, or public relations practitioners deal directly with the clients who pay their employers. They are quite literally the agents of their employers. Under a principle called *respondeat superior,* their employers can be held liable for their misconduct and may be forced to honor agreements they make with clients or news sources. Furthermore, newspapers, broadcast stations, advertising agencies, and public relations firms are very visible. They are, more than most businesses, the subject of suits in a litigious society. Therefore, it is essential for practitioners to know when their actions may create legal obligations for their media or communications employers or clients.

Employment at Will and Termination for Cause

Employment at will means simply that employees are employed solely at the discretion of their employers and may be fired at the will of the employer. Unless there is some legal prohibition or other exception, an employer may fire an employee simply because he or she does not like the employee or just to make an opening available for some other person, like his or her son-in-law. Obviously, there are civil rights prohibitions, but these do not apply to all businesses and they only prohibit discrimination against protected groups like those based on race, creed, color, national origin, or alienage, or suspect classifications like age and gender. If, for example, an employer treats all employees with equal contempt, regardless of their race, he or she has not violated the civil rights laws designed to prohibit racial discrimination.

Although employment is generally "at will," there are, obviously, exceptions. We have already noted the requirements to avoid discrimination based on protected or suspect classes. Other exceptions include the employer's obligation to honor contracts.[55] Contracts may be very specific written documents or they may be in the form of employee handbooks.[56] Even oral contracts and contracts that are implied by conduct and practice have been used to protect employees from wrongful termination. Oral contracts are particularly difficult to prove in court and most jurisdictions require that an oral contract contain very specific terms.[57] Also, the Statute of Frauds may require that an employment contract for more than 1 year be written. Implied contracts are difficult to prove and are usually created only when an employee has been with an employer for a long time and there have been consistent practices in place.[58] Employment contracts, regardless of their form, usually permit termination only for cause.

Termination for cause may be for business or economic reasons or for what is called just cause. Economic and business reasons include significant loss of business income, bankruptcy, or a change in the economy. Just cause is usually divided into the categories of misconduct or inadequate performance. Because an employee rarely has any control over the economic health of his or her employer, and we assume our readers will not engage in misconduct, we limit this discussion to the concept of inadequate performance.

Montana was the first state to create statutes specifically prohibiting wrongful discharge. That state's statute defines good cause as "reasonably job-related grounds . . . based on a failure to satisfactorily perform."[59] Frankly, such definitions of just cause or good cause are not very helpful. What really seems useful to know is how an employer may decide what is "satisfactory performance." Most people working in a mass communications field will be producing work products that are subject to subjective evaluation. Work products that are subject to taste, fancy, or subjective judgment are not sufficient so long as the person required to evaluate it honestly believes they are inadequate. Case law interpreting employment contracts follow this same principle. As long as the decision is not arbitrary and is "based on facts (1) supported by substantial evidence and (2) **reasonably believed** to be true," (emphasis added)[60] an employer is justified in terminating an employee even when there was a valid employment contract. This means you could be terminated, regardless of the objective quality of your work, if your employer reasonably believes there is evidence that your work is substandard.

Principal–Agent or Master–Servant

Some people are surprised and some offended to learn that employers have as much power as they do. Even more surprising and potentially offensive is the terminology used to describe some of the obligations that are created by the employment relationship. Specifically the terms *master* and *servant* label important concepts in employment law. Today, employees and workers would most likely be offended at being called servants and few employers would be comfortable with the title "master," but it may help to know why those terms are legally important.

Employees are often seen by clients and customers as representatives of their employer. This status of representative or spokesman for the employer has lead to the creation of an elaborate set of laws usually described today as agency law. Agency law began its evolution at a time when servants were quite common and when employers were thought of as the absolute master of the workplace. Historically, a tradesman selling goods to a household would negotiate the sale with a maid or butler. That servant was the representative of the home's "master" and the master was expected to honor the agreements made by his or her servant. Today, the progeny of the master–servant laws are called principal–agent law and they have evolved to cover all kinds of situations where one person acts as the representative or agent of a principal. Important terms in agency law are defined in Exhibit 11.4.

Today, the terms **master** and principal are used interchangeably. A **principal** is a person who "employs" an **agent** or **servant** to perform a service for him or her and who has control over that person's conduct in the performance of the service. The word *employ*, in this context, not only refers to a paid employee but can also refer to an unpaid intern, a volunteer worker, or even a family member who offers assistance.[61] The servant or agent is the other half of the relationship. He or she is the employee, intern, or volunteer who is performing some service for the principal. The reason the principal–agent relationship is legally important is the doctrine of *respondeat superior.* ***Respondeat superior*** is Latin for "let the master answer" and refers to the vicarious

Exhibit 11.4.   Terms of Art in Agency Law.

Term	Definition
Master or principal	One who employs a servant or agent to perform a service for him or her and has control or the right to control the conduct of the servant or agent
Servant or agent	One who is employed to perform a service and whose physical conduct in the performance of that service is controlled or is subject to a right of control by the master or principal
Vicarious liability	Legal responsibility for the misconduct or obligations of another person
Respondeat superior	Latin for "let the master answer." Refers to the vicarious liability of a principal or master for the misconduct or obligations of the servant or agent.
Fiduciary	A person who has a duty to act primarily for the benefit of another person

liability of the principal for the actions of the agent. The agent is obligated to act primarily for the benefit of the principal. Because the agent is acting on behalf of the principal, a number of laws have evolved that permit people doing business with the agent to assume the principal will stand behind the actions and agreements of the agent. This concept is particularly important for people working in public relations and advertising because in those fields agents of public relations or advertising firms are often the only people dealing directly with both clients and representatives of target publics. An advertising or public relations agent, therefore, really speaks for the firm and actually creates legally binding obligations for that firm.

Creation of an Agency Relationship

Before the law recognizes an individual as an agent, several requirements must be met. These requirements, listed in Exhibit 11.5, are, consent, control of the agent by the principal, action by the agent on behalf of the principal, and proof of the agency to third parties.

Consent

Both the agent and the principal must **consent** to the agent–principal relationship. The requirement for consent from the principal may be met in either of two ways. Either the principal must give actual consent or the principal must place the agent in a position that gives the impression of consent to third parties. This impression of consent is called **manifestation of consent**. A New York Appellate Court described this requirement by saying,

Exhibit 11.5.   Elements Required to Create an Agency Relationship.

Element	Explanation
Consent	Agent must consent to control of principal and principal must consent for agent to act on his or her behalf OR give impression of such consent
Control	Control of the agent by the principal OR the right of the principal to control the agent
On behalf of	Agent must be working primarily on behalf of the principal
Proof or notice	Third parties must be given some indication that the agent works for or represents the principal

Agency is a fiduciary relationship resulting from a manifestation of consent by one person (the principal) to another (the agent) that the other shall act in his behalf and subject to his control, together with the consent by the other to so act.[62]

Control

The second element of agency is **control**. It is not required that the principal physically control every behavior of the agent. In fact, there is not even a requirement for actual control of any behavior of the agent. What is required is the "right of control." If the principal has the legal right to control the significant behaviors or communications of the agent, then there is adequate control to create a principal–agent relationship.[63] It should be noted that the control need not be total but there must be control of the significant components of the agent's conduct. For example, the McDonalds corporation was found not to be in an agent–principal relationship with a meat supplier even though McDonalds was their only customer and exercised virtually total control over their product quality. The case dealt with an employee of the company killed in a meat grinder and the issue was whether McDonalds was legally liable for the death as a principal of the meat processing company. The court ruled that McDonalds did not control or have a right to control safety practices at the meat processing company. Therefore, the meat processing company was not McDonalds' agent and McDonalds was not liable for the employee's death.[64] As a general rule, a right to inspect a person's work does not make that person an agent.[65] There are policy reasons for particularly encouraging safety by allowing customers a right to inspect for safety without incurring the obligations of a principal–agency relationship.[66] Therefore, an advertising or public relations firm could hire an artist and retain the right to inspect that artist's work. The firm could even reserve a right to inspect the artist's studio for safety violations. These inspections do not rise to the level of control necessary to make the artist an agent of the firm.

Far less colorful or complicated are questions about the control of traditional employees by employers. Generally courts find that full-time employees are under the control of their employers and are therefore agents of the employer.[67] However, employees are not the only agents. Interns and even volunteer workers can be agents and can be subject to control. "One volunteering service without any agreement for or expectation of reward may be a servant of the one accepting such services."[68] If a principal issues instructions and the agent consistently obeys those instructions that is evidence of control. Payment is not necessary.

On Behalf of the Principal

In order for a legal principal–agent relationship to exist, the agent must be acting primarily on behalf of the principal. It is not necessary that the agent have absolutely no self-interest in his actions. Obviously, the typical employee has at least some self-interest in a paycheck, so to require total altruistic commitment to the principal would mean there could never be a legal principal–agent relationship. But, the agent must be primarily working for the benefit of the principal. Franchise holders, for example, have been held to be working primarily for their own profits and not "on behalf of" the franchisor.[69] Therefore, franchisees like the typical owners of chain restaurants and stores may not be the legal agents of the parent company. It also seems noteworthy that an individual may be the employee of one company but at the same time be working "on behalf of" another. For example, when an employee of a public relations agency is gathering information for a newspaper, at that moment the employee might actually be working on behalf of the newspaper.[70]

Proof or Notice

The element of proof or notice means that something about the conduct of the agent and/or principal gave a reasonable person the impression that the agent was the principal's representative. Something as simple as a sign outside a business identifying the principal as the business owner or manager can give proof or notice that the people working at that location are the principal's agents.[71] It is possible for the element of proof or notice to create an apparent agency. **Apparent agency** creates all the obligations of a principal–agent relationship even if the other elements are not present. If a principal creates or permits a situation that would give reasonable people the impression of a principal–agent relationship he or she may be just as liable as if all the elements of consent, control, and work on behalf of the principal were present. This liability can be based entirely on the appearance given to a third party. It does not depend on the actual agreement between the principal and agent.[72] To use an old colloquialism, if it walks like a duck, quacks like a duck, and looks like a duck, the courts will probably say it is a duck. If two people behave for others to see just as though they were agent and principal, the courts will treat them as agent and principal.

A classic example of this principle was used to resolve a lawsuit against Holiday Inn arising from a robbery at a franchise hotel in 1981. Some time before the robbery, the subject hotel had been sold to a franchisee. There was no consent for the hotel's new owner to continue as an agent of Holiday Inn and Holiday Inn did not exercise control over the new hotel owner. However, Holiday Inn did agree to permit the hotel's name to remain in the Holiday Inn directory. They permitted a sign outside the hotel identifying it as a Holiday Inn to remain and the Holiday Inn corporation continued advertising for the hotel. Guests at the hotel who were robbed and assaulted sued both the hotel and Holiday Inn. The Federal Appeals Court ruled that there was no consent, no control, and no action of the hotel on behalf of Holiday Inn. Still, they ruled that Holiday Inn had created an apparent agency by giving the impression of a principal–agent relationship. The court, therefore, did uphold Holiday Inn's liability for injuries to the hotel guests.[73]

In order to create an apparent agency, the party who pursues an action against the principal for the misconduct or obligations of the agent must have actually relied on that apparent agency. You cannot, for example, contract with a person and then after the contract fails try to find some person or company with greater wealth to sue. You must have understood that there was a principal–agent relationship and elected to do business with that agent because of some confidence in the assumed principal.[74] In this context, it seems obvious that a notice that there is no principal–agent relationship completely avoids the creation of an apparent agency.[75] If you own a communication business and do not want your clients or customers to think some contractors or other people have authority to act as your agent, you need to include an exculpatory clause in contracts with your customers or clients. An exculpatory clause is a statement that identifies who does, and more importantly who does not, have authority to act as your agent.

Business Contracts that May Create Principal–Agent Relationships

We have already explained that full-time salaried employees are almost always seen as agents of their employers. There are some other forms of business contracts that may create principal–agent relationships. Here, we discuss two such contracts or business forms that are often found in mass communications. First, we describe the somewhat complex rules that govern when an independent contractor is, or is not, an agent. Second, we describe the much simpler rules that govern the principal–agent status in business partnerships.

Independent Contractors

An **independent contractor** is "a person who contracts with another to do something for him but who is not controlled by the other nor subject to the other's right to control with respect to his physical conduct in the performance of the undertaking."[76] In most situations, the courts will rule that an independent contractor is not working primarily on behalf of the principal who hires him or her. Therefore, independent contractors are usually not agents and hiring one does not create a principal–agent relationship. There are exceptions to this rule that we discuss later, but first we need to explain how a court will decide who is an independent contractor and who is a traditional employee. The factors courts use to identify independent contractors are listed on Exhibit 11.6.

The Restatement of Agency identifies five factors to determine who is and who is not an independent contractor. These five factors are (a) who supplies the tools, (b) what level of skill is required, (c) whether payment is by task or time, (d) how long the agent or actor is employed, and (e) whether the work is part of the principal's regular business.

Exhibit 11.6. Factors to Identify Independent Contractors (Restatement of Agency 2D § 220).

- Who supplies tools
- What level of skill is required by the agent
- Whether payment is by task or by time
- How long the agent is employed
- Whether work is regular part of principal's business

It is important to note that no one of these factors, by itself, defines an independent contractor but the five factors, taken together, are used by courts to decide who is an independent contractor.

Because employees or agents are under the control of their principal or employer, the courts assume those employers will provide the tools needed to perform their jobs. An individual who supplies his or her own tools is usually seen as an independent contractor. If an advertising agency or public relations firm hires a Web designer and that designer provides his or her own computer and server, he or she is probably an independent contractor. If the designer uses the company's computer, he or she may be an employee and therefore an agent of the company. The more highly skilled a person, the more likely he or she is to be beyond the control of the person employing them. Therefore, highly skilled workers like advertising executives or public relations executives are more likely to be viewed as independent contractors.

The method of payment is probably the single most important factor. Regardless of who supplies the tools or how skilled an individual is, the courts generally assume that people who are salaried are not independent contractors.[77] Furthermore, the longer an individual is employed by one company, the more likely it is that he or she will be seen as an employee rather than an independent contractor. Finally, people who do work that is outside the principal's normal business are much more likely to be seen as independent contractors. If, for example, a manufacturing company hired an advertising designer that designer is much more likely to be viewed as an independent contractor than he or she would be if hired by an advertising firm.

Independent Contractors are Sometimes Agents. As with many things in law, there are exceptions to the exceptions. Usually, independent contractors are not agents and their employers are not liable for their misconduct or obligations but there are situations in which the courts have refused to allow employers to escape duties by assigning them to independent contractors. The two major areas where employers are still liable for the actions of independent contractors are (a) inherently dangerous activities, and (b) legal duties. If a public relations firm hired a skydiver to promote a client's product, that skydiver is engaged in an inherently dangerous activity and the firm may be held responsible if he or she injures others while working for it. The courts will not permit the firm to cause a dangerous act to occur and then to insulate itself from legal liability by hiring an independent contractor. Likewise, firms cannot escape legal obligations by hiring an independent contractor.[78] In this context, legal obligations are things one is required to do by law or by court order.

Partnerships

One of the most common forms of business organizations is a partnership. If two or more people create a business together without a contract or statute to impose some other form of business they are in a **partnership**. In other words, when you form a business with other people, unless you create a corporation or some other structure for your business you automatically become a partnership. The reason partnerships are important here is that "Every partner is an agent of the partnership for the purpose of its business."[79] As we discuss later, agents can create legal obligations for the principal. Because all partners are agents of the partnership, all the partners have the legal authority to bind the whole partnership and they can create debts for the entire business. This ability to bind the partnership can be restricted by a limited liability partnership agreement and it is limited by statute in some states. Here we provide some very general principles. Anytime you go into business with another person you should seek the advice of local legal counsel to ensure you know what liabilities you are creating for yourself and for others.

Rights and Obligations that Result from Agency

The primary reason for introducing you to contract law was to help you understand employment relationships and specifically the principal–agent relationship. The primary reason for explaining how principal–agent relationships are created is to help you understand the rights and obligations that such relationships create. As we have explained before, the vast majority of people working in mass communications are legally agents of some principal. That principal may be a newspaper, a broadcast network, an advertising agency, or a public relations firm. Those principals have obligations to their agents and the agents have obligations to the principals. Also, the existence of a principal–agent relationship means that the agents can create obligations for the principals to third parties like clients, customers, or news sources.

Even if a principal–agent relationship exists, the obligations we describe can only arise when the agent is working within the scope of his or her agency. For example, a reporter who is away from his or her newspaper acting entirely in his or her private life is not acting within the scope of his or her agency. However, that same reporter, even if "off duty," may step into the scope of agency if he or she sees a newsworthy event and begins to collect information. Also, even during the workday, a reporter or other mass communications professional may deviate from the tasks assigned. During those "detours" from his or her agency, the principal is not responsible for obligations or liabilities created by the agent. However, it should be noted that an agent who "detours" from his or her duty to the principal may later return to the scope of his or her agency. If he or she does so, the agent is again in a position to create obligations for the principal.[80]

Finally, remember that consent is one element of a principal–agent relationship. Therefore, the principal always has the authority to terminate the agency. He or she may simply fire the agent and thereby terminate the agent's ability to create obligations for the principal.[81]

So long as a principal–agent relationship exists and throughout the scope of employment or agency three kinds of legal obligations are created. They are obligations of the principal to the agent, obligations of the agent to the principal, and obligations to third parties. We discuss each of those three categories of obligations separately. Following the discussion of obligations of the agent to the principal, we also describe what are commonly called *whistleblower protections*. These are often misunderstood exceptions to the obligations of agents to principals.

Obligations of the Principal to the Agent

The obligations of the principal to the agent are fairly straightforward. A principal has an obligation to honor the contracts he or she forms with the agent or employee. These obligations do not change because of a principal–agent relationship and are identical to those discussed earlier under employment law. The principal has other obligations that seem to need no explanation. These include a duty to provide a safe workplace, a duty to hire competent co-workers, a duty to to provide compensation for injury, and a duty to deal fairly and in good faith with the agent or employee.[82]

The principal also has an obligation to provide reasonable compensation for the agent's services. For people in advertising or public relations, it may be useful to note that this obligation to pay for services includes an obligation to reasonably compensate agents for recruiting new clients or customers who will provide revenue to the principal.[83] One other observation about the obligation to pay for services that might prove useful is the idea that courts usually assume services performed by members of the principal's family are gifts for which the principal has no obligation of payment.[84] The test for whether you should be paid is a "reasonable expectation."[85] Therefore, if you are employed by a family member, it might be wise to protect yourself with a written contract detailing the rates of compensation.

The principal also has what is called a duty of indemnity. This means that the principal is obligated to defend an agent who is sued for any action that occurs while the agent is properly performing his or her job.[86] This duty of indemnity arises from "the general doctrine that an agent may recover any expenditures necessarily incurred in the transaction of his principal's affairs."[87] Applying these principles to the practices of mass communications, if a reporter is sued for defamation for a story he or she writes while working for a newspaper, that newspaper is obligated to pay for the legal defense of the reporter. In addition, if the reporter loses the lawsuit the newspaper is obligated to reimburse the reporter for any judgment against him or her. This, of course, is true only as long as the reporter was the agent of the newspaper, was working within the scope of his or her agency at the time of the alleged defamation, and did not deliberately create the liability. Similarly, if a client sues an advertising agent for failing to perform adequately or for loss of business the advertising agent's employing firm can be required to pay for legal defense and judgment so long as the advertising executive is acting within the scope of the principal–agent relationship.

Obligations of the Agent to the Principal

We discuss the obligations of the agent to the principal in two sections. First, we describe the specific duties owed by the agent to the principal. Then we describe how those duties can lead to ethical or even legal conflicts in the practices of journalism, advertising, or public relations.

The simplest obligation of the agent is also one that is potentially most offensive in our society. The agent is obligated to obey the principal. The whole principal–agent relationship depends on the principal's control or right to control the agent. In order for the principal to have a right to control, he or she must have the legal right to expect the agent to obey directives. If the agent does not obey the instructions of the principal, the agent has a legal duty to pay the principal for any negative results. This duty to pay for the result of a failure to follow instructions obtains whether the failure is deliberate or simply the act of negligence. Negligence is failing to behave like a reasonable person. If, for example, a public relations writer's employer tells him or her to be sure to run "spell check" on all news releases and the writer fails to do so, he or she could be held personally responsible for the cost of rewriting or reprinting all the releases that contained misspelled words. The writer did not obey and either deliberately did not run "spell check" or behaved unreasonably by not using the spelling tool. Therefore, he or she is liable for the resulting costs. Of course, the duty to obey does not extend to a duty to obey illegal directives.[88]

Two other duties of agents to their principal are conceptually related. There is a duty to disclose and a duty of loyalty. The duty to disclose means the agent has a legal obligation to tell the principal of anything he or she knows that might affect the principal's business. If, for example, you learn that a client of your employer's advertising or public relations agency is in financial trouble and may not be able to pay the agency's bill, you have a duty to tell the principal so he or she can stop advancing services for which she or he may not be paid.[89] Not only is an agent obligated to disclose bad news, like a client's impending bankruptcy, he or she is also obligated to tell the principal about business opportunities that might be used to advantage.[90] For example, an employee cannot learn of a public relations request for proposal, not tell his or her principal about that request, and write the proposal him or herself in the hopes of starting his or her own agency. Obviously, the agent is not obligated to tell the principal every piece of good news he or she hears. The agent is only obligated to disclose the information acquired in the course of work as the principal's agent that could impact the principal's business.[91]

The duty to disclose is similar to the duty of loyalty because both arise from the agent's obligation to act primarily on behalf of the principal. An agent cannot protect the client's reputation to the detriment of the principal's income and he or she cannot protect his or her own interest to the detriment of the principal's interest. Problems with this duty of loyalty most often arise in the context of employment changes. A practitioner in any field of mass communications may leave one employer for another as part of perfectly reasonable career advancement. A public relations practitioner, for example, may move to a competing public relations agency for a promotion or salary increase. That is not disloyal. But, it is disloyal for one to steal his or her current employer's clients and take them to the new employer's agency or to his or her own business.[92] Furthermore, an agent cannot use information gained in confidence to help a future employer. It is very common for agents to have access to campaign plans, customer lists, or other trade secrets. It would violate the agent's duty of loyalty to give that information to a competitor of his or her principal.[93] This duty to protect confidential information continues after the agent leaves the employ of the principal. Specifically, an agent cannot leave the employ of his or her principal and then use trade secrets, goodwill, or even extraordinary training or education that was provided by the principal in any way that harms the interests of the principal.[94] Of course, the agent is free to use the ordinary skills he or she developed during the principal–agent relationship so long as exercising those skills does not harm the principal.

Whistleblower Protections

The duty of loyalty can create ethical or legal problems when there is a conflict or perceived conflict between the public's interest and the interest of the employer. Despite what most of us would like to believe, there really are times when an agent has a legal obligation and maybe an ethical obligation to protect the interests of an unethical principal. This can happen in virtually every area of mass communications practice. Newspaper editors have been known to tell reporters to omit or fabricate facts, advertising agencies have told advertising copywriters to exaggerate or even lie about a product's characteristics, and public relations clients do tell their public relations agents to lie for them. Fortunately, these are rare situations but they can happen. In such situations, an agent may have a legal obligation, as part of his or her duty of loyalty, to comply with unethical instructions. Even if there is not a legal duty, the practitioner has to weigh two ethical obligations, one to his or her sense of propriety and one to his or her duty to the principal. This is not a text on ethics, so we focus on the legal duties that operate when a principal directs an agent to do something improper or asks the agent to remain silent about an illegal or unethical act.

First and most simply, remember there is usually no duty to obey an instruction that requires the agent to engage in illegal behavior.[95] A few jurisdictions have given principals the right to fire employees for refusing to engage in fairly minor violations of regulations,[96] but these are typically low-risk or temporary deviations from legal requirements. It may help guide your decisions about what directives to obey to know that if you do agree to assist your principal in a criminal act you may be legally liable as a conspirator.[97] If, for example, a producer of advertising knows that he or she is helping to sell fraudulent securities, he or she can be charged with securities fraud. "I was only following orders" is not a defense. If the action with which the principal instructs the agent to assist is not criminal but is subject to civil lawsuits, the agent can be named as a co-defendant and can be held liable for any judgment won. For example, a public relations practitioner who knowingly assists in the malicious defamation of a politician could be sued right along with the principal who asked him or her to design the malicious campaign.

In many jurisdictions, there also is no duty to obey an instruction that requires an agent to engage in unethical behavior. In this context, it is not the agent's judgment of what is ethical or unethical, it will be the judgment of the local courts. If the agent opts to take a stand it would be wise to check with local counsel to know exactly what he or she is risking before simply refusing to comply with an employer's instructions.

When an agent is instructed to do something illegal or unethical by the principal, the agent's decisions are comparatively easy. The agent, knowing he or she does not have to, may obey and suffer the possible consequences or may politely decline and risk having to pursue a wrongful discharge lawsuit. Where the decision becomes far more complex is when the agent knows of some illegal or unethical behavior by the principal. In this situation, the agent is not asked to do something improper, but he or she is asked to keep silent about the improper conduct of the principal. One of the most difficult legal duties to understand is the obligation to remain silent, called the duty of **confidentiality**. In most circumstances, when an agent is given information in confidence as part of the agent–principal relationship, he or she does have a duty to hold that information in confidence anytime sharing the information would harm the principal. Obviously, if an agent knows the principal is doing something illegal, revealing that information would harm the principal because he or she could be sued or prosecuted. If the agent knows the principal is doing something improper, he or she may also perceive an ethical duty to speak.

Many people in our society believe they are relieved of their duty of loyalty or duty of confidentiality by so-called **whistleblower** statutes. It is important to remember that these statutes are very complex and provide very little protection. We describe the federal protections and provide a brief summary of state laws.

Federal Whistleblower Protection.   Federal courts have ruled very specifically that other laws requiring reporting do not protect one who reports information gained in confidence[98] and that an employee's duty is to the person who pays him or her, not to the public or other entity with whom he or she deals.[99]

Contrasted with the duty to the employer, there are two groups of federal whistleblower protections. Both are very limited in terms of whom they protect and what must be done to qualify for protection. The first group of protections is created by a relatively new set of statutes designed to encourage federal employees to report illegal or dangerous conduct. The second set of protections is provided for what are called *qui tam relators*.

The statutes designed to protect federal employees prohibit retaliatory firing or demotion for some civil servants and government contract employees. These include, for example, specific protection for employees of the Department of Energy who report nuclear hazards,[100] protection for employees of the Federal Aviation Administration who report flight safety deficiencies,[101] and prohibitions of retaliation against hospital employees who report violations of emergency medical treatment requirements.[102] Each of these protections is limited to either federal employees or employees of companies that accept federal assistance. Also, to enjoy these protections, employees must report the covered misconduct through the appropriate agency or congressional channel. These statutes do not provide any protection for anyone who reveals confidential information to the media or the general public.

The second federal protection is that afforded *qui tam relators*. This protection applies to any citizen who initiates a legal action under the Federal False Claims Act.[103]

The phrase *qui tam* is an abbreviated form of *qui tam pro domino rege quam pro se imposo sequitur*, which means "If the king therefore himself commences this suit, he shall have the whole forfeiture." This odd expression means that the individual who initiates the suit, called the *qui tam relator*, is actually suing on behalf of the government in an action that would result in a judgment for the government had it brought the suit alone. *Qui Tam* laws have existed in the United Kingdom since the 14th century and were adopted in the United States by the First Continental Congress.[104] These laws provide a means of encouraging private citizens to report and prosecute fraud against the federal government. In order to enjoy statutory protection, *qui tam relators* must initiate legal action against a party who commits fraud against the government. The *qui tam relator* is only protected if he or she bases the suit on information that is not generally available to the public and that is not available from public records.[105] Further, in order to enjoy protection from retaliation by the employer or principal the *qui tam relator* must be the first to file. This means that the federal law only protects people who actually file lawsuits, it does not protect people who merely report misconduct. The federal law only protects people who are the first to file a suit based on some fraud against the U.S. government.

One additional limitation of the federal whistleblower law arises because of the sovereign immunity of state governments. When an agent of a branch of a state government is a defendant in a *qui tam* action the state government may assert its sovereign immunity from suit. This means the *qui tam relator's* suit is dismissed and the whistleblower may lose his or her protection under the federal statute.[106]

State Whistleblower Protections. In addition to the limited federal protections, approximately three fourths of the states have some whistleblower protection. These state laws vary widely. The differences include whether a report must first be made to the principal, whether the accusation must be true, and whether protection is limited to reports of illegal acts.

Two thirds of the state whistleblower statutes only protect public sector employees.[107] This means that in the vast majority of states there is no protection at all for agents of principals like newspapers, broadcasters, advertising firms, and public relations offices that are not in the public sector. Some examples of conduct that has resulted in action against agents may give you some idea of what kind of whistleblowing is not protected. In Virginia, an agent who simply testified at a fellow employee's discharge hearing was fired. The courts upheld that termination.[108] In Maine, an employee who reported his employer's contract violations was not protected by that state's whistleblower laws. The court ruled the law only protects reports of acts that are actually illegal.[109] The Texas whistleblower laws only protect individuals who report misconduct that would result in criminal penalties. They provide no protection for reporting acts that would result in civil penalties and no protection for honest mistakes in reports by the agent.[110] Indiana only protects whistleblowers if they would be personally liable for the conduct they report.[111]

One final example may be instructive. George Green was an architect for the Texas Department of Human Services. After reporting misconduct in that agency, he was fired for taking excess sick leave and for making a 13 cent private call on the agency's telephone. It took Green more than $130,000 in legal fees, 4 years, and the intervention of the state's lieutenant governor to finally secure a financial settlement. Much of that settlement went to pay lawyers, consultants, and creditors.[112] In summary, an agent does have a duty of loyalty and a duty of confidentiality to her or his principal and the protections for agents who violate those duties are much more limited than most people realize. Furthermore, even when legally protected for a breach of the duty of confidentiality, few agents have the financial or legal resources to effectively enforce their whistleblower protections.

Rights of Third Parties: Respondeat Superior

We have described obligations of principals to agents and agents to principals and we have discussed the limited situations in which whistleblower statutes provide exceptions to some of the agent's obligations to his or her principal. Finally, we describe how the actions of agents create rights in third parties. These actions create obligations for the principal to those third parties. The principal may be responsible to third parties because of the torts of the agent and he or she may also be liable for contractual obligations created by the agent.[113]

Torts are civil legal actions for intentional misconduct or negligence. Striking someone results in the tort of battery. Battery is an **intentional tort** and someone who commits battery can be compelled by a civil court to pay money damages to the person he or she battered. Accidentally hitting another car with your car is the unintentional tort of negligence. Because you failed to behave with the care a reasonable person would, you may be ordered by a court to pay for the damages to the car you hit. When an agent commits a tort while working for the principal, the principal may incur an obligation to pay for the resulting damages. This duty is called vicarious tort liability. It is different from the duty to indemnify the agent because the duty is not to pay the agent if he or she loses a lawsuit but it is a duty to pay the person who was injured. In other words, the third party who was injured has a right to sue the principal for the misconduct of the agent. Under the doctrine of *respondeat superior*, the master or principal must answer for the misconduct of his or her servant or agent. This obligation of the principal does not relieve the agent of his or her liability for misconduct. It is a right the third party has in addition to his or her right to sue the agent.

The vicarious liability of principals for the torts of their agents arose in English common law as early as 1698.[114] Originally, the principal was liable only if he or she had given specific instructions to the agent to do that which lead to the liability. Today, the principal may be liable for all actions of the servant so long as those actions are within the scope of the agent's duties while working for the principal. There are a number of policy arguments for imposing this liability on the principal. First, if a person is going to take advantage of having others work for them they should have to pay for that advantage. One cost of that advantage in business is the responsibility for the actions of agents. Some commentators have argued that the responsibility obtains because the principal selected the agents and the responsibility for their actions arises because of the obligation to carefully hire and supervise employees. The simplest argument may not come from law but from the old adage: "If you want something done right, do it yourself." Under the doctrine of *respondeat superior,* if you do not do it yourself you are at least liable if it is not done right.

Because of their vicarious liability, media principals have been successfully sued for virtually every communication tort of their agent reporters or writers.[115]

The notion that principals may be liable for the unintentional torts of their agents has some commonsense appeal. After all, when an employer hires someone the employer has to expect that the employee will have accidents and by placing agents in situations where their accidents will harm others the principal could expect to incur some liability. But, the vicarious liability of principals goes even further than this. Principals can be held liable for the intentional torts of their agents. A condominium owner had to pay a judgment to a tenant who was assaulted by an agent maintenance worker[116] and the Los Angeles Police Department was required to pay a judgment to the rape victim of a police officer.[117] Obviously, these principals did not give their agents instructions to assault tenants or citizens. They were held liable because the courts believed holding the principal liable would encourage them to be more careful in future hirings and because the principal had some duty to protect the interests of the third parties who were injured. This same reasoning can lead to liability for a newspaper, broadcast station, advertising agency, or public relations firm if their agent employee deliberately harms another, for example, by deliberately writing a dishonest news release or advertisement.

Principals have also been ordered to pay punitive damages because of agent misconduct. Particularly where the principal either specifically orders the agent's misconduct or helps hide the misconduct after it happens, the principal may be required to pay not only the cost of making the injured party whole but an additional judgment designed to punish the misconduct.[118] Because the purpose of these punitive damages is to deter recurrence it makes no sense to punish principals who did not know about the misconduct of their agents. Therefore, courts usually do not impose punitive damages on principals who were not aware of their agent's tortuous conduct.[119]

People who are injured are often more motivated to sue the principal than to sue the agent. Although vicarious liability does not eliminate the liability of the agent who committed the tort, most plaintiffs sue the principal and not the agent. The motivation is not legal—it is mercenary. Almost always, the media employer who is the principal has more money than does the reporter or other communications worker who is the agent. Injured third parties opt to sue the principal, not because they have committed the greatest wrong, but simply because they have more money. They would rather have a judgment against a wealthy newspaper or public relations firm than against a reporter or copywriter. Lawyers refer to this decision as selecting the **deep pockets** and it, more than any legal principle, guides decisions when lawsuits are filed.

In addition to vicarious liability for the torts of agents, principals are also liable to third parties for any contracts their agents create. This right of third parties to enforce contracts against principals arises in two situations. First, the agent may have express authority to contract for the principal. Second, the agent may have implied authority to contract. Express authority means the principal appointed the agent to act for him or her. Problems from this kind of authority are rare because the principal knows of the contract and usually protects himself or herself from abuse. Far more often, problems arise from an agent exercising implied authority.

Implied authority is related to the idea of notice or proof of agency. It arises when the principal creates or allows the creation of a situation wherein the third party is given the impression that the agent has authority to contract for the principal. These situations are common in the practice of mass communications. A subject who is offered payment for permission to take his picture by a photographer from a well-known newspaper may very reasonably assume that the photographer has the authority to promise payment from the newspaper. That reasonable assumption creates an implied authority. By allowing the photographer to carry a press pass or to identify him or herself as an employee of the newspaper, the newspaper has created a situation that gives the impression of authority to contract. Public relations firms often give their clients the impression that account executives have authority to contract for the firm. Advertising executives and newspapers may be placed in similar situations of implied authority by their employers. Generally, third parties may assume that people in a position have the authority normally associated with those positions.[120]

The simplest way to decide when an implied right to contract for the principal has been given to an agent is to remember that reality is irrelevant. It is appearance that matters. If, under the totality of circumstances, a naïve third party could reasonably assume the agent has the authority to contract for the principal, then the third party may have the legal right to hold the principal to a contract agreed to by the agent. This means that even without the express authority of their employers, reporters may bind newspapers to contracts of confidentiality, and public relations and advertising professionals may bind their agencies and firms to fee agreements or production time tables.

Almost nothing in law is as simple as one rule. There are exceptions to the rule that a reasonable impression left by their behavior may give an agent authority to bind his or her principal to contracts. The first exception is the duty of the third party to behave reasonably. Before entering into a contract the third party must use common sense.[121] The third party may be required to ask for identification or to question unusual contract terms. This obligation only extends to reasonable inquiry. The third party is entitled to assume someone introduced as a reporter or agent really has all the authority normally associated with those positions. Related to the obligation to behave reasonably is the obligation to honor known limitations on agency. Even if a photographer can usually offer payment for a release, if the third party has been told that one photographer does not have such authority, the third party cannot continue to assume the photographer can bind his or her principal.[122]

The next limitation on an agent's ability to bind his or her principals to contracts continues the Latin lesson. ***Delegates no potest delegare*** translates "a delegate cannot delegate." This means simply that an agent cannot appoint another agent for the principal. If the head of a public relations firm introduces an account executive to a client, that account executive cannot tell the same client that a copywriter or even a new account executive is now the principal's agent.

Finally, government agents have unique protection. A third party has an affirmative duty to determine the actual authority of a government agent.[123] A third party may be entitled to assume an account executive is an agent with authority to bind the public relations firm that is his or her principal. However, that same third party cannot assume a military public affairs officer has the authority to bind his or her principal—the Department of Defense.

As if the exceptions to rules of law were not complicated enough, in the case of third-party rights created by agents, there is at least one significant exception to the exceptions. If the principal ratifies the contract of an agent, the principal is bound by that agreement even when there were exceptions that might have allowed him or her to avoid any obligation. Ratification, in this context, means taking the benefit of the contract. Ratification can be as simple as sending a bill for a payment required under the contract.[124] Returning to the example of the photographer promising payment for a subject's release, if the photographer's newspaper, knowing of that agreement, uses the subject's photograph, then the newspaper has ratified the photographer's contract and is obligated to make the agreed payment to the subject.

All businesses, including the business of mass communications, run on contracts and the services of employees and agents. The information in this chapter was presented to help you understand how agreements like releases and employment contracts are regulated. The information on agency, in particular, was presented so that you may better understand what is required of the relationship between media employers and the employees who are their agents. We also want to help you understand that as an agent you create obligations for your employer or principal so that you may be more sympathetic with why your principal is motivated to inspect your work and control your behavior.

Practice Notes

Many people in mass communications believe they stand in some special place that permits them to avoid the operation of general laws. Here we explore one situation that demonstrates how all of us, within or outside the media, are bound by the general laws. Specifically, we explain that the First Amendment does not mitigate the duty to obey an employer. In the second practice note, we describe contacts not to compete because those agreements often impact careers in news, public relations, and advertising. Related to the area of contract law and agency law, we would remind you of the practice note in chapter 6 where we described how contract obligations may compete with the duty to honor a subpoena.

Conflict Between a Reporter's First Amendment Rights and the Duty to Obey: Who Owns the Right of Free Press?

Before beginning a discussion of the conflict between the duty to obey and the right of free press, we should remind you that this is a text on law, not ethics. We fully realize that most ethical journalists will cringe at the suggestion that economics or contractual obligations supercede their obligations as reporters of fact. However, we do feel an obligation to explain how the law treats these conflicts so that anyone making a decision about how to respond to an employer's directive to manipulate news coverage knows what rights they have. Obviously, such behaviors do not fit within the professional standards of journalism, public relations, or advertising, but business owners are offered favorable news coverage in exchange for advertising placements. Anyone who has worked in public relations cannot help but notice that some newspapers are more likely to use releases from or about clients who are heavy advertisers. A report published in the *Los Angeles Times* quoted the editor of another, unnamed, newspaper as telling his editorial page writers, "We do not hire opinion writers to trash advertisers. . . . No newspaper would do that."[125] Business considerations do influence news coverage and that is not illegal.

In order to understand the obligations associated with either an editor or advertiser's attempt to direct news, one must understand both the limitations on First Amendment rights and the obligations created by contracts and agency relationships. Simply put, the First Amendment provides no protection at all from either financial coercion or the directives of a principal. The First Amendment begins, "Congress shall make no law . . ." ". . . the United States Constitution guarantees freedom of expression only against infringement by the state, not by private actors."[126] Simply put, the First Amendment does not, in any way, restrict the actions of private advertisers or media owners.

The courts have upheld the right of commercial groups to use threats of boycotts and advertising revenue to try to influence the content of television stations[127] and the Federal Communications Commission has even used this right to justify reductions in governmental regulation of broadcast television content. The decrease in governmental regulation of programming content was justified by the observation, in Congress, that viewers can influence programming content through the influence of advertisers.[128] The U.S. Court of Appeals has even allowed government entities to avoid First Amendment entanglement by using private companies to regulate some media.[129]

Those of us committed to a free and open flow of communication may not be happy about it, but there simply is no First Amendment protection against private financial influence on media content. This fact, coupled with an agent's duty to obey, can make the assertion of a right of free speech very difficult for a journalist. If a newspaper's owner, who is usually the reporter's employer and principal, orders a reporter to kill a story or to produce a story with a bias in favor of a particular business or politician, that reporter is not free to ignore the principal's directive. We are not suggesting anyone abandon their sense of propriety or ethics, but we are saying you need to know that there are situations in which you can be fired for taking a moral stand against an unethical principal.

The Covenant Not to Compete

In virtually every field where employee talent is critical to an enterprise's success, covenants not to compete are used to prevent employees from taking their talents to the competition. Professional athletes and actors are often required to execute such contracts and today it is very common for newspapers, television stations, advertising agencies, and public relations firms to make such contracts part of their employment agreements.

A **covenant not to compete** is sometimes called a noncompetition agreement. It is simply a contract that exchanges a promise by the employer, usually for salary, for a promise by the employee not to work for a competitor. There is extraordinary variation in how different jurisdictions treat covenants not to compete. Some states outlaw them altogether[130] and some states specifically endorse their propriety,[131] but the general rule

Exhibit 11.7. Factors Used to Determine if Covenant Not to Compete is Overbroad (*Data Management, Inc. v. Greene*, 757 P.2d 62 [Alaska 1988]).

- Limitations of time and space.
- Whether the employee has trade secrets.
- Compare benefit to employer with detriment to former employee.
- Does the contract bar the employee's sole means of support?
- Does contract stifle the inherent skills and experience of the employee?
- Were employee's talents developed solely during employment with this employer?
- What were the circumstances of termination?

is that they can be enforced if they are not overbroad. **Overbroad** noncompetition agreements are those that impose so much restriction on the employee or agent that they operate as a restraint on trade. Factors that may make a covenant not to compete overbroad are listed in Exhibit 11.7.

There are no specific rules for what is and what is not an overbroad covenant not to compete but generally courts look at six factors. The first of these is the time and space covered by the covenant. Noncompetition agreements that prohibit employees from working in their profession for too long or in too great a geographic area are usually not enforced. Unfortunately, there are no clear standards for what is an appropriate time or area. Some idea of the appropriate limitations can be garnered from cases. For example, an agreement barring computer programmers from working anywhere in the State of Alaska for 5 years after leaving the employment of a data processing company was ruled overbroad and unenforceable[132] but an agreement barring a veterinarian from practicing for 5 years in the city of Toledo was upheld.[133] Generally, agreements for up to 6 months and in geographic areas where customers will travel from the old employer to the new employer are upheld.[134]

The employee's access to trade secrets of the employer is also a factor to consider. The courts are far more likely to uphold noncompetition agreements against employees who have private information that would give them an advantage in competition with the old employer. In this context, personal contact with clients and access to client lists are trade secrets.[135] Based on this factor, some states prohibit noncompetition agreements for employees but permit them for business owners and partners.[136] The logic seems to be that owners and partners are more likely to have trade secrets and client contact information.

The comparison of benefit to the employer with detriment to the employee is usually interpreted to mean that the noncompetition agreement will only be enforced if the restraint is no greater than necessary to protect the old employer. This limitation also means that the hardship on the employee must be considered.[137] Related to this balance is a factor that requires the court to consider whether the contract bars the old employee's sole means of support. Obviously, the needs of an employer must be extraordinary to justify preventing a former employee from making a living at all.

Finally, the courts consider what skill or talent is suppressed by the agreement. Noncompetition agreements almost always prohibit the old employee from practicing some profession, trade, or skill. If that skill was developed solely during employment with the old employer courts are much more likely to enforce a noncompetition agreement than they are if the skill is a natural talent or an inherent skill the employee had before entering into the noncompetition agreement.

The enforceability of noncompetition agreements is also influenced by the circumstances surrounding the termination of employment. Employees who are fired or wrongfully discharged are much more likely to escape the requirement not to work for a competitor than are employees who simply quit or who breach their duty to their employer. When the employer breaches the employment contract and wrongfully discharges the employee, the employee is usually released from any obligation not to compete but he or she still has a duty to protect the trade secrets of the old employer.[138] However, even wrongfully discharged employees may be held to the terms of their contractual agreements if the contracts were entered into voluntarily and are not overbroad.[139]

Finally, do remember that specific performance cannot be imposed for personal services contracts. This means that no principal can force any agent to work for him or her. All that a covenant not to compete can do is to prevent the former employee from taking his or her skills to a competitor. It is not legally possible for a principal to force you to do something you believe is unethical. The worst that can happen is that the unethical principal may fire you from a job where you were already uncomfortable.

Magic Words and Phrases

Acceptance	Disaffirm (a contract)
Agent	Duress (as contract defense)
Apparent agency	Duty to mitigate damages
Bare promise	Employment at will
Breach of contract	Executory contract
Capacity to contract	Expectation damages
Confidentiality	Fraud (as contract defense)
Consent (to agency)	Impossibility (as contract defense)
Consideration	Independent contractor
Contract	Intentional tort
Contract with minor	Liquidated damages
Control (of agent)	Lost bargain
Covenant not to compete	Manifestation of consent
Deep pockets	Master
Delegates no potest delegare	Meeting of the minds
Detrimental reliance	Mistake (as contract defense)

Mutual mistake	*Quantum meruit*
Novation	*Qui tam*
Offer	*Respondeat superior*
On behalf of principal	Scope of agency
Overbroad	Servant
Part performance	Specific performance
Partnership	Statute of Frauds
Principal	Termination for cause
Public sector employee	Whistleblower

Suggested Cases to Read and Brief

Bard v. Bath, 590 A.2d 152 (Me.1991)
Billups Petroleum Co. v. Hardin's Bakeries Corp., 217 Miss. 24, 63 So.2d 543 (1953)
Campbell v. Stanford, 817 F.2d 499 (1987)
Crinkley v. Holiday Inns Inc., 844 F.2d 156 (1987)
DeMuth v. Miller, 438 Pa.Super. 437, 652 A.2d 891 (1995)
Eden v. Spaulding, 218 Neb. 799, 359 N.W.2d 758 (1984)
Ferris v. Polarsky, 191 Md. 79, 59 A.2d 749 (1948)
Graphic Directions Inc. v. Bush, 862 P.2d 1020 (Colo.1993)
Hayman v. Ramada Inns Inc., 86 N.C.App. 274, 357 S.E.2d 395 (1987)
Jet Courier Services Inc. v. Mulei, 771 P.2d 486 (Colo.1989)
Loughry v. Lincoln First Bank, N.A., 67 N.Y.2d 369, 494 N.E.2d 70 (1986)
Reilly v. Waukesha County, 193 Wis.2d 527, 535 N.W.2d 51 (1995)
Shivers v. John H. Harland Co. Inc., 310 S.C. 217, 423 S.E.2d 105 (1992)
VanSteenhous v. Jacor Broadcasting of Colo. Inc., 958 P.2d 464 (Colo.1998)

Questions for Discussion

1. Draft a simple contract you might use to bind a release from a photography subject or one you could use to prevent an information source from suing you for publishing the information they provide. Explain what you would have to do to make these contracts binding if the person you want to sign them is 14 years old.

2. In most college courses students are given a syllabus the first day of class. That syllabus describes assignments and how grades will be assigned. Is the syllabus a contract between the teacher and the students? If you think it is a contract, why do you think that? If you think it is not a contract, explain your position. When making your decision, be sure to identify what consideration or mutual obligations the contract involves and whether the consideration is future or past consideration.

3. If you rent a dorm room, apartment, or house, does the rental agreement have to be in writing? If you think it has to be in writing, are there any exceptions or situations that can substitute for a written lease or rental agreement?

4. We described both the concept of employment at will and the idea that evaluations of matters involving taste only require honest judgment. That means an employer could hire you as a reporter or copywriter and fire you because he or she simply did not like the way you write. Is there anything you can do when you accept a job to ensure you will not be fired just because your employer or editor cannot write well him or herself?

5. If you received a job offer that you know was also made to several other people and the offer said, "the first person to accept this offer will get the job," what could you do to accept as quickly as possible?

6. Many contracts contain language like "If any clause or provision of this contract shall be deemed unenforceable, that ruling shall not affect the other requirements herein." Why do you think that language is included?

7. If you were starting an advertising or public relations business and you want to be sure that you are legally an independent contractor, what can you do to encourage that perception? If you do not want to be perceived as an independent contractor so that you can take advantage of your principals' duty to indemnify, what can you do to encourage the perception that you are NOT an independent contractor?

8. The decision in *Stanford v. Dairy Queen Prods.*[140] says that franchisees work primarily for their own profits and not "on behalf of" the franchisor. If that is true how can you explain the decision in *Crinkley v. Holiday Inns, Inc.*,[141] which held that Holiday Inns were liable for an assault at an independent hotel because it looked like a Holiday Inn?

9. What policy reasons or justifications can explain why principals are liable for the intentional torts of their agents?

10. We have explained that employees as agents usually do have a duty to obey their employers as principals. If you were a public relations or advertising professional who was told by your employer/principal to produce a message you knew violated Federal Trade Commission regulations, what would you do? What would you do if a client asked you to lie about their product? In both cases, what are the possible legal ramifications of your decision?

11. Assume you are working for a firm in one of the areas of mass communications and when you were hired you signed a covenant not to compete. You are now a few years into your career and realize you can seriously improve yourself by moving to a larger newspaper, public relations firm, advertising agency, or broadcast station. How can you make that move without violating a typical covenant not to compete?

Notes

1. Justice Roberts, *Associated Press v. National Labor Relations Board*, 301 U.S. 103, 132 (1937).
2. Henry C. Black, Black's Law Dictionary (4th ed. 1968).
3. *Carroll v. Lee*, 148 Ariz. 10, 712 P.2d 923 (1986).
4. *Whitfield v. Lear*, 751 F.2d 90 (2d Cir. 1984).
5. See, e.g., *Rhen Marshall v. Purolator Filter Div.*, 211 Neb. 306, 318 N.W.2d 284 (1982).

6. *Lefkowitz v. Great Minneapolis Surplus Store*, 251 Minn. 188, 86 N.W.2d 689 (1957).

7. *Petterson v. Pattberg*, 248 N.Y. 86, 161 N.E. 428 (1928).

8. *Langellier v. Schaeffer*, 36 Minn 361 (1887).

9. *Preston Farm & Ranch Supply v. Bio-Zyme Enters.*, 625 S.W.2d 295 (Tex.1981).

10. *Lyon v. Adgraphics*, 14 Conn.App. 252, 540 A.2d 398 (1988).

11. *Adams v. Lindsell*, 1 B. & Ald. 681, 106 Eng.Rep. 210 (K.B.1818).

12. See, e.g., *Brauer v. Shaw*, 168 Mass. 198, 46 N.E. 617 (1897).

13. *Cushing v. Thomson*, 118 N.H. 292, 386 A.2d 805 (1978).

14. See, e.g., *Morrison v. Thoelke*, 155 So.2d 889 (Fla.App.1963); *Postal Telegraph-Cable Co. v. Willis*, 93 Miss. 540, 47 So. 380 (1908).

15. *Lyon v. Adgraphics*, 14 Conn.App. 252, 540 A.2d 398 (1988).

16. See, *Harrison v. Cage*, 5 Mod. 411, 87 Eng.Rep 736 (K.B.1698), *Stonestreet v. Southern Oil Co.*, 226 N.C. 261, 37 S.E.2d 676 (1946).

17. *Schumm v. Berg*, 37 Cal.2d 174, 231 P.2d 39 (1951).

18. *Hamer v. Sidway*, 64 N.Y.Supp.Ct. (57 Hun. 229 (1890).

19. See, e.g., *Allen v. Bryson*, 67 Iowa 951, 25 N.W. 820 (1885).

20. AMERICAN LAW INSTITUTE, RESTATEMENT OF CONTRACTS 2D § 152 (1990).

21. *Aragon v. Boyd*, 80 N.M. 14, 450 P.2d 614 (1969).

22. *Hawley Fuel Coalmart v. Steag Handel GmbH*, 796 F.2d 29 (2d Cir. 1986).

23. *Goetz v. Hubbell*, 66 N.D. 491, 266 N.W. 836 (1936).

24. *Mid-South Packers v. Shoney's*, 761 F.2d 1117 (5th Cir. 1985).

25. *Clark v. Larekin*, 172 Kan. 284, 239 P.2d 970 (1952).

26. *Champion Home Builders Co. v. Jeffress*, 352 F.Supp. 1081 (E.D. Mich. 1973); *Jennings v. Ruidoso Racing Assn.*, 79 N.M. 144, 441 P.2d 42 (1968).

27. *Mann v. Commissioner*, 483 F.2d 673 (8th Cir. 1973).

28. *Howley v. Whipple* , 68 N.H. 487 (1869).

29. See, e.g., TEX. FAM. CODE § 31.01 (1995).

30. See, *Ware v. Mobley*, 190 Ga. 249, 9 S.E.2d 67 (1940), *McNaughton v. Granite City Auto Sales*, 108 Vt. 130, 183 A. 340 (1936).

31. *DelSanto v. Bristol County Stadium*, 273 F.2d 605, (1st Cir. 1960).

32. *Byers v. Lemay Bank & Trust Co.*, 365 Mo. 341, 282 S.W.2d 512 (1955); see contra, *DelSanto v. Bristol County Stadium*, 273 F.2d 605, (1st Cir. 1960).

33. *Lloyd v. Jordan*, 544 So.2d 957 (Ala.1989).

34. See, e.g., CONSUMER PROTECTION ACT of 1968, 15 U.S.C.A. §§ 1601–1665 (2002); MAGNUSON-MOSS WARRANTY-FEDERAL TRADE COMMISSION IMPROVEMENT ACT, 15 U.S.C. §§ 2301-2312 (2002).

35. *Ard Dr. Pepper Bottling Co. v. Dr. Pepper Co.*, 202 F2d 372 (5th Cir. 1953).

36. *Fursmidt v. Hotel Abbey Holding Co.*, 10 App.Div.2d 447, 100N.Y.S.2d 216 (1960).

37. See, *Ferris v. Polarsky*, 191 Md.79, 59 A.2d 749 (1948).

38. *Gibson v. Granage*, 39 Mich. 49 (1878).

39. AMERICAN LAW INSTITUTE, RESTATEMENT OF TORTS 2D § 411 (1990).

40. *Dallas Cowboys Football Club v. Harris*, 348 S.W.2d 37 (Tex.Civ.App.1961).

41. *Mieske v. Bartell Drug Co.*, 92 Wash.2d 40, 593 P.2d 1308 (1979).

42. See, e.g., *United States v. Behan*, 110 U.S. 338 (1884).

43. See, *Menzel v. List*, 24 N.Y.2d 91, 246 N.E.2d 742 (1969), for example of bargain value.

44. *Tony Down Food Co. v. United States*, 530 F.2d 367 (Ct.Cl.1976).

45. See, e.g., *Dover Pool & Racquet Club v. Brookings*, 366 Mass. 629, 322 N.E.2d 168 (1975).

46. *Sherwood v. Walker*, 66 Mich. 568, 33 N.W. 919 (1887).

47. AMERICAN LAW INSTITUTE, RESTATEMENT OF CONTRACTS 2D § 152 (1990).

48. See, e.g., *Boise Junior College Dist. v. Mattefs Constr. Co.*, 92 Idaho 757, 450 P.2d 604 (1969).

49. *Wasserman Theatrical Enter. v. Harris*, 137 Conn. 371, 77 A.2d 329 (1950).

50. See, e.g., *Taylor v. Caldwell*, 3 B. & S. 826, 122 Eng.Rep. 309 (K.B. 1863).

51. *Louisville & N.R.R. v. Mottley,* 219 U.S. 467 (1911).

52. See, e.g., *Florida Power & Light Co. v. Westinghouse Elec. Corp.*, 826 F.2d 239 (4th Cir. 1987).

53. *Winget v. Rockwood*, 69 F.2d 326 (8th Cir. 1934).

54. AMERICAN LAW INSTITUTE, RESTATEMENT OF CONTRACTS 2D §175(1) (1990).

55. See, e.g., *Shivers v. John H. Harlan Co.*, 310 S.C. 217, 423 S.E.2d 105 (1992).

56. *Toussant v. Blue Cross Blue Shield*, 408 Mich. 579, 292 N.W.2d 880 (1980).

57. *Rowe v. Montgomery Ward*, 473 Mich 627, 473 N.W.2d 268 (1991).

58. *Cleary v. American Airlines, Inc.,* 11 Cal.App3d 443, 168 Cal.Rptr. 722 (1980).

59. MONT. CODE ANN. §39-2-0-901 to 39-2-914 (2003).

60. *Baldwin v. Sisters of Providence,* 112 Wash.2d 127, 769 P.2d 298 (1989).

61. *Heims v. Hanke,* 5 Wis.2d 465, 93 N.W.2d 455 (1958).

62. *Meese v. Miller,* 436 N.Y.S.2d 496, 79 A.D.2d 237 (App. Div. 4th Dept. 1981).

63. *Ahn v. Rooney, Pace, Inc.* 624 F.Supp. 368 (S.D.N.Y.1985).

64. *Lavazzi v. McDonalds Corp.* 239 Ill.App.3d 403, 606 N.E.2d 845 (1992).

65. *Noonan v. Texaco,* 713 P.2d 160 (Wyo.1986).

66. *Eden v. Spaulding,* 218 Neb. 799, 359 N.W.2d 758 (1984).

67. *Cooke v. E.F. Drew & Co.*, 319 F.2d 493 (9th Cir. 1963).

68. *Heims v. Hanke*, 5 Wis.2d 465, 468, 93 N.W.2d 455 (1958).

69. *Stanford v. Dairy Queen Prods.* 623 S.W.2d 797 (Tex.App.1981).

70. See, e.g., *Thayer v. Pacific Elec. Rwy.* 55 Cal.2d 430, 360 P.2d 56 (1961).

71. *See, e.g., Crinkley v. Holiday Inns, Inc.,* 844 F.2d 156 (4th Cir. 1988).

72. AMERICAN LAW INSTITUTE, RESTATEMENT OF AGENCY 2D § 261 (1958).

73. *Crinkley v. Holiday Inns, Inc.,* 844 F.2d 156, 166-167 (4th Cir. 1988).

74. *Hayman v. Ramada Inn. Inc.*, 86 N.C.App. 274, 357 S.E.2d 394 (1987).

75. *Eamoe v. Big Bear Land & Water Co.*, 98 Cal.App.2d 370, 220 P.2d 408 (Cal.App.2 Dist.1950).

76. AMERICAN LAW INSTITUTE, RESTATEMENT OF AGENCY 2D § 2 (1958).

77. *Cooke v. E.F. Drew & Co.*, 319 F.2d 493 (9th Cir. 1963).

78. *Kleeman v. Rheingold*, 598 N.Y.S.2d 149, 614 N.E.2d 712 (1993).

79. UNIFORM PARTNERSHIP ACT § (9)(1) (1914).

80. *Fiocco v. Carver,* 234 N.Y. 219, 137 N.E. 309 (N.Y. 1922).

81. *Beebe v. Columbia Axle Co.*, 233 Mo.App. 212, 117 S.W.2d 624 (1938).

82. *Taylor v. Cordis Corp.,* 634 F.Supp. 1242 (S.D.Miss.1986).

83. *Roberts Associates Inc. v. Blazer Intern. Corp.,* 741 F. Supp. 650 (E.D. Mich.1990).

84. *Hartley v. Bohrer*, 52 Idaho 72, 11 P.2d 616 (1932).

85. *McCollum v. Clothier*, 121 Utah 311, 242 P.2d 468 (1952).

86. *Admiral Oriental Line v. United States*, 86 F.2d 201 (2d Cir. 1936).

87. *Bibb v. Allen*, 149 U.S. 481, 499 (1893).

88. *Ford v. Wisconsin Real Estate Examining Bd.*, 48 Wis.2d 91, 179 N.W.2d 786 (1970).

89. See, e.g., *Lindland v. United Business Investments*, 298 Or. 318, 693 P.2d 20 (1984).

90. See, e.g., *Meinhard v. Salmon,* 249 N.Y. 458, 164 N.E. 545 (1928); *Dixon v. Trinity Joint Venture*, 49 Md.App. 379, 431 A.2d 1364 (1981).

91. See, e.g., *Fuqua v. Taylor,* 683 S.W.2d 735 (Tex. App.1984).

92. See, e.g., *Graphic Directions Inc. v. Bush,* 862 P.2d 1020 (Colo.App.1993); but see *Jet Courier Service v. Mulei*, 771 P.2d 486 (Colo.1989).

93. AMERICAN LAW INSTITUTE, RESTATEMENT OF AGENCY 2D § 395 (1958).

94. *Robbins v. Finlay*, 645 P.2d 623 (Utah 1982).

95. See, *Petermann v. International Brotherhood of Teamsters*, 174 Cal.App.2d 184, 344 P.2d 25 (1959).

96. *Reilly v. Waukesaa County*, 193 Wis.2d 527, 535 N.W.2d 51 (Ct.App.1995), court upheld termination of employee who refused to supervise more children than day-care regulations permitted.

97. See, e.g., *Commonwealth v. Benesch*, 290 Mass. 125, 194 N.E. 905 (1935).

98. *Douglas v. DynMcDermott Petroleum Operations Co.*, 144 F.3d 364, 364 (1998).

99. *Id.* at 371.

100. 50 U.S.C.S. § 2702 (2004).

101. 49 U.S.C.S. § 42121 (2004).

102. 42 U.S.C.S. § 1395dd (2004).

103. FEDERAL FALSE CLAIMS ACT, (1863) Ch 67, 12 Stat. 696; codified at 31 U.S.C. § 3730 (2004).

104. *U.S. ex rel Stillwell v. Hughes Helicopters, Inc.* 714 F.Supp. 1084, 1086 (C.D. Cal. 1989).

105. False Claims Act §§ 3730 (e)(4)(A) & 3730 (b)(5) (2004).

106. See, e.g., *U.S. ex rel Foulds v. Texas Tech University*, 171 F.3d 279 (1999).

107. Mark A. Rothstein, Charles B. Craver, Elinor P. Schroeder & Elaine W. Shoben, EMPLOYMENT LAW § 8.17 (2d ed. 1999).

108. *Miller v SEVAMP Inc.* 234 Va. 462, 362 S.E.2d 915 (1983).

109. *Bard v. Bath Iron Works Corp.*, 590 A.2d 152 (Me., 1991).

110. *Sabine Pilot Svs. v. Haueck*, 687 S.W. 2d 733 (Tex.1985).

111. *Remington Freight Lines Inc. v. Larkey*, 644 N.E.2d 931 (Ind.App.1994).

112. L. Tucker Gibson, Jr. & Clay Robison, ADDENDUM TO GOVERNMENT AND POLITICS IN THE LONE STAR STATE 13-14 (4th ed. 2002).

113. Oliver W. Holmes, *Agency*, 5 HARV. L. REV. 1 (1891), *qui facit per alium facit per se*, "he who acts through another acts himself."

114. *Jones v. Hart*, 90 Eng.Rep. 1255 (Eng.1698).

115. See, e.g., *Philadelphia Newspapers, Inc. v. Hepps*, 475 U.S. 767 (1986); *New York Times v. Sullivan*, 376 U.S. 254 (1964); *Curtis Publishing v. Butts*, 388 U.S. U.S. 130 (1967); *Virgil v. Time, Inc.* 527 F.2d 1122, 1128 (9th Cir. 1975) *cert. denied* 425 U.S. 998 (1976); *Briscoe v. Reader's Digest Assn.*, 4 Cal.3d 529, 483 P.2d 34 (1971).

116. *Williams v. Feather Sound, Inc.*, 386 So.2d 1236 (Fla.App.1980).

117. *Mary M. v. City of Los Angeles*, 285 Cal.Rptr. 99, 814 P.2d 1341 (1991).

118. *Loughry v. Lincoln First Bank, N.A.*, 502 N.Y.S.2d 965, 494 N.E.2d 70 (1986).

119. *Campen v. Stone*, 635 P.2d 1121 (Wyo.1981).

120. *Bucher & Willis Consulting Engineers, Planners and Architects v. Smith*, 7 Kan.App2d 467, 643 P.2d 1156 (1982).

121. *Link v. Kroenke*, 909 S.W.2d 740 (Mo.App.W.D.1995).

122. *Bayless v. Christie, Manson & Woods Intern, Inc.*, 2 F.3d 347 (10th Cir.1993).

123. *Blake Const. Co. v. United States*, 296 F.2d 393 (D.C.Cir.1961).

124. See, e.g., *Evans v. Ruth*, 129 Pa.Super. 192, 195 A. 163 (1937); *Dempsey v. Chambers*, 154 Mass. 330, 28 N.E. 279 (1891).

125. B. Horovitz, *Advertisers Influence Media More, Report Says*, L.A. TIMES, Mar. 12, 1992, at B6.

126. *Christ's Bride Ministries, Inc. v. Southeastern Pennsylvania Transportation Authority*, 148 F.3d 242, 247 (3d Cir, 1998) citing *Hurley v. Irish-American Gay, Lesbian, and Bisexual Group of Boston,* 515 U.S. 557 (1995).

127. Patrick M. Fahey, *Advocacy Group Boycotting of Network Television Advertisers and Its Effects on Programming Content*, 140 U. PA. L. REV. 647 (1991).

128. Patrick M. Fahey, *Advocacy Group Boycotting of Network Television Advertisers and Its Effects on Programming Content*, 140 U. PA. L. REV. 647, 697 (1991).
129. *Maxwell v. Borough of New Hope*, 735 F.2d 85 (3d Cir.1984), city council used land owner to enforce ban on outdoor advertising.
130. See, e.g., MONT. CODE § 28-2-703 (2003).
131. See, e.g., FLA.STAT.ANN.§ 542.33 (2004).
132. *Data Management, Inc. v. Greene*, 757 P.2d 62 (Alaska 1988).
133. *Raiminde v. VanVerch*, 42 Ohio St.2d 21, 325 N.E.2d 544 (1975).
134. See, e.g., *The Phone Connection, Inc. v. Harbst,* 11 Ariz.App 145, 462 P.2d 838 (1969).
135. See, e.g., *General Commercial Packaging, Inc., v. TPS Package Engineering, Inc.*, 126 F.3d 1131 (9th Cir. 1997); *Blackwell v. E.M. Helides Jr., Inc.* 368 Mass 225, 331 N.E.2d 54 (1975).
136. *Bosley Medical Group v. Abramson,* 161 Cal.App.3d 284, 207 Cal.Rptr 477 (1984).
137. AMERICAN LAW INSTITUTE, RESTATEMENT OF CONTRACTS 2D § 188 (1990).
138. *Uncle B's Bakery, Inc. v. O'Rourke*, 920 F.Supp. 1405 (N.D.Iowa 1996).
139. See, *DeMuth v. Miller*, 438 Pa.Super. 438 Pa.Super. 437, 652 A.2d 891 (1995).
140. 623 S.W.2d 797 (Tex.App.1981).
141. *Crinkley v. Holiday Inns, Inc.*, 844 F.2d 156 (4th Cir.1988).

Commercial Communication: Rights and Regulations

[T]he suppression of advertising reduces the information available for consumer decisions and thereby defeats the purpose of the First Amendment.[1]

Overview
What Is Commercial Communication?
Rights Afforded Commercial Communication
Regulation of Commercial Communication: The Federal Trade Commission
Other Limitations on Commercial Communication
Practice Notes

Overview

Commercial messages are granted fewer rights and are subjected to more regulation than other forms of communication. In fact, until fairly recently most courts ruled that the First Amendment did not even cover messages proposing commercial transactions. The limited First Amendment protection of commercial messages results from the federal government's obligation to simultaneously protect both commerce and freedom of communication. Understanding how these obligations are balanced and the resulting treatment of business-related communication is particularly important to people practicing in commercial advertising. The concepts are also important to journalists covering business and to public relations practitioners working in the areas of investor relations or commercial product promotions.

In this chapter, we first define *commercial communication*. We then describe the limited rights of free speech that are afforded commercial messages. We also detail the extensive regulations on commercial communication that are imposed by the Federal Trade Commission (FTC) and explore actions in civil court for fraudulent messages. We also describe limitations on advertising to children, advertising about tobacco products, and advertising attorneys' services. We conclude with practice notes that describe media, client, and agency liabilities for false or dangerous advertising, and the restrictions on political advertising and lobbying. We realize that political advertising and lobbying are not commercial communication but feel this information is helpful to communications practitioners whose practice in commercial communication may overlap with political communication.

What Is Commercial Communication?

To facilitate understanding how the law balances obligations to commerce and to free speech, we begin by explaining the difference between commercial communication (sometimes called commercial speech) and advertising. Because not all advertising is commercial communication, FTC regulations do not apply to all advertising. However, those regulations do apply to some forms of mass communication that are not usually thought of as advertising.

We must be able to recognize "commercial advertising" before we can know which of our messages do not enjoy full First Amendment rights and which ones are subject to governmental regulations. **Commercial communication**, as legally defined, does include most advertising but it does not include all advertising. Furthermore, commercial communication, as legally defined, includes a great many messages that are not traditional advertisements. It may be helpful for mass communications students and practitioners to note that the courts and regulatory agencies usually use the term *commercial advertising* to label the advertising that is subject to regulations.

Communication Definition of Advertising

Those of us in mass communications were probably taught that we can define advertising based on how the medium of the communication was financed. We consider a message to be advertising and the practitioner who places it an advertiser if he or she purchased the newspaper space, Internet page, or broadcast time for the message. This definition of advertising has advantages. It allows us to easily differentiate between what we label advertising, public relations, or journalism. However, in order to understand the legal limitations on the rights of commercial communication and the governmental regulation of commercial communication it is essential for us to understand that the law uses a different and more complicated system of identification. The law not only considers whether the time or space for a message was purchased, the law also considers the intent of the message itself.

Because of the legal definition of commercial communication, rights of free speech can be restricted for advertisers, public relations practitioners, and even journalists. Free speech rights can be restricted for any communications practitioner if his or her communication activities have a commercial purpose. The FTC regulations that many people believe can only control those in the advertising profession can be applied with equal force to those in other mass communications professions when they produce commercial communication. Furthermore, not all advertising is subject to the regulation of the FTC.

Some pure advertising escapes FTC regulation and enjoys the full protection of the First Amendment.

Legal Definition of Commercial Communication

In 1964, in its decision in *New York Times v. Sullivan,* the U.S. Supreme Court had to determine if an advertisement placed in *The New York Times* was a commercial communication. In that decision the Court said: "That the Times was paid for publishing the advertisement is as immaterial in this connection as is the fact that newspapers and books are sold."[2] Almost 20 years later, the Court affirmed this position in *Bolger v. Young's Drug Products Corp.* In that case, the Court was trying to determine whether a postal regulation was constitutional. The regulation prohibited delivery of unsolicited pamphlets offering contraceptives for sale. There the Court ruled the federal regulation of speech would be constitutional only if the pamphlets were commercial communication. After determining the pamphlets were advertisements, the Court said, "The mere fact that these pamphlets are conceded to be advertisements does not compel the conclusion that they are commercial speech."[3] Very specifically, the U.S. Supreme Court has ruled that not all advertising is regulated as commercial communication. In the *Bolger* decision the Court did say that messages that do "no more than propose a commercial transaction" are at "the core" of commercial communication[4] but even messages that only proposed a commercial transaction have been ruled not to be commercial communication if the transaction is related to an activity that is traditionally protected by the First Amendment. Specifically, in both *Murdock v. Pennsylvania*[5] and *Jamison v. Texas,*[6] the Supreme Court ruled that advertisements offering religious books for sale were not commercial communication and enjoyed full First Amendment protection.

Similarly, the FTC's regulations do not apply to all advertising. Limitations of the FTC's authority to regulate commercial communication is seen in the 1931 case of *Federal Trade Commission v. Raladam*[7] and the 1938 amendment to the FTC's enabling statutes. Raladam advertised and sold an obesity cure and the FTC enjoined Raladam from advertising the product without adding a disclaimer to the advertisements. The U.S. Supreme Court unanimously ruled that the FTC's statutory authority was limited to protecting business competitors from unfair business practices and did not give the FTC authority to control false advertising to protect consumers. Responding to this decision, in 1938 the U.S. Congress amended 15 USC § 45 (a) (1). This section formerly gave the FTC authority to control "unfair practices." After the amendment it gave the FTC authority to control "unfair or **deceptive** practices in commerce" (emphasis added). The current FTC authority to regulate false advertising arises entirely from this clause and is limited to the regulation of "commercial" advertising.

It is obvious that not all advertisements are commercial communication. It is equally obvious that some messages not included in advertisements are commercial communication. One example of commercial communication that is not typically labeled advertising is in-person solicitation.[8] Other examples include letters, news releases, and editorials. News releases, editorials, and letters were the focus of the conflict between Marc Kasky and Nike, Inc. This case, perhaps more than any other, emphasizes the fact that some commercial communication falls outside the definition of advertising used by communications practitioners.

Nike, Inc. v. Kasky

"Beginning in 1996, Nike was besieged with a series of allegations that it was mistreating and underpaying workers at foreign facilities. Nike responded to these charges in numerous ways, such as by sending out press releases, writing letters to the editors of various newspapers around the country, and mailing letters to university presidents and athletic directors."[9] Clearly, press releases, letters to the editor, and letters to university officials do not use the paid media typically associated with advertising. Nike itself has characterized its actions as a public relations campaign. As part of its public relations campaign,

> In 1997, Nike commissioned a report by former Ambassador to the United Nations Andrew Young on the labor conditions at Nike production facilities. After visiting 12 factories, Young issued a report that commented favorably on working conditions in the factories and found no evidence of widespread abuse or mistreatment of workers.[10]

Nike publicized Young's report in news releases and letters.

In 1998, Marc Kasky sued Nike saying the company had violated California laws against unfair or deceptive business practices and false advertising. Nike responded to Kasky's suit with a legal response called a demurrer. In effect, Nike asked that the suit be dismissed and said that Kasky could not sue because the challenged messages were not commercial communication and were therefore not subject to laws governing false advertising or deceptive business practices. The trial court granted Nike's request to dismiss the case and the California Court of Appeals upheld that decision saying, "Our analysis of the press releases and letters as forming part of a public dialogue on a matter of public concern within the core area of expression protected by the First Amendment compels the conclusion that the trial court properly sustained the defendants' demurrer without leave to amend."[11] In more simple terms, the trial court and the appeals court both said the messages were not commercial communication and were therefore not subject to laws governing false advertising.

The California Supreme Court reversed and ruled that the news releases, editorials, and letters about labor practices and working conditions in factories where Nike products are made were "commercial speech."[12] In its decision, the Court said, "such representations, when aimed at potential buyers for the purpose of maintaining sales and profits, may be regulated to eliminate false and misleading statements because they are readily verifiable by the speaker and because regulation is unlikely to deter truthful and nonmisleading speech." The Court concluded, "contrary to the Court of Appeals, that Nike's speech at issue here is commercial speech."[13]

The California Supreme Court used the same rules articulated by the U.S. Supreme Court in its 1983 decision in *Bolger*. The California Supreme Court looked at three factors—advertising format, product references, and commercial motivation—that in combination supported a characterization of commercial communication in that case.[14]

The U.S. Supreme Court initially granted certiorari, agreeing to hear an appeal of the California Supreme Court's decision. Later, the Supreme Court reversed itself and ruled that the grant of certiorari had been "improvident." The Court gave several reasons for deciding not to hear the case. The first two of their reasons were based on arguments dealing with the Court's jurisdiction and are beyond the scope of this book. However, while explaining the third reason for its decision, the Court made several points that support the conclusion that news releases, editorials, or letters to university officials may be treated exactly like commercial advertising. In this explanation, the Court said, "This case presents novel First Amendment questions because the speech at issue represents a blending of commercial communication, noncommercial communication, and debate on an issue of public importance."[15] Apparently, the Court found that news releases, editorials, and letters could contain commercial communication because they involved "direct communications with customers and potential customers that were intended to generate sales—and possibly to maintain or enhance the market value of Nike's stock."[16]

The U.S. Supreme Court remanded the matter back to the California courts. Before the California courts could review the facts and determine whether Nike's communications were commercial or noncommercial, Nike settled with Kasky. For the time being, all we know for sure is that the kinds of media used by Nike in its campaign might be commercial communication if a court found they met the criteria described in *Bolger v. Youngs Drug Products.*[17]

The Bolger Test

The California Supreme Court, in *Kasky*, relied on the *Bolger* test to determine if Nike's communications were commercial. Since the Supreme Court's decision in *Bolger v. Youngs Drug Products* in 1983, the definition of commercial communication or commercial advertising has depended on the admittedly vague and imprecise test, which is summarized in Exhibit 12.1. In a preliminary step, the test says that communication that does "no more than propose a commercial transaction" is commercial communication.[18] However, if the communication mixes both commercial and noncommercial components or includes more than a proposal to sell a product then three factors are examined. The three factors are (a) advertising format, (b) product references, and (c) commercial motivation. What makes the test ambiguous is that the Court has not only rejected the notion that any of these factors is sufficient by itself, but it has also declined to hold that all of these factors in combination, or any one of them individually, is necessary to support a commercial communication characterization.[19]

A review of how courts have applied the ***Bolger* test** produces some limited clarification. It appears that communications that are in the format of advertisements must be reviewed but the fact that a message is in a purchased medium and in the format of an advertisement does not, by itself, mean that the message is commercial communication. Similarly, a reference to a specific product does not, by itself, make a message commercial and the fact that the speaker has an economic motivation for delivering the message is insufficient to turn a message into commercial communication. The combination of all three factors provides strong support that the message can be characterized as commercial communication.[20]

For those in advertising, public relations, journalism, or broadcasting this means that they must be careful about any message that meets any one of these criteria. Messages that look like advertisements or that mention specific products or in which practitioners

Exhibit 12.1. The *Bolger* Test Used to Determine if a Message is Commercial Communication.

Step 1	A. Can the communication be construed to propose a commercial transaction? If no, *stop here*. It is NOT commercial communication.
	B. Does the communication propose a commercial transaction and do nothing else? If so, *stop here*. It is commercial communication.
	If the communication does not fit either A or B, then proceed to Steps 2–3.
Step 2	Answer the following questions:
	A. Is the communication in the "format" of an advertisement?
	B. Does the communication include a reference to a specific product or service?
	C. Does the person or company creating the communication have a financial motivation for creating and delivering the message?
Step 3	Do the answers to the three questions in Step 2 lead a reasonable person to believe the communication is commercial? If yes, it is commercial. If no it is not.
	(Remember you do not have to answer all three questions "yes" to find that the combination of answers makes the message commercial communication, nor is a message commercial speech just because one or two of the questions was answered yes. It is a subjective and somewhat vague test.)

or their clients have a financial interest may not enjoy full First Amendment protection and may be subject to some government regulations. Of course, this does not mean practitioners cannot deliver messages that fit one, or all, of the above criteria. Journalists obviously cover stories about the stock prices of their newspapers, public relations practitioners deliver news releases about their client's products, and advertising professionals place their advertisements while complying with all legal restrictions and regulations. Even commercial communication enjoys some First Amendment protection.

Rights Afforded Commercial Communication

Current legal doctrine holds that any message fitting the definition of commercial communication is afforded less First Amendment protection than is given noncommercial communication. However, the First Amendment protects even purely commercial messages as long as the message is not false, misleading, potentially misleading, or coercive, and does not encourage an illegal act. The doctrine granting some limited First Amendment protection to commercial communication is fairly recent. Historically, commercial communication was totally subject to government regulations and enjoyed no First Amendment protection.

Historical Perspective

At one point, speech intended to generate marketplace transactions was governed by the principle of *caveat emptor* or "let the buyer beware." Under this principle, it was the buyer's responsibility to identify any deception in commercial communication. This doctrine encouraged self-serving deception by advertisers whose messages were often perceived as socially worthless. There was no social movement or governmental motivation to protect that kind of advertising. Not only was there no impetus to protect commercial communication, there was an opposite drive to protect consumers from fraud and deception. Commercial communication was, therefore, susceptible to virtually unlimited governmental regulation.

In 1942, the U.S. Supreme Court specifically said commercial communication was not protected by the First Amendment. This decision came in a conflict between Valentine, the police commissioner of New York, and Christensen, a Florida resident who sought to advertise tours of a submarine he had moored in New York Harbor. Initially, Christensen printed handbills announcing the tours. He was told the handbills violated a New York sanitary ordinance prohibiting handbills. The ordinance only permitted handbills about public protest. Christensen, being a dedicated entrepreneur, had the handbills reprinted. The new version of Christensen's handbills omitted the price of the tour and, on the reverse side, included a protest against the City of New York. Christensen argued that these new handbills either were not commercial advertising or that they so intermingled commercial and noncommercial messages that their distribution was protected by the First Amendment. Valentine said he would permit distribution of the handbill protesting the city's actions, but would not permit distribution of the handbill if even one side of it contained information about the submarine tours. Lower courts issued an injunction ordering the police commissioner to permit Valentine to distribute his handbills, complete with tour information. The U.S. Supreme Court reversed saying, in part:

> This court has unequivocally held that the streets are proper places for the exercise of
> the freedom of communicating information and disseminating opinion and that,
> though the states and municipalities may appropriately regulate the privilege in the
> public interest, they may not unduly burden or proscribe its employment in these public thoroughfares. We are equally clear that the Constitution imposes no such restraint
> on government as respects purely commercial advertising.[21]

The Court also noted it thought Christensen was trying to evade the anti-advertising ordinance by adding the protest. The Court said, "If that evasion were successful, every merchant who desires to broadcast advertising leaflets in the streets need only append a civic appeal, or a moral platitude, to achieve immunity from the law's command."[22]

Without citing any prior authority at all, the Court simply said that purely commercial advertising had absolutely no First Amendment rights. Furthermore, the Court found that even mixed commercial and noncommercial messages had no protection where some part of the message was intended to advance a commercial purpose. The police commissioner was allowed to prevent Christensen from distributing his handbill advertisements.

Beginning of Commercial Communication Protection

The U.S. Supreme Court first began to recognize some rights for commercial speech in its decision in *Bigelow v. Virginia.*[23] The Bigelow case dealt with advertisements placed in Virginia newspapers announcing that abortion services were available and legal in New York. A Virginia statute prohibited circulation of any message encouraging abortion. In its opinion, the U.S. Supreme Court ruled the Virginia statute unconstitutional because it suppressed speech that was protected by the First Amendment. The Court effectively reversed its earlier decision in *Valentine v. Christensen* saying that in their *Christensen* decision,

> The ordinance was upheld as a reasonable regulation of the manner in which commercial advertising could be distributed. The fact that it had the effect of banning a particular handbill does not mean that *Christensen* is authority for the proposition that all statutes regulating commercial advertising are immune from constitutional challenge.[24]

It might be noted the Court seemed unwilling to admit it was reversing itself. The decision in *Valentine v. Christensen* dealt with a challenge to an ordinance that only applied to commercial advertising and specifically exempted protest messages. A careful reading shows it was not the "time, place, and manner" restriction the Court claimed it had been. It seems obvious the Court, in *Bigelow*, was trying to find a way to grant First Amendment rights to some commercial advertising.

Within a year after the Supreme Court issued its decision in *Bigelow,* it found the courage to acknowledge First Amendment protection for commercial speech. In 1976, the Court reviewed a challenge to a Virginia law that prohibited advertising the price of prescription drugs. After finding the challenged messages were the purest form of commercial communications that did no more than propose a lawful commercial transaction, the Court said, "It is a matter of public interest that those economic decisions, in the aggregate, be intelligent and well informed. To this end, the free flow of commercial information is indispensable."[25] This decision effectively gave commercial advertising some First Amendment protection. It recognized that information about products and prices is essential for decisions by consumers and that such information also is valuable in a free enterprise system where government and concerned citizens can use the information to regulate or challenge commercial practices.

This decision was followed quickly by other decisions affirming the First Amendment rights of commercial communication. However, these decisions also made it obvious that commercial communication did not enjoy full First Amendment protection. The first of these cases was *Lindmark Associates, Inc. v. Township of Willingboro.*[26] The Township of Willingboro created an ordinance that prohibited real estate "for sale" signs. They prohibited the signs because they feared the signs in interracial neighborhoods would create "white flight." In its analysis, the Court said that the township's interest in protecting real estate values and residential integration could be met in other ways that did not require such a significant infringement on the First Amendment rights of those who wanted to sell their property.

The second of these cases is *Carey v. Population Services International.*[27] *Carey* addressed several issues related to the sale and advertising of birth control products. Part of that decision declared unconstitutional a New York statute prohibiting the advertisement of condoms. The Court did recognize a First Amendment right to distribute truthful information about condoms through advertising, but also said, "even a burdensome regulation may be validated by a sufficiently compelling state interest."[28] Later, the Court said that such regulation "may be justified only by compelling state interests, and must be narrowly drawn to express only those interests."[29] In effect, the Court held that, although commercial communication enjoys First Amendment protection, protection is not absolute. The Court said New York could regulate or limit a constitutional right if (a) it could demonstrate an adequate governmental interest, and (b) the restriction on constitutional rights was only as great as was necessary to meet the governmental interest.

After describing this logic, the Court applied it to the New York statute prohibiting advertising of condoms. It ruled that the complete suppression of truthful information about a lawful product was too broad to be constitutional even if New York had a legitimate interest in protecting its citizens from potentially offensive advertising."[30]

When *Virginia Pharmacy*, *Lindmark,* and *Carey* are all read together they do show that the Supreme Court had recognized some First Amendment rights for commercial speech, even commercial advertising. However, they also make it obvious that the Court was not giving commercial communication the same First Amendment protection that is enjoyed by noncommercial communication. This balance of protection and limitation was made a bit clearer by the Court's decision in what is commonly called the *Central Hudson* decision.

The Central Hudson *Test*

Three years after the decisions in *Virginia Pharmacy, Lindmark,* and *Carey* the Supreme Court decided a case brought by Central Hudson Gas and Electric against the New York Public Service Commission.[31] The case arose because a New York utility commission ordered Central Hudson to stop all advertising that promoted the use of electricity. The utility commission's decision was based on their belief that the New York electrical system did not have sufficient fuel stocks or electrical generation capacity to meet consumer demands. The ban on advertising was originally imposed because the commission anticipated particularly high demand for power during the winter of 1973–1974. However, the commission did not lift the ban after that winter because it thought advertising would encourage consumption contrary to its policy to conserve energy. Central Hudson challenged the order through the New York court system and lost at every level. The company then appealed to the U.S. Supreme Court saying that the public service commission's order violated the First and Fourteenth Amendments to the U.S. Constitution. The Supreme Court reversed the New York courts and held that the ban on energy advertising was unconstitutional. In this decision, the Court finally detailed specific rules that could guide future decisions about what First Amendment rights are given to commercial communication. First, the Court explained that commercial communication is not afforded the same First Amendment protection as is given to noncommercial communication. Justice Powell, writing for the Court, explained that,

> [t]wo features of commercial speech permit regulation of its content. First, commercial speakers have extensive knowledge of both the market and their products. Thus, they are well situated to evaluate the accuracy of their messages and the lawfulness of the underlying activity. In addition, commercial speech, the offspring of economic self-interest, is a hardy breed of expression that is not "particularly susceptible to being crushed by overbroad regulation."[32]

In other words, because those who produce commercial communication are unlikely to accidentally misstate facts and because they are so well motivated financially that they will not be easily deterred by regulations, the Court would permit greater regulation of commercial communication than noncommercial communication.

In addition to explaining why commercial communication could be more aggressively regulated than other forms of communication, the Court also explained when commercial messages would be afforded First Amendment protection. This four-part standard for balancing the First Amendment rights of commercial communication with other government interests that could justify restriction of First Amendment rights has come to be called the ***Central Hudson Test***.

The first step of the test is to determine whether the communication has any First Amendment protection at all. In order to even be considered for First Amendment protection, commercial communications must not promote an illegal product, service, or activity and it must not be false or misleading. Messages that promote illegal products or activities, or that are false or misleading simply are not given any First Amendment protection and for such messages it is not necessary to consider the next steps of the *Central Hudson* Test.

The second step of the *Central Hudson* Test is to determine if the governmental body that seeks to regulate the speech has asserted a substantial interest. This means that the state or other government entity that wants to restrict the free expression of the commercial speaker or advertiser must show it has some duty to protect that is important enough to justify a restriction on free expression. For example, the government entity may say that it has a duty to protect its citizens from being exposed to offensive images.

The third step in the *Central Hudson* Test is to assess whether the restriction on free expression actually will advance the asserted governmental interest. Here the Court asks, for example, if citizens will actually be protected from offensive images by the restriction of free expression.

The fourth step requires the Court to determine if the restriction on free expression is no greater than necessary to meet the governmental interest. Continuing the example of a government trying to protect its citizens from offensive images, the Court would ask if there is another way to protect the citizens that does not require as much restriction of free expression.

The *Central Hudson* Test has the advantage of giving some rules that may guide a state or regulatory agency trying to decide whether it may limit commercial communication. However, the test still has major weaknesses. Each of the four steps requires very subjective judgments and even justices of the U.S. Supreme Court have noted the test cannot be consistently applied and its results cannot be predicted. The difficulty of applying the test can be seen in the Court's decision in *Metromedia, Inc. v. San Diego,*[33] which was decided just 1 year after the *Central Hudson* decision. In *Metromedia,* the justices wrote five separate opinions, each attempting to apply the logic of the *Central Hudson* Test to an ordinance that banned most outdoor advertising. Ultimately, they concluded that the ordinance was unconstitutional. However, in his dissent, Justice Rehnquist called the decision a "tower of Babel." The confusion over how to apply the *Central Hudson* Test was further exacerbated a few years later when in its decision in *City Council v. Taxpayers for Vincent,*[34] the Supreme Court ruled that an ordinance banning political signs on public land was constitutional. In 3 years, applying the same test, the Court found commercial signs could not be restricted by city ordinance but that political signs could be restricted. These holdings are particularly confusing because the rulings seem inconsistent with the governmental interests advanced and the type of communication involved. In *Metromedia* the city of San Diego asserted its ban on off-site billboards advanced a governmental interest in "eliminating hazards to pedestrians and motorists brought about by distracting sign displays, and to preserve and improve the appearance of the city." In *Vincent,* the city of Los Angeles asserted an interest in "esthetics and in preventing visual clutter." Application of the second stage of the *Central Hudson* Test would seem to favor the city of San Diego yet the ordinance was declared unconstitutional, while the Los Angeles ordinance challenged in *Vincent* was upheld. The decisions are even more puzzling when one considers that the ordinance in Vincent addressed political signs and political messages have traditionally received the highest First Amendment protections.

Application of the *Central Hudson* Test was made more difficult in 1986 when the Court decided *Posadas de Puerto Rico Associates v. Tourism Company of Puerto Rico.*[35] The legislature of Puerto Rico passed a law prohibiting advertising of casino gambling that was directed to the local residents. That same legislature passed laws making casino gambling legal and making it legal to advertise for the casinos as long as the advertisements targeted only tourists or prospective tourists. In its decision, the Court ruled that the government of Puerto Rico had a substantial interest in limiting corruption and crime that would attend increases in gambling by locals. Furthermore, the Court ruled there was a connection between advertising and demand by local residents for gambling, but the Court did not consider whether any alternative that imposed lesser restrictions on free expression could advance the governmental interest. The Court simply did not require any support for the third or fourth steps of the *Central Hudson* Test. Complicating the decision even further was the Court's observation that the Puerto Rican legislature had the power to completely ban casino gambling and that the power to ban an activity included the lesser power to ban advertising of the activity.[36] This last assertion has led many to believe the *Central Hudson* Test need not be applied to commercial messages about any activity that could be prohibited by government.

More confusion followed in 1999 when in *Greater New Orleans Broadcasting Association v. United States*[37] the Court ruled that advertisements for legal casinos in Louisiana and Mississippi could not be banned. The Court ruled the state failed to meet the third step of the *Central Hudson* Test because its asserted interest in the control of social costs like crime, corruption, and financial burdens on the poor was not supported by a ban on advertising. Not only is the *Central Hudson* Test itself vague and subjective, there are even serious questions about whether it will always be applied.

Clarification of Central Hudson *Test—Maybe?*

There have been some attempts to clarify or even operationalize some of the *Central Hudson* Test steps. These are summarized in Exhibit 12.2. In 1989, in *Board of Trustees of the State University of New York v. Fox,*[38] the Court offered some explanation of what it meant by the phrase "no greater than necessary to meet the governmental interest" as that phrase is used in the fourth step of the *Central Hudson* Test. The case arose in a challenge to a State University of New York (SUNY) regulation banning most commercial enterprises from its campuses. Enforcing this regulation, the SUNY police broke up a Tupperware party in a university dorm. Fox and other students at SUNY sought a court order challenging the regulation.

The courts reviewed several issues, one of which was whether a total ban on commercial activity was "greater than necessary to meet the governmental interest." The governmental interests asserted by SUNY were (a) promoting an educational rather than a commercial atmosphere on the university's campuses, (b) promoting safety and security, (c) preventing commercial exploitation of students, and (d) preserving residential tranquility.[39] One question presented to the Court was whether some narrower restriction like controlling the hours during which parties could be held might still meet these interests. Justice Scalia, writing for the Court, simply redefined the word "necessary" and said what is required to meet the fourth step of the *Central Hudson* Test is not the least abridgment of free expression "necessary" but only a "fit" between the regulation abridging free expression and the asserted governmental interest. He explained further that what is required to meet the fourth step is,

> not necessarily the least restrictive means but . . . a means narrowly tailored to achieve the desired objective. Within those bounds we leave it to governmental decisionmakers to judge what manner of regulation may best be employed.[40]

The decision in *Board of Trustees of the State University of New York* does not completely vitiate the fourth step of the *Central Hudson* Test. In 1993, the U.S. Supreme Court in *City of Cincinnati v. Discovery Network, Inc.,*[41] ruled that the "fit" between the restriction on free expression and the governmental interest must be substantial. In *City of Cincinnati,* the Court reviewed a decision by Cincinnati authorities to revoke the Discovery Network's right to place newsracks on the city's property. The city's decision was based on an ordinance prohibiting commercial handbills. The Court found that the city did permit other newsracks and that the number of newsracks used for commercial handbills was small in comparison to the total number of newsracks. The Court ruled that the city's interest in safety and esthetics could be adequately met by regulating the number of racks or their size and location. A total ban on newsracks for commercial handbills was ruled unconstitutional. As recently as 2003, in *Atlanta Journal and Constitution v. City of Atlanta Department of Aviation,*[42] the court of appeals supported such a conclusion by declaring the city's power to cancel a publisher's airport newsrack license unconstitutional.

It appears that even though the fourth step of the *Central Hudson* Test was modified, it must still be met before a governmental agency can restrict the free expression of commercial communication.

Social Conformist Applications

The Supreme Court has never specifically said it uses a **social conformist** approach when deciding what is and what is not commercial communication. Nor has it offered such a philosophical explanation for its decisions regarding the propriety of government regulation of commercial communication. However, neither the *Bolger* Test nor the *Central Hudson* Test can be applied with the kind of precision that an absolutist or literalist approach makes possible. A review of how the *Central Hudson* Test has been applied suggests an unspoken rule. The Court does appear to use the social function component of the social conformist approach to constitutional interpretation. Speech

---

Exhibit 12.2.   The *Central Hudson* Test Used to Determine Whether Commercial Speech May Be Subjected to Government Regulation.

Step 1   A. Does the communication promote an illegal product, service, or activity? If yes, stop here; it has no First Amendment protection and is subject to government regulation.

B. Is the communication false or misleading? If yes, stop here; it has no First Amendment protection and is subject to government regulation.

If the answer to Questions A and B are both no, the communication may have some First Amendment protection; go to Steps 2–4.

Step 2   Does the government body attempting to regulate the commercial communication assert a substantial and legitimate government interest? If no, stop here; the regulation probably does violate the First Amendment. If yes, go to Step 3.

Step 3   Is the government interest described in Step 2 advanced or helped by the proposed regulation of the commercial communication? If no, stop here; the regulation probably does violate the First Amendment. If yes; go to Step 4.

Step 4   Is there a substantial "fit" between the regulation and the government interest described in Step 2? (This does not mean that the regulation is absolutely "necessary" to meet the government interest but it cannot be a much broader or more invasive regulation than is needed to meet the government interest.) If no, stop here; the regulation probably does violate the First Amendment. If yes, the regulation probably does not violate the First Amendment.

---

that advances goals the Court sees as socially important is given greater First Amendment protection than is communication that does not have a socially important function.

Decisions regarding government impositions on commercial communication follow a rough pattern from the middle 1970s to the late 1990s. Beginning with the Supreme Court's decision in *Roe v. Wade*,[43] the Court apparently found protecting personal decisions about health, particularly reproductive health, an important social goal. Many of the cases that imposed limits on governmental control of commercial communication after that date all seem to advance the goal of protecting personal decisions about health. The first case to restrict governmental impositions on commercial communication was *Bigelow v. Virginia*, a case dealing with information about abortion availability. The other major cases granting greater constitutional protection to commercial communication in the 1970s addressed similar health issues. For example, in 1976 the Court protected drug price advertising and in 1977 it protected messages about contraceptives. The other major area where constitutional protection was expanded was real estate advertising and in those cases racial integration, another important social function, was being protected.

Restrictions on the protection of commercial communication can also be seen to follow a social function approach. After granting extensive protection to commercial communication in the 1970s, the Court began to limit those protections in a series of cases that addressed other important social functions like the government's ability to control gambling, and liquor consumption. In 1977, the Court reasoned that prohibitions against attorney advertising should be overturned to meet the social goal of encouraging access to the legal system.[44]

Regulation of Commercial Communication: The Federal Trade Commission

The **Federal Trade Commission** Act was passed in 1914 with the specific social function of preventing unfair competition in commerce. Section 5 of the FTC Act included the phrase: "Unfair methods of competition in . . . commerce . . . are . . . declared unlawful."[45]

Shortly after its creation, the Commission interpreted the provision of the FTC Act barring unfair methods of competition to give it power to control exaggerated or misleading claims. The FTC ordered an underwear manufacturer to "show cause" why it should not be prevented from labeling its goods as "natural wool" when, in fact, the underwear was only 10% wool. The manufacturer responded that the FTC Act did not give the Commission the authority to control labeling or advertising. On review, the Second Circuit Court of Appeals agreed with the manufacturer saying that the FTC's authority was limited to controlling acts of unfair competition. The U.S. Supreme Court, in *Federal Trade Commission v. Winsted Hosiery Co.*,[46] ruled that any communication calculated to deceive consumers was an act of "unfair competition" and could be regulated by the FTC. This case did not give the FTC blanket authority to regulate advertising but did say that if a label or other representation was deliberately inaccurate and gave one business an unfair advantage over its competitors, the FTC could take action against the deceptive practice. This decision did not give the FTC any authority to protect consumers; it only addressed the rights of other businesses to be free from unfair competition.

In 1931, the Court ruled the FTC did not have any authority to protect consumers. Its authority was limited to the protection of commerce and commercial competitors. This decision came in the case of *Federal Trade Commission v. Raladam.*[47] Raladam was a marketer of a claimed "obesity cure," which uncontested evidence showed had no ability to control obesity. The FTC brought an action against Raladam but the Supreme Court ruled that even though the product was misrepresented, the FTC did not have authority to act because Raladam did not injure any competitor. Specifically, the Court said,

> Findings of the Commission justify the conclusion that the advertisements naturally would tend to increase the business of respondent; but there is neither finding nor evidence from which the conclusion legitimately can be drawn that these advertisements substantially injured or tended thus to injure the business of any competitor.[48]

In effect, although consumers were deceived and Raladam made money, because no competitor was injured the FTC did not have the authority to act.

Acting with typical "speed," 7 years later Congress passed the Wheeler-Lea Act amending Section 5 to permit regulation of "unfair or deceptive acts or practices in commerce" that injure consumers. For the first time, this act gave the FTC authority to protect consumers from false or misleading advertisements.[49] Elsewhere in the same act, Congress gave the federal courts the authority to impose monetary damages for violations of FTC orders to stop deceptive or misleading advertising.[50]

Before the FTC would have the authority we think of today, there was one more major issue to address. The FTC was created specifically to protect interstate commerce. The first paragraph of the section dealing with unfair business practices makes it absolutely clear the FTC was never intended to address international trade issues. It says the FTC has the "power to prohibit unfair practices; inapplicable to foreign trade."[51] In addition, because the FTC is an agency of the federal government it is seen as only having authority over interstate commerce. In 1941, the U.S. Supreme Court made this limitation clear when it ruled the FTC had no authority over trade practices that were completed entirely within one state.[52] Again, it took Congress some time to address this deficiency. In 1982, in Section 101 of the Magnuson-Moss Warranty Federal Trade Commission Improvement Act, Congress gave the FTC authority over local business that can impact interstate commerce. That section says, in part,

> [t]he term "commerce" means trade, traffic, commerce, or transportation
> (A) between a place in a State and any place outside thereof, *or*
> (B) which affects trade, traffic, commerce, or transportation described in
> subparagraph (A). (emphasis added)[53]

Except for some commercial communication dealing with very small businesses and entirely foreign commercial enterprises, the FTC is now charged with protecting consumers in the United States from false or misleading commercial advertising. It is important to remember, however, that even with its current broad powers, the FTC does not have the authority to regulate "advertising." Its authority is limited to "[U]nfair methods of competition in or *affecting commerce,* and unfair or deceptive acts or practices in or *affecting commerce*" (emphasis added).[54] Advertising that is not connected with commerce is not subject to FTC regulations.

Today, the FTC has basically two tasks. First, it protects people and companies doing business in the United States from unfair competition. Second, it protects consumers from personal and economic injury, including injuries resulting from deceptive or misleading commercial advertising.

Structure of the FTC

The Federal Trade Commission is administered by a board with five members. Each member is appointed for a 7-year term by the president. The board must be bipartisan and no more than three members can be appointed from any one political party. The **Division of Advertising Practices**, within the **Bureau of Consumer Protection**, is charged with enforcing FTC policies against deceptive, unsubstantiated, and/or unfair commercial advertising.

What Is Deception?

The FTC can pursue legal or administrative action against a commercial advertiser for false or deceptive messages. Therefore, it is helpful for advertisers to know specifically how the FTC defines false or misleading communication. In 1983, in response to a request for such a definition from Representative John Dingell, the then chairman of the FTC James Miller explained a three-step procedure the FTC uses to define deceptive advertising. These steps are listed in Exhibit 12.3.

First, there must be a representation, omission, or practice that is likely to mislead a consumer. Second, the deception must be viewed from the perspective of a **reasonable consumer**. Third, the deception must be **material**.[55]

The first element can be met if the advertisement or commercial communication misrepresents facts, offers misleading price claims, fails to disclose a consistently defective product, or it involves tactics like bait-and-switch or failure to meet warranty requirements.

The second element can be met only if the alleged misstatement, omission, or practice would deceive a reasonable person. In other words, statements that any reasonable person would know are not true are not prosecuted by the FTC. Practices typically

Exhibit 12.3. FTC Elements of Deceptive Advertising (all three elements must be met for a commercial communication to be defined as deceptive under FTC standards).

Element 1	*Representation, omission*, or *practice* likely to mislead a consumer
Element 2	Must mislead a *reasonable person*
Element 3	Must be *material* to a decision to buy a product or service

protected by this element are obvious **puffery** or absurd statements. For example, statements like "our cookies are baked by elves," although presumably not true are not prosecuted by the FTC because any reasonable person would know they are not true and would not rely on the assertion to make a commercial decision.

The third element requires that the assertion be material. At law, a material assertion is one that actually impacts the quality, price, or reliability of the product or service described. Materiality can best be tested by asking if the assertion or omission would affect a purchasing decision. Statements that are irrelevant to a purchasing decision by a reasonable person, even if they are false, are not seen as deceptive.

What Is Unfairness?

In addition to actions for messages delivered through media of mass communication, the FTC is also charged with protecting consumers from unfair commercial practices that may be used at the point of sale. The elements of these enforcement actions are described here primarily because they give broader power to the FTC and may be used in actions against advertisers or other practitioners in mass communications when their messages become part of a larger pattern of sales techniques that harm consumers. It is difficult to operationalize the concept of "unfair" practice, but the FTC has made an effort. Maybe because the very concept of "unfairness" is vague, the FTC's rules in this area are more than a little ambiguous and it is difficult to accurately predict exactly what is and what is not an unfair practice.

When assessing whether a sales technique is unfair, the FTC generally applies two criteria. First, the practice must injure consumers and second, the practice must violate some public policy. The first of these elements is further subdivided. Before a practice will be found to injure consumers:

1. The injury must be substantial or important enough to justify FTC action.
2. The injury must not be outweighed by some benefit to the consumer or to competition in the marketplace.
3. The injury must be one the consumer him or herself could not have reasonably foreseen and avoided.

The second criterion requires that the practice must violate some public policy. It is important to note that, according to the FTC, public policy can be created by statute, common law, or even industry practices. Under these circumstances, it may be very easy to violate a "public policy" if one's client is using a new, creative, or unpopular sales technique.

Remedies and Actions of the FTC

A Federal Trade Commission investigation can be initiated by a complaint from a competitor or a consumer. Investigations can also be initiated by a request from another governmental entity or they can be initiated internally within the FTC. After the investigation, if the FTC has reason to believe there has been an act of unfair competition or an unfair or deceptive commercial communication, it can proceed in three different ways. First, the

FTC usually attempts to persuade the offending advertiser to comply with the rules voluntarily and enter into a "consent order." A **consent order** is a negotiated agreement in which the offending advertiser agrees to stop the conduct that violated FTC rules.

If this negotiation fails, the FTC may either initiate an administrative hearing or take the complaint directly to the U.S. District Court. Decisions of the FTC usually do not go to the District Court. However, **Trade Regulations** have the force of statutes because Congress has delegated its authority to the FTC to make rules that define specific acts or practices that have an unfair impact on commerce.[56] Because of this delegation, the FTC has the option of taking its complaint directly to the U.S. District Courts to request injunctions or other enforcement of its trade rules without first conducting an internal administrative hearing.

The more common practice is for the FTC to begin formal proceedings before an administrative judge. This procedure is not conducted in a court of law but it does involve some opportunities to present evidence. Decisions from these hearings may be appealed to the full five-member FTC Board and the decisions of the Board can be appealed directly to the U.S. Court of Appeals.

Hearing Procedure

Administrative actions are begun by notifying the person or company responsible for the unfair business practice. That notice gives the offending person or company 30 days to respond and describes the required reply. Typically, the notice says that the person or company must appear at a specified place for hearing and explain why the Commission should not enter an order forcing the person or company to stop the deceptive practice.[57]

At the hearing, the accused person or company has the option of being represented by an attorney. The accused can also present legal arguments, testimony, or evidence showing why the communication or practice challenged by the FTC is not unfair or deceptive. One of the options available to a person or company accused of unfair or deceptive practice is substantiation. Substantiation simply means proving or "substantiating" that the claims made in the advertisement are true.

Substantiation Policy

Proving that the speaker had a reasonable belief that the assertions in an advertisement are true is called **substantiation**. It may appear odd to refer to substantiation as a defense because a commercial speaker must have had reason to believe his or her assertions were true before making them. However, there is no reason or opportunity to demonstrate substantiation until after someone challenges a claim made in an advertisement or other commercial message.

After several years of case-by-case interpretation of this requirement, the FTC has formalized the requirements for substantiation. The FTC standard begins with the requirement that the advertiser have a reasonable belief that any assertion is true. There are several different criteria for showing a reasonable belief, each applied to a particular type of advertising claim.

Express or specific claims of support for the product advertised are held to a high standard. For example, an advertisement that says, "9 out of 10 doctors recommend Widget" must have the advertised level of support. For such a claim, the advertiser must be able to prove that he or she has actually surveyed physicians or has some concrete evidence that 9 out of 10 doctors really do recommend the product.

When an advertisement implies support, the advertiser must be able to show the amount of support implied in its communication with consumers. In this context, such evidence as expert testimony and consumer surveys can be considered. Experts might testify about what claims a consumer hearing an advertisement could infer and surveys can be used to show what the majority of consumers thought they were being told in the advertisement.

Whether the assertions have to do with claims of support for the product or descriptions of a product's attributes, an advertiser "should not say what it cannot prove."[58] Claims of specific endorsements, support, or product qualities can be the subject of action by the FTC and in some instances it has ruled that scientific testing may be required to establish a reasonable belief in a claim.[59]

One area of claim sometimes seen as an exception to the requirement for substantiation is "puffery." Objective claims of support or endorsement or that describe specific product attributes must be substantiated, but subjective claims that describe the product's beauty, virtue, or superiority are often excused as puffery. The key difference between objective claim and puffery is whether the claim or assertion can be objectively verified. Such things as beauty are so subject to individual interpretation that there is no objective way to measure or substantiate them.[60]

Cease and Desist Orders

After its hearing, if the FTC finds there is deception or an unfair practice, it can issue what is called a **cease and desist order**.[61] These orders have the force of law and a company ordered to 'cease and desist' that continues to run the offending advertisement can be charged in a federal court. The penalty for violations of a cease and desist order can be as much as $10,000 for each violation of the order. Each day that an offending advertisement continues to run after the cease and desist order is a new violation, so the fines can be as much as $10,000 per day. The FTC can also ask for other penalties, including orders for corrective advertising.[62]

Corrective and Affirmative Advertising

One problem with cease and desist orders is that they do nothing to protect the consumers who have already heard a false or deceptive advertisement. An advertiser could use a false advertisement to create the impression that its product is superior or to "position" the product and then do nothing to correct the mis-impressions created even if a cease and desist order is entered. In order to counteract this unfair advantage, the FTC can order advertisers to place corrective or affirmative advertising.

Corrective advertising is new advertising that the FTC requires the offending company run. This new advertising must specifically correct the misrepresentations of earlier messages. For example, in 1977 the FTC required Warner-Lambert, the manufacturer of Listerine mouthwash, to design and place advertisements that specifically said Listerine does not cure or prevent colds. The FTC imposed this requirement because Waner-Lambert had, for years, advertised that Listerine did cure or prevent colds and the FTC thought many consumers purchased the mouthwash in reliance on this belief. In that case, the only way to correct the unfair competitive advantage of Warner-Lambert was to force the company to use corrective advertising to say the product did not prevent colds.[63]

Affirmative advertising refers to a requirement that any future advertising include disclaimers or detailed explanations. A company ordered to use affirmative advertising is not required to correct the messages in earlier advertisements but must either stop using the message or add a disclaimer explaining more carefully or noting information not included in the original advertisements. For example, in *National Comm'n on Egg Consumption v. Federal Trade Comm'n,* the advertisers for the National Commission on Egg Consumption were ordered to include information that many health experts believe egg consumption may increase the risk of heart attack in any future advertisement touting the health benefits of eating eggs.[64]

Judicial Remedies

In addition to its authority to issue cease and desist orders and to direct corrective or affirmative advertising, the FTC may ask the district court to order other remedies against offending advertisers. These **judicial remedies** include injunctions, criminal penalties, or restitution to consumers. **Injunctions** are court orders directing, in this case, an advertiser to stop delivering an offensive message. These court orders are used when there is a fear that continuing the message even during the time of the FTC's investigation and hearing will cause harm to the consumers.

Criminal penalties are limited to false advertising of food, drugs, cosmetics, or devices that may harm consumers' health. The penalty for this kind of harmful advertising is $5,000 and up to 6 months in jail for a first offense and a fine up to $10,000 and as much as 1 year of imprisonment for a second offense.

The FTC is charged with protecting consumers. The FTC realizes that cease and desist orders and fines do little to correct harm already done to the victims of false advertising. For this reason, the FTC may apply to the federal district courts to modify contracts with consumers and for payments to deceived consumers. These actions may be pursued by the FTC but the FTC is not required to take them and they should not be viewed as a substitute for civil actions by aggrieved consumers.[65]

Of course, consumers are free to pursue actions against advertisers outside of the FTC's rules. Actions for fraud and contract enforcement may be pursued by individual consumers against any person or company that engages in deceptive business practices or lies in its advertising.

Other Limitations on Commercial Communication

In addition to civil lawsuits for fraud or contract violation, individual citizens may bring actions to enforce the FTC's rules under the Lanham Act.

Lanham Act

The **Lanham Act** is very broad legislation that protects against infringement on trademarks and trade dress as well as unfair business practices. Typically, Sections 1051 through 1127 of Title 15 of the U.S. Code are referred to as the Lanham Act. It is one small portion of those sections that gives rise to the right of private citizens to sue for violation of FTC regulations. A subsection titled "Civil Actions" says, in part:

> Any person who . . . in commercial advertising or promotion, misrepresents the nature, characteristics, qualities, or geographic origin of his or her or another person's goods, services, or commercial activities . . . shall be liable in a civil action by any person who believes that he or she is or is likely to be damaged by such act.[66]

On its face this would appear to give any person who has been harmed by some violation of FTC advertising regulations the right to bring a suit against the offending advertiser. However, like most laws, the provisions are much more complicated than they first appear.

The most important of these complications is determining who is "likely to be damaged." Consistently, the courts have ruled that only competitors, and not consumers, are allowed to bring actions using the Lanham Act. In order to sue an advertiser for violation of an FTC regulation under the Lanham Act, the courts have required that the plaintiff be a member of a commercial class. Although investors and at least one contractual employee have been permitted to sue under the Lanham Act, a consumer has never been allowed to use the act to press a claim for any unfair business practice. In effect, the laws that created the FTC and the Lanham Act, in particular, are intended to protect those **in commerce** and not the general consumer.[67]

Although consumers are not given the authority to bring actions under the Lanham Act, business competitors of an advertiser may bring such actions. Obviously, that is a population highly motivated to aggressively pursue any false advertising claim. For competitors to win an action they must plead and prove five elements. First they must prove that the defendant actually made false statements of fact about their own product or the competitor's product. Second, they must show that the false statements actually deceived or could have deceived a significant number of purchasers. Third, they must prove that the false statement was material and could have influenced a purchasing decision. The second and third elements are necessary to show that the plaintiff actually lost or could have lost business to the false advertiser. Fourth, it must be shown that the goods or services advertised were in interstate commerce. The FTC was created to protect interstate commerce and plaintiffs under the Lanham Act must show that the FTC would have had jurisdiction over the challenged advertising. Finally, the plaintiff must show that he, she, or it was, or was likely to be, financially harmed by the deceptive advertising. The elements required for a Lanham Act suit are listed in Exhibit 12.4.

Although the plaintiff must prove all five of these elements, the Lanham Act gives plaintiffs some very real advantages over traditional civil lawsuits for fraud or unfair competition. A qualified plaintiff may secure both an injunction ordering the defendant to stop using the offending advertisements or business practices and monetary damages up to triple the amount of money actually lost.

One of the largest awards made in a Lanham Act suit was in *U-Haul International v. Jartran*.[68] A description of this suit illustrates how the Lanham Act gives some advantages to plaintiffs who have been wronged by a competitor's false advertising.

Exhibit 12.4.   Elements of Lanham Act Suit (the plaintiff must prove all five elements to win a suit under the Lanham Act).

Element 1	Defendant made false statement of fact about their product or competitor's product
Element 2	False statement actually deceived purchasers
Element 3	False statement was material to decision to buy
Element 4	Goods lied about must have been in interstate commerce
Element 5	Plaintiff was harmed or was likely to be harmed by false statement. *It is not enough to be harmed as a "simple consumer." The harm must result from some commercial relationship with the defendant.*

U-Haul is the largest company in the U.S. truck rental business. Jartran, which is owned largely by James Ryder, entered the rental truck market in 1979. During 1979 and 1980 Jartran engaged in a nationwide newspaper campaign that compared cost, fuel efficiency, and appearance of Jartran and U-Haul trucks. The campaign won a "Gold Effie" award from the American Marketing Association and during the campaign, income for Jartran rose from $7 million to $80 million, while the revenue for U-Haul declined from $395 million to $378 million. In 1980, U-Haul sued Jartran for false advertising. The District Court agreed with U-Haul's contentions and ruled that Jartran had deliberately misrepresented both its products and those of U-Haul. The District Court issued an injunction ordering Jartran to stop advertising by comparing its trucks to those of U-Haul. After litigation, the court awarded U-Haul $40 million.[69] The $40 million was determined by adding together the $6 million that Jartran spent on its advertising campaign to the $13.6 million U-Haul spent on advertising to correct the false impressions. The Court then doubled that total under a section of the Lanham Act that permits damages up to three times the actual damages to punish deliberately deceptive practices.[70]

In this case, U-Haul was able to use the Lanham Act to stop the offending advertising and to recover their cost of corrective advertising. Because of the punitive award, U-Haul was also able to more than recover all its lost profits. Jartran, on the other hand, was severely punished for its deceptive comparison advertising. It appears the "Gold Effi" award did not impress the Court.

State Fraud and Deceptive Practice Laws

Although the FTC and Lanham Act do impose significant regulation on unfair commercial communication, they are not always available. Some deceptive advertising or unfair commercial communication may not impact interstate commerce. Sometimes the people harmed by false advertising are individual consumers who cannot pursue Lanham Act suits, and the FTC is simply too overwhelmed to correct every unfair commercial communication.

Other systems for protecting consumers involve regulation or control of commercial communication. Most states have created an office of consumer protection and/or have assigned their attorney general or other official with the responsibility for hearing and prosecuting consumer complaints. It would be impossible to summarize all of these local and state laws impacting commercial communication here. It is, however, possible to provide some general rules that govern state and local communication regulation. Of course, if you need specific information on local communication regulation, you should consult an attorney licensed in your geographic area who is expert in this area of practice.

The first of the general rules is that no local law may take away rights guaranteed under the U.S. Constitution. Very simplistically stated, the Fourteenth Amendment requires the state and local governments to honor First Amendment rights. State laws can give you more rights than does the U.S. Constitution but they can never take away or limit constitutional rights. Refer back in this chapter to the *Central Hudson* Test. Any state or local law that violates that test also probably violates your rights as a commercial communicator. Applying the *Central Hudson* Test, we can anticipate that state or local laws that really do protect an important government interest are enforceable. Thus, laws that regulate the placement of billboards in order to protect visibility and traffic safety are most likely to be constitutional. Also permissible are local laws that prohibit and/or punish deceptive advertising or unfair business practices, or that punish the advocacy of illegal activities or products. These state and local procedures that prohibit deception in business or communication advocating illegal acts are often called '**baby FTC**' or 'mini-FTC' laws because they are usually modeled after the FTC regulations and prohibit the same conduct the FTC restricts.

State and local laws that protect government interests may not violate the constitutional rights of commercial speakers. In addition, there are some state, local, and federal laws that regulate advertising for legal but dangerous products, that are designed to protect groups of people who are particularly susceptible to persuasion, or that are designed to limit the use of some advertising media. The next section summarizes some trends in restricting commercial communications, directed to children, the advertisement of highly regulated products, and a heavily regulated service.

Audience, Product, and Service-Specific Restrictions

Advertising Directed to Children

There has long been a belief that children are particularly susceptible to influence. Congresspeople and their constituents have consistently shown that they believe television has almost magical powers over children. The belief that television can influence children, coupled with the governmental interest in protecting children, has precipitated a number of laws and regulations restricting advertisements directed to children.

One of the earliest official actions was the issuance of FCC guidelines in 1974. These guidelines were proffered in response to pressure from "Action for Children's Television," a citizen organization that filed petitions and letters demanding action from the FCC. Although there was no empirical evidence to support the influence of advertising on children, the FCC did produce a policy statement advising broadcasters to limit advertising on children's programming to 12 minutes per hour during the week and 9.5 minutes per hour on weekends. In 1978, the FCC issued another notice to determine if the broadcasters were complying with these guidelines. During the Reagan administration, regulation of broadcasting was significantly decreased and even these guidelines were eliminated. This deregulation was challenged by Action for Children's Television and, in 1987, the Federal Circuit Court in Washington, DC, ordered the FCC to "explain the elimination of its children's television advertising guidelines."[71] The FCC initiated an inquiry but did not create new guidelines for advertising directed to children.

In 1988, Congress passed legislation requiring limitations on children's advertising that were nearly identical to the original FCC guidelines.[72] However, President Reagan declined to sign the bill and it never became law. In 1990, another bill regulating advertising to children did pass under President George H.W. Bush. The **Children's Television Act of 1990** limited advertising on children's television programming to 12 minutes per hour during the week and 10.5 minutes per hour on weekends. The law also required the FCC to use broadcast stations' compliance with this requirement to determine the propriety of issuing or renewing broadcast licenses.[73] The Congressional record shows that, when discussing the constitutionality of this law, the House Energy and Commerce Committee used a *Central Hudson* Test analysis.[74] The committee found that even though children's advertising may be truthful, the government has a substantial interest in shielding children from overcommercialization. The committee also thought that limiting the amount of advertising on children's television advanced this interest and that there was a reasonable "fit" between the limits on children's advertising and the government interest.

Highly Regulated Products

Commercial communication about some legal products or activities in the United States is heavily regulated. Such products include firearms, alcoholic beverages, and tobacco. Communication about gambling is also heavily regulated even where gambling is legal. We have chosen the restrictions on communication about tobacco products as an example because these regulations can be used to illustrate almost all types of restrictions imposed on legal but undesirable products or activities.

Many of the restrictions on tobacco advertising do overlap with limitations on advertising to children but some of the restrictions seem to arise from the government's ambivalent attitude toward the product itself. Some evidence indicates that tobacco products cause the death of more than 250,000 U.S. citizens each year and the government does impose limitations on tobacco advertising in an attempt to control consumption, particularly among children. That same government seems unwilling to ban the manufacture, sale, or consumption of tobacco. In short, tobacco is a legal product that is economically important but there seems to be a governmental interest in limiting its use. Thus, there are significant limitations on commercial communication about tobacco and even affirmative requirements specifying the content of communication about tobacco. Some of these government restrictions have been upheld, while others have been found to be unconstitutional abridgements of the First Amendment rights of commercial advertisers. Analysis of each of these rules may help us understand the limits of government regulation of commercial communication about socially or politically unattractive products.

Advertising Tobacco Products to Children.   Some of the most restrictive laws ever imposed on commercial communication addressed advertising of tobacco to children. Food and Drug Administration (FDA) regulations prohibited outdoor advertising of cigarettes or smokeless tobacco within 1,000 feet of a playground, park, or school.[75] This same regulation, in another section, attempted to limit advertisement to black text on a white background unless the advertisements are on vending machines that could not be viewed from outdoors.[76] The regulation even prohibited the use of music or sound effects for fear these would influence children.[77]

Although the government certainly does have a substantial interest in protecting the health of children, it appears these restrictions are not consistent with the *Central Hudson* Test. In *Lorillard Tobacco Co. v. Reilly,*[78] the U.S. Supreme Court ruled that similar laws in Massachusetts were too broad to be constitutional. Because they impact adult consumers of legal tobacco products, these rules do not have the substantial "fit" with the governmental interest required by the fourth step in the *Central Hudson* Test. Other cases in the U.S. Court of Appeals have upheld some limitations on outdoor tobacco advertising when these limits were narrowly tailored to protect children.[79] As of 2005, it appears some limitations on advertising tobacco to children are legal but it is not clear how extensive those limitations may be.

Media-Specific Restrictions on Tobacco Advertising.   The restrictions on advertising tobacco on television are even broader than the restrictions on advertising other products to children in that medium. Both the Federal Cigarette Labeling and Advertising Act and the Comprehensive Smokeless Tobacco Health Education Act impose a complete ban on the advertising of cigarettes, little cigars, and smokeless tobacco products in any electronic media under the jurisdiction of the FCC. On its face, this total ban on advertising of tobacco on radio and television seems just as defective as the restrictions on display advertising that were ruled unconstitutional in *Lorillard Tobacco Co. v. Reilly.*[80] However, when the rules prohibiting radio and television advertising were challenged by Capital Broadcasting in 1971 they were upheld by the U.S. District Court in the District of Columbia. That court ruled that the ban on tobacco advertising in electronic media was within the authority given the government in the Commerce Clause and did not violate the First or Fifth Amendments. This decision was upheld by the U.S. Supreme Court in 1972.[81] It should be noted that these decisions both took place 4 years before the First Amendment rights of commercial communication were acknowledged in *Virginia Pharmacy*[82] and 8 years before the creation of the *Central Hudson* Test.[83] Given the changes in treatment of commercial communication since 1972, it is nearly impossible to predict how the ban on broadcast advertising of tobacco products would be treated today. Furthermore, because there has been a settlement agreement between the tobacco industry and most states' attorneys general there is little likelihood we will ever know how today's courts would judge the constitutionality of a total ban on broadcast advertising of tobacco.

All we can say with certainty is that the ban on advertising of most tobacco products in media controlled by the FCC is in place and is being enforced. This reality suggests that bans on advertising of specific products may be upheld and that bans are particularly likely in media that already require a governmental license.

Affirmative Content Requirements.   Cigarettes and smokeless tobacco labels are required to carry warning statements that tell consumers about the hazards of using the products.[84] Failure to use the label warning statements can result in fines up to $10,000 and injunctions against the product itself.[85] These warning labels are analogous to corrective advertising imposed without a specific finding of prior deceptive advertising. Although a number of appellate courts have ruled that such corrective advertising is constitutional[86] the Supreme Court has not yet ruled on the issue. Since the requirements have been in place for four decades without a successful challenge, it seems unlikely they will be repealed any time soon.

A Regulated Service: Advertising for Attorneys

Historically, professions like law, medicine, and the clergy had ethical prohibitions against advertising. Some of these ethical prohibitions manifest themselves as laws against advertising. Since the majority of legislators and judges are attorneys, the law has always reflected an unusual concern for the reputation of the legal profession. Here, we analyze the change in laws regarding attorney advertising because they seem instructive for those considering advertising for either attorneys or other service professions where advertising has been either illegal or a violation of some professional prohibition.

Prior to 1977, many influential attorneys and bar associations protected the status quo within the legal business by prohibiting all advertising. This prohibition virtually guaranteed that new lawyers and solo practitioners could not compete for clients. It also operated to discourage those not familiar with lawyers from seeking assistance in the justice system. Some commentators suggest a different motivation for the prohibition. These authors note that the number of lawyers increased dramatically prior to 1977. For example, from 1952 to 1971 the number of lawyers increased by 326%.[87] These authors have argued that the prohibitions on attorney advertising really existed to protect old established law firms and to "freeze out" the large number of new lawyers.[88]

Regardless of their real motivation, the prohibitions were challenged in 1977 by John Bates and Van O'Steen who were recent law school graduates. Both graduated near the top of their class and were admitted to the bar. When they began their partnership they placed an advertisement in the *Arizona Republic* offering to provide legal services for "very reasonable fees." The advertisement also featured a graphic of the scales of justice. They were disciplined by the Arizona Bar Association, which, like all bar associations and attorney disciplinary commissions of the time, prohibited attorney advertising. Bates and O'Steen appealed and the Arizona Supreme Court upheld the disciplinary action. Their appeal was based on arguments that the prohibitions against advertising violated the noncompetition clauses of the Sherman Anti-Trust Act and that it abridged their First and Fourteenth Amendment rights. The appeal ultimately reached the U.S. Supreme Court, which ruled against Bates and O'Steen on the Sherman Anti-Trust argument but in favor of the young lawyers on the First and Fourteenth Amendment arguments.[89]

In the U.S. Supreme Court, the Arizona Bar Association argued, in part, that (a) advertising by attorneys would place too great a burden on the justice system by encouraging litigation, (b) advertising would increase the cost of attorney services because lawyers would have to increase their clients' fees in order to cover the cost of advertising, (c) that attorneys would cut the quality of their services in order reduce costs so they could advertise lower fees, (d) that permitting advertising makes the law appear to be a trade rather than a profession, and (e) that the general public is not sophisticated enough to be able to evaluate attorney advertising. Justice Blackmun, writing for the Supreme Court, did not consider the image of lawyers a significant issue but rather ruled against the prohibition of advertising because advertising would attract new clients and therefore level the economic field for new lawyers. The Court also said, "[a]dvertising is the traditional mechanism in a free-market economy for a supplier to inform a potential purchaser of the availability and terms of exchange."[90]

Since the Bates decision, there has been a growth in attorney advertising and some would say the concerns of the Arizona Bar Association have proven true because the image of the legal profession has been tarnished. Regardless of these perceptions, attorney advertising is clearly a reality. Most attorneys spend about $2,500 a year on advertising[91] and 94% of the U.S. population is familiar with attorney advertising.[92]

Since the *Bates* decision, several cases have upheld some restrictions on attorney advertising but have permitted most traditional advertising by attorneys. For example, the Supreme Court has upheld prohibitions against attorneys soliciting clients who are under stress or otherwise unable to make careful decisions, such as while hospitalized after an accident.[93] The Court has struck down, as unconstitutional, prohibitions against advertising specializations[94] and mailed advertisements, letters, or announcements.[95]

The discussions of tobacco product advertising and attorney advertising are not presented to make you an expert in the regulation of commercial communication about one product or one service. Rather, they are presented to provide some insight into how products and services that are subject to unusual scrutiny can be treated within the existing framework of protection for commercial communication. We do not provide any details but it should be noted that there are similar restrictions on other products like firearms and alcohol and on services like gambling and adult entertainment. In addition, public and political pressure can create a government interest in the regulation or outright prohibition of some advertising forms. The drives to restrict telemarketing and e-mail solicitation are examples of this.

Practice Notes

Obviously, those mass communications professionals in the field of advertising should find it useful to know what messages are prohibited by the FTC and when their First Amendment rights can supercede local restrictions on commercial communication. However, this information should also be valuable to those in public relations, broadcasting, and journalism. Professionals in those fields, often with some financial interest, produce news releases, articles, or other messages about commercial products or services. In this final section, we address four questions that may impact people in each of the subfields of mass communications. Those questions are:

1. When does the conduct of an advertising agent or public relations practitioner create liability for his or her client?

2. Can a public relations practitioner or advertising agent be held liable for delivering false or deceptive information if he or she was given the information by the client?

3. Can a newspaper or broadcast station refuse to accept an advertisement?

4. Can a newspaper or broadcast station be held liable for delivering an untrue advertisement or a message advocating an illegal product or service?

Each of these questions can be answered by exploring the interaction between commercial communication doctrine and other forms of legal liability.

We conclude the practice notes with a discussion of limitations on political advertising and lobbying. Although these activities usually are not commercial communication, they can be. In early 2005, a bill titled the Federal Propaganda Prohibition Act was introduced to Congress. This act was a reaction to government expenditures for publicity and payments to reporters for news coverage. It emphasizes the relationship between commercial speech lobbying and political advertising.[96]

Client Liability for Advertising or Public Relations Agent Misconduct

Under the doctrine of *respondeat superior* the advertising client or employer may be held liable for the conduct of the advertising or public relations agent even if the client did not know that his or her advertising or public relations agency was producing improper commercial messages. *Respondeat superior*, which was explained in chapter 11, literally means, "let the master answer." As applied in most courts, this doctrine imposes liability on the employer for the misconduct of the employee. For the employer or client to be liable, the advertising or public relations agent must be acting within the scope of his or her duties as an employee and the person who is harmed must understand that the agent is the representative of the client.[97] These requirements are met in most situations where an advertising agency delivers an advertising message for a client to the media or where a public relations practitioner writes a news release for a client. An advertising agent or public relations practitioner who creates a false, misleading, or illegal message on behalf of a client can cause that client to lose a lawsuit for the improper communication even if the client did not know about the message or its improper content. Needless to say, clients placed in this situation are very unhappy and advertising agents and public relations practitioners who create such liability rarely keep their jobs.

Advertising or Public Relations Agent Liability for Client Misconduct

The reciprocal of the aforementioned situation can be created if the advertising agent or public relations practitioner relies on inaccurate information provided by the client. There appears to be no law or rule that insulates the advertising or public relations professional from liability. An employee cannot defend misconduct simply by saying he or she was acting under the orders of his or her boss or client. However, virtually every law creating liability for commercial communication requires some element of knowledge that the communication was improper. The concepts of knowledge, scienter, and mens rea were explained earlier. As applied in this situation, they mean that the advertising or public relations agent cannot be held liable for a false or misleading message unless he or she knew or had some reason to know that the information contained in his or her advertisement or news release was not true or might reasonably be expected to cause harm to others.[98]

Generally, an advertising agent or public relations practitioner is not required to independently check all the information provided to him or her by a client. However, if the agent actively participated in the fraud by creating false information, modifying camera angles, or manipulating evidence, he or she can certainly be sued for false advertising or fraud. Furthermore, it should be noted that the agent does not have to actually know the information is untrue. The agent may be held liable if he or she should have known the information was not true or was dangerous. Many courts have held that if a reasonable person would suspect information is not true, there is a duty to confirm its veracity before using it in a commercial communication.[99]

The Media's Right to Reject Commercial Messages

Many students and practitioners simply forget that the First Amendment imposes no obligation at all on the media. It only prohibits governmental actions that restrict free speech. Just as an auditorium owner may refuse to rent his or her facility to an unpopular speaker, a newspaper or broadcaster cannot be required to sell space or time for any commercial message. Responding to an argument that newspapers have a monopoly on the distribution of information and should be required to carry political advertisement, the U.S. Supreme Court ruled, "A newspaper is more than a passive receptacle or conduit for news, comment, and advertising."[100] Newspapers are business and are free to accept or reject advertising, including editorial advertising.[101]

These same rulings that permit newspapers to reject advertising or to reject news releases also apply to broadcasters. Some have argued that because broadcasting is regulated and licensed by the government the broadcasting industry has an obligation to protect free speech. This argument would impose upon broadcasters the First Amendment obligation to "make no law" restricting free speech. The Supreme Court has summarily dismissed this argument. In its decision in *CBS, Inc. v. Democratic National Committee*, the Court reviewed a challenge to broadcast network's decision not to sell time for an editorial advertisement. The Court said, "Editing is what editors are for; and editing is selection and choice of material."[102] Simply put, newspapers and broadcasters are free to accept or to refuse advertising or news releases from any source as long as they do not violate specific laws like those that prohibit discrimination based on race or creed.

The media must, however, honor their contracts and assume liability for the decisions they make. In effect, with the right to reject advertising comes with some responsibility for the advertising that is accepted.

Liability of Newspapers and Broadcasters for Advertising Content

As long as it does not impose liability without fault, a state may constitutionally hold a publisher liable for falsehood that injures an individual.[103] Just like newspapers or broadcast stations can be sued for defamation or invasion of privacy in their news stories, they can also be sued for liabilities arising from the advertisements they carry. However, they must have been at fault—had some knowledge, scienter, or mens rea — before they can be held liable. In chapter 4 we described some basic principles of tort law and introduced the use of the incitement standard in civil litigation. Those concepts will help you understand the liability described here.

A review of three similar cases involving *Soldier of Fortune* magazine will provide a useful summary of the legal requirements for publisher or broadcaster liability. In each of these cases, a plaintiff sued *Soldier of Fortune* alleging it was liable for an injury to the plaintiff because of advertising carried in the magazine. The advertisements are shown in Exhibit 12.5.

Survivors or relatives of victims who had been attacked by the mercenaries who were hired because of their advertisements in *Soldier of Fortune* brought each of the lawsuits. The theories of liability in these cases included negligent incitement, wrongful death, and intentional infliction of emotional distress. In each case, one key issue was whether the First Amendment protected the publisher from suit. Similar questions would be raised if the publisher had been sued for fraud or some other commercial tort associated with false or deceptive advertising.

Exhibit 12.5.   Advertisements from *Soldier of Fortune* (copy from public court records).

Norwood v. Soldier of Fortune, 651 F. Supp 1397, 1398 (W.D.Ark,1987)

GUN FOR HIRE: 37-year-old professional mercenary desires jobs. Vietnam Veteran. Discreet and very private. Bodyguard, courier, and other special skills. All jobs considered. Phone [deleted]

and

GUN FOR HIRE. NAM sniper instructor. SWAT. Pistol, rifle, security specialist, body guard, courier plus. All jobs considered. Privacy guaranteed. Mike [phone number deleted].

Eimann v. Soldier of Fortune, 880 F.2d 830, 831 (5th Cir.1989) *cert denied* 493 U.S. 1024 (1990)

EX-MARINES – 67–69 'Nam Vets, Ex-DI, weapons specialist—jungle warfare, pilot, M.E., high-risk assignments, U.S. or overseas. [phone number deleted]

Braun v. Soldier of Fortune, 968 F.2d 1110, 1112 (11th Cir.1992) *cert denied* 506 U.S. 1070 (1993)

GUN FOR HIRE: 37-year-old professional mercenary desires jobs. Vietnam Veteran. Discrete [*sic*] and very private. Bodyguard, courier, and other special skills. All jobs considered. Phone [deleted] (days) or [deleted], or write: [address deleted] Gatlinburg, TN 37738.

In the first of these cases, *Norwood v. Soldier of Fortune*, the Federal District Court was asked to review a summary judgment that said, in effect, no matter what *Soldier of Fortune* did the First Amendment protected them from liability. The Federal District Court ruled that a jury should hear the case to determine if the advertisements "had a substantial probability of ultimately causing harm to some individual."[104] Because this case went back to the trial court and was not appealed again all we know is that the Federal District Court said it was, at least, possible that *Soldier of Fortune* could be liable if its advertisement ultimately caused harm.

The second and third cases are more helpful because they lay out a standard that can be applied to determine when a publisher can be held liable for advertisements it carries. In *Eimann v. Soldier of Fortune*,[105] the U.S. Court of Appeals for the Fifth Circuit reversed a $9.4 million jury verdict for a wrongful death action against *Soldier of Fortune*. In that case, the Court of Appeals ruled that jury instructions had been so broad they violated the First Amendment rights of *Soldier of Fortune*. The court said, "The standard of conduct imposed by the district court against *Soldier of Fortune* is too high; it allows a jury to visit liability on a publisher for untoward consequences that flow from his decision to publish any suspicious, ambiguous ad that might cause serious harm."[106] Explaining this ruling, in dicta the court said, "Peanut butter advertising cannot be banned just because someone might someday throw a jar at the presidential motorcade."[107]

Three years later, in *Braun v. Soldier of Fortune*,[108] the Court of Appeals for the 11th Circuit upheld a $4.375 million judgment against the magazine. The major difference between the decisions in *Eimann* and *Braun* were variations in the jury instructions given at the two trials. In the *Eimann* case, the jury was told it could find *Soldier of Fortune* liable if, considering the context of other advertisements, articles, the magazine's typical reader, and other factors, the publisher could reasonably infer the advertisement involved illegal activities.[109] In *Braun*, the trial judge "instructed that the jury could hold [*Soldier of Fortune*] liable for printing [the] advertisement only if the advertisement on its face would have alerted a reasonably prudent publisher to the clearly identifiable unreasonable risk of harm to the public that the advertisement posed."[110]

Comparing the decisions in *Eimann* and *Braun*, it is apparent that publishers may be held liable for the illegal results of advertisements they carry but the publisher is not required to conduct any investigation at all. The publisher is not even liable for looking at the advertisement in context. Publisher liability attaches to the publisher only if the advertisement "on its face" would alert a reasonably prudent publisher that the message presents an unreasonable risk of harm.

Political Advertising and Lobbying

There may be no more misunderstood and maligned specializations in mass communications than political advertising and lobbying. Neither is regulated as commercial communication and both have a reputation for deviations from the truth. However, both specializations can be performed ethically and both are required for the functioning of a democracy. Political advertising helps voters understand issues and gives a sense of the candidates' personalities and positions. Lobbying provides information and input for legislators and government executives without direct taxpayer support.

Although the content of political advertising and lobbying communication are not subject to legal regulation, there are restrictions on both activities. Here, we describe the spending limits imposed on political advertising and the registration requirements imposed on lobbyists.

Political Advertising

Before specifically addressing the limitations on political campaign spending, we mention the one other significant restriction on political campaign communication. The restriction on direct involvement in politics by elected officials and government employees began in 1939 with the Hatch Act. The Hatch Act was created to promote government neutrality and to improve citizen trust in politics. It has been modified several times, most recently in the 1990s. Today, the Hatch Act prohibits government employees from engaging in any political activity while they are on duty, while they are in government offices, while wearing uniforms or government insignia, and while using a government vehicle. Simply put, the act tries to avoid the use of taxpayer money for campaigning or the creation of any implied endorsement of a political position by the government.[111]

Federal Limits on Campaign Spending.   More directly related to our purpose here are the Taft Hartley Act of 1947 and the Federal Election Campaign Act of 1971. These laws are designed to limit the influence of wealth on U.S. politics. Some commentators argue that the limits on campaign spending and advertising are motivated by an attempt to provide a "level playing field" for less wealthy politicians. Others very cynically note that politicians only want to save the financial burden of expensive advertising campaigns. Regardless of the motivation, the campaign-spending limits must be considered when planning any significant political advertising or public relations campaign.

The 1947 Taft Hartley Act prohibited spending by corporations and unions advocating election or defeat of a "clearly identified candidate."[112] These restrictions have been modified to create the contemporary election spending limits. Today, the Federal Election Campaign Act imposes limitations on how much can be given by individuals or groups and sets reporting requirements.[113] In addition to the limitations on contributions and reporting requirements, the act originally also imposed limits on how much candidates could spend and on how much other organizations could spend on behalf of candidates. The provisions limiting expenditures were overturned as unconstitutional by the U.S. Supreme Court in the 1976 decision in *Buckley v. Valeo*.[114] The decision is summarized in Exhibit 12.6.

The *Buckley v. Valeo* decision effectively created the Political Action Committee (PAC) loophole for campaign spending. Although candidates may only accept a limited amount of cash contributions, PACs may spend as much as they are able advancing their political ideas or agendas. The freedom of PACs to make their own expenditures on behalf of a political point of view was confirmed by the U.S. Supreme Court 10 years after the *Buckley v. Valeo* decision, in *Federal Election Commission v. Mass. Citizens for Life, Inc.*[115] That case arose because the Federal Election Commission charged the

Exhibit 12.6.   Federal Campaign Expenditure Limitations (Federal Election Campaign Act, 2 USCS 441a; *Buckley v. Valeo*, 424 U.S. 1 [1976]).

Constitutional? *Buckley v. Valeo,* 424 U.S. 1 (1976)	Limitation
Yes	Limit contributions by an individual or group to one candidate to $1,000
Yes	Limit contributions by a political committee to one candidate to $5,000
Yes	Limit total contribution by one contributor to one candidate to $25,000 per year
No	Limit expenditures by individual or group advocating election or defeat of a candidate to $1,000 per year
No	Limit spending by candidate per year and per election, amount varies with office
Yes	Committees required to report names of contributors of over $10 & provides for public inspection of reports of names of people who contribute more than $100 per year
Yes	People other than committee or candidate required to report contributions or expenditures over $100 per year
Yes	Provides for public financing of presidential nominating conventions and some campaigns

Citizens for Life with violation of a provision in the Federal Election Campaign Act that prohibited corporations from making donations to political candidates.[116] Citizens for Life, Inc., published a newsletter that urged its readers to vote "pro-life." The newsletter also contained photographs of candidates who supported the organization's pro-life agenda. The Supreme Court held the newsletter did violate the applicable section of the Federal Election Campaign Act[117] but the act, in this case, violated the First Amendment rights of the group. Specifically, the Court ruled that political spending by corporations like Citizens for Life could not be limited. The characteristics of Citizens for Life, Inc. that the Court found significant were (a) the corporation was formed for the express purpose of promoting political ideas, (b) it had no shareholders to claim corporate earnings, (c) it was not established by a business or union, and (d) it did not accept contributions from a business or union.[118]

State Limits on Campaign Finance.   The Federal Election Campaign Act only limits donations supporting candidates for federal office. Some individual states have created similar provisions limiting campaign contributions and/or requiring a report of campaign donations and spending. Massachusetts, for example, had a statute that prohibited banks and other business corporations from spending corporate funds for the purpose of influencing a vote on a referendum unless the referendum related to the business of the corporation. The U.S. Supreme Court ruled that law unconstitutional saying there could be no broad prohibition against political speech by corporations.[119] However, the Supreme Court has upheld some state restrictions on political spending by corporations. In *Austin v. Michigan State Chamber of Commerce,* the Court ruled that a Michigan prohibition against expenditures for or against political candidates was constitutional.[120] The Michigan law that was upheld by the Supreme Court prohibited spending except from segregated funds that were donated or created for political purposes. The Court ruled the law was narrowly tailored to meet a compelling government interest in preventing wealthy organizations from influencing elections or trading contributions for preferential treatment by politicians. Anyone representing a candidate or issue in a state or local election would be well advised to explore local limitations on campaign spending.

Lobbying

The term *lobbying* was coined because people who sought to influence legislators would gather in the lobby of the legislative hall to present their pleas as the legislators passed through on the way to vote. Today, lobbying involves far more sophisticated communication, but the goal is still to influence legislators' votes. Until the Lobbying Registration Act of 1946 there were virtually no legal limitations on the practices of lobbyists. Even today, the act only requires that the lobbyists register and report their activities.[121]

The Lobbying Registration Act defines a lobbyist as anyone who spends more than 20% of his or her time trying to influence policy decisions by the president, the vice president, senior members of the executive branch, senior military officers, congresspeople, senators, or senior members of the legislative staffs.[122] Lobbying itself is defined as any oral or written communication intended to influence policy or legislation on behalf of a principal. The word *principal*, here, is used exactly as described in the discussion of the principal–agent relationship in chapter 11.

Lobbyists are required to register with the Clerk of the House and Secretary of the Senate within 45 days of being hired if they spend more than $20,000 in any 1 year or if they are paid more than $5,000 in 1 year. They must also file semi-annual reports describing the nature of their efforts and identifying the issues and bills they seek to influence. The reports must also identify the branches of government contacted. They are not required to list the names of specific people with whom the lobbyist met. Grassroots lobbying groups and tax-exempt organizations like religious congregations are not required to register. This exemption is quite significant since some of the largest lobbying organizations have religious or moral foci.

For practitioners in the field of public relations, it is important to note that the U.S. Supreme Court has ruled lobbying is limited to direct communications with government officials. Efforts to influence either government officials or public opinion through books, periodicals, and other traditional tools of public relations are not regulated as lobbying.[123]

Although "attempts to saturate the thinking of the community" through the tools of public relations are not regulated,[124] there are some situations in which public relations practitioners and publicists do have to register. Although it does not really address lobbying, the Foreign Agents Registration Act seems worthy of mention. It says agents working for foreign principals must register with the Office of the U.S. Attorney General.[125] This act very specifically includes public relations counsel for foreign companies and governments[126] and publicity agents.[127] The act does exempt foreign news media[128] and diplomatic officials.[129]

Magic Words and Phrases

Advertising	Federal Trade Commission
Affirmative advertising	In commerce
Baby FTC	Injunctions
Bolger Test	Judicial remedies
Bureau of Consumer Protection	Lanham Act
Caveat emptor	Material assertion
Cease and desist order	Puffery
Central Hudson Test	Reasonable consumer
Children's Television Act of 1990	Social conformist
Commercial communication	Substantiation
Consent order	Trade Regulations
Corrective advertising	Unfair commercial practices
Division of Advertising Practices	

Suggested Cases to Read and Brief

Bigelow v. Virginia, 421 U.S. 809 (1975)
Board of Trustees of the State University of New York v. Fox, 492 U.S. 469 (1989)
Bolger et. al. v. Youngs Drug Products Corp., 463 U.S. 60 (1983)
Braun v. Soldier of Fortune, 968 F.2d 1110 (11th Cir.1992) *cert. denied* 506 U.S. 1070 (1993)
Braun v. Armour & Co. 254 N.Y. 514, 173 N.E. 845 (1930)
Capital Broadcasting Co. v. Mitchell, 33 F.Supp 582 (DDC1971)*, aff'd Capital Broadcasting v. Acting Attorney General*, 405 U.S. 1000 (1972)
CBS, Inc. v. Democratic National Committee, 412 U.S. 94 (1973)
Central Hudson Gas & Elect. Corp. v. Public Service Comm'n, 447 U.S. 557 (1980)
City Council v. Taxpayers for Vincent, 466 U.S. 789 (1984)
City of Cincinnati v. Discovery Network, Inc., 507 U.S. 410 (1993)
Eimann v. Soldier of Fortune, 880 F.2d 830 (5th Cir.1989) *cert denied* 493 U.S. 1024 (1990)
Federal Trade Commission v. Bunte Bros., 312 U.S. 349 (1941)
Federal Trade Commission v. Raladam, 283 U.S. 643 (1931)
Federal Trade Commission v. Winsted Hosiery Co., 258 U.S. 483 (1922)
Gertz v. Robert Welch, Inc., 418 U.S. 323, 346 (1974)

Lorillard Tobacco Co. v. Reilly, 533 U.S. 525 (2001)

Marc Kasky v. Nike, Inc., 27 Cal. 4th 939, 968 (2002) 45 P. 3d 243

Metromedia, Inc. v. San Diego, 453 U.S. 490 (1981)

Miami Herald Publishing Co. v. Tornillo, 418 U.S. 241 (1974)

Nike, Inc. v. Kasky, 539 U.S. 654 (2003)

U-Haul International v. Jartran, 793 F.2d 1034 (1986)

Valentine v. Christensen, 316 U.S. 52, 54 (1942)

Virginia State Bd. of Pharmacy v. Virginia Citizens Consumer Council, Inc., 425 U.S. 748 (1976)

Warner-Lambert Co. v. Federal Trade Comm's 562 F.2d 749, 753 (D.C.Cir 1977)

Questions for Discussion

1. Applying the *Bolger* Test, are there any times when an advertisement for a charity could be commercial communication? For example, does an advertisement asking for contributions to "feed starving children" meet the *Bolger* Test definition of commercial communication if the charity making the appeal pays its employees from contributions or if the advertising agency that produced and placed the advertisement is paid a percentage of the contributions it secures?

2. In both *Murdock v. Pennsylvania* and *Jamison v. Texas,* the Supreme Court ruled that advertisements offering religious books for sale were not commercial communication and enjoyed full First Amendment protection. However, in both of these cases, the books were either offered for free or at very low cost. Would the ruling have been the same if the books had been offered at a price that generated a large profit for the advertiser or seller?

3. In the second step of the *Bolger* Test, you are asked if the communication is in the "format of an advertisement." Can a messages that is not in the format of an advertisement be a commercial communication and be subject to regulation? For example, should personal letters written by a soap manufacturer to potential customers be treated as commercial communication? What about editorials or letters to the editor written by a corporate CEO about his or her company's business practices if the objective of the editorial is to improve consumer perception of the company and thereby increase sales?

4. Do you agree that the Supreme Court's rulings on what commercial communication deserves First Amendment protection varies with social pressure or social objectives? Can you find examples in case decisions that argue for the social conformist perspective? Can you find examples that argue against this perspective?

5. If a university wanted to discourage drinking by its students, could the university forbid the student newspaper to carry advertising for bars or liquor stores? Does this meet the *Central Hudson* Test? Could the university prohibit distribution of the paper on its campus if its objective was to discourage underage drinking?

6. Who are qualified plaintiffs under the Lanham Act? What arguments can you make for permitting consumers to be plaintiffs under the act? What arguments can you make for denying consumers the right to sue under the Lanham Act?

7. Find some examples of "puffery" in contemporary advertising. If everyone knows this is just puffery, why do advertisers use it?

8. Traditionally, the U.S. government has provided greater protection for people who are incapacitated or unable to protect themselves. Does the FTC definition of deceptive communication that requires the message to deceive a "reasonable person" violate this principle? Should a consumer who is mentally disabled be able to prosecute an advertiser if he or she really believed a cookie was "baked by elves" and based a purchasing decision on that belief?

9. Under the FTC rules defining unfair business practices, "bait-and-switch" sales tactics have been successfully prosecuted. Bait-and-switch means advertising a low-cost product that either is not available, is in short supply, or is known to be undesirable and then trying to switch consumers to a higher price product when they come to the store. Should "loss-leader" advertising also be prosecuted? Loss-leader advertising is offering a low-cost product for sale to lure customers into a store so that they may buy other higher priced products.

10. Explain the difference between corrective and affirmative advertising. If you represented a product whose advertisements were found to be deceptive by the FTC, would you rather be required to do corrective advertising or affirmative advertising?

11. If you are a manufacturer of soap and your competitor's advertisements falsely say your soap causes premature aging, what remedy would you pursue? What advantages and disadvantages are there to FTC enforcement, Lanham Act suits, and state court suits for fraud?

12. If you are a public relations practitioner and a client pharmaceutical company says they have found a drug that guarantees "eternal youth," how much research must you do before you can write and place a press release saying the drug cures old age?

13. If you are a journalist and you receive the news release saying a drug cures old age, how much research must you do before you can put that release in your newspaper?

Notes

1. *Central Hudson Gas & Elect. Corp. v. Public Service Comm'n*, 447 U.S. 557, 567 (1980).
2. *New York Times Co. v. Sullivan*, 376 U.S. 254, 265 (1964).
3. *Bolger et. al. v. Youngs Drug Products Corp.*, 463 U.S. 60, 65 (1983).
4. *Id.* at 66.
5. *Murdock v. Pennsylvania*, 319 U.S. 105 (1943).
6. *Jamison v. Texas*, 318 U.S. 413 (1943).
7. *Federal Trade Commission v. Raladam*, 283 U.S. 643 (1931).
8. *Ohralik v. Ohio State Bar*, 436 U.S. 447 (1978).
9. *Nike, Inc. v. Kasky*, 539 U.S. 654 (2003).
10. *Id.* at 656.
11. *Marc Kasky v. Nike, Inc.*, 79 Cal. App. 4th 165, 178 (2000).
12. *Id.* at 968.
13. *Id.* at 970.

14. *Id.* at 957.
15. *Nike, Inc. v Kasky*, 539 U.S. 654, 663 (2003).
16. *Id.* at 664.
17. *Bolger v. Youngs Drug Products*, 463 U.S. 60 (1983).
18. *Id.* at 66.
19. *Marc Kasky v. Nike, Inc.*, 27 Cal. 4th 939, 957, 45 P. 3d 243 (2002).
20. *Bolger*, 463 U.S. at 66–67.
21. *Valentine v. Christensen*, 316 U.S. 52, 54 (1942).
22. *Id.* at 55.
23. *Bigelow v. Virginia*, 421 U.S. 809 (1975).
24. *Id.* at 819–820.
25. *Virginia State Bd. of Pharmacy v. Virginia Citizens Consumer Council, Inc.*, 425 U.S 748, 765 (1976).
26. *Lindmark Associates, Inc. v. Township of Willingboro*, 431 U.S. 85 (1977).
27. *Carey v. Population Services International*, 431 U.S. 678 (1977).
28. *Id.* at 686.
29. *Id.*
30. *Id.* at 700.
31. *Central Hudson Gas & Elect. Corp. v. Public Service Comm'n*, 447 U.S. 557 (1980).
32. *Id.* at 564 n.6.
33. *Metromedia, Inc. v. San Diego*, 453 U.S. 490 (1981).
34. *City Council v. Taxpayers for Vincent*, 466 U.S. 789 (1984).
35. *Posadas de Puerto Rico Associates v. Tourism Company of Puerto Rico*, 478 U.S. 328 (1986).
36. *Id.* at 346.
37. *Greater New Orleans Broadcasting Association v. United States*, 527 U.S. 173 (1999).
38. *Board of Trustees of the State University of New York v. Fox*, 492 U.S. 469 (1989).
39. *Id.*
40. *Id.* at 480.
41. *City of Cincinnati v. Discovery Network, Inc.,* 507 U.S. 410 (1993).
42. *Atlanta Journal and Constitution v. City of Atlanta Department of Aviation*, 322 F.3d 1298 (11th Cir.2003).
43. *Roe v. Wade*, 410 U.S. 113 (1973).
44. *Bates v. State Bar of Arizona*, 433 U.S. 350 (1977).
45. The original FTC act was passed on September 26, 1914, as Chapter 311 § 5. It is codified at 15 U.S.C. § 45 (2004).
46. *Federal Trade Commission v. Winsted Hosiery Co.*, 258 U.S. 483 (1922).
47. *Federal Trade Commission v. Raladam*, 283 U.S. 587 (1931).
48. *Id.* at 652.
49. 15 U.S.C.A. § 45 (a)(1) (2004).
50. 15 U.S.C.A. § 45 (m)(l) (2004).
51. 15 U.S.C.A. § 45 (2004).
52. *Federal Trade Commission v. Bunte Bros.*, 312 U.S. 349 (1941).
53. 15 U.S.C.A. §§ 2301–2312 (2004).
54. 15 U.S.C.A. § 45 (a) (2004).
55. Letter to Rep. John Dingell from James Miller, III, October 143, 1983, as reprinted in Appendix to *In re Cliffdale Associates, Inc.*, 103 F.T.C. 110, 174–184 (1984).
56. 15 U.S.C.A. § 57 (a) (1) (B) (2004).

57. 15 U.S.C.A. 45 (b) (2004).
58. *Thompson Medical Co., Inc. V. Federal Trade Comm'n*, 791 F.2d 189, 197 (D.C. Cir. 1986).
59. *Porter & Dietsch v. Federal Trade Comm'n*, 605 F.2d 294, 302 (7th Cir. 1979).
60. See, e.g., *U.S. Healthcare, Inc. v. Blue Cross of Greater Philadelphia*, 898 F.2d 914 (3d Cir.), *cert denied*, 498 U.S. 816 (1990).
61. 15 U.S.C.A. 45 (b) (2004).
62. 15 U.S.C.A. § 45 (m) (2004).
63. *Warner-Lambert Co. v. Federal Trade Comm'n*, 562 F.2d 749, 753 (D.C.Cir 1977).
64. *National Comm'n on Egg Consumption v. Federal Trade Comm'n*, 570 F.2d 157, 159 (7th Cir.1977).
65. See, e.g., *Federal Trade Comm'n v. H.N. Singer, Inc.*, 668 F.2d 1107 (9th Cir. 1982); *Federal Trade Comm'n v. National Business Consultants, Inc.*, 781 F. Sup. 1136 (E.D. La. 1991); and *Warner-Lambert Co. v. Federal Trade Comm'n* 562 F.2d 749, 753 (D.C.Cir 1977).
66. 15 U.S.C.A. § 1125 (a) (1) (2004).
67. See, e.g., *Colligan v. Activities Club of New York, Ltd.*, 442 F.2d 686 (2d Cir, 559), *cert. denied* 404 U.S. 1004 (1971). Compare *Thorn v. Reliance Van Co., Inc.*, 736 F.2d 929 (3d Cir.1984); *Smith v. Montoro*, 648 F.2d 602 (9th Cir.1981).
68. *U-Haul International v. Jartran*, 793 F.2d 1034 (1986).
69. The District Court used two different methods to calculate the award but only one of these methods is relevant to our discussion of the Lanham Act.
70. 15 U.S.C.A. 1117(a) (2004).
71. *Action for Children's Television v. F.C.C.*, 821 F.2d 741, 750 (D.C.Cir.1987).
72. H.R. 3288 100th Cong. 1st Sess. (1987).
73. 47 U.S.C.A. § 303 (2004).
74. H. Rep. No. 385, 101st Cong., 2d Sess. 9–11 (1989).
75. 61 Fed. Reg. 44617 (1996*)*.
76. 61 Fed. Reg. 44617 (1996).
77. 61 Fed. Reg. 44617 (1996).
78. *Lorillard Tobacco Co. v. Reilly*, 533 U.S. 525 (2001).
79. See, *Federation of Advertising Industry Representatives v. City of Chicago*, 189 F.3d 633 (7th Cir. 1999), *cert. denied*, 529 U.S. 1066 (2000) and *Consolidated Cigar Corp. v. Reilly*, 218 F. 3d 30 (1st Cir. 2000).
80. *Lorillard*, 533 U.S. 525.
81. *Capital Broadcasting Co. v. Mitchell*, 33 F.Supp 582 (DDC1971*)*, *aff'd Capital Broadcasting v. Acting Attorney General*, 405 U.S. 1000 (1972).
82. *Virginia State Bd. of Pharmacy v. Virginia Citizens Consumer Council, Inc.*, 425 U.S 748, 765 (1976).
83. *Central Hudson Gas & Elect. Corp. v. Public Service Comm'n*, 447 U.S. 557 (1980).
84. 15 U.S.C.A. §§ 1331–1334 (2004).
85. 15 U.S.C.A. §§ 1338–1339 (2004).
86. See, *Porter & Dietsch v. Federal Trade Comm'n* 605, F.2d 294, 304–307 (7th Cir.1978); *Grolier Inc. v. Federal Trade Comm'n*, 699 F.2d 983, 988 (9th Cir.1983); *Warner-Lambert Co. v. Federal Trade Comm'n*, 562 F.2d 749, 758–759 (D.C.Cir 1977).
87. R.H. Sanders & E.D. Williams, *Why are There So Many Lawyers*? 14 LAW AND SOCIAL INQUIRY 447 (1989).
88. See, e.g., J.S. Auerback, *UNEQUAL JUSTICE: LAWYERS AND SOCIAL CHANGE IN MODERN AMERICA* (Oxford University Press 1978).
89. *Bates v. State Bar of Arizona*, 433 U.S. 350 (1977).

90. *Id.* at 375.
91. Lauren Bowen, *Advertising and the Legal Profession*, 18 THE JUSTICE SYSTEM JOURNAL 47 (1995).
92. Richard B. Schmitt, *Lawyers Try In-Your-Face Pitches*, WALL STREET JOURNAL, Jan. 12, 2001 at B1.
93. *Ohralik v. Ohio State Bar Association*, 436 U.S. 447 (1978).
94. *Peel v. Attorney Registration and Disciplinary Commission of Illinois*, 496 U.S. 91 (1990).
95. *In re Primus*, 436 U.S. 412 (1978); *In re RMJ*, 455 U.S. 191 (1982); *Shapero v. Kentucky Bar Association*, 486 U.S. 466 (1988).
96. See, Erica Iacono, *New Propaganda Evidence Spurs PR Legislation on Hill*, PR WEEK, Jan. 31, 2005, at 1.
97. See, *Delaware L. & W.R. Co. v. Pittinger*, 293 F. 853, 855 (3d Cir.1923).
98. See *United States v. Greenbaum*, 138 F2d 437, 438 (3d Cir.1943); *In re American Home Products Co*rp., 98 F.T.C. 136 (1981).
99. See *Braun v. Armour & Co.* 254 N.Y. 514, 173 N.E. 845 (1930); *Kerby v. Hal Roach Studios*, 53 Cal. App.2d 207, 127 P.2d 577 (1942).
100. *Miami Herald Publishing Co. v. Tornillo*, 418 U.S. 241 (1974).
101. *Chicago Joint Board, Amalgamated Clothing Workers of America, AFL-CIO v. Chicago Tribune Co.*, 435 F.2d 470 (7th Cir.1970), *cert. denied*, 402 U.S. 973 (1971).
102. *CBS, Inc. v. Democratic National Committee*, 412 U.S. 94, 124 (1973).
103. *Gertz v. Robert Welch, Inc.*, 418 U.S. 323, 346 (1974).
104. *Norwood v. Soldier of Fortune*, 651 F.Supp 1397, 1403 (W.D.Ark.1987).
105. *Eimann v. Soldier of Fortune*, 880 F.2d 830 (5th Cir.1989), *cert. denied* 493 U.S. 1024 (1990).
106. *Id.* at 838.
107. *Id.* at 837.
108. *Braun v. Soldier of Fortune*, 968 F.2d 1110 (11th Cir.1992), *cert. denied* 506 U.S. 1070 (1993).
109. *Eimann*, 880 F.2d at 833.
110. *Braun*, 968 F.2d at 1115.
111. 5 U.S.C. § 7323 (2002).
112. 2 U.S.C. § 441b(a) (2002).
113. 2 U.S.C.S. 441a (2002).
114. *Buckley v. Valeo*, 424 U.S. 1(1976).
115. *Federal Election Commission v. Mass. Citizens for Life, Inc.*, 479 U.S. 238 (1986).
116. 2 U.S.C.S. 441b (2002).
117. 2 U.S.C.S. 441b (2002).
118. *Mass. Citizens for Life, Inc.*, 479 U.S. at 264.
119. *First National Bank of Boston v. Belotti*, 435 U.S. 765 (1977).
120. *Austin v. Michigan State Chamber of Commerce*, 494 U.S. 652 (1990).
121. See 2 U.S.C.S. §§ 1602 & 1610 (2002).
122. 2 U.S.C.S. § 1602 (2002).
123. *United States v. Rumely*, 345 U.S. 41 (1953).
124. *Id.* at 47.
125. 22 U.S.C.S. § 612 (1999).
126. 22 U.S.C.S. §611(g) (2002).
127. 22 U.S.C.S. § 611 (h) (2002).
128. 22 U.S.C.S. §611 (2002).
129. 22 U.S.C.S. § 613 (2002).

13

Investor Relations and Financial Press Regulations

A business corporation is organized and carried on primarily for the profit of the stockholders.[1]

Overview
Introduction to Investor Relations
What Are Securities?
What Is a Corporation?
How Is a Corporation Organized and Administered?
Securities Exchange Commission Regulation
State Regulations and Actions
Practice Notes

Overview

Perhaps because communication is so important to establishing the price of securities, investor relations and financial reporting are two of the most lucrative areas of communication practice. Also, in the recent past the legal and ethical misconduct of practitioners in these areas has received significant public attention.

This chapter builds from the information on commercial speech presented in chapter 12. It begins with a very brief introduction to investor relations. It follows with a description of the structure and purpose of corporations and an explanation of how communication practitioners are central to the function and success of corporations. Of course, in this brief chapter we cannot begin to explain all the nuances of corporate structure. We limit the discussion to a brief introduction of corporate structure and an equally brief description of the corporate decision-making procedures that are most affected by mass communications. Continuing this focus on communication by and about corporations, we explain the anti-fraud provisions of the Securities and Exchange Commission's

(SEC's) regulations and summarize recent changes in this area of law, particularly the Sarbanes–Oxley Act. In the practice note at the end of this chapter, we describe potential personal liabilities of financial reporters and practitioners in investment relations.

Introduction to Investor Relations

Stocks or shares of corporations, along with bonds and other records of investments, are called **securities**. Reporting about stocks, advertising the sale of bonds, and communicating about all kinds of securities are important tasks for communication practitioners because communication has an extraordinary impact on the value of the securities themselves. Stocks and bonds differ from most commodities that can be bought or sold because they have no intrinsic value. A purchaser or seller cannot look at a security instrument and decide how valuable it is. The buyer or seller must rely on information about the security to determine what it is worth. Most goods are produced and sold to be consumed and government regulation of communication about those goods is designed to protect consumers and enforce fair business practices. Securities instruments are created only to be sold and they cost virtually nothing to produce. A purchaser must have accurate information to even know what he or she is buying.

Accurate information about securities has a profound impact on their value but delivering accurate information about them is difficult because the language used to describe them is alien to many publics. The language of business is accounting and when describing stocks this language takes two major forms—the profit and loss (P & L) statement and the balance sheet. Grossly oversimplified, the **profit and loss statement** reports revenue, expenses, and income and is based on the mathematical formula:

Revenue − Expenses = Income

Equally simplified, the **balance sheet** describes assets, liabilities, and the net worth of a corporation or other business entity. The balance sheet is based on the formula:

Assets − Liabilities = Net Worth

Although the formulas of the profit and loss statement and balance sheet appear very simple they are subject to interpretation and manipulation and there is extraordinary temptation to misrepresent the information in them. For example, the revenue included in the profit and loss statement includes accounts receivable. Reporting large accounts receivable makes a company look more profitable and may positively influence its stock values. Accounts receivable are debts owed to the company and they may never actually be paid. The decision to include a debt in the profit and loss statement as an account receivable or to omit that debt is just one example of the many communication decisions that must be made by practitioners in investor relations.

What Are Securities?

Just like the Federal Trade Commission only regulates commercial communication, the **Securities and Exchange Commission** only regulates communication about securities.

"Congress, in enacting the security laws, did not intend to provide a broad federal remedy for all fraud."[2] Therefore, before one can understand SEC regulation of communication, one must first be able to identify a security. A **security** is a document that shows a debt or financial obligation. Using this simple definition, think of a personal check written on a local bank account as a security. It is a document you created that shows your promise to pay the amount indicated when it is presented to your bank. However, most securities regulations only address securities that are both much larger than the typical bank check and that are created as a profit-making investment. Security is defined in the Securities Act of 1933 as:

> any note, stock, treasury stock, bond, debenture, evidence of indebtedness, certificate of interest or participation in any profit-sharing agreement, collateral-trust certificate, preorganization certificate or subscription, transferable share, investment contract, voting-trust certificate, certificate of deposit for a security, fractional undivided interest in oil, gas or other mineral rights, or, in general, any interest or instrument commonly known as a "security," or any certificate of interest or participation in, temporary or interim certificate for, receipt for, guarantee of, or warrant or right to subscribe to or purchase, any of the foregoing.[3]

Frankly, this is too much information to be useful. For our purposes, securities are stocks, stock options, stock futures, and investment contracts. **Stocks** are shares or proportionate ownership interests in a corporation.

Even when the security involved is the sale of an entire business, that sale is covered by security regulations if the business ownership was held in the form of shares or stocks in the business.[4] The vast majority of regulated communication about securities addresses concerns about these stocks or shares.

One form of stock or note not considered a security is a note secured by a mortgage on a home. Other documents excluded from the definition of a security include currency and any note that becomes payable within 90 days.

Some of the confusion about what is and what is not a security was resolved by the U.S. Supreme Court in 1990. That year, in *Reves v. Ernst & Young*, the Supreme Court adopted a standard for defining securities that was originally proposed by the Court of Appeals for the Second Circuit.[5] The *Reves* decision dealt with an investment scheme by a cooperative association in Arkansas. The investments were needed to acquire funding for a gasohol plant. The investments were described in the cooperative's newsletter with the language:

> YOUR CO-OP has more than $11,000,000 in assets to stand behind your investments. The Investment is not Federal [sic] insured but it is . . . Safe . . . Secure . . . and available when you need it.[6]

Despite these assurances, the cooperative filed for bankruptcy and left 1,600 investors holding $10 million in worthless notes. Bob Reves was one of several investors who lost money after investing in demand notes. The investors sued Ernst & Young accounting company, claiming the company had misrepresented the financial situation of the

Exhibit 13.1. Family Resemblance Test to Determine What is a Security (From *Bob Reves v. Ernst & Young*, 494 U.S. 56 [1990] and *Chemical Bank v. Arthur Andersen & Co.* 726 F.2d 930 [1984]).

Begin with presumption that any note or paper with a term of more than 90 days is a security unless it is on, or resembles something on, this list:

Mortgage on a home
Short-term note secured by lien on a small business
"Character" or signature loan to a bank
Open account debt incurred in the ordinary course of business

To determine if an item resembles something on the list or should be added to the list ask four questions:

Question	Item is a security if:	Item is not a security if:
What are the motives that would prompt a reasonable seller and buyer to enter into this agreement?	The seller's purpose is to raise money for a business enterprise or to finance substantial investments and the buyer is interested primarily in profit	It is exchanged only to facilitate the purchase and sale of a minor asset or consumer good or to correct short-term cash flow problems
What is the plan for distribution of the instrument?	There is common trading and speculation among a large number of people	It is a private exchange between two people or a very small group of people
What is the reasonable expectation of the investing public?	The public expected it to be protected as a security and based their purchase decisions on such expectations	The public perceived the instrument as a private agreement and not as a security
Is there some factor that reduces the risk of investment and renders the protections of the Securities Acts unnecessary?	There is no factor that reduces the risk	There is a factor (or factors) that significantly reduces the risk to the investing public

cooperative. Reves claimed Ernst & Young had violated provisions of the federal securities laws and Arkansas state securities laws. One of Ernst & Young's defenses was simply to assert that the notes were not securities and therefore the securities regulations did not apply. After the appellate court granted Ernst & Young's motion to dismiss, the U.S. Supreme Court reversed saying the notes did meet the definition of a security and therefore were covered by the securities regulations.

The test used by the Supreme Court to reach this decision, often called the **family resemblance test**, begins with the assumption that any note or document that can be sold or requires a payment more than 90 days beyond its issuance is a security. The test then offers a list of exceptions and says any note or paper that bears a "family resemblance" to something on the list is not a security. The test also includes four steps or questions to ask when trying to determine what is a security.[7] These steps are explained in Exhibit 13.1.

Stock options, puts, and calls are all agreements addressing the future sale of stocks. *Options* are an agreement allowing one party to purchase shares at some future date at a specific price. A *put* is a privilege of delivering, or not delivering, the stock for sale and a *call* is a privilege of calling for or demanding the sale.[8] These agreements are treated as securities and any proposal or offer to sell such agreements are controlled by the regulations we discuss in this chapter. Finally, investment contracts are regulated as securities and are defined as any agreement whereby a "person invests his money in a common enterprise and is led to expect profits solely from the efforts of the promoter or a third party."[9]

Some securities are exempt from regulation. Most notable among these exceptions are obligations issued or guaranteed by the U.S. government and securities that mature in less than 9 months. Therefore, if you are advertising or promoting the purchase of U.S. savings bonds, the communication regulations we discuss here do not apply.

What Is a Corporation?

Most securities are stocks or ownership shares of a corporation so understanding securities requires some understanding of corporations. There are a number of misconceptions about the purpose and legal status of corporations. Knowing why corporations are formed and how they are structured is essential to understanding the need for legal restrictions on communication by and about corporations. Therefore, we present a brief history and description of corporations.

Business and trade organizations that are similar to corporations can be found as far back as the time of Hammurabi, in ancient Greece and in the Roman Empire. But the modern corporation really did not begin until the industrial and trade revolution. By the middle of the 18th century in Britain only the Crown could grant corporate status. This tradition of governmental license influenced the formation of corporate law in the United States, where states still control the formation and recognition of corporations. Early in U.S. history, individual states passed laws permitting incorporation by groups of investors. For example, North Carolina had such a law in 1795 and Massachusetts adopted one in 1799. Initially, these laws only allowed corporations to be formed for purposes beneficial to the public. Usually the corporations were formed to build a bridge, or operate a canal or toll road. In 1837, Connecticut adopted statutes permitting the formation of corporations for "any lawful purpose." This statute is the forerunner of modern corporate structure.

Most **corporations** can be divided into three types: (a) corporations for-profit, (b) not-for-profit corporations, and (c) government-owned corporations, but there are some other forms of corporations. For example, most states require professionals like physicians and attorneys who want to incorporate to do so under professional corporation acts or as "limited corporations" and some industries such as banking and insurance are subject to special statutes. One other form is the close corporation that is only created when there is a very small number of shareholders. Each of these corporation types has its own legal idiosyncrasies and any communication professional reporting on or representing a corporation should consult legal counsel to identify the restrictions associated with specific forms of incorporation. For the purpose of this chapter, we focus on publicly held, for-profit corporations. These tend to be the largest corporations and are the ones subject to the greatest public interest and the most extensive communication regulation.

Simply put, the purpose of for-profit business corporations is to generate and protect wealth for their owners. They are not public interest organizations or quasi-governmental systems. The Supreme Court of Michigan best described the purpose of business corporations when it said:

> A business corporation is organized and carried on primarily for the profit of the stockholders. The powers of the directors are to be employed for that end. The discretion of directors is to be exercised in the choice of means to attain that end and does not extend to a change in the end itself, to the reduction of profits or to the nondistribution of profits among stockholders in order to devote them to other purposes.[10]

In addition to generating income for the shareholders, another major reason for forming a publicly held, for-profit corporation is limiting the liability of shareholders for the corporation's debts. As the individual states adopted and modified their corporate statutes, they gradually limited the liability of corporation owners or shareholders for the debts of the corporation. Today, there are very few instances wherein a shareholder can be held liable to pay any part of a corporate debt. The reciprocal is also true. The corporation cannot be sued or held liable for the personal debts of its shareholders. In effect, the corporation has become a legal "person" with a financial identity independent of its shareholder owners. This status as an independent legal "person" means that the corporation continues to exist even if a shareholder dies and that shareholders may sell their interests in the corporation without affecting the corporation's ability to create contracts, collect obligations, and pay its debts.

Corporations differ from other forms of business enterprise and are attractive systems for organizing business because they insulate owners from business debt and because their shares are transferable. These advantages can be seen when corporation structures are compared to other forms of business. A sole proprietorship is a business run by an individual and a partnership is a business created and managed by a group of individuals who form their relationship through a formal or informal agreement among themselves. Sole proprietors and business partners are usually personally liable for the debts of their business and their business assets can be taken to pay their personal debts. It may be helpful to recall that in our discussion of agent–principal law we explained that partners are all agents of the partnership. In their status as agents of the partnership, partners can create debts and liabilities for the entire partnership. Furthermore, when a sole proprietor dies or leaves his or her business, that business ceases to exist. When any one partner dies or leaves a business, it often forces the other partners to dissolve the partnership and either leave business altogether or reorganize the enterprise.

Because corporations are more permanent than either sole proprietorships or partnerships, they are more attractive to customers and financers. Because corporations do

Exhibit 13.2. Characteristics of Corporations.

- **Created by permission of government.**

- **Legal "person."** It is legally independent of its shareholders and unaffected by retirement or death of owners.

    It can be sued and it can sue.

    It can buy, hold, and sell property in its own name.

    It has constitutional protection like equal protection and due process.

    It has a legal domicile and/or residence.

- **Individual shareholders have no right or duty to manage the corporation.** Collectively, all of the shareholders do have the right to manage the corporation, but only through their actions as a group.

- **Ownership interest is transferable.** Shareholders are free to buy and sell stock.

- **Limited liability of shareholders.** Owners of shares are not obligated to pay the corporation's debts from their private funds.

- **Tax liability.** Since the corporation is a legal "person," it is obligated to pay taxes on its income.

not subject their individual shareholder owners to personal debt liability they are attractive to individual investors. Such individual investors are, of course, a major source of capital investment for the corporation. Because the corporation is a legal "person" and, perhaps, because it insulates its owners from some debts, it must be created by government license or charter and it is subject to extensive government regulation. These regulations not only cover how the corporation is organized, they also cover how the corporation can communicate. We focus on the regulations that limit how those of us in mass communications can talk or write about corporations. In order to understand the limitations on communication, it is necessary to have some basic understanding of how the corporation is owned and how its owners make decisions about how to run the corporation. The characteristics of a corporation are listed in Exhibit 13.2.

How Is a Corporation Organized and Administered?

The person or group who forms a corporation is called a *promoter*. The promoter usually discovers a business or an idea that can be profitably developed. He or she recruits people willing to invest in the corporation, helps create the initial corporate bylaws, and arranges to have the corporation licensed. Those initial investors are the first shareholders. Shareholders own a "share" of the corporation in proportion to their investment in its creation. It is those shares that can later be purchased and sold as stock. The prices at which the shares are sold help determine the value of the corporation.

The shares not only determine how much of the corporation the individual shareholders own, they also determine the magnitude of control the individual shareholders have in the administration of the corporation. When the most important decisions are made in a corporation, the shareholders vote to make those decisions. In these corporate elections one share equals one vote, so the larger the number of shares or the larger portion of the corporation an individual owns, the greater his or her voice in the operation of the corporation. For the sake of simplicity, we limit our discussion here to common stock. Preferred stock and other classes of stocks may be treated differently.

Share ownership in a corporation is important for two reasons. First, owning a share entitles a shareholder to a portion of the corporation's profits and second owning a share entitles a shareholder to a voice in the corporation's decision making. Communication by and to shareholders, therefore, is important because it can influence both the distribution of money and the allocation of power. Money and power are the source of many disagreements and influencing the distribution of money and power creates extraordinary temptations to use communication to deceive and to manipulate others. Almost all regulation of communication about corporations is designed to control this temptation and to force accurate disclosure of information.

How Decisions Are Made

The individual shareholders of the corporation do not have a right to manage the business of the corporation simply because they own shares of the enterprise. Having all the shareholders of a major corporation participate in all decisions would simply be too cumbersome and inefficient. Generally, the shareholders are only asked about major decisions that involve some change in their ownership interest like dissolution or merger and to select a board of directors. The day-to-day management of the corporation is entrusted to a board of directors so the selection of the board is one of the most important decisions in corporate management.

The shareholders make their collective decisions by "voting their shares" in special elections or at an annual meeting. The corporate elections are analogous to political elections except that they follow the principle of one share–one vote. The more shares a shareholder owns the more influential his or her vote in corporate decision making. It should also be noted that there are variations in how shares can be voted. Straight voting is common but many corporations also use a system called cumulative voting in which each shareholder may have multiple votes depending on how many members of the board of directors are being elected. There may also be variations in voting rights based on classes of shares, voting trusts, and voting agreements, none of which would be permissible in traditional political elections.

Because the shareholders must vote to decide how the corporation is administered and to choose the board that will manage the corporation, the availability of accurate information about corporate affairs is essential. Only well-informed shareholders are in a position to select the best board and to choose board members who reflect the shareholders' views of how the corporation should be administered.

Typically, the board of directors is elected at annual shareholders' meetings. At these meetings, the shareholders are also usually asked to approve the corporation's independent auditors, to ratify stock option plans for management, and to vote on shareholder proposals. Most states follow the **Model Business Corporations Act** (MBCA), which specifies that annual shareholder meetings must be held at a time and place specified by the corporation's bylaws. These meetings may be held anywhere permitted by the bylaws. Some corporations hold the meetings in the city where their headquarters are located. Some rotate the meeting locations for the convenience of the shareholders and some even hold meetings in deliberately inconvenient locations to discourage attendance. Under the MBCA, other meetings for elections can be called if 10% of the shareholders request the meeting. Such meetings are often called to remove a director or an entire board of directors when the shareholders are unhappy with the corporation's performance. One function of communication in these elections is the distribution of notice that ensures all shareholders are given the opportunity to vote.

Obviously, not all shareholders can physically attend shareholder meetings to vote their shares. These individuals may not vote or they may select a proxy. A **proxy** is someone appointed by the shareholder to vote for him or her at the shareholder meeting. Often, the current board of directors will ask shareholders to allow them to vote their shares. These and similar requests, including requests by those who oppose the existing board, are called **proxy solicitations**. A major function of communication in shareholder elections is the solicitation of proxies. Communication regarding these solicitations is heavily regulated.

Those in mass communications may be called on to produce the documents and other communications used to encourage stock purchases, to report the activities of the corporation, and to influence the elections that determine how corporations will be managed. Both state and federal laws regulate these communications activities. Obviously, those in the subfields of investor relations or financial reporting must be familiar with these regulations.

Securities Exchange Commission Regulation

One of the most significant economic disasters in U.S. history was the stock market crash of 1929. Students of the crash have identified two major reasons for this breakdown in the economic fabric of the country. First, investors lacked the information they needed to make informed decisions about the purchase and sale of securities. Second, the claims about securities' values being made by sellers were dishonest. These claims were so out of control that some sellers were even able to sell stock in companies that did not exist.

To prevent another economic collapse, the U.S. Congress considered two options. These options were called merit registration and the disclosure scheme. **Merit registration** had been adopted by some states and required any seller of securities to secure approval from the government before the stocks were sold. The government would appoint auditors or analysts to determine if the stocks were actually worth the proposed sale price. Stocks not deemed to be good investments simply could not be sold. This approach assumed that individual investors were not sophisticated enough to distinguish between good and bad investments.

The **disclosure scheme** assumed individual investors could make intelligent decisions about how to invest their money if they were given enough accurate information.

Basically, it assumes investors need government help to obtain information but that investors do not need government help to evaluate the information or to make actual investment decisions. Based on the disclosure scheme, Congress enacted the Securities Act of 1933 and the Securities Exchange Act of 1934.[11] These two acts are the foundation of all current investor relations regulation. They have three basic objectives, all of which are based on an **affirmative duty to disclose** important information. The objectives are

1. To require disclosure of relevant information about a security (stock or share) and the corporation itself to allow investors to make intelligent and informed investment decisions.
2. To impose liability on those who fail to fully disclose relevant information or who give false or misleading information.
3. To require registration of issuers, insiders, professional sellers, and securities exchanges.

In 1940, two additional acts were passed. The Investment Company Act added a requirement for the registration of publicly owned companies that engage in investing and trading securities, and the Investment Advisers Act required registration and regulation of people selling advice about investments.

Although it may seem that the regulation of communication about securities is very similar to the FTC regulation of communication about commercial products, there is a profound difference. The FTC prohibits the distribution of false or misleading information while securities regulations actually requires disclosure of unfavorable information. By analogy, if the securities regulation requirements were imposed on advertising of all commercial products it would create a requirement that companies actually run negative advertising describing the weaknesses and potential problems with their products. When communicating about securities one must not only tell the truth, one must actually volunteer negative information. It is this requirement to volunteer negative information that is called the affirmative duty to disclose.

A Note on Rules, Regulations, and Statutes

As you read the descriptions of regulations and laws that restrict communication about securities and investor relations, it may be helpful to note that those practicing in this area of law have adopted an odd nomenclature to describe laws and regulations. Here, we occasionally use the word *rule* followed by a section number. Statutes are usually identified as *Acts* and when they are organized into codes, statutes are identified with their title, chapter, and section. Regulations that are created by administrative agencies authorized by statutes are divided into titles, parts, and sections. The word *rule* is not usually used to identify any federal law or regulation.

The Securities Act of 1933 and Securities Exchange Act of 1934 appear in the U.S. Code in Title 15, Chapter 2A and Chapter 2B, respectively. Chapter 2A begins with Section 77a and ends with Section 77aa. Chapter 2B begins with Section 78a and ends with

Section 78mm. Many of these sections are worded as they were in the original 1933 and 1934 act but the section numbers do not correspond. However, the section numbers in the Code of Federal Regulations in Title 17, Part 240 do have section numbers that correspond with the original 1933 and 1934 act. The word "rule" is used in this area of practice to refer to sections within Title 17, Part 240 of the Code of Federal Regulations and to sections within the original Securities Act of 1933 and Securities Exchange Act of 1934. For example, Rule 10b-5, refers to 17 C.F.R. 240.10b-5 in the Code of Federal Regulations and to Section 10b-5 of the Securities Exchange Act of 1934. However, as of this writing, the same provision or "rule" is found in the U.S. Code at 17 U.S.C. 77j.

Fraud, Deception, and Manipulation

Most of the specific prohibitions of the Securities Act of 1933 and the Securities Exchange Act of 1934 grow from the duty for affirmative disclosure and the prohibitions against fraud, deception, and manipulation of the securities markets. The provision of the Securities Exchange Act that most broadly covers these prohibitions is Rule 10b-5.[12] Rule 10b-5 is summarized in Exhibit 13.3. Other language prohibiting any deception or manipulation of the market can be found in Rule 14a, Rule 14e, and Rule 15c-1.[13] However, because Rule 10b-5 is the most all-encompassing of these provisions, we focus on its requirements in the hope that anyone communicating about securities who avoids violating this provision will also avoid violation of any of the more specific provisions. Of course, this information cannot substitute for the advice of qualified legal counsel.

In Connection with the Purchase of Sale of any Security

Under this regulation it is illegal to say or do anything that could deceive someone considering a stock purchase. The language is so broad it not only prohibits deception, it affirmatively requires the communicator to provide damaging information. Even though the regulation's language is broad, the courts have given the rule even broader

---

Exhibit 13.3.   Securities Exchange Act Rule 10b-5 (See, 17 C.F.R. 240.10b-5 [2003]).

It shall be unlawful for any person, directly or indirectly, by the use of any means or instrumentality of interstate commerce, or of the mails, or of any facility of any national securities exchange

> To employ any device, scheme, or artifice to defraud,

> To make any untrue statement of a material fact or to omit to state a material fact necessary in order to make the statements made, in the light of circumstances under which they were made, not misleading, or

> To engage in any act, practice, or course of business which operates or would operate as a fraud or deceit upon any person

In connection with the purchase or sale of any security.

■

application. For example, the regulation, on its face, would appear to apply only to communication about the sale or purchase of a security. Of course, this includes offers to sell or buy stock and such negotiations as bids to take over an entire corporation. It also covers much more than these very specific communications about stock purchases or sales. The courts have said that any information about a corporation whose stocks are in the market can influence stock prices and therefore any such information is "in connection with the purchase or sale of" a security. An example of a prosecution under Rule 10b-5 that is particularly applicable in the field of mass communications is the case of *Texas Gulf Sulfur*.

In 1963 and 1964, Texas Gulf Sulfur discovered copper and silver ore on property it owned in Canada. The company began purchasing more land in the area and a report of the exploration and land purchases appeared in *The New York Times* on April 11, 1964. Texas Gulf Sulfur responded to *The New York Times* article by issuing a press release on April 12, 1964. The press release did not specifically say there were no valuable minerals on the land but described the earlier *New York Times* article as a rumor and said that analysis of the site was not complete. The SEC brought an action against officers of Texas Gulf Sulfur and the Court of Appeals ruled the press release did violate the requirements of Rule 10b-5.[14] The ruling is extensive and involves several issues. It includes a statement that the failure to completely disclose that the mine site showed extraordinary promise as a source of copper and silver operated as fraud or deceit.[15] The court also said that because the press release was issued by a publicly traded corporation the information could influence stock prices and this was enough to be "in connection with the purchase or sale of any security."[16] All mass communications professionals could be similarly liable if they profit from knowingly misstating or failing to state completely information that would lead a reasonable investor to change a stock purchase or sale decision.

To Omit to State a Material Fact

Rule 10b-5 not only prohibits actions that would deceive, like deliberate misstatements or lying about a stock's value, it also imposes the affirmative duty to disclose information. Whenever a mass communications professional representing a corporation issues any statement about the corporation's stock, value, or business future, he or she not only has to avoid misstatements, he or she must also volunteer negative information. With this requirement one might assume there are times when it is best simply not to say anything at all but the SEC rules prohibit even the strategy of silence. Sections 12, 13, and 14 of the Securities Exchange Act of 1935 require an annual report, a quarterly report, and a report for any month in which a significant change in the corporation's management, finances, or income potential changes. The requirement for these reports has been expanded and the penalties for errors in the reports were made more severe by the recent Sarbanes–Oxley Act. That act is described in more detail later in this chapter.

Penalties for failing to make these reports or for making false statements in the reports can be severe. For example, under the Securities Exchange Act §18 "any person who makes or causes to be made, a false or misleading statement in any report" can be held liable for the losses of any other person who buys stocks in reliance on that information. In other words, although it is usually the corporation that "pays for the mistake," a mass communications professional who actually makes the report could be held personally liable for misstatements that motivate stock sales or purchases.

In 1964, Belock Instrument Corporation produced several reports and news releases that described high corporate profits. These reports failed to include the information that much of the corporation's profits came from overcharging the U.S. government for contracts with federal agencies. Shareholders who purchased stock based on these favorable reports later sued Belock and some of its agents and employees when the stock prices fell after the government discovered the overcharges. The Court of Appeals ruled that Belock and its agents were liable for the investors' losses even though the intent of the misstatements was to defraud the government, not to defraud the investors.[17]

What Does "To Defraud" Mean?

Rule 10b-5 prohibits the use of any device, scheme, or artifice to defraud. At law, **fraud** means "an intentional perversion of the truth for the purpose of inducing another to part with something of value."[18] Put another way, fraud is delivering false information in order to make a profit.

Insider Trading.   **Insider trading** is the classic example of fraud or deceit in investment communication. It is also the form of securities fraud or deceit most often committed or confronted by mass communications professionals. Insider trading refers to the use of information only available to those inside an organization to guide purchasing or sale decisions. In *Speed v. Transamerica Corp.*,[19] a U.S. District Court described insider trading. The court said:

> It is unlawful for an insider, such as a majority stockholder, to purchase the stock of a
> minority stockholder without disclosing material facts affecting the value of the stock,
> known to the majority stockholder by virtue of his inside position but not known to
> the selling minority stockholder, which information would have affected the judgment
> of the sellers.[20]

Insider trading, therefore, does not require some private exchange of information between those inside the corporation and those outside the organization. Officers or employees of a corporation who base their own stock purchase or sale decisions on information they have because of their confidential relationship with the corporation are guilty of insider trading.

One of the first examples of a prosecution for insider trading came during World War II when corporate officers of Ward LaFrance Truck Company purchased shares of their own corporation in the "over-the-counter" market without revealing that they knew there would be a substantial improvement in the company's earnings. They did not lie or deliver false information; they simply failed to share the fact that the company's fortunes were improving. The SEC ruled that this failure to disclose would operate to deceive those who sold the stock.[21]

It is not uncommon for mass communications professionals to have similar inside information. Public relations or advertising professionals are often given information to help them prepare releases, advertisements, or reports. Until this information is actually published and available to the public, it is insider information. In 1980, an employee of a printer was doing the markup of documents to be distributed to shareholders proposing a merger. Although his employer masked the names of the companies until the night before the documents were to be distributed, the employee was able to determine the names of the companies and purchase stock in the company being acquired. After the stock prices went up following the merger, he sold the stocks. The trial court rendered judgment against him and that judgment was upheld by the court of appeals. The U.S. Supreme Court reversed saying the insider "duty arises from a specific relationship."[22] The printer's employee did not have a legal relationship with the trading companies, therefore his information was not "insider" information. By implication, this means that because management of a company, public relations counsel for the company, or the company's advertising agency have a legal relationship with the company, they could all be held liable for insider trading if they make a stock purchase based on information given them because of their relationship with the company.

In *Dirks v. S.E.C.*,[23] the SEC prosecuted an employee of a company that was misrepresenting its income. The employee gave the information to shareholders and even sent a release to a newspaper that declined to print the story. The trial court and court of appeals rendered judgment against the employee for violating Rule 10b-5 because some of the people to whom he gave the information based purchase and/or sale decisions on the insider information. Judgment against him was reversed by the U.S. Supreme Court because his motivation was to expose fraud rather than to defraud. The Court noted particularly that he did not himself buy or sell stock based on the information and therefore did not make money with the information. The Court also noted his attempt to make the information public by giving it to a newspaper. The fact that the Supreme Court considered Dirks' motivation or intent suggests that a deliberate intention to misuse information may be a required element of insider trading.

Can You Accidentally "Defraud"?   If fraud involves the communication of false information or the failure to share important information, can a person accidentally commit fraud or is the intention to misuse information a required element? For example, can a reporter who is given information by a reliable source commit fraud if he or she repeats that information in print? More to the point here, could a public relations professional commit fraud if he or she included information in a press release that was provided by the corporation? The courts have wrestled with similar questions and concluded that an essential element of fraud is scienter or knowledge. In order to commit fraud or to violate Rule 10b-5, the communicator must know that the information he or she is delivering is not true or does not include all the material facts. When reversing a judgment against a brokerage manager who failed to correct the misstatements of employees, the U.S. Supreme Court said, "Scienter is a necessary element of a violation of section 10(b)5."[24] In another place in the same case, the Court defined scienter as "[a]n intent on the part of the defendant to deceive, manipulate, or defraud."[25] It might appear one cannot accidentally commit fraud or violate Rule 10b-5 while using information from a reliable source.[26] However, the U.S. Supreme Court in *Aaron* did say that it had no reason to determine whether the requirement for scienter could be met if a defendant was simply reckless in his or her pursuit of the truth. That question has only been addressed by the courts of appeal.

In *Sanders v. Nuveen*, the Seventh Circuit Court of Appeals reviewed a 10b-5 action against an underwriter who had honestly relied on the inaccurate statements by his certified public accountant (CPA). In its decision, the court said, "In certain areas of the law recklessness is considered to be a form of intentional conduct."[27] Elsewhere, in the same case, the court said it could find enough intent or scienter on the part of the defendant if he either knew or "with the exercise of reasonable care" could have known that the information given him by the CPA was false.[28] Later, the court actually described the kind of recklessness that would be enough to justify a ruling against a defendant who honestly relied on false information given him or her by another. The court said a defendant whose conduct was "highly unreasonable and . . . an extreme departure from the ordinary standard of care"[29] could be held liable for violating Rule 10b-5. For reporters, public relations practitioners, and advertising professionals alike, everyone who deals with investor relations has a duty to verify information carefully before making it public.

Proxy Solicitations

The SEC's prohibitions against fraud and requirements for affirmative disclosure not only apply to communication in connection with the purchase or sale of any security, the same prohibitions against deception and the affirmative duty to disclose information are imposed on communication about the governance of the corporation. Because many shareholders in large corporations cannot attend shareholder meetings to vote, the government of a corporation is often at the mercy of proxy solicitations. Section 14 of the Securities Exchange Act makes it unlawful for a registered corporation to solicit proxies from its shareholders unless those solicitations contain full disclosure.

What Is False or Misleading?

Rule 10b-5 deals with the requirement for disclosure in the sale or transfer of stock ownership. Rule 14a deals with the requirement for disclosure in proxy solicitations. The elements of Rule 14a actions are listed in Exhibit 13.4. Whereas Rule 10b-5 provides

---

Exhibit 13.4.   Elements or Cause of Action under Section 14(a) (See, *Epic Enterprises, Inc. v. Brothers*, 395 F. Supp. 773, 775 [N.D. Okla. 1975]; *Jacobs v. Airlift International, Inc.*, 440 F. Supp. 540, 542 [S.D. Fla. 1977]).

A proxy solicitation,

That contains false or misleading statement or omission,

The statement or omission is material, and

The statement or omission causes injury to the plaintiff.

---

a defense for a communicator who honestly relies on the statements of others, Rule 14a provides no such defense. For example, in the case of *Dasho v. Susquehanna Corp.*, the U.S. Court of Appeals for the Seventh Circuit ruled, "Knowledge of the falsity or misleading character of a statement and a bad faith intent to mislead or misrepresent are not required to prove a violation of the statute upon which a civil remedy for damages will lie."[30] In that case, some of the defendants relied on representations from their accounting firm and a history of stock values to describe the financial advantages of a merger. The description appeared in their proxy solicitation asking shareholders to allow them to vote for the proposed merger. Although they did not actually know what they said was not true, the court ruled they could be held liable. The court did not impose the requirement for a highly unreasonable departure from an ordinary standard of care described in *Sanders v. Nuvey*.[31] The court said that in a proxy statement all that had to be shown was a "lack of diligence . . . or negligent conduct."[32]

The circuit courts seem to believe that a corporation must have knowledge of its situation and its agents and therefore cannot be ignorant. The Seventh Circuit Court of Appeals in *Dasho* found that lack of diligence or negligent conduct was enough to justify a ruling against someone soliciting proxies. The Second Circuit also has said, "Negligence alone either in making a misrepresentation or in failing to disclose a material fact in connection with proxy solicitation is sufficient to warrant recovery."[33] In short, simply being sloppy in checking your facts can lead to liability when drafting or issuing a proxy solicitation.

What Is Material?

Information is material if it would have an effect on the voting decision of the person whose proxy is solicited. However, it is not necessary to show that the misstatement actually caused the person solicited to vote one way or the other.[34] In fact, the U.S. Supreme Court has ruled that a statement or omission could be material if "it *might* have been considered important by a reasonable shareholder who was in the process of deciding how to vote" [emphasis added].[35] It would appear any kind of information that might influence a shareholder to vote could be material. The only real exception to this very broad definition of what is material is a ruling that says information that would influence shareholders whose votes were not necessary is not material. Applying this rule in *Virginia Bankshares v. Sandberg*,[36] the U.S. Supreme Court addressed a case where the group of shareholders who prepared a proxy solicitation was so large that their votes alone could carry the election. In that context, the Court ruled information that would mislead the minority shareholders was not material. It appears the definition of what is material depends on whether the misrepresentation or omission of the information could actually influence the outcome of an election.

A great many topics have been found to be material. Exhibit 13.5 lists 11 of these topics. They include such vague concepts as the honesty or character of the person or group soliciting the proxy and such concrete information as an explanation of how prices and values used in the solicitation were calculated.

Exhibit 13.5. Subjects Included in Proxy Solicitations (From *Central Foundry Co. v. Gondelman*, 166 F. Supp. 429 [S.D.N.Y. 1958]; *Gerstle v. Gamble-Skogmo Inc.*, 478 F.2d 121 [2d Cir. 1973]; *Dillon v. Berg*, 326 F.Supp. 214 [D. Del. 1971], *aff'd per curium*, 453 F.2d 867 [3d Cir. 1971]; *Swanson v. American Consumer, Inc.*, 415 F.2d 1326 [7th Cir. 1969]; *Scott v. Multi-Amp Corp.*, 386 F. Supp. 44 [D.N.J. 1974]; *Norte & Co. v. Huffines*, 304 F.Supp. 1096 [S.D.N.Y. 1968]; *Gruss v. Curtis Publishing Co.*, 361 F. Supp 58 [S.D.N.Y. 1973, *revd* 534 F2d 1396; 1976]; *Dasho v. Susquehanna Corp.*, 461 F.2d 11 [7th Cir. 1972], *cert. denied*, 408 U.S. 925 [1972]; *Union Pac. Col. v. Chicago & N.W.Ry. Co.*, 226 F. Supp. 400 [N.D. Ill. 1964]; *SEC v. Okin*, 58 F. supp. 20 [SD.N.Y. 1944]).

The following subjects have been required to be reported accurately in proxy solicitations:

- The character of the person soliciting the proxy.

- Future plans of those soliciting the proxy.

- Description of the directors proposed in the proxy.

- Positions as directors or board members in other corporations.

- Conflicts of interest among the proposed directors.

- Any current litigation.

- The minority shareholder's right to secure an appraisal.

- An explanation of the price, including any premium, paid for acquiring shares of a target corporation in a merger or takeover.

- The value of the stock acquired in past or proposed merger or takeover.

- The earnings and financial condition of the corporation(s) involved.

- Any allegation that any corporate assets have been wasted or of excess payments to directors or others.

Waiting Periods and Preclearance Rules

Regulation of communication about securities is so extensive that some rules appear to violate the First Amendment prohibition against prior restraint. For example, when proxy solicitations ask for approval to vote for anything more than shareholder proposals or the routine actions of approving accounting statements or election of corporate officers they must be filed with the SEC 10 days before they are to be mailed to shareholders.[37] During this 10-day **preclearance** period, the SEC can review the proxy solicitation and recommend changes. Although the SEC does not actually censor the solicitation, the 10 days of review can produce recommendations or outright threats of action that have the same effect. Similar, although certainly not identical, requirements are imposed on proposals for the sale of stocks in a new company or newly incorporated company and for "take-over bids." Take-over bids are proposals to buy stocks that would result in one person or group owning more than 5% of the controlling interest in a corporation.

Informal Rules and Private Rights of Action

Obviously, a massive body of very detailed rules governs communication about securities, but even a thorough knowledge of the formal rules cannot adequately prepare a communication practitioner for investor relations work. The SEC often communicates its views or requirements in the form of "releases." These documents, somewhat like traditional public relations news releases, state the Commission's views or policies and are distributed to the news media, companies, securities traders, and others. In addition to its "releases," the SEC will also issue "no-action letters." **No-action letters** are responses to an individual investor or trader's private inquiry. They are called no-action letters because typically the private inquiry describes how an investor or trader plans to conduct his or her business. The letter then says that if the transaction is conducted as described the Commission will take no action. In effect, the Commission is saying it will not object to or take action to prevent the transaction described by the investor or trader.

The SEC is not the only party whose action or lack of action is important to investor relations practitioner. Private investors can sue for misconduct or fraud. Courts have ruled that SEC rules, particularly Rule 10b-5, were created to protect the investing public and that any private person whose interests are damaged by a violation of the rules has a right to sue.[38] This **private right of action** applies both to misstatements involving stock sales and to fraudulent or inaccurate statements in proxy solicitations.[39] However, not just anyone can sue for violations of Rule 10b-5. The plaintiff must be an owner, purchaser, or seller of stock because only those people actually involved in the sale or corporate management can be legally injured by inaccurate communication about the company or its stocks.[40]

Sarbanes–Oxley Act

In Fall 2001, Enron was found to have violated the trust of its shareholders. Later scandals involving WorldCom, Tyco, ImClone, Adelphia, Global Crossing, and others became public. Thereafter, a number of other corporations issued earnings restatements. These restatements, in effect, said the companies had overreported the profits they expected to make. Although earning restatements are not novel, it was the number of corporations issuing such restatements that really frightened the investing public. The increasing number of earnings restatements are shown in Exhibit 13.6.

The combination of corporate scandal and the increasing number of earnings restatements led to a serious loss of investor confidence that, at least in part, led to a dramatic drop in stock prices. In late July 2002, Congress adopted the **Sarbanes–Oxley Act**. The extent of the pressure on Congress can be seen in the speed and near unanimity with which the act passed. The Senate passed the bill by a vote of 99 to 0 and the vote in the House of Representatives was 423 to 3.

The Sarbanes–Oxley Act has as its goal the promotion of full, fair, timely, and accurate disclosure. In effect, it seeks to guarantee the transparency sought by the original

Exhibit 13.6. Earnings Restatements prior to Sarbanes–Oxley [Troy A. Paredes, *F. Hodge O'Neal Corporate and Securities Law Symposium: After the Sarbanes-Oxley Act: The Future of the Mandatory Disclosure System*, 81 Wash. U.L.Q 229, 230 [2003].)

Year	Earnings Restatements Issued
1997	116
1998	158
1999	234
2000	258
2001	305

Securities Exchange Act. Provisions of the Sarbanes–Oxley Act include mandating new disclosure requirements, tougher penalties for securities fraud, and a requirement that corporate officers certify the accuracy of financial statements. The act also created a new Public Company Accounting Oversight Board.

Some provisions of the Sarbanes–Oxley Act may indirectly impact communications practitioners. These provisions include an extension of the statute of limitations for private rights of action and stiffer criminal penalties. The extended statute of limitations makes it easier for shareholders who are victims of deceptive communication to sue communications professionals. The stiffer criminal penalties would impact those investor relations practitioners whose conduct is truly egregious. We do not address these changes in detail because we assume our readers will not intentionally violate the requirements for honest disclosure of financial information.

The provisions of the Sarbanes–Oxley Act that seem most worthy of note for honest investor relations communicators are the increased requirements for disclosure and a change in the rules for dealing with one-time expenses or income. The disclosure requirements have been expanded to now require specific descriptions of loans to corporate officers, and publication of reports each time there is some significant change in the corporation's financial situation. Loans to corporate officers must be reported largely because granting and forgiving such loans was a strategy that precipitated some of the corporate scandals and investor losses of the late 1990s and early 2000s.

Quarterly reports, called 10-Q reports, were required prior to Sarbanes–Oxley. The new report, called an **8-K report**, is required each time there is a significant change in the corporation's income, losses, or business within a quarter. The goal of these reports is to keep investors constantly apprised of changes in the corporation's financial potential. Section 409 of the Sarbanes–Oxley Act says that the corporation should disclose "on a rapid and current basis, . . . additional information concerning material changes in the financial condition or operations of the issuer." This provision suggests that any change in the financial conditions or operation of a corporation that could impact an investing decision should be disclosed immediately.

Historically, the financial portion of corporate reports has followed a set of rules called Generally Accepted Accounting Principles (GAAP). However, expense and income that are not recurring are often reported in ways that do not follow these principles. Perfectly honest accountants may have separated out these expense or income items because they do not help accurately predict the long-term financial performance of a company. This practice of treating some financial information differently is called "pro-forma accounting." Pro-forma accounting has been used by some accountants to hide debt or to exaggerate the financial potential of a corporation. Under the provisions of Sarbanes–Oxley, any pro-forma figure must not contain any untrue statement or omit any material facts. Pro-forma figures must also be reconciled back into the GAAP report.

Some investor relations practitioners may resist the provisions of the Sarbanes–Oxley Act. The act does make their job more difficult and complex, but its provisions, when properly understood and uniformly applied, simply add to the information available to guide investment decisions.

State Regulations and Actions

Although most discussions of securities law focuses on the federal SEC, state laws also impact communication about securities. In 1996, the federal government did preempt significant areas of state securities regulation with the "National Securities Markets Improvement Act"; however, each of the 50 states has some system for regulating communication about business ventures in its jurisdiction. More than 30 states have adopted a **uniform securities act**.[41] Even with this uniform act, securities laws still vary widely from state to state but most prohibit fraud and require registration of securities, stockbrokers, and dealers in securities. Of course, any communications practitioner should consult an attorney who is familiar with his or her state's specific regulations but it can be noted that most state anti-fraud provisions are patterned after Rule 10b-5. That rule's very broad definition of fraud covers virtually every imaginable misstatement or omission.

In addition to a state's securities laws or regulations, its citizens may also be able to pursue a common law action in fraud against any communications practitioner who uses his or her skills to manipulate investing decisions. Fraud is a common law remedy. In order to win an action in fraud a plaintiff must be able to prove:

there was a false representation of facts
the facts were known, or could have been known by the defendant
the defendant knew the assertion was false or that he or she asserted it was true
    without knowing whether or not it was true.
the defendant intended the plaintiff to act on the false information
the plaintiff actually did act in reliance on the false information
the plaintiff suffered some damage that was caused by the misrepresentation.[42]

It should be noted that the requirements for common law fraud look very similar to the requirements for a Rule 10b-5 violation. One major difference is that fraud requires an affirmative statement. In other words, unlike Rule 10b-5, there is no common law penalty for omitting important information unless the defendant makes some assertion that his or her communication contains all the pertinent information. In this respect, fraud is more difficult to prove than a Rule 10b-5 violation. However, in another respect, fraud may be easier to prove. For fraud, there is no requirement to prove intent to deceive. In other words, if the defendant knew or could have known the information disseminated was not true and only expected people to act on it, then the plaintiff does not have to prove that the defendant actually intended to deceive the plaintiff. Many states do not require this level of intent; some do not even require that the defendant knew the information delivered was not true.[43]

Practice Notes

One of the arguments against professional licensing for communications professionals is that such a license would subject the practitioner to a higher standard of legal liability. Accountants, because they are members of a recognized profession, can be held legally liable for deviation from generally accepted accounting standards or principles. For those in investor relations or business reporting there is no such standard and therefore they are not usually susceptible to suits for failing to perform. However, they can be legally liable for violating their duties to their employers and their contractual obligations.

Public relations or advertising practitioners may be held liable for deviation from their professions' standards. They often have access to insider information when they prepare proxy solicitations and reports. It may be more difficult to understand that journalists can be legally liable for coverage of investment news. Under a principle called **misappropriation theory**, journalists have been held liable for the misuse of information about securities or corporations.

As early as 1961, there were administrative rulings from the SEC holding brokers and others outside of corporate structure responsible for insider trading.[44] However, in 1980 it appeared that the U.S. Supreme Court stopped that trend with its decision in *Chiarella v. U.S.*[45] In *Chiarella*, which was discussed earlier in this chapter, the Court ruled that only people who were in some financial relationship with a corporation were "insiders," and that only such insiders could be charged with violation of Rule 10b-5.[46] The Court ruled Chiarella was not liable for insider trading even though he essentially stole the information he used to make his stock purchases.

Since 1980, several circuit court cases, including one decision that the U.S. Supreme Court refused to review, have found ways to hold "outsiders" liable for deception or manipulation of information associated with stock sales. This line of cases is based on a concept called misappropriation theory and the theory has been used to support convictions of reporters in the financial media who leak confidential information or who misuse information obtained in their profession. Misappropriation theory is based on the duty of the reporter or other corporate outsider to protect confidential information given him or her by an employer.

The U.S. Court of Appeals for the Second Circuit first applied misappropriation theory in a prosecution for violation of the Securities Exchange Act in *U.S. v. Newman*.[47] James Newman's co-conspirators were employed by Morgan Stanley and Kuhn Loeb. They gave Newman information that had been entrusted to them by their employers. Newman then passed the information on to confederates who used foreign bank accounts to purchase stocks in companies that were the targets of merger or takeover by clients of Morgan Stanley. Because of the inside information, Newman knew that the value of these stocks would soon increase and could be sold for a significant profit. One of the charges against Newman was that he had violated Rule 10b-5. He argued that he was not an "insider" and had no duty to the people from whom the stock was purchased. The District Court dismissed the indictment against him but the Court of Appeals reversed saying that Newman owed a duty to people other than the actual sellers of the stock.[48] The Court of Appeals noted, "Rule 10b-5 makes it unlawful for any person to engage in any act or practice which operates as a fraud or deceit upon *any person*" [emphasis added].[49] Based on this logic, the court ruled that Newman had violated Rule 10b-5 because he helped his co-conspirators violate the duty of honesty, loyalty, and silence they owed to their employers.

Moving closer to the communications professions, the U.S. Court of Appeals for the Second Circuit found a proofreader for a financial printing company had violated the Securities Exchange Act when he bought stocks based on information he gained while working for his employer. The Court of Appeals found that Anthony Materia, the proofreader, had violated a duty of confidentiality he owed to his employer and was therefore liable for violation of Rule 10b-5. Materia was ordered to pay $99,862.50 and was permanently enjoined from such stock trades.[50]

This same logic has also been used to find reporters guilty of violating Rule 10b-5. In 1985, two reporters for *The Wall Street Journal* used information about the content of that newspaper to make stock purchase and sale decisions. R. Foster Winans was a reporter at *The Wall Street Journal* and one of the writers for a column titled "Heard on the Street." Winans knew that stock prices were often affected by statements in the column and because he was writing the column he knew its contents before it appeared in print. Winans would leak information to a stockbroker about the timing, subject, and tenor of the "Heard on the Street" columns. The broker would then use that information to make stock purchases. Winans and his confederates then split the profits. Although Winans apparently never altered the content of his column to influence stock prices, he used his advance information to make a profit from the purchase and sale of stock. The court, in its decision to impose criminal penalties on Winans, said, "We hold that such activity falls squarely within the fraud or deceit language of the Rule."[51] It should be noted that *The Wall Street Journal* does have a confidentiality policy and the court ruled very specifically that Winans violated his obligation to his employer when he violated that policy. It was his violation of this duty to his employer that the court used to justify his conviction.

In earlier chapters, we described employee duties to employers and how these can be enforced under contract law. The application of the misappropriation theory and SEC rules creates another avenue for employers to enforce agreements with employees including reporters and other communication professionals.

Magic Words and Phrases

8-K report	Preclearance
Affirmative duty to disclose	Private right of action
Balance sheet	Profit & loss statement
Board of directors	Proxy
Bonds	Proxy solicitation
Corporation	Recklessness
Disclosure scheme	Sarbanes–Oxley Act
Family resemblance test	Securities
Fraud	Securities and Exchange Commission (SEC)
Insider trade	
Letter of no-action	Shareholder
Limited liability	Shareholder meeting
Material fact	Shares
Merit registration	Stocks
Misappropriation theory	Uniform Securities Act
Model Business Corporations Act	Waiting period

Suggested Cases to Read and Brief

Aaron v. SEC, 446 U.S. 680 (1980)

Blue Chip v. Manor, 421 U.S. 723 (1975)

Bob Reves v. Ernst & Young, 494 U.S. 56, 59 (1990)

Chiarella v. U.S., 455 U.S. 222, 232 (1980)

Dasho v. Susquehanna Corp. 461 F.2d 11, 19 (7th Cir. 1972), *cert. denied* 408 U.S. 925 (1972)

Dirks v. SEC, 463 U.S. 646 (1983)

Hansen v. Ford Motor Co., 278 F.2d 586, 591 (8th Cir. 1960)

Heit v. Weitzen, 402 F.2d 909 (2d Cir. 1968)

Herman & MacLean v. Huddleston, 459 U.S. 375 (1983)

Marine Bank v. Weaver, 455 U.S. 551, 556 (1982)

Sanders v. Nuveen, 554 F.2d 790 (7th Cir. 1977)

SEC v. Materia, 745 F.2d 197 (2nd Cir. 1984)

SEC v. National Securities, 398 U.S. 453 (1969)

SEC v. Texas Gulf Sulfur, 401 F.2d 833 (2d Cir. 1968)

SEC v. W.J. Howey Co., 328 U.S. 293, 299 (1946)

Speed v. Transamerica Corp., 99 F.Supp 808 (D.Del. 1951)

U.S. v. Newman, 664 F2d 12 (2d Cir. 1981)

U.S. v. Winans, 612 F.Supp. 827 (S.D.N.Y., 1985)

Questions for Discussion

1. In this chapter, we described some advantages of incorporation. If you were planning to start a business would you form a corporation or some other form of business organization? Do you see any disadvantages to forming a corporation? If so, what are those disadvantages?

2. It has been argued that the "language" of business is accounting. Do you believe most investors understand that "language"? If investors do not understand accounting, will providing them more information or even absolutely accurate information help them make better investment decisions?

3. If most investors do not understand the nuances of accounting and business reporting, what advantages are there to forcing corporations to provide accurate information? When answering this question consider whether you agree with the concept of "merit registration" or a "disclosure scheme."

4. If you think a "merit registration" system for protecting investors is the best approach, then explain why you think the government should or could decide what investments are best. If you think a "disclosure scheme" is best for protecting investors, explain why the requirement for full disclosure did not prevent investment disasters like Enron.

5. Does the government's imposition of an "affirmative duty to disclose" violate the First Amendment? Why or why not?

6. Why should the level of intent or scienter be different for communications advocating stock purchases and for proxy solicitations? (Remember that for communication advocating a stock sale, §10(b)5 requires the knowledge or scienter before a communications professional can be held liable while §14a has been interpreted to say someone issuing a proxy solicitation is liable for inaccurate information simply for being negligent in checking their facts.)

7. Because communication about stocks or securities for sale really is "commercial speech," why do these communications need their own set of regulations under the SEC? Why aren't the FTC regulations enough to control stock fraud and investment manipulation?

8. If you were a public relations practitioner hired to write a report about a corporation, what would you do to ensure that your report did not violate Rule 10b-5? If you were in charge of the investor relations staff or public relations office for a corporation, how would you ensure that no one on your staff violated Rule 10b-5?

9. If you were hired to write a proxy solicitation and you knew that the individual asking for the proxy had served a prison sentence for embezzlement, would you have to volunteer that information in the proxy solicitation? If you believe you have to volunteer the information, what would you say in the solicitation?

10. Some legal scholars have argued that the preclearance rules violate the First Amendment prohibition against prior restraint. Do you believe that requiring a proxy solicitation be given to the SEC for 10 days before it is mailed to shareholders is censorship? Why or why not?

11. What concerns justify allowing private citizens to sue for violation of Rule 10b-5? Why isn't the SEC able to adequately enforce the rule?

12. Do you believe the Sarbanes–Oxley Act will make investments safer for the average shareholder? If that Act had been in place prior to 2000, would it have prevented the investment losses associated with Enron, WorldCom, Tyco, ImClone, Adelphia, or Global Crossing? Explain why or why not?

13. Because the SEC regulations are very broad and prohibit virtually every possible kind of investor relations miscommunications, why do you think states still have laws that try to protect investors? What investment situations can you think of where it would be helpful to have a state investment law or a state-enforced common law against fraud?

14. If you were a managing editor of a newspaper what could you do to ensure your business reporters never violated any securities regulations?

Notes

1. *Dodge v. Ford Motor Co.*, 204 Mich. 459, 506 (1919) 170 N.W. 668, 684 (Mich., 1919).
2. *Marine Bank v. Weaver*, 455 U.S. 551, 556 (1982).
3. 15 U.S.C. § 77b(a)(1) (2004).
4. *Landreth Timber Co. v. Landreth*, 471 U.S. 681 (1985).
5. *Bob Reves v. Ernst & Young*, 494 U.S. 56, 59 (1990).
6. *Id.* at 59.
7. See, *Chemical Bank v. Arthur Andersen & Co.*, 726 F.2d 930 (2nd Cir, 1984); *Bob Reves v. Ernst & Young*, 494 U.S. 56 (1990).
8. *Pixley v. Boynton*, 79 Ill. 351 (1875).
9. *SEC v. W.J. Howey Co.*, 328 U.S. 293, 299 (1946).
10. *Dodge v. Ford Motor Co.* 204 Mich. 459, 506 (1919) 170 N.W. 668, 684 (1919).
11. The Securities Act of 1933, codified at 15 U.S.C. §§ 77a–77aa (2003). The Securities Exchange Act of 1934, codified at 15 U.S.C. §§ 78a–78mm (2003).
12. 17 C.F.R. 240.10b-5 (2004).
13. 17 C.F.R. §§ 14a, 14e & 15c-1 (2004), §14a deals with proxy solicitations, §14e with tender offers, and §15c with registration requirements.
14. *SEC v. Texas Gulf Sulfur*, 401 F.2d 833 (2d Cir. 1968).
15. *SEC v. Texas Gulf Sulfur*, 401 F.2d 833, 862 (2d Cir. 1968).
16. *Id.* at 860.
17. *Heit v. Weitzen*, 402 F.2d 909 (2d Cir. 1968).
18. *Pauly Jail Bldg. & Manufg. Co. v. Hemphill County*, 62 F. 698, 704 (5th Cir. 1893).
19. *Speed v. Transamerica Corp.*, 99 F.Supp 808 (D.Del. 1951).
20. *Id.* at 829.
21. *Ward La France Truck Corp.*, 13 S.E.C. 373 (1943).
22. *Chiarella v. U.S.*, 455 U.S. 222, 232 (1980).
23. *Dirks v. S.E.C.*, 463 U.S. 646 (1983).
24. *Aaron v. S.E.C.*, 446 U.S. 680, 695 (1980).
25. *Id.*
26. See, also, *Ernst and Ernst v. Hochfelder*, 425 U.S. 185 (1976).
27. *Sanders v. Nuveen*, 554 F.2d 790, 792 (7th Cir. 1977).

28. *Id.*
29. *Id.* at 793.
30. *Dasho v. Susquehanna Corp.*, 461 F.2d 11, 19 (7th Cir. 1972), *cert. denied* 408 U.S. 925 (1972).
31. *Sanders*, 554 F.2d at 793.
32. *Dasho v. Susquehanna Corp.*, 461 F.2d 11, 19 (7th Cir. 1972), *cert. denied* 408 U.S. 925 (1972).
33. *Gerstle v. Gamble-Skogmo*, 478 F.2d 1281, 1298 (2d Cir. 1973).
34. *Mills v. Electric Auto-Lite,* 396 U.S. 375 (1970).
35. *TSC Industries v. Northway*, 426 U.S. 438, 447 (1976).
36. *Virginia Bankshares v. Sandberg,* 501 U.S. 1083 (1991).
37. 17 C.F.R. 240.14a-6 (2004).
38. *Kardon v. National Gypsum,* 69 F.Supp. 512 (E.D.Pa. 1946*).*
39. *SEC v. National Securities*, 398 U.S. 453 (1969); *Herman & MacLean v. Huddleston,* 459 U.S. 375 (1983).
40. *Blue Chip v. Manor*, 421 U.S. 723 (1975).
41. Uniform Securities Act, 1956.
42. See, *Hansen v. Ford Motor Co.*, 278 F.2d 586, 591 (8th Cir. 1960).
43. See, e.g., *Williams v. Bedenbaugh*, 215 Ala. 200, 110 So. 286 (1926); *Klapmeier v. Peat, Marwick, Mitchell & Co.*, 363 F.Supp 1212, 1215 (D. Minn. 1973); *Cameron v. First Nat. Bank of Galveston*, 194 S.W. 469 (Tex.Civ.App. 1917); *Peake v. Thomas*, 222 Ky. 405, 300 S.W. 885 (1927).
44. See, e.g., *In re Cady, Roberts & Co.*, 40 S.E.C. 907 (1961).
45. *Chiarella v. U.S.*, 455 U.S. 222 (1980).
46. *Id.* at 232.
47. *U.S. v. Newman*, 664 F2d 12 (2d Cir. 1981).
48. *Id.* at 15.
49. *Id.* at 16–17.
50. *SEC v. Materia*, 745 F.2d 197 (2d Cir. 1984) *cert denied* 471 U.S. 1053 (1985).
51. *U.S. v. Winans*, 612 F.Supp. 827, 841–842 (S.D.N.Y. 1985).

Appendix A

How to Find and Brief a Case

There are as many procedures for briefing cases as there are people who perform the task. Furthermore, the word "brief" can be used to label either a case brief or a document prepared to present a legal argument to a court. Here we provide instructions for preparing case briefs. These documents summarize a court's rulings and do not add any argument or analysis from the author. They are an important first step to complete before beginning any argument or analysis. We have found success with the approach in this appendix when preparing for appellate argument. We believe following this procedure will minimize your workload and, at the same time, guarantee that you find and understand the most important parts of the case. There are many people who approach this task differently. Therefore, we suggest you check with whomever assigned you to brief a case before using this approach.

Purpose

A case brief is not an act of creativity; it is more analogous to a scavenger hunt. In fact, a well-written case brief may not contain one original word from its author. Its purpose is not to demonstrate your legal skills or to present your opinions; rather its purpose is to cull out the excess verbiage of the court to expose the rules of law contained therein.

Learning to properly brief a case is important for a number of reasons. Most errors made by journalists reporting about legal decisions arise because they do not know how to properly "read" or analyze the reports of judicial decisions. Briefing a case forces a reader to organize his or her thoughts and to demonstrate a proper analysis or "reading" of the case. If you properly brief a case you will:

1. know you are properly "reading" the case for relevant legal meaning and that you are capable of discerning the important parts of each case.
2. develop a file or catalogue of cases to avoid duplication and to recognize trends in judicial decisions. These trends chart the development of case law.
3. be able to distinguish dicta, argument, dissent, and other less important parts of the case from the actual judgment of the court.

How to Proceed

Find the Case

Historically, you would have used a set of books called a digest to search by topic and then used the references therein to find the case in another set of books called reporters. There are some advantages to using these tools even today, but unless you are interested in spending an extraordinary amount of time trying to find obscure cases, we recommend you consider two Internet sources—LexisNexis or FindLaw.

LexisNexis

LexisNexis is a database placed online by Reed Elsevier, Inc. Access to the database depends on payment of a license fee. Unless you plan very extensive searches, the academic version of LexisNexis is more than adequate and many college and university libraries do subscribe to the service. It may be linked off your library's Web page. If it is not, we suggest you contact your university or library to see if you may use the service.

Once you access LexisNexis, follow the links to "legal research." From there, the easiest way to find a specific case is to enter the case citation. If you do not have the citation there is also an option to search by case party names.

The case reports posted on LexisNexis include head notes, a syllabus or case summary, and other introductory information that may help you understand and brief the case. This material is prepared by the publisher's editors and is not part of the case itself. Also included in the LexisNexis case reports are parallel citations to other reporters. These are explained in the sample brief in Appendix B.

FindLaw

A student version of FindLaw is online at http://www.findlaw.com/casecode/. If your library does not subscribe to LexisNexis, this database is an excellent substitute. To use the FindLaw database you will need to move through links for the court that made the decision but once in the appropriate court's search page you may search by year, citation, or party name. There is also a provision to search the cases' text. FindLaw does not include many of the helpful supplements that are included in LexisNexis but the cases posted there do include the entire corpus of the official case decision.

Neither LexisNexis nor FindLaw provides a system to search by U.S. *Law Week* citation. Therefore, you will have to search for very current cases using the party names.

Copy the Case

Copy the complete case. Do not try to complete a brief by merely reading it off your computer screen. You will not get a comprehensive understanding of the case and you may miss major points. Remember, judges typically do not report the case in a neat brief order. You may have to search through the case for important information.

Read the Case

Read the entire case. The case does not begin until you see the words, "Opinion by Justice (or Judge) _____ . . . ." The case ends when you see the words, "Judgment . . ." or "It is so ordered. . . ." The head notes, syllabus, and lists of counsel and judges are not part of the case. Concurring opinions and dissenting opinions also are not part of the opinion.

Although you will want to know the "vote count" to determine the weight of the opinion, do not give the names of the justices, except for the justice who actually wrote the opinion of the court. Do not list the names of attorneys or witnesses. Include only the names of the appellant(s) and appellee(s) in this case.

Mark the Major Points

Find and mark the seven major points listed here.

Heading

The heading should include the case title and official citation. Do not include parallel citations unless those are required by the *Uniform System of Citations*. The heading includes the case name and the citation to a reporter where the case was printed. The case name is always in italics or underlined and is the name of the appellant followed by "v." and the name of the appellee. The names of the appellee and appellant are shortened following a set of rules for abbreviation. These rules for abbreviation and the reporter citation to be used are established by the *Uniform System of Citations*. Each state has its own set of rules, but generally state cases cite both the official state reporter and then a regional reporter. U.S. Supreme Court cases cite to only one reporter and always in this order: First, U.S.; if the case does not appear in U.S. then to S.Ct., L.Ed., and U.S.L.W., in that order. Never cite to Media Law Reporter.

For example, the case in which an unmarried woman, identified only as "Jane Roe," and several physicians and civil rights groups were the appellants and the District Attorney of Dallas County was the appellee was decided on January 22, 1973. The decision is reported on page 113 of volume 410 of U.S. Reports. It is also reported in the Supreme Court Reporter and the Lawyer's Edition. All of this information is summarized in the following heading:

Roe v. Wade, 410 U.S. 113 (1973)

For decisions made in state courts or lower U.S. courts an identification of which court made the decision will precede the year in the parenthesis at the end of the citation. For example, a decision made by the U.S. Court of Appeals for the Ninth Circuit might look like this:

Smith v. Montoro, 648 F.2d 602 (9th Cir.1981)

Judicial History

The judicial history is a description of prior court actions, not a description of facts or investigation results. It is absolutely essential to understand the judicial history because the ultimate judgment will be a response to this judicial history. For example, if the court affirms, you will not know what it is affirming unless you have a firm grasp on the judicial history and the decisions in lower courts.

The judicial history is usually stated near the beginning of a case but sometimes it is scattered throughout other parts of the case. Under judicial history, you should include a brief summary of everything that has happened in the courts below, from the first court pleading or filing to this point of the case. The defendant, plaintiff, appellant, appellee, and any other parties should be identified as well as the results of any hearings, trials, or prior appeals.

Remember it is both judicial and it is history. Because it is judicial, you do not repeat evidence. Evidence refers to events that happened outside of the courtroom. Save major points of evidence for the section titled "facts." Do not use people's names, except for the parties. After identifying the parties you may use the terms *plaintiff, defendant, petitioner, complainant, defendant, respondent, appellant,* and *appellee,* but be absolutely sure you are using those terms correctly. You may use abbreviations like P. or Π for the plaintiff and D. or Δ for the defendant.

Because this section is a history, do not describe the decisions of the court being reported. Those decisions are in the "present" and are not appropriately part of a history.

Facts

The facts, or factual history, are the evidence or information on which the first court based its finding. This section should include a brief but complete summary of actual elements of the case as found or proven at trial. You should also include events that lead to the arrest or charging of a criminal defendant or any alleged actions by a civil defendant. Pick out key words and phrases to describe circumstances of the case.

Outline the events that led up to trial in chronological order. Wherever possible, use the court's own summary of the evidence or testimony at trial. This section should explain what the defendant did to get himself or herself sued or charged in the first place. Also, explain what happened during the investigation or trial if those facts are important to understand the issues or rulings. Do not repeat the judicial history here.

Issues

The issues are the questions of law that are being answered or decided in this case. You should list each issue separately and number them even if they were "run together" as one issue or general sentence by the appellate court. Issues could be identified by specific statutes, constitutional provisions, or principles of common law. They might also be identified with individual elements of a tort or crime. Use the court's own wording as a "hint" that the issue is being presented or phrased for the reader. Look for such words as:

"The issue(s) is (are) . . ."
"The question(s) is (are) . . ."
"The issue or question in this case is whether or not . . ."

Do use the court's own words verbatim to describe the issues. This is not a time to be creative. The judges or justices should tell you exactly what they thought they were deciding. If, for some reason, the court's statement of the issues is confusing, you may state it and then attempt a simple explanation. Do not use the words of any lower court. The issues identified by lower courts may or may not be the issue as seen by this court.

It may be helpful to note that an issue is always a question. The holding always answers the question posed by the issue. Each question or issue must have an answer or holding. There must always be the same number of issues and holdings.

Reasoning

The reasoning is the points of law selected and applied by this court to resolve the issues or questions before it. You might think of it as the court "arguing with itself" to reach a decision. There are two parts to this process.

First, the court will begin listing rules of law and include quotations from statutes, constitutions, or cases on which it will rely when answering questions or deciding issues in this case. List at least four of the cases or statutes the court cites and for each one give a very brief statement of law for which the case stands.

Second, the court will begin selecting salient facts from this case (the case at bar) and applying the principles of law it has selected as relevant to the facts to arrive at its "solution," "holding," or "decision." Describe briefly how the court applied the principles of law from cases it cited to the facts.

Courts often present points of law that support both sides of a controversy. It may help to edit the reasoning to first locate the holding and then to select those points of law or logics that support the court's ultimate decision.

Holding or Decision

The terms holding and decision are used interchangeably with or in addition to "the rule of the case." This is a summary conclusion of the court's reasoning process which states the "principle of law," "law finding," or "rule of law" in relation to each issue in this specific case. **You should have as many holdings as you do issues** in each case. The court often marks the holding or decision with wording such as: "We find . . .," "We conclude . . ." or, "We hold. . . ."

Quote the court's holdings **verbatim**. This should be a very brief and specific statement, usually located in the last one or two paragraphs of the case. It is the holding that becomes precedent for the future so you must be absolutely accurate in reporting it. Never quote holdings from the summary, syllabus, or head notes. These were written by clerks or editors and not by the court.

Judgment or Decision

Be sure to list the final judgment or outcome of this particular case. Was the lower court affirmed or reversed, was the decision vacated or voided, was it remanded with instructions? It is also useful to note the "vote" or number of judges who concurred or dissented in the judgment. The holding is often followed by words like "It is so ordered."

The court's judgment may be as brief as one word. It should always be quoted **verbatim**. *Per curium* or plurality opinions should be noted because these do not carry full precedential weight.

Be Sure the Case is "Good Law": Shepardize

Before you cite a case in support of a legal argument or to explain a principle of common law, you must be sure the holding in that case has not been reversed, overturned, or modified. Cases that are mandatory authority and that have not been altered by other courts are said to be "good law." To identify good law, you must review every subsequent decision by equal or superior courts that reference the same issue. Although this task may sound daunting or even impossible, there is a relatively simple way to do it. Because lawyers have to check the reliability of holdings they cite, publishers have developed ways to meet that need. The most common of the publications for verifying holdings is called *Shepard's Citations*.

Shepard's Citations is available in any good law library and the system for verifying citations is available online. The academic version of Lexis/Nexis, for example, includes a listing from *Shepard's* for U.S. Supreme Court cases.

To use the printed version, first check the "codes" listed in the front of each volume. Then look up the case whose decision you seek to verify. Under the citation for that case there will be a table of other citations, each preceded by one of the "codes" from the front of the book. To the untrained eye *Shepard's Citations* looks like a table of random numbers and symbols but with some experience it can be used to find whether a decision is good law.

The online version looks less like an obscure code. From the Lexis/Nexis legal research page, click the "Shepard's" symbol. Then enter the citation for the case whose holding you want to verify. The program will then list all subsequent cases that referenced your case. The subsequent cases that reversed, overruled, or modified the decision will be marked with a red dot.

Of course, any issue that has been reversed or overruled should not be cited as legal authority.

Suggestions

It Is a Brief, Not a Length

Case briefs should be no more than three pages and may be in outline form or presented as bulleted headings. The whole reason for writing a case brief is to learn how to read cases for salient and pertinent points so that you may report them accurately and omit the irrelevant material.

Never Confuse Ratio Decidend with Obiter Dictum

Ratio decidend is Latin for "the ground of decision" and *obiter dictum* is Latin for "a remark by the way." *Obiter dictum* is a remark made or an opinion expressed by a judge in his or her decision making or reasoning. It is a statement or several statements included in the reasoning of the court said by the way or in passing that is incidentally or collaterally made and is not directly on the issues or questions before the court. These statements are sometimes referred to as "dicta" and are introduced by the court in illustration, analogy, or argument to itself. Dicta relates to extraneous information or speculation about other circumstances. These **are not part of the decision**, but they do make up the vast majority of copy in most case reports. The single most common error by journalists and scholars in mass communications law is the confusion of dicta and decision. It is only the decision or holding of the court that is authoritative or binding in similar cases. Dicta have no bearing at all on precedent or *stare decisis*.

Never Cite Dissenting or Concurring Opinions

Often, the judges whose opinions did not sway their "brethren" write dissenting or concurring opinions. These are essentially arguments for why the court should have ruled some other way. Dissenting opinions explain why the court should have reached another judgment and concurring opinions explain why their author thinks the court should have reached the same judgment by different reasoning. These are **never** part of the decision. In fact there is a common saw among appellate lawyers—"the only people who read dissenting opinions are the lawyers who lost the case and morons."

Appendix B

Sample Brief of *Branzburg v. Hayes,* 408 U.S. 665 (1972)

Report of case as it appears in Lexis

Reprinted with the permission of LexisNexis. Copyright © 1972 Lexis Nexis, a division of Reed Elsevier Inc. All rights reserved. No copyright is claimed as to any part of the original work prepared by a government officer or employee as part of that person's official duties.

BRANZBURG v. HAYES ET AL., JUDGES

No. 70-85

SUPREME COURT OF THE UNITED STATES

408 U.S. 665; 92 S. Ct. 2646; 33 L. Ed. 2d 626; 1972 U.S. LEXIS 132; 24 Rad. Reg. 2d (P & F) 2125; 1 Media L. Rep. 2617

February 23, 1972, Argued
June 29, 1972, Decided *
* Together with No. 70-94, In re Pappas, on certiorari to the Supreme Judicial Court of Massachusetts, also argued February 23, 1972, and No. 70-57, United States v. Caldwell, on certiorari to the United States Court of Appeals for the Ninth Circuit, argued February 22, 1972.

Recommended Case Brief

Heading
Branzburg v. Hayes, **408 U.S. 665 (1972)**

Explanation

This is the heading.

Cite only the required plaintiff and defendant, and only one reporter. The preferred order of citation is U.S., S.Ct. L.Ed., U.S.L.W.

NEVER cite Media L. Rep. [UNIFORM SYSTEM OF CITATION 183 (17th ed. 2000)].

Some state courts require citation to state reporter and to West regional reporter. You will have to review the requirements for each state.

[UNIFORM SYSTEM OF CITATION 189-241 (17th ed. 2000)].

PRIOR HISTORY:
CERTIORARI TO THE COURT OF APPEALS OF KENTUCKY.

Not part of the brief.

DISPOSITION: No. 70-85, 461 S. W. 2d 345, and Kentucky Court of Appeals judgment in unreported case of Branzburg v. Meigs; and No. 70-94; 358 Mass. 604, 266 N. E. 2d 297, affirmed; No. 70-57, 434 F.2d 1081, reversed.

Do not include "prior history," disposition," or "Summary" in the brief.

SUMMARY: The United States Supreme Court granted certiorari in three cases to consider newsmen's constitutional privilege from giving grand jury testimony. In No. 70-85, the Kentucky Court of Appeals denied a newsman's petition for prohibition and mandamus against the Kentucky state trial judge's order that the newsman identify before a grand jury the individuals he had seen possessing marijuana and making hashish from marijuana (461 SW2d 345); and denied the newsman's petition for prohibition and mandamus to quash a summons directing his appearance before a grand jury investigating narcotics violations. In No. 70-94, the Supreme Judicial Court of Massachusetts affirmed the denial of a newsman's motion to quash a summons directing him to appear before a grand jury (266 NE2d 297). In No. 70-57, the United States Court of Appeals for the Ninth Circuit reversed the contempt commitment of a newsman who refused to appear before a federal grand jury (434 F2d 1081).

This information may help you understand the case but it is not part of the court's decision and should not be cited in any way in the brief.

On certiorari, the United States Supreme Court affirmed in Nos. 70-85 and 70-94, and reversed in No. 70-57. In an opinion by White, J., expressing the views of five members of the court, it was held that the First Amendment accords a newsman no privilege against appearing before a grand jury and answering questions as to either the identity of his news sources or information which he has received in confidence.

Powell, J., while concurring in the court's opinion, filed a separate opinion emphasizing the limited nature of the court's decision.

Douglas, J., dissented on the grounds that a newsman has an absolute right not to appear before a grand jury.

Stewart, J., joined by Brennan and Marshall, JJ., dissented on the grounds that before a newsman is asked to appear before a grand jury and reveal confidences, the government must show (1) probable cause to believe that the newsman has information clearly relevant to a specific probable violation of law, (2) that the information cannot be obtained by alternative means less destructive of First Amendment rights, and (3) a compelling and overriding interest in the information.

LAWYERS' EDITION HEADNOTES:

[***HN1]
CONSTITUTIONAL LAW §935.5

WITNESSES §70
free press — newsmen's privilege —

Headnote: [1A]
[1B]
Requiring newsmen to appear and testify before state or federal grand juries does not abridge the freedom of speech and press guaranteed by the First Amendment.
Headnotes 2 through 42 omitted

[***HN43]
WITNESSES §70
newsman's privilege —

Headnote: [43]
A newsman has no privilege to refuse to appear before a grand jury until the government demonstrates some "compelling need" for his testimony.

Not part of the brief.

The head notes are useful tools for finding specific rulings or points of dicta in the corpus of the case but they are not themselves part of the court's decision.

SYLLABUS: The First Amendment does not relieve a newspaper reporter of the obligation that all citizens have to respond to a grand jury subpoena and answer questions relevant to a criminal investigation, and therefore the Amendment does not afford him a constitutional testimonial privilege for an agreement he makes to conceal facts relevant to a grand jury's investigation of a crime or to conceal the criminal conduct of his source or evidence thereof. Pp. 679–709.

Not part of the brief.

The syllabus may help you understand the case but it is a summary written by an editor and is not part of the case.

COUNSEL: Edgar A. Zingman argued the cause for petitioner in No. 70-85. With him on the briefs was Robert C. Ewald. E. Barrett Prettyman, Jr. argued the cause for petitioner in No. 70-94. With him on the briefs was William H. Carey. Solicitor General Griswold argued the cause for the United States in No. 70-57. With him on the briefs were Assistant Attorney General Wilson, Assistant Attorney General Petersen, William Bradford Reynolds, Beatrice Rosenberg, and Sidney M. Glazer.

Edwin A. Schroering, Jr., argued the cause for respondents in No. 70-85. With him on the brief was W. C. Fisher, Jr. Joseph J. Hurley, First Assistant Attorney General, argued the cause for respondent, Commonwealth of Massachusetts, in No. 70-94. With him on the brief were Robert H. Quinn, Attorney General, Walter H. Mayo III, Assistant Attorney General, and Lawrence T. Bench, Deputy Assistant Attorney General. Anthony G. Amsterdam argued the cause for respondent in No. 70-57. With him on the brief were Jack Greenberg, James M. Nabrit III, Charles Stephen Ralston, and William Bennett Turner.

William Bradford Reynolds argued the cause for the United States as amicus curiae urging affirmance in Nos. 70-85 and 70-94. With him on the brief were Solicitor General Griswold, Assistant Attorney General Wilson, and Beatrice Rosenberg.
[Amicus curia briefs omitted]

Not part of the brief.

One of the most common mistakes of students writing briefs is to list the counsel and the judges. This information is not part of the case and should not be part of the brief.

JUDGES: White, J., wrote the opinion of the Court, in which Burger, C. J., and Blackmun, Powell, and Rehnquist, JJ., joined. Powell, J., filed a concurring opinion, post, p. 709. Douglas, J., filed a dissenting opinion, post, p. 711. Stewart, J., filed a dissenting opinion, in which Brennan and Marshall, JJ., joined, post, p. 725.

OPINION BY: WHITE
OPINION: [*667] [***631] [**2649] Opinion of the Court by MR. JUSTICE WHITE, announced by THE CHIEF JUSTICE.

The issue in these cases is whether requiring newsmen to appear and testify before state or federal grand juries abridges the freedom of speech [**2650] and press guaranteed by the First Amendment. We hold that it does not. [***HR1A] [1A]

Issue

The issue in these cases is whether requiring newsmen to appear and testify before state or federal grand juries abridges the freedom of speech and press guaranteed by the First Amendment.

The case report begins with the "Opinion."

Remember the specific words, "the issue is" and "whether," which are both markers of the issue.

Also, recall that the case components may not appear in the same order as the brief points. You will have to rearrange the contents.

Here there is a summary holding but a more complete one is located later in the case.

[**2650] indicates the location in the case verbiage where page 2650 of the second cited reporter begins. In this instance the second cited reporter was 92 S. Ct. 2646.

[***HR1A] [1A] indicated where, in the case copy, the principle in Headnote 1A is located – Later references to Head notes are omitted.

I

The writ of certiorari in No. 70-85, *Branzburg v. Hayes* and *Meigs*, brings before us two judgments of the Kentucky Court of Appeals, both involving petitioner Branzburg, a staff reporter for the Courier-Journal, a daily newspaper published in Louisville, Kentucky.

On November 15, 1969, the Courier-Journal [***632] carried a story under petitioner's byline describing in detail his observations of two young residents of Jefferson County synthesizing hashish from marijuana, an activity which, they asserted, earned them about $5,000 in three weeks. The article included a photograph of a pair of hands working above a laboratory table on which was a substance identified by the caption as hashish. The article stated that petitioner had promised not to [*668] reveal the identity of the two hashish makers. n1 Petitioner was shortly subpoenaed by the Jefferson County grand jury; he appeared, but refused to identify the individuals he had seen possessing marijuana or the persons he had seen making hashish from marijuana. n2 A state trial court judge n3 ordered petitioner to answer these questions and rejected his contention that the Kentucky reporters' privilege statute, Ky. Rev. Stat. § 421.100 (1962), n4 the First Amendment of the United States Constitution, or §§ 1, 2, and 8 of the Kentucky Constitution authorized his refusal to answer. Petitioner then sought prohibition and mandamus in the Kentucky Court of Appeals on the same grounds, but the Court of Appeals denied the petition. *Branzburg* v. [*669] *Pound*, 461 S. W. 2d 345 (1970), as modified on denial of rehearing, Jan. 22, 1971. It held that petitioner had abandoned his First Amendment argument in a supplemental memorandum he had filed and tacitly rejected his argument based on the Kentucky Constitution. It also construed Ky. Rev. Stat. § 421.100 as affording a newsman the privilege of refusing to divulge the identity

Judicial History

- Decision involves four cases all with same issue to be heard by Supreme Court.
- Two similar cases involve petitioner Branzburg.

Case 1

- Branzburg subpoenaed by grand jury of Jefferson County, Ky.
- Appeared but refused to identify criminal suspects whose hands he had photographed with what he identified in article as marijuana.
- State trial judge ordered Branzburg to answer.
- Branzburg appealed to Kentucky Court of Appeals seeking prohibition & Mandamus.
- Kentucky Court of Appeals denied motion.

Case 2

- Grand jury subpoenaed Branzburg about observations and conversations with unnamed drug users about use and sale of drugs detailed in a second article about drugs in Franklin County.

Very often the court will mark or identify sections of their opinion. Here the roman numeral I sets off a description of the cases involved.

This section does mix the factual and judicial history. The court's description is complicated by the fact that it has combined four cases.

Two of the cases involve Branzburg. They are *Branzburg v. Hayes* and *Branzburg v. Meigs*. The name Pound appears because Pound was a judge in Jefferson County who was later replaced by Meigs.

The other two cases are *In re Pappas* and *United States* v. *Caldwell*.

All four cases are so similar that the court renders only one opinion to cover all four cases.

Here we only brief the cases involving Branzburg. Therefore, the case material referring to Pappas and Caldwell is omitted.

of an informant who supplied him with information, but held that the statute did not permit a reporter to refuse to testify about events he had observed personally, including the identities of those persons he had observed. **[Footnotes 1–4 omitted]**

The second case involving petitioner Branzburg arose out of his later story published on January 10, 1971, which described in detail the use of drugs in Frankfort, Kentucky. The article reported that in order to provide a comprehensive survey of the "drug scene" in Frankfort, petitioner had "spent two weeks interviewing several dozen drug users in the capital city" and had seen some of them smoking marijuana. A number of conversations with and observations [***633] of several unnamed drug users were recounted. Subpoenaed to appear before a Franklin County grand jury "to testify in the matter of violation of statutes concerning [**2651] use and sale of drugs," petitioner Branzburg moved to quash the summons; n5 the motion was denied, although [*670] an order was issued protecting Branzburg from revealing "confidential associations, sources or information" but requiring that he "answer any questions which concern or pertain to any criminal act, the commission of which was actually observed by [him]." Prior to the time he was slated to appear before the grand jury, petitioner sought mandamus and prohibition from the Kentucky Court of Appeals, arguing that if he were forced to go before the grand jury or to answer questions regarding the identity of informants or disclose information given to him in confidence, his effectiveness as a reporter would be greatly damaged. The Court of Appeals once again denied the requested writs, reaffirming its construction of Ky. Rev. Stat. § 421.100, and rejecting petitioner's claim of a First Amendment privilege. It distinguished *Caldwell* v. *United States*, 434 F.2d 1081 (CA9 1970), and it also announced its "misgivings" about that

- **Prior to grand jury appearance Branzburg moved to quash summons.**
- **Motion to quash denied by trial court.**
- **Protective order issued permitting Branzburg to protect confidential sources and associations but requiring answer by him about criminal acts he observed directly.**
- **Prior to grand jury date Branzburg sought mandamus and prohibition from Kentucky Court of Appeals. It was denied.**
- **Branzburg sought Writ of Certiorari from both judgments of Kentucky Court of Appeals from U.S. Supreme Court.**
- **Motion for certiorari granted.**

Factual History

Case 1
- **Branzburg was a staff reporter for Courier-Journal, a Louisville, KY. newspaper.**
- **He wrote and published a story about two residents synthesizing hashish from**

decision, asserting that it represented "a drastic departure from the generally recognized rule that the sources of information of a newspaper reporter are not privileged under the First Amendment." It characterized petitioner's fear that his ability to obtain [*671] news would be destroyed as "so tenuous that it does not, in the opinion of this court, present an issue of abridgement of the freedom of the press within the meaning of that term as used in the Constitution of the United States."
[Footnote 5 omitted]

Petitioner sought a writ of certiorari to review both judgments of the Kentucky Court of Appeals, and we granted the writ. n6 402 U.S. 942 (1971).
[Footnote 6 omitted]

[*672] [***634] *In re Pappas*, No. 70-94, originated when petitioner Pappas, a television newsman-photographer working out of the Providence, Rhode Island, office of a New Bedford, Massachusetts, television station, was called to New Bedford on July 30, 1970, to report on civil disorders there which involved fires and other turmoil.
[Copy from here to page 676 only refers to Pappas. It has been omitted]

United States v. *Caldwell*, No. 70-57, arose from subpoenas issued by a federal grand jury in the Northern District of California to respondent Earl Caldwell, a reporter for the New York Times assigned to cover the Black Panther Party and other black militant groups.
[Copy from here to page 680 only refers to Caldwell. It has been omitted]

II
Petitioners Branzburg and Pappas and respondent Caldwell press First Amendment claims that may be simply put: that to gather news it is often necessary [**2656] to agree either not to identify the source of information published or to publish only part of the facts revealed, or

marijuana. In the story he said the residents were earning $5,000 in 3 weeks.
- **The article included a photograph of the residents' hands.**
- **Grand jury subpoenaed Branzburg and asked him to identify people whose hands were shown.**

Case 3
- **Branzburg published later story describing, in detail, use of drugs in Franklin County, KY.**
- **Story said he spent 2 weeks interviewing several dozen drug users and had seen some smoking marijuana. He described observations and conversations with several drug users.**
- **Branzburg was subpoenaed to appear before grand jury to testify about violation of state statutes prohibiting use and sale of drugs.**

Reasoning

Branzburg **408 U.S. @ 682-683.**
"It is clear that the First Amendment does not invalidate every

In the reasoning, pick out sources or authority cited by the court. We suggest four or five cases, statutes, rules, or constitutional provisions that are presented to justify both; that if the reporter is nevertheless [*680] forced to reveal these confidences to a grand jury, the source so identified and other confidential sources of other reporters will be measurably deterred from furnishing publishable information, all to the detriment of the free flow of information protected by the First Amendment. Although the newsmen in these cases do not claim an absolute privilege against official interrogation in all circumstances, they assert that the reporter should not be forced either to appear or to testify before a grand jury or at trial until and unless sufficient grounds are shown for believing that the reporter possesses information relevant to a crime the grand jury is investigating, that the information the reporter has is unavailable from other sources, and that the need for the information is sufficiently compelling to override the claimed invasion [***639] of First Amendment interests occasioned by the disclosure. Principally relied upon are prior cases emphasizing the importance of the First Amendment guarantees to individual development and to our system of representative government, n17 decisions requiring that official action with adverse impact on First Amendment rights be justified by a public interest that is "compelling" or "paramount," n18 and those precedents establishing the principle that justifiable governmental goals may not be achieved by unduly broad means having an unnecessary impact [*681] on protected rights of speech, press, or association. n19 The heart of the claim is that the burden on news gathering resulting from compelling reporters to disclose confidential information outweighs any public interest in obtaining the information. n20 **[Footnote 17–20 omitted]**

We do not question the significance of free speech, press, or assembly to the country's welfare. Nor is it suggested that news gathering does not qualify for First Amendment protection; without some protection for seeking out the news, freedom of the press could

incidental burdening of the press that may result from the enforcement of civil or criminal statutes of general applicability. Under prior cases, otherwise valid laws serving substantial public interests may be enforced against the press as against others, despite the possible burden that may be imposed. The Court has emphasized that "the publisher of a newspaper has no special immunity from the application of general laws. He has no special privilege to invade the rights and liberties of others." Associated Press v. NLRB, 301 U.S. 103, 132-133 (1937).

Branzburg 408 U.S. @ 684
"It has generally been held that the First Amendment does not guarantee the press a constitutional right of special access to information not available to the public generally." Zemel v. Rusk, 381 U.S. 1, 16-17 (1965)

Branzburg 408 U.S. @ 685
". . . the great weight of authority is that

or explain the ultimate holding.

The ones presented here are examples. Of course, you may choose to include other components of the court's reasoning or examples of authorities it cites.

be eviscerated. But these cases involve no intrusions [**2657] upon speech or assembly, no prior restraint or restriction on what the press may publish, and no express or implied command that the press publish what it prefers to withhold. No exaction or tax for the privilege of publishing, and no penalty, civil or criminal, related to the content of published material is at issue here. The use of confidential sources by the press is not forbidden or restricted; reporters remain free to seek news from [*682] any source by means within the law. No attempt is made to require the press to publish its sources [***640] of information or indiscriminately to disclose them on request.

The sole issue before us is the obligation of reporters to respond to grand jury subpoenas as other citizens do and to answer questions relevant to an investigation into the commission of crime. Citizens generally are not constitutionally immune from grand jury subpoenas; and neither the First Amendment nor any other constitutional provision protects the average citizen from disclosing to a grand jury information that he has received in confidence. n21 The claim is, however, that reporters are exempt from these obligations because if forced to respond to subpoenas and identify their sources or disclose other confidences, their informants will refuse or be reluctant to furnish newsworthy information in the future. This asserted burden on news gathering is said to make compelled testimony from newsmen constitutionally suspect and to require a privileged position for them.
[Footnote 21 omitted]

It is clear that the First Amendment does not invalidate every incidental burdening of the press that may result from the enforcement of civil or criminal statutes of general applicability. Under prior cases, otherwise valid laws serving substantial public interests may be enforced against the press as against others, despite [*683] the possible burden that may be imposed. The Court has emphasized that "the publisher of a

newsmen are not exempt from the normal duty of appearing before a grand jury and answering questions relevant to a [2659] criminal investigation. At common law, courts consistently refused to recognize the existence of any privilege authorizing a newsman to refuse to reveal confidential information to a grand jury." See, e. g., *Ex parte Lawrence*, 116 Cal. 298, 48 P. 124 (1897) . . .**

Branzburg **408 U.S. @ 689-690**
"A number of States have provided newsmen a statutory privilege of varying breadth, but the majority have not done so, and none has been provided by federal statute. Until now the only testimonial privilege for unofficial witnesses that is rooted in the Federal Constitution is the Fifth Amendment privilege against compelled self-incrimination."

Branzburg **408 U.S @ 695-696**
". . . the privilege claimed is that of the reporter, not the

newspaper has no special immunity from the application of general laws. He has no special privilege to invade the rights and liberties of others." *Associated Press* v. *NLRB*, 301 U.S. 103, 132-133 (1937). It was there held that the Associated Press, a news-gathering and disseminating organization, was not exempt from the requirements of the National Labor Relations Act. The holding was reaffirmed in *Oklahoma Press Publishing Co*. v. *Walling*, 327 U.S. 186, 192-193 (1946), where the Court rejected the claim that applying the Fair Labor Standards Act to a newspaper publishing business would abridge the freedom of press guaranteed by the First Amendment. See also *Mabee* v. *White Plains Publishing Co*., 327 U.S. 178 (1946). *Associated Press* v. *United States*, 326 U.S. 1 (1945), similarly overruled assertions that the First Amendment precluded application of the Sherman Act to a newsgathering and disseminating organization. Cf. *Indiana Farmer's Guide Publishing Co*. v. *Prairie Farmer Publishing Co*., 293 U.S. 268, 276 (1934); *Citizen Publishing Co*. v. *United States*, 394 U.S. 131, 139 (1969); *Lorain Journal Co*. v. *United States*, 342 U.S. 143, 155-156 (1951). Likewise, a newspaper may be subjected [***641] to nondiscriminatory forms of general taxation. *Grosjean* v. *American Press Co*., 297 U.S. 233, 250 [**2658] (1936); *Murdock* v. *Pennsylvania*, 319 U.S. 105, 112 (1943).

The prevailing view is that the press is not free to publish with impunity everything and anything it desires to publish. Although it may deter or regulate what is said or published, the press may not circulate knowing or reckless falsehoods damaging to private reputation without subjecting itself to liability for damages, including punitive damages, or even criminal prosecution. See *New York Times Co*. v. *Sullivan*, 376 U.S. 254, [*684] 279-280 (1964); *Garrison* v. *Louisiana*, 379 U.S. 64, 74 (1964); *Curtis Publishing Co*. v. *Butts*, 388 U.S. 130, 147 (1967) (opinion of Harlan, J.,); *Monitor Patriot Co*. v.

informant . . . Historically, the common law recognized a duty to . . . report felonies to the authorities . . . "Whoever, having knowledge of the actual commission of a felony cognizable by a court of the United States, conceals and does not as soon as possible make known the same to some judge or other person in civil or military authority under the United States, shall be [guilty of misprision]." 18 U. S. C. § 4. n36

Roy, 401 U.S. 265, 277 (1971). A newspaper or a journalist may also be punished for contempt of court, in appropriate circumstances. *Craig* v. *Harney*, 331 U.S. 367, 377-378 (1947).

It has generally been held that the First Amendment does not guarantee the press a constitutional right of special access to information not available to the public generally. *Zemel* v. *Rusk*, 381 U.S. 1, 16-17 (1965); *New York Times Co.* v. *United States*, 403 U.S. 713, 728-730 (1971), (STEWART, J., concurring); *Tribune Review Publishing Co.* v. *Thomas*, 254 F.2d 883, 885 (CA3 1958); *In the Matter of United Press Assns.* v. *Valente*, 308 N. Y. 71, 77, 123 N. E. 2d 777, 778 (1954). In *Zemel* v. *Rusk, supra*, for example, the Court sustained the Government's refusal to validate passports to Cuba even though that restriction "render[ed] less than wholly free the flow of information concerning that country." *Id.*, at 16. The ban on travel was held constitutional, for "the right to speak and publish does not carry with it the unrestrained right to gather information." *Id.*, at 17. n22 **[Footnote 22 omitted]**

Despite the fact that news gathering may be hampered, the press is regularly excluded from grand jury proceedings, our own conferences, the meetings of other official bodies gathered in executive session, and the meetings of private organizations. Newsmen have no constitutional right of access to the scenes of crime or [*685] disaster when the general public is excluded, and they may be prohibited from attending or publishing information about trials if such restrictions are necessary to assure a defendant a fair trial before an impartial tribunal. In *Sheppard* v. *Maxwell*, 384 U.S. 333 (1966), for example, the Court reversed a state court conviction where the trial court failed to adopt "stricter [***642] rules governing the use of the courtroom by newsmen, as Sheppard's counsel requested," neglected to insulate witnesses from the press, and made no "effort to control the release of leads, information, and

Holding

Branzburg **408 U.S. @ 690-691**
"On the records now before us, we perceive no basis for holding that the public interest in law enforcement and in ensuring effective grand jury proceedings is insufficient to override the consequential, but uncertain, burden on news gathering that is said to result from insisting that reporters, like other citizens, respond to relevant questions put to them in the course of a valid grand jury investigation or criminal trial."

The holding is a statement that answers the question posed by the issue or issues. It is very common for the holding to be embedded in the reasoning. Of course, it can also come in a conclusion at the end of the reasoning.

gossip to the press by police officers, witnesses, and the counsel for both sides." *Id.*, at 358, 359. "The trial court might well have proscribed extrajudicial statements by any lawyer, party, witness, or court official which divulged prejudicial matters." *Id.*, at 361. See also *Estes* v. *Texas*, 381 U.S. 532, 539-540 (1965); *Rideau* v. *Louisiana*, 373 U.S. 723, 726 (1963).

It is thus not surprising that the great weight of authority is that newsmen are not exempt from the normal duty of appearing before a grand jury and answering questions relevant to a [**2659] criminal investigation. At common law, courts consistently refused to recognize the existence of any privilege authorizing a newsman to refuse to reveal confidential information to a grand jury. See, *e.g., Ex parte Lawrence*, 116 Cal. 298, 48 P. 124 (1897); *Plunkett* v. *Hamilton*, 136 Ga. 72, 70 S. E. 781 (1911); *Clein* v. *State*, 52 So. 2d 117 (Fla. 1950); *In re Grunow*, 84 N. J. L. 235, 85 A. 1011 (1913); *People ex rel. Mooney* v. *Sheriff*, 269 N. Y. 291, 199 N. E. 415 (1936); *Joslyn* v. *People*, 67 Colo. 297, 184 P. 375 (1919); *Adams* v. *Associated Press*, 46 F.R.D. 439 (SD Tex. 1969); *Brewster* v. *Boston Herald-Traveler Corp.*, 20 F.R.D. 416 (Mass. 1957). See generally Annot., 7 A. L. R. 3d 591 (1966). In 1958, a news gatherer asserted for the first time that the First Amendment [*686] exempted confidential information from public disclosure pursuant to a subpoena issued in a civil suit, *Garland* v. *Torre*, 259 F.2d 545 (CA2), cert. denied, 358 U.S. 910 (1958), but the claim was denied, and this argument has been almost uniformly rejected since then, although there are occasional dicta that, in circumstances not presented here, a newsman might be excused. *In re Goodfader*, 45 Haw. 317, 367 P. 2d 472 (1961); *In re Taylor*, 412 Pa. 32, 193 A. 2d 181 (1963); *State* v. *Buchanan*, 250 Ore. 244, 436 P. 2d 729, cert. denied, 392 U.S. 905 (1968); *Murphy* v. *Colorado* (No. 19604, Sup. Ct. Colo.), cert. denied, 365 U.S. 843 (1961) (unreported, discussed in *In re*

Continue reading until you find the judgment.

Goodfader, supra, at 366, 367 P. 2d, at 498 (Mizuha, J., dissenting)). These courts have applied the presumption against the existence of an asserted testimonial privilege, *United States* v. *Bryan*, 339 U.S. 323, 331 (1950), and have concluded that the First Amendment interest asserted by the newsman was outweighed by the general obligation of a citizen to appear before a grand jury or at trial, pursuant to a subpoena, and give what information he possesses. The opinions of the state courts in *Branzburg* and *Pappas* are typical of the prevailing view, although a few recent cases, such as *Caldwell*, have recognized and given effect to some form of constitutional newsman's privilege. See *State* v. *Knops*, 49 Wis. 2d 647, 183 N. W. 2d 93 (1971) (dictum); *Alioto* v. *Cowles Communications, Inc.*, C. A. No. 52150 (ND Cal. 1969); *In re Grand Jury Witnesses*, 322 F.Supp. 573 (ND Cal. 1970); *People* v. *Dohrn*, Crim. No. 69-3808 (Cook County, Ill., Cir. Ct. 1970).

 [***643]

The prevailing constitutional view of the newsman's privilege is very much rooted in the ancient role of the grand jury that has the dual function of determining if there is probable cause to believe that a crime has been committed and of protecting citizens against unfounded [*687] criminal prosecutions. n23 Grand jury proceedings are constitutionally mandated for the institution of federal criminal prosecutions for capital or other serious crimes, and "its constitutional prerogatives are rooted in long centuries of Anglo-American history." *Hannah* v. *Larche*, 363 U.S. 420, 489-490 (1960) (Frankfurter, J., concurring in result). The Fifth Amendment provides that "no person shall be held to answer for a capital, or otherwise infamous crime, unless on a presentment or indictment of a Grand Jury." n24 The adoption [**2660] of the grand jury "in our Constitution as the sole method for preferring charges in serious criminal cases shows the

high place it held as an instrument of justice."
Costello v. *United States*, 350 U.S. 359, 362
(1956). Although state systems of criminal procedure differ greatly among themselves, the
grand jury is similarly guaranteed by many
state constitutions and plays an important role
in fair and effective law enforcement in the
overwhelming [*688] majority of the States.
n25 Because its task is to inquire into the existence of possible criminal conduct and to return
only well-founded indictments, its investigative
powers are necessarily broad. "It is a grand in-
quest, a body with powers of investigation and
inquisition, the scope of whose inquiries is not
to be limited narrowly by questions of propriety
or forecasts of the probable result of the investigation, or by doubts whether any particular individual will be found properly subject to an
accusation of crime." *Blair* v. *United States*,
250 U.S. 273, 282 (1919). Hence, the grand
jury's authority to subpoena witnesses is
[***644] not only historic, *id.*, at 279-281, but
essential to its task. Although the powers of the
grand jury are not unlimited and are subject to
the supervision of a judge, the longstanding
principle that "the public . . . has a right to
every man's evidence," except for those persons
protected by a constitutional, common-law, or
statutory privilege, *United States* v. *Bryan*, 339
U.S., at 331; *Blackmer* v. *United States*, 284
U.S. 421, 438 (1932); 8 J. Wigmore, Evidence
§ 2192 (McNaughton rev. 1961), is particularly
applicable to grand jury proceedings. n26
[Footnote 23–26 omitted]

[*689]
A number of States have provided newsmen a
statutory privilege of varying breadth, n27 but the
majority have not [**2661] done so, and none
has been provided by federal statute. n28 Until
now the only testimonial privilege for unofficial
witnesses that is rooted in the Federal Constitution [*690] is the Fifth Amendment privilege
against compelled self-incrimination. We are
asked to create another by interpreting the First

Amendment to grant newsmen a testimonial privilege that other citizens do not enjoy. This we decline to do. n29 Fair and effective law enforcement aimed at providing security for the person and property of the individual is a fundamental function [***645] of government, and the grand jury plays an important, constitutionally mandated role in this process. On the records now before us, we perceive no basis for holding that the public interest in law enforcement and in ensuring effective grand jury proceedings is insufficient to override the consequential, but uncertain, burden on news gathering that is said to result from insisting that reporters, like other citizens, respond to relevant [*691] questions put to them in the course of a valid grand jury investigation or criminal trial.
[Footnotes 27–29 omitted]

This conclusion itself involves no restraint on what newspapers may publish or on the type or quality of information reporters may seek to acquire, nor does it threaten the vast bulk of confidential relationships between reporters and their sources. Grand juries address themselves to the issues of whether crimes have been committed and who committed them. Only where news sources themselves are implicated in crime or possess information relevant to the grand jury's task need they or the reporter be concerned about grand jury subpoenas. Nothing before us indicates that a large number or percentage of *all* confidential news sources falls into either category and would in any way be deterred by our holding that the Constitution does not, as it never has, exempt the newsman from performing the citizen's normal duty of appearing and furnishing [**2662] information relevant to the grand jury's task.

The preference for anonymity of those confidential informants involved in actual criminal conduct is presumably a product of their desire to escape criminal prosecution, and this preference, while understandable, is hardly deserving of constitutional protection. It would be frivolous to assert – and no one does in these cases – that the First Amendment, in the interest of securing news or otherwise, confers a license on either the reporter or his news sources to violate valid criminal laws. Although stealing documents or private wiretapping could provide newsworthy information, neither reporter nor source is immune from conviction for such conduct, whatever the impact on the flow of news. Neither is immune, on First Amendment grounds, from testifying against the other, before the grand jury or at a criminal trial. The Amendment does not reach so far as to override the interest of the public in ensuring [*692] that neither reporter nor source is invading the rights of other citizens through reprehensible conduct forbidden to all other persons. To assert the contrary proposition

"is to answer it, since it involves in its [***646] very statement the contention that the freedom of the press is the freedom to do wrong with impunity and implies the right to frustrate and defeat the discharge of those governmental duties upon the performance of which the freedom of all, including that of the press, depends. . . . It suffices to say that, however complete is the right of the press to state public things and discuss them, that right, as every other right enjoyed in human society, is subject to the restraints which separate right from wrong-doing." *Toledo Newspaper Co.* v. *United States*, 247 U.S. 402, 419-420 (1918). n30
[Footnote 30 omitted]

Thus, we cannot seriously entertain the notion that the First Amendment protects a newsman's agreement to conceal the criminal conduct of his source, or evidence thereof, on the theory that it is better to write about crime than to do something about it. Insofar as any reporter in these cases undertook not to reveal or testify about the crime he witnessed, his claim of privilege under the First Amendment presents no substantial question. The crimes of news sources are no less reprehensible and threatening to the public interest when witnessed by a reporter than when they are not.

[*693] There remain those situations where a source is not engaged in criminal conduct but has information suggesting illegal conduct by others. Newsmen frequently receive information from such sources pursuant to a tacit or express agreement to withhold the source's name and suppress any information that the source wishes not published. Such informants presumably desire anonymity in order to avoid being entangled as a witness in a criminal trial or grand jury investigation. They may fear that disclosure will threaten their job security or personal safety or that it will simply result in dishonor or embarrassment.

The argument that the flow of news will be diminished by compelling reporters to aid the grand jury in a criminal investigation is not irrational, nor are the records before us silent on the matter. But we remain unclear how often and to what extent informers are actually deterred from furnishing information when newsmen are forced to testify before a grand jury. The available data [**2663] indicate that some newsmen rely a great deal on confidential sources and that some informants are particularly sensitive to the threat of exposure and may be silenced if it is held by this Court that, ordinarily, newsmen must testify pursuant to subpoenas, n31 but the evidence fails to demonstrate that there would be a significant constriction of the flow of news to the public if this Court reaffirms the prior common-law and [***647] constitutional rule regarding the testimonial obligations of newsmen. Estimates of the inhibiting effect of such subpoenas on the willingness of informants to make disclosures to newsmen are widely divergent and [*694] to a great extent speculative. n32 It would be difficult to canvass the views of the informants themselves; surveys of reporters on this topic are chiefly opinions of

predicted informant behavior and must be
viewed in the light of the professional self-
interest of the interviewees. n33 Reliance by
the press on confidential informants does not
mean that all such sources will in fact dry up
because of the later possible appearance of the
newsman before a grand jury. The reporter may
never be called and if he objects to testifying,
the prosecution may not insist. Also, the relationship of many informants to the press is a
symbiotic one which is unlikely to be greatly
inhibited by the threat of subpoena: quite often,
such informants are members of a minority political or cultural group that [*695] relies heavily
on the media to propagate its views, publicize
its aims, and magnify its exposure to the public.
Moreover, grand juries characteristically conduct
secret proceedings, and law enforcement officers
are themselves experienced in dealing with
informers, and have their own methods for
protecting them without interference with the
effective administration of justice. There is little
before us indicating that informants whose interest in avoiding exposure is that it may threaten
job security, personal safety, or peace of mind,
would in fact be in a worse position, or would
think they would be, if they risked placing their
trust in public officials as well as reporters. We
doubt if the informer who prefers anonymity
but is sincerely interested in furnishing evidence
of crime will always or very often be deterred by
the prospect of dealing with those public authorities characteristically charged with the duty to
protect the public interest as well as his.
[Footnotes 31–33 omitted]

Accepting the fact, however, that an undeter-
mined number of informants not themselves
implicated in crime will nevertheless, for
whatever reason, refuse to talk to newsmen if
[**2664] they fear identification by a reporter
in an official investigation, we cannot accept
the argument that the public interest in possible
future news about crime from undisclosed,
unverified sources must take precedence

[***648] over the public interest in pursuing and prosecuting those crimes reported to the press by informants and in thus deterring the commission of such crimes in the future.

We note first that the privilege claimed is that of the reporter, not the informant, and that if the authorities independently identify the informant, neither his own reluctance to testify nor the objection of the newsman would shield him from grand jury inquiry, whatever the impact on the flow of news or on his future usefulness as a secret source of information. More important, [*696] it is obvious that agreements to conceal information relevant to commission of crime have very little to recommend them from the standpoint of public policy. Historically, the common law recognized a duty to raise the "hue and cry" and report felonies to the authorities. n34 Misprision of a felony – that is, the concealment of a felony "which a man knows, but never assented to . . . [so as to become] either principal or accessory," 4 W. Blackstone, Commentaries * 121, was often said to be a common-law crime. n35 The first Congress passed a statute, 1 Stat. 113, § 6, as amended, 35 Stat. 1114, § 146, 62 Stat. 684, which is still in effect, defining a federal crime of misprision:

"Whoever, having knowledge of the actual commission of a felony cognizable by a court of the United States, conceals and does not as soon as possible make known the same to some judge or other person in civil or military authority under the United States, shall be [guilty of misprision]." 18 U. S. C. § 4.

[*697] It is apparent from this statute, as well as from our history and that of England, that concealment of crime and agreements to do so are not looked upon with favor. Such conduct deserves no encomium, and we decline now to afford it First Amendment protection by denigrating the duty of a citizen, whether reporter or informer, to respond to grand jury subpoena and answer relevant questions put to him.
[Footnotes 34–36 omitted]

Of course, the press has the right to abide by its agreement not to publish all the information it has, but the right to withhold news is not equivalent to a First Amendment exemption from the ordinary duty of all other citizens to furnish relevant information to a grand jury [***649] performing an important public function. Private restraints on the flow of information are not so favored by the First Amendment that they override all other public interests. As Mr. Justice Black declared in another context, "freedom of the press from governmental [**2665] interference under the First Amendment does not sanction repression of that freedom by private interests." *Associated Press* v. *United States*, 326 U.S., at 20.

Neither are we now convinced that a virtually impenetrable constitutional shield, beyond legislative or judicial control, should be forged to protect a private system of informers operated by the press to report on criminal conduct, a system that would be unaccountable to the public, would pose a threat to the citizen's justifiable expectations of privacy, and would equally protect well-intentioned informants and those who for pay or otherwise betray their trust to their employer or associates. The public through its elected and appointed [*698] law enforcement officers regularly utilizes informers, and in proper circumstances may assert a privilege against disclosing the identity of these informers. But "the purpose of the privilege is the furtherance and protection of the public interest in effective law enforcement. The privilege recognizes the obligation of citizens to communicate their knowledge of the commission of crimes to law-enforcement officials and, by preserving their anonymity, encourages them to perform that obligation." *Roviaro* v. *United States*, 353 U.S. 53, 59 (1957).

Such informers enjoy no constitutional protection. Their testimony is available to the public when desired by grand juries or at criminal trials; their identity cannot be concealed from the defendant when it is critical to his case. *Id.*, at 60-61, 62; *McCray* v. *Illinois*, 386 U.S. 300, 310 (1967); *Smith* v. *Illinois*, 390 U.S. 129, 131 (1968); *Alford* v. *United States*, 282 U.S. 687, 693 (1931). Clearly, this system is not impervious to control by the judiciary and the decision whether to unmask an informer or to continue to profit by his anonymity is in public, not private, hands. We think that it should remain there and that public authorities should retain the options of either insisting on the informer's testimony relevant to the prosecution of crime or of seeking the benefit of further information that his exposure might prevent.

We are admonished that refusal to provide a First Amendment reporter's privilege will undermine the freedom of the press to collect and disseminate news. But this is not the lesson history teaches us. As noted previously, the common law recognized no such privilege, and the constitutional argument was not even asserted until 1958. From the beginning of our country the press has operated without constitutional protection [*699] for press informants, and the press has flourished. The existing constitutional rules have not been a serious obstacle to either the development or retention of confidential news sources by the press. n37 **[Footnote 37 omitted]**

It [***650] is said that currently press subpoenas have multiplied, n38 that mutual distrust and tension between press and officialdom have increased, that reporting styles have changed, and that there is now more need for confidential sources, particularly where the press seeks news about minority cultural and political groups or dissident organizations suspicious of the law and public officials. These developments, even if true, are treacherous grounds for a far-reaching [**2666] interpretation of the First Amendment fastening a nationwide rule on courts, grand juries, and prosecuting officials everywhere. The obligation to testify in response to grand jury subpoenas will not threaten these sources not involved with criminal conduct and without information relevant to grand jury investigations, and we cannot hold that the Constitution places the sources in these two categories either above the law or beyond its reach.

[Footnote 38 omitted]

The argument for such a constitutional privilege rests heavily on those cases holding that the infringement of protected First Amendment rights must be no broader than necessary to achieve a permissible governmental purpose, see cases cited at n. 19, *supra*. We do not deal, however, with a governmental institution that has abused [*700] its proper function, as a legislative committee does when it "expose[s] for the sake of exposure." *Watkins* v. *United States*, 354 U.S. 178, 200 (1957). Nothing in the record indicates that these grand juries were "prob[ing] at will and without relation to existing need." *DeGregory* v. *Attorney General of New Hampshire*, 383 U.S. 825, 829 (1966). Nor did the grand juries attempt to invade protected First Amendment rights by forcing wholesale disclosure of names and organizational affiliations for a purpose that was not germane to the determination of whether crime has been committed, cf. *NAACP* v. *Alabama*, 357 U.S. 449 (1958); *NAACP* v. *Button*, 371 U.S. 415 (1963); *Bates* v. *Little Rock*, 361 U.S. 516 (1960), and the characteristic secrecy of grand jury proceedings is a further protection against the undue invasion of such rights. See Fed. Rule Crim. Proc. 6 (e). The investigative power of the grand jury is necessarily broad if its public responsibility is to be adequately discharged. *Costello* v. *United States*, 350 U.S., at 364.

The requirements of those cases, see n. 18, *supra*, which hold that a State's interest must be "compelling" or "paramount" to justify even an indirect burden on First Amendment rights,

are also met here. As we have indicated, the
investigation of crime by the grand jury implements a fundamental governmental role of
securing the safety of the person and property
of the citizen, and it appears to us that calling
reporters to give testimony [***651] in the
manner and for the reasons that other citizens
are called "bears a reasonable relationship to the
achievement of the governmental purpose asserted as its justification." *Bates* v. *Little Rock,
supra*, at 525. If the test is that the government
"convincingly show a substantial relation
between the information sought and a subject
of overriding and compelling state interest,"
Gibson v. *Florida Legislative Investigation
Committee*, [*701] 372 U.S. 539, 546 (1963),
it is quite apparent (1) that the State has the
necessary interest in extirpating the traffic in
illegal drugs, in forestalling assassination attempts on the President, and in preventing the
community from being disrupted by violent
disorders endangering both persons and property; and (2) that, based on the stories Branzburg
and Caldwell wrote and Pappas' admitted
conduct, the grand jury called these reporters
as they would others — because it was likely
that they could supply information to help the
government determine whether illegal conduct
had occurred and, if it had, whether there was
sufficient evidence to return an indictment.

Similar considerations dispose of the reporters'
claims that preliminary to requiring their grand
jury appearance, the State must show that a
crime has been committed and that they possess relevant information not available from
other sources, for only the grand jury itself can
make this determination. The role of the grand
jury as an important instrument of effective law
enforcement necessarily includes an investigatory function with respect to determining
[**2667] whether a crime has been committed
and who committed it. To this end it must call
witnesses, in the manner best suited to perform

its task. "When the grand jury is performing its investigatory function into a general problem area . . . society's interest is best served by a thorough and extensive investigation." *Wood* v. *Georgia*, 370 U.S. 375, 392 (1962). A grand jury investigation "is not fully carried out until every available clue has been run down and all witnesses examined in every proper way to find if a crime has been committed." *United States* v. *Stone*, 429 F.2d 138, 140 (CA2 1970). Such an investigation may be triggered by tips, rumors, evidence proffered by the prosecutor, or the personal knowledge of the grand jurors. *Costello* v. *United States*, 350 U.S., at 362. It is [*702] only after the grand jury has examined the evidence that a determination of whether the proceeding will result in an indictment can be made.

"It is impossible to conceive that in such cases the examination of witnesses must be stopped until a basis is laid by an indictment formally preferred, when the very object of the examination is to ascertain who shall be indicted." *Hale* v. *Henkel*, 201 U.S. 43, 65 (1906).

See also *Hendricks* v. *United States*, 223 U.S. 178 (1912); *Blair* v. *United States*, 250 U.S., at 282-283. We see no reason to hold that these reporters, any more than other citizens, should be excused from furnishing information that may help the grand jury in arriving at its initial determinations.

The privilege claimed here is conditional, not absolute; given the suggested [***652] preliminary showings and compelling need, the reporter would be required to testify. Presumably, such a rule would reduce the instances in which reporters could be required to appear, but predicting in advance when and in what circumstances they could be compelled to do so would be difficult. Such a rule would also have implications for the issuance of compulsory process to reporters at civil and criminal trials and at legislative hearings. If newsmen's confidential sources are as sensitive as they are claimed to be,

the prospect of being unmasked whenever a judge determines the situation justifies it is hardly a satisfactory solution to the problem. n39 For [**2668] them, it would appear [***653] that only an absolute privilege would suffice.
[Footnote 39 omitted]

[*703]
We are unwilling to embark the judiciary on a long and difficult journey to such an uncertain destination. The administration of a constitutional newsman's privilege [*704] would present practical and conceptual difficulties of a high order. Sooner or later, it would be necessary to define those categories of newsmen who qualified for the privilege, a questionable procedure in light of the traditional doctrine that liberty of the press is the right of the lonely pamphleteer who uses carbon paper or a mimeograph just as much as of the large metropolitan publisher who utilizes the latest photocomposition methods. Cf. *In re Grand Jury Witnesses*, 322 F.Supp. 573, 574 (ND Cal. 1970). Freedom of the press is a "fundamental personal right" which "is not confined to newspapers and periodicals. It necessarily embraces pamphlets and leaflets. . . . The press in its historic connotation comprehends every sort of publication which affords a vehicle of information and opinion." *Lovell* v. *Griffin*, 303 U.S. 444, 450, 452 (1938). See also *Mills* [*705] v. *Alabama*, 384 U.S. 214, 219 (1966); *Murdock* v. *Pennsylvania*, 319 U.S. 105, 111 (1943). The informative function asserted by representatives of the organized press in the present cases is also performed by lecturers, political pollsters, novelists, academic researchers, and dramatists. Almost any author may quite accurately assert that he is contributing to the flow of information to the public, that he relies on confidential sources of information, and that these sources will be silenced if he is forced to make disclosures before a grand jury. n40
[Footnote 40 omitted]

[**2669] In each instance where a reporter is subpoenaed to testify, the courts would also be embroiled in preliminary factual and legal determinations with respect to whether the proper predicate had been laid for the reporter's appearance: Is there probable cause to believe a crime has been committed? Is it likely that the reporter has useful information gained in confidence? Could the grand jury obtain the information elsewhere? Is the official interest sufficient to outweigh the claimed privilege?

[***654] Thus, in the end, by considering whether enforcement of a particular law served a "compelling" governmental interest, the courts would be inextricably involved in [*706] distinguishing between the value of enforcing different criminal laws. By requiring testimony from a reporter in investigations involving some crimes but not in others, they would be making a value judgment that a legislature had declined to make, since in each case the criminal law involved would represent a considered legislative judgment, not constitutionally suspect, of what conduct is liable to criminal prosecution. The task of judges, like other officials outside the legislative branch, is not to make the law but to uphold it in accordance with their oaths.

At the federal level, Congress has freedom to determine whether a statutory newsman's privilege is necessary and desirable and to fashion standards and rules as narrow or broad as deemed necessary to deal with the evil discerned and, equally important, to refashion those rules as experience from time to time may dictate. There is also merit in leaving state legislatures free, within First Amendment limits, to fashion their own standards in light of the conditions and problems with respect to the relations between law enforcement officials and press in their own areas. It goes without saying, of course, that we are powerless to bar state courts from responding in their own way and construing their own constitutions so as to recognize a newsman's privilege, either qualified or absolute.

In addition, there is much force in the prag-
matic view that the press has at its disposal
powerful mechanisms of communication and is
far from helpless to protect itself from harassment or substantial harm. Furthermore, if what
the newsmen urged in these cases is true – that
law enforcement cannot hope to gain and may
suffer from subpoenaing newsmen before grand
juries – prosecutors will be loath to risk so much
for so little. Thus, at the federal level the
Attorney General has already fashioned a set of
rules for federal officials in connection [*707]
with subpoenaing members of the press to testify before grand juries or at criminal trials. n41
These rules are a [***655] major step in the
direction the reporters [**2670] herein desire
to move. They may prove wholly sufficient to
resolve the bulk of disagreements and controversies between press and federal officials.
[Footnote 41 omitted]

Finally, as we have earlier indicated, news
gathering is not without its First Amendment
protections, and grand jury investigations if
instituted or conducted other than in good
faith, would pose wholly different issues for
resolution under the First Amendment. n42
Official harassment of the press undertaken not
for purposes of law enforcement but to disrupt
a reporter's relationship [*708] with his news
sources would have no justification. Grand
juries are subject to judicial control and subpoenas to motions to quash. We do not expect
courts will forget that grand juries must operate
within the limits of the First Amendment as
well as the Fifth.
[Footnote 42 omitted]

III
We turn, therefore, to the disposition of the
cases before us. From what we have said, it
necessarily follows that the decision in *United
States* v. *Caldwell*, No. 70-57, must be reversed.
If there is no First Amendment privilege to

Judgment

Branzburg **408 U.S.
@708**
**"The decisions in No.
70-85,** *Branzburg* **v.**

To find the judgment, look
for the specific words:
"affirmed," "reversed," or
"it is so ordered."

refuse to answer the relevant and material questions asked during a good-faith grand jury investigation, then it is *a fortiori* true that there is no privilege to refuse to appear before such a grand jury until the Government demonstrates some "compelling need" for a newsman's testimony. Other issues were urged upon us, but since they were not passed upon by the Court of Appeals, we decline to address them in the first instance.

The decisions in No. 70-85, *Branzburg* v. *Hayes* and *Branzburg v. Meigs*, must be affirmed. Here, petitioner refused to answer questions that directly related to criminal conduct that he had observed and written about. The Kentucky Court of Appeals noted that marihuana is defined as a narcotic drug by statute, Ky. Rev. Stat. § 218.010 (14) (1962), and that unlicensed possession or compounding of it is a felony punishable by both fine and imprisonment. Ky. Rev. Stat. § 218.210 (1962). It held that petitioner "saw the commission of the statutory felonies of unlawful possession of marijuana and the unlawful conversion of it into hashish," in *Branzburg* v. *Pound*, 461 S. W. 2d, at 346. Petitioner may be presumed to have observed similar violations of the state narcotics laws during the research he did for the story that forms the basis of the subpoena in *Branzburg* v. *Meigs*. In both cases, if what petitioner wrote was true, [*709] he had direct information to provide the grand jury concerning the commission of serious crimes.

The only question presented at the present time in *In re Pappas*, No. 70-94, is whether petitioner Pappas must appear before the grand jury to testify pursuant to subpoena. The Massachusetts Supreme Judicial Court characterized the record in this case as "meager," and it is not clear what petitioner will be asked by the grand jury. It is not even clear that he will be asked to divulge information received in confidence. We affirm the decision of the Massachusetts

Hayes and *Branzburg* v. *Meigs*, **must be affirmed.**"

OR simply

"**Affirmed**"

The reason the judicial history was important was to know that here what is being affirmed is the Kentucky Court of Appeals decision to deny Branzburg's motion for mandamus. In other words, he is ordered to honor the subpoena. He must testify.

You may want to add the Court's vote. In this case, the vote was 5–4.

White wrote the opinion of the Court.
Powell filed a concurring opinion criticizing Stewart's dissent.
Stewart wrote a dissenting opinion that was joined (or endorsed) by Brennan and Marshall.
Douglas filed a separate dissenting opinion.

Supreme Judicial Court and hold that petitioner
must appear before the grand jury to answer
the questions put to him, subject, of course,
[***656] to the supervision of the presiding
judge as to "the propriety, purposes, and scope
of the grand jury inquiry and the pertinence of
the probable testimony." 358 Mass., at 614,
266 N. E. 2d, at 303-304.

So ordered.

CONCUR BY: POWELL
[concurring opinion omitted]

DISSENT BY: DOUGLAS; STEWART
[dissenting opinions omitted]

Concurring and dissenting
opinions are not part of
the decision and usually
are not briefed.

Appendix C

Sample Documents

These sample documents are provided to give the reader some idea of how contracts may appear. They are not intended for use. Before entering into any legal agreement or engaging in any conduct that might result in legal liabilities or obligations, **always** consult with legal counsel who is familiar both with your profession and the laws of the jurisdiction where you work.

Here we present three contracts—a release for a photography subject, an employment contract, and a covenant not to compete—as examples of the types of wording and phrases one might see in such documents.

Sample Release for Photography Model or Subject

In consideration of _____ dollars ($ _____), in hand paid, and other good and valuable consideration, the receipt and sufficiency of which to bind this agreement being acknowledged, I _____, hereinafter referred to as "Subject," hereby give _____, her or his assigns, successors, heirs, licensees, and representatives, hereinafter collectively referred to as "photographer," the irrevocable right to use:

My likeness,

My name and likeness

A pseudonym or fictional name in, and in association with, any photograph made this _____ (date) in all forms and in all media and in all manners, without any restrictions as to the fees, charges, or alterations of the image; for advertising, trade, promotion, exhibition, or any other lawful purposes, and including written copy that may be created and appear therewith. *[HERE insert any limitations, such as an exception for alterations of the image, use of the image in combination with other images or a right to approve the final image.]*

I hereby release and agree to hold photographer harmless from any liability for use of the above described name or likeness, specifically including any liability for optical illusion, distortion, defect, alteration, or use in composite form whether intentional or otherwise that may occur or be produced in the taking of the photographs, or any development or other processing *[OPTIONAL – unless it can be shown that the defects or alterations and the publication thereof were maliciously produced and published solely for the purpose of subjecting me to conspicuous ridicule, scandal, reproach and indignity]*

I agree that photographer owns the copyright in these images and I hereby waive any claim or right of recovery I may have based on any use of the photographs or works derived therefore, including, but not limited to, claims for invasion of privacy, defamation, or my right of publicity.

I am of full age, suffer from no legal disability, and am competent to sign this release. *[OMIT this sentence for minors]*

I agree that this release shall be binding on me, my legal representatives, heirs, and assigns.

I have read this release, am familiar with and understand its contents, and all the obligations created and rights waived herein.

Signed: _____ (subject)

Printed name and address:

_____

_____

Date: _____

Signed: _____ (photographer)

Printed name and address:

_____

_____

Date: _____

[NOTE, Some jurisdictions will add a requirement to have the signature witnessed. If a witness is required, be sure the witness actually sees the subject sign the release and have him or her sign it and provide contact information on the release itself.]

[If the subject is a minor delete the sentence about being of full age and add the following.]

I am the parent or guardian, and the legal representative of the minor named above and herein referred to as "subject." I hereby certify that I have the legal authority to execute the above release.

I approve the foregoing release and waive any rights, for myself and on behalf of the above named minor, in the premises.

I have read this release, am familiar with and understand its contents. and all the obligations created and rights waived herein.

Signed: _____

Printed name and address:

_____

_____

Date: _____

Employment Agreement

This agreement is made as of _____ (date) by and between _____, an *[individual, unincorporated association, partnership, or corporation]* with its principal offices at _____ *[be sure to include enough information that you can be located and to indicate the state for jurisdiction]* doing business under the laws of the state of _____, hereinafter for convenience referred to as "Employer"; and _____ of _____ *[residence of employee]*, hereinafter referred to as "Employee."

WITNESSETH
Whereas Employer wishes to employ Employee as a staff writer and Employee is willing to serve in that capacity; and

Whereas Employer and Employee wish to set the terms and conditions of that employment.

Therefore, in consideration of the promises and mutual agreements contained herein and for other good and valuable consideration, the receipt and sufficiency of which are hereby acknowledged, Employer and Employee agree as follows:

This agreement shall be subject to the laws of the state of _____ and its construction, execution, and interpretation shall be governed by the laws of that state, without giving effect to the conflict or choice of law provisions thereof.

EMPLOYMENT
Employer hereby agrees to employ Employee as a staff writer and Employee agrees to be employed by Employer on the terms and conditions set forth herein.

Employer shall report to _____ *[Specify a job title but not an individual's name, who will be the employee's supervisor]* and shall have the duties, responsibilities, and authority commensurate with that position. *[Here the contract may include specific duties such as research and writing of news releases or research, reporting and writing articles. Often work hours are also included here.]*

Employee will dedicate all of his or her professional skill, time, and effort to the duties described above and will faithfully serve Employer. This obligation will not prevent Employee from participating in pro bono work and other activities that do not interfere with Employee's obligations to Employer created hereby.

TERM OF EMPLOYMENT
[NOTE- this may be as simple as saying Employee will serve at the will of Employer, or it may be more specific.]

Unless terminated earlier for reasons specified in the paragraph titled "termination" below, Employee will begin employment for Employer on _____ (date), and Employee's employment will continue for a term of _____ years.

Employee's employment for Employer will be automatically renewed for successive _____ _____ -year terms unless either party gives written notice to the other at least _____ *[term of weeks or months]* prior to the expiration of any then existing employment term.

TERMINATION

Employee's employment under this agreement will terminate immediately upon any of the following events:

[Here is typically listed conduct that would make the Employee unacceptable. This conduct may include criminal convictions, revealing Employer trade secrets, violating a non-competition clause, failure to perform, or actions inconsistent with the interest of Employer. Often also included are the death of the Employee and/or significant changes in Employer's financial situation. One other clause is often included and that is one that permits the Employer to terminate without cause with some period of notice. This final clause is included to permit employers to terminate employees without having to actually prove misconduct or malfeasance.]

COMPENSATION

As compensation for his or her services under this Agreement, Employer will pay Employee a base salary of $_____ per _____. *[Here often the employer will include a schedule for payment and a description of evaluations for any salary increases and/or bonuses. Here also are typically listed such things as benefit packages and vacation time.]*

REQUIREMENT FOR CONFIDENTIALITY AND NON-COMPETITION

Employee hereby enters into a non-disclosure and non-competition agreement the effective dates of which are _____ *[The dates usually begin upon employment or agreement and continue well after termination. Also, many employers use a separate covenant not to compete and will use language that incorporates that covenant into the employment contract.]*

INDEMNIFICATION

During the employment of Employee by Employer, Employer will indemnify Employee to the greatest extend permitted by law against any judgments, fines, or reasonable settlement expenses, including attorney's fees and other costs associated with any claim, civil action, or criminal action against Employee that arises from Employee's work within the scope of his or her employment by Employee. Employee and Employer specifically agree that this indemnification does not apply to any action or claim against Employee by Employer, whether or not that claim or action arises from Employee's work within the scope of his or her employment by Employer.

REPRESENTATION

Employee represents and warrants that he or she is not prohibited or limited by any contractual or other obligation from committing to and honoring each and all of the agreements contained herein.

SEVERABILITY

Any term or provision of this agreement that is invalid or unenforceable in any jurisdiction shall not render invalid or unenforceable the remaining terms and provisions of this agreement nor shall it affect the validity or enforceability of any of the terms or provisions of this agreement in any other jurisdiction.

NOTICE

All notices required or described herein shall be in writing and shall be deemed to have been duly given when delivered by hand, or through the U.S. Postal Service to *[here specify addresses for delivery and indicate if the postal delivery must be by a particular means such as express or certified.].*

THE PARTIES HERETO understand and agree that this document contains the full and complete understanding of the parties hereto and that it supersedes any and all prior agreements, whether oral or written. Each party to this Agreement acknowledges that no representations, inducements, promises, or agreements, oral or otherwise, have been made by either party, or anyone acting on behalf of either party, which are not embodied herein.

THE PARTIES FURTHER understand and agree that this agreement shall be binding upon and inure to the benefit of Employee and his or her heirs, distributes, and shall be binding upon and inure to the benefit of Employer, its successors, and assigns; and that this agreement may not be assigned by Employee. Employer may assign this agreement only in connection with a merger or a sale by Employer of all or substantially all of its assets, and then only provided that the assignee specifically assumes in writing all of Employer's obligations hereunder.

IN WITNESS WHEREOF, Employer has caused this Agreement to be duly executed Employee has hereunto set his or her hand as of the date first set forth above.

Employer:

By: _____ [usually an executive of the company]

Employee: _____

[Note that some jurisdictions will require witnesses. If that is the case, ensure the witnesses actually see the parties sign and that they include contact information so they may be found if their testimony is needed.]

Covenant Not To Compete

This agreement entered into between _____, hereinafter referred to as Employer and _____, hereinafter referred to as Employee, on the _____ day of _____, _____.

A. Employee agrees not to directly or indirectly compete with the business of Employer during the term of his or her employment and for a period of _____ months [*or years*] following the termination of employment, regardless of who initiated the termination.

1. Employee specifically agrees not to be employed by, own, manage, consult with, service, or contract with any individual or company that usually conducts business with Employer.
2. Employee specifically further agrees not to be employed by, own, manage, or consult with a business that is either similar to or competes with the business of Employer. This restriction shall be limited to the geographic areas in which Employer usually conducts his or her business.

B. Employee also agrees not to directly or indirectly disclose or use any confidential information about or acquired from Employer or his or her business, except in the execution of his or her duties as an employee of Employer.

1. Employee agrees that confidential information includes, but is not limited to, client lists, client files, trade secrets, financial data, sales and marketing data, plans, campaign proposals, and the like.
2. Employer and Employee agree that confidential information does not include any information that Employer voluntarily discloses to the public.

In consideration for Employee's agreements contained herein Employer will compensate Employee as follows:

[Here list the compensation. It may be a cash payment, a promise of future employment, or any other thing of value. Remember that an already existing agreement or a past act cannot be consideration. Therefore, the employer cannot use, as consideration, the existing employment contract with the employee.]

This agreement is binding on Employer, Employee, and their heirs, successors, assigns, and personal representatives. Furthermore, this writing constitutes the entire understanding and its terms may not be modified except in writing signed by both parties.

Any waiver of any term herein shall not be construed as a waiver of the other provisions of this contract. This agreement will be governed by the laws of the State of

_____ .

Signed:

_____ Employer

_____ Printed name and title

_____ Employee

_____ Printed name

[Note that some jurisdictions will require witnesses. If that is the case, ensure the witnesses actually see the parties sign and that they include contact information so they may be found if their testimony is needed.]

Appendix D

Sample Jury Instructions

Here we provide a copy of the jury instructions used to explain to juries how they are to make a decision regarding the offense of copyright infringement. These instructions cover both the federal misdemeanor offense of willful copyright infringement and the federal felony offense of willful copyright infringement. These instructions would be given along with several others that explain concepts like burden of proof.

The first instruction would be given only in a case involving misdemeanor copyright infringement. The second instruction would be given only in a case involving felony copyright infringement. The remaining instructions are used to further explain concepts used in the first two.

1. Elements of the Offense of Misdemeanor Willful Infringement of Copyright
(17 U.S.C. § 506(a) and 18 U.S.C. § 2319(b)(3))

The defendant is charged in [Count _____ of] the indictment with criminal copyright infringement in violation of Section 506 of Title 17 and Section 2319(b)(3) of Title 18 of the United States Code. In order for the defendant to be found guilty of this charge, the government must prove each of the following elements beyond a reasonable doubt:

First, that there exists a valid copyright for [describe work in question];

Second, that at the time and place alleged, the defendant infringed the copyright in [the work] by [reproducing] [distributing] [performing publicly] [preparing a derivative work] [displaying publicly] copies of [the work];

Third, that the defendant, in infringing the copyright, acted willfully;

Fourth, that the act of infringement was for the purpose of commercial advantage or private financial gain.

2. Elements of the Offense of Felony Willful Infringement of Copyright
(17 U.S.C. § 506(a) and 18 U.S.C. § 2319(b)(1))

The defendant is charged in [Count _____ of] the indictment with criminal copyright infringement in violation of Section 506 of Title 17 and Section

2319(b)(1) of Title 18 of the United States Code. In order for the defendant to be found guilty of this charge, the government must prove each of the following elements beyond a reasonable doubt:

First, that there exists a valid copyright for [describe work(s) in question];

Second, that at the time and place alleged, the defendant infringed the copyright(s) in [the work(s)] by [reproducing] [distributing] copies of [the work];

Third, that the defendant, in infringing the copyright(s), acted willfully;

Fourth, that the acts of infringement were for the purpose of commercial advantage or private financial gain;

Fifth, that at the time and place alleged, the defendant, in infringing the copyright(s), [reproduced] [distributed] at least 10 [copies] [phonorecords] of [the work];

Sixth, that the copies or phonorecords [reproduced] [distributed] had a retail value of more than $2,500.

3. Validity of the Copyright

The first of these elements is that there exists a valid copyright in [the work(s) in question].

With respect to the first element of the offense charged, you are instructed that a copyright may be obtained in [the work in question]. A person who holds a copyright is entitled to a certificate of registration from the Copyright Office. This certificate is "prima facie evidence" of the facts stated therein. "Prima facie evidence" means sufficient evidence to establish that (the work) has a valid copyright, unless outweighed by other evidence in the case.

The evidence in this case includes the certificate of registration for [the work in question]. The certificate is Government's Exhibit No. _____. You are instructed that the certificate is prima facie evidence that there is a valid copyright in [the work in question].

4. Elements of the Offense — Infringement

The second element of the offense charged is infringement. An infringement of a copyright occurs whenever someone who is not the copyright owner and who has no authorization from the owner does an act which is the exclusive right of the copyright owner to do. Among the exclusive rights given to the owner of a valid copyright are the rights to [reproduce, distribute] the copyrighted work. In this case, the Government alleges that the defendant infringed the copyright by [reproducing, distributing] [the work in question].

If you find that the defendant [reproduced, distributed] [the work in question] without the authorization of the copyright owner, then you may find that the defendant infringed the copyright in [the work in question].

5. Elements of the Offense — Willfulness

Prosecutors may rely upon the appropriate pattern jury instructions in their circuit to define "willful."

6. Elements of the Offense — Commercial Advantage or Private Financial Gain

The fourth element of a copyright infringement is that the alleged infringement was done for the purpose of commercial advantage or private financial gain. With respect to this element, you are instructed that the Government need not prove that the defendant actually received a profit from the infringement. The Government need only show that the defendant acted with the hope or expectation of some commercial advantage or financial gain.

If you find that the defendant infringed the copyright in [the work in question] with the hope or expectation of some financial gain, then you may find that the defendant's infringement was done for the purpose of commercial advantage or private financial gain.

The Constitution
of the United States

We the People of the United States, in Order to form a more perfect Union, establish Justice, insure domestic Tranquility, provide for the common defense, promote the general Welfare, and secure the Blessings of Liberty to ourselves and our Posterity, do ordain and establish this Constitution for the United States of America.

Article I

Section 1.

All legislative Powers herein granted shall be vested in a Congress of the United States, which shall consist of a Senate and House of Representatives.

Section 2.

The House of Representatives shall be composed of Members chosen every second Year by the People of the several States, and the Electors in each State shall have the Qualifications requisite for Electors of the most numerous Branch of the State Legislature.

No Person shall be a Representative who shall not have attained to the Age of twenty-five Years, and been seven Years a Citizen of the United States, and who shall not, when elected, be an Inhabitant of that State in which he shall be chosen.

Representatives and direct Taxes shall be apportioned among the several States which may be included within this Union, according to their respective Numbers, which shall be determined by adding to the whole Number of free Persons, including those bound to Service for a Term of Years, and excluding Indians not taxed, three fifths of all other Persons. The actual Enumeration shall be made within three Years after the first Meeting of the Congress of the United States, and within every subsequent Term of ten Years, in such Manner as they shall by Law direct. The Number of Representatives shall not exceed one for every thirty Thousand, but each State shall have at Least one Representative; and until such enumeration shall be made, the State of New Hampshire shall be entitled to chuse three, Massachusetts eight, Rhode-Island and Providence Plantations one, Connecticut five, New York six, New Jersey four, Pennsylvania eight, Delaware one, Maryland six, Virginia ten, North Carolina five, South Carolina five, and Georgia three.

When vacancies happen in the Representation from any State, the Executive Authority thereof shall issue Writs of Election to fill such Vacancies.

The House of Representatives shall chuse their Speaker and other Officers; and shall have the sole Power of Impeachment.

Section 3.

The Senate of the United States shall be composed of two Senators from each State, chosen by the Legislature thereof for six Years; and each Senator shall have one Vote.

Immediately after they shall be assembled in Consequence of the first Election, they shall be divided as equally as may be into three Classes. The Seats of the Senators of the first Class shall be vacated at the Expiration of the second Year, of the second Class at the Expiration of the fourth Year, and of the third Class at the Expiration of the sixth Year, so that one third may be chosen every second Year; and if Vacancies happen by Resignation, or otherwise, during the Recess of the Legislature of any State, the Executive thereof may make temporary Appointments until the next Meeting of the Legislature, which shall then fill such Vacancies.

No Person shall be a Senator who shall not have attained to the Age of thirty Years, and been nine Years a Citizen of the United States, and who shall not, when elected, be an Inhabitant of that State for which he shall be chosen.

The Vice President of the United States shall be President of the Senate, but shall have no Vote, unless they be equally divided.

The Senate shall chuse their other Officers, and also a President pro tempore, in the Absence of the Vice President, or when he shall exercise the Office of President of the United States.

The Senate shall have the sole Power to try all Impeachments. When sitting for that Purpose, they shall be on Oath or Affirmation. When the President of the United States is tried, the Chief Justice shall preside: And no Person shall be convicted without the Concurrence of two thirds of the Members present.

Judgment in Cases of Impeachment shall not extend further than to removal from Office, and disqualification to hold and enjoy any Office of honor, Trust or Profit under the United States: but the Party convicted shall nevertheless be liable and subject to Indictment, Trial, Judgment and Punishment, according to Law.

Section 4.

The Times, Places and Manner of holding Elections for Senators and Representatives, shall be prescribed in each State by the Legislature thereof; but the Congress may at any time by Law make or alter such Regulations, except as to the Places of chusing Senators.

The Congress shall assemble at least once in every Year, and such Meeting shall be on the first Monday in December, unless they shall by Law appoint a different Day.

Section 5.

Each House shall be the Judge of the Elections, Returns and Qualifications of its own Members, and a Majority of each shall constitute a Quorum to do Business; but a smaller Number may adjourn from day to day, and may be authorized to compel the

Attendance of absent Members, in such Manner, and under such Penalties as each House may provide.

Each House may determine the Rules of its Proceedings, punish its Members for disorderly Behaviour, and, with the Concurrence of two thirds, expel a Member.

Each House shall keep a Journal of its Proceedings, and from time to time publish the same, excepting such Parts as may in their Judgment require Secrecy; and the Yeas and Nays of the Members of either House on any question shall, at the Desire of one fifth of those Present, be entered on the Journal.

Neither House, during the Session of Congress, shall, without the Consent of the other, adjourn for more than three days, nor to any other Place than that in which the two Houses shall be sitting.

Section 6.

The Senators and Representatives shall receive a Compensation for their Services, to be ascertained by Law, and paid out of the Treasury of the United States. They shall in all Cases, except Treason, Felony and Breach of the Peace, be privileged from Arrest during their Attendance at the Session of their respective Houses, and in going to and returning from the same; and for any Speech or Debate in either House, they shall not be questioned in any other Place.

No Senator or Representative shall, during the Time for which he was elected, be appointed to any civil Office under the Authority of the United States, which shall have been created, or the Emoluments whereof shall have been increased during such time; and no Person holding any Office under the United States, shall be a Member of either House during his Continuance in Office.

Section 7.

All Bills for raising Revenue shall originate in the House of Representatives; but the Senate may propose or concur with Amendments as on other Bills.

Every Bill which shall have passed the House of Representatives and the Senate, shall, before it become a Law, be presented to the President of the United States: If he approve he shall sign it, but if not he shall return it, with his Objections to that House in which it shall have originated, who shall enter the Objections at large on their Journal, and proceed to reconsider it. If after such Reconsideration two thirds of that House shall agree to pass the Bill, it shall be sent, together with the Objections, to the other House, by which it shall likewise be reconsidered, and if approved by two thirds of that House, it shall become a Law. But in all such Cases the Votes of both Houses shall be determined by Yeas and Nays, and the Names of the Persons voting for and against the Bill shall be entered on the Journal of each House respectively. If any Bill shall not be returned by the President within ten Days (Sundays excepted) after it shall have been presented to him, the Same shall be a Law, in like Manner as if he had signed it, unless the Congress by their Adjournment prevent its Return, in which Case it shall not be a Law.

Every Order, Resolution, or Vote to which the Concurrence of the Senate and House of Representatives may be necessary (except on a question of Adjournment) shall be presented to the President of the United States; and before the Same shall take Effect, shall be approved by him, or being disapproved by him, shall be repassed by two thirds of the Senate and House of Representatives, according to the Rules and Limitations prescribed in the Case of a Bill.

Section 8.

The Congress shall have Power To lay and collect Taxes, Duties, Imposts and Excises, to pay the Debts and provide for the common Defence and general Welfare of the United States; but all Duties, Imposts and Excises shall be uniform throughout the United States;

To borrow Money on the credit of the United States;

To regulate Commerce with foreign Nations, and among the several States, and with the Indian Tribes;

To establish a uniform Rule of Naturalization, and uniform Laws on the subject of Bankruptcies throughout the United States;

To coin Money, regulate the Value thereof, and of foreign Coin, and fix the Standard of Weights and Measures;

To provide for the Punishment of counterfeiting the Securities and current Coin of the United States;

To establish Post Offices and post Roads;

To promote the Progress of Science and useful Arts, by securing for limited Times to Authors and Inventors the exclusive Right to their respective Writings and Discoveries;

To constitute Tribunals inferior to the supreme Court;

To define and punish Piracies and Felonies committed on the high Seas, and Offences against the Law of Nations;

To declare War, grant Letters of Marque and Reprisal, and make Rules concerning Captures on Land and Water;

To raise and support Armies, but no Appropriation of Money to that Use shall be for a longer Term than two Years;

To provide and maintain a Navy;

To make Rules for the Government and Regulation of the land and naval Forces;

To provide for calling forth the Militia to execute the Laws of the Union, suppress Insurrections and repel Invasions;

To provide for organizing, arming, and disciplining the Militia, and for governing such Part of them as may be employed in the Service of the United States, reserving to the States respectively, the Appointment of the Officers, and the Authority of training the Militia according to the discipline prescribed by Congress;

To exercise exclusive Legislation in all Cases whatsoever, over such District (not exceeding ten Miles square) as may, by Cession of particular States, and the Acceptance of Congress, become the Seat of the Government of the United States, and to exercise like Authority over all Places purchased by the Consent of the Legislature of the State in which the Same shall be, for the Erection of Forts, Magazines, Arsenals, dock-Yards, and other needful Buildings;—And

To make all Laws which shall be necessary and proper for carrying into Execution the foregoing Powers, and all other Powers vested by this Constitution in the Government of the United States, or in any Department or Officer thereof.

Section 9.

The Migration or Importation of such Persons as any of the States now existing shall think proper to admit, shall not be prohibited by the Congress prior to the Year one thousand eight hundred and eight, but a Tax or duty may be imposed on such Importation, not exceeding ten dollars for each Person.

The Privilege of the Writ of Habeas Corpus shall not be suspended, unless when in Cases of Rebellion or Invasion the public Safety may require it.

No Bill of Attainder or ex post facto Law shall be passed.

No Capitation, or other direct, Tax shall be laid, unless in Proportion to the Census or enumeration herein before directed to be taken.

No Tax or Duty shall be laid on Articles exported from any State.

No Preference shall be given by any Regulation of Commerce or Revenue to the Ports of one State over those of another; nor shall Vessels bound to, or from, one State, be obliged to enter, clear, or pay Duties in another.

No Money shall be drawn from the Treasury, but in Consequence of Appropriations made by Law; and a regular Statement and Account of the Receipts and Expenditures of all public Money shall be published from time to time.

No Title of Nobility shall be granted by the United States: And no Person holding any Office of Profit or Trust under them, shall, without the Consent of the Congress, accept of any present, Emolument, Office, or Title, of any kind whatever, from any King, Prince, or foreign State.

Section 10.

No State shall enter into any Treaty, Alliance, or Confederation; grant Letters of Marque and Reprisal; coin Money; emit Bills of Credit; make any Thing but gold and silver Coin a Tender in Payment of Debts; pass any Bill of Attainder, ex post facto Law, or Law impairing the Obligation of Contracts, or grant any Title of Nobility.

No State shall, without the Consent of the Congress, lay any Imposts or Duties on Imports or Exports, except what may be absolutely necessary for executing its inspection Laws: and the net Produce of all Duties and Imposts, laid by any State on Imports or Exports, shall be for the Use of the Treasury of the United States; and all such Laws shall be subject to the Revision and Control of the Congress.

No State shall, without the Consent of Congress, lay any Duty of Tonnage, keep Troops, or Ships of War in time of Peace, enter into any Agreement or Compact with another State, or with a foreign Power, or engage in War, unless actually invaded, or in such imminent Danger as will not admit of delay.

Article II

Section 1.

The executive Power shall be vested in a President of the United States of America. He shall hold his Office during the Term of four Years, and, together with the Vice President, chosen for the same Term, be elected, as follows:

Each State shall appoint, in such Manner as the Legislature thereof may direct, a Number of Electors, equal to the whole Number of Senators and Representatives to which the State may be entitled in the Congress: but no Senator or Representative, or Person holding an Office of Trust or Profit under the United States, shall be appointed an Elector.

The Electors shall meet in their respective States, and vote by Ballot for two Persons, of whom one at least shall not be an Inhabitant of the same State with themselves. And they shall make a List of all the Persons voted for, and of the Number of Votes for each; which List they shall sign and certify, and transmit sealed to the Seat of the Government of the United States, directed to the President of the Senate. The President of the Senate shall, in the Presence of the Senate and House of Representatives, open all the Certificates, and the Votes shall then be counted. The Person having the greatest Number of Votes shall be the President, if such Number be a Majority of the whole Number of Electors appointed; and if there be more than one who have such Majority, and have an equal Number of Votes, then the House of Representatives shall immediately chuse by Ballot one of them for President; and if no Person have a Majority, then from the five highest on the List the said House shall in like Manner chuse the President. But in chusing the President, the Votes shall be taken by States, the Representation from each State having one Vote; A quorum for this purpose shall consist of a Member or Members from two thirds of the States, and a Majority of all the States shall be necessary to a Choice. In every Case, after the Choice of the President, the Person having the greatest Number of Votes of the Electors shall be the Vice President. But if there should remain two or more who have equal Votes, the Senate shall chuse from them by Ballot the Vice President.

The Congress may determine the Time of chusing the Electors, and the Day on which they shall give their Votes; which Day shall be the same throughout the United States.

No Person except a natural born Citizen, or a Citizen of the United States, at the time of the Adoption of this Constitution, shall be eligible to the Office of President; neither shall any Person be eligible to that Office who shall not have attained to the Age of thirty-five Years, and been fourteen Years a Resident within the United States.

In Case of the Removal of the President from Office, or of his Death, Resignation, or Inability to discharge the Powers and Duties of the said Office, the Same shall devolve on the Vice President, and the Congress may by Law provide for the Case of Removal, Death, Resignation or Inability, both of the President and Vice President, declaring what Officer shall then act as President, and such Officer shall act accordingly, until the Disability be removed, or a President shall be elected.

The President shall, at stated Times, receive for his Services, a Compensation, which shall neither be increased nor diminished during the Period for which he shall have been elected, and he shall not receive within that Period any other Emolument from the United States, or any of them.

Before he enter on the Execution of his Office, he shall take the following Oath or Affirmation:—"I do solemnly swear (or affirm) that I will faithfully execute the Office of President of the United States, and will to the best of my Ability, preserve, protect and defend the Constitution of the United States."

Section 2.

The President shall be Commander in Chief of the Army and Navy of the United States, and of the Militia of the several States, when called into the actual Service of the

United States; he may require the Opinion, in writing, of the principal Officer in each of the executive Departments, upon any Subject relating to the Duties of their respective Offices, and he shall have Power to grant Reprieves and Pardons for Offences against the United States, except in Cases of Impeachment.

He shall have Power, by and with the Advice and Consent of the Senate, to make Treaties, provided two thirds of the Senators present concur; and he shall nominate, and by and with the Advice and Consent of the Senate, shall appoint Ambassadors, other public Ministers and Consuls, Judges of the supreme Court, and all other Officers of the United States, whose Appointments are not herein otherwise provided for, and which shall be established by Law: but the Congress may by Law vest the Appointment of such inferior Officers, as they think proper, in the President alone, in the Courts of Law, or in the Heads of Departments.

The President shall have Power to fill up all Vacancies that may happen during the Recess of the Senate, by granting Commissions which shall expire at the End of their next Session.

Section 3.

He shall from time to time give to the Congress Information of the State of the Union, and recommend to their Consideration such Measures as he shall judge necessary and expedient; he may, on extraordinary Occasions, convene both Houses, or either of them, and in Case of Disagreement between them, with Respect to the Time of Adjournment, he may adjourn them to such Time as he shall think proper; he shall receive Ambassadors and other public Ministers; he shall take Care that the Laws be faithfully executed, and shall Commission all the Officers of the United States.

Section 4.

The President, Vice President and all civil Officers of the United States, shall be removed from Office on Impeachment for, and Conviction of, Treason, Bribery, or other high Crimes and Misdemeanors.

Article III

Section 1.

The judicial Power of the United States shall be vested in one supreme Court, and in such inferior Courts as the Congress may from time to time ordain and establish. The Judges, both of the supreme and inferior Courts, shall hold their Offices during good Behaviour, and shall, at stated Times, receive for their Services a Compensation, which shall not be diminished during their Continuance in Office.

Section 2.

The judicial Power shall extend to all Cases, in Law and Equity, arising under this Constitution, the Laws of the United States, and Treaties made, or which shall be made, under their Authority;—to all Cases affecting Ambassadors, other public Ministers and Consuls;—to all Cases of admiralty and maritime Jurisdiction;—to Controversies to which the United States shall be a Party;—to Controversies between two or more States;—between a State and Citizens of another State;—between Citizens of different States;—between Citizens of the same State claiming Lands under Grants of different States, and between a State, or the Citizens thereof, and foreign States, Citizens or Subjects.

In all Cases affecting Ambassadors, other public Ministers and Consuls, and those in which a State shall be Party, the supreme Court shall have original Jurisdiction. In all the other Cases before mentioned, the supreme Court shall have appellate Jurisdiction, both as to Law and Fact, with such Exceptions, and under such Regulations as the Congress shall make.

The Trial of all Crimes, except in Cases of Impeachment, shall be by Jury; and such Trial shall be held in the State where the said Crimes shall have been committed; but when not committed within any State, the Trial shall be at such Place or Places as the Congress may by Law have directed.

Section 3.

Treason against the United States, shall consist only in levying War against them, or in adhering to their Enemies, giving them Aid and Comfort. No Person shall be convicted of Treason unless on the Testimony of two Witnesses to the same overt Act, or on Confession in open Court.

The Congress shall have Power to declare the Punishment of Treason, but no Attainder of Treason shall work Corruption of Blood, or Forfeiture except during the Life of the Person attainted.

Article IV

Section 1.

Full Faith and Credit shall be given in each State to the public Acts, Records, and judicial Proceedings of every other State. And the Congress may by general Laws prescribe the Manner in which such Acts, Records and Proceedings shall be proved, and the Effect thereof.

Section 2.

The Citizens of each State shall be entitled to all Privileges and Immunities of Citizens in the several States.

A Person charged in any State with Treason, Felony, or other Crime, who shall flee from Justice, and be found in another State, shall on Demand of the executive Authority of the State from which he fled, be delivered up, to be removed to the State having Jurisdiction of the Crime.

No Person held to Service or Labour in one State, under the Laws thereof, escaping into another, shall, in Consequence of any Law or Regulation therein, be discharged from such Service or Labour, but shall be delivered up on Claim of the Party to whom such Service or Labour may be due.

Section 3.

New States may be admitted by the Congress into this Union; but no new State shall be formed or erected within the Jurisdiction of any other State; nor any State be formed by the Junction of two or more States, or Parts of States, without the Consent of the Legislatures of the States concerned as well as of the Congress.

The Congress shall have Power to dispose of and make all needful Rules and Regulations respecting the Territory or other Property belonging to the United States; and nothing in this Constitution shall be so construed as to Prejudice any Claims of the United States, or of any particular State.

Section 4.

The United States shall guarantee to every State in this Union a Republican Form of Government, and shall protect each of them against Invasion; and on Application of the Legislature, or of the Executive (when the Legislature cannot be convened), against domestic Violence.

Article V

The Congress, whenever two thirds of both Houses shall deem it necessary, shall propose Amendments to this Constitution, or, on the Application of the Legislatures of two thirds of the several States, shall call a Convention for proposing Amendments, which, in either Case, shall be valid to all Intents and Purposes, as Part of this Constitution, when ratified by the Legislatures of three fourths of the several States, or by Conventions in three fourths thereof, as the one or the other Mode of Ratification may be proposed by the Congress; Provided that no Amendment which may be made prior to the Year One thousand eight hundred and eight shall in any Manner affect the first and fourth Clauses in the Ninth Section of the first Article; and that no State, without its Consent, shall be deprived of its equal Suffrage in the Senate.

Article VI

All Debts contracted and Engagements entered into, before the Adoption of this Constitution, shall be as valid against the United States under this Constitution, as under the Confederation.

This Constitution, and the Laws of the United States which shall be made in Pursuance thereof; and all Treaties made, or which shall be made, under the Authority of the United States, shall be the supreme Law of the Land; and the Judges in every State shall be bound thereby, any Thing in the Constitution or Laws of any State to the Contrary notwithstanding.

The Senators and Representatives before mentioned, and the Members of the several State Legislatures, and all executive and judicial Officers, both of the United States and of the several States, shall be bound by Oath or Affirmation, to support this Constitution; but no religious Test shall ever be required as a Qualification to any Office or public Trust under the United States.

Article VII

The Ratification of the Conventions of nine States, shall be sufficient for the Establishment of this Constitution between the States so ratifying the Same.

The Word, "the," being interlined between the seventh and eighth Lines of the first Page, the Word "Thirty" being partly written on an Erazure in the fifteenth Line of the first Page, The Words "is tried" being interlined between the thirty-second and thirty-third Lines of the first Page and the Word "the" being interlined between the forty-third and forty-fourth Lines of the second Page.

Attest William Jackson Secretary

Done in Convention by the Unanimous Consent of the States present the Seventeenth Day of September in the Year of our Lord one thousand seven hundred and Eighty seven and of the Independence of the United States of America the Twelfth In witness whereof We have hereunto subscribed our Names,

The Preamble to The Bill of Rights

Congress of the United States

begun and held at the City of New York, on Wednesday the fourth of March, one thousand seven hundred and eighty nine.

THE Conventions of a number of the States, having at the time of their adopting the Constitution, expressed a desire, in order to prevent misconstruction or abuse of its powers, that further declaratory and restrictive clauses should be added: And as extending the ground of public confidence in the Government, will best ensure the beneficent ends of its institution.

RESOLVED by the Senate and House of Representatives of the United States of America, in Congress assembled, two thirds of both Houses concurring, that the following Articles be proposed to the Legislatures of the several States, as amendments to the Constitution of the United States, all, or any of which Articles, when ratified by three fourths of the said Legislatures, to be valid to all intents and purposes, as part of the said Constitution; viz.

ARTICLES in addition to, and Amendment of the Constitution of the United States of America, proposed by Congress, and ratified by the Legislatures of the several States, pursuant to the fifth Article of the original Constitution.

Amendment I

Congress shall make no law respecting an establishment of religion, or prohibiting the free exercise thereof; or abridging the freedom of speech, or of the press; or the right of the people peaceably to assemble, and to petition the Government for a redress of grievances.

Amendment II

A well-regulated Militia, being necessary to the security of a free State, the right of the people to keep and bear Arms, shall not be infringed.

Amendment III

No Soldier shall, in time of peace be quartered in any house, without the consent of the Owner, nor in time of war, but in a manner to be prescribed by law.

Amendment IV

The right of the people to be secure in their persons, houses, papers, and effects, against unreasonable searches and seizures, shall not be violated, and no Warrants shall issue, but upon probable cause, supported by Oath or affirmation, and particularly describing the place to be searched, and the persons or things to be seized.

Amendment V

No person shall be held to answer for a capital, or otherwise infamous crime, unless on a presentment or indictment of a Grand Jury, except in cases arising in the land or naval forces, or in the Militia, when in actual service in time of War or public danger; nor shall any person be subject for the same offence to be twice put in jeopardy of life or limb; nor shall be compelled in any criminal case to be a witness against himself, nor be deprived of life, liberty, or property, without due process of law; nor shall private property be taken for public use, without just compensation.

Amendment VI

In all criminal prosecutions, the accused shall enjoy the right to a speedy and public trial, by an impartial jury of the State and district wherein the crime shall have been committed, which district shall have been previously ascertained by law, and to be informed of the nature and cause of the accusation; to be confronted with the witnesses against him; to have compulsory process for obtaining witnesses in his favor, and to have the Assistance of Counsel for his defence.

Amendment VII

In suits at common law, where the value in controversy shall exceed twenty dollars, the right of trial by jury shall be preserved, and no fact tried by a jury, shall be otherwise reexamined in any Court of the United States, than according to the rules of the common law.

Amendment VIII

Excessive bail shall not be required, nor excessive fines imposed, nor cruel and unusual punishments inflicted.

Amendment IX

The enumeration in the Constitution, of certain rights, shall not be construed to deny or disparage others retained by the people.

Amendment X

The powers not delegated to the United States by the Constitution, nor prohibited by it to the States, are reserved to the States respectively, or to the people.

Amendment XI

Passed by Congress March 4, 1794. Ratified February 7, 1795.

Note: Article III, section 2, of the Constitution was modified by amendment 11.

The Judicial power of the United States shall not be construed to extend to any suit in law or equity, commenced or prosecuted against one of the United States by Citizens of another State, or by Citizens or Subjects of any Foreign State.

Amendment XII

Passed by Congress December 9, 1803. Ratified June 15, 1804.

Note: A portion of Article II, section 1 of the Constitution was superseded by the 12th amendment.

The Electors shall meet in their respective states and vote by ballot for President and Vice-President, one of whom, at least, shall not be an inhabitant of the same state with themselves; they shall name in their ballots the person voted for as President, and in distinct ballots the person voted for as Vice-President, and they shall make distinct lists of all persons voted for as President, and of all persons voted for as Vice-President, and of the number of votes for each, which lists they shall sign and certify, and transmit sealed to the seat of the government of the United States, directed to the President of the Senate;—the President of the Senate shall, in the presence of the Senate and House of Representatives, open all the certificates and the votes shall then be counted;—The person having the greatest number of votes for President, shall be the President, if such number be a majority of the whole number of Electors appointed; and if no person have such majority, then from the persons having the highest numbers not exceeding three on the list of those voted for as President, the House of Representatives shall choose immediately, by ballot, the President. But in choosing the President, the votes shall be taken by states, the representation from each state having one vote; a quorum for this purpose shall consist of a member or members from two-thirds of the states, and a majority of all the states shall be necessary to a choice. [And if the House of Representatives shall not choose a President whenever the right of choice shall devolve upon them, before the fourth day of March next following, then the Vice-President shall act as President, as in case of the death or other constitutional disability of the President.—]* The person having the greatest number of votes as Vice-President, shall be the Vice-President, if such number be a majority of the whole number of Electors appointed, and if no person have a majority, then from the two highest numbers on the list, the Senate shall choose the Vice-President; a quorum for the purpose shall consist of two-thirds of the whole number of Senators, and a majority of the whole number shall be necessary to a choice. But

Superseded by section 3 of the 20th amendment.

no person constitutionally ineligible to the office of President shall be eligible to that of Vice-President of the United States.

Amendment XIII

Passed by Congress January 31, 1865. Ratified December 6, 1865.

   Note: A portion of Article IV, section 2, of the Constitution was superseded by the 13th amendment.

Section 1.

Neither slavery nor involuntary servitude, except as a punishment for crime whereof the party shall have been duly convicted, shall exist within the United States, or any place subject to their jurisdiction.

Section 2.

Congress shall have power to enforce this article by appropriate legislation.

Amendment XIV

Passed by Congress June 13, 1866. Ratified July 9, 1868.

   Note: Article I, section 2, of the Constitution was modified by section 2 of the 14th amendment.

Section 1.

All persons born or naturalized in the United States, and subject to the jurisdiction thereof, are citizens of the United States and of the State wherein they reside. No State shall make or enforce any law which shall abridge the privileges or immunities of citizens of the United States; nor shall any State deprive any person of life, liberty, or property, without due process of law; nor deny to any person within its jurisdiction the equal protection of the laws.

Section 2.

Representatives shall be apportioned among the several States according to their respective numbers, counting the whole number of persons in each State, excluding Indians not taxed. But when the right to vote at any election for the choice of electors for President and Vice-President of the United States, Representatives in Congress, the Executive and Judicial officers of a State, or the members of the Legislature thereof, is denied to any of the male inhabitants of such State, being twenty-one years of age,* and citizens of the United States, or in any way abridged, except for participation in rebellion, or other crime, the basis of representation therein shall be reduced in the proportion which the number of such male citizens shall bear to the whole number of male citizens twenty-one years of age in such State.

---

*Changed by section 1 of the 26th amendment.

Section 3.

No person shall be a Senator or Representative in Congress, or elector of President and Vice-President, or hold any office, civil or military, under the United States, or under any State, who, having previously taken an oath, as a member of Congress, or as an officer of the United States, or as a member of any State legislature, or as an executive or judicial officer of any State, to support the Constitution of the United States, shall have engaged in insurrection or rebellion against the same, or given aid or comfort to the enemies thereof. But Congress may by a vote of two-thirds of each House, remove such disability.

Section 4.

The validity of the public debt of the United States, authorized by law, including debts incurred for payment of pensions and bounties for services in suppressing insurrection or rebellion, shall not be questioned. But neither the United States nor any State shall assume or pay any debt or obligation incurred in aid of insurrection or rebellion against the United States, or any claim for the loss or emancipation of any slave; but all such debts, obligations and claims shall be held illegal and void.

Section 5.

The Congress shall have the power to enforce, by appropriate legislation, the provisions of this article.

Amendment XV

Passed by Congress February 26, 1869. Ratified February 3, 1870.

Section 1.

The right of citizens of the United States to vote shall not be denied or abridged by the United States or by any State on account of race, color, or previous condition of servitude—

Section 2.

The Congress shall have the power to enforce this article by appropriate legislation.

Amendment XVI

Passed by Congress July 2, 1909. Ratified February 3, 1913.

Note: Article I, section 9, of the Constitution was modified by amendment 16.

The Congress shall have power to lay and collect taxes on incomes, from whatever source derived, without apportionment among the several States, and without regard to any census or enumeration.

Amendment XVII

Passed by Congress May 13, 1912. Ratified April 8, 1913.

Note: Article I, section 3, of the Constitution was modified by the 17th amendment.

The Senate of the United States shall be composed of two Senators from each State, elected by the people thereof, for six years; and each Senator shall have one vote. The electors in each State shall have the qualifications requisite for electors of the most numerous branch of the State legislatures.

When vacancies happen in the representation of any State in the Senate, the executive authority of such State shall issue writs of election to fill such vacancies: *Provided*, That the legislature of any State may empower the executive thereof to make temporary appointments until the people fill the vacancies by election as the legislature may direct.

This amendment shall not be so construed as to affect the election or term of any Senator chosen before it becomes valid as part of the Constitution.

Amendment XVIII

Passed by Congress December 18, 1917. Ratified January 16, 1919. Repealed by amendment 21.

Section 1.

After one year from the ratification of this article the manufacture, sale, or transportation of intoxicating liquors within, the importation thereof into, or the exportation thereof from the United States and all territory subject to the jurisdiction thereof for beverage purposes is hereby prohibited.

Section 2.

The Congress and the several States shall have concurrent power to enforce this article by appropriate legislation.

Section 3.

This article shall be inoperative unless it shall have been ratified as an amendment to the Constitution by the legislatures of the several States, as provided in the Constitution, within seven years from the date of the submission hereof to the States by the Congress.

Amendment XIX

Passed by Congress June 4, 1919. Ratified August 18, 1920.

The right of citizens of the United States to vote shall not be denied or abridged by the United States or by any State on account of sex.

Congress shall have power to enforce this article by appropriate legislation.

Amendment XX

Passed by Congress March 2, 1932. Ratified January 23, 1933.

Note: Article I, section 4, of the Constitution was modified by section 2 of this amendment. In addition, a portion of the 12th amendment was superseded by section 3.

Section 1.

The terms of the President and the Vice President shall end at noon on the 20th day of January, and the terms of Senators and Representatives at noon on the 3rd day of January, of the years in which such terms would have ended if this article had not been ratified; and the terms of their successors shall then begin.

Section 2.

The Congress shall assemble at least once in every year, and such meeting shall begin at noon on the 3rd day of January, unless they shall by law appoint a different day.

Section 3.

If, at the time fixed for the beginning of the term of the President, the President elect shall have died, the Vice President elect shall become President. If a President shall not have been chosen before the time fixed for the beginning of his term, or if the President elect shall have failed to qualify, then the Vice President elect shall act as President until a President shall have qualified; and the Congress may by law provide for the case wherein neither a President elect nor a Vice President shall have qualified, declaring who shall then act as President, or the manner in which one who is to act shall be selected, and such person shall act accordingly until a President or Vice President shall have qualified.

Section 4.

The Congress may by law provide for the case of the death of any of the persons from whom the House of Representatives may choose a President whenever the right of choice shall have devolved upon them, and for the case of the death of any of the persons from whom the Senate may choose a Vice President whenever the right of choice shall have devolved upon them.

Section 5.

Sections 1 and 2 shall take effect on the 15th day of October following the ratification of this article.

Section 6.

This article shall be inoperative unless it shall have been ratified as an amendment to the Constitution by the legislatures of three-fourths of the several States within seven years from the date of its submission.

Amendment XXI

Passed by Congress February 20, 1933. Ratified December 5, 1933.

Section 1.

The eighteenth article of amendment to the Constitution of the United States is hereby repealed.

Section 2.

The transportation or importation into any State, Territory, or Possession of the United States for delivery or use therein of intoxicating liquors, in violation of the laws thereof, is hereby prohibited.

Section 3.

This article shall be inoperative unless it shall have been ratified as an amendment to the Constitution by conventions in the several States, as provided in the Constitution, within seven years from the date of the submission hereof to the States by the Congress.

Amendment XXII

Passed by Congress March 21, 1947. Ratified February 27, 1951.

Section 1.

No person shall be elected to the office of the President more than twice, and no person who has held the office of President, or acted as President, for more than two years of a term to which some other person was elected President shall be elected to the office of President more than once. But this Article shall not apply to any person holding the office of President when this Article was proposed by Congress, and shall not prevent any person who may be holding the office of President, or acting as President, during the term within which this Article becomes operative from holding the office of President or acting as President during the remainder of such term.

Section 2.

This article shall be inoperative unless it shall have been ratified as an amendment to the Constitution by the legislatures of three-fourths of the several States within seven years from the date of its submission to the States by the Congress.

Amendment XXIII

Passed by Congress June 16, 1960. Ratified March 29, 1961.

Section 1.

The District constituting the seat of Government of the United States shall appoint in such manner as Congress may direct:

A number of electors of President and Vice President equal to the whole number of Senators and Representatives in Congress to which the District would be entitled if it were a State, but in no event more than the least populous State; they shall be in addition to those appointed by the States, but they shall be considered, for the purposes of the election of President and Vice President, to be electors appointed by a State; and they shall meet in the District and perform such duties as provided by the twelfth article of amendment.

Section 2.

The Congress shall have power to enforce this article by appropriate legislation.

Amendment XXIV

Passed by Congress August 27, 1962. Ratified January 23, 1964.

Section 1.

The right of citizens of the United States to vote in any primary or other election for President or Vice President, for electors for President or Vice President, or for Senator or Representative in Congress, shall not be denied or abridged by the United States or any State by reason of failure to pay poll tax or other tax.

Section 2.

The Congress shall have power to enforce this article by appropriate legislation.

Amendment XXV

Passed by Congress July 6, 1965. Ratified February 10, 1967.
Note: Article II, section 1, of the Constitution was affected by the 25th amendment.

Section 1.

In case of the removal of the President from office or of his death or resignation, the Vice President shall become President.

Section 2.

Whenever there is a vacancy in the office of the Vice President, the President shall nominate a Vice President who shall take office upon confirmation by a majority vote of both Houses of Congress.

Section 3.

Whenever the President transmits to the President pro tempore of the Senate and the Speaker of the House of Representatives his written declaration that he is unable to discharge the powers and duties of his office, and until he transmits to them a written declaration to the contrary, such powers and duties shall be discharged by the Vice President as Acting President.

Section 4.

Whenever the Vice President and a majority of either the principal officers of the executive departments or of such other body as Congress may by law provide, transmit to the President pro tempore of the Senate and the Speaker of the House of Representatives their written declaration that the President is unable to discharge the powers and duties of his office, the Vice President shall immediately assume the powers and duties of the office as Acting President.

Thereafter, when the President transmits to the President pro tempore of the Senate and the Speaker of the House of Representatives his written declaration that no inability exists, he shall resume the powers and duties of his office unless the Vice President and a majority of either the principal officers of the executive department or of such other body as Congress may by law provide, transmit within four days to the President pro tempore of the Senate and the Speaker of the House of Representatives their written declaration that the President is unable to discharge the powers and duties of his office. Thereupon Congress shall decide the issue, assembling within forty-eight hours for that purpose if not in session. If the Congress, within twenty-one days after receipt of the latter written declaration, or, if Congress is not in session, within twenty-one days after Congress is required to assemble, determines by two-thirds vote of both Houses that the President is unable to discharge the powers and duties of his office, the Vice President shall continue to discharge the same as Acting President; otherwise, the President shall resume the powers and duties of his office.

Amendment XXVI

Passed by Congress March 23, 1971. Ratified July 1, 1971.

   Note: Amendment 14, section 2, of the Constitution was modified by section 1 of the 26th amendment.

Section 1.

The right of citizens of the United States, who are eighteen years of age or older, to vote shall not be denied or abridged by the United States or by any State on account of age.

Section 2.

The Congress shall have power to enforce this article by appropriate legislation.

Amendment XXVII

Originally proposed Sept. 25, 1789. Ratified May 7, 1992.

   No law, varying the compensation for the services of the Senators and Representatives, shall take effect, until an election of representatives shall have intervened.

Table of Cases

References are to page of text on which the case reference appears.

Aaron v. S.E.C., 429, 431

Abercrombie & Fitch Co. v. Hunting World, Inc., 320, 325

Abrams v. U.S., 107, 109

Action for Children's Television v. F.C.C., 148, 152, 405

Adams v. Lindsell, 1 B. & Ald. 363

Adamson v. California, 81

Admiral Oriental Line v. U.S., 364

Adobe Systems v. Southern Software, Inc., 323

Ahn v. Rooney, Pace, Inc., 364

Alfred Bell & Co. v. Catalda Fine Arts, Inc., 320, 323

Allen v. Bryson, 363

Allied Maintenance Corp. v. Allied Mechanical Trades, Inc., 325

Allstate Insurance Co. v. Allstate, Inc., 3325

American Institute of Architects v. Fenichel, 324

American International Pictures, Inc. v. Foreman, 320, 324

Apple Computer, Inc. v. Franklin Computer Corp., 320, 323

Apple Computer, Inc. v. Microsoft Corp., 321, 322, 323, 326

Aragon v. Boyd, 363

Ard Dr. Pepper Bottling Co. v. Dr. Pepper Co., 363

Arkansas AFL-CIO v. FCC, 151

Ashcroft v. ACLU, 148, 152

Ashcroft v. Free Speech Coalition, 110

Ashwander v. Tennessee Valley Authority, 25, 27

Associated Press v. National Labor Relations Board, 362

Associated Press v. U.S., 150

Associated Press v. Walker, 268, 270, 289, 292, 293

Atlanta Journal and Constitution v. City of Atlanta Department of Aviation, 378, 404

Austin v. Michigan State Chamber of Commerce, 400, 406

Ayeni v. Mottola, 191

Baker v. Carr, 25, 27

Baker v. Selden, 320, 323

Baldwin v. Sisters of Providence, 364

Ballew v. Georgia, 58

Balmetto Broadcasting Co., 152

Barber v. Time, Inc., 293, 294

Bard v. Bath Iron Works Corp., 361, 365

Barnes v. Glen Theatre, Inc., 82

Baron v. The Mayor and City Council of Baltimore, 80

Barr v. Matteo, 289, 292, 296

Bates v. State Bar of Arizona, 404, 405

Batista v. Chrysler Corp., 296

Bayer Co. v. United Drug Co., 325

Bayless v.Christie, Manson & Woods Intern, Inc., 365

Bechtel v. FCC, 148, 150

Becker v. FCC, 148, 152

Beebe v. Columbia Axle Co., 364

Beech-Nut packaging Co. v. P. Lorillard Co., 326

Bell v. Ohio, 257

Benton v. Maryland, 65, 67, 78, 81

Berger v. New York, 231

Berlin v. E.C. Publications, Inc., 324

Bibb v. Allen, 364

Bichler v. Union Bank & Trust Co., 295

Bigelow v. Virginia, 87, 108, 374, 380, 401, 404

Billups Petroleum Co. v. Hardin's Bakeries Corp., 361

Blackwell v. E.M. Helides Jr., Inc., 366

Blake Const. Co. v. U.S., 365

Bleistein v. Donaldson Lithographing Co., 324

Blue Chip v. Manor, 429, 432

Board of Trustees of the State University of New York v. Fox, 378, 401, 404

Bob Reves v. Ernst & Young, 410, 429, 431

Boiling v. Sharpe, 78

Boise Junior College Dist. v. Mattefs Constr. Co., 364

Bolger et. al. v. Youngs Drug Products Corp., 369, 371, 401, 403, 404

Booth v. Curtis Pub., Co., 295

Borreca v. Fasi, 164, 189, 190, 192, 193

Bosley Medical Group v. Abramson, 366

Bradwell v. Illinois, 78, 80, 82

Brandenberg v. Ohio, 78, 81, 87, 108

Brandywine-Main Line Radio, Inc. v. FCC, 80

Branzburg v. Hayes, 183, 184–185, 188, 189, 191, 192, 193, 248, 258, 440–469

Brauer v. Globe Newspaper Co., 294

Brauer v. Shaw, 363

Braun v. Armour & Co., 401, 406

Braun v. Flynt, 294

Braun v. Soldier of Fortune Magazine, Inc., 107, 108, 109, 396, 397, 401, 406

Bridges v. California, 202, 227, 229, 230

Bridges v. Wixon, 213, 227, 231

Bright Tunes Music Corp. v. Harrisongs Music, Ltd., 320, 324

Briscoe v. LaHue, 292

Briscoe v. Reader's Digest Ass'n., 293, 294, 365

Bromberg v. Carmel Self Service, Inc., 325

Brown Bag Software v. Symantec Corp., 323

Brown Instrument Co. v. Warner, 323

Brown v. Board of Education, 78, 80

Brown v. Louisiana, 109

Bucher & Willis Consulting Engineers, Planners and Architects v. Smith, 365

Buckley v. Fitzsimmons, 292

Buckley v. Valeo, 398, 399, 406

Burrow-Giles Lithographic Co. v. Sarony, 320, 323

Burson v. Freeman, 189, 190, 191, 193

Bush v. Gore, 531 U.S. 98 (2000).

Busse Broadcasting Corp. v. FCC, 149

Butchers' Benevolent Assoc. v. Crescent City Livestock Landing and Slaughterhouse Co., 80

Butterworth v. Smith, 201, 204, 227, 229, 230, 231

Byers v. Lemay Bank & Trust Co., 363

Cafeteria & Restaurant Workers Union v. McElroy, 161, 165, 189, 191, 192

Cain v. Hearst Corp., 294

California First Amendment Coalition v. Calderon, 250, 255, 257

California First Amendment Coalition v. Woodford, 249, 252, 254, 255, 257, 258

Cameron v. First Nat. Bank of Galveston, 432

Campbell v. Acuff-Rose Music, Inc., 320. 324

Campbell v. Blodgett, 249, 255, 258

Campbell v. Stanford, 361

Campen v. Stone, 365

Canessa v. J.I. Kislak, Inc., 295

Cantrell v. Forest City Publishing Co., 289, 294

Cape Publications, Inc., v. Bridges, 293

Capital Broadcasting Co. v. Mitchell, 401, 405

Carey v. Population Services International,404

Carroll v. Lee, 362

CBS v. Democratic Nat'l Committee, 158, 151, 395, 401, 406

CBS, Inc. v. FCC, 453 U.S., 148, 151

Central Hudson Gas & Elect. Corp. v. Public Service Comm'n., 82, 109, 375, 379, 401, 403, 404, 405

Century Communications Corp. v. FCC, 150

Chamberlain v. Feldman, 320, 323

Champion Home Builders Co. v. Jeffress, 363

Chandler v. Florida, 242, 243, 255, 257

Chemical Bank v. Arthur Andersen & Co., 410, 431

Cher v. Forum Int'l., Ltd., 289, 295

Chiarella v. U.S.,427, 429, 431

Chicago Joint Board, Amalgamated Clothing Workers of America, AFL-CIO v. Chicago Tribune Co., 406

Chinese Exclusion Case, 212, 227, 230

Christ's Bride Ministries, Inc. v. Southeastern Pennsylvania Transportation Authority, 363

Cinel v. Connick, 277, 293, 294

City Council v. Taxpayers for Vincent , 377, 401, 404

City of Cincinnati v. Discovery Network, Inc., 378, 401, 404

Clark v. Larekin, 1363

Cleary v. American Airlines, Inc., 364

Cmty. For Creative Non-Violence v. Reid, 320, 326

Coca-Cola Co. v. Seven Up Co., 320, 325

Cohen v. California, 82

Cohen v. Cowles Media Co., 192, 193

Coker v. Georgia, 257

Colegrove v. Green, 25, 27

Colligan v. Activities Club of New York, Ltd., 405

Columbia Broadcasting System, Inc. v. DeCosta, 305, 320, 323

Commonwealth v. Benesch, 365

Complaint by Julian Bond, 152

Complaint of Syracuse Peace Council Against Television Station WTVH, Syracuse, New York, 151

Computer Associates International, Inc. v. Altai, Inc.,323

Consolidated Cigar Corp. v. Reilly, 405

Cooke v. E.F. Drew & Co., 364

Cornelius v. NAACP Legal Defense & Educational Fund, Inc., 109

Cox Broadcasting Corp. v. Cohn, 289, 293

Craig v. Harney, 227, 230

Craig v. Boren, 78, 82

Crinkley v. Holiday Inns, Inc., 361, 362, 364, 366

Crump v. Beckley Newspapers, Inc., 289, 294

Curtis Publishing Co. v. Butts, 268, 270, 289, 292, 293, 365

Cushing v. Thomson, 363

Daily Herald Co. v. Munro, 159, 190, 191, 193

Daily Times Democrat v. Graham, 293, 294

Dallas Cowboys Football Club v. Harris, 363

Dasho v. Susquehanna Corp., 422, 423, 429, 432

Data management, Inc. v. Greene, 359, 366

De Funis v. Odegaard, 416 U.S. 312 (1974).

Dean v. Dearing, 264, 292

Delaware L. & W.R. Co. v. Pittinger, 406

Dellar v. Samuel Goldwin, Inc., 324

DelSanto v. Bristol County Stadium, 363

Dempsey v. Chambers, 365

DeMuth v. Miller, 361, 366

Dennis v. U.S., 78, 81, 107, 109, 227, 229

Denver Area Educational Telecommunications Consortium, Inc. v. FCC, 145, 148, 152

Detroit Free Press v. Ashcroft, 214, 216, 227, 230, 231

Devlin v. Greiner, 294

Diaz v. Oakland Tribune, Inc., 293

Dietemann v. Time, Inc., 189, 191, 295

Dirks v. S.E.C , 420, 429, 431

Dixon v. Trinity Joint Venture, 364

Dodge v. Ford Motor Co., 431

Douglas v. DynMcDermott Petroleum Operations Co., 365

Douglass v. Hustler Magazine, Inc., 295

Dover Pool & Racquet Club v. Brookings, 363

Dreamland Ball Room v. Shapiro, Bernstein & Co., 324

Dun & Bradstreet, Inc. v. Greenmoss Builder, Inc., 289, 292

DuPont Cellophane Co. v. Waxed Products Co., 325

Eamoe v. Big Bear Land & Water Co., 364

Eden v. Spaulding, 361, 364

Eimann v. Soldier of Fortune, 396, 397, 401, 406

El Vocero de P.R. v. Pureto Rico, 230

Encyclopedia Britannica Educational Crop v. Crooks, 324

Entertainment Network, Inc. v. Lappin, 250, 255, 258

Ernst and Ernst v. Hochfelder, 431

Estes v. Texas, 239, 255, 256, 257

Evans v. Ruth, 365

Ex rel.Mezei, 231

F.C.C. v. Midwest Video Corp., 150

F.C.C. v. League of Women Voters of California, 151

F.C.C. v. National Citizens Comm. for Broadcasting, 148, 150

F.C.C. v. Pacifica Foundation, 108, 140, 148, 152
F.C.C. v. Pottsville Broadcasting Co., 115, 148, 149
F.C.C. v. Sanders Bros. Radio Station, 149
F.T.C. v. Bunte Bros., 401. 404
F.T.C. v. H.N. Singer, Inc., 405
F.T.C. v. National Business Consultants, Inc., 405
F.T.C. v. Raladam, 369, 381, 401, 404
F.T.C. v. Winsted Hosiery Co., 380, 401, 404
Farmers Educational & Cooperative Union of America v. WDAY, 148, 151
Fawcett Publications, Inc. v. Morris, 289, 292
Federal Election Commission v. Mass. Citizens for Life, Inc., 398, 406
Federation of Advertising Industry Representatives v. City of Chicago, 405
Feiner v. New York, 79, 81
Feist v. Rural Telephone Service Co., Inc., 321, 323
Ferguson v. National Broadcasting Co., 321, 324
Ferris v. Polarsky, 1361, 363
Fiocco v. Carver, 364
First National Bank of Boston v. Belotti, 406
Firstamerica Dev. Corp. v. Daytona Beach News-Journal Corp., 292
Fiske v. Kansas, 79, 81, 82
Florida Power & Light Co. v. Westinghouse Elec. Corp., 364
Florida Star v. B.J.F., 191
Florida Star v. B.J.F., 229
Ford v. Wisconsin Real Estate Examining Bd., 364
Forsher v. Bugliosi, 293
Forsyth County, Georgia v. Nationalist Movement, 79, 81
Fort Wayne Books, Inc. v. Indiana, 110
Fortnightly Corp. v. United Artists Television, Inc., 148, 150
Froelich v. Werbin, 295
Frontiero v. Richardson, 77, 79, 82
Fuqua v. Taylor, 364
Fursmidt v. Hotel Abbey Holding Co., 363

G.D. Searle & Co. v. Chase Pfizer & Co., 325
G.Ricordi & Co. v. Mason, 324
Gannett Co. v. DePasquale, 197, 198, 205, 227, 229, 230
Gannett Co., Inc. v. Re, 292
Garrett v. Estelle, 248, 255, 257
Garrison v. Louisiana, 292
Garvis v. Employers Mut.Cas.Co., 191
Garziano v. E.I. DuPont De Nemours & Co., 292, 296
General Commercial Packaging, Inc., v. TPS Package Engineering, Inc.363
Gentile v. State Bar of Nevada, 231
Gerstle v. Gamble-Skogmo, 423, 431
Gertz v. Robert Welch, Inc., 269, 270, 289, 292, 293, 401, 406
Gibson v. Grannge, 363
Gill v. Curtis Pub. Co., 294
Gitlow v. New York, 79, 81, 82, 93, 107, 108, 109
Globe Newspaper Co. v. Superior Court, 199, 203, 215, 216, 227, 230
Goesaert v. Cleary, 79, 82
Goetz v. Hubbell, 363
Goldstein v. California, 321. 323
Goldwater v. Carter, 25, 27
Gonzales v. Southwestern Bell Tel. Co., 295
Gonzalez v. Avon Products, Inc., 296
Gram v. Richardson, 79, 82
Graphic Directions Inc. v. Bush, 364
Greater New Orleans Broadcasting Association v. U.S., 377, 401
Greer v. Spock, 161, 189, 191
Gregoire v. G.P. Putnam's Sons, 289, 292, 293
Grolier Inc. v. F.T.C. 405
Guglielmi v. Spelling-Goldberg Prods., 295
Hague v. CIO, 109
Hamer v. Sidway, 363
Hanlon v. Berger, 189, 191
Hanover Star Milling Co. v. Metcalf, 321, 325
Hansen v. Ford Motor Co., 429, 432
Harms v. Miami Daily News, Inc., 295
Harper & Row Publishers, Inc. v. Nation Enterprises, Inc., 321, 324
Harrison v. Cage, 363
Hartley v. Bohrer, 364

Hawkins by and through Hawkins v. Multimedia, Inc., 293, 294
Hawley Fuel Coalmart v. Steag Handel GmbH, 363
Hayburn's Case, 79, 81
Hayman v. Ramada Inn. Inc., 361, 364
Heffron v. International Society for Krishna Consciousness, 109
Heims v. Hanke, 364
Heit v. Weitzen, 431
Herbert v. Lando, 193
Herbert v. Shanley Co., 321, 324
Herceg v. Hustler Magazine, Inc., 107, 109
Herman & MacLean v. Huddleston, 429, 432
Hinerman v. Daily Gazette Co., Inc., 289, 293
Hinish v. Meier and Frank Co., 295
Holden v. State of Minnesota, 245, 247, 248, 255, 257, 258
Holtzman v. Schlessinger, 25, 27
Hoover v. Intercity Radio Co., 148, 149
Howley v. Whipple, 363
Hoyiton v. U.S., 79
Hurley v. Irish-American Gay, Lesbian and Bisexual Group of Boston, 365
Hurtado v California, 58, 81
Hutchinson v. Proxmire, 271, 289, 292
Illinois v. Abbott & Assoc., Inc., 204, 228, 230
In re American Home Products Corp., 406
In re Cady, Roberts & Co., 432
In re E.I. DuPont DeNemours & Co., 321, 325
In re Gault, 57
In re Hutchinson Technology, Inc., 325
In re Primus, 406
In re Riverbank Canning Co., 325
In re RMJ, 406
In re Sealed Case (Espy), 178, 190, 192
In re Sociedade Agricola E. Comercial Dos Vihnos Mesias, S.A.R.L., 325
In re Societe Generale Des Eaux Minerales De Vittel, 321, 325
In re Winship, 57
In re Yardley, 323
In re: Petition of Post-Newsweek Stations, Florida, Inc., for Change in Code of Judicial Conduct, 257

International Kennel Club v. Mighty Star Inc., 325

International Society for Krishna Consciousness v. Lee, 109

Jacobellis v. Ohio, 110

James v. Meow Media, Inc., 109

Jamison v. Texas, 369, 402, 403

JB Pictures, Inc. v. D.O.D., 162, 190, 191, 193, 252, 258

Jennings v. Ruidoso Racing Assn., 363

Jet Courier Services Inc. v. Mulei, 361, 364

Jewelers Circular Publishing Co. v. Keystone Pub. Co., 323

Johnson Controls, Inc. v. Phoenix Control Systems, Inc., 323

Jones v. Hart, 365

Jurek v. Texas, 257

Kapellas v. Kofman, 293

Kardon v. National Gypsum, 432

Katz v. U.S., 231

Keeton v. Hustler Magazine, Inc., 267, 289, 292

Kennedy for President v. FCC, 148, 151

Kent v. U.S., 57

Kerby v. Hal Roach Studios, 406

Kimbrough v Coca-Cola/USA, 295

Klapmeier v. Peat, Marwick, Mitchell & Co., 432

Kleeman v. Rheingold, 364

Korematsu v. U.S., 79, 82

Lamprecht v. FCC, 148, 150

Landmark Communications, Inc. v. Virginia, 201, 228, 229

Landon v. Plasencia, 213, 228, 230

Landreth Timber Co. v. Landreth, 431

Langellier v. Schaeffer, 363

Lavazzi v. McDonalds Corp., 364

Lavin v. New York News Inc., 293

Lee v. A.R.T. Co. 323, 324

Lee v. Nash, 294

Lefkowitz v. Great Minneapolis Surplus Store, 363

Leverton v. Curtis Pub. Co., 294

Lindland v. United Business Investments, 364

Lindmark Associates, Inc. v. Township of Willingboro, 374, 404

Link v. Kroenke, 365

Livsey v. Salt Lake County, 294

Lloyd v. Jordan, 363

Lorillard Tobacco Co. v. Reilly, 391, 402, 405

Loughry v. Lincoln First Bank, N.A., 361, 365

Louisville & N.R.R. v. Mottley, 364

Lyon v. Adgraphics, 363

Machleder v. Diaz, 293

MacMillan v. King, 324

Macon Telegraph Pub. Co. v. Tatum, 293

Mann v. Commissioner, 363

Mapp v. Ohio, 79, 81

Marbury v. Madison, 15, 26, 27, 72, 79, 81

Marc Kasky v. Nike, Inc., 402, 403, 404

Marine Bank v. Weaver, 429, 431

Mark v. King Broadcasting Co., 295

Mark v. Seattle Times,295

Mary M. v. City of Los Angeles, 365

Masson v. New Yorker Magazine, 287, 289, 292, 296

Mastandrea v. Lorain Journal Co., 293

Matthew Bender & Co. v. West Publishing Co., 323

Maxwell v. Borough of New Hope, 366

Maxwell v. Dow, 81

Mayflower Broadcasting Corp., 151

Mazur v. Stein, 300, 321, 323

McCabe v. Village Voice, Inc., 294

McCollum v. Clothier, 364

McCutcheon v. State, 292

McGautha v. California, 257

McIntire v. William Penn Broadcasting Co., 149

McKeiver v. Pennsylvania, 57

McNaughton v. Granite City Auto Sales, 363

McSurely v. McClellan, 289, 294

Mead Data Central Inc. v. Toyota Motor Sales, U.S.A., 321, 325

Meeropol v. Nizer, 324

Meese v. Miller, 364

Meinhard v. Salmon, 364

Melvin v. Reid, 289, 293, 294

Menzel v. List, 363

Metro Broadcasting, Inc. v. FCC, 150

Metromedia, Inc. v. San Diego , 377, 402, 404

Miami Herald Publishing Co. v. Tornillo, 402, 406

Mid-South Packers v. Shoney's, 363

Mieske v. Bartell Drug Co., 363

Milkovich v. Lorain Journal Co., 272, 287, 289, 293, 295

Miller Brewing Co. v. Falstaff Brewing Corp., 325

Miller v SEVAMP Inc. 365

Miller v. California, 102, 103, 104, 105, 110

Miller v. National Broadcasting Co., 295

Mills v. Electric Auto-Lite, 432

Mirage Editions, Inc. v. Albuquerque A.R.T. Co., 323

Miranda v. Arizona, 79, 81

Modular Cinemas of America, Inc. v. Mini Cinemas Corp., 325

Moore v. Big Picture Co., 294

Morgan v. Hustler Magazine, Inc., 294

Morrison v. Thoelke, 363

Morrissey v. Proctor & Gamble Co., 321, 323

Mosley v. Rusk, 166, 192

Muller v. Oregon, 79, 82

Murdock v. Pennsylvania, 369, 402, 403

Namath v. Sports Illustrated, 295

National Broadcasting Co. v. U.S., 150

National Broadcasting Co., Inc. v. Cleland, 190, 191, 193

National Comm'n on Egg Consumption v. F.T.C., 386, 405

National Socialist Party of America v. Skokie, 81

NBC Subsidiary (KNBC-TV), Inc. v. Superior Court of Los Angeles County, 230

Near v. Minnesota, 63, 67, 79, 81, 82, 86, 98, 100, 107, 108, 109, 139, 140, 152, 199, 228, 229, 256

Nebraska Press Association v. Stuart, 200, 228, 229

Neff v. Time, Inc., 293

Neiman Marcus v. Lait 289, 292

New York Times Co. v. Roxbury Data Interface, Inc., 324

New York Times Co. v. U.S., 99, 107, 108, 109, 228

New York Times Co., v. Sullivan, 264, 268, 272, 290, 292, 293, 365,369, 403

New York v. Ferber, 104, 107, 110

Nichols v. District Court, 256

Nichols v. Universal Pictures Corp., 324

Nicholson v. McClatchy Newspapers, 295

Nike, Inc. v. Kasky, 404

Nixon v. Warner Communications, 242, 257

Nixon v. Warner Communications, Inc., 211, 228, 230

Noonan v. Texaco, 364

North Jersey Media Group, Inc. v. Ashcroft, 228, 231

Norwood v. Soldier of Fortune, 6396, 397, 406

Ohralik v. Ohio State Bar Association, 403, 406

Oklahoma Publishing Co. v. Oklahoma County Dist. Court, 201,

Ollman v. Evans, 286–287, 295

Onassis v. Christian Dior-New York, Inc., 290, 295

Osborne v. Ohio, 110

Palko v. Connecticut, 65, 75, 79, 81, 82

Park'N Fly, Inc. v. Dollar Park & Fly, Inc., 325

Paulsen v. FCC, 148, 151

Pauly Jail Bldg. & Manufg. Co. v. Hemphill County, 431

Pavesich v. New England Life Ins. Co., 295

Peake v. Thomas, 432

Pearson v. Dodd, 286, 290, 295

Peay v. Curtis Pub. Co., 294

Peel v. Attorney Registration and Disciplinary Commission of Illinois, 406

Pell v. Procunier, 165, 190, 191, 192, 248, 256, 258

Pennekamp et al. v. Florida, 230

Perry Education Assoc. v. Perry Local Educators' Assoc., 109

Petermann v. International Brotherhood of Teamsters, 365

Petterson v. Pattberg, 363

Philadelphia Newspapers, Inc. v. Hepps, 261, 290, 292, 365

Phillips v. The Evening Star Newspaper Co., 292

Pixley v. Boynton, 431

Planned Parenthood v. American Coalition of Life Activists, 81

Plessy v. Ferguson, 79, 80

Police Department of the City of Chicago v. Mosley, 164, 190

Polin v. Dun and Bradstreet, Inc., 294

Pope v. Illinois, 102, 110

Porter & Dietsch v. F.T.C, 405

Posadas de Puerto Rico Associates v. Tourism company of Puerto Rico, 377, 404

Postal Telegraph-Cable Co. v. Willis, 363

Powell v. McCormack, 25, 27

Prescott v. Bay St. Louis Newspapers, Inc., 294

Press Enterprise Co. v. Superior Court, 205, 206–207, 209, 228, 230

Preston Farm & Ranch Supply v. Bio-Zyme Enters., 363

Prestwick, Inc. v. Don Kelly Buliding Co., 325

Prince Albert v. Strange, 273, 293

Pruneyard Shopping Center v. Robins, 109

Quincy Cable TV, 150

Rafferty v. Hartford Courant Co., 295

Raiminde v. VanVerch, 366

Rawlins v. Hutchinson Pub. Co., 295

Rawls v. Conde Nast Pub., Inc., 295

Red Lion Broadcasting Co, Inc. v. FCC, 115, 148, 149, 151

Reddy Communications v. Environmental Action Foundation, 321, 325

Reed v. Ponton, 294

Reed v. Reed, 79, 82

Regents of University System of Georgia v. Carroll, 149

Reilly v Waukesaa County, 365

Remington Freight Lines Inc. v. Larkey, 365

Reno v. ACLU, 148, 151, 152

Reno v. American-Arab Anti-Discrimination Committee, 231

Renwick v. News & Observer Pub. Co., 294

Rhen Marshall v. Purolator Filter Div., 362

Rice v. Paladin Enterprises, Inc, 107, 108, 109

Richmond Newspapers v. Virginia,197–198, 199, 203, 207, 211, 216, 222, 228, 229, 230

Ritzmann v. Weekly world News, Inc., 295

Robbins v. Finlay, 365

Roberson v. Rochester Folding Box Co., 295

Roberts Associates Inc. v. Blazer Intern. Corp., 364

Robertson v. Batten, Barton, Durstine & Osborne, Inc., 324

Roe v. Wade, 23, 25, 27, 81, 380, 404, 435

Rosenberger v. Rector & Visitors of the University of Virginia, 109

Rosenblatt v. Baer, 269, 292

Roshto v. Hebert, 294

Ross v. Midwest Communications, Inc., 293

Roth v. U.S., 110

Rowan v. Post Office Dept., 110

Rowe v. Montgomery Ward, 354

Roy Export Co. v. Trustees of Columbia University, 321, 324

S.E.C v. W.J. Howey Co., 429, 431

S.E.C. v. Materia, 429, 432

S.E.C. v. National Securities, 429, 432

S.E.C. v. Texas Gulf Sulfur, 418, 429, 431

Sabine Pilot Svs. v. Haueck, 365

Sable Communications of California, Inc. v. FCC, 142, 148, 152

Salinger v. Random House, Inc., 324

Sanders v. Nuveen, 421, 429, 431

Sanford v. Boston Herald-Traveler Corp., 292

Satellite Broadcasting v. FCC, 148, 150, 151

Saxbe v. Washington Post Co., 248, 258

Scarves by Vera, Inc. v. Todo Imports Ltd., 325

Schenck v. U.S., 81, 91–92, 107, 108, 109, 202, 228

Schiavone Constr. Co. v. Time, Inc., 292

Schumm v. Berg, 363

Scott Paper Co. v. Scott's Liquid Gold Inc., 325

Shapero v. Kentucky Bar Association, 406

Shapiro, Bernstein & Co. v. Jerry Vogel Music Co., 321, 323

Sheila's Shine Products Inc. v. Sheila Shine, Inc., 326

Sheppard v. Maxwell, 3240, 256

Sherrill v. Knight, 165–166, 190, 191, 192, 193, 256

Sherwood v. Walker, 363

Shivers v. John H. Harland Co. Inc., 361, 364

Sid & Marty Kroft Television Productions, Inc. v. McDonalds Corp., 321, 324

Sidis v. F-R Pub. Corp., 277, 290, 293, 294

Smith v. Daily Mail, 201, 228, 229

Smith v. Montoro, 405, 435

Snyder v. Ringgold, 166, 167, 190, 192

Sony Corp. of America v. Universal City Studios, Inc., 321, 324

Spahn v. Julian Messner, Inc., 294

Special Force Ministries v. WCCO T.V., 190, 191

Speed v. Transamerica Corp., 419, 429, 431

Stahl v. Oklahoma, 190, 191

Stanford v. Dairy Queen Prods., 362, 364

Stanford v. Kentucky, 57

Stanley v. Georgia, 107, 110

Stonestreet v. Southern Oil Co., 363

Stowe v. Thomas, 324

Strada v. Connecticut Newspapers, Inc., 262, 292

Strauder v. West Virginia, 79, 82

Stroble v. California, 231

Syracuse Peace Council v. FCC, 148, 151

Tacket v. Delco Remy Div., 296

Taylor v Caldwell, 364

Taylor v. Cordis Corp., 364

Terminiello v. Chicago, 82

Thayer v. Pacific Elec. Rwy., 364

The Free Speech Coalition v. Reno, 110

The Phone Connection, Inc. v. Harbst, 366

Thomas v. Collins, 82

Thompson Medical Co., Inc. v. F.T.C., 405

Thompson v. Oklahoma, 57

Thorn v. Reliance Van Co., Inc., 405

Thornburgh v. Abbott, 255

Thrifty Rent-A-Car System v. Thrift Cars, Inc., 321, 325

Time, Inc. v. Bernart Geis Associates, 325

Time, Inc. v. Firestone, 292

Time, Inc. v. Hill, 294

Time, Inc. v. Motor Publications, Inc., 325

Times Mirror v. U.S., 228, 230

Tony Down Food Co. v. U.S., 363

Toprosyan v. Boehringer Ingelheim Pharmaceuticals, Inc., 296

Toussant v. Blue Cross, Blue Shield, 364

TSC Industries v. Northway, 432

Tureen v Equifax, Inc., 294

Turner Broadcasting System, Inc. v. FCC, 126–127, 148, 150

Turner v. Safley, 255, 258

Twining v. New Jersey, 81

U.S. v. Behan, 363

U.S. v. Corbitt, 207, 208, 228, 230

U.S. v. Grace, 109

U.S. v. Progressive, Inc., 99–100, 109

U.S. ex rel Foulds v. Texas Tech University, 365

U.S. ex rel Stillwell v. Hughes Helicopters, Inc., 365

U.S. Healthcare, Inc. v. Blue Cross of Greater Philadelphia, 405

U.S. v. 12–20 Ft. Reels, 110

U.S. v. Dennis, 109

U.S. v. Greenbaum, 406

U.S. v. Lindh, 217, 228, 231

U.S. v. Newman, 428, 429, 432

U.S. v. O'Brien, 150

U.S. v. Playboy Entertainment Group, Inc., 148, 152

U.S. v. Rumely, 406

U.S. v. Steffens, 321, 325

U.S. v. U.S. District Court, 231

U.S. v. Winans, 429, 432

U-Haul International v. Jartran, 387, 402, 405

Uncle B's Bakery, Inc. v. O'Rourke, 366

Universal City Studios, Inc. v. Nintendo Co., Ltd., 321, 325

Valentine v. Christensen, 374, 402, 404

VanSteenhous v. Jacor Broadcasting of Colo. Inc., 361

Virgil v. Time, Inc. 293, 294, 365

Virginia Bankshares v. Sandberg, 422, 432

Virginia State Bd. of Pharmacy v. Virginia Citizens Consumer Council, Inc., 87, 108, 402, 404, 405

Wainwright Securities, Inc., v. Wall Street Transcript Corp., 324

Waller v. Georgia, 206, 228, 230

Waller v. Osbourne, 109

Walt Disney Productions v. Air Pirates, 5321, 324

Wandt v. Hearst's Chicago American, 294

Ward La France Truck Corp., 431

Ward v. Rock Against Racism, 109

Ware v. Hoylton, 79, 81

Ware v. Mobley, 363

Warner Brothers Pictures, Inc. v. Majestic Pictures Corp., 324

Warner-Lambert Co. v.F.T.C., 402, 405

Wasserman Theatrical Enter. v. Harris, 364

Watchtower Bible and Tract Society of New York v. Village of Stratton, 109

Weeks v. U.S., 79, 81

Wehling v. Columbia Broadcasting System, 293

Welch v. Mr. Christmas, Inc.,295

WGBH Educational Foundation, 152

White v. Fraternal Order of Police, 290, 293, 294

Whitfield v. Lear, 362

Whitney v. California, 81, 107, 108, 109

Williams & Wilkins v. U.S., 321, 324

Williams v. Bedenbaugh, 432

Williams v. Feather Sound, Inc., 365

Williams v. Florida, 58

Williams v. New York, 228, 230

Wilson v. Layne, 190, 191

Winget v. Rockwood, 364

Winter v. G.P. Putnam's Sons, 109

Wolston v. Reader's Digest Ass'n, Inc., 292

Wood v. Georgia, 228, 230

Wood v. Hustler Magazine, Inc., 290, 294

Yates v. California, 107, 108

Yates v. U.S., 79, 81

Zacchini v Scripts-Howard Broadcasting Co., 295, 321, 325

Zadvydas v. Davis, 231

Zamora v. CBS, 107, 109

Zemel v. Rusk, 164, 166, 190, 191, 192, 233, 248, 256, 258

Index

8-K report, 425

A
A la Carte rule, 129
ABA Model Rules of Professional
  Responsibility, 225, 226, 229
Abandonment of trademark, 317
Absolute Immunity, 270
Absolutist, 69, 83–85
Abstention doctrine, 22–24
Acceptance in contract, 328, 330–331
Acquittal, 40
Adjudication, 48
Admonished, 42
Adversarial judicial system, 195
Advertising defined, 368–369
Affirm, 21
Affirmative advertising, 385–386
Affirmative defense, 38, 155, 181–182,
  261, 270, 282, 286, 287
Affirmative duty to disclose, 416, 418
    in proxy statement, 421
Agent, 341, 342–346
American Jurisprudence, 59
American Law Institute, 363, 364, 365,
  366
Answer, 49, 50
Antidilution of trademark, 315–316
Apparent agency, 345–346
Apparent government authority test,
  269
Appeals de novo, 12
Appellate judgments/dispositions, 24
Appellate jurisdiction, 10, 12
Appellate procedure, 51
Appropriation, 282–284
ARPANET, 130
Arraignment, 34
Array, 40
Ascertainment study, 118, 121
Auerback, J.S., 405
Authority, 2, 3

B
Baby FTC, 389
Balance sheet, 408
Balancing test, 163, 185
Bar, 236

Bare promise, 331
Baum, L., 26, 58
Beeson, A., 231
Bench, 236
Bench trial, 35, 40, 44, 51, 54
Berne Convention, 297, 298, 302
Bifurcated hearing, 48
Bifurcated supreme courts, 12
Bill
    of indictment, 33
    of particulars, 38
Bill of Rights, 61–64, 490–492
Black, H. L., 69, 81
Black, H. C., 328, 362
Black's Law Dictionary, 328
Blackstone, W., 292
Blanket statutory closure rule, 203
Board of directors, 414–415
Bolger test, 371–372
Bonds, 408
Bowen, L., 406
Brandeis, L. D., 291, 293
Breach of contract, 336, 338
Bureau of Consumer Protection, 382
Business Wire, 293

C
California-style preliminary hearings,
  205
Capacity to contract, 338
Carry-one, carry-all rule, 129
Case & controversy, 22
Case law, 5, 20
Case of first impression, 52
Case-by-case fairness, 64
Caveat emptor, 373
Cease and desist order, 385
Central Hudson test, 375–379
Challenges for cause, 41
Children's Television Act of 1990, 390
Civil contempt, 186–187
Civil laws & procedures, 49
Civil liberties, 60–63
Civil rights, 60–63
Clear and present danger test, 71, 84,
  87, 91–93
Closing statements, 43
Codes, 7, 9

Collegial body, 168
Colorado Rules of Professional
  Responsibility, 231
Commercial communication, 368–369
Commercial interests in trials, 235
Common carriers, 127, 129–130, 142
Common law, 4, 29
Common law right of access to records,
  207
Communication or publication in
  defamation, 266
Compelling state interest test, 73,
  75–76
Compensatory damages, 96
Concurrent jurisdiction, 19
Concurring opinion, 22
Confidentiality, duty of, 352, 354
Consent as defense, 279–280
Consent order, 384
Consent to agency, 343–344
Consideration, 328, 331–332
Consolidated court system, 9, 12
Constitution, 2, 3, 4, 481–499
Constitutionality, 72, 74–75
Consumer Protection Act of 1968, 363
Contempt, 186
Contempt power, 96
Contract, 327–340
    samples, 471–477
    with minor, 327, 334
Control of agent, 342–343, 344–345
Copyright, 298, 302
Core programming, 137, 147
Corollary to the "equal access
  doctrine," 166
Corporation defined, 411–413
Corrective advertising, 385–386
Counterclaim, 50
Covenant not to compete, 358–360
Creativity in copyright, 298, 299–302,
  305
Creppy directive, 212, 214–217
Criminal
    complaint, 31
    contempt, 186
    law, 29, 45
    procedure, 30
Cross-examination, 35, 42

Cross-petition, 50
Cruel and unusual punishment, 245
Cullman corollary, 132–133

D
Damage, 94, 96
De novo, 54–55
Deep pockets, 355
Defamation, 260–273
Defense, 270
Delegates no potest delegare, 356
Demurrer, 49
Denning, B. P., 82
Deportation hearings, 209, 212,
    214–220
Depositions, 50
Derivative use immunity, 181
Derivative work, 304, 305–306
Descriptive terms in trademark, 314–315
Designated public forum, 88–89
Deterrence of death sentence, 245, 254
Detrimental reliance, 337
Dicta, 433
Dingell, J., 382, 404
Disaffirm a contract, 334
Disclosure scheme, 415–416
Discovery, 38, 50
Discretionary jurisdiction, 18
Dispositional hearing, 48
Dissenting opinion, 21, 22
Distribution in copyright, 305, 306
Diversity jurisdiction, 16, 17
Division of Advertising Practices, 382
Dual network rule, 125
Ducat, C. R., 27, 81, 109
Due process clause of Constitution, 75
Due process of law, 36
Duopoly rule, 124
Duration of copyright, 303–304
Duress as contract defense, 338, 340
Duty to mitigate damages, 338
Dye, T. R., 36, 58, 230

E
Easton, S. D., 257
Economic effect of copyright
    infringement, 309, 311
Electronic simultaneous Multiple-round
    auctions, 119, 121
Empanelled, 41
Employee communication defense to
    defamation, 287–288

Employment at will, 341
Entry by misrepresentation, 157
Equal opportunities rule, 132–134, 136
Equality of access doctrine, 164–166
Equitable remedies, 7
Equity, 7
Exaggerated response to access to
    executions, 247
Exception, 155, 175, 182
Exclusive jurisdiction, 19
Executory contract, 332
Exemption, 155, 165, 175, 178, 180,
    182
Expectation damages, 337
Express consent, 156, 279, 280, 283
Extra-judicial tribunals, 11

F
Fahey, P. M., 365, 366
Fair comment, 272
Fair use, 305, 309–311
Fairness doctrine, 131–134
False light, 280–282
Falsehood in defamation, 261
Family resemblance test for securities,
    410–411
Federal democratic republic, 3, 4
Federal False Claims Act, 352, 365
Federal governmental system, 2
Federal Judicial Center, 26
Federal Register, 170
Federal Reporter, 52
Federal rules of Criminal Procedure, 242
Federal Supplement, 52
Federal Trade Commission, 382–386
Federalism, 243
Felonies, 30–31
Financial benefit in appropriation,
    282–284
Find Law, 434
First appearance, 34
First Sale Doctrine, 306
FISA courts, 217–220
Flack, H. E., 81
Fragmented court system, 13
Fraud and securities, 409, 417, 418
    defined, 419
Fraud as contract defense, 338, 340
Freedom of Information Act, 155,
    171–174
Fundamental rights, 75
Funnel effect, 36

G
Gag order, 199, 202
General jurisdiction, 7, 16
Gibson, L. T., 365
Grand jury, 31–32
Gravamen, 278
Guardian ad litem, 47

H
Habeas corpus, 44
Hacking in intrusion, 285
Harm in defamation, 260,
    264–266
Harrison, J. B., 230
Heightened scrutiny, 73, 76
Hill, M. G., 26
Holmes, O. W., 365
Homo economicus, 113
Homo politicus, 113
Horovitz, B., 365

I
Iacono, E., 406
Immunity, 155, 177, 180–181
Immunity in defamation, 270–272
Implied consent, 156
    in appropriation, 283
    in defamation, 280
Implied endorsement, 284
Impossibility as contract defense, 338,
    339–340
In commerce, 387
Incidental use in appropriation,
    284
Incitement test, 94, 97
Indecency, 84, 86, 101
Independent contractor, 346–348
Independent public interest test, 269
Indictment, 31–33
Injunctions, 386
Inquisitorial judicial system, 195
Insanity as a defense, 38
Insider trade defined, 419
Intellectual property, 298
Intentional intrusion, 285
Intentional misconduct, 96
Intentional tort, 354, 355
Intermediate appellate courts, 12, 14,
    15
Intermediate scrutiny, 73, 76
Interrogatories, 50
Intrusion by deception, 285

Invasion
 of personal space or information,
 285–286
 of property, 278
Issues in case report, 436–437

J
Joint work and copyright, 304
Journalistic interests, 235
Judgment, 434–435, 437
Judgment non obstante verdicto, 43
Judicial history, 435–436
Judicial remedies, 386
Judicial review, 5, 6, 20, 61, 66, 68, 71,
 72, 74
Jurisdiction, 1, 4, 5, 7, 9, 11
Jury box, 236
Jury instructions, 42–43
 sample, 478–479
Justiciability, 1, 22, 23
Juvenile delinquency laws, 29–30,
 46–47

K
Keeton, W. P., 292

L
Lanham Act, 386–388
Lassiter, C., 257
Leased access channels, 127, 145
Legal duty, 95
Legally true, 262
Letter of no-action, 424
Lexis/Nexis, 434
Libel, 260, 264–266
 per quod, 265–266
 per se, 265–266
Limited liability and corporations,
 413
Liquidated damages, 337
Literalist, 69
Loathsome disease in defamation,
 265–266
Local public inspection file, 122
Local radio multiple ownership rule,
 124
Local TV multiple ownership rule,
 124
Long-arm statutes, 49
Look-alike, 283
Lost bargain, 337
Lowest unit charge, 132

M
Magnuson-Moss Warranty-Federal
 Trade Commission Improvement
 Act, 363
Major courts, 11
Majority opinion, 22
Malice, actual and legal, 282–288
Mandatory authority, 15, 22
Mandatory jurisdiction, 12, 18
Manifest weight of the evidence, 54
Manifestation of consent, 343, 344
Marshall, J., 1
Master, 342
Material assertion in adverting, 383
Material fact in securities defined,
 422–423
McHugh, J. T., 26
McLaughlin, J. A., 295
Means of access to trials, 233
Media Bureau, 116–117
Meeting of the minds, 328, 329,
 330–331
Meikeljohn, A., 81
Memorandum of understanding, 217
Mens rea, 38, 95
Merit registration, 415
Metaphysical forum, 89
Mill, J. S., 80
Miller, J., 382, 404
Minor courts, 11
Misappropriation theory and securities
 reporting, 427
Misdemeanors, 31
Mistake as contract defense, 338, 339
Model Business Corporations Act,
 415
Modern communications torts,
 259–260
Modified negligence standard, 97
Modify a judgment, 2, 21
Montana Annotated Code, 364
Mootness, 22
Moral turpitude in defamation, 265
Motion
 for a re-trial, 44
 for declaratory judgment, 51
 for directed verdict, 42
 for jury trial, 38
 to reconsider, 44
 for summary judgment, 50
Multiple-round auctions, 119, 121
Must-carry rule, 126

Mutual mistake, 339
Muzzle order, 199

N
Narrowly tailored court closure, 199,
 203
National TV multiple ownership rule,
 124
National/federal court system, 9
Negligence, 95, 268
Negligent incitement, 96
Newspaper/broadcast cross-ownership
 rule, 124
Newsworthy in private facts, 275–278
No bill of indictment, 33
Nolo contendere, 34
Nominal damages, 96
Non-disclosure order, 225
Non-public forum, 89
Not guilty, 34
Novation, 337

O
Obiter dictum, 438–439
Objections, 42
Offensive to a reasonable person,
 275–276
Offer, 328, 329
Official record of trials, 242
On behalf of principal, 343–345
Opening statements, 41
Opinion defense, 272, 286–287
Ordinances, 5–7, 9
Original jurisdiction, 9–12, 17
Overbroad, 359–360
Overrule a motion, 42

P
Parody in copyright, 309, 310,
 311–312
Part performance, 333–334
Partnership, 346, 348
Patents, 298, 300, 312
PEG channels, 127
Pember, D., 295
Per curiam opinion, 21–22
Performance and copyright, 305, 306
Personal attack corollary, 132
Personal jurisdiction, 16
Personal service, 49
Persuasive authority, 15, 20
Petition or complaint, 31, 33

Petition
  for change of venue, 38
  for joinder, 38
  for severance, 38
  for speedy jury trial, 38
  to suppress evidence or
    confession, 39
Petty offenses, 30–31
Plea bargain, 35
Pleadings, 50
Plurality opinion, 21–22
Police powers, 19
Political question, 23
Pollocks, F. 256
Post conviction relief, 44–45
Post-trial motions & appeals, 44
Power, 2
Precedent, 4
Preclearance rules and securities, 423
Pre-emptory challenges, 41
Preferred freedoms, 74–75
Preliminary hearing, 33
Preponderance of the evidence, 29
Pre-sentence investigation, 208
Presidential privilege, 178–179
Press pool, 248
Prima facie case, 42
Primary authority, 20
Principal, 342–343
Prior restraint, 199
Privacy Act of 1974, 155
Private facts, 273–280
Private right of action
  for false advertising, 386–388
  for securities fraud, 424
Privilege, 155, 175–179, 270, 287
Privileges and immunities, 63–64, 177
Procedural due process, 195–196
Procedural law, 29
Professional incompetence in
  defamation, 265
Profit & loss statement, 408
Proportion taken and fair use,
  309– 310–311
Prosecutor's information, 31
Prosecutorial grant of immunity, 181
Prosser, W. L., 292
Protected classification, 75
Protection, 155, 175, 181
Protective orders, 216–217
Proxy defined, 415
Proxy rules, 421–425
Proxy solicitation defined, 415

Public figure, 261–262, 268–270
Public forum, 88–89
Public interest directive, 114–115
Public matter, 269–270
Public meeting, 171
Public official, 268, 269–270
Public records in private facts, 276
Public sector employee and
  whistleblowers, 353
Publicity, 275, 279–281
Puffery, 383, 385
Punitive damages, 96
Pure idea in copyright, 301, 302
Pure speech, 69

Q
Quantum meruit, 337
Qui tam or qui tam relator, 352–353

R
Radio/TV cross-ownership rule, 124
Ratio decidend, 438–439
Rational relationship test, 75
Reasonable access rule, 134
Reasonable consumer, 382
Reasonable doubt, 29
Reasonableness standard, 74, 76–77
Rebuttal witness, 42
Reckless disregard for the truth, 268,
  272, 279
Recklessness in securities fraud, 431
Recognized by the general public in
  appropriation, 283
Redacting, 208
Regulations, 5–7, 19
Remand, 21
Removal hearings, 214
Reply, 50
Respondeat superior, 341, 342–343
Restatement of Agency, 346, 347, 364
Restatement of Contracts, 332, 363
Restatement Second of Torts, 279, 293,
  363
Restraining order, 199–200
Restrictive order, 119, 202
Retraction statute, 273
Reverse a judgment, 21
Reverse blocking, 142
Reverse proportionality in copyright,
  311
Right of privacy, 155
Ripeness, 23
Rothstein, M. A., 365

Rules, 4, 5
Rutenberg, J., 152

S
Safe harbor, 138, 144
Sanders, R.H., 405
Sarbanes-Oxley Act, 424–426
Schmidt, S. W., 26, 109
Schmitt, R. B., 406
Scope of agency, 348
Secondary authority, 20
Securities Act of 1933, 416–417, 431
Securities defined, 408–411
Securities Exchange Act of 1934,
  416–418, 421, 431
Securities Exchange Commission, 415
Seitel, F., 231
Selective incorporation, 61, 64–65
Selective incorporation "plus," 65
Sentencing hearing, 40, 44, 47
Seriatim opinion, 21
Servant, 342
Service mark, 298, 312
Shakespeare, W., 256
Shapiro, R., 231
Shareholder meeting, 415, 421
Shareholder rights and liabilities,
  412–413
Shares defined, 408–409
Shepardize, 438
Shield law, 181–182, 203
Siegel, L. J., 58
Single publication rule, 267
Slander, 260
Smith, J. C., 231
Social conformist, 70–71
Social conformist and commercial
  communication, 379
Social effects, 69–71
Social function, 69–71
Sound-alike, 283
Sovereignty, 2–3, 158
Special interest cases, 214
Special or limited jurisdiction, 11–12,
  16
Specific performance, 336, 360
Speech "plus," 69
Spence, G., 291, 292
Sponsorship identification, 134–136
Standards of judicial review, 54, 61, 68,
  72, 74
Standing, 22–23
Stare decisis, 4, 6

State court systems, 11
State statutory privilege, 179, 182–183
Statue of Frauds, 332, 333–334
Status offenses, 46–48
Statute, 6–7, 12, 16
Statute of limitations, 39
Statutory copyright license, 128–129
Statutory interpretation, 5
Stipulated bench trial, 35
Stocks defined, 408–409
Strict scrutiny standard, 74–76
Subject matter jurisdiction, 16
Subpoena, 155, 169, 178, 183, 184–189
Subpoena duces tecum, 186
Substantiation, 384–385
Substantive law, 29, 40
Summons, 47, 49
Sunshine Act, 168–170
Suppression hearings, 197, 206
Supremacy Clause, 3
Surrebuttal, 42
Surrogates of The People, 234, 254

T
Tangible form in copyright, 298, 299,
    300, 301–302
Termination for cause, 341–342
Termination of transfer of copyright, 304
Texas Family Code, 363

Tie-breaker lotteries, 119
Tort, 259
Total incorporation, 66
Total incorporation "plus," 66
Totality of circumstances clear error, 54
Trade dress, 298, 312
Trade Regulations, 384
Trademark, 312–318
Transactional immunity, 180
Treaty, 10, 16, 19
Trespass to private property, 156
Trial broadcast fee, 244
Trial closure order, 198
Trial Handbook, 58
Trier of fact, 39, 40, 54, 276, 281, 286
True bill of indictment, 33
Truth as defense in defamation, 261

U
U.S. Department of Justice, 58
Unalienable rights, 62
Unanimous opinion, 21
Unchastity of a woman in defamation,
    265
Unfair commercial practices, 383
Unified court system, 15
Uniform Partnership Act, 364
Uniform Securities Act, 426
Unitary governmental system, 2

United States Reports, 52
Uphold a judgment, 21
Use immunity, 181
Utilitarian and copyright, 299–300

V
Vacate a judgment, 21
Venire men & women, 40
Vicarious infringement, 308
Viewpoint discrimination, 163
Voir dire, 40

W
Waiting period for stock sales and
    proxies, 424
Waiver
    in false light, 282
    in private facts, 280
Warren, S. D., 291, 293
Whistleblower, 351–354
Witness box, 236
Witness protection laws, 203
Work for hire, 318–320
Writ of certiorari, 18–19
Writ of mandamus, 7–8

Z
Zapple doctrine, 132–133, 135
Zieske, W. F., 231